Vietnam Travel Guide

The Top 10 Highlights in Vietnam

Table of Contents

Introduction to Vietnam 6

1. Hoi An..9

2. Ha Long Bay..12

3. Hanoi..16

4. Ho Chi Minh 19

5. The Southern Beaches 21

6. Hai Van Pass 23

7. Mekong River Delta......................................25

8. Sa Pa...27

9. Hue..29

10. Ninh Binh...31

Introduction to Vietnam

A country with a long history and ancient traditions, Vietnam makes for one amazing tourist destination. Stretching down the southeastern coast of Asia, Vietnam boasts spellbinding emerald mountains, delicious food and a rich culture all waiting to be explored.

Most travelers who head to Vietnam are drawn by the spectacular natural beauty of the green northern rice fields and the intriguing bustle of the south's Mekong River Delta. This combined with the numerous old temples and historical landmarks makes Vietnam a must-see for every traveler.

Ninh Binh is home to Nha Trang, a seaside town situated along the country's second most beautiful bay. The scuba diving center of Vietnam, Nha Trang features fantastic beaches with clean, fine sand and crystal clear ocean waters.

The life-blood of Vietnam, the Mekong River Delta is a very rich, lush area that's covered in rice fields that produce half of the country's total agricultural output. Visitors can explore the vibrant floating markets, lush sugarcane and coconut plantations found here.

Vietnam boasts a number of spectacular beaches. Phu Quoc is the largest of Vietnam's islands, which boasts pristine tropical forests, unspoiled coral reefs and amazing beaches, including Bai Dai which was selected as one of the world's 5 cleanest and most beautiful beaches. In addition to its great beaches, Mui Ne boasts a vast sandy expanse of dunes that offer great panoramic views particularly at sunset.

Once a small fishing village, Hoi An is today one of Vietnam's main attractions. The heart of this city is the Old Quarter which is characterized by Chinese-style shops, winding lanes and narrow canals cutting through the town.

Hanoi is the Vietnamese capital where new and old Asia collide, but get along just fine. Hanoi has managed the rarest of feats: sensitive and elegant modernization characterized by hip restaurants and nightclubs sitting adjacent to ancient pagodas and temples, harmoniously blended together. While in Hanoi, be sure to visit Hoan Kiem Lake, a scenic spot that's popular with the locals.

Ha Long Bay is home to thousands of islands, each topped by thick jungle vegetation to form a majestic seascape of limestone pillars. Some of the islands are hollow and have enormous caves; while others have lakes that support the floating fishing villages.

A former royal capital, Hue is divided into two by the Perfume River, with the Citadel and old city on one side and the new town with its restaurants on the other. The imperial past of Vietnam is well on display in Hue, as seen in its plethora of stately colonial palaces, pagodas and tombs.

The Vietnamese town of Sa Pa is positioned perfectly to provide incredible views across a valley of pine forests and rice paddy fields. Set against a backdrop of thick bamboo woodlands, the famous Sa Pa rice terraces provide sustenance to dozens of Vietnam's ethnic minor groups inhabiting the area, each with their own dialect, customs and dress.

From intrepid explorers to tropical-paradise beach lovers, few can resist the charms of Vietnam. With so much to see and do in Vietnam, it's no wonder that the country attracts thousands of visitors every year - and these are just a few reasons why you should be one of them.

1. Hoi An

Wandering the narrow, cobbled streets of Hoi An is like stepping back in time. The old town of Hoi An comprises brick alleys, narrow streets and ancient structures partially restored. Many cafes and tailor shops now dominate the Old Town which still gives a feeling of its historic buzz in the air.

Up until the 17th century, Hoi An served as a major trading stop in Vietnam for Chinese, Japanese, Indian and Dutch traders. Today, Hoi An caters to a large tourist crowd who come to have custom clothing made or simply to enjoy locally-brewed beers by the river.

The old clan houses, charming footbridges and rich culture make Hoi An an interesting stop on the well-beaten north-south tourist trail. It's very easy to get around Hoi An on foot, which is the best way to appreciate the city vibe, particularly at night.

Built in the 1600s, the Japanese Bridge is a landmark in Hoi An, which crosses a small canal situated on the town's western edge. Close by is a quiet street that is dominated by art galleries and handicraft shops. The arched footbridge crosses the river, serving as a photogenic focal point within the old town, as well as providing access to the restaurants across the river on the An Hoi Peninsula.

During the night, the old town's streets are dimly lit by lantern only, which gives a warm and pleasant atmosphere for an evening stroll. The thousands of colorful lanterns are what make Hoi An so enjoyable at night. The lanterns also make for perfect souvenirs and gift items. Cross the footbridge to the peninsula and then turn left where you will find a large cluster of shops that sell lanterns.

Many cafés and restaurants line the narrow Thu Bon River. The old town of Hoi An is interesting enough for simply taking a stroll around. Visitors can tour the city's 18 museums, temples, communal houses and other attractions such as the Tan Ky House.

In addition to wandering around the old town, shopping is another thing that draws tourists to Hoi An. The town is famous for its custom clothing, with many tailor shops that make shoes, suits and other clothing items on order. Prices in the tailor shops are open to negotiation.

Both traditional and modern artwork is widely available around Hoi An. Cross the Japanese Bridge then take a stroll down the Nguyen Thi Minh Khai Street where you can appreciate the numerous art galleries.

Kim Bong is a historic woodworking village that has been crafting fine wooden sculptures since the 16th century. The mastery of the town's artisans in the woodworking craft is on display at the village where you can also purchase some unique wooden sculptures. The village is situated about a half hour boat ride from the old town.

There is also the New Market, an outdoor market that sells produce, animals and souvenirs. To access it, walk on the Bach Dang Street along the river to the town's eastern edge.

Hoi An has plenty of eateries, some of which serve great options for vegetarians. Many of the restaurants along the river have pleasant upstairs seating with a view. Be sure to sample the tasty Vietnamese dish, Pho.

Other delicious local specialties include Hoi An pancakes which comprise sheets of firm rice paper, salad greens and an egg omelet which you fold into a spring roll. Also try the White Rose which is a plate of inverted dumplings, with the noodle folded neatly below the pork or shrimp in the shape of a rose. And then there's Cao Lau which features firm noodles with a tasty broth, thinly-sliced pork and salad.

2. Ha Long Bay

A picturesque body of water, Ha Long Bay offers the perfect convergence of water, sky and rock, and amazing views of more than 3,000 undulating karst outcrops and islands that in ancient times reminded the Vietnamese of the backs of dragons emerging from the sea. While the topography of Ha Long is entirely the result of natural processes, it's difficult to shake the feeling that it appears out of this world.

The bay is situated in Quang Ninh province. If the weather and your timing is right, you will get a view of Ha Long Bay from the deck of your boat that will be absolutely worth the long drive it took to get there. The Bay offers more than breathtaking ocean views. Visitors can explore the grottoes and caves lurking on the sides of the many islands that dot the bay.

Eons of weather activity have sculpted the limestone outcrops into fantastic shapes. Some of the islands derive their names from the animals they are supposed to resemble. For instance, the Ga Choi islet supposedly resembles two fighting roosters.

The islets and islands in Ha Long Bay rise to between 160 and 300 feet. Most of the islands are uninhabited. In fact, many are inaccessible due to their comprising sheer limestone cliffs. The larger islands have beaches and caves, while the biggest island Cat Ba offers a diverse landscape ideal for adventure travel.

The karst and seawater landscape of Ha Long Bay offers an ideal playground for the adventure-minded traveler. Visitors can explore the hiking trails inside the Cat Ba National Park, or go kayaking through a limestone cave into a secluded cover. With more than 300 islands within the Cat Ba National Park alone, you will have plenty of room to blaze your own adventure trail in Ha Long Bay.

The Cat Ba National Park is a nature reserve that covers more than 15,000 hectares of sea and jungle. The forests shelter more than 700 species of plants and trees, along with 20 mammalian species and more than 70 bird species. The beaches and trails of the park offer some of the best images of Ha Long Bay, so be sure to bring your camera along.

One of the more challenging hiking trails in the Cat Ba National Park will take you 6-8 hours to complete, and winds through one of the island mountains before returning to Viet Hai, a village situated just outside the park. Most hiking trails through the park end at Viet Hai from where you can hire a boat to return you to Cat Ba town. Shorter and more pleasant hikes are also available.

Your guide will help you to spot the unique flora and fauna of the park including langurs, hornbills and hedgehogs moving amid the forest cover.

Butterfly Valley is the number one stop for serious rock climbers. The site features a limestone cliff close to the pleasant Lien Minh Village situated on the island of Cat Ba. This 160-foot-high unpolished karst wall has approximately 50 individual climbing routes, with a top-rope system installed to ensure you complete your climb in one piece.

For deepwater soloing, venture out to Polish Pillar and Tiger Beach. The former is a limestone spire rising out of the sea with a slim base where the seawater erodes the limestone; while the latter is a massive crag on Lan Ha Bay which is accessible by kayak. Always check the tide before you venture out to climb as you want to ensure there's enough water below to break your fall.

Moody Beach is a secluded sand slip close to Tiger Beach which is only accessible by boat. The crag is a relatively easy gray limestone face that rises up from the sand.

To experience Ha Long Bay just as nature intended it; get a kayak to explore its secret beaches, hidden lagoons and rustic fishing villages. The calm bay waters provide a hospitable environment for kayakers as they sail past the local fishermen who eke their living from Ha Long Bay, while residing in floating houses and cultivating fish and clams for the local crabs and shrimp.

The karst landscape with its tucked way corners and low ceilinged caves almost seem designed to be explored via kayak. Luon Grotto - a tunnel in the side of Bo Hon Island, leading into a secluded, tree-lined lagoon that's bordered by steep limestone walls - is a great example.

Ho Ba Ham Cave is another popular spot with kayakers. Set inside the western face of Dau Be Island, the cave is an inlet reaching into 3 lakes. Other favorite kayaking destinations including Lan Ha Bay, Ba Trai Dao Lagoon, and the Light and Dark Caves.

3. Hanoi

Hanoi is the capital and one of the major cities of Vietnam that well captures the breadth of the country's historical and cultural experience. For a long time a jewel in the Vietnamese crown, Hanoi served as the royal capital and seat of learning for a millennium, and today has many monuments that celebrate the long and glorious history of the city.

Begin your tour of Hanoi with a visit to Hoan Kiem Lake. The historic Hoan Kiem Lake is the site of a foundational legend in Vietnam. "Ho Hoan Kiem" means "Lake of the Returned Sword" and this alludes to the legend of a future emperor who received a sword from a magic turtle at the edge of the lake. The emperor would later use the sword to drive the Chinese out of Vietnam.

Today, the lake serves as a charming cultural and social center for the citizens of Hanoi. A graceful, red wooden bridge leads up from the lakeside into Ngoc Son Temple where devotees continue performing their religious duties as they have been doing for close to 1,000 years.

Next visit the Temple of Literature, a 1,000 year-old temple to education and the site of the oldest university in Vietnam.

The Temple is laid out in a sequence of 5 courtyards from north to south, spanned by 3 pathways. The last and northernmost courtyard is the site of the former university for mandarins known as Quoc Tu Giam, which translates to "Temple of the King Who Distinguished Literature" and was established in 1076.

The Old Quarter of Hanoi is also worth a visit. Situated a short walk from Hoan Kiem Lake, this is the ultimate shopping hotspot in the city. Its maze of streets offer an abundance of shopping options and delicious foods. The Old Quarter has worn its age well with visitors encountering narrow sidewalks and shops selling fine silk shirts, lacquer-ware and a range of other items.

Ho Chi Minh Mausoleum is the final resting place of Ho Chi Minh. The huge mausoleum is situated on Ba Dinh Square adjacent to the Presidential Palace that's closed to visitors except for its garden and the Ho Chi Minh stilt house within. There is also the One Pillar Pagoda and a Ho Chi Minh Museum nearby that were erected in his memory.

Inside the Mausoleum, the preserved body of Ho Chi Minh lies in state underneath a glass case with a military honor guard watching as visitors file past.

Hoa Lo Prison was built in the 1880s by the French and maintained until the end of the Vietnam War. The southern part of the prison features grisly exhibits that show the suffering of the Vietnamese prisoners of war.

Hanoi Opera House is a beautiful Art Nouveau building situated in the French Quarter of Hanoi. Built in 1911, the

Opera House continues today as a performance venue for the high arts scene of Hanoi. Tours are not permitted inside unless you are there to watch an opera.

4. Ho Chi Minh

Still known to many as Saigon, Ho Chi Minh City is the largest city in Vietnam and its cultural hub. A bustling urban sprawl of interesting sights and busy roundabouts, the city offers plenty of attractions to please every traveler.

The tradition of water puppetry in Vietnam dates from the 11th century and watching a show will be well worth your while. The best performances are held exclusively in Vietnamese, but this should not hinder your enjoyment. Musicians sit on the sides of the stage to provide the soundtrack using traditional instruments, as well as the voices of the puppets.

Some of the puppets are heavy and large and are used to enact village life scenes, all on top of a pool of water. How the puppets are controlled is a closely guarded secret, so attend a performance to see if you can figure it out! The Golden Dragon Water Puppet Theater is the most popular venue for water puppet shows in Ho Chi Minh City.

The Reunification Palace is the site at which the Vietnam War ended. On the morning of April 30, 1975, a North Vietnamese tank crashed through the wall of the palace which was used as a war command center. Strategic maps and war-related objects are today on display in the palace. Visitors can tour the building and its grounds to see highlights such as the presidential office and the command bunker.

Ben Thanh Market is a cramped area featuring a labyrinth of stalls that sell everything from pigs' feet to trinkets. A full-on sensory experience, the Market is ideal for souvenir hunters, photographers or travelers who just want to take a whirl in one of Asia's most bustling markets.

An odd place, the War Market comprises of cages in a basement with artifacts and relics dug up from the American and French wars in Vietnam. Also on sale are plenty of other Chinese-made army surplus items including ribbons, uniforms, dog tags and unidentifiable items lost by soldiers or taken out of helicopter wrecks.

At the War Remnants Museum, visitors can see exhibits of unexploded ordinance, artifacts and photography depicting the horrors of war that many Vietnamese have had to live with for decades.

The Notre Dame Cathedral in Saigon was constructed between 1863 and 1880 and is also worth a look.

A Bia Hoi is a simple sidewalk café that offers local beer and Vietnamese foods such as pho. Great for socializing, the bia hois have plastic stools on which you can sit and watch Vietnamese life go by. Bu Vien Street is the busiest and most popular street for enjoying a bia hoi experience.

5. The Southern Beaches

Sprawling rice fields, blindingly-white beaches and a landscape as dramatic as its history, Vietnam boasts a long coastline that measures over 3,400km. The coastline is characterized by fine sandy beaches with infinite stretches of warm blue waters, lovely lagoons, hidden coves and tropical islands with even more spectacular beaches.

The idyllic tropical beaches of Vietnam have long been a favorite among locals and intrepid travelers. The turquoise waters and unique diving opportunities along the southern and central coasts continue to draw beach lovers in droves from around the world. Vietnam's best beaches are found in the southern region: from Hue all the way south to Phan Thiet you will find a stretch of fantastic beaches.

The beaches at Cape Mui Ne are popular with both tourists and locals. A 13-mile stretch of beach, Mui Ne offers interesting red sand dunes that rise above the village to create a mysterious desert vibe and great photo-taking opportunities.

Ong Dia beach is the jewel of Mui Ne's beaches and is famous for its gold and red dunes which you can ride over or board down. Or simply stand on top of one and enjoy the sea breeze sweeping your face as you watch coconut palms sway in the sunset.

Situated off the west coast of the Mekong Delta, Phu Quoc is an island that boasts diverse topography of natural forest land, peppered plantations and sparkling white sandy beaches backed by lush jungle. The island has managed to maintain some of its unspoiled charm with quiet shores, dirt roads and limited tourist facilities.

One of the most beautiful islands of Vietnam, Phu Quoc is famous for having the whitest sands in the country and some of the most stunning sunsets in the entire Asia. Its popular beach is Bai Sao, which is ringed by bright white sands. Be sure to sample the islands famous seafood dish, the fermented fish sauce. Bai Dai is another beach, beautifully remote with sparkling white sands and picturesque vistas.

Phan Thiet is a fishing village situated a 3-hour drive from Saigon, which makes for a quick weekend getaway from the city. The beaches here are lovely and well worth the trip over.

Thanks to their isolated location off the coast of Vietnam, the Con Dao islands also offer a host of idyllic beaches. The remote location of the islands has protected them from the ravages of tourism and left them unspoiled. Therefore, visitors who go here can enjoy some of the most pristine beachfront property in the entire Vietnam.

6. Hai Van Pass

For a memorable adventure, an incredible journey and fabulous views in Vietnam, look no further than the Hai Van Pass. The Hai Van Pass is a mountain pass connecting the cities of Hue and Da Nang. Measuring 21 km long, the Pass is a deserted ribbon of perfection that is widely regarded as the most scenic route in Vietnam. Every corner of this stunning pass will unveil even more spectacular views.

To get to the Pass, you will need to drive around Da Nang Bay taking Nguyen Tat Thanh Street all the way up, crossing the railway track up into the clouds. The steep mountain path winds its way up the cliff edge peaks and jungle, opening up to breathtaking views at every 90 degree corner until you hit its peak that's littered with fortifications. Stop here to explore by foot and grab some refreshments.

Weave in and out of the Hai Van Pass, with the stunning coastline and the East Sea to one side, and the jungle trails to the other. Stop by the waterfalls. The slow climb upwards will take you about an hour or longer if you frequently stop to admire the views, while the winding route downhill makes for an adventurous experience.

From the fortifications, you can continue down the other side. As the road levels out at the bottom, a left turn off will take you around a magical, oyster-farming lagoon. The lagoon is a stunning site of wood and tin houses stilted over the tranquil waters. Do a loop around the lagoon before breaking off for lunch at one of the oyster shacks that surround the area and enjoy some tasty charcoal-grilled oysters.

7. Mekong River Delta

To some, Mekong River brings back old images of Vietnam during the war. Today, the river continues to serve as a lifeline for the Vietnamese.

The tenth longest river in the world, Mekong is approximately 2,700 miles long, with its source lying in the mountains of Tibet. The river crosses China before snaking its way through 5 other countries in Southeast Asia. After leaving China, Mekong flows briefly through Myanmar before forming part of the border between Thailand and Laos. It then dissects Cambodia, entering the South China Sea near Saigon.

A cruise on the Mekong River in Vietnam is well worth it. Much of the river's route in Vietnam passes through lush tropical areas, rural landscapes, small villages, towns and cities. The cruise focuses on the history and culture of the region, to provide you with an in-depth look at the country. You will embark and disembark in Ho Chi Minh City.

During your cruise, stop by the Cai Rang floating market in Can Tho. Here you will find boats overflowing with watermelon, pineapple and cabbage that is sold wholesale to locals who cruise up in smaller vessels. The market begins at 6am and ends around 9am.

Visit here to experience the hustle and bustle of floating market merchants and see the homes of the Vietnamese found along the estuaries of Mekong. This area makes for a superb boat trek along the riverbank on a fine day.

8. Sa Pa

A colorfully beautiful and hilly town in northwest Vietnam, Sa Pa is one of the country's favorite tourist spots. A laid back mountain town that's blessed with cool climate throughout the year, Sa Pa is dominated by the Hoang Lien Mountain range that offers a dramatic backdrop for numerous scenic treks.

Every Saturday, the local ethnic groups head into town for the main market to buy and sell fresh produce, meat, livestock as well as handicrafts and clothing. Visitors can go trekking in the local villages and beyond where spectacular scenery abounds.

For stunning scenery, you will need to get out to the Tram Ton Pass, the highest in Vietnam, which connects Sa Pa to Lai Chau. All around you will see near vertical rice paddy field terraces and stunning mountain peaks with mist constantly hovering above them. Plan your visit during the harvest season in Sa Pa so you can see the golden color of the rice fields.

Situated on the same route is the spectacular Thac Bac waterfall where you can go to indulge in a refreshing mist of water.

If you are very fit and have time, take a hike to the top of Fansipan, the highest peak in Indochina which rises to 3143m. If you are up for the challenge, the rewards will be breathtaking with majestic views over the Hoang Lien mountain range. Fansipan is also the last major peak of the Himalayan range.

If you're not fit enough for Fansipan, opt for Mount Ham Rong which enables you to see the town from a different angle. The mountain also has a colorful flower garden that's worth a peek.

A stroll through the streets of Sa Pa will leave you with images that will be forever carved in your heart. Sa Pa has some of the longest and most fascinating walking destinations in the world. You can walk dozens of miles from dawn till dusk, through villages, towns, rice paddy fields, over bridges and through streams. Take a walk to live slower. Observe and learn from the life and culture of the locals.

If old world charm is your thing, do not miss out on a trip to the Sa Pa museum where you can enjoy an educational day viewing exhibitions on the town's rich history, culture, ethnic groups, customs and traditional crafts.

9. Hue

The former feudal and imperial capital of Vietnam, Hue is the capital of the surrounding Binh Tri Thien province. To appreciate Hue, you need to understand that the town has played a significant role in the history of Vietnam for the last several hundred years. History is what makes Hue tick.

With its new town situated on one side of the Huong or "Perfume" River, and a collection of old pagodas, tombs and imperial buildings on the other, Hue is famous for its numerous royal structures, most notably the Forbidden Purple City which was home to the Nguyen Emperors.

The southern half of Hue city is a quiet, bustling community with old charming 19th century houses and a scattering of temples. The northern half is dominated by the Forbidden Purple City and the Imperial Citadel. Shopping areas have sprung up around the Dong Ba Market which is situated next to the Citadel.

The Citadel has high stone walls and measures about 520 hectares in size. The interior of the Citadel features plenty of wide open spaces where the imperial buildings used to stand.

The Royal Tombs of Hue all bear common elements derived from feng shui, aimed at maximizing the auspicious standing of the structure with the universe. Of the 7 imperial tombs, the most popular are the tombs of Minh Mang, Khai Dinh and Tu Duc.

The Thien Mu Pagoda is one of the city's oldest historical sites and comprises a hilltop temple overlooking the northern bank of Perfume River.

Situated inside the Citadel is the Museum of Royal Fine Arts which is worth a visit. The museum houses everyday items from the Forbidden Purple City during its heyday including sedan chairs, gongs, utensils and clothing. Here you will also see finely crafted bronze ware, chinaware, court finery and ceremonial weaponry that offer insights into the extraordinary lives of the Nguyen courtiers.

The Museum building dates from 1845, and is notable for its unique architecture, a traditional type that features sloping successive roofs supported by 128 pillars. The walls have been inscribed with brushed letters in the traditional script of Vietnam.

The history of Hue as an imperial power center is tied closely to the history of the prominent families in the area, the majority of whom built ornate garden houses in the city.

Visitors can enjoy a tour of some of the garden houses including Lac Tinh Vien, Princess Ngoc Son and Y Thao. Every garden house covers an area of about 2,400 square yards and has common aspects such as a lush garden surrounding the house, a tile-covered gate at the front of the house, a small rock garden and a traditional house.

10. Ninh Binh

Famous for its beautiful karst limestone formations, Ninh Binh offers a more peaceful and natural side to Vietnam. Situated to the north of the country, the city doesn't offer a lot to do but makes for the perfect base for exploring the natural beauty of the surrounding countryside.

Nha Trang is a busy beach area famous for its endless days of sunshine. Snorkelers and divers will enjoy the soft and hard coral reefs, caves and sea walls that offer some of the best diving spots in the South China Sea. Above-water adventures include kite surfing, wakeboarding and banana boat rides. You can also relax by the sea while adventure-lovers head to the countryside and mountains nearby.

Then go explore the wonders of Tan Coc. This beautiful area features impressive limestone formations that are similar to those found at Ha Long Bay. A boat will take you through waterways to see the rock formations close up. The surroundings of Tam Coc are also very scenic and make for good exploration on a bicycle.

Also visit the Grottoes of Trang An which enable you to explore natural caves. You will need to rent a boat and hire a guide to take you on a trip through the grottoes.

Then venture into the Cuc Phuong National Park, a beautiful park of lush, green tropical forest. Established in 1962, the park is home to numerous hidden grottoes and rich in wildlife and natural beauty.

The park has numerous scenic trails as well as an Endangered Primate Rescue Center that provides sanctuary to about 130 monkeys. Visitors can walk around a loop trail that will take you to the 1,000 year old tree or stay overnight in the park.

Next, marvel at the Bich Dong Pagoda. The 15th century pagoda was built on a steep mountainside with temples that are built right into the caves. A relaxing and beautiful place, the pagoda's highest temple has a spot with rocks where you can climb and enjoy views of the city.

Copyright © 2015. All rights reserved.

Except as permitted under the United States Copyright Act of 1976, reproduction or utilization of this work in any form or by any electronic, mechanical, or other means, now known or hereafter invented, including xerography, photocopying, and recording, and in any information storage and retrieval system, is forbidden without written permission.

The ideas, concepts, and opinions expressed in this book are intended to be used for educational and reference purposes only. Author and publisher claim no responsibility to any person or entity for any liability, loss, or damage caused or alleged to be caused directly or indirectly as a result of the use, application, or interpretation of the material in this book.

Printed in Great Britain
by Amazon

The Ind... Hostel G...

England
Wales
Scotland

Edited by
Sam Dalley and Alice Lockett

Independent Hostels UK

Independent Hostel Guide 2015: England, Wales and Scotland
24th Edition, Editors: Sam Dalley and Alice Lockett
British Library Cataloguing in Publication Data. A Catalogue record for this book is available at the British Library ISBN 978-0-9565058-4-2
Published by: The Backpackers Press, Speedwell House, Upperwood, Matlock Bath, Derbyshire, DE4 3PE. Tel: +44 (0) 1629 580427.
© Independent Hostels UK, 2015

Printed by: Sterling Solutions, www.sterlingsolutions.co.uk
Cover Photos by Whole Picture www.wholepicture.co.uk

Front Cover Photographs: Mwnt coast path close to Piggery Poke Hostel (pg 324) and Cambrian Mountains close to Mid Wales Bunkhouse (pg 336). **Back Cover Photographs:** Piggery Poke Hostel (pg 324).

Internal Photographs: Title page: Millhouse Hostel (pg 440). Photo on pg 521 taken at Piggery Poke Hostel. Photo Credits: page 434 credited to Highland Photos, page 378 credited to Tony Jones, pg 318 credited to Claire Eaton Photography. Other pages contain photos provided by the bunkhouses and hostels.

Distributed in the UK by Cordee Books and Maps, 3a De Montfort Street, Leicester, LE1 7HD. Tel: (0116) 2543579

ISBN 978-0-9565058-4-2

CONTENTS

Contents	3
Key to Symbols	4
Holiday Ideas	7
Maps and Hostels :	
England	34
Wales	288
Scotland	386
Jersey	38
Isle of Man	287
Hostel Networks and Associations	514
Join your accommodation to IHUK	521
Become a Travel Writer	524
Index (by name)	525

INDEPENDENT HOSTELS UK

Independent Hostels UK is a network of 350 bunkhouses, hostels and group accommodation centres. These businesses provide a unique form of accommodation ideal for groups and for individuals and families who enjoy good company, travel and the outdoors.

KEY

- Mixed dormitories
- Single sex dormitories
- Private rooms
- Family rooms
- Blankets or duvets provided
- Sheets required
- Sleeping bags required
- Hostel fully heated
- Some areas heated
- Drying room available
- Showers available
- Cooking facilities available
- Shop at hostel
- Meals provided at hostel (with notice)
- Breakfast only at hostel (with notice)
- Meals available locally
- Clothes washing facilities available
- Facilities for less-able people
- Computer with internet facilities
- WiFi available
- Within 1 mile, 3 miles, 5 miles of a NCN cycle route
- Bike Shed
- Affiliated to Hostelling International
- Simple accommodation. Clean, friendly and basic

KEY

GROUPS ONLY	Accommodation for groups only
	Dog Friendly
	VisitScotland Quality Assured
	VisitWales Quality Assured
	VisitEngland Quality Assured
	Bronze, Silver or Gold Green Tourism Business Award
pp	per person
GR	Ordnance Survey grid reference

INDEPENDENT HOSTELS

Hostels have shared areas, such as self-catering kitchens, and they often have sleeping accommodation in bunks. Bunkhouses, camping barns, city centre hostels and group accommodation centres are all types of hostels.

Unique Qualities of Independent Hostels:-

▲ Self-catering facilities available

▲ You can stay for just one night

▲ There are private bedrooms, en suite rooms and dorms

▲ Great wild locations for outdoor activities

▲ Great city centre locations for independent travellers

▲ Families, individuals and groups are all welcome

▲ Hostels can be booked 'sole-use' for get-togethers

▲ No membership required

▲ Independent Hostels are privately owned (around 5% are also affiliated to the YHA or SYHA marketing schemes).

If you enjoy the outdoors or travel and, like us, you think hostels are great, you might like to join our team of bloggers. To find out more see:-

IndependentHostels.co.uk/travel-writer

Write about you adventures and stay for free.

HOLIDAY IDEAS

The Independent Hostels' website has an active and popular blog, written by IHUK's team of travel writers.

The holiday ideas on the following pages are extracts from the blog, you can read the full posts on:-

www.independenthostels.co.uk

New holiday ideas and special offers are added to our website every day. Follow our social media to keep informed.

fb.com/independenthostelguide

@indiehostelsuk

@Indiehostelsuk

IndependentHostels YouTube

ESCAPE TO

The Gilfach Nature reserve, five minutes' drive, along quiet lanes, was deserted on the sunny Sunday we visited. Swishing grass, a backdrop of heather clad hillsides and the babbling of the river Marteg cascading over waterfalls and through shady glens, it was perfect for picnics and paddling. We walked along a shady disused railway, part of the Wye Valley Walk, for a swim the Wye.

I was hoping we would catch a glimpse of the Red Kites that Rhyder is famous for, but I was not expecting them to be a constant feature in the skies. We watched them hovering, the characteristic kite shaped tail constantly twitching as the bird balanced, and then a glimpse of stunning red as it banked.

THE CAMBRIANS

By Sam Dalley

We had a brilliant few days in this quiet part of Wales, thanks to our hosts at Mid Wales Bunkhouse.

In the Cambrian mountains you escape from the pressure of everyday life, no traffic, no hordes of tourists, just beautiful scenery, abundant wildlife and the peace and welcome of Mid Wales Bunkhouse.

The bunkhouse is set amidst a wildlife garden, its wooden veranda overlooking a lawn clucking with chickens and ducks and pockets of wild flowers with tiny safe pools and tall trees reaching up into the sky.

When we arrived in Mid Wales, to find the quite lanes and endless tracks and bridleways, we wished we had bought our bikes. There are loads of challenging cycle routes on the Cambrian Mountains but we opted for an easy trail along on an old railway track from Rhayader, where we hired our bikes, to the Elan Valley Visitors Centre. After cake at the centre, we explored the quiet lakeside roads beyond the dam, up through woods and deep into the mountains. We never met another cyclist and hardly a car in all those miles of scenery.

CYCLING THE

Millhouse hostel was lovely with its fresh spring colours and bright rooms with the sun shining down through velux windows. A perfect base.

Each day we set off for the beach later and later frequently not coming back until it was nearly dark. A few days on Tiree and we were so relaxed we were regularly cooking dinner at 10pm. Corresponding late mornings and plenty of spring sunshine and fresh breezes put us in the perfect frame of mind for days of kite surfing, beach combing and evenings watching the wildlife.

INNER HEBRIDES

By Sam Dalley

Coll and Tiree are remote unspoilt Scottish islands in the inner Hebrides. Surprisingly easy to reach with a relaxed journey by ferry from Oban. We left the cars in Oban, making the ferry very economically and the whole holiday a healthy breath of fresh air.

We docked first on the Isle of Coll where we stayed for 3 nights, allowing us to explore this sparsely populated island with fabulous white sandy beaches, empty except for us and the seals. We stayed at Coll bunkhouse, close to both the ferry and the only bar on the island. Perfect for a group to self-cater and with ideal family sized rooms.

A few days later we were back on the ferry for the short journey to Tiree. We landed at the small village of Scarinish, a positive metropolis of tiny white cottages and a supermarket!

It was a 5 mile ride to Millhouse Bunkhouse, which was close to the famous kite surfing beaches on the north side of the island. We passed huge tame hares on the roadside but very few cars.

EXOTIC

Intertwining history, culture, shopping and a first rate university are just some of the city's most notable characteristics. The shopping precinct of 'Princesshay' lies within the city walls; remnants preserved at every twist and turn. A plaque can be seen on one stretch reading "Built by the Romans about 200 A.D, since repaired by others."

The city's student fraternity contribute much to Exeter's multicultural and energetic feel. I happened upon a street performance by the Footlights Company.

Such creativity is also the likely reason why a diverse mix of retro, curio and craft shops pepper the walk down towards the Quayside and the River Exe. The Quayside offers its own collection of shops, restaurants and outdoor activities, which blend with 17th and 18th century warehouse buildings that in yesteryear would have been a hive of trading activity. Today, the hustle and bustle comes from weekenders trying to secure one of the prime seats outside the Quayside coffee shops to watch the ebb and flow of Exeter life.

CHARMS OF EXETER

By Ramy Salameh

Stepping from the train at Exeter Central, I heard the calm reassuring sound of seagulls squawking overhead. Exeter is a place that immediately wooed me with its quaint cobbled pathways, wonky medieval architecture and ornate cathedral that remains head and shoulders above the city landscape.

I stayed at Globe Backpackers. Housed in an 18th century townhouse in the very heart of Exeter, it has a magnificent façade where period features are mixed with fun murals.

Back in 1268 when the city and Cathedral were constantly at odds, a wall and several gatehouses were erected to keep the two separated, now a few narrow and cobbled alleyways branch out into the modern city beyond. This remarkable landmark, together with the medieval houses enclosing the Cathedral grounds, provide a quintessentially English scene

CEREDIGION

Neighbour to the Pembrokeshire Coastal Path the Ceredigion Coastal Path is beautiful and less visited. The paths are part of the Wales Coast Path and meet at Cardigan, the county town of old Cardiganshire (now Ceredigion).

The Ceredigion Coastal Path travels from Cargidan to Ynys-Las (just north of Aberystwyth) in 7 documented sections. Our adventure includes the first three sections and we changed the location of the first night's break, to make an even daily mileage and to walk to the door of the hostel on the first night. You can find details of the route on the blog of the Independent Hostels website.

The key to the trip is the Cardi Bach coastal bus service operated by Green Dragon Buses. This runs twice a day along the coast from Cardigan to New Quay and twice a day it returns. Seats on the bus can be booked in advance and the bus will collect you from any road in the coastal zone along the route. Perfect for walking a linear route along the coast and returning to the same base each night. The Cardi Bach bus runs 6 days a week from May-Sept and bookings must be made before 12pm the day before you travel. This route was devised using the 2014 summer bus timetable. Please check the bus timetable for your travel dates before you make your plans.

COASTAL PATH

By Sam Dalley

Our base for the whole trip was Piggery Poke Hostel, four-star, self-catering accommodation in the old farmyard at Cardigan Coastal Cottages. At the hostel you can book a private bedroom for you and your group or book a bed in a shared room.

All the rooms have en suite showers and toilets. The shared, self-catering kitchen and lounge are a great place to meet other walkers.

WALK AND CYCLE

The Moray Coast Cycle Route makes an easy 2 day cycling holiday for a family or anyone who enjoys stopping off en route. With 29 miles to cycle there is plenty of time to watch for dolphins and otters or to sample the produce of the local fishing industry.

Cullen Harbour Hostel is on the eastern end of the Cycle Route which travels along a flat railway bed from Cullen to Buckie. From Buckie the route continues on quite roads to Elgin after which is goes off road to the coast at Lossiemouth. There is one section on a quiet B road to Hopeman before the last section off road to Burghead.

Cullen Harbour Hostel can be used for both nights by making use of the bus routes to Elgin. Elgin also has a train station so can be a good starting point for those wanting to holiday by bike and public transport.

There is an option for a third day using an additional 18 mile stretch (not part of the Moray Coast Cycle Route) along quiet flat roads from Burghead to Findhorn. Findhorn is seaside village with accommodation available for groups at Findhorn Village Hostel.

THE MORAY COAST

By Sam Dalley

At Cullen Harbour Hostel an artistic feel this flows through the fabric of the building. Rebuilt from a fisherman's store on the water's edge, the hostel has a smell of warm wood and sea air. With skylights in the slate roof and no ceilings you see the sky framed by the internal wood of the building. There are chunky bunkbeds and deep thick drapes, a farmhouse kitchen with Aga, piano and dresser. Mix this with the sound of the sea and you get the feel of this unique place.

The 50 mile Moray Coastal Trail footpath hugs the coast from Cullen Harbour all the way to Findhorn and beyond.

This route can be completed in four days using public transport to overnight at both hostels. Passing long sandy beaches, fishing town harbours, along the rugged coastline famous for its dolphins, this is an excellent route for those who enjoy seascapes and wildlife.

ADVENTURE IN

We ate, laughed and chatted our way through the first evening, the kids having a great game of hide and seek - inside and out, before heading off for bed. The two bunk rooms were great - we split into boys and girls and with everyone so tired from the walking we all got to sleep easily.

After breakfast we did a circular walk stopping for a picnic and getting back to the Reckoning House mid afternoon for a nap. More family arrived this time bringing dinner with them.

DERBYSHIRE

By Bridget McCrea

When Aunty Mary comes to stay from Canada she likes to do something different. The challenge was to find somewhere unusual where various members of the family could all stay together. We needed a place for approximately 12, good for kids and close by.

We looked through the Independent Hostel Guide and struck gold with The Reckoning House. Unbelievably the exact two nights we wanted were available and we could walk there from my house! So Aunts, Uncles, Mums, Dads and Kids all gathered together and set off from Matlock on the Limestone Way heading towards Over Hadden.

The walk was a fantastic idea, the Canadians were very impressed by the beautiful little villages along route and how friendly everyone was. We arrived exhausted but happy and were delighted with the Reckoning House. Lots of area to cook - everything we needed and loads of table space (as more family came for meals).

EXPLORE THE

Conwy Valley Backpackers, run by organic livestock farmer Claudia Bryan, is ideally positioned to explore Conwy valley as well as Snowdonia, which is just a short drive away. On consecutive evenings we sat by the log fire of Ye Olde Bull, an easy walk from the barn, with pints of the excellent J.W. Lees ale before prizing ourselves out into the dark night where hooting owls and vivid constellations saw us back down the hill to bed.

Conwy is the UK's most complete medieval walled town and it is linked by an estuary cycle trail to the west shore of Llandudno. We walked down to Conwy quay, past the UK's smallest house (which by the way is smaller than you'd imagine) and found a staircase up to the city walls. The views from the walls over the sea and mountains were impressive even with an icy wind taking the skin off my nose. From our vantage point you could see the peninsular of Llandudno, the mountains of Snowdoina and back up the Conwy Valley, towards the Backpackers Barn.

CONWY VALLEY

By Harry Drysdale-Wood

The Conwy Valley stretches from the heart of Snowdonia out to the north west coast of Wales and is an ecologically precious area rich in ancient history. Most people head here to enjoy the spectacular walking in the National Park, yet there is so much more to this pocket of North Wales than simply Snowdonia. Visitors really looking to get the most from the region must take the time to explore among others the 12th century walled city of Conwy, the amazing Bodnant Gardens and the eccentric seaside town of Llandudno with its wacky pier, and cable car up the famous Great Orme.

The National Trust owned Bodnant Gardens in the Conwy Valley have surreal beauty and total tranquility. The fact we were there in early March meant that only the most hardy species were on show (mostly rhododendrums), but this was easily offset by the view of the distant snow capped mountains from the Lily Terrace. I could have easily spent a day gazing at the extraordinary Californian Redwoods, planted in 1886, and climbing to 45m, utterly mesmerising. We wandered around the vast grounds for several hours followed by tea in the Magnolia tea-room, before stocking up on local cheese and fresh bread from the farm shop.

SCOTLAND'S

Castle Rock Hostel is a fantastic base from which to explore:- a 30 second walk from the iconic Royal Mile and the Castle entrance just a short walk up the steps across the road. The hostel has a relaxed feel – there is a 'chill' room where technology, bad vibes and shoes are banned ! The common room offers a great space for socialising – we had numerous games of pool with many different nationalities and these interesting characters really made our stay.

At night, the city is alive with excitement, with great restaurants and pubs buzzing with life. In the old town the quirky wynds, such as Advocates Close, offer a relaxing refuge from the bustle of the Royal Mile and it is a joy to soak up the history and oddities of a time gone by.

CAPITAL CITY

23

By Hadyn Park-Patterson

Steeped in a rich history, culture and whisky. Edinburgh is one of the most picturesque and interesting cities in the United Kingdom. Full of little alleyways and quirky corners, you are never far from street theatre or live music.

There are plenty of things to do during the day, it's easy to spend more than a few hours marvelling at the 200 year old Camera Obscura and the frankly quite terrifying and weird illusions found over 5 floors at the World of Illusions exhibition, both close to the Castle. If that's not your thing then the old town has lots of quirky independent shops and cafes and the new town, while different to the old, still retains a certain charm and offers a great selection of high street shops.

Photos taken using a 1980's film camera

HOSTELS FOR

Family accommodation in Wales includes Piggery Poke Hostel, just a quarter mile from the stunning Ceredigion coast and the secluded Mid Wales Bunkhouse, set in its own wildlife garden complete with goal and trampoline.

To help families choose the hostel that's right for them, the Independent Hostel Guide website allows users to filter for accommodation with family rooms. Look for the Requirements logo on the top search bar.

FAMILY HOLIDAYS

By Pat Edgar

Family rooms offer the privacy of a multi bed room, sometimes with a double bed, often en suite and ideal for any family size. Self-catering facilities make it simple to cook for kids. Gardens and social areas provide space for the children to meet up and play. All these make Independent Hostels ideal for family holidays.

There's a good choice of family friendly hostels throughout the UK. Palace Farm Hostel in the North Kent Downs AONB offers family rooms surrounding an attractive courtyard garden, bikes are available to hire to explore the local area which is great for wildlife spotting.

Friends of Nature, one of Europe's oldest environmental groups, offer family accommodation in a picturesque Victorian cottage in the peaceful village of Kirk Yetholm, Roxburghshire.

RETRO YOUTH

As the evening moved on food was shared, as if this was the most natural thing. Warmth and plenty spread through the room. One person announced there was live music in the village and a group of friends, who were strangers just hours before, left together to enjoy it. The rest of us continued by the fire, until in dribs and drabs we found our ways to bed.

The future of Corris Hostel is under threat, so if you have memories of happy times spent at youth hostels in the past, visit Corris Hostel this year and relive them while you can.

HOSTEL EXPERIENCE

By Sam Dalley

Corris Hostel left the Youth Hostel Association years ago and before this it was independent place; artistic, quirky and caring. It was converted with input from the Centre of Alternative Technology, before the environment was much talked about elsewhere. It was designed to provide holidays of fresh air and exercise high up in the Welsh Mountains by Michael Parish, who is still welcoming guests 20 years on.

In the words of Michael, *Don't expect sleek glamour with packaged courtesy gestures, here you will find only old fashioned fellowship and a real welcome, warmth and peace.*

We came to Corris Hostel and had an evening just like the youth hostel experiences of my youth. As soon as we walked through the door we were welcome. The warden introduced us to the other guests and I could tell immediately that everyone felt they belonged. There were children playing board games. A visiting dog was quietly bedded down by the fire. No one was a nuisance. Conversation sprouted up between strangers and fell into a comfortable ease. Within minutes of arrival each new guest was enveloped into the group.

WOOD FUELED

It is no mean feat for a remote eco hostel to maintain such warmth in an old solid stone building but Rob and Val have achieved it by installing a waste wood biomass system. Rob says it was a substantial investment in 2006, but it has repaid itself more than twice over in eight years. Energy Performance Certificates rate both buildings as a reasonable E for energy efficiency, and a very impressive B for environmental (CO_2) impact. Burning five broken pallets a day in the depths of winter and only a few a week in warm weather, a thousand pallets a year provide hot water and generous central heating for three lighthouse keeper's apartments and Rob and Val's own home.

ECO HOSTEL

By Sam Dalley

What you need most of all when sleeping in a lighthouse keeper's apartment on the east coast of the North Sea, is solid construction and warmth! That is what we found when we arrived at Rattray Head Eco Hostel one evening in freezing fog.

Next day the dunes, ruins and seals of Rattray Head kept us out and about as we enjoyed the peace and history of the location. Come evening there was endless hot water to shower off the sand and a cosy sitting room with kitchen. There was no need to light the wood burning stove (fired by chunks of waste wood from broken pallets) but we turned the radiators down and lit it anyway, just to enjoy the glow.

HOSTELS FOR

Situated in the heart of the Lake Districy, overlooking Derwent Water and two miles from Keswick, Derwentwater Independent Hostel is a popular destination for school groups of all ages.

Cedar House School visited Beatrix Potter's former home, The Wordsworth Museum and the Theatre by the Lake in Keswick. We were delighted to help them plan these visits. Both schools also experienced the delights of the Keswick Launch, viewing the hostel and the surrounding fells from the middle of Derwent Water, and the teenage South African students were particularly thrilled to see snow !

SCHOOL GROUPS

By Fiona McCarthy

No two school groups are the same and staff at Derwentwater Independent Hostel were fascinated to see how students from two very different parts of the globe enjoyed their visit.

Arriving at the Grade II listed Georgian mansion from very different parts of the globe, the recent visits of Ashfield Primary School (Cumbria) and Cedar House School (South Africa) reveal the fascinating variety of residential visits hosted by Derwentwater Independent Hostel. Both groups agreed that their visits had been a big adventure, despite the very different distances travelled

Ashfield Primary School based their activities in the hostel grounds, helped by the Cumbria Wildlife Trust. Full of excitement on their first residential, the pupils explored our extensive woodland, going on a mini beast hunt, building a den in the trees, and sketching the waterfall that cascades through the grounds.

With space for large groups, indoor social areas and outdoor activities, many Independent Hostels are a great choice for schools. The Group Enquires facility on the Independent Hostel's website makes it easy to contact hostels of the right size and in the right location.

YORKSHIRE

The climbing wall in Ingleton requires your own equipment. So, we went to the Lakeland Climbing Centre in Kendal. We had an hour and a half in the Crazy Climb room which was full of varied and challenging climbs – including a series of stacks where, you ended up leaping to a punch bag suspended from the ceiling.

Before heading home we did a circuit of the Yorkshire Peaks. First stop was Sedburgh for book shops, followed by a trip down the idyllic Dent valley with quaint 'shires' views around every bend. We stopped at the Ribblehead viaduct just as a train was chugging over and lunch was sausage, egg and chips and a mug of tea at the Pen-y-Ghent Café in Horton in Ribblesdale. Feeling completely rejuvenated, we drove home, planning to return to do the myriad of things left undone.

PEAKS HOLIDAY

By Clare Hollands

The village of Ingleton nestles between the Yorkshire Three Peaks of Inglebrough, Whernside and Pen-y-Ghent, so the scenery is simply stunning. There are fabulous views in every direction. Secreted down Sammy Lane is Ingleton's Independent Hostel "Greta Towers" which is also affiliated to the YHA.

Stopping at Booth's (an upmarket supermarket) in Kirkby Lonsdale en route, we arrived at the hostel to make our tea. The dining room was shared by diners and self-caterers which made for a friendly atmosphere and the hostel's license meant that we could have a relaxing drink.

From the window of our comfortable en suite family room, we spotted Ingleton's outdoor heated swimming pool and made a note to visit later. The bright sunshine put a spring in our steps so we pottered down to the Ingleton Waterfalls' Trail.

This is an absolute must, there are eight beautiful waterfalls on this spectacular walk. By the time we'd completed the four and half mile, up and down trip we most definitely deserved a visit to Frumenty and Fluffin, Ingleton's most special tea shop.

South England

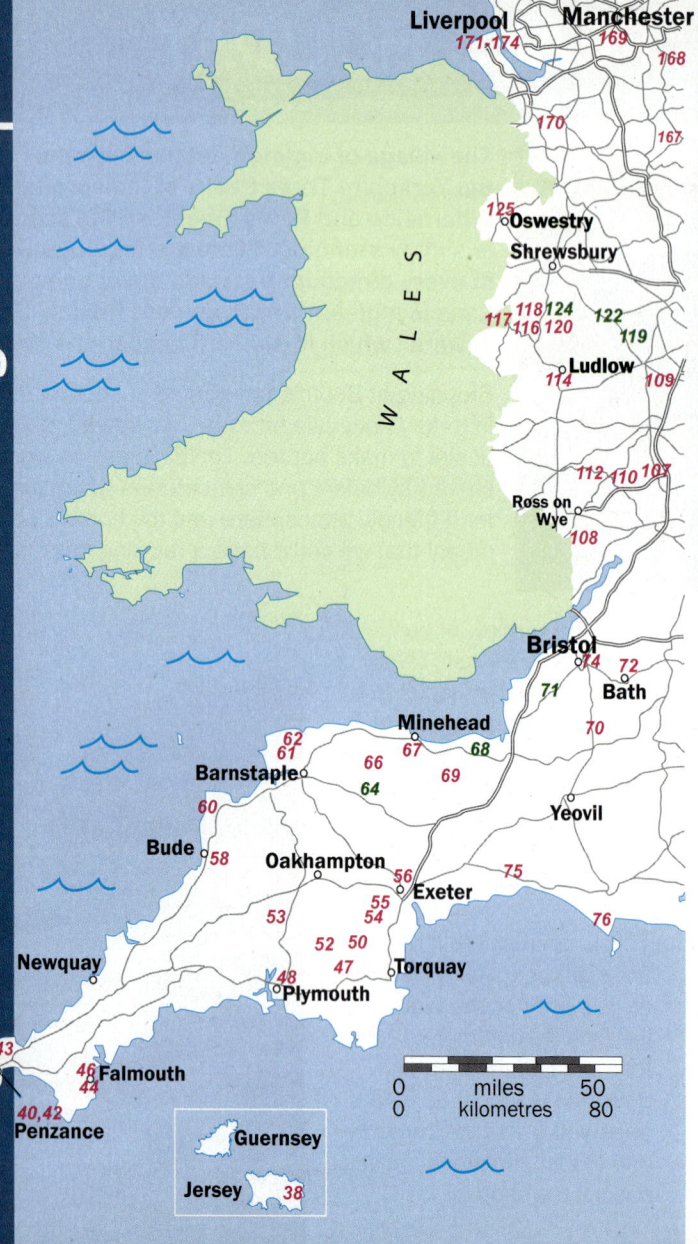

34

- Liverpool *171–174*
- Manchester *169, 168, 170, 167*
- Oswestry *125*
- Shrewsbury
- *117, 118, 124, 122*
- *116, 120, 119*
- Ludlow *114, 109*
- *112, 110, 107*
- Ross on Wye *108*
- Bristol *74, 72*
- Bath
- *71, 70*
- Minehead *67, 68*
- *62, 61, 66, 69*
- Barnstaple *64*
- *60*
- Yeovil
- Bude *58*
- Oakhampton *56, 75*
- *55, 54*
- Exeter
- *53, 52, 50, 76*
- Newquay *47*
- Torquay
- *48* Plymouth
- *43*
- *39* *46* Falmouth
- *44*
- *40, 42* Penzance
- Guernsey
- Jersey *38*

0 miles 50
0 kilometres 80

South England

Sheffield *160* *153* *158* *164* *156* *146* *148* *166* *154* *162* *152* *151* *138* *142* *140* *136* *150* *144*

Derby

Nottingham *127*

Lincoln *128*

Skegness

Leicester

King's Lynn *132* *130, 133, 134*

135 **Norwich**

Birmingham *126*

Coventry

Northampton

Peterborough

Cambridge

Ipswich

104 *106* **Colchester**

Luton

95

London *96 to 103*

Oxford *86*

Reading

90 *92* *94* **Canterbury** Dover

84 Guildford

Salisbury

81 *80*

82 *88*

Portsmouth **Brighton** Hastings

Bournemouth

78 *77*

KEY

45 - **Hostel page number**

45 - **Page number of group only accommodation**

North England

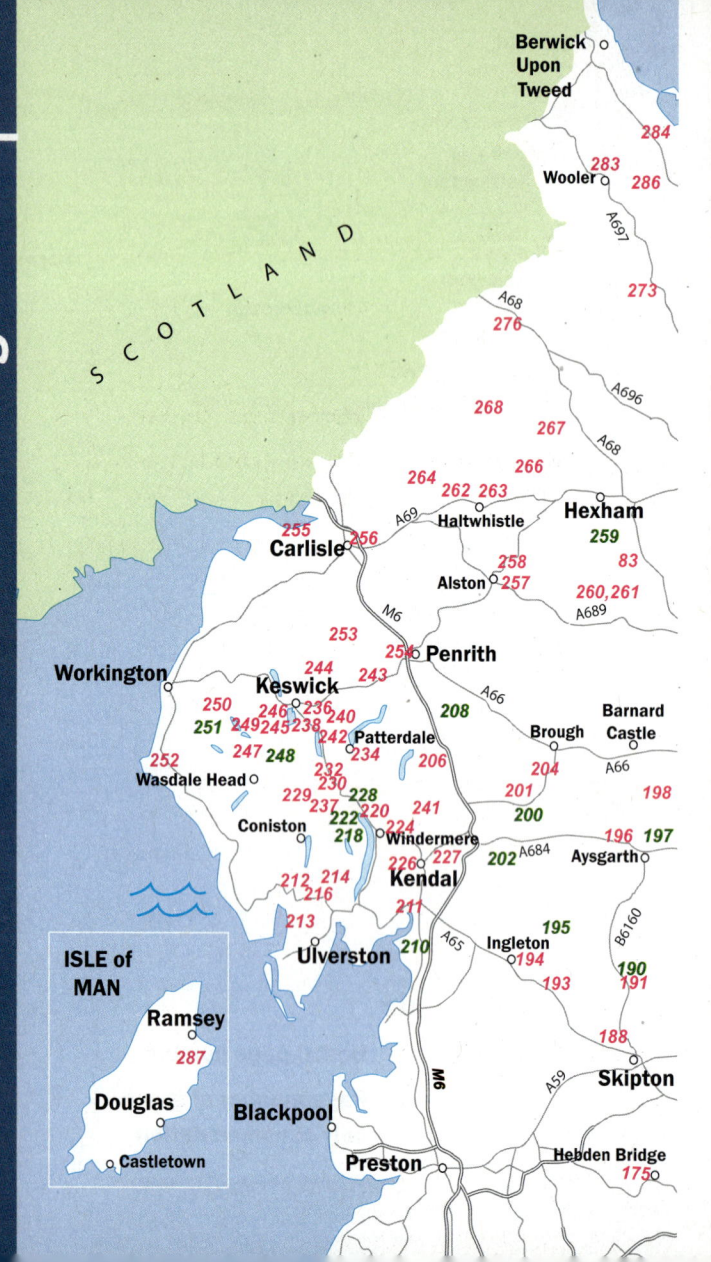

36

Berwick Upon Tweed

284
283
Wooler 286

273

276
268
267
266
264 262 263
Haltwhistle **Hexham**
255 259
Carlisle 256
258 83
Alston 257
260, 261

253
250 **Penrith**
Workington 244 254
Keswick 243
246 236 **Barnard Castle**
250 240 208 **Brough**
251 249 245 238 204 198
247 248 242 **Patterdale** 201
252 234 206 200
Wasdale Head 232 241
230 228 196 197
229 224 202 **Aysgarth**
237 222 220 227
Coniston 218 **Windermere**
226 **Kendal**
212 214 211 195
216 **Ingleton**
213 194
210 190
Ulverston 193 191

188
ISLE of MAN
Ramsey **Skipton**
287
Douglas
Blackpool
Castletown **Hebden Bridge**
Preston 175

North England

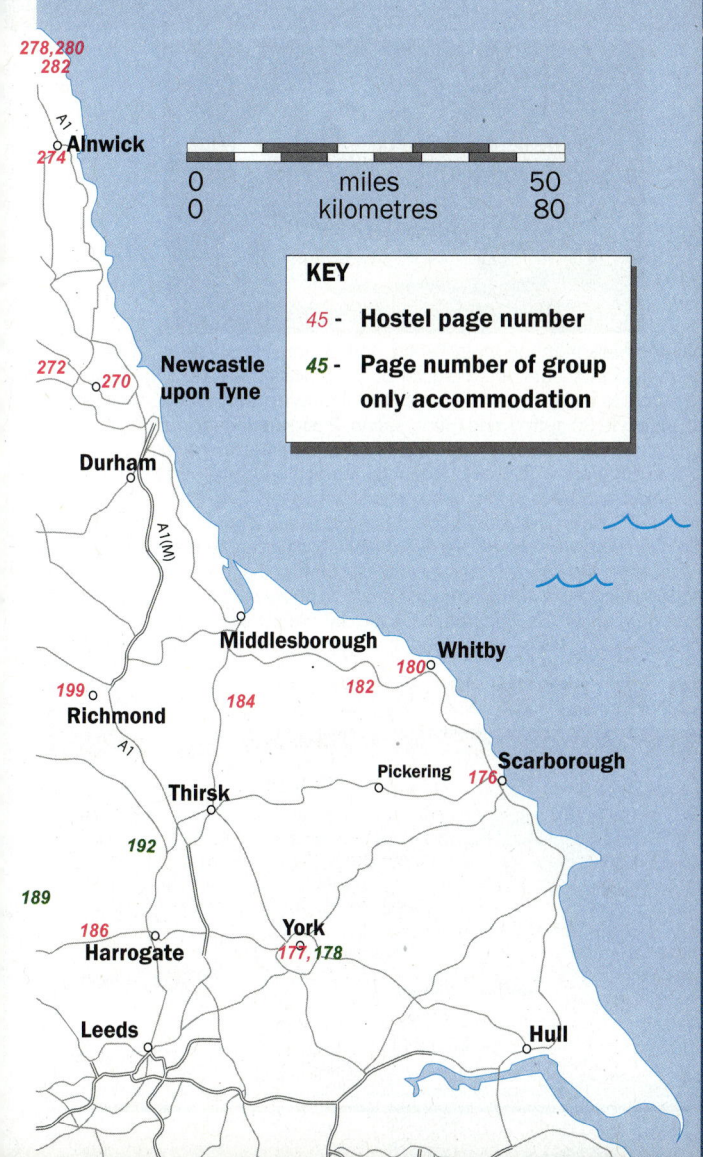

KEY

- *45* - Hostel page number
- *45* - Page number of group only accommodation

278, 280
282
274 Alnwick

272 *270* Newcastle upon Tyne

Durham

Middlesborough
180 Whitby
184 *182*
199 Richmond
Pickering Scarborough
Thirsk *176*
192
189
186 York
Harrogate *177, 178*

Leeds
Hull

JERSEY ACCOMMODATION AND ACTIVITY CENTRE

ENGLAND

A 5 minutes' walk from the pretty fishing port of Gorey in St Martin which has several restaurants, bars and a regular bus to St Helier, the JAAC has a wide range of rooms including private en suites and dorms with shared showers. Facilites include 60 seat dining room, sauna, 2 large lounges, laundry, drying room and extensive outside space. Ball and board games are available as well as a TV and separate DVD player. Ideal for families and larger groups who can often be accommodated in the same area of the hostel. Single sex dorms can be provided. Breakfast included, packed lunches and a 2 course evening meals available. Camping with electric hook-up, running water and a shower and toilet block available. On-site activities include climbing wall and zip wire for under 12s, archery, bush craft and an all ages obstacle course. Off-site a wide range of outdoor pursuits or "Escape from a Castle" by completing a range of physical and problem solving tasks. Beds, food, transport & activity packages available.

DETAILS

- **Open** - All year, 8.30 - 20.00
- **Number of beds** - 110 (Bunk 1x10 6x8 1x6 4x4) (En suite 1x6 2x4 2x3 4x2 2x1)
- **Booking** - First night deposit required. Full payment if less than 10 days before arrival. 20% deposit for group bookings.
- **Price per night** - Breakfast included. Bunks £25-£30pp Singles and en suite bunk £27-£32pp, Twin en suites £52-£63pp, Family 3 4 & 6 en suites £72.00 - £135 /room.
- **Public Transport** - No 1 bus from Liberty Station, St Hellier to Gorey Pier or No 13 bus to Ramsons Garden centre. 5 minute walk to hostel.
- **Directions** - Follow directions to The East and then Gorey. From Gorey Pier continue up the hill past the church take the next right, JAAC is 200m on your right.

CONTACT: Anna Stammers
Tel: 00 44 1534 498636
info@jerseyhostel.co.uk   www.jerseyhostel.co.uk
La Rue de La Pouclee et Des Quatre Chemins, Faldouet, St Martins, Jersey, Channel Islands JE3 6DU

LAND'S END
HOSTEL AND B&B
ENGLAND

39

Land's End Hostel and B&B provides friendly, family run accommodation in an idyllic location. Located in the heart of Trevescan Hamlet, just a quarter of a mile from Land's End, this converted Mill Barn has views across Land's End to the Isles of Scilly. The accommodation is ideal for a self-catering holiday, with a fully equipped kitchen and the opportunity to source local food. 'Breakfast in a Basket' is available for £5 per head. The reception area has a TV/DVD and a selection of books to borrow. The hostel rooms are spacious and some private rooms are available. All the beds are dressed with duvets and bath sheet sized towels can be hired. The hostel is double glazed and centrally heated. There are 3 large bathrooms with showers, complimentary WiFi, private parking and cycle storage. Outside is a courtyard with table & chairs, and washing facilities for wet suits, surf boards and getting rid of the sand.

DETAILS

- **Open** - All year, all day
- **Number of beds** - 14: 2x2, 2x4, 1x2 super king B&B room en-suite, adjacent to hostel with breakfast bar and private alcove
- **Booking** - 50% deposit required. Please book by phone or email or online booking inquiry form.
- **Price per night** - £25 per person, per night. Use of self-catering kitchen from £5 per day. B&B en suite room from £75 per night.
- **Public Transport** - Bus stop 50 yards away, including open top tourer
- **Directions** - GR SW 355 248. Take the B3315 from the A30 Land's End for quater of a mile. The hostel is on the left.

CONTACT: Susie or David
Tel: 07519309908/07773846131
susie@landsendhostelaccommodation.co.uk www.landsendhostelaccommodation.co.uk
Mill Barn, Trevescan, Sennan, Nr Lands End, Penzance, TR19 7AQ

PENZANCE BACKPACKERS

Penzance, with its mild climate, its wonderful location looking across to spectacular St Michael's Mount, with all the coach and rail services terminating here, is the ideal base for exploring the far SW of England and the Scilly Isles.

Whether you are looking for sandy beaches and sheltered coves, the storm lashed cliffs of Land's End, sub-tropical gardens, internationally acclaimed artists, the remains of ancient cultures, or simply somewhere to relax and take time out, Penzance Backpackers is for you. Situated in a lovely tree-lined road close to the sea front, with the town centre, bus station and railway station only a short walk away. Accommodation is mostly in small bunk-bedded rooms with bed linen. Fully equipped self-catering kitchen, hot showers, comfortable lounge, lots of local information and a warm welcome all included.

DETAILS

- **Open** - All year, 10.00-12.00, 18.00-22.00
- **Number of beds** - 30: 2 double, 1x 4 (double + 2 bunks), 3x6, 1x7.
- **Booking** - It's best to email or phone.
- **Price per night** - From £16 per person.
- **Public Transport** - Penzance has a train station and National Express service. 15 mins' walk from train/bus station or catch buses 1, 1a, 5a or 6a from Tourist Information/bus/train station. Ask for top of Alexandra Road.
- **Directions** - From Tourist Information/bus/train station either follow quay and Promenade to mini-roundabout, turn right up Alexandra Rd, we are a short way up on the left; or follow main road through town centre until second mini-roundabout, turn left down Alexandra Rd; we are on right.

CONTACT: Mathew
Tel: 01736 363836
info@pzbackpack.com www.pzbackpack.com
The Blue Dolphin, Alexandra Road, Penzance, TR18 4LZ

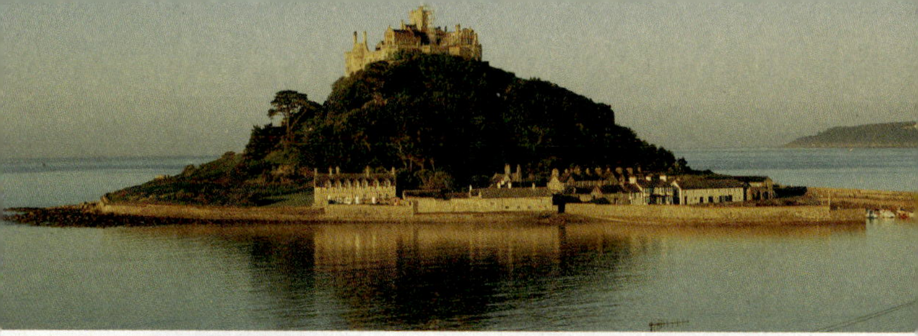

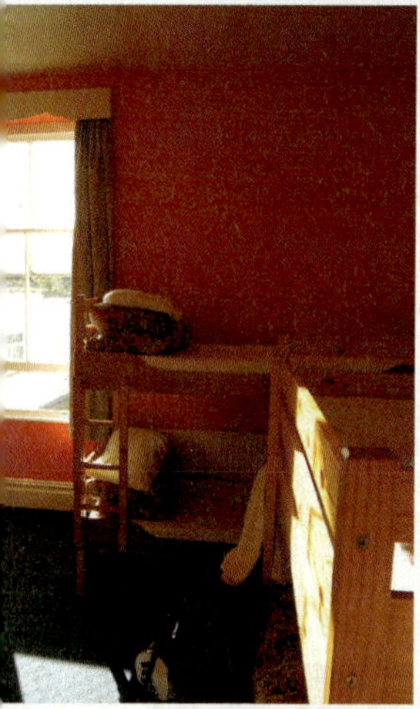

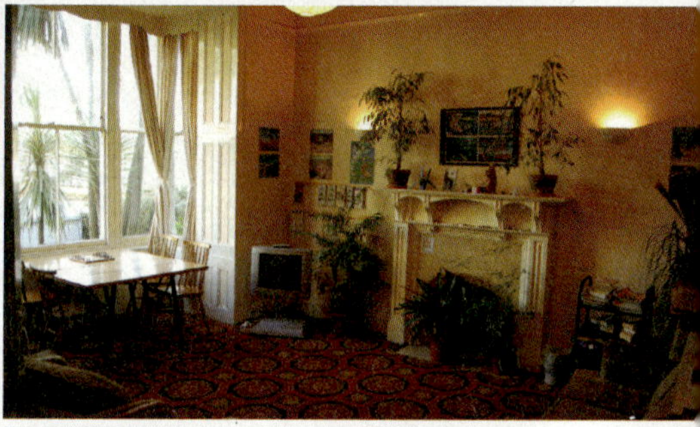

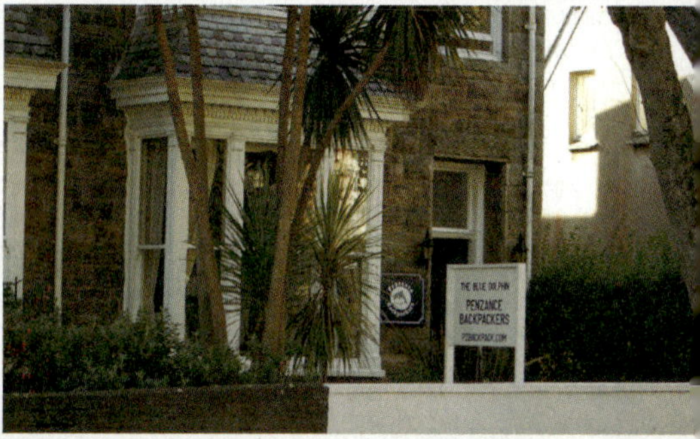
THE BLUE DOLPHIN
PENZANCE
BACKPACKERS

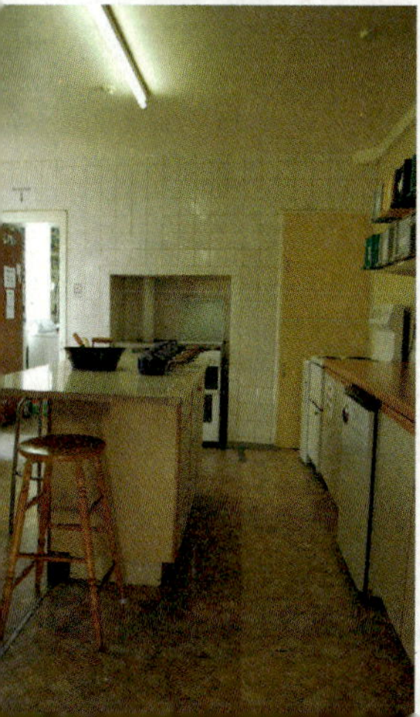

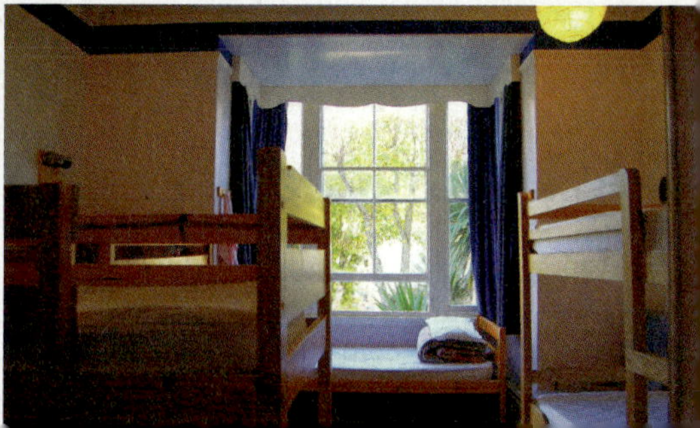

YMCA CORNWALL
PENZANCE

ENGLAND

West Cornwall is famous for its rugged coastlines, secret coves and long sandy beaches. It offers the chance to relax and unwind, to surf, walk, deep sea dive, horse ride and to visit galleries, small harbours and villages.

The YMCA is more than just a hostel, it also offers sporting and conference facilities. It is these facilities that provide the ideal location for school/youth groups of any size, for short weekends or for longer holidays. Latest improvements include free WiFi in bedrooms, and the a new coffee shop. The YMCA has been serving the community of Penwith since 1893, providing an ideal base for you to discover all the area has to offer.

Now available: Isle of Scilly parking from just £6.50 a day!!

DETAILS

- **Open** - All year, 8am to 10pm (except by prior arrangement)
- **Number of beds** - 54:
- **Booking** - booking not essential but advisable in summer
- **Price per night** - Dorm from £15.50pp, single from £23.00, twin from £40.00, family rooms from £51.30. inc. light breakfast. Discount for parties of 15+.
- **Public Transport** - Penzance train station 15 min walk. Penzance bus station bus service numbers 6A and 6B. Taxi from Penzance centre approx £3.
- **Directions** - From the train / bus stations, turn left towards the centre of town onto Market Jew Street. Turn left and follow Market Jew Street until it becomes Alverton Road. Go straight over the roundabout until you see our sign on the left (approx 200m).

CONTACT: Reception Team
Tel: 01736 334820
penzanceadmin@ymcacornwall.org.uk   www.ymcacornwall.org.uk
International House, The Orchard, Alverton, Penzance, TR18 4TE

LOWER PENDERLEATH [43]
ST IVES FARM HOSTEL ENGLAND

Just three miles from St Ives' beaches and 5 miles from Penzance, Lower Penderleath Farm Hostel near St Ives provides self-catering accommodation in four twin rooms, one room with an alpine dormitory for 12 (large room with mattresses) and a family maisonette. All rooms are private and lockable, three rooms have twin beds and the fourth has a bunk bed. No bedding is provided. The hostel has a fully equipped kitchen. A dining room adjoins the kitchen and there are plenty of showers and toilets. Heating is by oil filled towel radiators and drying racks are provided. The self contained family maisonette has a small kitchen and private shower and toilet. The water on site is natural mineral water sold as bottled mineral water in 1989 and now visitors can cook, drink and shower in it. A picturesque footpath leads to the village of Cripples Ease just ten minutes' walk away where there is a pub that serves meals. The village of Halsetown, with its own pub, is also in walking distance.

DETAILS

- **Open** - Easter to Oct incl, Open all day. Leave by 11am arrive between 2pm-8pm.
- **Number of beds** - 24: 4x2, alpine platform of 12, 1x4 self contained maisonette
- **Booking** - Please book by email. Pay on arrival. Office open from 8.30am-9pm.
- **Price per night** - £17pp. £34 twin room. £80 maisonette. 0-2years half price, bring your own cot. 2yrs+ full price One person per bed. Bring your sleeping bag and pillow
- **Public Transport** - Local busses pass the road end three quarters of a mile from the hostel. Service runs four times a day between St Ives and Penzance.
- **Directions** - Pass Penderleath camping park on left and 300m further on right hand side you will find Lower Penderleath Farm and Hostel.

CONTACT: Russell Rogers
Tel: 0772 3014567
rusrogers@hotmail.com www.stivescampingandhostel.com
Lower Penderleath Farm, Towednack, St.Ives, Cornwall, TR26 3AF

FALMOUTH BACKPACKERS

ENGLAND — 44

Falmouth's beautiful natural harbour provides a picturesque background to the main street of charming shops, restaurants, cafés and pubs. Voted the 2nd best coastal town, Falmouth is renowned for its sandy beaches, Pendennis Castle, exotic gardens, Arts Centre and the Princess Pavilion. Go sightseeing on ferries to St Mawes, Truro, Flushing and the Helford Passage. On a rainy day visit National Maritime Museum and the Ships and Castle leisure pool. Take advantage of watersports, fishing trips, sailing, diving, with tuition and equipment hire. New owner Judi has moved back from Grenada in the West Indies, to take over Falmouth Lodge. Judi welcomes guests to enjoy all Cornwall has to offer and has added her own character and flavour to the hostel. Relaxed, friendly and clean, Falmouth Lodge Backpackers is just two minutes' walk from the Blue Flag beach of Gyllyngvase and the South West Coast Path and eight minutes' walk into town and the harbour. Free WiFi and internet facilities. Free parking. No curfew. Complimentary tea, coffee and breakfast. Well-equipped kitchen and cosy lounge with TV/DVD and games.

DETAILS

- **Open** - All year, 9am to 12 noon and 5pm to 10pm
- **Number of beds** - 28: 2 x 2/3, 3 x 4/5, 1 x 6/7, 1 double en suite (some seaviews)
- **Booking** - Telephone or email in advance. Walk-ins also welcomed.
- **Price per night** - From £19 per person
- **Public Transport** - Train - change at Truro for Falmouth town station 250 mtrs. National Express to Falmouth. By air - London Stansted/Gatwick to Newquay
- **Directions** - On A39 look for Gyllyngvase Rd on right, then left to Gyllyngvase Ter.

CONTACT: Judi
Tel: 01326 319996, mobile 07525 722808, Fax: 0132631999
judi@falmouthlodge.co.uk www.falmouthbackpackers.co.uk
9 Gyllyngvase Terrace, Falmouth, Cornwall, TR11 4DL

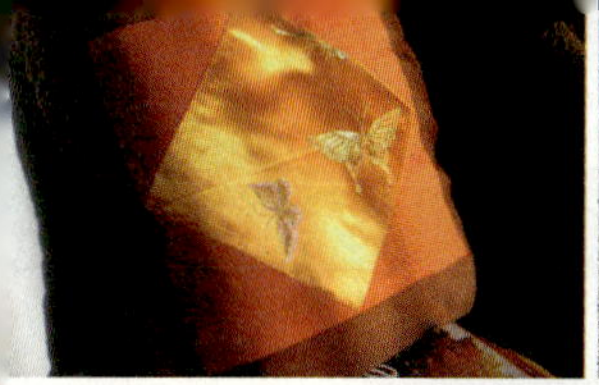
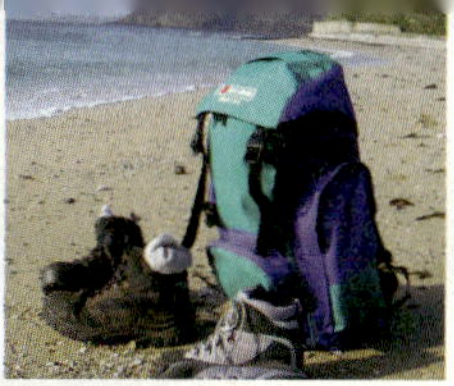
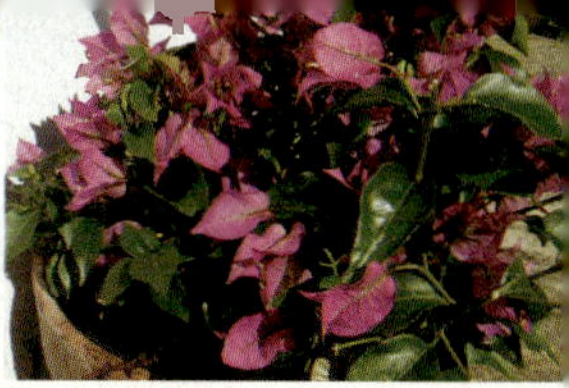
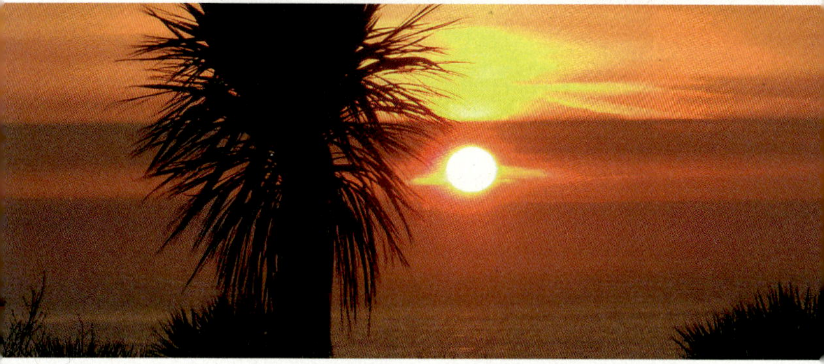
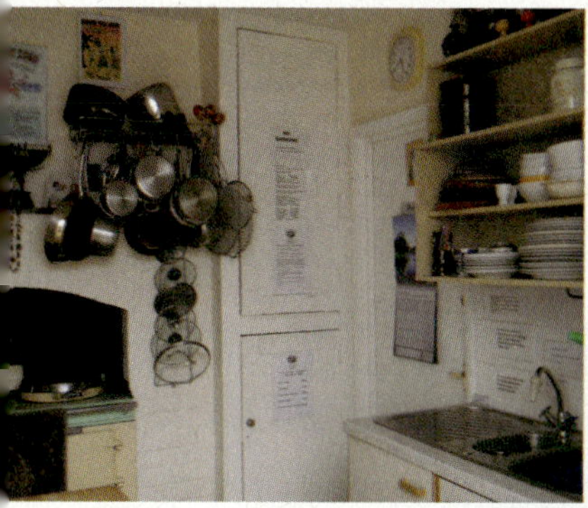
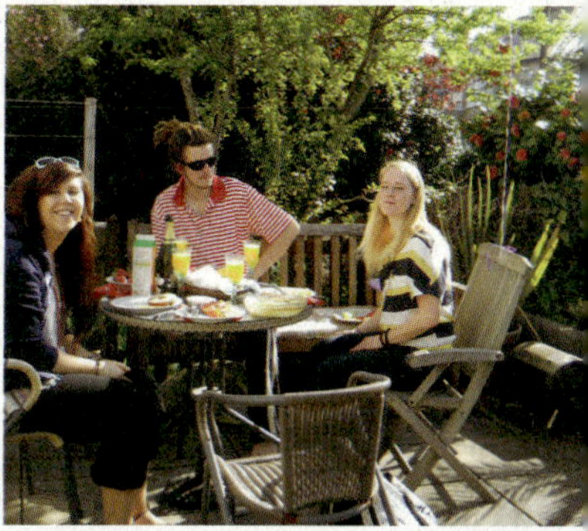
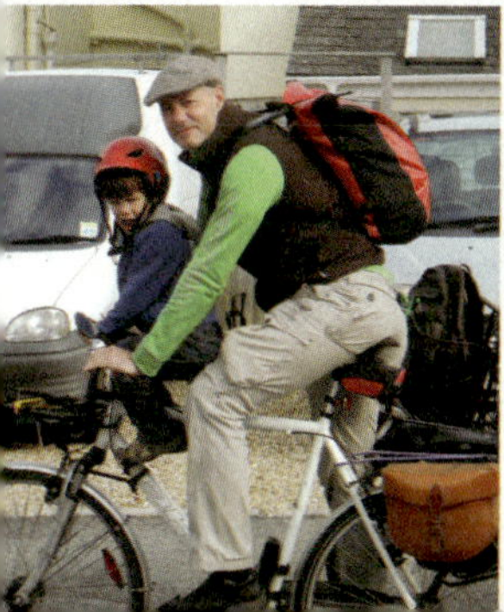
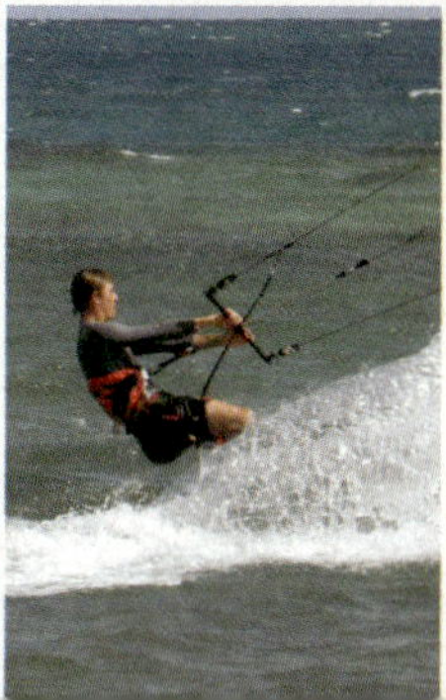
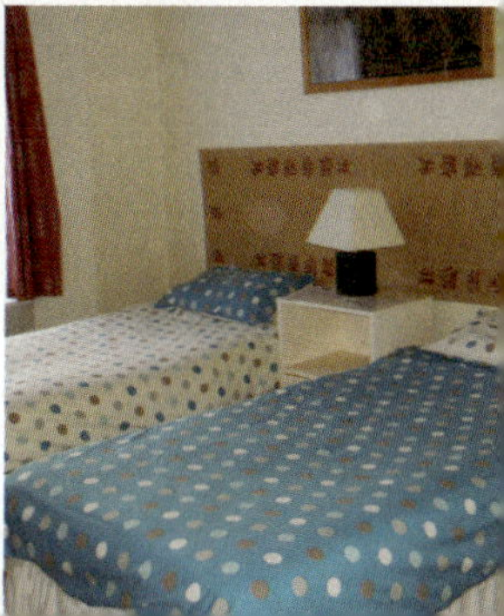

… ENGLAND

TREGEDNA LODGE

Tregedna Lodge offers comfortable, spacious accommodation. The Lodge has been converted to a high standard, yet keeping much of its originial charm and character. There are 24 bedspaces in a range of five bedrooms - single occupancy or shared. You can book a little space or the whole lot. All the facilities have disabled access and include; a shared, fully equipped kitchen and open dining area, a relaxing lounge with comfy chairs, laundry room with coin operated washer/dryer, separate showers and toilets. Bed linen is provided and towels are available to hire. There is ample parking for cars and boats and a secure area for bikes etc. The South West Coastal footpath is adjacent for walks with spectacular views and Maenporth beach, only half a mile away, offers a safe, clean, sandy beach. Nearby Falmouth has a wide range of restaurants, pubs, places of interest. Ideally located to explore the many delights of Cornwall, Tregedna Lodge has a 4-star grading by VisitEngland.

DETAILS

- **Open** - All year, all day (please phone between 9am-8pm)
- **Number of beds** - 24: 1x8, 1x6, 1x2, 2x4 / family (double bed and bunk bed)
- **Booking** - Booking essential. 25% deposit.
- **Price per night** - £20pp in dormitory style rooms, Family rooms £50. Enquire for group rates.
- **Public Transport** - Trains at Falmouth (1.5 miles). Buses run past Tregedna hourly during summer months, less frequently during winter months.
- **Directions** - By car from Truro take the A39 to Falmouth. At the ASDA roundabout go straight across. At the Hillhead roundabout turn right, go straight over the next two roundabouts and continue on this road for approx 2 miles. Tregedna is on your right.

CONTACT: Liz
Tel: 01326 250529 / 07979645946
tregednafarm@btinternet.com www.tregednafarmholidays.co.uk/lodge.html
Tregedna Farm, Maenporth, Falmouth, Cornwall, TR11 5HL

HARFORD
BUNKHOUSE & CAMPING ENGLAND

Harford Bunkhouse & Camping offers comfortable budget accommodation on the edge of South Dartmoor. An ideal choice if you are planning to start the Two Moors Way walk from south to north.

Run alongside a working Dartmoor farm, the bunkhouse offers dormitory style accommodation with bunk beds in each of the rooms. A kitchen, large seating area, toilets and showers are all within the bunkhouse.

The camp site is divided between two of the farms meadows. Campers can use the toilets and showers located within the bunkhouse buildings. Facilities include a wash up area, drying room, laundry facilities and disabled access. There are also two camping pods and a cabin in the meadows. These sleep up to 6 people each and have the same facilities as camping. Small campfires and BBQs are allowed at the farm's discretion. Children and dogs welcome.

DETAILS

- **Open** - All year, Open all hours
- **Number of beds** - 40-50 beds
- **Booking** - Phone or email.
- **Price per night** - From £15pp. Camping pods and cabin £50 each.
- **Public Transport** - Yes, train or bus nearby
- **Directions** - From Ivybridge take Harford Road. Bunkhouse is 1.5 miles from Ivybridge in The Dartmoor National Park.

CONTACT: Julie Cole
Tel: 01752691883 or 07968566218
julie.cole6@btinternet.com www.harfordbunkhouse.com
West Combeshead, Harford, Ivybridge, Devon, PL21 0JG

PLYMOUTH
GLOBE BACKPACKERS

ENGLAND

Globe Backpackers Plymouth is located just five minutes' walk from the ferry port where boats leave for Roscoff and Santander. The hostel is close to all amenities and a short stroll to the famous Barbican waterfront, Mayflower Steps and city centre. Also near to the bus and railway stations. Excursions to Dartmoor, canoeing on the Tamar River, local boat trips, sailing and walking the coastal paths can be arranged from Plymouth. The theatre, sports/leisure centre, ice-skating rink and National Aquarium are a short walk from the hostel. Globe Backpackers Plymouth has 4, 6 and 8 bed dorms, plus 2 double rooms. Bedding and linen are included in the price. Fully equipped self-catering kitchen, TV lounge, separate social room and courtyard garden. Free WiFi. Free tea and coffee. Brits and overseas visitors all need to produce valid ID.

DETAILS

- **Open** - All year (Christmas stays available by special arrangement), daily check ins from 3.30-11pm only. No curfew.
- **Number of beds** - 38
- **Booking** - Please phone ahead to make a secure booking.
- **Price per night** - Dorms: From £16.50pppn. Weekly rates available. Private rooms from £38. There is a 50p surcharge for debit/credit card payments.
- **Public Transport** - National Express, local buses and various rail networks.
- **Directions** - From train station walk up Saltash Road to North Croft roundabout, turn right along Western Approach to Pavilions on your left. From bus station walk up Exeter Street, across roundabout to Royal Parade, cross road to Union Street, Pavilions on your left. From Plymouth Pavilions walk towards the Hoe, turn left up Citadel Road, the hostel is in 100 metres on the right hand side.

CONTACT:
Tel: 01752 225158
info@plymouthbackpackers.co.uk www.plymouthbackpackers.co.uk
172 Citadel Road, The Hoe, Plymouth, PL1 3BD

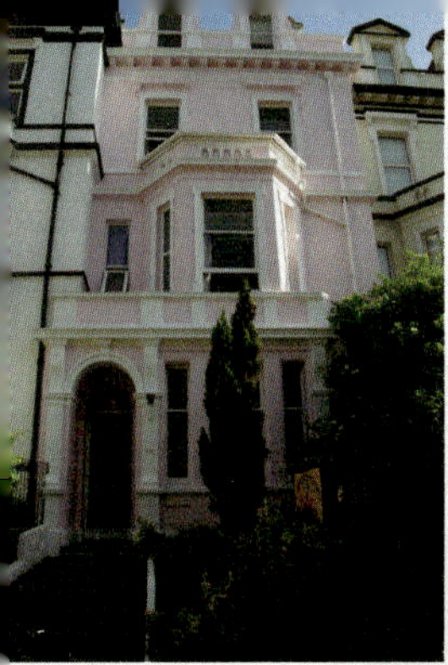

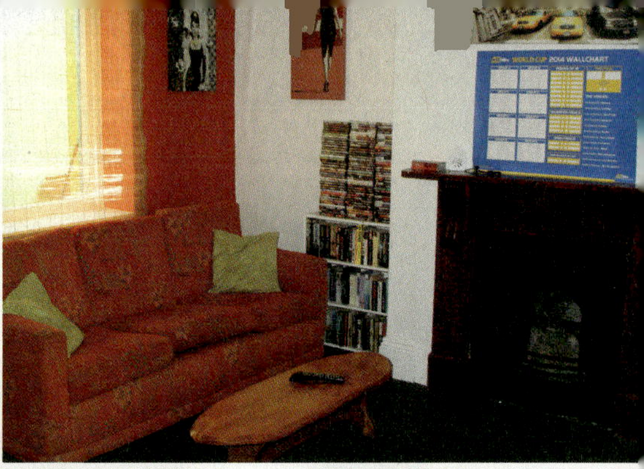
WORLD CUP 2014 WALLCHART

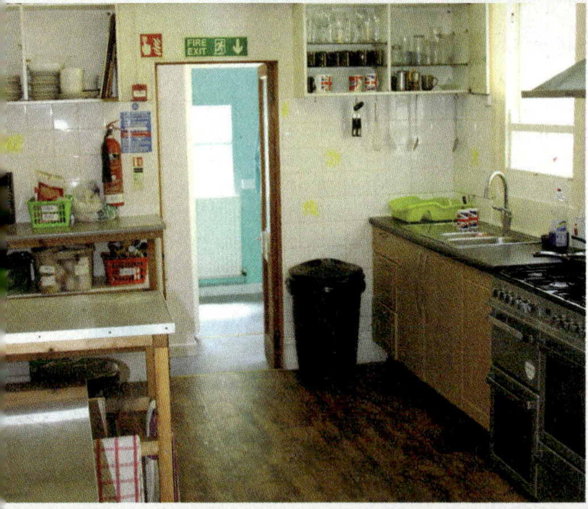
FIRE EXIT

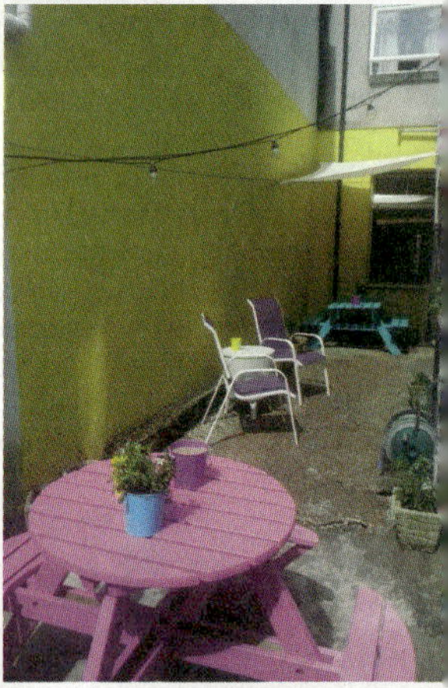

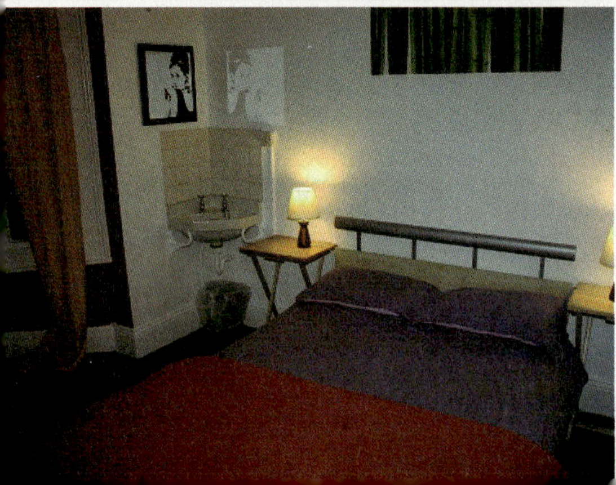

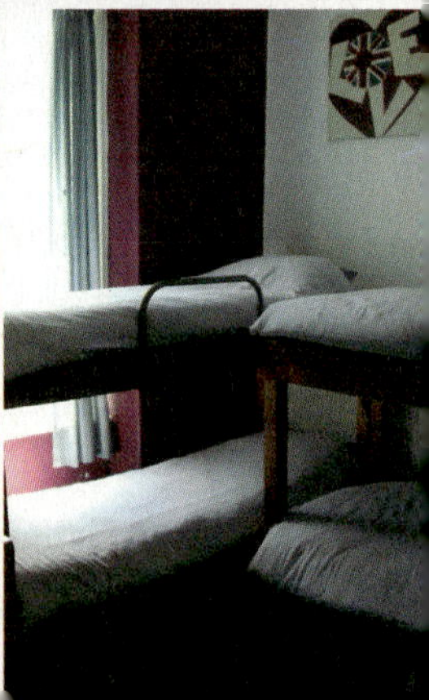

DARTMOOR EXPEDITION CENTRE

ENGLAND

Great for walking, climbing, canoeing, caving, archaeology, painting or visiting places of interest nearby, Dartmoor Expedition Centre has two 300-year-old barn bunkhouses with cobbled floors and thick granite walls. Simple but comfortable accommodation for groups, with bunk beds and a wood burning stove, radiant heaters (two in each area) and night storage heating (one in each barn). Kitchen area equipped with 2 fridges, water heater, electric stoves and kettles. All crockery and pans provided, and there is freezer space available. Electric appliances are coin operated (£1 coins). Solar hot water system for free showers in wash rooms. House Barn has the living area downstairs and upstairs sleeps 9 plus 5 in an inner cubicle. Gate Barn sleeps 11 downstairs and 10 upstairs. There are three upgraded rooms (2 double, 1 twin). Beds provided with sheet/pillow/pillowcase, sleeping bags needed.

DETAILS

- **Open** - All year, 7.30 am to 10.30 pm
- **Number of beds** - 39; 1 x 1, 2 x 2, 1 x 8, 1 x 5, 1 x 11, 1 x 10
- **Booking** - Book in advance with 25% deposit.
- **Price per night** - £14.50 pp (£16.50 in upgraded room). £350 per night exclusive. Discounts for longer lets depending on numbers.
- **Public Transport** - Nearest train station Newton Abbot. Summer buses to Widecombe (1.5 miles from hostel). Taxi fare from station £30.
- **Directions** - GR 700 764. Come down Widecombe Hill into the village. Turn right 200yds after school and travel up a steep hill past Southcombe onto the open moor. Continue for one mile until you reach crossroads. Turn right and take first left after 400yds. Hostel is 200yds on left.

CONTACT: John Earle
Tel: 01364 621249
johnearle@dartmoorbase.co.uk www.dartmoorbase.co.uk
Widecombe-in-the-Moor, Newton Abbot, Devon, TQ13 7TX

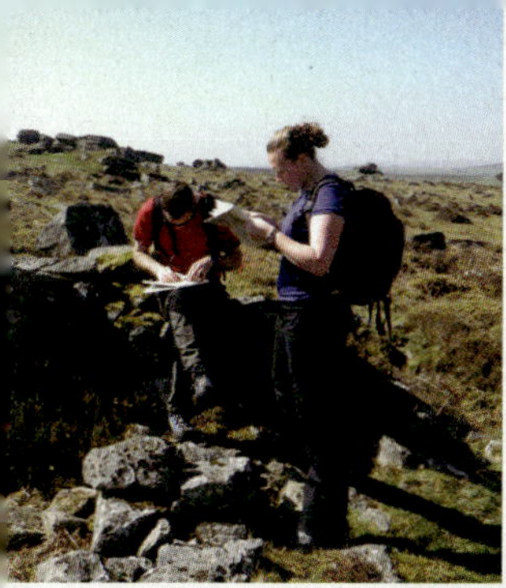
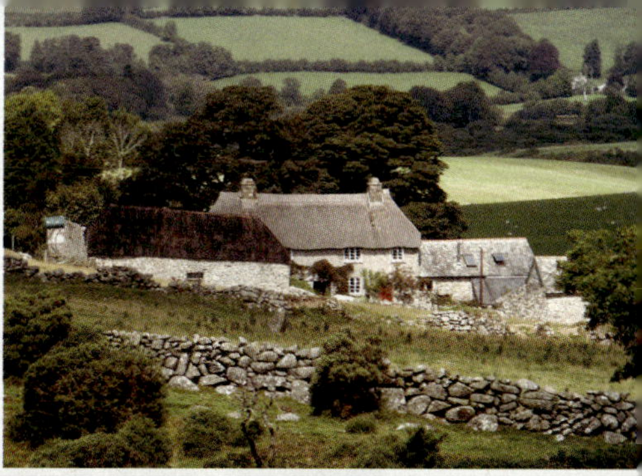
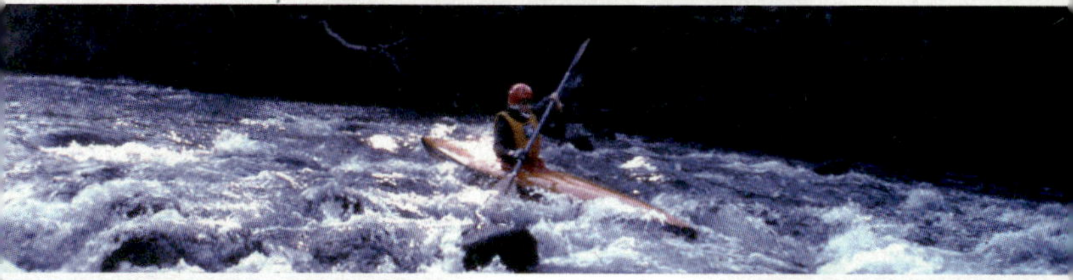
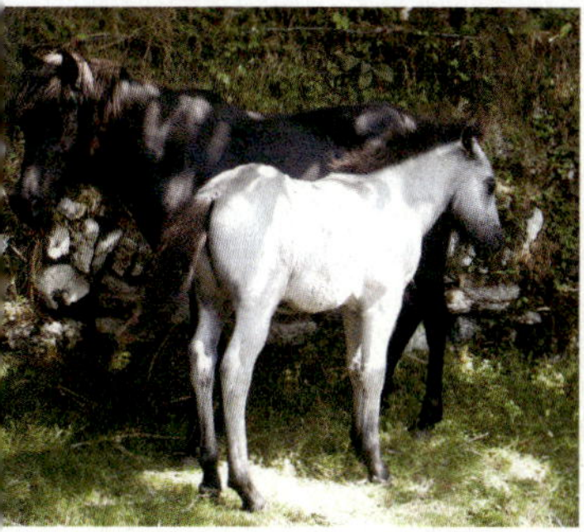
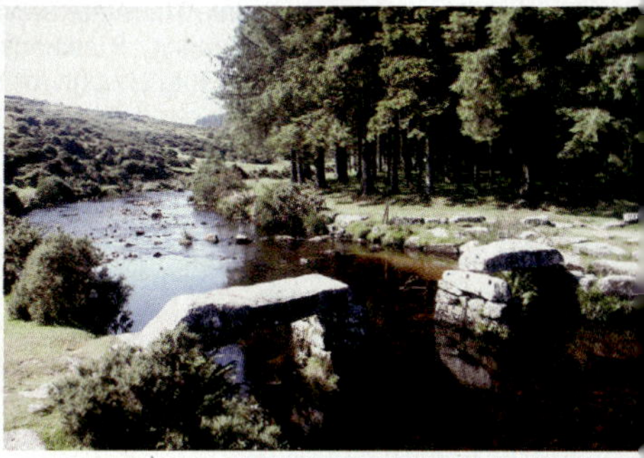
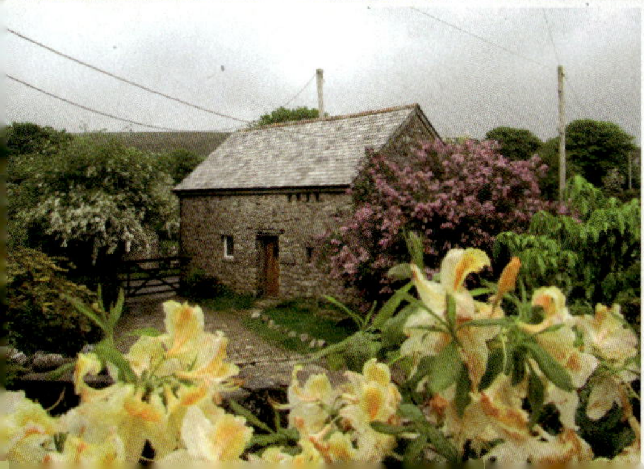
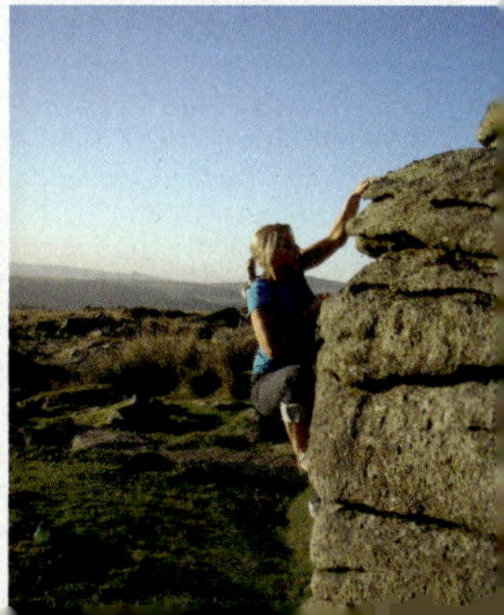

FOX TOR CAFÉ AND BUNKHOUSE

ENGLAND

Princetown in Dartmoor is an ideal base for anyone wishing to spend time on Dartmoor whether it is to walk, climb, cycle, kayak or just relax and enjoy the spectacular scenery. Fox Tor Café Bunkhouse is situated near the centre of the village and offers self-catering accommodation for up to 12, in 3 rooms of 4. It is newly decorated, has central heating and a kitchen equipped with microwave, fridge, kettle, toaster and sink. There are separate male and female showers and toilets with under-floor heating. Bunkhouse guests have the option to use the drying room / store room (big enough for bicycles) and can book packed lunches and breakfasts for an early start. The café has a wood burning stove and hosts seasonal events and activities such as Christmas wreath making. Guided walks and off road mountain biking are available and outdoor adventure holidays can be arranged to your requirements. WiFi and cycle hire now available. Contact Abbi or Dave for more details

DETAILS

- **Open** - All year, all day. Arrive from 4.30pm, leave by 10.30am.
- **Number of beds** - 12: 3 x 4
- **Booking** - Advisable with 50% deposit.
- **Price per night** - From £10.50 pp. £32.00 for 1 person in a private room. £35.00 for 2 in a private room. £38.50 for 3 in a private room. £42.00 for 4 in a private room.
- **Public Transport** - Trains at Exeter and Plymouth. Devon Bus 98 Tavistock-Princetown. Devon Bus 82 Exeter-Plymouth. First 272 Gunnislake-Newton Abbot.
- **Directions** - GR 591 735. Just off the mini roundabout in the centre of Princetown on the Two Bridges road (B3212). 20 mins' drive from Tavistock, 15 mins' Yelverton, 35 mins Ashburton.

CONTACT: Abbi or Dave
Tel: 01822 890238, Fax: 441822890238
enquiries@foxtorcafe.com www.foxtorcafe.co.uk
Two Bridges Road, Princetown, Dartmoor, Devon, PL20 6QS

GALFORD SPRINGS
HOLIDAY FARM

53

ENGLAND

Galford Springs Holiday Accommodation is situated in rural Devon on a 300 acre farm nestled in the Lew Valley, overlooking some of England's most stunning scenery. It is ideal for families, groups, schools and clubs. Situated next to a 17th century Devon longhouse, the hostel is a recent conversion and contained within the same building is a free-to-use 15m indoor swimming pool and sauna. The main area is large and ideal for holding meetings and events as the furniture can be moved into a variety of configurations. This area also contains bunkbeds for 10 people and two single beds. In addition there are three en suite double bedrooms two of which also have a single bed in them. The hostel features all modern conveniences including a pool table, table tennis and skittle alley. Outside there is a basket ball and barbeque area. Hostel breakfasts available by arrangement. Farmhouse B&B also available with double en suite rooms.

DETAILS

- **Open** - All year,
- **Number of beds** - 16: 1x12, 2x3 (family room en-suite), 2x2 (double en-suite)
- **Booking** - Recommended
- **Price per night** - £20 pp. Minimum of £120 (6 persons or more). B&B £30pp.
- **Public Transport** - Bus route to Lewdown village which is about one and half miles from accommodation on the old A30.
- **Directions** - Turn left off A30 at Sourton Services. Turn right at end of slip road then immediately left towards Lewdown. Follow for 6 miles then turn left, signposted Chillaton. After reaching Lewtrenchard Manor, turn left and further down the road take the right turn to Lew Mill. Turn left at T junction, Galford Springs is on the right.

CONTACT: Mr F. Harding
Tel: 01566 783264
claire_taylor1@btconnect.com www.galfordsprings.co.uk
Galford Farm, Lewdown, Okehampton, Devon, EX20 4PL

SPARROWHAWK BACKPACKERS

ENGLAND — 54

Sparrowhawk is a small, friendly eco-hostel in the centre of Morehampstead, popular with cyclists, hikers, bikers, artists and photographers, located within the breathtaking Dartmoor National Park. Moretonhampstead is 14 miles west of Exeter and can be reached easily by frequent direct bus. Accommodation is in a beautifully converted, fully equipped stable, with solar-heated showers and a secure bike shed. High open moorland is close by for great hiking, cycling and off-road mountain biking, while the rocky tors rising up on the hilltops offer climbers a challenge. Wild swims in the rivers amongst woodlands or out on the moor are a must for the adventurous traveller. Magnificent stone circles, dwellings and burial sites of ancient civilizations together with wild ponies, buzzards, flora and fauna are all here to be explored. Moretonhampstead has shops, cafés, art gallery/studios and pubs serving good food/ beer/ music/ cabaret/comedy nights. CTC/ Cicerone LeJoG cycle routes are on the doorstep.

DETAILS

- **Open** - All year, all day
- **Number of beds** - 18: 1 x 14 plus double / family room
- **Booking** - Book ahead if possible by phone or email.
- **Price per night** - Adults £17. Under 14 £8. Double/family room £38/ £8 per child.
- **Public Transport** - Direct from Exeter Bus 359, indirect 178. From Okehampton or Newton Abbot Bus 173 or 179. Enquires Tel 0870 6082608.
- **Directions** - From Exeter, take the B3212 signposted on the one-way system at Exe Bridges. From Plymouth head towards Yelverton and then B3212. The hostel is on Ford Street (A382) 100 metres from tourist office.

CONTACT: Alison
Tel: 01647 440318 - 07870 513570
ali@sparrowhawkbackpackers.co.uk www.sparrowhawkbackpackers.co.uk
45 Ford Street, Moretonhampstead, Dartmoor, Devon, TQ13 8LN

BLYTHESWOOD
HOSTEL
ENGLAND

Blytheswood Hostel is a detached wooden chalet in secluded woodland overlooking the Teign Valley on the eastern edge of Dartmoor. It is an ideal base for exploring rugged high Dartmoor and the delightful lower slopes rich in wild flowers, butterflies and birds. The surrounding native woodland and nature reserve are home to badgers, deer and otters. There are walks straight from the door (come and see the daffodils in spring) and fishing, golf and cycling nearby. Local attractions include Castle Drogo, The Miniature Pony Centre, Canonteign Falls and picturesque thatched villages. The cathedral city of Exeter is 8 miles away and the beaches of South Devon are 40 minutes' drive. Blytheswood Hostel provides flexible accommodation in cosy rooms sleeping between 2 and 8 people in bunks. It is ideal for use by families and groups who can book sole use of the whole hostel. There is a fully equipped self-catering kitchen, lounge/dining room, drying room and picnic areas. Duvets and linen provided.

DETAILS

- **Open** - All year, reception open 8-10.30am and 5-8pm (hostel is closed between 10.30am and 5pm, unless arranged).
- **Number of beds** - 24: 1x2, 2x4, 1x6, 1x8
- **Booking** - Booking is essential. Deposit required.
- **Price per night** - £14pp. Children under 18 £8. Whole hostel £200 per night.
- **Public Transport** - Trains Exeter. Bus 359 from Exeter + 82 on summer wknds
- **Directions** - On the B3212 between Exeter and Moretonhampstead, 1mile outside Dunsford. Approx 100m from Steps Bridge, opposite car park. Please use car park when staying at the hostel.

CONTACT: Patrick and Tracey
Tel: 01647 252435
blytheswood@blueyonder.co.uk www.blytheswood.co.uk
Steps Bridge, Dunsford, Exeter, Devon, EX6 7EQ

EXETER GLOBE BACKPACKERS
ENGLAND

A city centre hostel within easy walk of the beautiful old port, cathedral, shopping district and a wonderful mix of pubs, clubs, live music, restaurants and café scene. Great for the young and "young at heart" who enjoy a vibrant city centre. Twenty minutes drive to Exmouth with its 2 mile sandy beach for all sail sports, and the same to Dartmoor National Park for walking, climbing, cycling and horse riding. Exeter is an excellent place to find work and is just 2½ hours by train to London. In addition to male, female and mixed dorms there are new private rooms and three large double rooms with additional bunks, sitting area, tea/coffee making facilities, hair dryer and towels. One of these can be used as a twin room and another has a four poster bed. The new 5 star wet rooms are going down a treat! Free WiFi for guests with devices. Not suitable for hen and stag groups, DSS, unaccompanied under 18s and families. ID required from all.

DETAILS

- **Open** - All year (Christmas stays available by special arrangement). Check in 3.30pm-11pm only, closed 12-3.30pm, check out 8.30 -11am, earlier by arrangement.
- **Number of beds** - 46-52: 1x10, 3x8, 1x6, 3x4 (can also be used as dbl or twin)
- **Booking** - To secure a booking please phone ahead.
- **Price per night** - Dorms from £17.50pp or £75pp per week. Private rooms from £45 for two people, £75 for four people. 50p for card payments. £5 key deposit.
- **Public Transport** - National Express, local bus companies and rail networks.
- **Directions** - Bus station: over main road, take first turning on left "Southernhay East". Stay on LHS walk until you reach the Southgate Hotel. Hostel is diagonally opposite. From Central Station: take Queen St to High St, turn right then, at 1st lights turn left South St. Continue to large junction at bottom of hill. Cross at lights.

CONTACT: Duty Manager
Tel: 01392 215521, Fax:
info@exeterbackpackers.co.uk www.exeterbackpackers.co.uk
71 Holloway Street, Exeter, EX2 4JD

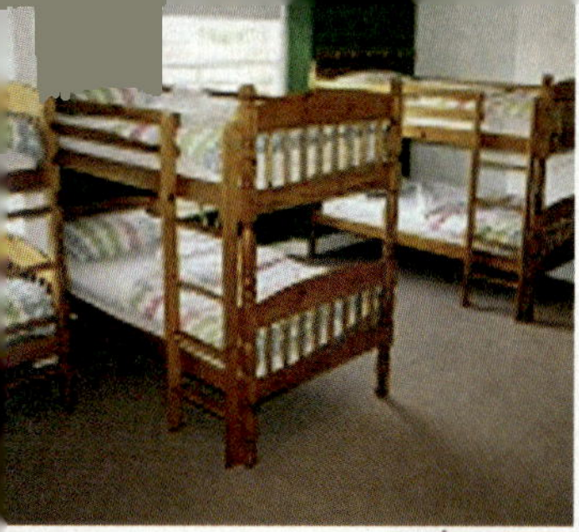
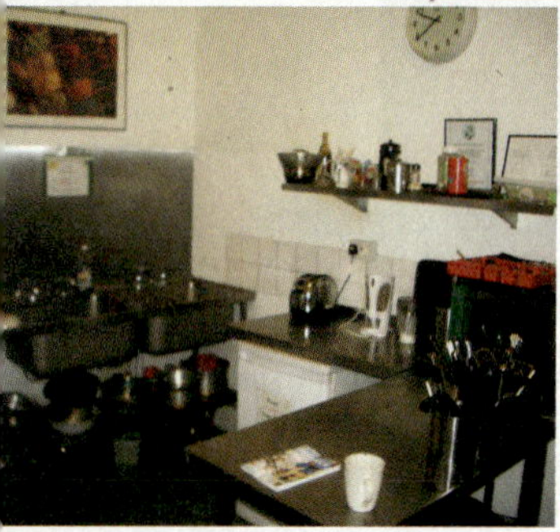
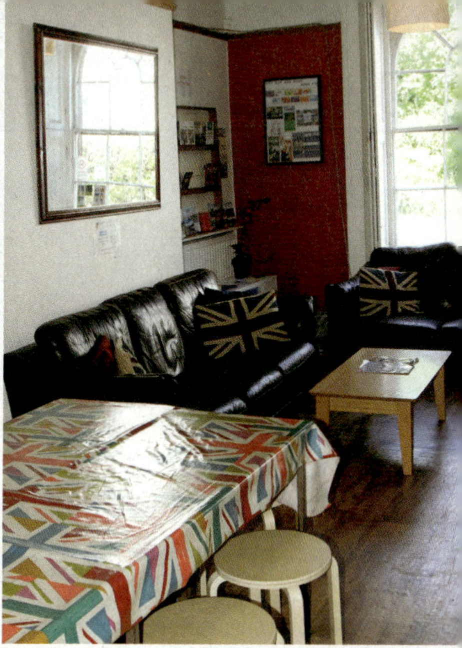
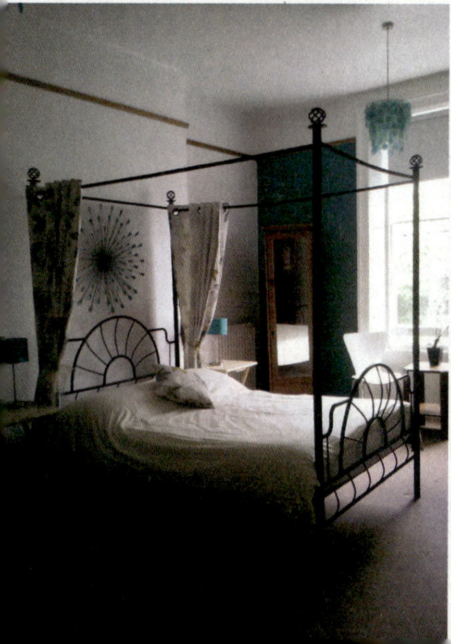
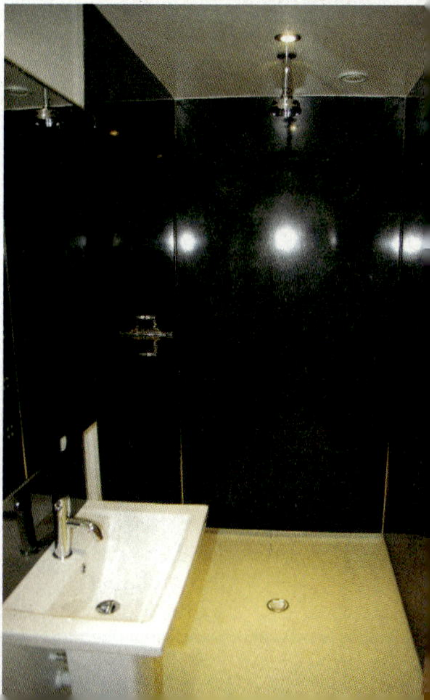

NORTHSHOREBUDE
ENGLAND

A relaxed place with a variety of bedrooms and large garden.

Close to town, beaches and South West Coastal Path.

No stag groups please. An ideal base to see the South West's attractions: The Eden Project, Tintagel Castle, The Tamar Lakes, Dartmoor and Bodmin Moor. There are competition standard surfing beaches nearby. Families with children aged over 5 welcome. Meet old friends or make new ones, on the deck, in the lounge or around the dining room table after cooking up a storm in the fully fitted kitchen. You can make your stay whatever you want it to be.

DETAILS

- **Open** - All year except Christmas week, 8.30am to 1pm and 4.30pm to 10.30pm
- **Number of beds** - 39: 2x6, 4x4, 1x3, 1x2, 3xdbl
- **Booking** - Advisable, credit card secures booking. Photo ID at check in. (Groups 6 or more by prior booking) No stag groups. At least one adult (18+) per booking.
- **Price per night** - From £16pp dorm rooms (single night supplement)
- **Public Transport** - To Bude: From Exeter via Okehampton buses X9, 599. From Newquay X10 (changing at Okehampton). From Bideford 85.
All buses- First Bus Company. There are train and bus links from London to Exeter.
- **Directions** - From A39, head into Bude down Stratton Rd past Morrisons on your right, follow the road down past Esso garage. Take the second road on the right, Killerton Road (before the Bencollen Pub). Continue up to the top of the road and Northshorebude is on the corner on your left. Turn into Redwood Grove and parking is the first on the left.

CONTACT: Sean or Janine
Tel: 01288 354256 or 07970 149486, Fax: 441288308776
northshorebude@uk2.net www.northshorebude.com
57 Killerton Road, Bude, Cornwall, EX23 8EW

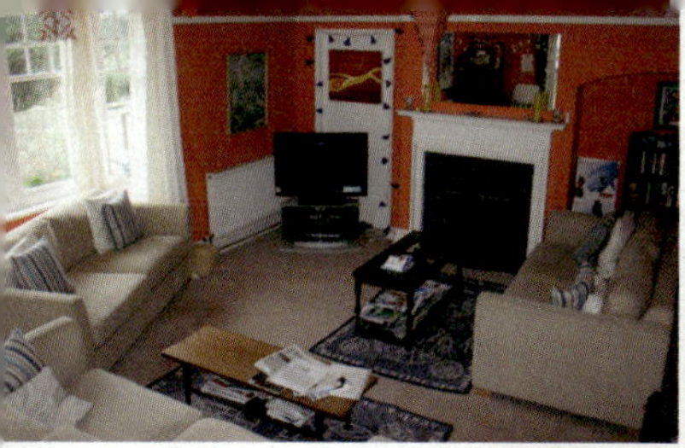
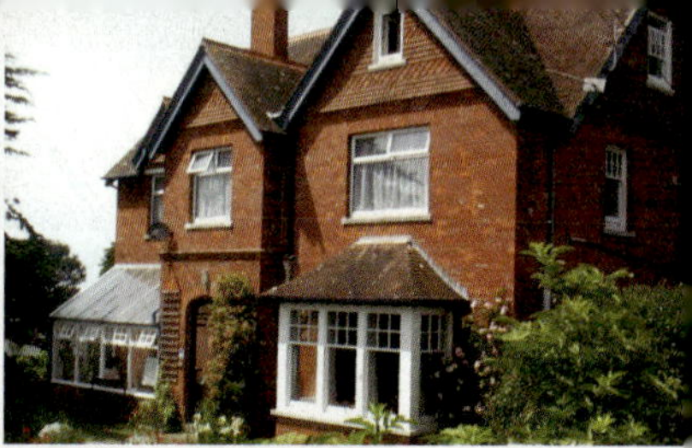
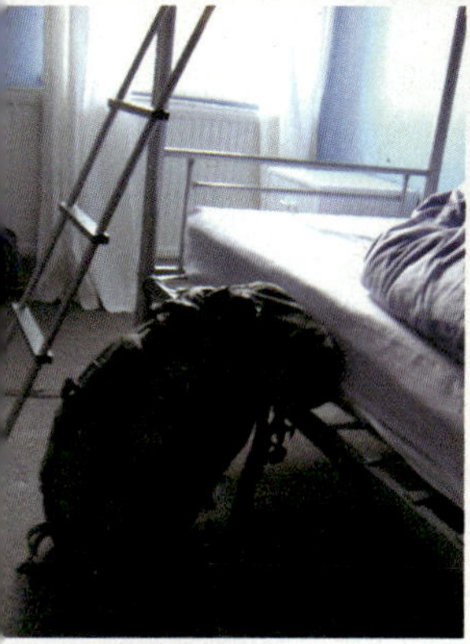
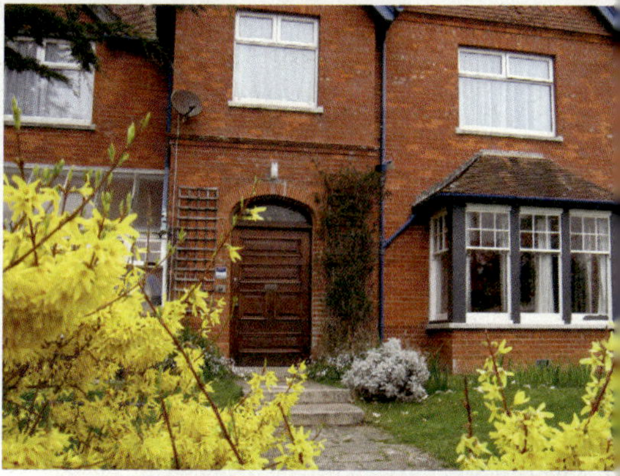
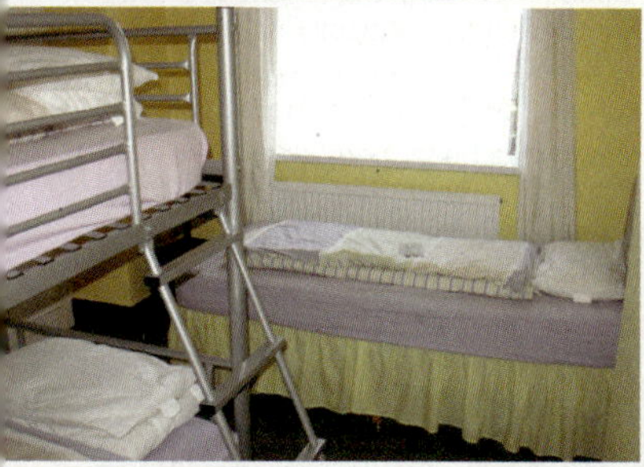
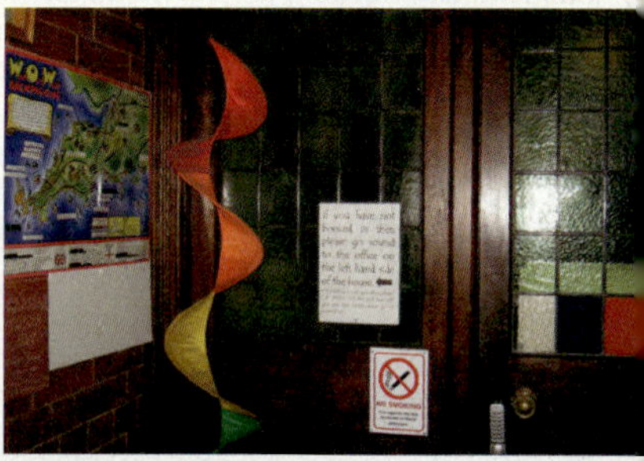
W.O.W.
NO SMOKING
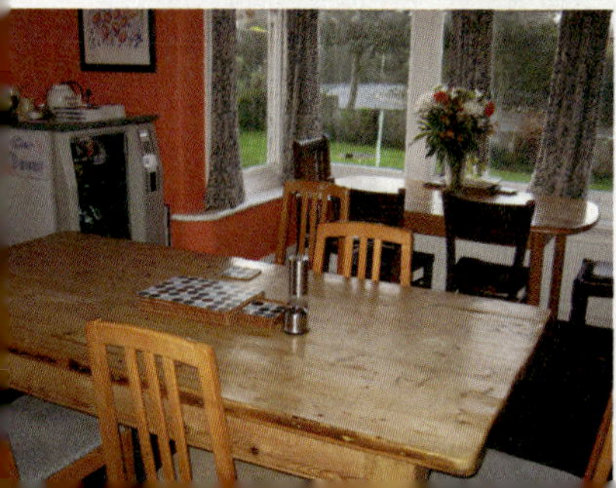
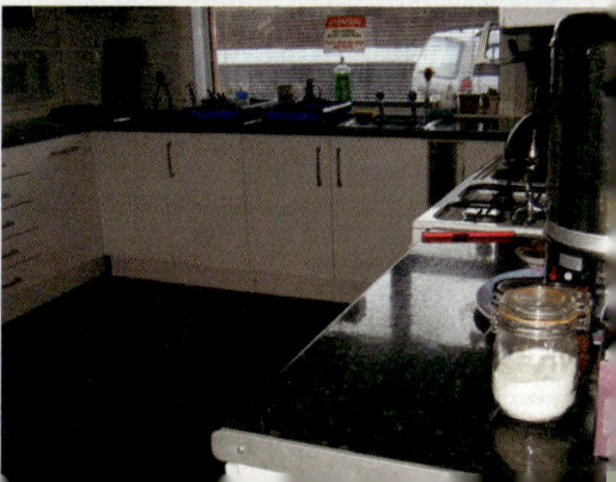

ELMSCOTT HOSTEL

ENGLAND

Elmscott, a former Victorian school, offers a next-to-nature retreat, surrounded by unspoilt coastline with sea views of Lundy Island.

Great for walking, cycling, surfing and bird watching, there are amazing rock formations and many quiet lanes to explore. The famous fishing village of Clovelly is a few miles away with its cobbled streets and pretty harbour. Also nearby is Hartland Abbey where Sense and Sensibility was filmed. Elmscott is a few minutes' walk from the South West Coast Path which passes many spectacular coves and river mouths. The accommodation is in one unit of 20 beds and another of 12. It has mixed dorms, single sex dorms and private rooms. In winter accommodation is only available for groups (up to 35 people). There is a kitchen, a well stocked shop in summer and a games room close by.

DETAILS

- **Open** - All year (winter for groups only), hostel opens each afternoon at 5pm.
- **Number of beds** - 32 (35 in winter): 1 unit of 20: 2x6, 2x4; 1 unit of 12: 1x6, 1x4, 1x2. Extra 3 bed room available for sole use bookings in winter.
- **Booking** - In summer book direct with the hostel by phone or email. In winter book via the YHA website, or for last minute sole use bookings call the owners.
- **Price per night** - Adult £16 to £20, under 18s £13 to £16 (discounts for YHA members). Enquire for special prices for groups or longer stays.
- **Public Transport** - Nearest trains Barnstaple (25 miles). Buses from Barnstaple to Hartland (4 miles from hostel). Phone hostel for taxi service.
- **Directions** - The hostel is in the small hamlet of Elmscott 4 miles from the village of Hartland. Grid Ref 231 217.

CONTACT: John & Thirza Goaman
Tel: Hostel 01237 441367/ House 01237 441276, Fax: 01237 441076
john.goa@virgin.net www.elmscott.org.uk
Elmscott, Hartland, Bideford, Devon, EX39 6ES

MULLACOTT FARM
CAMPING BARN
ENGLAND

61

Set in 30 acres on the coastal preservation area of North Devon, the farm boasts sea views overlooking Woolacombe, Lundy Island, Lee Bay, Ilfracombe, and the welsh coast on a clear day. The camping barn is a former stable block with all accommodation on ground level with raised sleeping areas. Each platform has mattresses at no extra charge, bring your own sleeping bag or bedding as well as warm clothing. There are air curtain heaters throughout the barn. Accommodation includes a dining area and well-fitted kitchen with electric full-size oven, hob, fridge-freezer, microwave, toaster, kettle, sinks with hot water from a water heater (all coin-operated) and basic cooking equipment and cutlery. A tumble dryer has also recently been added. Candles are NOT allowed, as they are a fire risk. A picnic and BBQ area are adjacent and a toilet block with ladies and gents toilets and electric shower (coin-operated) is a few steps away; as is a covered storage area for rucksacks, cycles, surfboards etc. Sorry no stag/hen groups. Mullacott Farm also provides B&B, camping and static caravan accommodation.

DETAILS

- **Open** - All Year, all day
- **Number of beds** - 20
- **Booking** - By phone or email
- **Price per night** - Barn: £7.50 per person per night. Sole use: by arrangement
- **Public Transport** - Train to Barnstable, No 21 bus to Mullacott Cross 300m walk.
- **Directions** - A361 towards Ilfracombe. 300m from Mullacott Cross turn left into Mullacott Farm drive. Follow the signs, up to the farmhouse on the rhs.

CONTACT: Alison and Adrian Homa
Tel: 01271 866877
relax@mullacottfarm.co.uk www.mullacottfarm.co.uk
Ilfracombe, Devon, EX34 8NA

…

OCEAN BACKPACKERS

ENGLAND

Ocean Backpackers is situated close to Ilfracombe's picturesque harbour. This cool, clean and friendly hostel offers excellent facilities for walkers, cyclists, surfers, divers as well as families, schools and activity groups. Facilities include a self-catering kitchen, dining area, communal lounge with free internet/WiFi, large storage basement, patio area and free car park. Nestled in an area of Outstanding Natural Beauty, Ilfracombe has many shops, galleries, pubs and restaurants. The harbour became home to Damien Hirst's statue "Verity" in 2012 and is fastly becoming an "arts destination." Ilfracombe is the start of the Route 27 Coast-to-coast ride to Plymouth and the South West Coast Path provides wonderful walks with stunning scenery that take your breath away! It is just a short drive to the sandy surf beaches of Woolacombe, Croyde and Saunton and the spectacular Exmoor National Park. We welcome groups of all sizes that enjoy the buzz of a Backpackers and have a love of the great outdoors! Weekly discounts are available and the whole hostel can be hired for exclusive use.

DETAILS

- **Open** - All year, reception 9-12pm and 4pm-10pm No curfew.
- **Number of beds** - 56:- 1x8, 5x6, 1x4, 1x twin, 2 x double, 2 x double & bunk.
- **Booking** - Booking advised but not essential.
- **Price per night** - Dorm beds £13.00-£18.50. Double rooms £40-£45 per room.
- **Public Transport** - Direct coaches from London Victoria/Heathrow/Plymouth/Exeter. By train take the Tarka line to Barnstaple then bus to Ilfracombe.
- **Directions** - Ocean Backpackers is by the harbour opposite the bus station. For more detailed directions go to our website and click on directions.

CONTACT: Chris and Abby
Tel: 01271 867835
info@oceanbackpackers.co.uk www.oceanbackpackers.co.uk
29 St James Place, Ilfracombe, Devon, EX34 9BJ

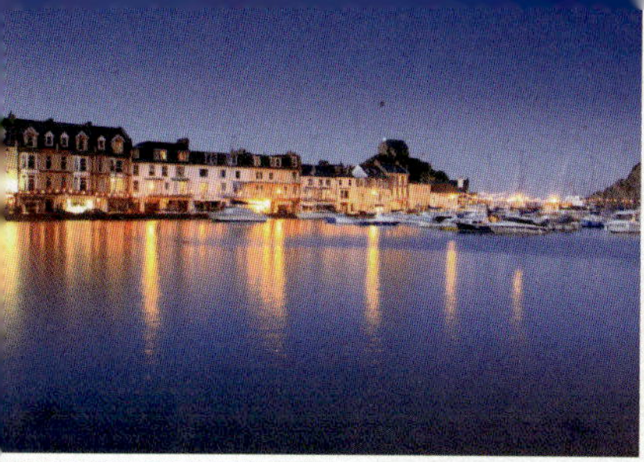
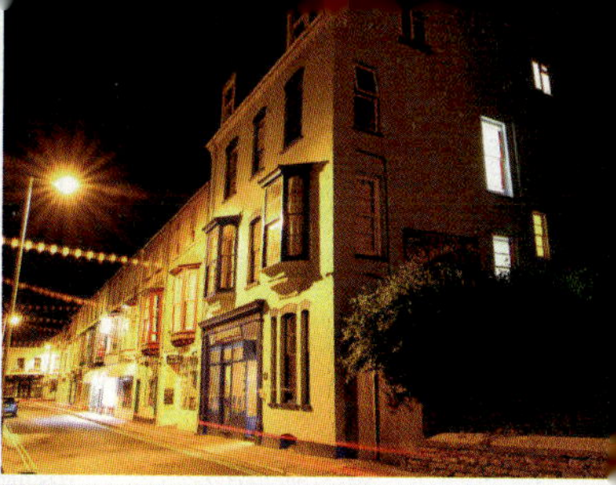
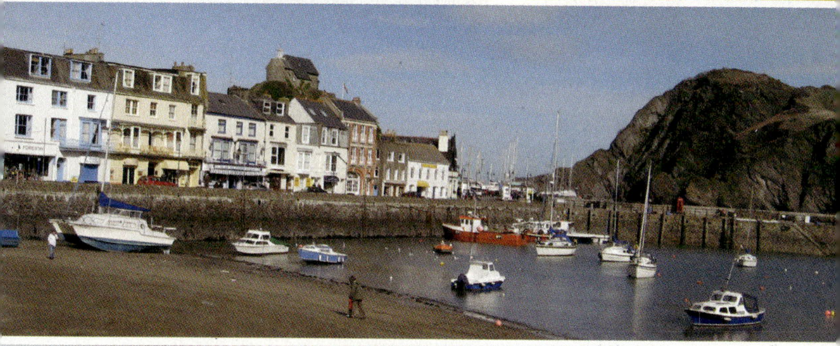
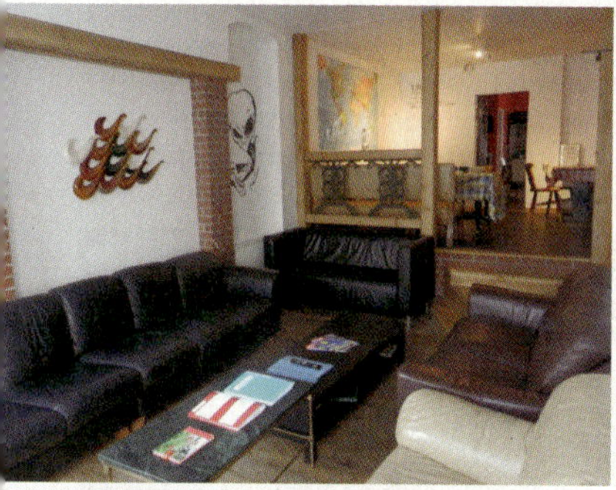
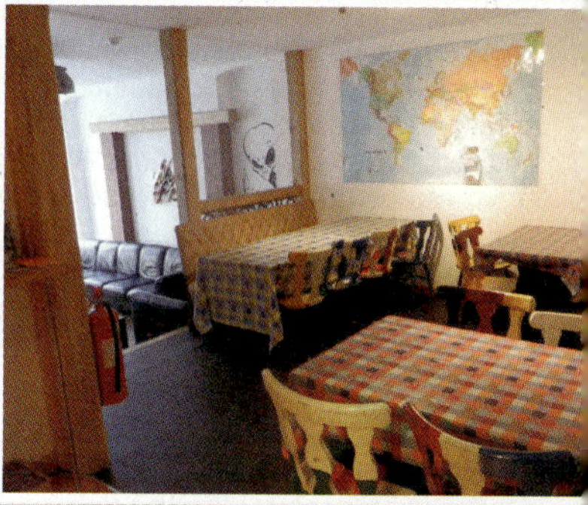
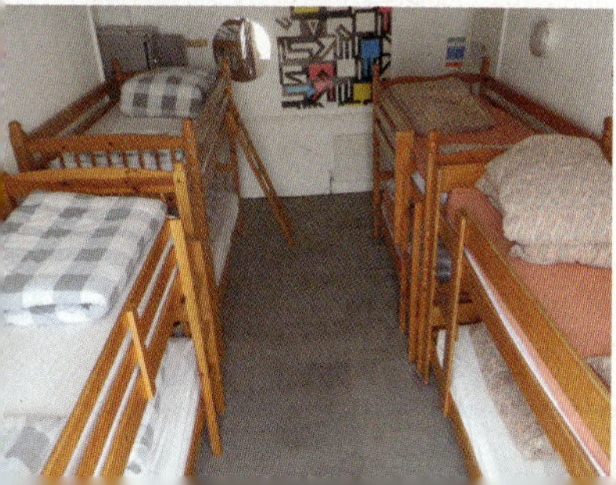
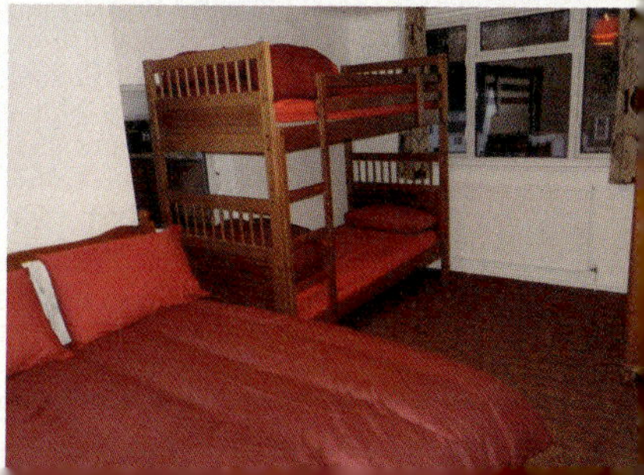

ROCK AND RAPID BUNKHOUSE

ENGLAND

An ideal place to come for an adventurous or relaxing break. The Rock and Rapid Adventure Centre is an AALA registered centre that offers activities such as climbing, coasteering, canoeing and surfing. The bunkhouse can be rented out for sole use, for an activity package or a full programme, including food, can be put together for your group.

The North Devon coastline is only 15 minutes' away from the centre, and surfing lessons and other water sports are on offer. On-site there is an indoor climbing and bouldering wall where climbing lessons are available for the beginner or climbers can register and use the wall themselves. The bunkhouse lends itself to groups wanting good quality but cheap accommodation. Being in a rural setting there are no neighbours; therefore it is ideal for groups such as hen and stags, as well as family or school groups wanting a quiet escape.

DETAILS

- **Open** - All Year, 24 Hours
- **Number of beds** - 40: 2 x 18, 2 x 2
- **Booking** - Email or phone us for any more information and for a booking form.
- **Price per night** - £200 per night sole use
- **Public Transport** - Railway station in either Tiverton or Barnstaple with buses or taxis easily available to South Molton.
- **Directions** - Rock and Rapid Bunkhouse is based at the Rock and Rapid Adventures Ltd centre in North Devon. Only 15 minutes' from the North Devon coastline and minutes from the Exmoor National Park.

CONTACT: Keith Crockford
Tel: 0333 600 6001, Fax: 0333 600 6002
info@rockandrapid.co.uk www.rockandrapidadventures.co.uk
Hacche Mill, South Molton, EX36 3NA

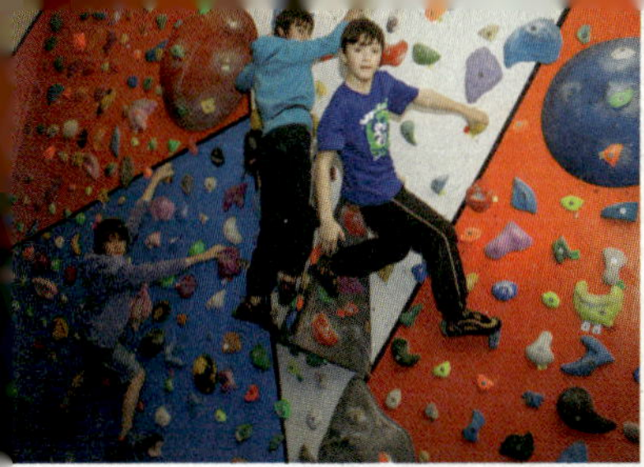

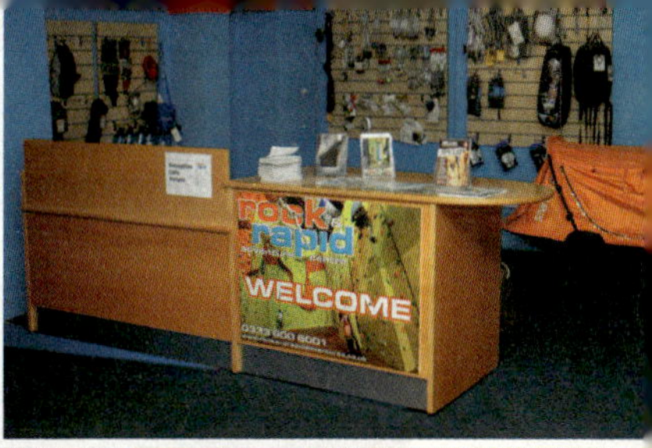
rock rapid
WELCOME

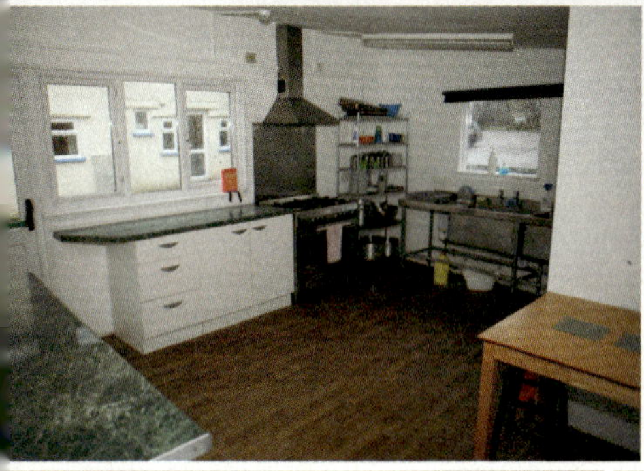

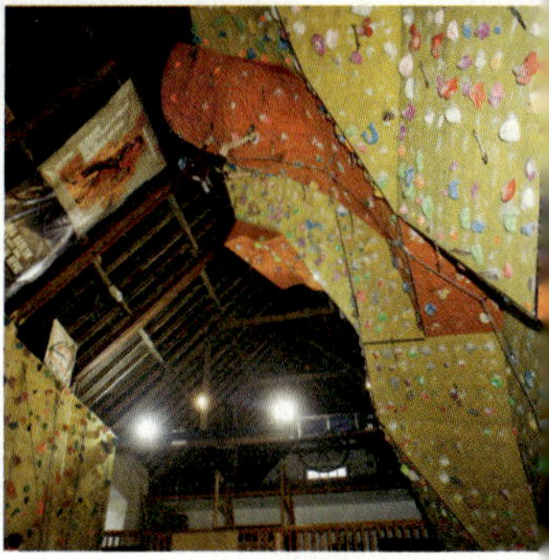

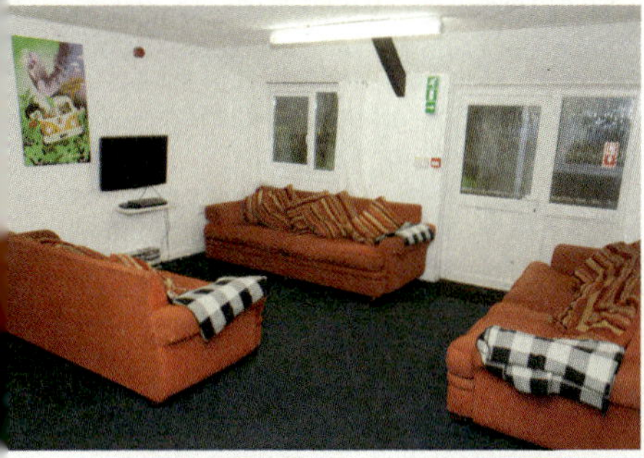

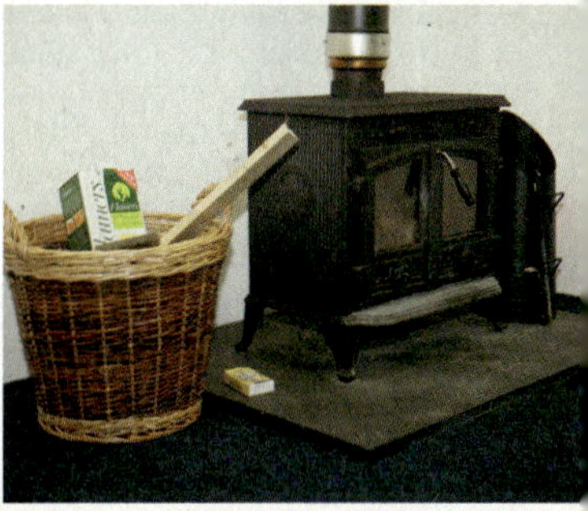

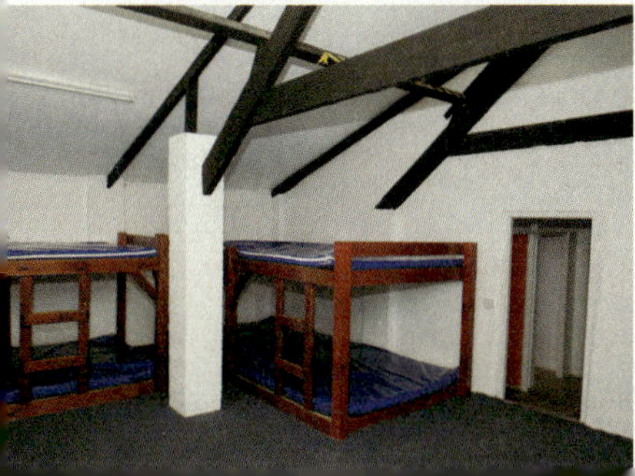

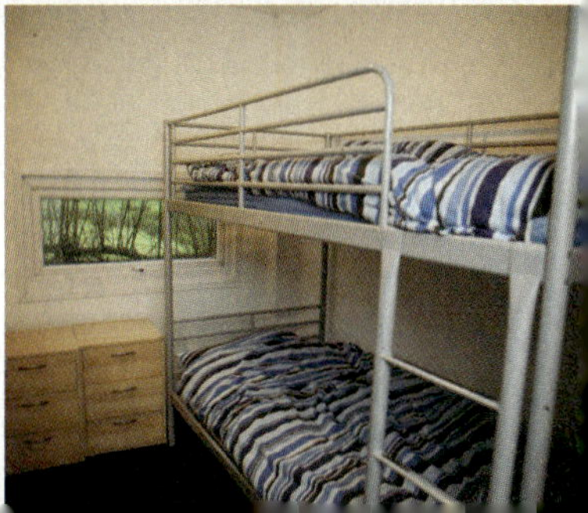

BLINDWELL
BUNKHOUSE

ENGLAND

Bunkhouse on traditional Exmoor hill farm, with far reaching views of Devon and Dartmoor with high quality comfortable bunks and mattresses, including drying/ laundry room and secure cycle/equipment lockup. Bunkhouse has hot water and underfloor heating from biomass boiler, solar panels supplementing electricity all included. Half a mile from Sustrans cycle route 3, off road mountain bike trails nearby and many beautiful walking trails. Set at the top of a secluded valley with lots of wildlife including red deer, buzzards, Exmoor ponies. Many Exmoor beauty spots within easy reach. 16 beds in three rooms The Mole x 6 ,The Danesbrook x 4 and ground floor The Barle x 6 with disabled access. Shared toilets and showers with underfloor heating and disabled facilities. Outside toilet facilities. Traditional local pubs near by, groceries can be ordered through local shop or supermarkets with prior notice.

DETAILS

- **Open** - all year,
- **Number of beds** - 16 1x6,1x6,1x4
- **Booking** - Booking via website or telephone 01598740246
- **Price per night** - £20 ppn including bedding, Group rates any night whole bunkhouse £280, Weekend Fri/Sat £540, Christmas and New Year by arrangement
- **Public Transport** - Trains to Taunton, Tiverton or Barnstaple. Buses to South Molton and Dulverton. Local Taxis service see website
- **Directions** - From A361 at South Molton turn right and go through North Molton towards Withypool after 4miles at the top of the hill turn right towards Twichen cross the next cross roads then take sharp back right immediately before cattle grid Blindwell Farm is half a mile on right hand side

CONTACT: Carol Delbridge
Tel: 01598740246, Fax: 447889475001
Delbridge.Carol@googlemail.com   www.blindwellbunkhouse.co.uk
Blindwell Farm, Twitchen, Sandyway, South Molton, EX36 3LT

BASE LODGE

ENGLAND

Base Lodge is ideally situated for exploring Exmoor, the Quantocks and the North Devon coast by mountain bike or foot. Excellent off and on road mountain biking for all levels. Guided mountain biking and secure lock up facilities. Exmoor affords excellent scenic moor and coastal views and the 600+ mile long South West Coastal Path starts here in Minehead. Other activities can be arranged including mountain biking, navigational training, climbing, surfing, pony-trekking and natural history walks and talks.

Base Lodge is clean, comfortable and friendly, providing a shared fully equipped kitchen and dining room. Local pubs and restaurants are all within walking distance.

DETAILS

- **Open** - All year, all day access once booked (reception open from 3pm).
- **Number of beds** - 22: 2x2, 1x7, 1x6, 1x5
- **Booking** - Booking advisable, bookings taken by phone or email or take a chance and call in. Deposit required for groups or exclusive use.
- **Price per night** - Dorms £15, private single £5 supplement, twin/ double £36. Exclusive use of Base Lodge from £250. Family room discount.
- **Public Transport** - Coach station 5 min walk. Buses from Taunton, Exeter and Tiverton. Train station: Taunton (26 miles). Steam railway from Taunton to Minehead.
- **Directions** - With the sea behind you, drive/walk up The Parade until you reach Park Street, continue straight on until you reach a fork. Take the right fork into The Parks (Baptist Church on your right). Only limited parking is available.

CONTACT: Wendy or Graham
Tel: 01643 703520 or 0773 1651536
togooutdoors@hotmail.com http://www.togooutdoors.co.uk/BaseLodge/Base%20Lodge%20Web-page.html
16 The Parks, Minehead, Somerset, TA24 8BS

CAMPBELL ROOM
GROUP ACCOMMODATION
ENGLAND

The Campbell Room offers self-catering group accommodation for youth organisations, schools and universities, training courses and groups of walkers, cyclists and others. Sheltered at the mouth of a rural valley on the edge of the Quantock Hills AONB, the building offers a main activity hall which can also sleep 18 on comfortable mattresses, 2 bedrooms each sleeping 3, a multi-use cabin, fully equipped kitchen, washrooms, showers, drying room, campfire area and space for 1 or 2 tents. Many walking, hiking and mountain biking routes pass close to the centre, a swimming pool is nearby and the forest is within 10 minutes' walk. Other attractions and activities in the area include horse riding, high ropes, water sports, beaches with rock pools and fossils, the coastal resort of Minehead, the West Somerset Railway, Wells Cathedral, Glastonbury Tor, Wookey Hole, Cheddar Gorge, Dunster Castle, Tropiquaria Animal and Adventure Park, Exmoor and the county town of Taunton.

DETAILS

- **Open** - All Year, by arrangement. Check current availability on our website.
- **Number of beds** - 24 recommended (but see website). 2x3, 1x18 max, 1x8 max
- **Booking** - Essential one month in advance with deposit. Bridgwater YMCA, Friarn Avenue, Bridgwater, Somerset, TA6 3RF.
- **Price per night** - £4.50 pp (2 leaders free for groups over 12), min £54 per night.
- **Public Transport** - Buses Mon to Sat from Bridgwater. Details on website.
- **Directions** - 10 miles from the M5 (junction 23 or 24). Centre is at T junction west of Aley, 1.5 miles south of Nether Stowey (on the A39 Bridgwater to Minehead road). GR ST187381. TA5 1HB / TA5 1HN. Full directions on our website.

CONTACT: Ask for Sam Budd
Tel: 01278 726 000
info@campbellroom.org.uk   www.campbellroom.org.uk
Campbell Room Group Accommodation, Aley, Over Stowey, Somerset.

CHITCOMBE FARM
CAMPING BARN
ENGLAND

Chitcombe is a small family run farm in West Somerset, on the edge of Exmoor. Providing inexpensive basic accommodation, with an emphasis on a warm and dry place to stay after a day out in the locality. So if you're looking to have a day hiking on Exmoor, or training for the UK 70.3 IRONMAN, or just spending time in the countryside this could be the place for you. The Hay Barn, is a dormitory style open plan barn with bunks, two bathrooms with showers, a kitchen and seating area for a maximum of 12 people, more by prior arrangement. It is centrally heated, with hot and cold running water no extra charge. The Cart Shed is more of an open plan chalet with a kitchen, bathroom with shower, seating area and bunks for four people, if you require extra beds for this barn there is a sofa bed (double). Also centrally heated with hot and cold running water. You will need to bring everything as if you were camping, Mattresses are provided but no pillows

DETAILS

- **Open** - All year,
- **Number of beds** - 16 The Hay Barn 12, The Cart Shed 4
- **Booking** - Book via website or phone
- **Price per night** - The Hay Barn £15pp, sole use £160, £1000/week. The Cart Shed: £15pp, sole use £50, £350/week
- **Public Transport** - Train to Taunton, local buses
- **Directions** - Don't use sat nav. From B3190 Raleigh's Cross to Bampton road: at crossroads take turning for Huish Champflower and Wiveliscombe, Chitcombe is the 2nd left 300 yards from cross roads, about half a mile down a steep bumpy lane.

CONTACT: Sam Kennen
Tel: 01398 371274 or 07866 852 699.
jekennen@hotmail.com chitcombebarns.co.uk/
Chitcombe Farm, Huish Champflower, Taunton, Somerset, TA4 2EL

MENDIP BUNKHOUSE

ENGLAND

Larkshall (Mendip Bunkhouse) is the Cerberus Spelaeological Society's headquarters and offers excellent modern facilities. As well as for members it is available for use by guest individuals or groups wanting accommodation on Mendip. It makes an ideal base for caving as well as many other outdoor activities including walking, cycling, climbing etc. It is also a good base for anyone wanting to explore the Somerset countryside and within very easy reach are the famous tourist attractions of Wells, Wookey Hole, Cheddar Gorge and caves, and the city of Bath. The accommodation provides all the home comforts with a kitchen/dining room, large lounge, showers and changing facilities. For anyone so inclined the central corridor can be traversed using the climbing holds fitted along the wall. There are two guest communal bunkrooms sleeping 12 and 19 respectively, with ample space to sleep large groups in comfort. For those that prefer, it is possible to camp. There is a large car park.

DETAILS

- **Open** - All year, 24 hours. Key available by prior arrangement.
- **Number of beds** - 31 (1 x 12 + 1 x 19). Unlimited camping available.
- **Booking** - Advisable. Email preferred, deposit required. Availability on website.
- **Price per night** - £5 per person. Sole use of bunkrooms £60 and £95. Minimum charge £10 per person per stay.
- **Public Transport** - There is a bus stop near the crossroads in Oakhill on the A367. Taxis are available in Shepton Mallet, Wells and Frome
- **Directions** - Larkshall is 4 miles north of Shepton Mallet and 15 miles south of Bath off the A367. At the crossroads in Oakhill take road to Stoke St Michael. Larkshall is about one mile from Oakhill on the right (ST 6505 4720).

CONTACT:
Tel: 0845 475 0954
hostelbookings@cerberusspeleo.org.uk www.cerberusspeleo.org.uk
Cerberus Spelaeological, Larkshall, Fosse Road, Oakhill, Somerset, BA3 5HY

GOBLIN COMBE
LODGE

ENGLAND

71

Just 10 miles outside Bristol, Goblin Combe Lodge is set in 8 acres of its own grounds with stunning views across the Severn Estuary and beyond. Set in 130 acres of woodlands, rich in history and geology with 80 acres designated as a site of special scientific interest, it offers something for everyone. The timber framed building is clad in larch and has a biomass central heating system, rainwater harvesting and a sewage treatment plant. Groups of up to 38 can be accommodated in 10 bedrooms sleeping 2, 4 & 6 people. The cottage alongside the Lodge provides a lounge, dining and catering facilities and is the ideal place to relax and warm yourself after a long day of activities or to prepare for an exciting night walk where you might meet the resident owls. The 18ft yurt is a great place for a drumming workshop, a day of meditation or just a get-together.

Fire pits and a BBQ area are included in the price. Smaller groups may be accommodated, camping available for the overspill of larger groups - please contact for information

DETAILS
- **Open** - All year, Please contact for opening times
- **Number of beds** - 38
- **Booking** - By phone/email. Booking address Plunder Street, Cleeve, BS49 4PQ.
- **Price per night** - £350-£495. No min stay. Reductions for charities and schools.
- **Public Transport** - The bus X1 between Bristol & Weston Super Mare stops at the end of Cleeve Hill Road on the A370. Nearest train station - Yatton - 3 miles.
- **Directions** - Detailed directions to the site will be given upon booking

CONTACT:
Tel: 01934 833723
enquiries@goblincombe.org.uk   www.goblincombe.org.uk
Goblin Combe Lodge, Cleeve Hill, North Somerset, BS40 5PP

BATH
YMCA

Bath YMCA offers a warm welcome and the best value accommodation. From its central location all the sights of this World Heritage City are easily reached on foot. Bath is also an ideal base for the explorer. Staying longer brings Stonehenge, Wookey Hole caves, Cheddar Gorge, the southern reaches of the Cotswolds, and more exciting destinations all within reach. With a total of 210 beds, Bath YMCA has a great deal of experience in making guests feel comfortable. There is a fully air conditioned lounge area with TV. Laundry, lockers, pool and football table, fax and internet facilities are available. The Health and Fitness suite provides a steam and sauna room with up to date equipment and qualified staff who work hard to provide 'Fitness with Fun'. Couples, families, groups and backpackers are all welcome. All these facilities and the YMCA's traditional sense of community will make your stay a truly memorable one. Awarded 3 stars by VisitBritain.

DETAILS

- **Open** - All year, 24-hour reception
- **Number of beds** - 210: Dorms: 2x10, 2x12, 1x14, 1x18. Rooms: 7 x quad, 6 x triple, 29 x twin, 5 x double, 9 x single
- **Booking** - Credit card guarantees.
- **Price per night** - From: Dorm £21pp. Single £32pp. Twin £28pp. Double £30pp. Triple £23pp. Quad £22pp. Includes light breakfast.
- **Public Transport** - Bath has a train station and is served by National Express.
- **Directions** - Located approximately ½ mile from rail and bus station. Broad Street is located near the Podium Shopping Centre off Walcott Street.

CONTACT: Reception
Tel: 01225 325900, Fax: 01225 462065
stay@bathymca.co.uk www.bathymca.co.uk
International House, Broad Street Place, Bath, BA1 5LH

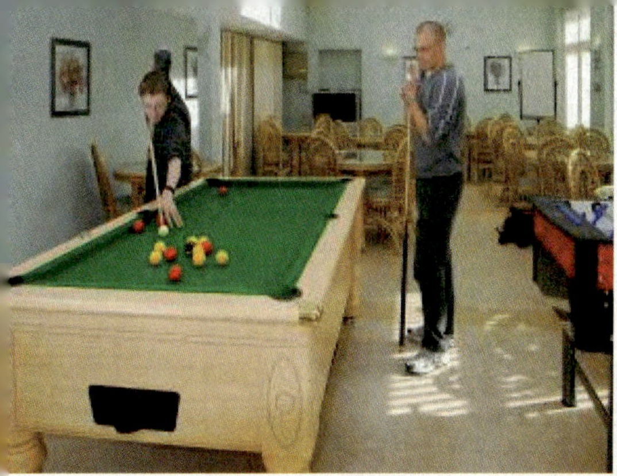
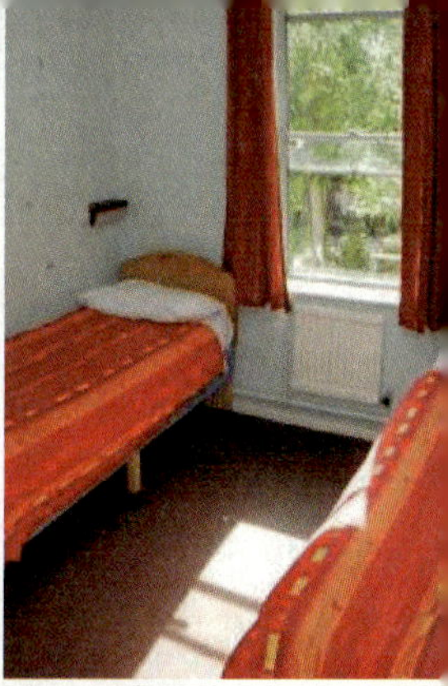
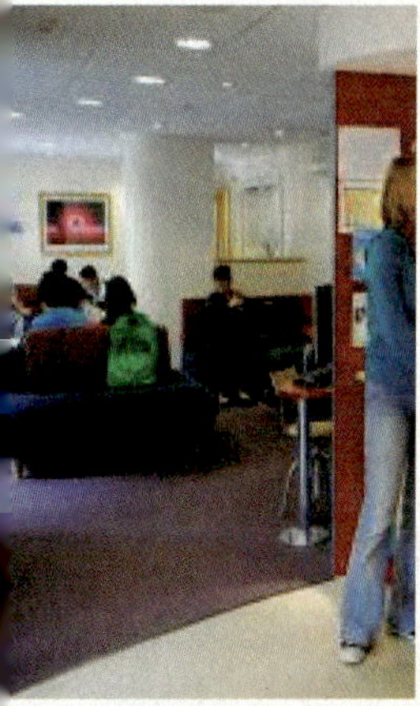
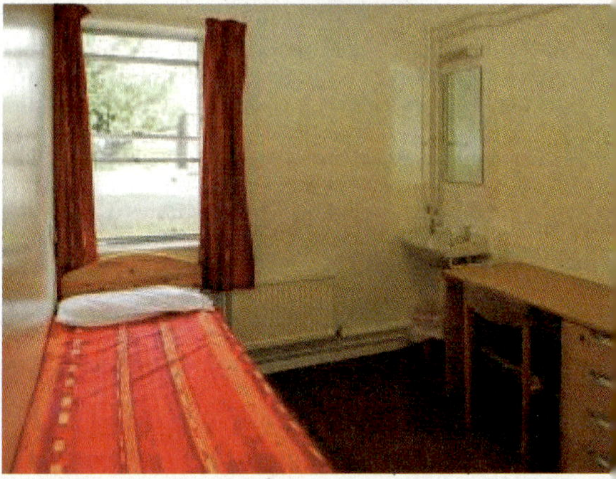
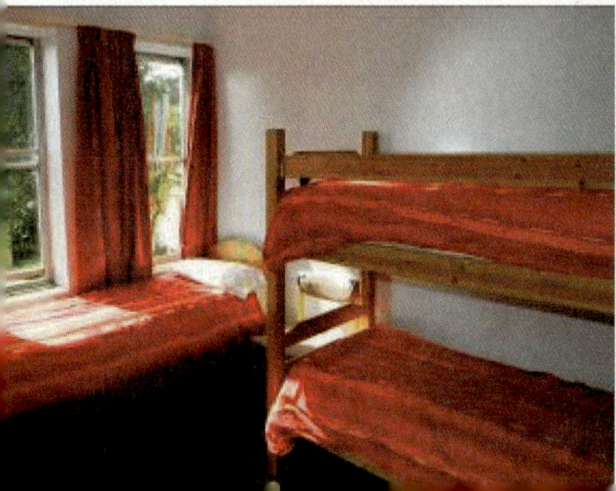
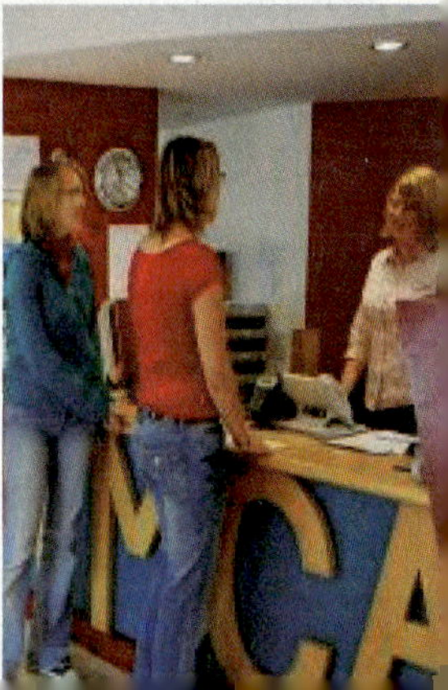

BRISTOL BACKPACKERS HOSTEL

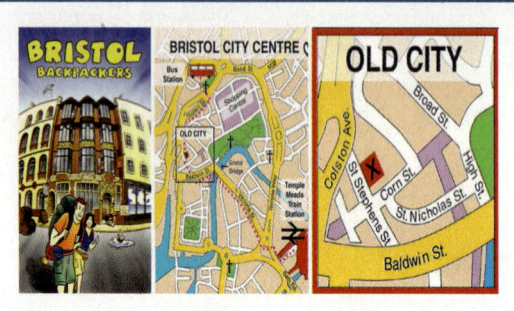

ENGLAND

Bristol's most central backpacker hostel - clean & comfy beds - mixed/single sex dorms - private rooms - individual bathrooms & free hot showers - free linen - large kitchen - free tea, coffee & hot chocolate - indoor bicycle storage.

Late night basement bar - piano & guitar room - DVD lounge - cheap internet machines - free WiFi - luggage storage room - laundrette.

Run by backpackers for backpackers - no curfew after check in.

DETAILS

- **Open** - All year, reception hours 9am -11.30pm (no curfew)
- **Number of beds** - 90: Bunk bed accommodation in private twin, private triple or 6, 8 and 10 bed dorms.
- **Booking** - Most cards, phone or walk in.
- **Price per night** - £17pp. Private rooms from £39. See website for discounts.
- **Public Transport** - See below.
- **Directions** - Located in 'Old City', the historic centre of Bristol. From Bristol Central Bus Station (Marlborough St) 7 minutes' walk. Follow pedestrian signs to 'Old City' then see map above. From Bristol Temple Meads train station 12 minutes' walk. Follow pedestrian signs to 'Old City' then see map above. Or take bus number 8 or 9 to the 'Centre Promenade'. Disembark at The Bristol Hippodrome. From Airport take the 'Shuttle' to the Central Bus Station. By road follow signs for Baldwin Street in the city centre.

CONTACT:
Tel: 0117 9257900
info@bristolbackpackers.co.uk www.bristolbackpackers.co.uk
17 St Stephen's Street, Bristol, BS1 1EQ

MONKTON WYLD COURT

ENGLAND

Set in a secluded Dorset valley just 3 miles from Axminster, Lyme Regis and Charmouth, Monkton Wyld Court is an education centre for sustainable living run by a resident community with the help of volunteers. The Court was built in 1848, originally as a rectory, and has been a hotel and a school before becoming an education centre. As well as B&B and hostel accommodation the centre offers courses, mainly land-based, and events for families, groups and individuals. Bring a sleeping-bag to take advantage of hostel rates. Accommodation is in shared rooms. Vegetarian lunches, evening meals, breakfasts, and picnic lunches, are available. We also cater for special dietary requirements such as gluten free, vegan etc. Meals are served in the Gothic dining room. Camping is an option at certain times of the year. The court is also available to hire as a venue.

DETAILS

- **Open** - Open all year round, please phone to check availability, 9am - 6pm daily
- **Number of beds** - 35 – single/double rooms or dormitory accommodation
- **Booking** - Email or phone for any more information and to book
- **Price per night** - £15 dormitory price
- **Public Transport** - Train to Axminster. The 31 bus from the station (Axminster to Lyme Regis) stops at the Hunters' Lodge pub in Raymonds Hill, a pleasant thirty minutes' walk away from the centre.
- **Directions** - Three miles from Charmouth, Axminster and Lyme Regis. Monkton Wyld is signposted from the A35 halfway between Charmouth and Axminster. You will find the Court just opposite St Andrews' Church.

CONTACT: Office Coordinator
Tel: 01297 560342
info@monktonwyldcourt.org www.monktonwyldcourt.co.uk
Elsdon Lane, Charmouth, Bridport, Dorset, DT6 6DQ

BUNKHOUSE PLUS

ENGLAND

Located in the heart of Weymouth, the gateway to the beautiful and exciting Jurassic coastline and the host of the 2012 Olympic Games, Bunkhouse Plus has a mixture of bunk rooms with the 'Plus' of double en suites rooms making it a versatile accommodation for your stay. Children over 5 are welcome accompanied and supervised by adults. Situated close to the beach and town centre with safe waters to swim, whilst the old harbour hosts tall ships and channel island ferries. Why not get involved in wind and kite surfing, fishing, sailing, diving or rock climbing? Whatever your sport or hobby, the friendly hostel staff are more than happy to link you to venues and organisers to help make your stay as exciting or peaceful as you wish. The building is available for exclusive use. Sleeps either 15 (winter) or 25 all year round. Facilities include large self-catering kitchen with free tea/coffee/sugar, lounge with TV and dining area . No curfew. Bedding & linen included, with towel hire available. A room for equipment wash down and drying available.

DETAILS

- **Open** - Open all year round, Reception times 4pm to 11pm daily
- **Number of beds** - 22: 2x4, 2x3, 2x2, 2x double en suites
- **Booking** - via website, email or telephone.
- **Price per night** - Double from £20pp. Dorm from £18pp self-catering only
- **Public Transport** - Trains, bus and coach from all areas.
- **Directions** - 5 minute walk from train/bus station. Follow Ranelagh Road to Walpole Street on right. From sea front head north, at Queen Victoria statue turn left into William Street across crossroads then bear to the left into Walpole Street.

CONTACT: Colin House
Tel: 01305 775228, Fax: 01305 775228
bunkhouseplus@gmail.com www.bunkhouseplus.co.uk
Bunkhouse Plus, 47 Walpole Street, Weymouth, DT4 7HQ

DAVID DONALD
FIELD STUDIES BASE ENGLAND

Offering accommodation for educational, family and other groups, this converted 1940 RAF radar station has been renovated with central heating and double glazing. It sleeps 24 but up to 40 if some wish to camp and share the indoor facilities. There is a well equipped kitchen, a spacious community room, a drying room, picnic area, BBQ / campsite area, a games area and lots of parking. There are ramps to the main building and adapted toilets for wheelchair users, but for these the drive to the centre is very difficult without a car. This is an outstanding area for environmental studies and is also popular with groups or families enjoying a relaxing break, reunions, walking, outdoor actvities and other social events. It is within an SSSI, and has Lulworth Cove, Durdle Door, The Arne Nature Reserve, Purbeck Marine Reserve, Corfe Castle, Swanage Heritage Railway, Poole Harbour and lots of other interesting sites nearby.

DETAILS

- **Open** - All year.
- **Number of beds** - 24: 1x2, 1x4 en suite, 1x8, 1x10
- **Booking** - Booking required with £200 deposit. Phone for availability. Forms can then be downloaded from website and returned to P&D Adv Centre, 37 Commercial Road Poole, Dorset. BH14 0HU
- **Price per night** - Whole centre £315 plus £5 per person for numbers exceeding 24. Bedding set hire £5 per person. Winter fuel supplement (Oct-Mar) £5 per night.
- **Public Transport** - Train to Wareham. Wilts & Dorset Buses to Worth Matravers.
- **Directions** - Arriving in Worth Matravers from Kingston bear right by duck pond into Pikes Lane. After Renscombe Farm road turns sharp right then left onto Renscombe Rd. 200m further the driveway to the base is on the right. OS SY967777

CONTACT: Poole & Dorset Adventure Centre
Tel: 01202 710701, Fax: 01202 710701
enquiries@dorsetadventure.co.uk www.dorsetadventure.co.uk
Off Renscombe Rd, Worth Matravers, Isle of Purbeck, Dorset. BH19 3LL

SWANAGE AUBERGE BUNKHOUSE

ENGLAND

Swanage Auberge, the bunkhouse that cares, is a refuge for climbers, walkers and divers, situated at the eastern end of the Jurassic Coast with excellent walking, diving and rock climbing on the doorstep. The bunkhouse is in the centre of Swanage town, a stone's throw from the South West Coast Path and all local amenities - pubs, shops, restaurants etc. Swanage Auberge is family run and self-contained with central heating, fully equipped self-catering kitchen, drying and laundry facilities and a meals service if required. There are two bunk rooms, one with 4 standard bunks and the other with 6 alpine style places (3 and 3). There is also a 5 bed dorm in the adjoining house. Towel, plus pillows are provided and bedding is included. There are three showers, loos and washrooms and an area to hang and wash wet-suits. Once booked in, the Auberge is available 24 hours a day. Parking is available for 2 vehicles and is allocated on a first come, first served basis. Price includes cereal breakfast and beverages. Packed lunches available (see website for further details).

DETAILS

- **Open** - All year. Arive 5.30pm (phone mobile to arrive earlier). Access all day.
- **Number of beds** - 15: 1x6, 1x4, 1x5
- **Booking** - by phone (mobile in day time), email or online. Deposit required
- **Price per night** - £20pp (one night), £18 if staying more than one night. Includes bedding, cereal breakfast, tea or coffee. Group rates available. No credit cards.
- **Public Transport** - Trains to Bournemouth, Poole or Wareham, bus to Swanage
- **Directions** - Turn left off High Street (opposite Earth Lights Café) into Mount Pleasant Lane. First left into Hardy Close. Swanage Auberge is at the end on the left.

CONTACT: Pete or Pam
Tel: 01929 424368, mobile 07711 117668
bookings@swanageauberge.co.uk   www.swanageauberge.co.uk
45 High Street, Swanage, Dorset, BH19 2LX

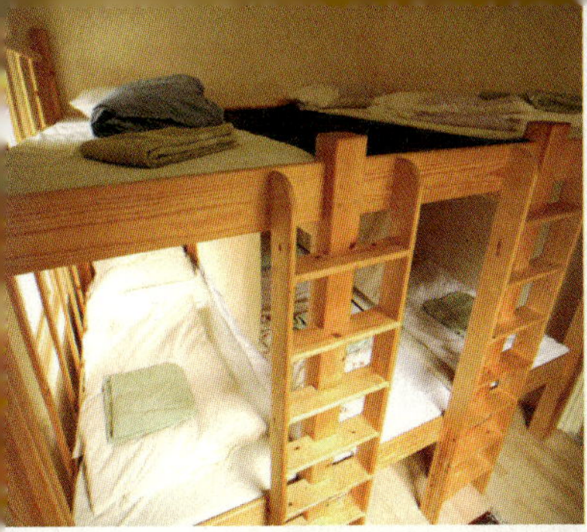

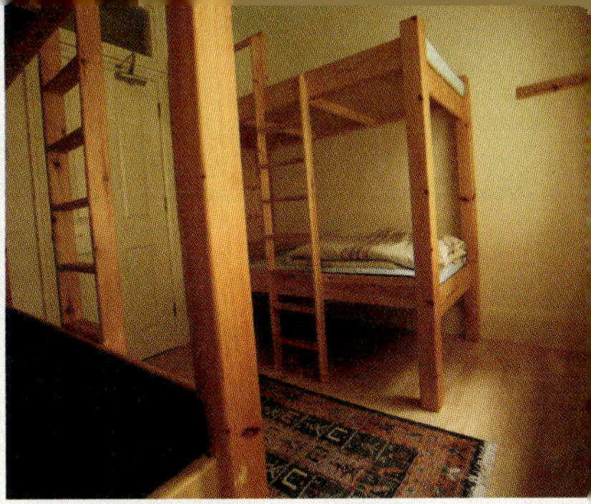

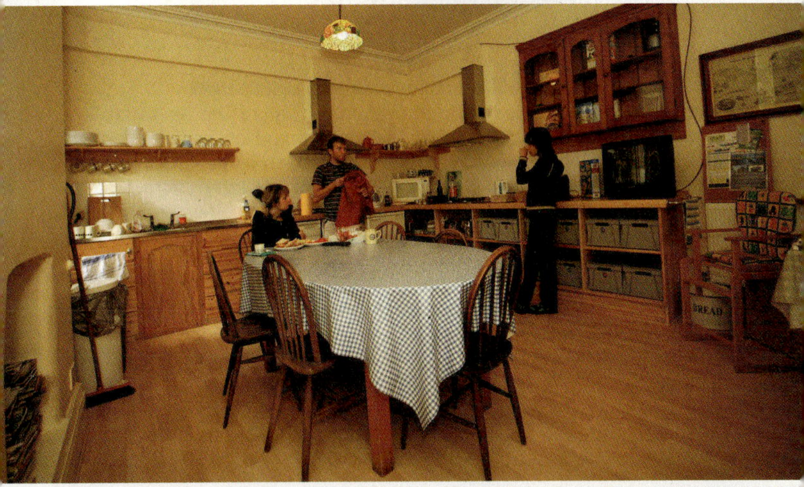
BREAD

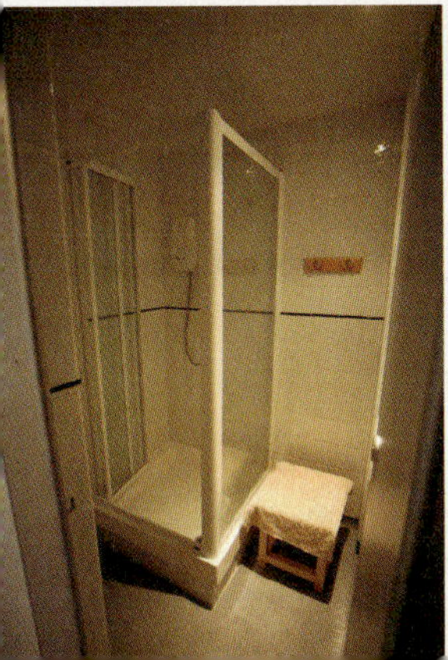

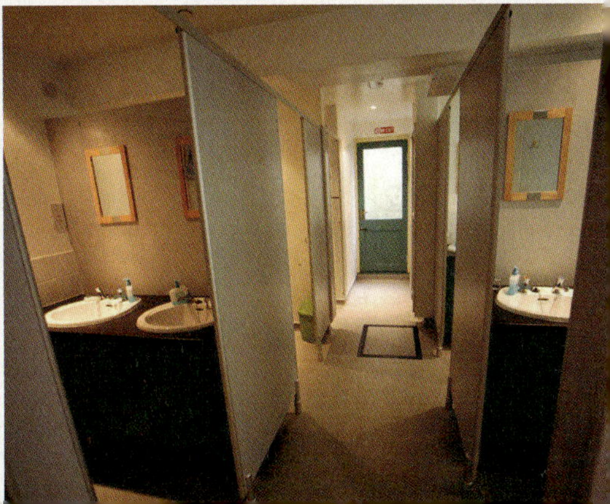

WETHERDOWN LODGE AND CAMPSITE

ENGLAND

An award winning example of eco-renovation and part of The Sustainability Centre which promotes environmental awareness and low impact living in the heart of the South Downs National Park. Just a few steps from the South Downs Way National Trail and ideal for walkers, cyclists, business away-days and family get-togethers. The Lodge has a fully equipped self-catering kitchen, a communal area, comfortable bedrooms with linen & towels provided, and shared bathrooms/toilets. A 'help yourself' breakfast is included. Packed lunches and evening meals can be pre-ordered from the on-site Beech Café. The Centre has large grounds with woodland trails and a café open every day. The Campsite has tipis and yurts, as well as fire pits, secluded woodland pitches and solar showers, offering a peaceful real camping experience. Within 2 miles there are country pubs, local shops, and take-aways/deliveries.

DETAILS

- **Open** - Lodge: All year (except Christmas/New Year). Campsite: April -October. Reception: 8.30am-7pm April-October; 9am-5pm November - March
- **Number of beds** - 38: 10 x 3, 4 x 2
- **Booking** - Book by telephone / email.
- **Price per night** - From £23 adult, £18 child (5-15). Inc linen and breakfast. Exclusive use available. Camping: £11/adult £6/child Lge Yurts: £25/adults; £10/child. Tipis/Mini Yurt: £20/adult, £10/child Under 5s free. Discount for arrivals on foot or bike
- **Public Transport** - Trains at Petersfield, 6 miles (£20-25 by taxi). 38 bus to Clanfield, 67 to East Meon, 41 bus to Clanfield from Portsmouth Harbour .
- **Directions** - GR 676 189. From A3 take Clanfield turn (brown sign). Turn right after Rising Sun in Clanfield. At top of hill, turn left signed Droxford.

CONTACT: Angie or Sara
Tel: 01730 823549, Fax: 01730 823168
accommodation@sustainability-centre.org www.sustainability-centre.org
The Sustainability Centre, Droxford Road, East Meon, Hampshire, GU32 1HR

THE PRIVETT CENTRE

ENGLAND

Situated mid-way between Alton and Petersfield in glorious Hampshire countryside, the Privett Centre offers lowest cost, comfortable short-stay accommodation in a unique rural setting. The centre is a picturesque converted Victorian school and schoolhouse located next to the church in a farming hamlet which lies within the East Hampshire 'Area of Outstanding Natural Beauty'. Sleeping a maximum of 26 dormitory style with 1 twin bedroom (with disabled access en suite) and one single room, the centre is designed to accommodate small to medium-sized groups who prefer the freedom of hiring a small centre all to themselves. The centre provides the basics – a self-catering kitchen, bunk beds mainly in bedrooms, a large common room, games room and shower rooms all under one roof. Outside a large paddock and asphalt playground provide secure and spacious recreational and parking space. Available for weekday, weekend and day use all year, the Privett Centre is an ideal residential setting.

DETAILS

- **Open** - All year,
- **Number of beds** - 29: 1x1, 1x2, 2x4, 1x6, 1x12
- **Booking** - Phone or email
- **Price per night** - From £13 pppn with a minimum charge of £150 per night. (please contact the centre for exact prices applicable to your group)
- **Public Transport** - Nearest train station - Petersfield, approx 6 miles from centre.
- **Directions** - From the A272 follow signs to Petersfield. Go straight across crossroads, centre is signposted on left after approx 2 miles.

CONTACT: Angela Grigsby
Tel: 01730 828238
info@privettcentre.org.uk www.privettcentre.org.uk
Church Lane, Privett, Hampshire, GU34 3PE

GUMBER BOTHY

Gumber Bothy is a converted Sussex flint barn on a working sheep farm within the National Trust's Slindon Estate. It provides simple overnight accommodation or camping for walkers, horse riders and cyclists, just off the South Downs Way, or a tranquil and remote location to get away from it all.

Five minutes' walk from Stane Street, the Roman Road that crosses the South Downs Way at Bignor Hill, facilities include sleeping platforms in 3 dorms sleeping up to 25, basic kitchen and bathroom facilities, BBQ, drying room, bike racks, payphone. Wheelchair accessible (please phone for details).

Sorry, but as the bothy is on a sheep farm, no dogs and most definitely NO CARS. Not suitable for under fives.

DETAILS

- **Open** - March to October (inclusive), ,flexible opening hours
- **Number of beds** - 25: 1 x 16, 1 x 5, 1 x 4 plus overflow area
- **Booking** - Booking by phone or email. Booking required for groups with 50% deposit.
- **Price per night** - £10 (adults), £5 (under 16s).
- **Public Transport** - Train stations, Arundel (urban) 5 miles, Amberley (rural) 5 miles, Chichester (8 miles). National Express stop at Chichester. Buses 84 and 85 from Chichester, stop at Fontwell and then it is a 3 mile walk to the Bothy. Taxi fare from Arundel to Northwood Farm is approx £10, followed by a 2 mile country walk.
- **Directions** - OS Map LR197 or E121 GR 961 119. Nearest car park GR 973 129. No vehicular access. One mile off South Downs Way on Stane Street bridleway

CONTACT: Bothy Ranger
Tel: 01243 814484
gumberbothy@nationaltrust.org.uk
Slindon Estate Yard, Slindon, Arundel, West Sussex, BN18 0RG

EDMUNDBYERS
YOUTH HOSTEL
ENGLAND

83

Edmundbyers Youth Hostel, now owned by a local farming family, offers friendly accommodation as part of the YHA and Independent Hostels networks. The hostel is former 17th century inn in the centre of the village, with wooden beams and a cosy open fire. A self-catering kitchen is available and the local pub, The Punch Bowl Inn, serves home cooked meals and locally brewed beer. The village of Edmundbyers lies in moorland close to the boundary between Nothumberland and County Durham, with fine views over Edmundbyers and Muggleswick Commons. It is two miles from Derwent Reservoir, where sailing and fishing are available, and within an Area of Outstanding Natural Beauty. The location is ideal for walking holidays, and there are prehistoric remains to explore. The village is on the Sea-to-Sea cycle route and for a day out you could visit Hadrian's Wall or the Beamish outdoor museum. The hostel has a campsite within a walled garden, with mature trees and stunning views. Campers can use the hostel showers, toilets and kitchen. Roadside parking available.

DETAILS

- **Open** - All year (camping Apr-Oct). Check in 5-10pm and check out 8-10am.
- **Number of beds** - 28: 2x6, 2x5,1x4,1x3. Eight pitches for camping.
- **Booking** - Book by email, phone or online.
- **Price per night** - From £23 (adult), £19 (under 18). Discounts for YHA members: £3 adult, £1.75 under 18. Room for 3 £60, for 4 £70, for 5 £80 and for 6 £90.
- **Public Transport** - Service 773 from Consett to Townfield calls at Edmunbuyers. Operated twice a day by Weardale Travel.
- **Directions** - Opposite the shop at the centre of the village of Edmunbyers.

CONTACT:
Tel: 01207 255651
lowhousehaven@outlook.com www.lowhousehaven.co.uk
Low House, Consett, Durham, DH8 9NL

PUTTENHAM ECO CAMPING BARN

ENGLAND

Puttenham Eco Camping Barn offers simple overnight accommodation and a warm welcome for walkers and cyclists - individuals, families or groups - in the Surrey Hills Area of Outstanding Natural Beauty.

Located on the North Downs Way and Sustrans NCN22 cycle route, the Barn has a fully equipped self-catering kitchen, a shower, toilets and foam covered sleeping platforms, as well as a garden with picnic benches. Electricity and hot water included but bring your own towel and sleeping bag (or hire one - £3 a stay). Evening meals are available in the village. The Barn has many sustainable features including solar panels and rainwater collection for flushing toilets. NO CARS ON SITE. Excellent cycle shed. Young people are welcome but must be accompanied by a responsible adult. The Barn is wardened.

DETAILS

- **Open** - Easter to October, arrive after 5pm leave before 10am.
- **Number of beds** - sleeping platforms for 11
- **Booking** - booking is essential
- **Price per night** - £15 adults; £12 under 18 (accompanied by adult). Sole use by arrangement. £4 `green` discount if arriving by foot, bicycle or public transport.
- **Public Transport** - Trains (08457 484950) at Wanborough (3.5 km), Guildford (7 km) and Farnham (9 km). Bus 65 (0845 1210190) from Guildford and Farnham stops within 1 km of Barn - alight Puttenham Hogs Back café & walk south to village; or bus 46 to Watts Gallery, Compton & follow North Downs Way 2 miles west.
- **Directions** - GR SU 933 479. In Puttenham village (halfway between Farnham and Guildford) the Camping Barn is on 'The Street' - opposite the church.

CONTACT: Bookings
Tel: 01629 592 700 or 0800 0191 700, Fax: 01629 592627
bookings@puttenhamcampingbarn.co.uk www.puttenhamcampingbarn.co.uk
The Street, Puttenham, Nr Guildford, Surrey, GU3 1AR

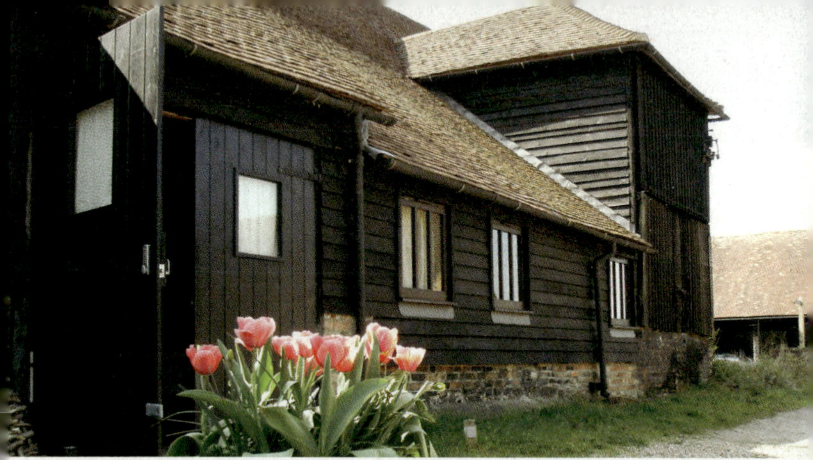

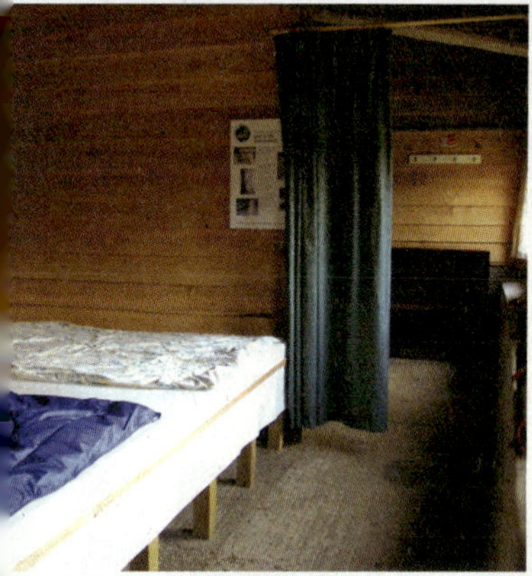

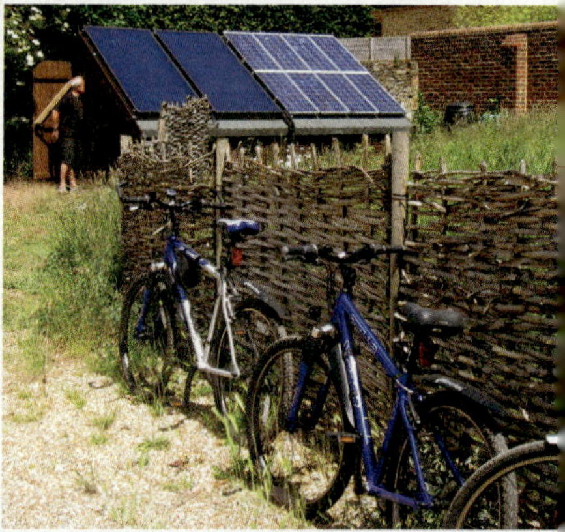

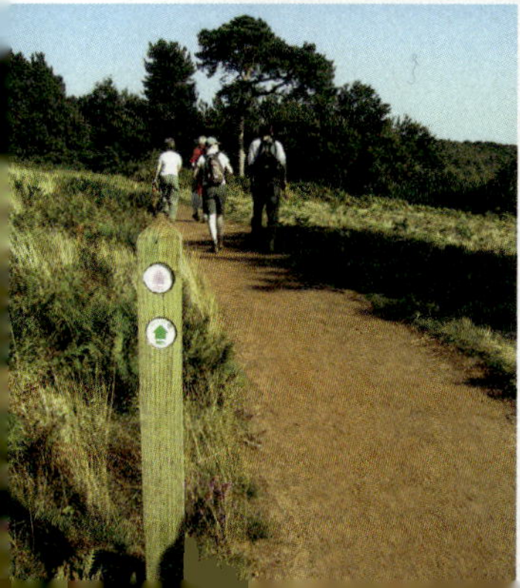

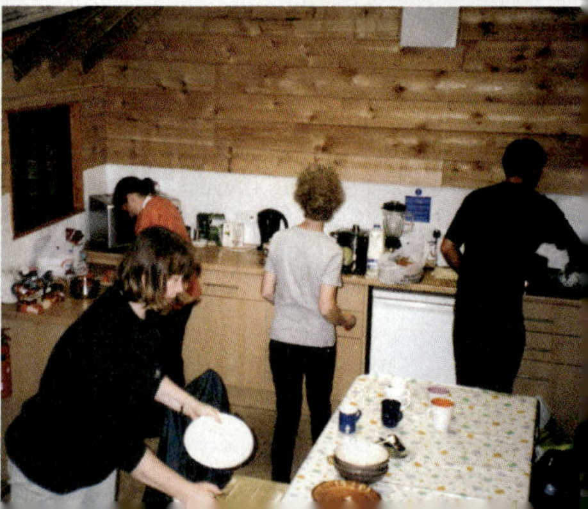

COURT HILL CENTRE

ENGLAND

Just 2 miles south of Wantage, and only a few steps from the historic Ridgeway National Trail, The Court Hill Centre enjoys breathtaking views over the Vale of the White Horse.

Reclaimed barns surround a pretty courtyard garden, on the site of a disused rubbish dump! Offering accommodation to families, groups and individuals, a popular year-round destination.

The centre offers evening meals, breakfasts, and picnic lunches. Meals are served in the beautiful high-roofed dining room which retains the impressive proportions and atmosphere of the old barn. There is also the option to self-cater. There is a small sunken lounge to relax in. Camping is an option. A meeting/classroom is also available.

DETAILS

- **Open** - Open all year round. To check availability please call 01235 760253.
- **Number of beds** - 59: 1x15, 1x9, 1x6, 1x5, 6x4, 1x2
- **Booking** - Essential 24 hours in advance.
- **Price per night** - Adult £18.50. Under 18 £14.50
- **Public Transport** - Train, Didcot Parkway 10 miles. Stagecoach, 32/A, X35,36 from Didcot Parkway to Wantage 2 miles. There is no direct connection to the centre.
- **Directions** - From the M4 Jct 14, follow signs to Wantage. From Oxford A420 and A338 through Wantage. The Court Hill Ridgeway Centre is accessed from the A338 close to Letcombe Regis

CONTACT: Reception
Tel: 01235 760253
info@Courthill.org.uk www.Courthill.org.uk
Court Hill, Letcombe Regis, Wantage, OX12 9NE

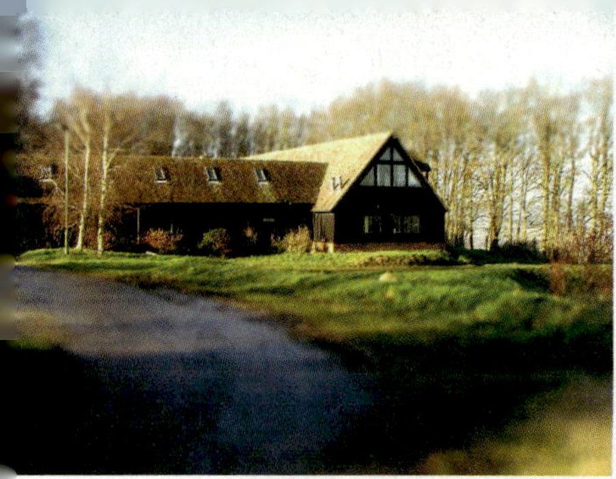
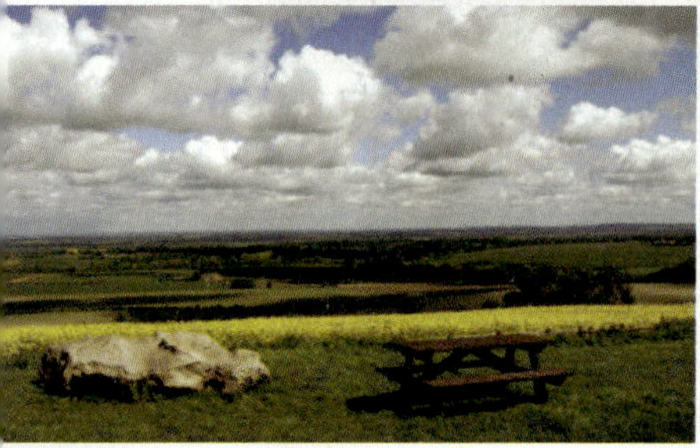
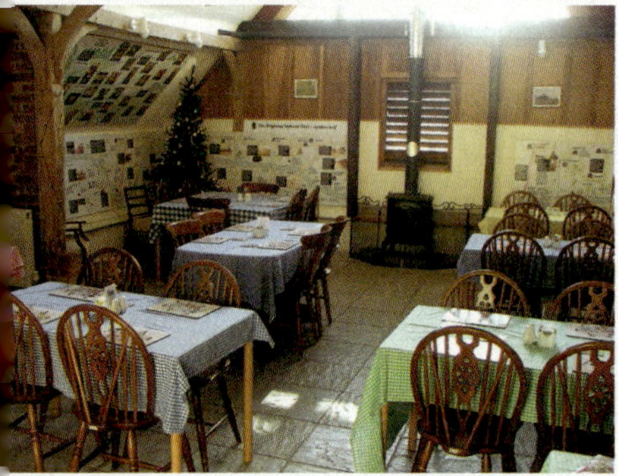
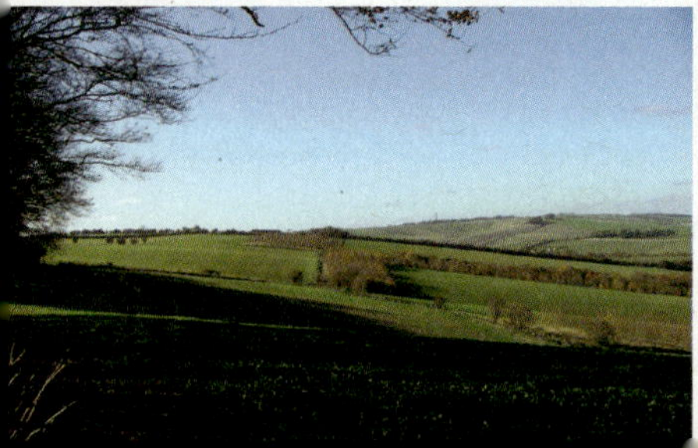
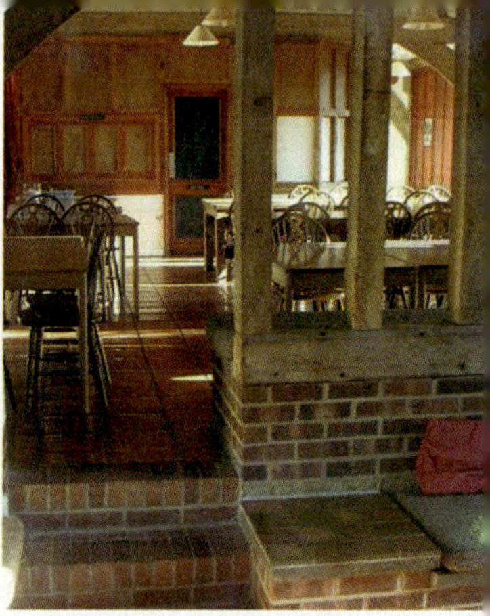
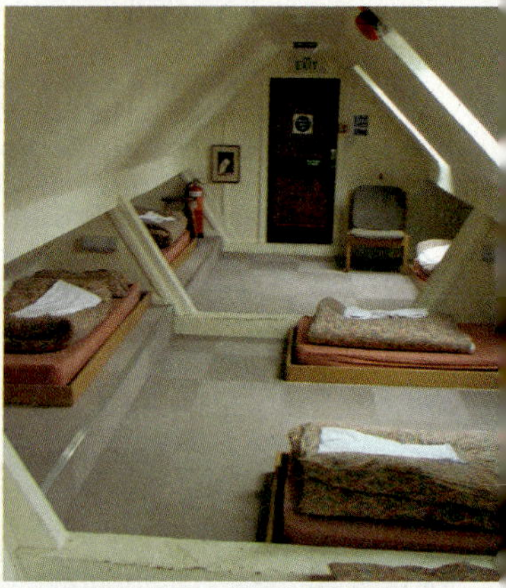
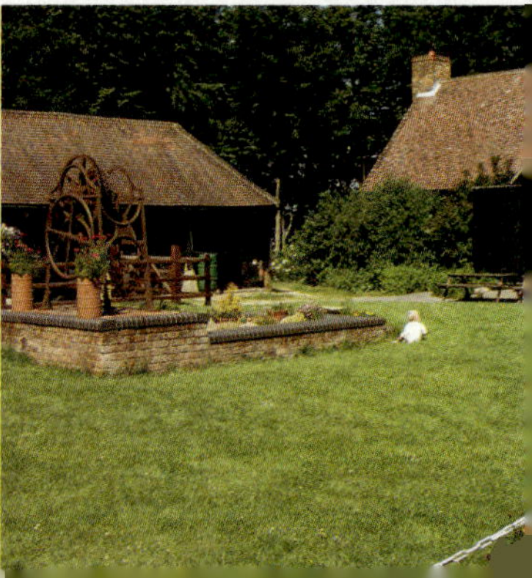

KIPPS BRIGHTON

Kipps Brighton is in the centre of Brighton, with views of the Royal Pavilion, close to the attractions, the pier and beach. Guests can relax on the roof terrace or in the lounge area and enjoy a continental breakfast in the dining room or a drink at the bar. Kipps Brighton has eight quality, well equipped private bedrooms all featuring TV, clock radio, CD player and wash basin. There are also two en suite dormitory rooms for groups or individuals. The hostel has a self-catering kitchen and offers nightly events and friendly knowledgable staff.

Kipps also have a hostel in Canterbury, a short walk from the town centre and historic attractions. See page 92 for details.

DETAILS

- **Open** - All year, reception 8am-11pm – No Curfew
- **Number of beds** - 47: 1x1, 6x dbl, 4x twin, 2x3, 2x10.
- **Booking** - Please book by phone, email or online (5% discount if booked online).
- **Price per night** - Dormitory rooms From £15 per person per night. private rooms from £21 per person.
- **Public Transport** - We are close to Brighton train station and bus station. From train station: exit and walk ahead down the main street for a few minutes, turn into Church Street (on your left) and walk along Church Street until the end, the hostel is opposite. From bus station: exit onto Old Steine Road and turn left towards the Royal Pavilion. At the far end of the Pavilion and opposite is the hostel.
- **Directions** - Take the M23, then A23 towards Brighton town centre. The hostel is opposite the Royal Pavilion on Grand Parade.

CONTACT: Reception
Tel: 01273 604182
kippshostelbrighton@gmail.com www.kipps-brighton.com
76 Grand Parade, Brighton, BN2 9JA

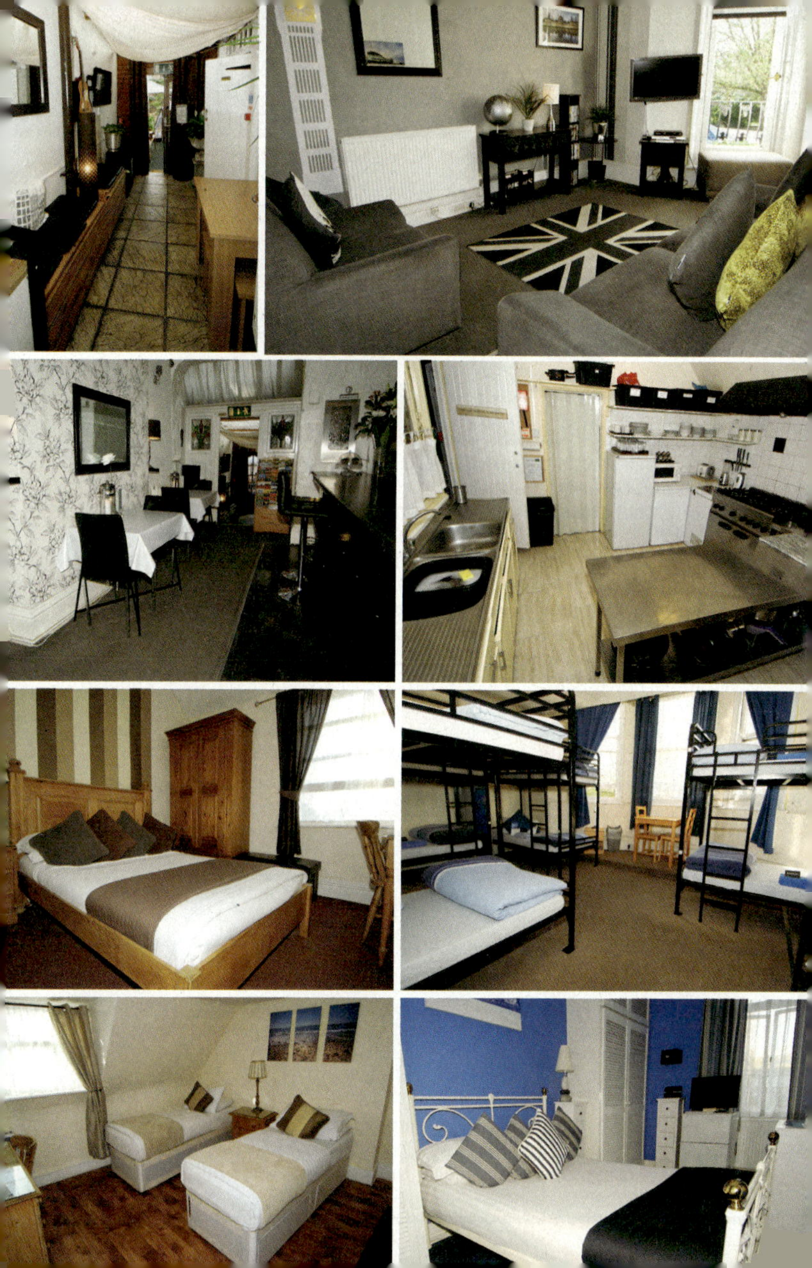

PALACE FARM HOSTEL

ENGLAND

Palace Farm Hostel is a relaxing and flexible four star hostel on a family run arable and fruit farm. It is situated in the village of Doddington, which has a pub, in the North Kent Downs Area of Outstanding Natural Beauty. The area is great for walking, cycling (cycle hire available £5 a day) and wildlife. The location is central for exploring Canterbury, Rochester, Chatham, Leeds Castle and the many other historic towns, villages and castles in Kent. The accommodation, in converted farm buildings, consists of ten fully heated en suite rooms sleeping up to 39 guests. The rooms surround an attractive courtyard garden with lawns, patio and barbecue area, ideal for families and groups. The en suite rooms cater for all age groups and those with disabilities. There are quality double beds, single beds & 3ft bunk beds. Duvets, linen and continental breakfast are included. There is also a small tent only campsite. Green Tourism Business Scheme GOLD Award winner.

DETAILS

- **Open** - All year, 8am to 10pm flexible, please ask
- **Number of beds** - 39: 1x8, 1x6, 2x5, 1x4, 1x3 and 4x2
- **Booking** - Advised.
- **Price per night** - From £16 to £30 (all private en suite rooms). Reduction for groups, see website.
- **Public Transport** - Trains: Sittingbourne (London Victoria to Dover). Buses from Sittingbourne station to Doddington two hourly (Mon-Sat), last buses 16.30 & 17.30.
- **Directions** - From A2 between Sittingbourne and Faversham turn south at Teynham, signed to Lynsted. Go through Lynsted and over M2 bridge, take 2nd turning right into Down Court Rd. Farm is 90 metres on left.

CONTACT: Graham and Liz Cuthbert
Tel: 01795 886200
info@palacefarm.com   www.palacefarm.com
Down Court Road, Doddington, Sittingbourne / Faversham, Kent, ME9 0AU

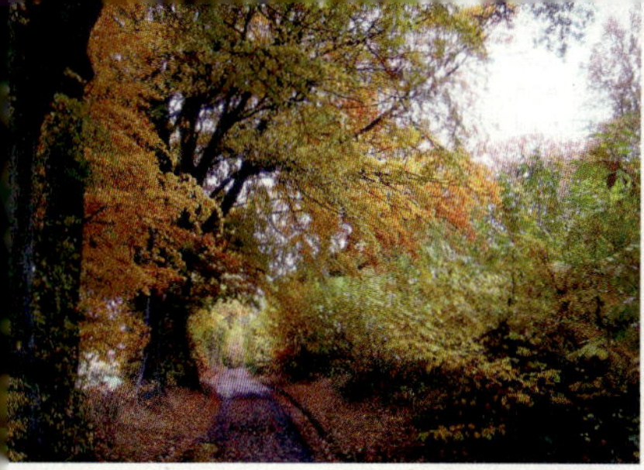
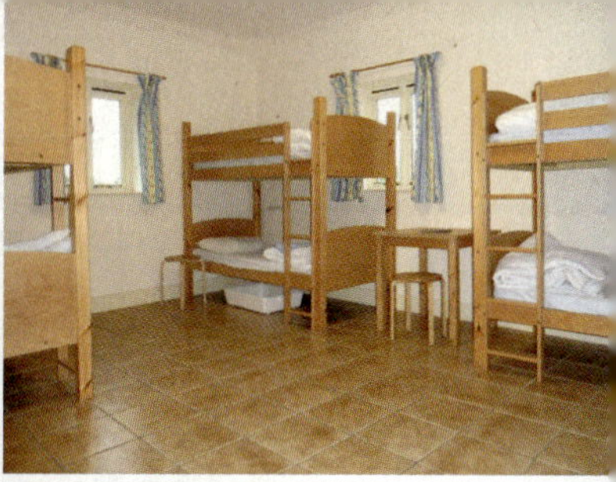
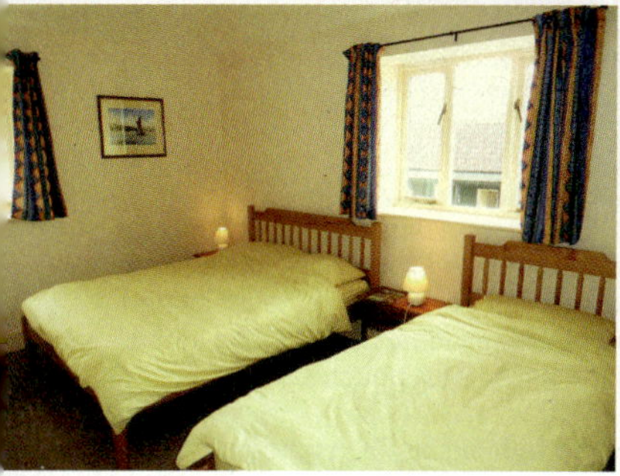
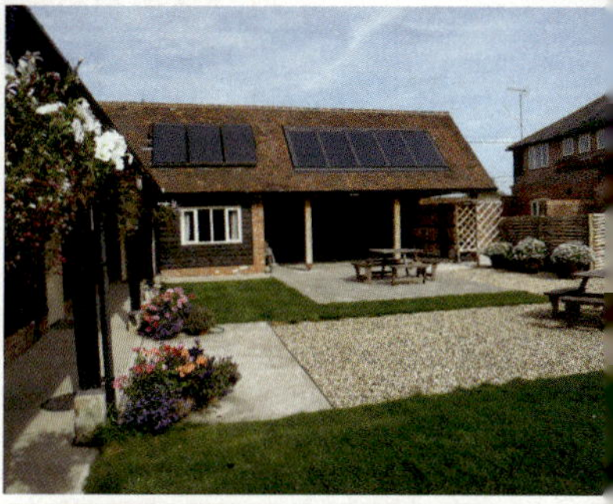
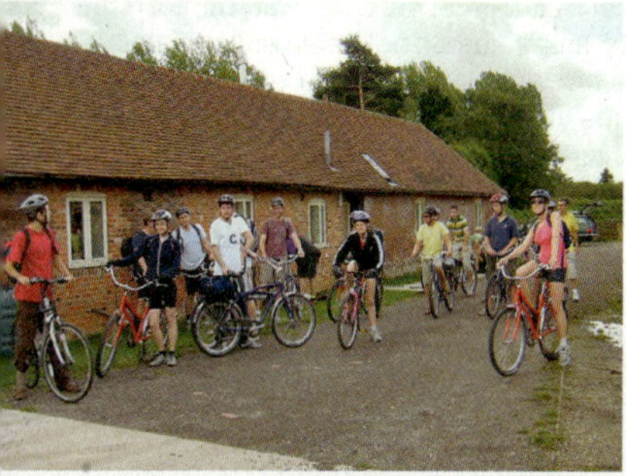
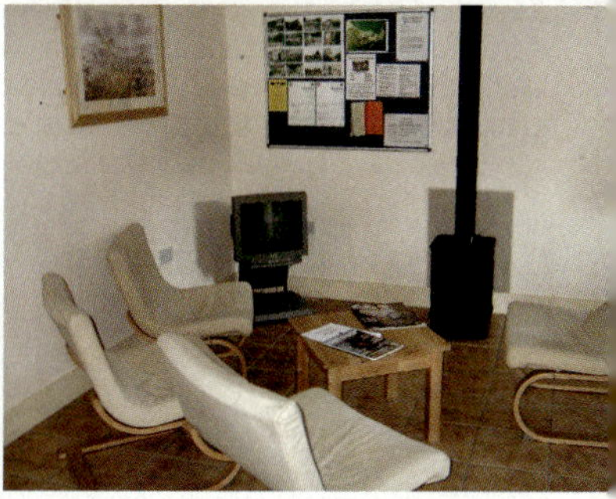
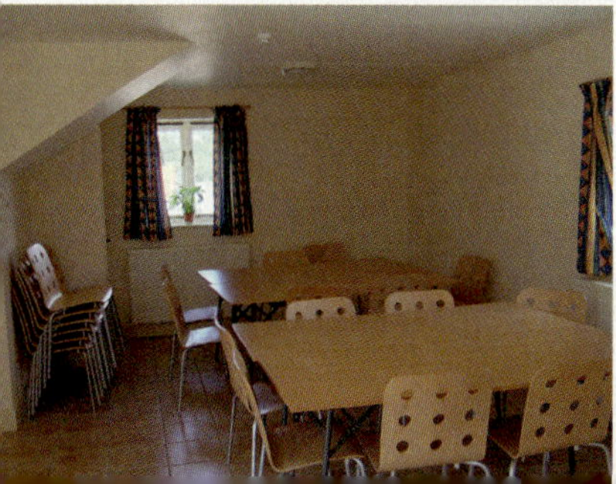
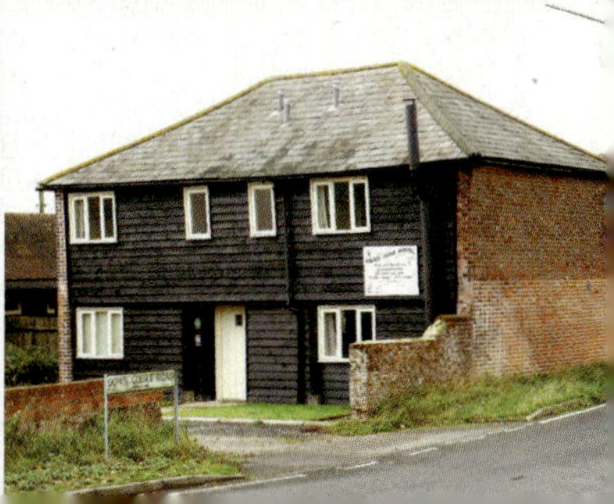

KIPPS CANTERBURY

Kipps is an ideal home-from-home for backpackers, visitors or small groups looking for self-catering budget accommodation in Canterbury. It is a short walk to the town centre and the historic attractions including the renowned Canterbury Cathedral. Canterbury also makes an ideal base for day trips to Dover, Leeds Castle and the many local beaches.

Facilities include dining room, TV lounge with digital TV, a garden, a fully equipped kitchen, a small shop offering breakfast and other food items, bicycle hire. Free WiFi & broadband access. Rooms include single/double/twin/family & dorms of up to 8 beds (most en suite). Camping available in summer. Free on-street parking. Kipps also have a hostel / hotel in Brighton, opposite the Royal Pavilion and close to town. See page 88.

DETAILS

- **Open** - All year, no curfew, reception 7.30am to 11pm
- **Number of beds** - 51:- 2x1, 2x2, 1x3, 1x5, 1x6, 1x7, 2x8, 1x9
- **Booking** - Advance booking recommended. Book online.
- **Price per night** - Prices from dorms £16pp, singles £22pp, doubles £37, quads £50. Weekly and winter rates available. Credit cards accepted.
- **Public Transport** - Canterbury East train station on London Victoria to Dover line, is ½ mile by footpath (phone hostel for directions). The local C4 bus stops by the door of the hostel. Taxi from coach/rail stations is £3.
- **Directions** - By car :- Take B2068 to Hythe from City Ring Road (A28). Turn right at first traffic lights by church. Kipps is 300 yds on left.

CONTACT: Reception
Tel: 01227 786121
kippshostel@googlemail.com www.kipps-hostel.com
40 Nunnery Fields, Canterbury, Kent, CT1 3JT

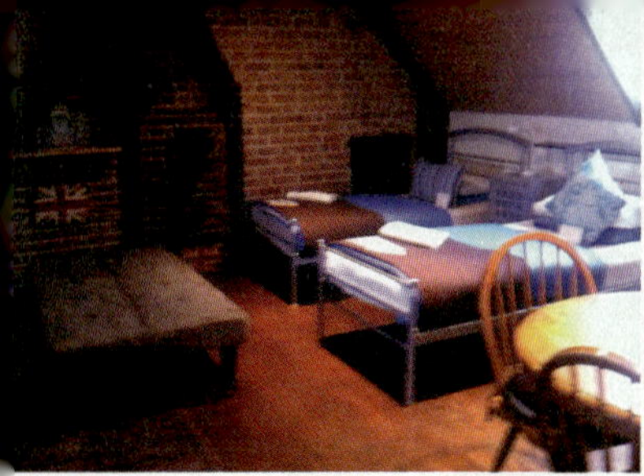
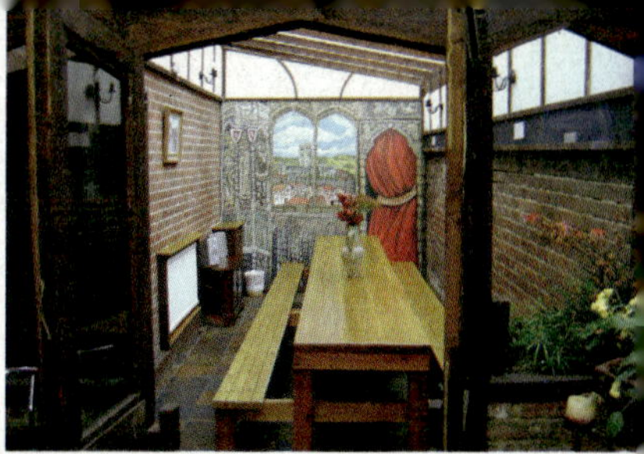
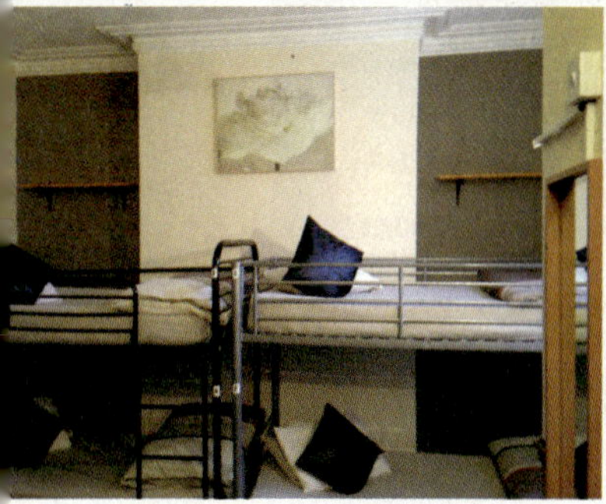
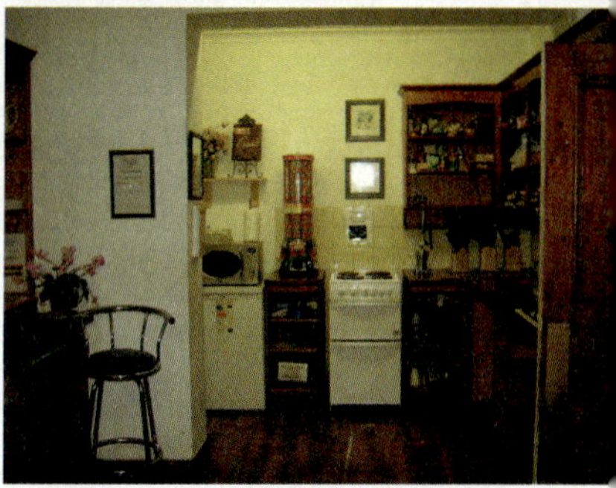
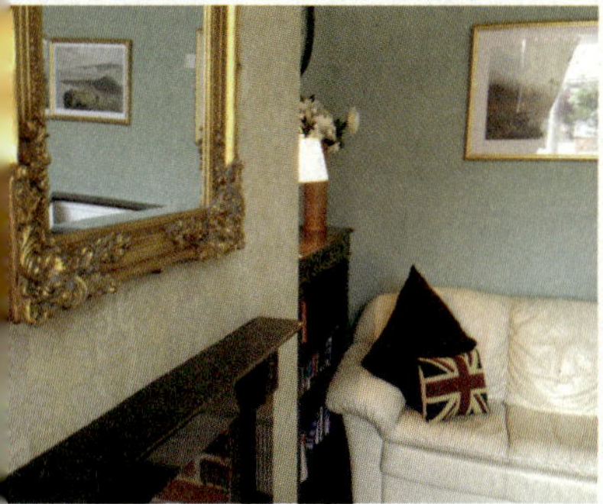
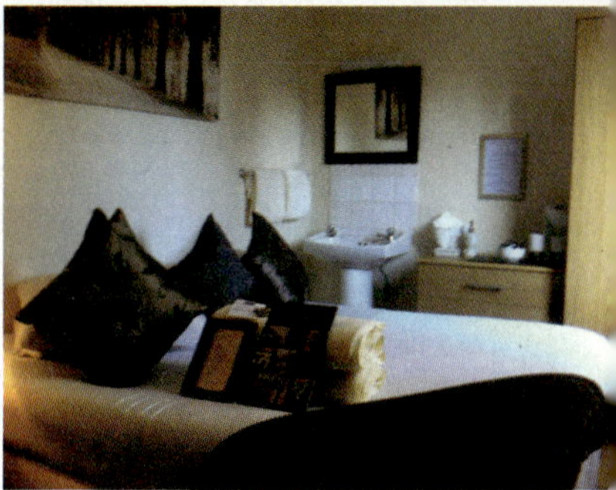
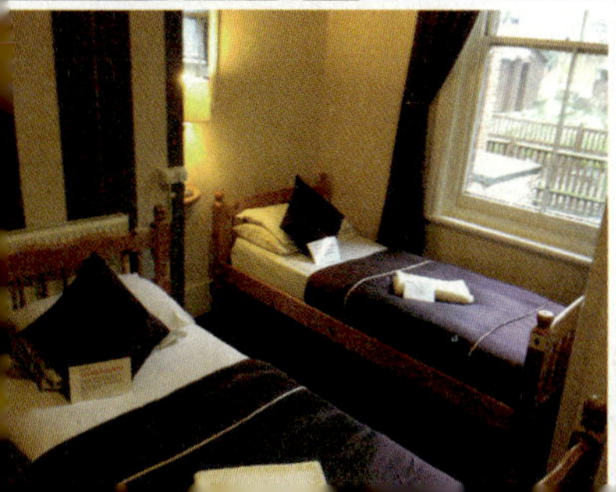
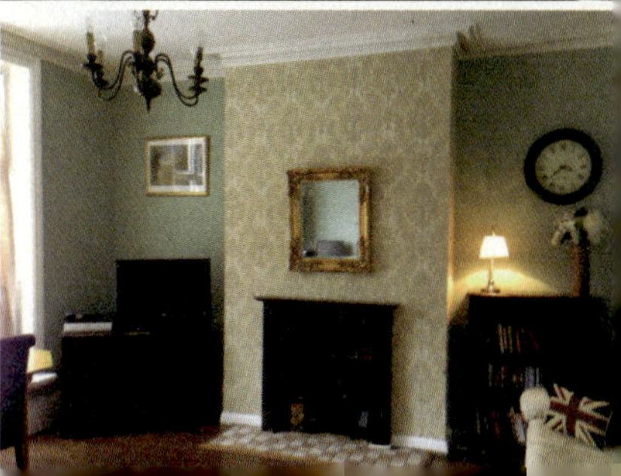

ALPHA HOSTEL

ENGLAND

A hostel by the sea. next to the Viking way for walkers and cyclists and just 50m from a Blue Flag, Safe Swimming beach, Alpha Hostel has been providing great budget accommodation in a friendly flexible atmosphere for over 20 years. Children love the beach which is only 50m from the front door- so parents be ready to help build those sand castles! The beach is also used by a number of different water sports enthusiasts. Facilities include; two lounges, a dining room, and large self-catering kitchen, washbasins in rooms, en suite family rooms. Secure bike storage. On street car/coach parking. Risk assessed for council, European schools and group use. Catering available for large groups (20+) exclusive hostel use with classroom available. Group self-catering also an option. Families and individuals also welcome. Why not visit the area or just stay on your way to Europe (1/2 hour to Dover by car)?

DETAILS

- **Open** - All year, 08.00 to 10.00hrs 17.00 to 22.30 hrs
- **Number of beds** - 60 .2x6, 2x5, 4x5, 2x3, 6x2
- **Booking** - Individuals/families: 25% deposit via website, balance on arrival, Groups: 25% deposit, balance 1 month before arrival.
- **Price per night** - Adult £16, under 18 £12.50, accommodation only groups please call/email hostel direct with requirements for meals etc. to obtain the best price.
- **Public Transport** - Train to Margate, bus to central Margate - Stagecoach, taxi, local buses and private hire. 10 minute walk to stations and town centre.
- **Directions** - By car: From A28 follow brown hostel signs. By foot from Margate walk to sea front. Turn left (to the west) and follow the prom. Take second set of stairs to the higher walkway. Hostel is across the road 25m away.

CONTACT: Suzy Shears
Tel: 01843 221616, Fax: 01843 229539
info@margatehostel.com www.margatehostel.com/
3 Royal Esplanade, Westbrook Bay, Margate, Kent CT9 5DL

HARLOW
INTERNATIONAL HOSTEL ENGLAND

95

Harlow International Hostel is situated in the centre of a landscaped park and is one of the oldest buildings in Harlow. The town of Harlow is the ideal base from which to explore London, Cambridge and the best of South East England.

The journey time to central London is only 35 minutes from the hostel door and it is the closest hostel to Stansted Airport. National Cycle Route 1 passes the front door. There are a range of room sizes from single to eight bedded including two rooms with double beds. Self-catering facilities, refreshments and a small shop are all available. During your visit you can relax with a book or game from our large collection. A children's zoo, orienteering course and outdoor pursuit centre are available in the park as well as pleasant river walks. Meals can be provided for groups.

DETAILS

- **Open** - All year, 8am-12 noon (check in 4-10.30pm)
- **Number of beds** - 30: 2x1, 5x2, 1x4, 1x6, 1x8
- **Booking** - Advance booking is recommended (can be taken 18 months in advance).
- **Price per night** - Please check our website for all prices.
- **Public Transport** - Harlow Town rail station is only 800m from hostel with direct links to London, Cambridge & Stansted Airport. Buses connect to London and airports.
- **Directions** - J7 of M11 take A414 into Harlow. At the 4th roundabout take 1st exit (First Ave). Drive to 4th set of traffic lights. Immediately after lights turn right (School Lane). Hostel is on left of Greyhound Pub.

CONTACT: Richard Adams
Tel: 01279 421702, Fax: 01279 421702
mail@h-i-h.co.uk www.h-i-h.co.uk
13 School Lane, Harlow, Essex, CM20 2QD

DOVER CASTLE
HOSTEL AND FLATSHARES
ENGLAND

Dover Castle Hostel and Flatshares, located close to London Bridge in Central London (Zone 1), offers backpackers great value, short and long stay accommodation. Located in the centre of the city. It is walking distance to sights such as Tower Bridge, St Paul's Cathedral, London Dungeon, Shakespeare's Globe, Tate Modern and the London Eye. Prices include free breakfast and free WiFi. The hostel has a guest kitchen and common room, free luggage room, a laundry service as well as a late guest bar with pool table and super drink offers. Guests wanting to stay in London for longer can rent rooms in Dover Castle house / flatshares. These furnished houses and flats are a short bus ride to London Bridge in Zone 2 (South East London). Single occupancy double rooms cost £140 per week and twin rooms cost £85 per week per person inclusive of bills and WiFi for a 6 week minimum stay. See www.london99.com for more info on the flatshares. Short or long term guests can find their home in London with Dover Castle!

DETAILS

- **Open** - All year, 24 hours. No Curfew
- **Number of beds** - 68: 1x4, 2x6, 1x8, 2x10, 2x12
- **Booking** - Booking advisable. Credit card secures bed.
- **Price per night** - £14-£24 pp incl. breakfast. Discounted weekly rates available
- **Public Transport** - Nearest main line station is London Bridge. Take underground Northern Line to Borough. The hostel is opposite Borough underground station between London Bridge and Elephant and Castle. 10 mins from Waterloo Station.
- **Directions** - From Borough tube, cross to Great Dover Street, 1 min walk on right.

CONTACT: Reception
Tel: 020 74037773, Fax: 020 75825247
stay@dovercastlehostel.com   www.dovercastlehostel.com
6 Great Dover Street, Borough, London, SE1 4XW

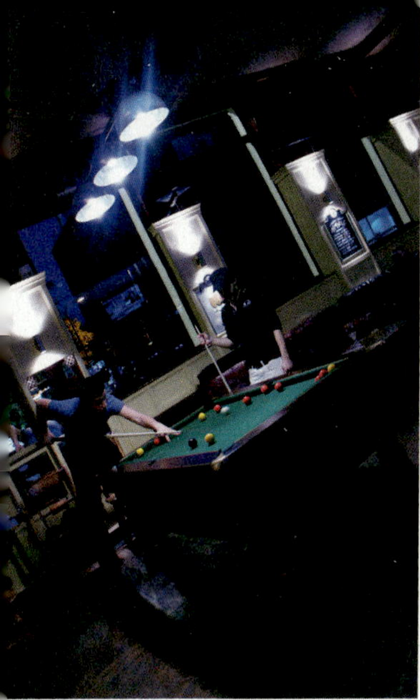
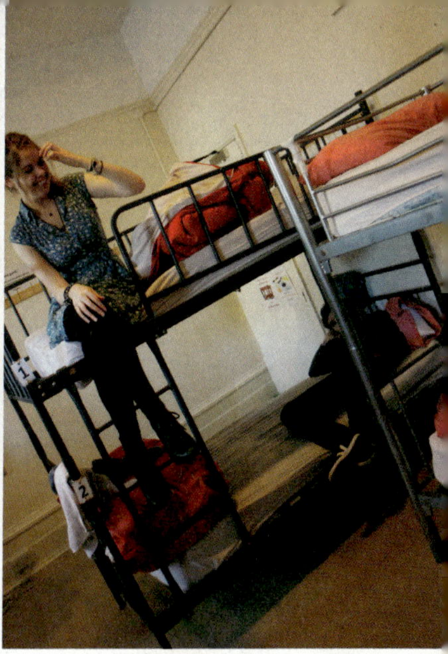
1
2
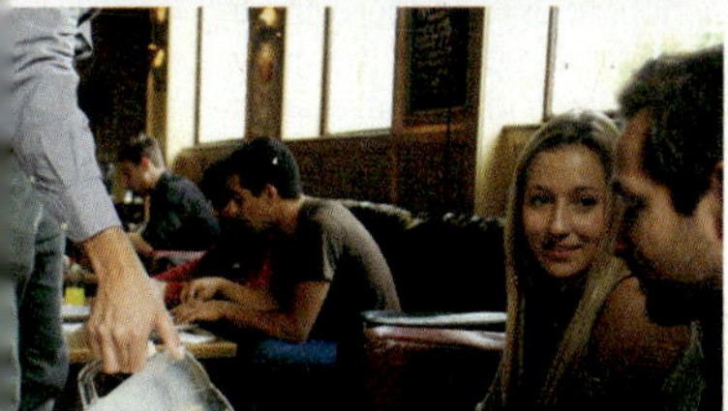
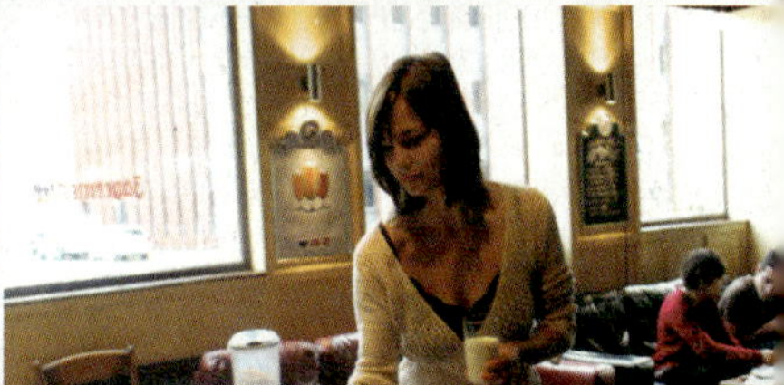
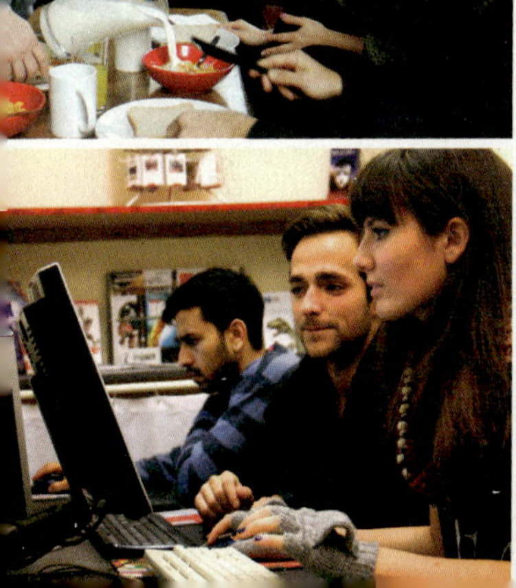
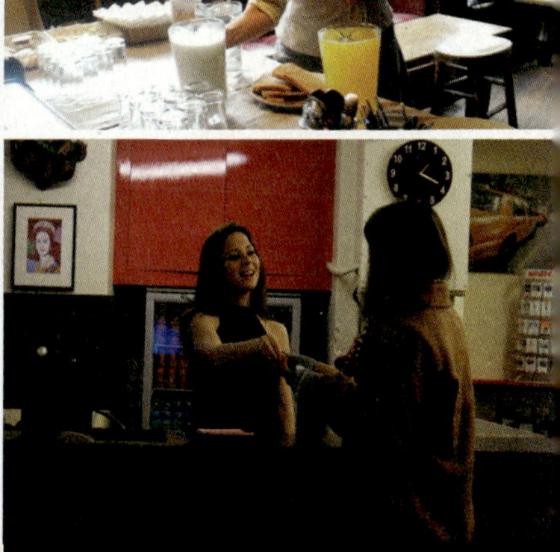

CLINK78

ENGLAND

Clink78 is a hip, modern backpackers hostel in the cool and hip streets of London King's Cross. Set in a 200-year-old magistrates' court house where Charles Dickens was inspired to write Oliver Twist and where The Clash stood trial, the building is truly a part of London's history. Restored to create a unique backpackers' retreat, it combines history with edgy and cool design. It's not a generic hostel! Facilities are modern, beds clean and cosy and the international staff friendly and fun!. The atmosphere is lively with a mix of young travellers meeting in the famous Clash bar for happy hour, music and fun; sharing food and tales in our modern self-catering kitchen; playing pool in the games area and chilling in front of the TV. Try innovative pod beds in dorms of varying sizes or book a private room, some en suite. The authentic Prison Cells and deluxe female dorms are recently refurbished with warmth and humour. So while visiting London, come and get locked-in at Clink and judge for yourself!

DETAILS

- **Open** - All year, 24 hours - no curfew or lockouts
- **Number of beds** - 500:4-16 bedded, triple, twin, single, en suite, cell rooms(for 2)
- **Booking** - online, by email or phone. with full payment by Credit or Debit Card.
- **Price per night** - From £13pp incl FREE breakfast, FREE bed linen, FREE WiFi and FREE London walking tour. Group discounts.
- **Public Transport** - Round the corner from King's Cross-St Pancras with direct links to Heathrow, Luton, Gatwick, Victoria, Eurostar and one change to Stansted.
- **Directions** - King's Cross station is 10 minutes away by foot. Exit the station, walk down King's Cross Road for 500m and you'll find Clink78 on your left.

CONTACT: Reservations
Tel: 020 7183 9400, Fax: 020 7713 0735
reservations78@clinkhostels.com   www.clinkhostels.com
78 Kings Cross Road, King's Cross, London, WC1X 9QG

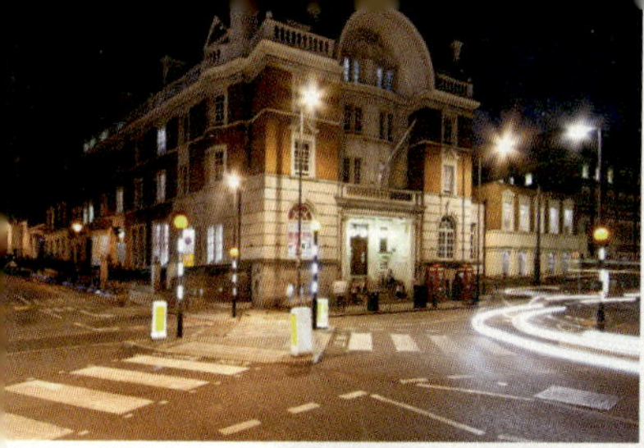

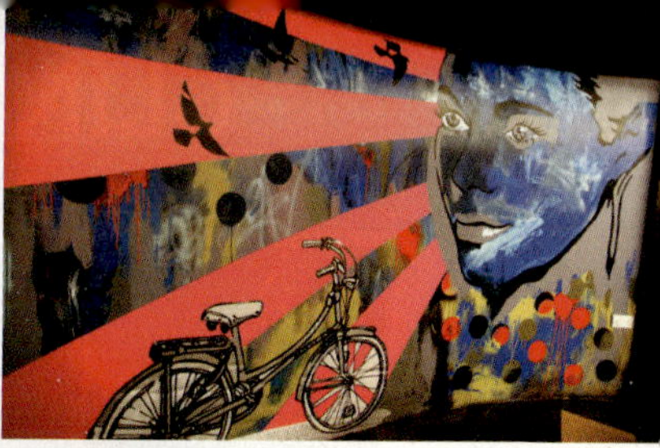

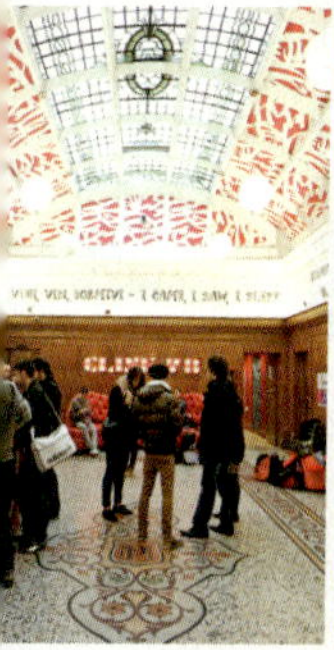

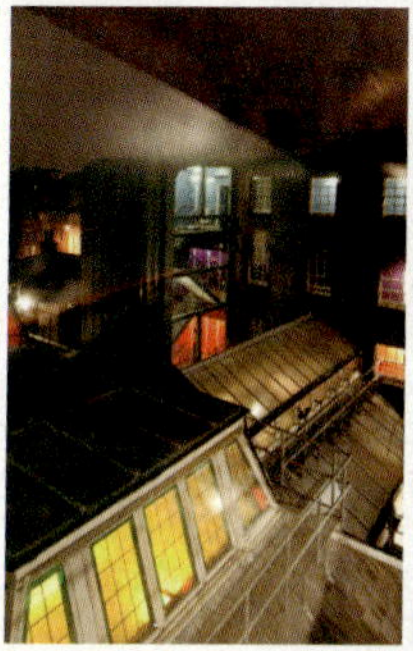

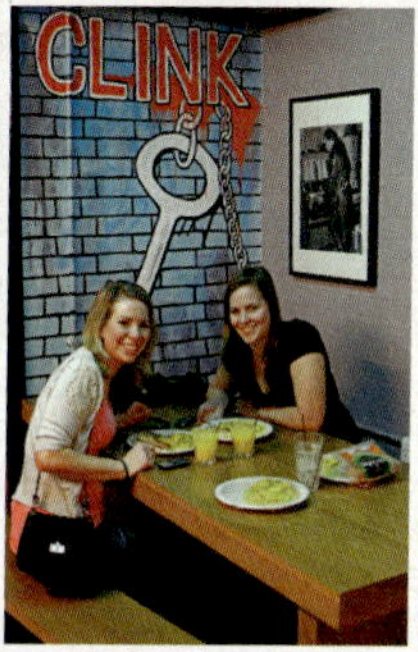
CLINK

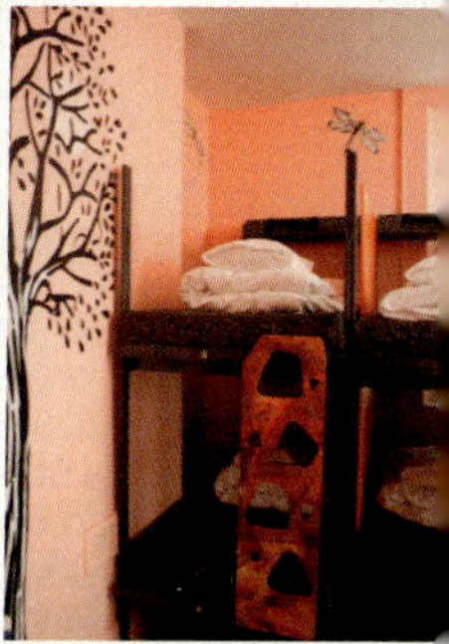

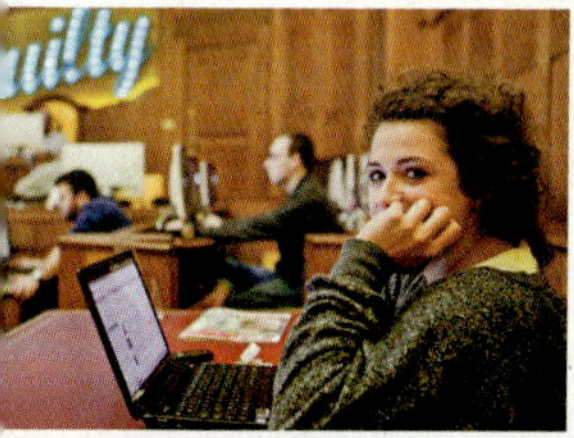

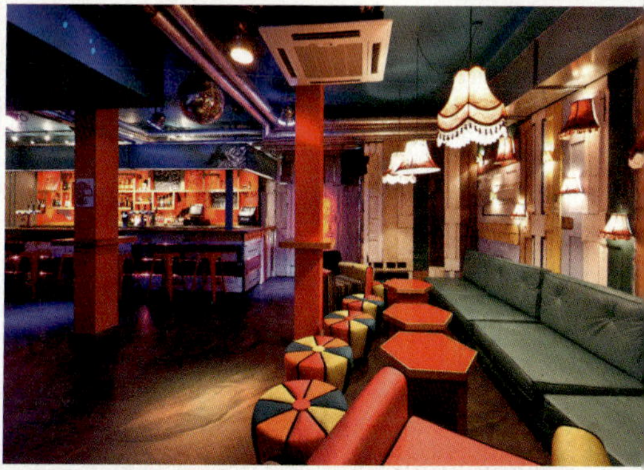

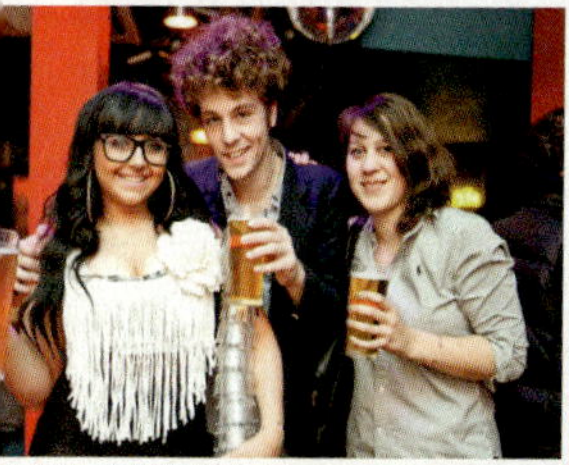

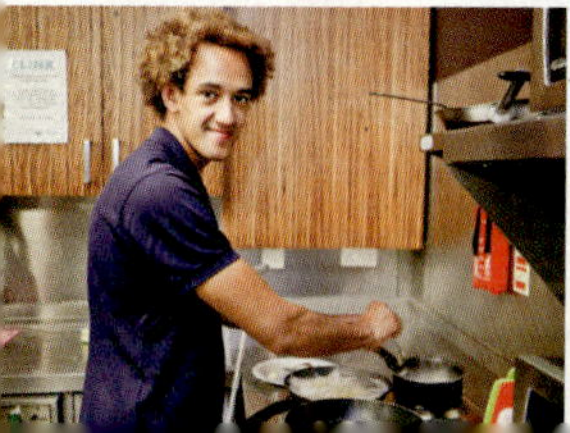

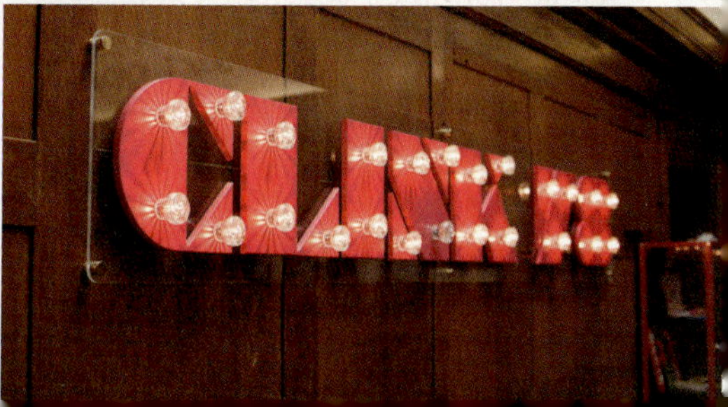
CLINK

CLINK261

ENGLAND

Clink261 is one of London's best established independent backpacker youth hostels, offering trendy and stylish accommodation in the very centre of London. This rather glamorous boutique hostel offers a very cosy and intimate atmosphere, combined with a personalised service. Clink261 attracts a diverse mix of individual and group travellers of all ages from around the world. You'll also find yourself a stone's throw from the British Museum, Covent Garden, Bloomsbury and Camden Market or just minutes away from the bright lights of Piccadilly Circus and Leicester Square on the tube. An improved security system gives you key card access to the building, your room and the self-catering kitchen and the tour desk will ensure you have everything you need for a great and unforgettable stay in London! All beds were upgraded in summer 2014 with LED lighting, power sockets and USB charge points.

DETAILS

- **Open** - All year (except for Christmas), 24 hours - no curfew or lockouts
- **Number of beds** - 170: 4-6 8-10 & 18 bed dorms 4 private rooms (up to 3 beds)
- **Booking** - Advanced booking recommended.
- **Price per night** - From £13pp including FREE breakfast & WiFi. Group discounts.
- **Public Transport** - Just beside King's Cross / St.Pancras which houses the Eurostar station and has UK mainline trains, underground, local buses and direct links with all major airports - Heathrow, Gatwick, Luton and Stansted. .
- **Directions** - Only 3 mins' walk from Kings Cross / St Pancras. From the station take the Gray's Inn Road exit, Keeping McDonald's on your right, walk straight ahead, past an exchange bureau, the police station and KFC. Gray's Inn Road curves to the right - the hostel is on the right 200m further on, opposite the hospital.

CONTACT:
Tel: 020 7833 9400, Fax: 020 7833 9677
reservations261@clinkhostels.com   www.clinkhostels.com
261-265 Gray's Inn Road, King's Cross, London, WC1X 8QT

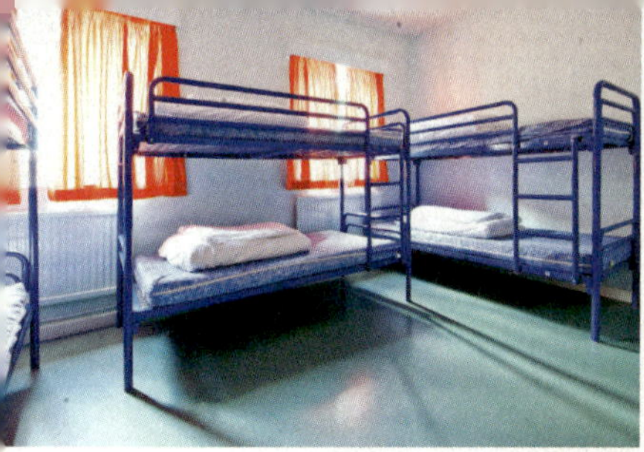

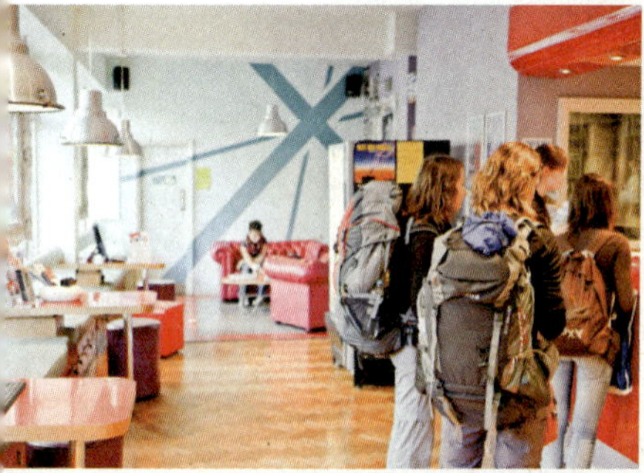

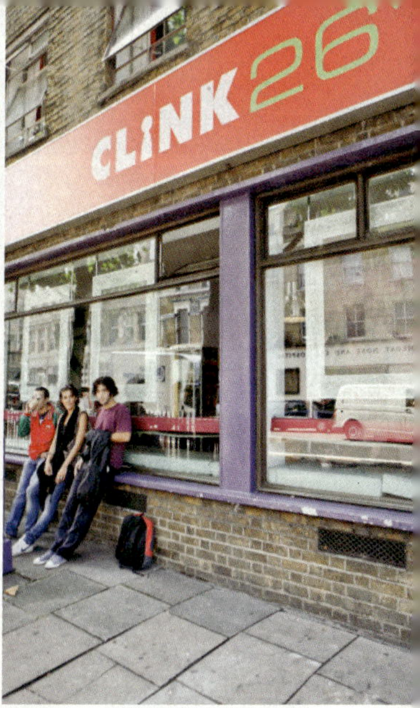
CLiNK 26

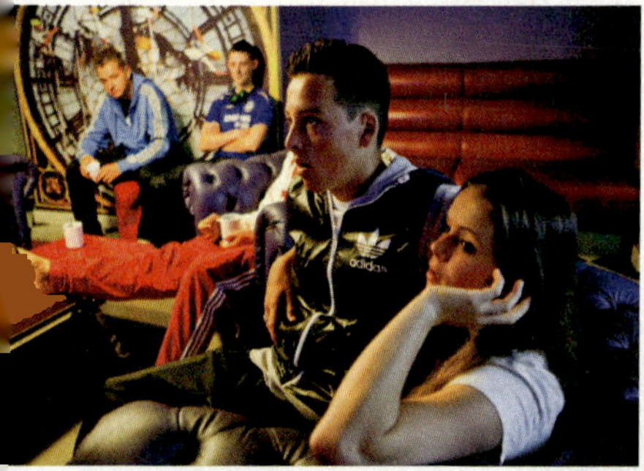
adidas

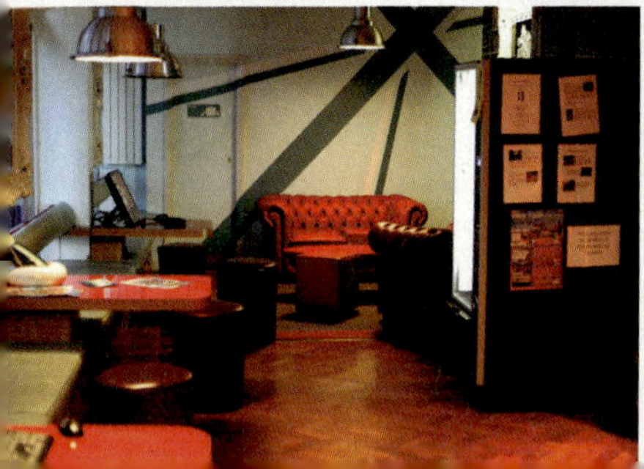

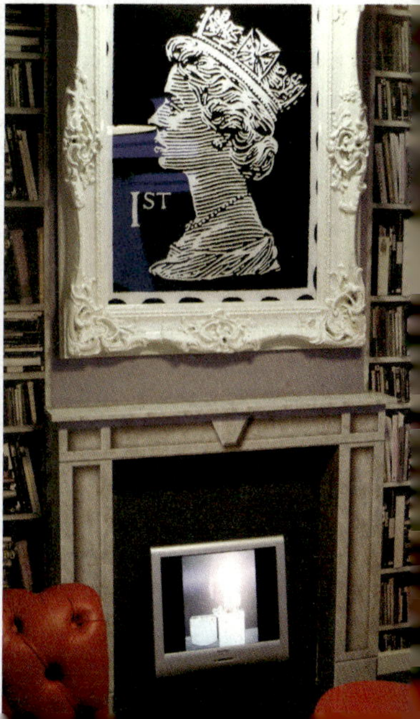
1ST

TRAVEL JOY HOSTEL

ENGLAND

Travel Joy Hostels are relaxed and chilled-out hostels which focus on personal service. Travel Joy is the only London hostel overlooking the river, centrally located between Chelsea and The Houses of Parliament. There is bicycle dock and a 24-hour bus outside the door that goes every ten minutes to Victoria Station, Houses of Parliament, Trafalgar Square, Soho, Oxford Street and Camden. On-site European restaurant and tour/theater-tickets desk. PCs in the lounge area (small fee) and € exchange with no commission/spread. Free tea/coffee/soft drinks at all times, free linen/towels, free WiFi in the entire building and free continental breakfast. There are no hidden costs. Other facilities include post, card phones, washing machine/dryer/iron, hair dryers, on-street parking and free luggage storage.

The hostel has a large bar, a great place to relax and socialize, with guest drink specials. You can BBQ on the terrace or hang out in the common room.

DETAILS

- **Open** - All year, reception open 24/7 except Sundays.
- **Number of beds** - 70:
- **Booking** - Booking recommended. By email, phone or online.
- **Price per night** - Dorm beds from £18. Includes breakfast, bed linen & towel.
- **Public Transport** - Pimlico tube station (Victoria Line) is 5-7 minutes' walk away. Victoria Station 10-15 minutes' walk. Bus 24 runs into central London 24 hours a day.
- **Directions** - From Pimlico tube take Bessborough St South exit, follow Lupus St, turn left onto Claverton St and then right onto Grosvenor Rd. Look for King William IV.

CONTACT: Reception
Tel: 0207 834 9689, Fax: 0207 834 0747
info@traveljoyhostels.com   www.traveljoyhostels.com
111 Grosvenor Rd. London SW1V 3LG

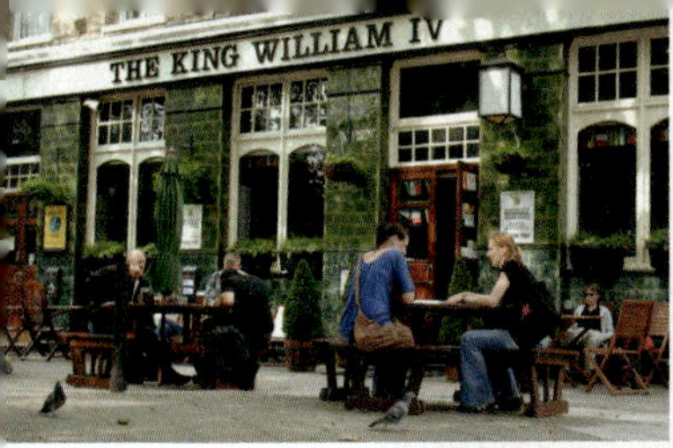
THE KING WILLIAM IV

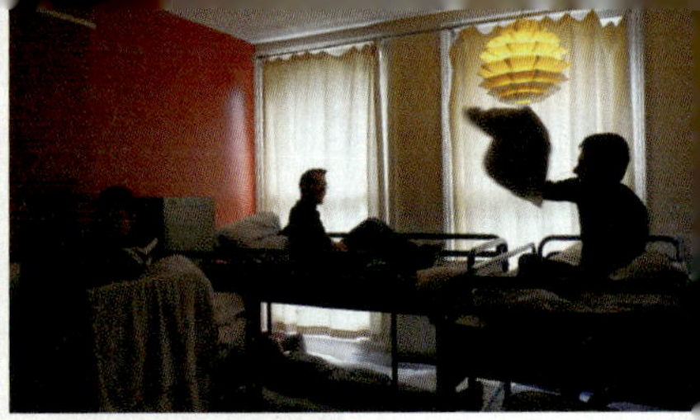

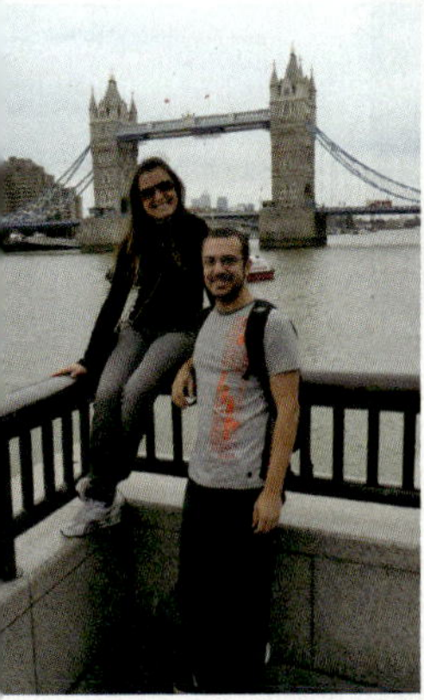

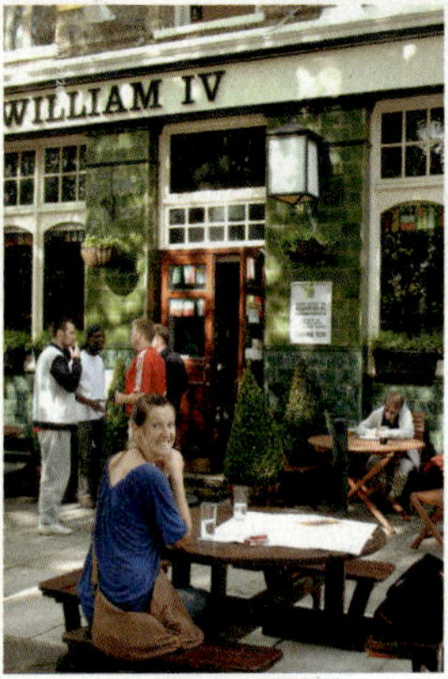
WILLIAM IV

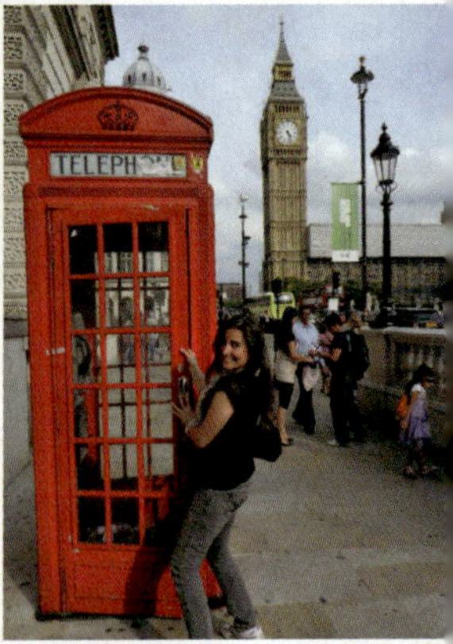

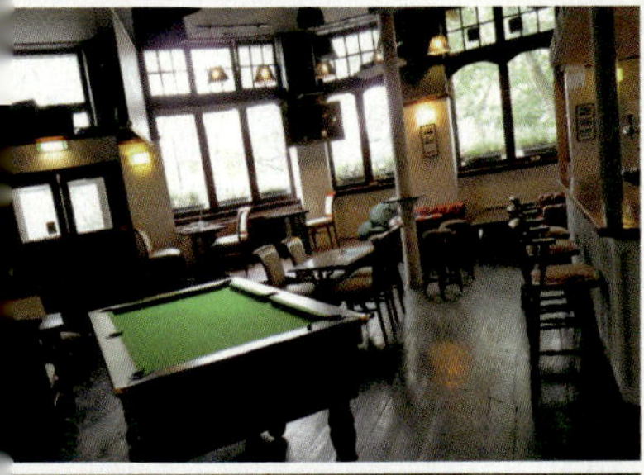

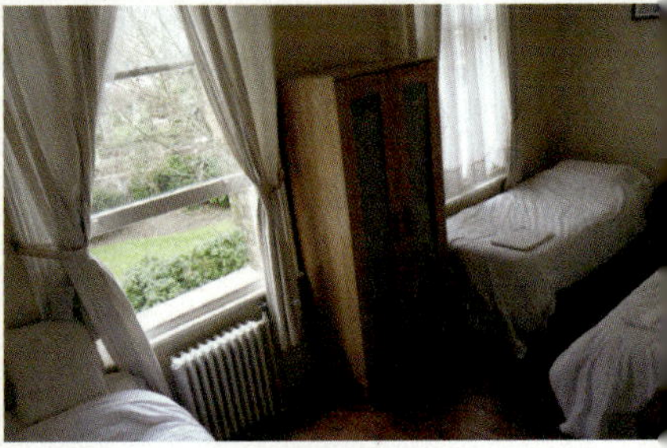

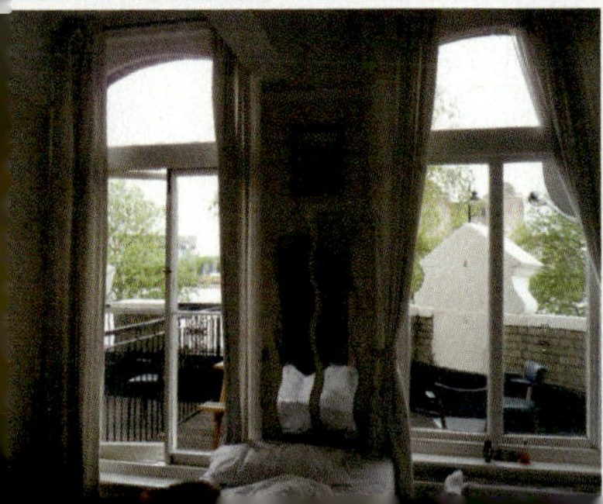

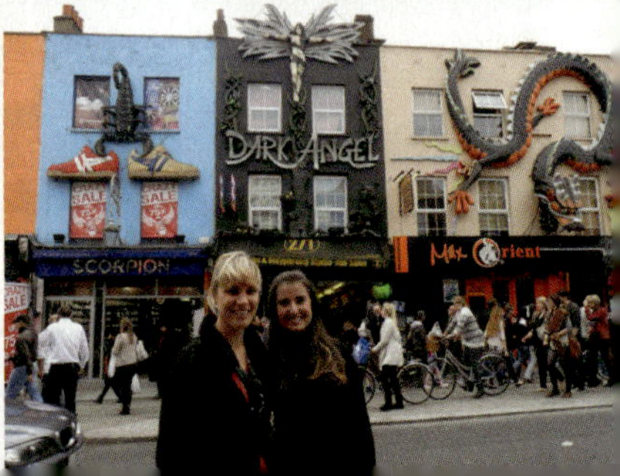
DARK ANGEL
SCORPION

STOUR VALLEY BUNKHOUSE

ENGLAND

Opened in 2007, and fitted with a wide range of modern facilities, Stour Valley Bunkhouse is set in peaceful surroundings on an historic 1000 acre working farm, an ideal base for exploring Constable Country. Close to the Stour Estuary, there are excellent opportunities for bird watching, walking and cycling on the doorstep. Alton Water is only 3 miles away for sailing and windsurfing. Ipswich is 6 miles away. For children of all ages there is a huge choice of local attractions, such as Jimmy's Farm or Colchester Castle. Colchester Zoo and Sutton Hoo are good options for a wet day, and there are excellent beaches at Dovercourt, Frinton and Walton. The bunkhouse sleeps up to 20 in 5 rooms. It is self-catering, with a shop and pub within a mile. The bunkhouse is unsuitable for stag parties or groups that are likely to be very noisy or drink heavily.

DETAILS

- **Open** - All year round (sole use groups only). Arrivals 4pm-9pm, depart by 10 am.
- **Number of beds** - 20 beds: 2 x 6, 1 x 4, 2 x 2
- **Booking** - Advance booking essential. Sole use group bookings only.
- **Price per night** - 2 nights from £430 - £639, 3 nights from £530 - £844 for a maximum of 20 guests.
- **Public Transport** - Manningtree Station 2.4 miles (less using bridle path) with regular service to London Liverpool St (1hr), Harwich Port and Ipswich. Taxis from Manningtree Station about £6.
- **Directions** - Grid Reference: TM120340. Six miles south of Ipswich on A137. Look out for The Bull pub, then cross the railway bridge and turn left after 200 yards, between white railings. Follow the drive to the crossroads, turn left and the bunkhouse is on the right hand side.

CONTACT: Caroline
Tel: 01473 327090 / 07857 630692
stourvalley@yha.org.uk   www.yha.org.uk/hostel/stour-valley-bunkhouse
Brantham Hall, The Chase, Brantham, Nr Manningtree, Suffolk, CO11 1PT

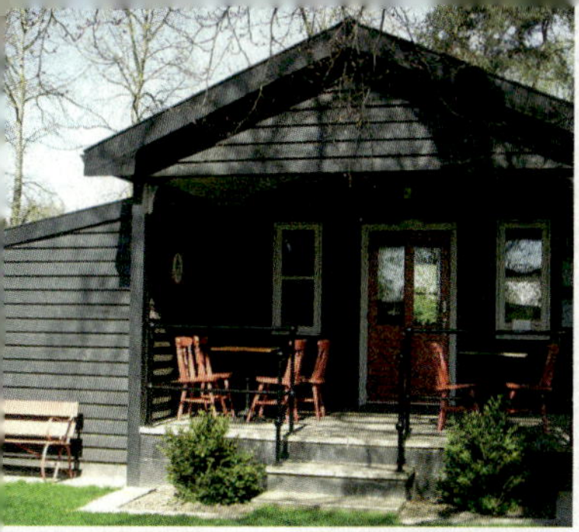
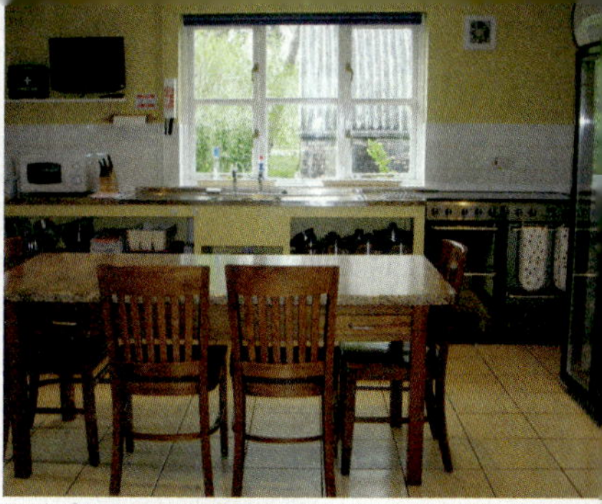
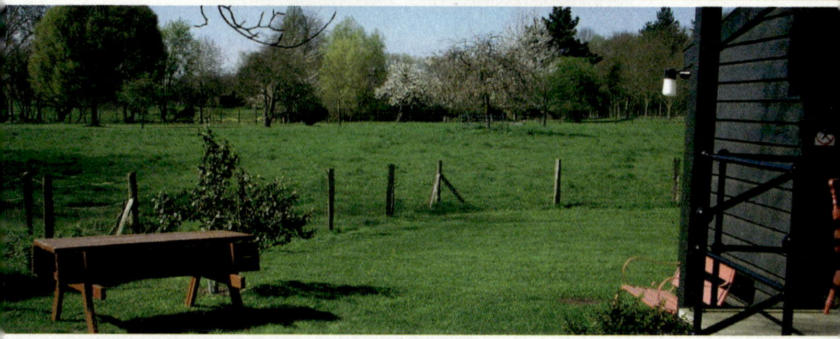
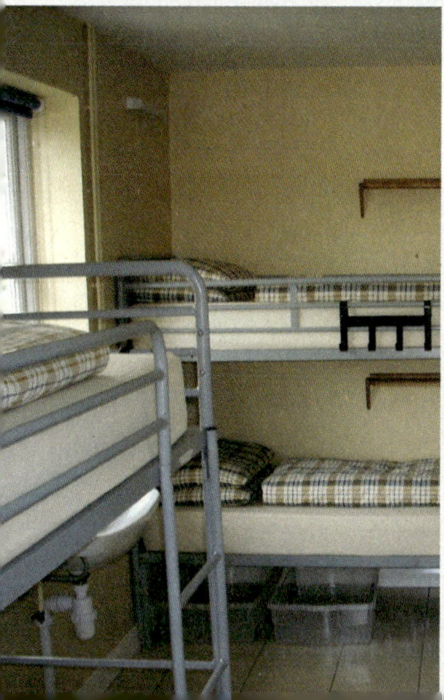
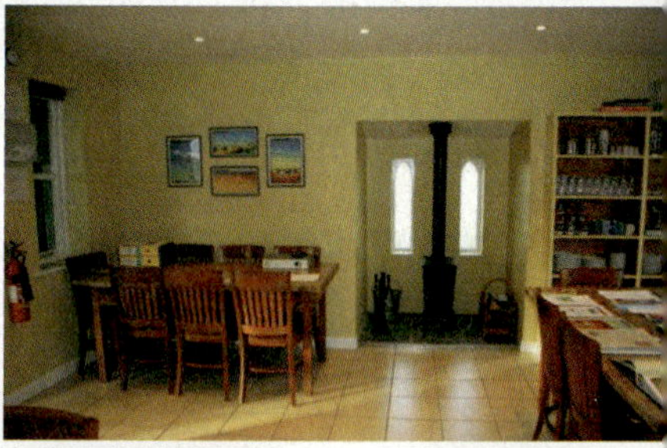
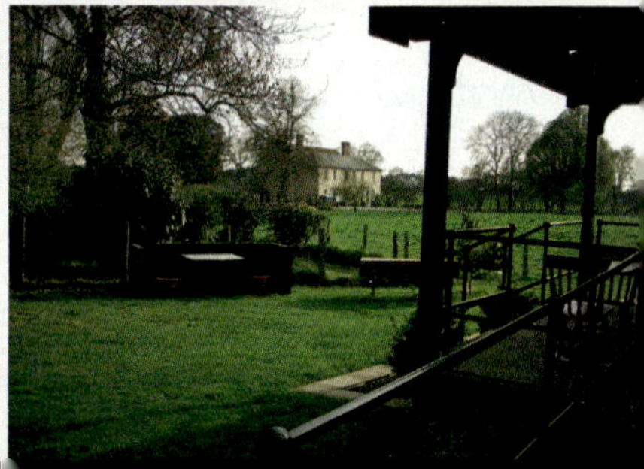

1912 CENTRE

ENGLAND

The 1912 Centre is the former town Fire Station situated within the heart of the Harwich Conservation area and just 50m from the sandy beach and promenade. Harwich owes much of its charm to its medieval origins, the grid pattern on which the original 13th century town was built still survives; there are over 200 listed buildings within half a square mile. The centrally heated hostel is laid out around the old engine garage, which now forms the central dining and recreational area. The upper floor has access to four cabin style sleeping areas, whilst additional beds are available on the ground floor allowing access for the disabled. All cabins have bunk beds. Facilities include a fully equipped kitchen, showers, a drying room. Visiting groups can bring their own sleeping bags, or can hire duvets from the Centre. The Centre is compact and easily managed, groups are expected to undertake certain domestic duties during their stay, and are responsible for leaving the Centre in a clean and tidy condition.

DETAILS

- **Open** - All year apart from 24th-27th December, Centre users have all day access.
- **Number of beds** - 26: 3 x 6, 2 x 2, 1 x 4.
- **Booking** - Sole use groups only. No stag groups. Pre booking essential.
- **Price per night** - Friday - Sunday (2 nights) £450, 1 Night - £240, 5 Nights - £900, 7 Nights - £1150. Other prices on application
- **Public Transport** - Harwich Town Station is a short walk from the Centre, direct trains to London Liverpool Street. The bus station is also within walking distance.
- **Directions** - Follow A120 to Harwich Quay, follow the road round past the Navy Yard Wharf. The Centre is on the right (adjacent to the Electric Palace Cinema).

CONTACT: Debbie Rotchell
Tel: 01255 552010
d.rotchell@harwichconnexions.co.uk www.harwichconnexions.co.uk
Cow Lane, Off Kings Quay Street, Harwich CO12 3ES

CROFT FARM WATERPARK

ENGLAND

Croft Farm is located just outside Tewkesbury in the scenic River Avon Valley, with a caravan and camping park adjacent to our own lake. The wide range of watersports activities and tuition on offer provide added interest for those wanting a more active holiday. A footpath meanders through the meadow to the River Avon, and free river fishing is available to all our camping guests. Accomodation is in Cabins, a Pod Village, Chalets and Camping. Croft Farm is ideally placed as a centre for touring, with the Cotswolds, Malverns, Bredon Hill and the Forest of Dean within easy reach. Local towns include Pershore, Evesham, Cheltenham, Gloucester and Tewkesbury.
We also offer a full range of activity holidays and events, from corporate team-building events to stag and hen groups.

DETAILS

- **Open** - All Year Round, 0900-2100
- **Number of beds** - 218: 50x4 9x2
- **Booking** - £15 deposit on individual bookings. £20 deposit on groups.
- **Price per night** - Bed £12, B&B £18, half board £24, full board £30
- **Public Transport** - Bus stop 100 yards from site entrance. Train station 2 miles Ashchurch for Tewkesbury
- **Directions** - M5 jnct 9. towards Tewkesbury. Turn right at the lights, (Shannon Way). At next lights turn right and go over the motorway bridge. Take the first turning left, through housing estate and over the motorway again. Turn right onto the B4080 and then first left into Croft Farm. From Tewkesbury take the B4080 north (Bredon). Croft Farm is on the left hand side after about 1.5 miles.

CONTACT: Martin Newell
Tel: 01684772321
alan@croftfarmleisure.co.uk   www.croftfarmleisure.co.uk
Bredons Hardwick, Near Tewkesbury, Gloucestershire GL20 7EE

YE OLD FERRIE INN BUNKHOUSE

108 ENGLAND

This beautiful riverside pub has been standing on the banks of the River Wye since the 15th Century. With charming traditional features, warming open fires and stunning views across the valley, Ye Old Ferrie Inn is the ideal base for your explortion of the Wye Valley.

Ye Old Ferrie Inn Bunkhouse, adjoining the inn, is the perfect place for you to hang up your rucksack, kick off your walking boots and relax. There are two bunkrooms, sleeping 6 and 12, which are cosy, practical and affordable. You can watch the world float by on the two riverside terraces and meals are available in the inn which serves traditional pub food, locally sourced.

The inn also has double B&B rooms with riverside views. The area is ideal for canoeing, walking and rock climbing.

DETAILS

- **Open** - All year, all day
- **Number of beds** - 20 (1x14, 1x6) plus double B&B rooms
- **Booking** - Book by phone or email.
- **Price per night** - From £15 per person. For sole use please ring to enquire.
- **Public Transport** - Train stations at Newport, Lydney, Hereford or Gloucester. Regular buses from Monmouth or Ross-on-Wye.
- **Directions** - From A40 Ross-on-Wye to Abergavenny road take junction signed Whitchurch/Symonds Yat West (B4164). Stay on B4164 and take slight left at Ferrie Lane and continue onto Washings Lane.

CONTACT: Jamie
Tel: 01600 890 232, Fax: +441600890232
hello@yeoldferrieinn.com www.yeoldferrieinn.com
Ferrie Lane, Symonds Yat West, Herefordshire HR9 6BL

HAYE FARM
SLEEPING BARN

ENGLAND

Located on a working family farm, Haye Farm Sleeping Barn offers bunkhouse accommodation finished to a very high standard. It has a fully equipped self-catering kitchen, dining room and lounge. Bedrooms range from double/twin en suite to a 6 bedded dormitory. The barn is central heated throughout. Covered decking, patio, lawn and a BBQ provide ample opportunity to enjoy the quiet rural location. A great location to enjoy the surrounding countryside, the Wyre Forerst being one of the largest remaining ancient forests in England. The Worcestershire Way footpath follows the boundary of the farm and both the Severn Way and Mercian Way (NCN route 45) pass through Bewdley.

The georgian town of Bewdley located on the river Severn is just 1 mile away, the West Midland Safari Park and Severn Valley Railway are also very close

DETAILS

- **Open** - Open all year, 24 hour access
- **Number of beds** - 15: 1x2, 1x3, 1x4, 1x6
- **Booking** - advance booking required
- **Price per night** - From £15pp. Can book bed in dormitory, private room or exclusive use of whole barn. Visit website for full prices
- **Public Transport** - Train station Kidderminster 4 miles. Bus stop Bewdley 1 mile
- **Directions** - One mile from Bewdley town centre, within 30 minutes' drive of both the M5 and M42. From Bewdley town centre take the B4194 southbound for ½ mile. At top of bank turn right (signposted Heightington/outdoor centre). Farm entrance on the right after ½ mile

CONTACT: Stuart Norgrove
Tel: 01299 403371
enquiries@haye-farm.co.uk   www.haye-farm.co.uk
Haye Farm, Ribbesford, Bewdley, Worcestershire, DY12 2TP

# BERROW HOUSE
ENGLAND BUNKHOUSE & CAMP SITE

Berrow House is situated between Rugged Stone Hill and Midsummer Hill in the Malvern Hills. An Area of Outstanding Natural Beauty close to the Forest of Dean, the Welsh border and the start of the Worcestershire Way Walk. In the garden around Berrow House there is a selection of simple accommodation and camping with a wildlife picnic area, woodland, star gazing and grass sledging to explore. The Bunkhouse has two rooms and shares the toilets and showers in the yard with the campsite. Its kitchen has a table and benches, hot water, fridge freezer, microwave and a cooker. Its sitting room has easy chairs, four beds and steps leading up to a low ceiling loft with mattresses for 3 small people. The Fold has a toilet and shower and two small bunkrooms each sleeping two. Just outside is a kitchenette with fridge, toaster, small cooker and utensils. The Bandsaw Barn is a meeting room for use by groups on request. Overflow accommodation for 3 on camp beds is available in the Bandshaw Barn and there is a double and a single bed in a caravan. This is simple accommodation heated by fan heaters, bring your on sleeping bag.

DETAILS

- **Open** - All year, 24 hours
- **Number of beds** - 7 (Bunkhouse), 4 (Fold), 3 (Bandsaw), 3 (Caravan) and 8 tents.
- **Booking** - Not required for individuals
- **Price per night** - £13 per person
- **Public Transport** - Nearest public transport is in Ledbury, 3 miles from the hostel.
- **Directions** - Take A449 from Ledbury towards Malvern. Turn right on to A438 through Eastnor. Berrow House is behind phone box in Hollybush (yellow sign).

CONTACT: Bill or Mary Cole
Tel: 01531 635845, Fax: 01531 635845
berrowhouse@tiscali.co.uk www.berrowhouse.co.uk
Hollybush, Ledbury, Herefordshire, HR8 1ET

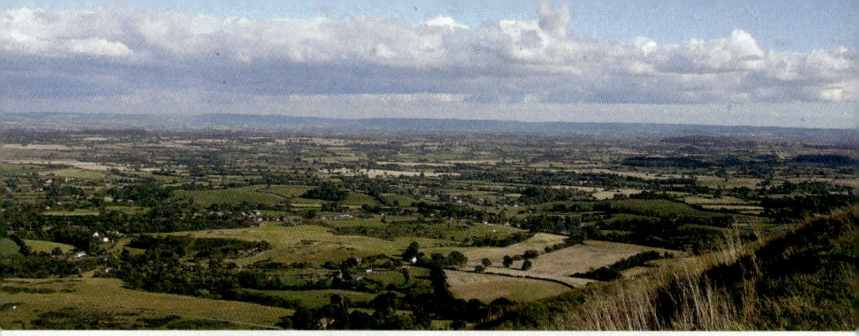

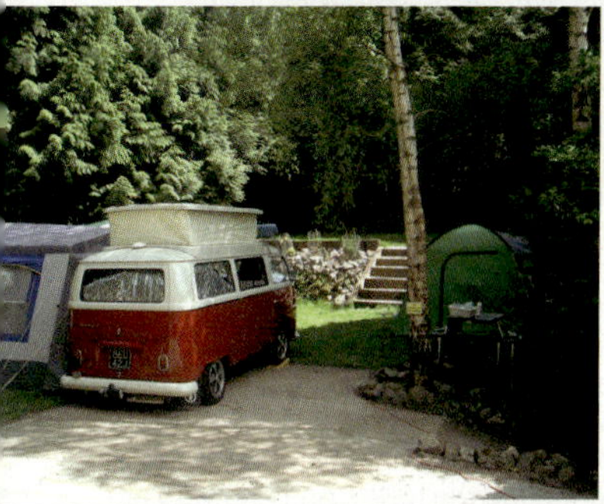

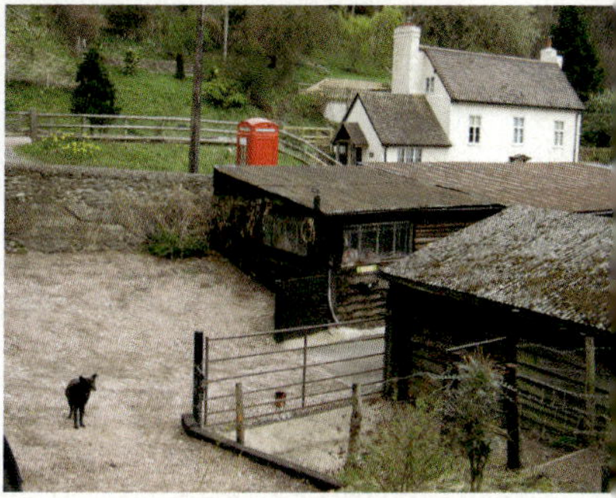

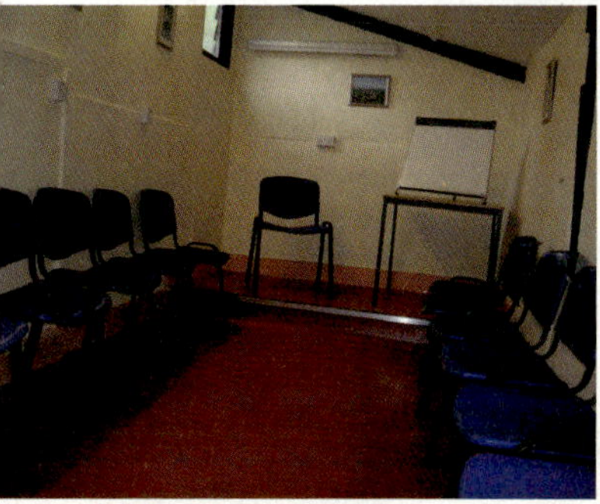

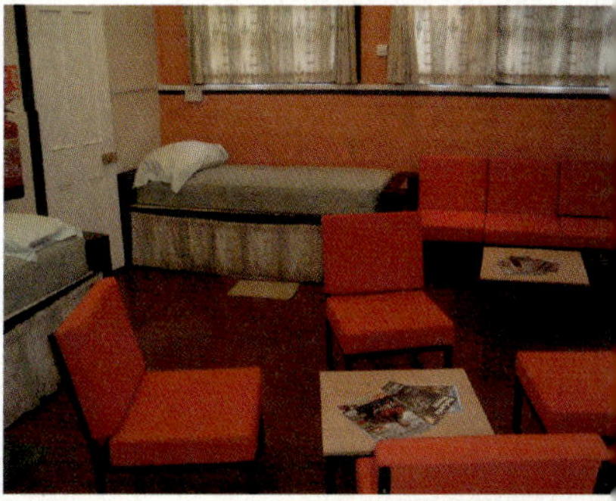

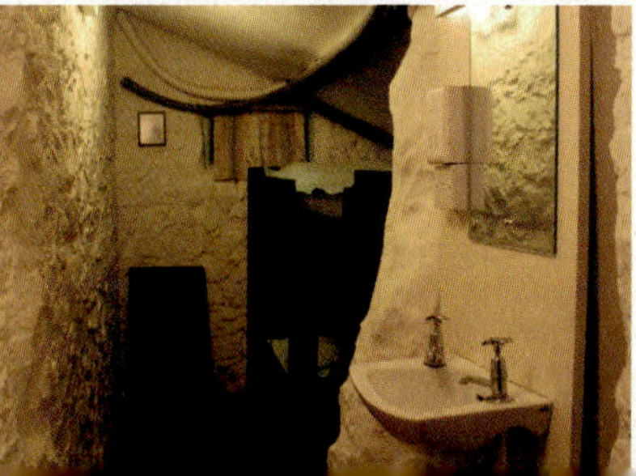

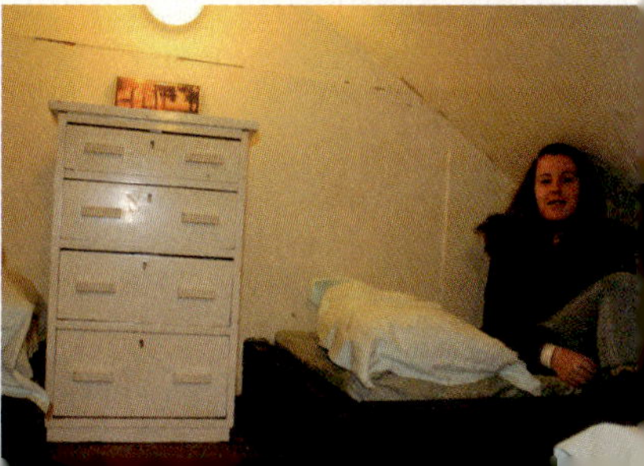

WOODSIDE LODGES BUNKHOUSE

ENGLAND

Woodside Lodges is a landscaped park with lakes, grass and woodland managed to encourage wildlife. In addition to the Scandinavian lodges, campsite and camping pods there is a modern barn converted into 5 self-catering units. 3 units sleep 2, 1 unit sleeps 3 and 1 unit sleeps 4 (additional camp beds are available). Each unit has a cooking area with kettle, toaster, microwave, 2 electric rings, fridge and basic utensils. Electricity is by coin meter and bedding can be provided for an extra charge (or bring your own sleeping bag). The bunkhouse has a small common room, the toilets and showers are shared with the campsite. Close to the Herefordshire Trail, the Malvern Hills and the Forest of Dean the area is ideal for walkers. Nature lovers will enjoy the site with its backcloth of mixed woodland, wild flowers, pools and waterfalls where fishing, wild swimming and picnics can be enjoyed. The nearby town of Ledbury is famous for its black and white buildings, cobbled streets and Poetry Festival.

DETAILS

- **Open** - All year, All day
- **Number of beds** - 13 : 3x2, 1x3, 1x4 (max 20 using camp beds)
- **Booking** - Booking in advance advised.
- **Price per night** - From £12.50 pp based on 4 sharing a room, weekend supplement, phone/website for full prices. Can be booked for exclusive use.
- **Public Transport** - Public transport is available within 1/2 mile.
- **Directions** - From Junction 2, M50 take the A417 to Ledbury. At the first roundabout turn left following Leadon Way (the by-pass). At the third roundabout turn left into Little Marcle Road. Go past the factory and take the right turn signposted Falcon Lane & Baregains Lane. Woodside Lodges is the sixth entrance on the right.

CONTACT: Woodside Lodges Country Park
Tel: 01531 670269, Fax: 0560 115 3922
info@woodsidelodges.co.uk www.woodsidelodges.co.uk
Woodside Lodges, Falcon Lane, Ledbury, Herefordshire, HR8 2JN

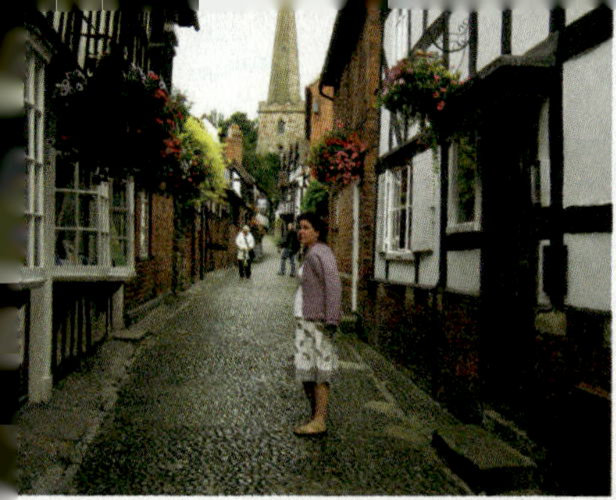
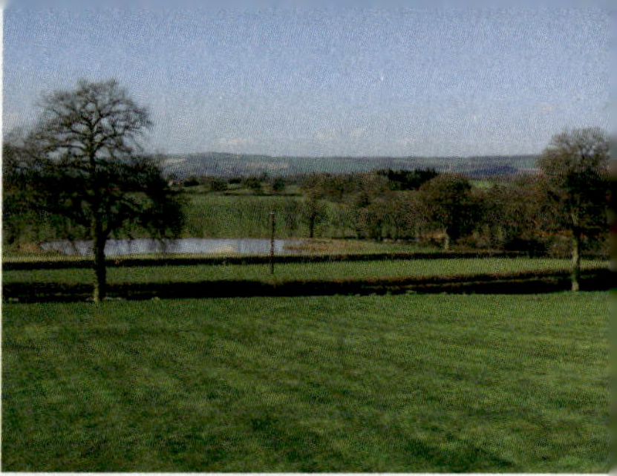
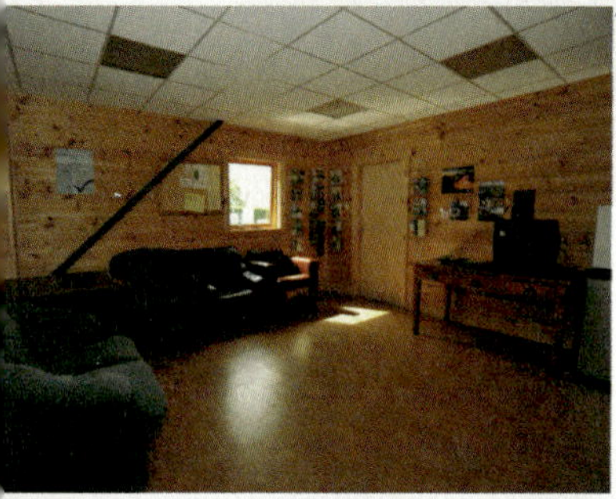
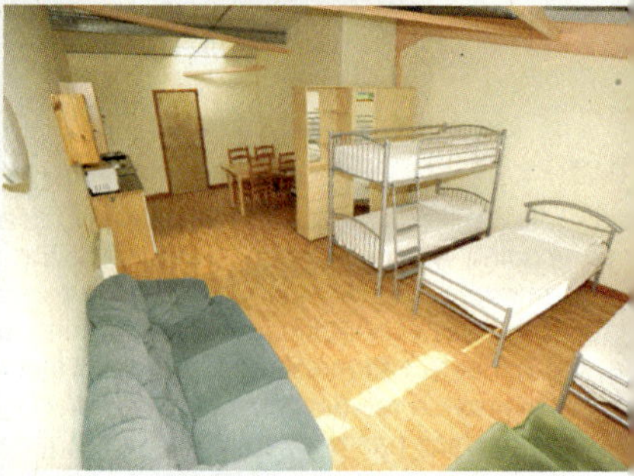
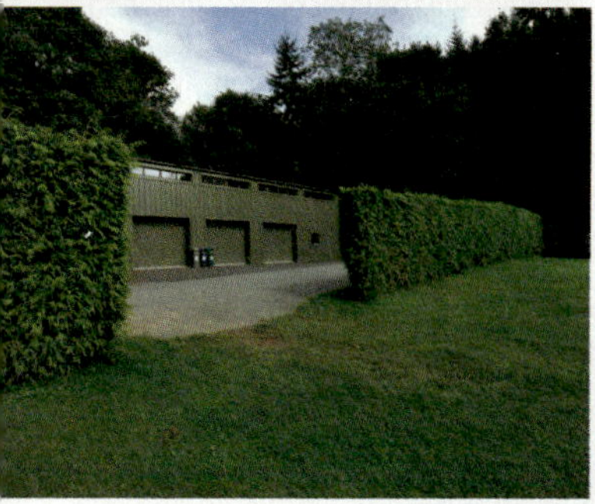
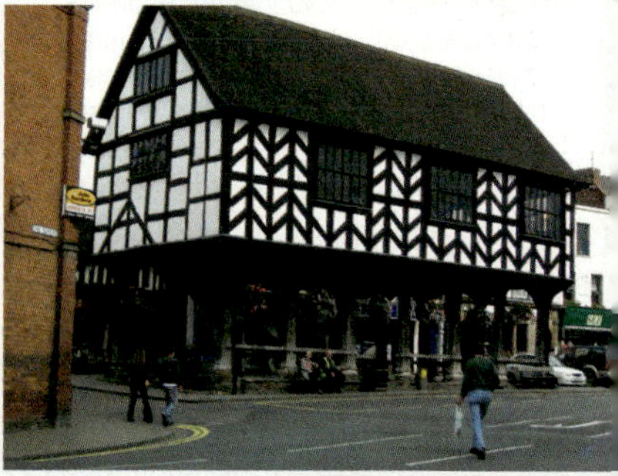
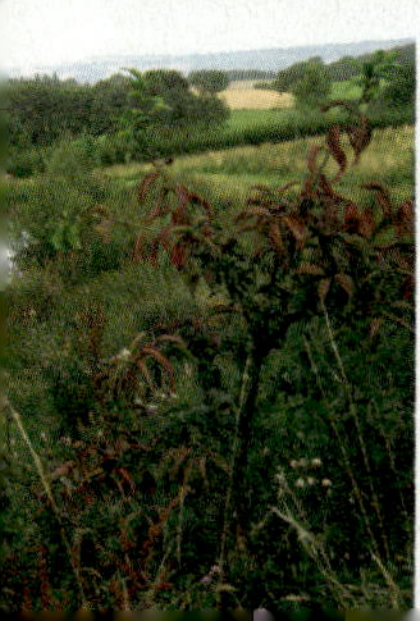
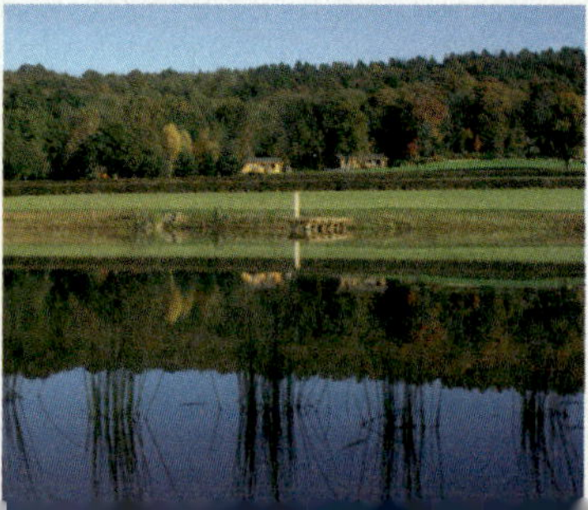
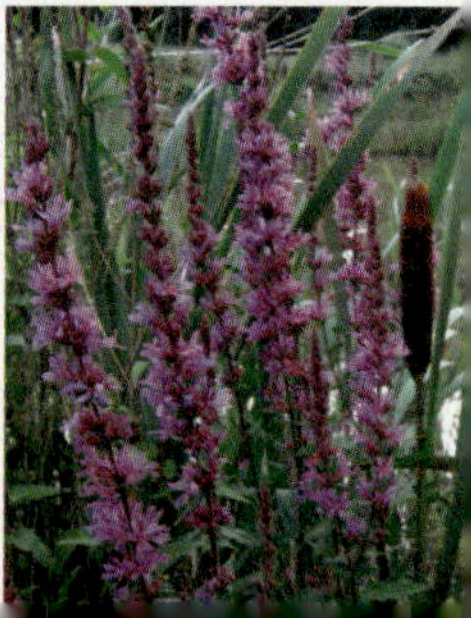

LUDLOW MASCALL CENTRE

ENGLAND

Located in the heart of this beautiful market town, with ample free parking, Ludlow Mascall Centre is within walking distance of the restaurants, markets, shops, pubs, museum, castle and church. The Shropshire Hills are close by, with miles of beautiful countryside and stunning landscapes to explore. Built in 1857 as a national school, this beautiful Victorian building has been extended to provide residential accommodation with twin rooms, a family room, and a room which has been designed for those with limited mobility in mind. All rooms have en suite toilets, basins and showers. Continental breakfasts are included and home cooked breakfasts using locally sourced produce are available for a small extra charge. Packed lunches, half board and full board are also available by arrangement. Tea and coffee making facilities are available in the residents lounge along with a television. The pretty courtyard garden with seating, won 'Best Community Garden' during 'Ludlow in Bloom 2012'. Guided cycling routes are available by prior arrangement.

DETAILS

- **Open** - Open all year except Christmas.
- **Number of beds** - 19: 7x2, 1x1, 1x4
- **Booking** - Bookings taken via telephone, email or website.
- **Price per night** - From £32 pppn B&B
- **Public Transport** - Ludlow railway station is five minutes' walk away.
- **Directions** - From A49 take Sheet Road towards Ludlow (The first roundabout from the South and second from the North) Continue along Sheet Road towards the town centre. The Centre is on the left hand side after the police station.

CONTACT:
Tel: 01584 873882
info@ludlowmascallcentre.co.uk www.ludlowmascallcentre.co.uk
Lower Galdeford, Ludlow, Shropshire SY8 1RZ

WALKERS WELCOME

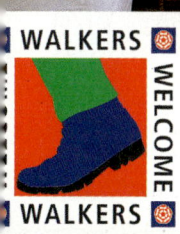

CYCLISTS WELCOME

FOXHOLES CASTLE BUNKHOUSE
ENGLAND

Foxholes Castle Bunkhouse at Bishops Castle is situated within a relaxed, family-run campsite, surrounded by glorious views of South West Shropshire's beautiful hill country. Within a few minutes' walk of the Shropshire Way, Offa's Dyke Path, the Sustrans cycle network and the lively town of Bishop's Castle it is ideal for families, couples, walkers, cyclists and photographers. The bunkhouse is heated, divided in half by a partition with an open doorway. There is a single bed and 3 sets of bunks (no bedding is provided) and television. In a heated buildings next to the bunkhouse (shared with the campsite) you will find 3 wet rooms, and a room with fridge, kettle and washing-up sink. A second set of showers and toilets are 30 seconds' walk away. There is good accessibility for wheelchair users. There is an outside table seating area and space for a BBQ. There are no cooking facilities but there are lots of pubs, restaurants, cafés and take-aways 5 minutes' walk away in Bishops Castle.

DETAILS

- **Open** - All year, 24 hours
- **Number of beds** - 7
- **Booking** - Bookings by phone or send an email.
- **Price per night** - £10 per person or £50 for whole bunkhouse (sleeps 7).
- **Public Transport** - Trains at Craven Arms (12 miles). Buses from Shrewsbury to Bishops Castle (5 minutes' walk from bunkhouse) every 2 hours.
- **Directions** - Bishops Castle is on the A488 about 20 miles south of Shrewsbury, and 35 miles from the M54. Foxholes is on the B4385 Montgomery Road just north of the town. Look for our sign, and follow our driveway for half a mile. GR SO 324 897

CONTACT: Chris or Wendy Jones
Tel: 01588 638924, mobile 07890 231351
foxholes.castle@googlemail.com   www.foxholes-castle.co.uk
Foxholes Camping, Montgomery Rd, Bishops Castle, Shropshire, SY9 5HA

BROUGHTON BUNKHOUSE

ENGLAND

Broughton Bunkhouse offers comfortable accommodation in 17th century barn with a wealth of exposed beams and full of character. The bunkhouse is clean and cosy, central heating, hot water and showers are all inclusive. There is a fully-equipped kitchen with cookers, fridge-freezer, dishwasher and all the utensils you will need. Clothes washing and drying facilities are also provided.

Broughton Bunkhouse is just outside Bishops Castle in South Shropshire, an excellent area for walking on the nearby Stiperstones and Long Mynd, cycling around Clun or just enjoying the real ale brewed in two of Bishop Castle's own pubs.

DETAILS

- **Open** - All year, 24 hours
- **Number of beds** - 12 : 2 x 6
- **Booking** - Check availability and arrange check-in. Deposit required for advance bookings.
- **Price per night** - From £10pp. Can be hired for sole use by groups per night or per week. Please telephone for prices.
- **Public Transport** - Train station at Craven Arms (12 miles). Taxi or bus service to Bishops Castle or pick up from hostel for £10 fee. National Coach stop in Shrewsbury. Local bus service to Bishops Castle, free pick-up to hostel from Bishops Castle.
- **Directions** - GR 313 906. From Bishops Castle take B4385 (signed Montgomery). Lower Broughton Farm is 2 miles out of town on the right (on the B4385).

CONTACT: Kate
Tel: 01588 638393, Fax: 01588 638393
lbrfarm@fastmail.co.uk   www.broughtonfarm-shropshire.co.uk
Lower Broughton Farm, Nr Bishops Castle, Montgomery, Powys SY15 6SZ

BRIDGES LONG MYND YOUTH HOSTEL

ENGLAND

This small hostel, once the old village school, is tucked away in the Shropshire hills with the Long Mynd to the east and Stiperstones to the west. It is an ideal spot for ramblers with the Shropshire Way passing close by and a great network of uncrowded paths to explore. Ideally situated for the End to End cycle route and plenty of mountain biking opportunities. The nearby small towns of Church Stretton, Ludlow, Much Wenlock, Bishops Castle and sleepy Montgomery are all worth a visit. There's also the Acton Scott working farm museum and Snailbeach former lead mines close by. The hostel has a good kitchen, lounge with wood fire, books and games, a drying room, a food shop and a large garden. One en suite room has some facilities for the disabled, phone to discuss your requirements. Meals are available, camping is allowed and there is a pub nearby.

DETAILS

- **Open** - All year, reception 8-10 am, 5-10 pm. Hostel closes at 11pm.
- **Number of beds** - 38: 2x4 en suite, 1x6 or 8, 1x10, 1x12
- **Booking** - Telephone to book. No credit or debit cards accepted. Cheques must be made payable to Bridges Youth Hostel not YHA.
- **Price per night** - Adults £16, plus £3 for non YHA members. Under 18's £11.50 plus £1.50 for non YHA members. Camping £8.
- **Public Transport** - Trains at Church Stretton (5 miles) with a shuttle bus to Bridges at weekends from April to September.
- **Directions** - From Church Stretton, take 'The Burway' road uphill. Take right fork at top of Long Mynd. From Shrewsbury take road via Longden and Pulverbatch, then left by Bridges Pub. Access from Church Stretton over the Long Mynd Hill is not advisable in bad weather during winter.

CONTACT: Bridges Youth Hostel
Tel: 01588 650656, Fax: 01588 650531
Ratlinghope, Shrewsbury, Shropshire, SY5 0SP

BIG MOSE BASECAMP

ENGLAND

Situated on the Dudmaston Estate, a National Trust property 4 miles east of Bridgnorth, Big Mose Basecamp accommodates groups of up to 20 people in 4 bunkrooms of varying sizes. The converted Tudor Farmhouse offers a large living area with a TV/DVD and lots of games for those rainy days, a dining area where everyone can sit together and enjoy reflecting on the day's adventures and a fully equipped kitchen area. Sleeping bags required.

Situated next to the Basecamp is a large camping area which, with the outside toilet block attached to the Basecamp, can accommodate additional members to your group. Having your annual meeting where you decide your events for the year? Then why not hire the meeting room, this beautiful airy room is perfect for all occasions.

DETAILS

- **Open** - All year.
- **Number of beds** - Basecamp 20: 1x2, 1x4, 1x6, 1x8.
- **Booking** - Essential
- **Price per night** - £550.00 per week (Mon - Fri 4 nights) £300.00 per weekend (Friday to Sunday 2 nights) £137.50 per night.
- **Public Transport** - Train stations at Telford, Wolverhampton or Kidderminster.
- **Directions** - From Bridgnorth take A458 towards Stourbridge. Travel 3 miles and after a small pine wood on right, take right hand turning to Mose. Approx 1/4 mile along take a left down a track with a small National Trust sign leading to the basecamp.

CONTACT: Nicola Hook
Tel: 01746 780866
bigmosebasecamp@nationaltrust.org.uk   www.nationaltrust.org.uk/dudmaston-estate
Big Mose Basecamp, Quatford, Bridgnorth, Shropshire, WV15 6QR

ALL STRETTON BUNKHOUSE

All Stretton Bunkhouse offers comfortable self-catering accommodation with underfloor heating for individuals and small groups of up to 10 people. It has easy access to the Long Mynd which offers walks and bike rides for all levels of fitness. It is within easy reach of the busy town of Church Stretton and all its facilities, and just 10 minutes' walk from the local pub (but please always book meals as it is not very big). Take-away food is available in Church Stretton.

There are three bedrooms in the bunkhouse: Synalds and Cardoc have two bunks (sleeping 4) and Novers has two singles. A cot is also available. The well-equipped kitchen has cooker, microwave, toaster, kettle and fridge. There is a shower, two toilets and a tumble dryer. The track up to the property is steep and rough so wheelchair access is difficult. Groups booking the complete bunkhouse may bring dogs.

DETAILS

- **Open** - All year, 5pm to 10.30pm. Reception 5pm to 9pm.
- **Number of beds** - 10 plus 1 cot.
- **Booking** - Book by phone, post or online.
- **Price per night** - Starting from £18.00
- **Public Transport** - Trains to Church Stretton from Shrewsbury, Hereford and Cardiff. Station 1.2 miles walk (or taxi) from bunkhouse. National Express buses to Shrewsbury, hourly local buses from Shrewsbury to Church Stretton via All Stretton.
- **Directions** - 300m on right going up Batch Valley bridleway (off the B5477, a mile north of Church Stretton).

CONTACT: Frankie Goode
Tel: 01694 722593   Mob: 0781 5517482, Fax: 01694722593
info@allstrettonbunkhouse.co.uk   www.allstrettonbunkhouse.co.uk
Meadow Green, Batch Valley, All Stretton, Shrops, SY6 6JW

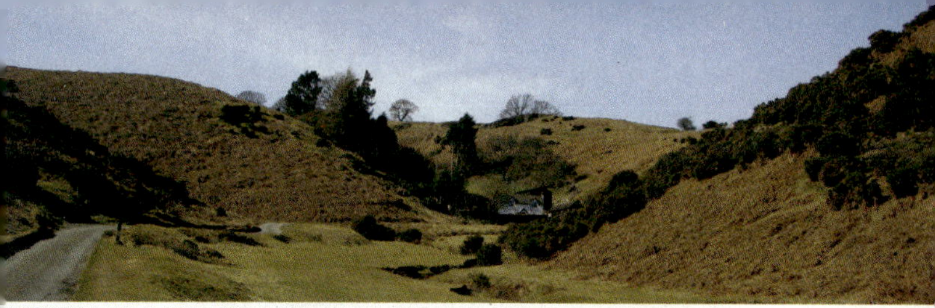

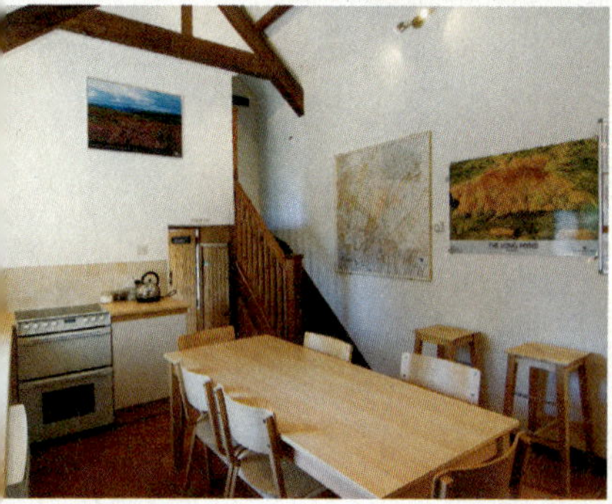

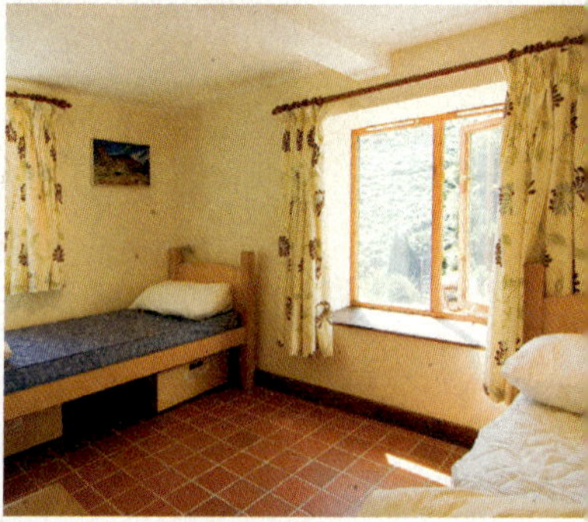

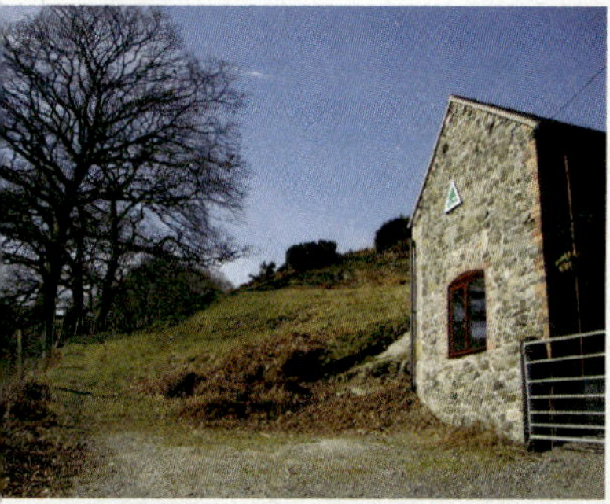

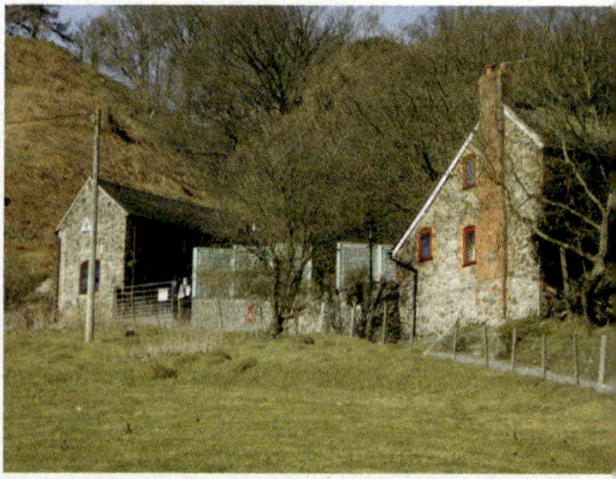

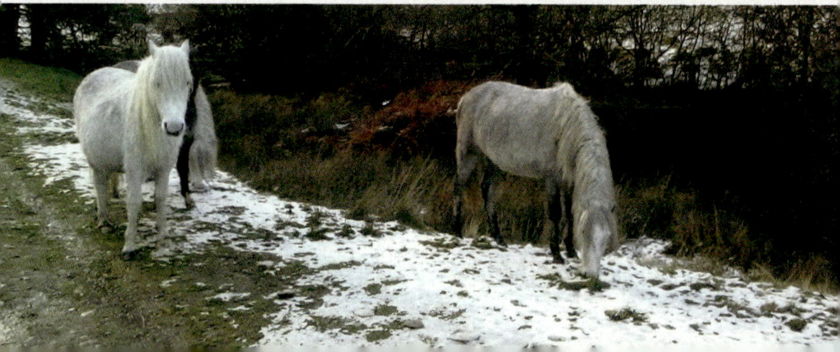

STOKES BARN BUNKHOUSES

ENGLAND

Stokes Barn is located on top of Wenlock Edge, an Area of Outstanding Natural Beauty, in the heart of Shropshire countryside. Two bunkhouses are available; the Threshing Barn (sleeping 28) and the Granary (sleeping 16).

These offer comfortable, centrally heated, dormitory accommodation for a wide range of groups and provide an ideal base for corporate groups, field study groups, universities, schools, stag and hen parties, walkers or just a relaxing reunion with friends or family. The Ironbridge World Heritage Site is only 6 miles away and is a great attraction. Walk to the historic town of Much Wenlock to visit shops, pubs and sports facilities. Situated only a few miles from Church Stretton and the Long Mynd the barn is in a walking / cycling haven. Many activities available. Have a relaxing and enjoyable stay.

DETAILS

- **Open** - All year, all day
- **Number of beds** - Threshing Barn 28: 1x12,1x10,1x6 Granary 16: 1x10,1x4,1x2
- **Booking** - Deposit required. Minimum stay 2 nights.
- **Price per night** - Minimum of two nights. Barn £540 two nights mid week, £840 two nights weekend. Granary: £384 two nights mid week, £580 two nights weekend.
- **Public Transport** - Trains at Telford (10 miles) and Shrewsbury (10 miles). National Express coaches call at Shrewsbury from London, call 0839 142348 for information. Midland Red buses stop in Much Wenlock, enquires 01952 223766.
- **Directions** - GR 609 999. From the M6 take M54 Telford following Ironbridge Gorge signs. A4169 to Much Wenlock, joining A458 for Shrewsbury. The Barn is signed at Newton House Farm (TF13 6DB) on the Much Wenlock to Shrewsbury Rd.

CONTACT:
Tel: 01952 727491 ext 2
info@stokesbarn.co.uk   www.stokesbarn.co.uk
Stokes Barn, Newtown Farm, Much Wenlock, Shropshire, TF13 6DB

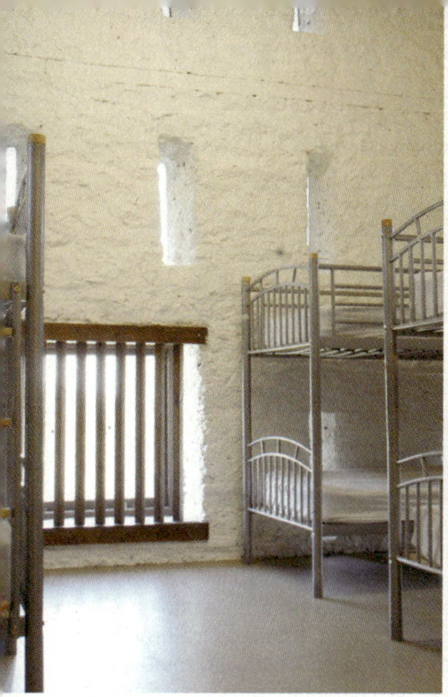
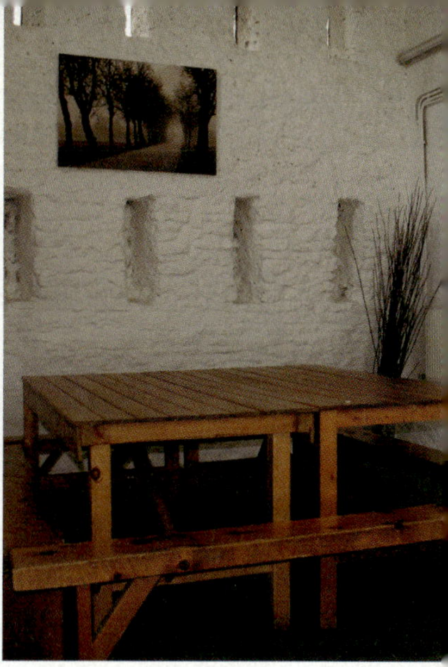
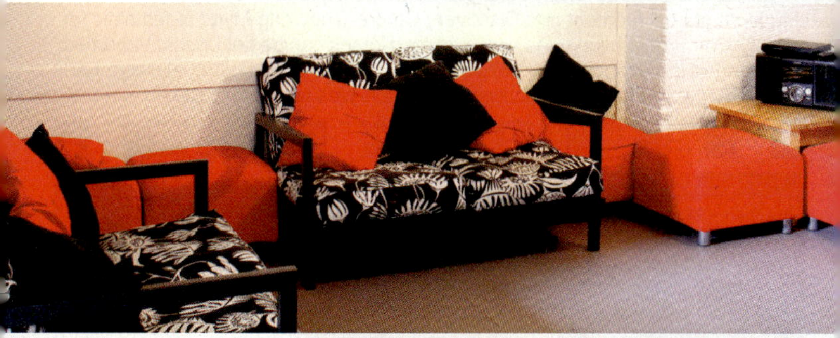
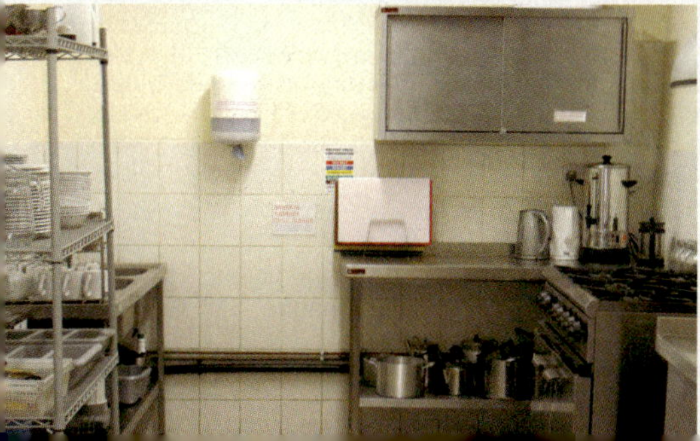
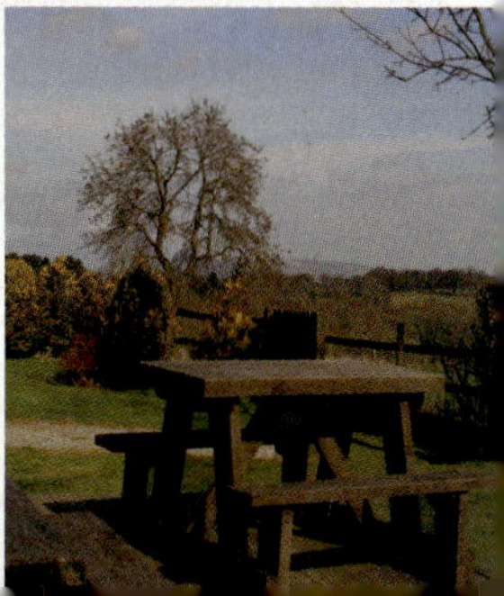

WOMERTON FARM BUNKHOUSE

ENGLAND

Womerton Farm Bunkhouse is situated right next to the Long Mynd, an Area of National Beauty in the heart of the Shropshire Hills. It offers small select accommodation to sleep eight; six in bunks downstairs and two in a double sofa bed upstairs. There is a fully equipped kitchen and living area upstairs. The bunkhouse is 3 miles from Church Stretton, 12 miles from historic Shrewsbury and 15 miles from Ludlow, food capital of Shropshire. There are many local attractions such as Acton Scott Working Farm Museum, Stokesay Castle, Museum of Lost Content and Discovery Centre. The Long Mynd is fantastic for walking, mountain biking and horse riding. Horses can be field-accommodated if arranged in advance. Well behaved dogs that are not moulting allowed. For photo gallery, directions and details please visit website.

DETAILS

- **Open** - All year, all day. Closed from 11 am to 4pm on change over days.
- **Number of beds** - 8: 1x6, plus double sofa bed in living area
- **Booking** - Booking recommended to guarantee a place.
- **Price per night** - £80 Christmas / New Year, £80 Easter to Sept, £60 off peak. Stay 3 nights get next 1 to 3 nights half price. Phone or email for midweek offers.
- **Public Transport** - Nearest train and bus station is Church Stretton (3 miles). Taxi fare is about £10.
- **Directions** - From Church Stretton follow A49 north. Past coffee shop and craft centre take a left turn signed Lower Wood. From Shrewsbury on A49 south, pass though Leebotwood then take the right turn signed Lower Wood. Follow this road for 1 mile, cross a cattle grid onto the Long Mynd and we are the first farm on the right.

CONTACT: Ruth or Tony
Tel: 01694 751260, Fax: 01694751260
ruth@womerton-farm.co.uk www.womerton-farm.co.uk
Womerton Farm, All Stretton, Church Stretton, Shropshire, SY6 6LJ

SPRINGHILL FARM
BUNKHOUSE

125
ENGLAND

Springhill Farm Bunkhouse is on a hill farm at 1475ft above sea level, near the Welsh/Shropshire border with beautiful views over the Ceiriog Valley and Berwyn Mountains. Great for walking and activity breaks or just to relax.

The main bunkhouse sleeps around 21 and the 2 smaller self-catering cottages can sleep up to 12 more. There is also a separate large room with its own kitchen which can be used for meetings or as a camping barn. The bunkhouse has under-floor heating, entrance hall with w/c and drying room, large kitchen, dining room and sitting room. There are 5 bedrooms sleeping 1-8 people. Outside is a large patio and lawn, BBQ and hot tub. Available onsite are cycle hire, archery and horse riding. Your own horse and pets welcome on request.

DETAILS

- **Open** - All year, all day (please don't phone after 9pm)
- **Number of beds** - 30+: 20 (bunkhouse) + two cottages + camping barn
- **Booking** - Advisable, deposit required
- **Price per night** - £20pp (including bedding but not towels)
- **Public Transport** - Nearest train station Chirk (8 miles). Nearest bus service is in the village Glyn Ceiriog (2.5 miles). Transfer can be arranged.
- **Directions** - GR SJ 210 346. On the A483 from Wrexham, take the third exit on the first roundabout (McDonalds). At the next roundabout take the first exit, continue into Chirk, and then turn right for Glyn Ceiriog. After 6 miles you will arrive at Glyn Ceiriog. At the mini roundabout turn left, go over the bridge, and then straight away turn right into a small lane. Continue up the hill for about two miles, do not turn off.

CONTACT: Sue Benbow
Tel: 01691 718406
sue@springhillfarm.co.uk www.springhillfarm.co.uk
Springhill Farm, Selattyn, Oswestry, Shropshire, SY10 7NZ

HATTERS
BIRMINGHAM

Your ideal choice for city central accommodation, Hatters Birmingham has combined hotel quality en suite rooms with the social atmosphere of an international travellers' hostel. Catering for groups of all sizes and independent travellers, you can enjoy the comforts of FREE WiFi, breakfast, en suite rooms, large communal areas and enthusiastic, informative staff. Full board or half board options are available for groups of over 15 people. Conveniently located for all city centre attractions and transport links, ask our reception staff about discounts to Cadbury World, Warwick Castle, Sealife Centre, and many other FREE adventures, including our FREE City Walking Tours and Quiz nights. If you are into the outdoors we have the largest bouldering complex just around the corner, or try out your mountain biking skills at Cannock Chase (30 mins' drive). So come and stay with us and we'll show you what's fun in Brum.

DETAILS

- **Open** - All year. Reception available, 24 hours. Check in 2pm, check out 11am.
- **Number of beds** - 100: single, double, twin, triple, 4, 6, 8 and 12 bed rooms.
- **Booking** - Booking not essential but recommended, especially at weekends. Photo ID (ie passport, ID card or driving license) required at check in.
- **Price per night** - From £14.50 dorms, from £35 private rooms, inc b/fast & linen. For group prices and bookings contact groups@hattersgroup.com
- **Public Transport** - Easy walking distance from all public transport hubs: New Street Station 15mins, Snow Hill Station 5mins, Digbeth Coach Station 20mins. Local taxi service @ £5.00 for all city centre travel. Taxi service: BB's Taxi 0121 693 3333
- **Directions** - Please contact the hostel reception for directions.

CONTACT: Reception
Tel: 0121 236 4031, Fax: 0121 2366694
birmingham@hattersgroup.com www.hattersgroup.com/#bham
92-95 Livery Street, Birmingham, B3 1RJ

IGLOO
BACKPACKERS HOSTEL ENGLAND

Located within 10 minutes' walk of the town square, the Igloo is Nottingham's most popular choice for budget-minded travellers. It offers a clean, safe and warm overnight stay from just £17 per night. Facilities include fully-equipped self-catering kitchens, power showers, lockers in dorms, free WiFi, a lounge with internet access and laundry facilities. 'Igloo Annexe' across the road offers single, double/twin, triple and family rooms with Freeview TV, WiFi and memory foam mattresses in all rooms. Our new addition, Igloo Pods, with boutique private rooms opened in 2014 and is inspired by lots of travelling, fellow explorers and a real passion for value. Created using mainly locally sourced, up-cycled and secondhand furniture (with added touches of personality and top notch comfort), all rooms feature local street art murals and secondary glazing.

DETAILS

- **Open** - All year, all day
- **Number of beds** - 46 (3x6, 3x4) + Singles/doubles/twins/triples and family rooms
- **Booking** - Essential - especially during summer months. Groups must confirm by email or by phone with deposit.
- **Price per night** - Dorms: £17pp. £85 per week after 10 nights stay. Singles £32.00. Other private rooms from £18 pp. Seasonal discounts.
- **Public Transport** - Direct, regular trains from London etc. National Express to Broadmarsh bus station. From stations 20 mins' walk, £4 taxi ride or catch the FREE Centrelink bus to Victoria Station - we are 1 minute by foot from there.
- **Directions** - From the Tourist Info Centre (Market Square) turn right, take next left onto Clumber Street, walk straight on for 10 mins, past the Victoria Shopping centre. Hostel is on the left just before the Golden Fleece pub on the opposite corner.

CONTACT: Igloo Backpackers Hostel & Annexe
Tel: 0115 9475250
reception@igloohostel.co.uk www.igloohostel.co.uk
100 Mansfield Road, Nottingham, NG1 3HL

BROOK HOUSE BARN

ENGLAND

Comfortable, self-catering accommodation ideally suited for families, groups or individuals. This high standard barn conversion has a fully equipped kitchen/dining area, drying room, utility, and a large lounge with panoramic views over the Wolds countryside. There are 2 bedrooms on the ground floor and 3 bedrooms and a small lounge on the first floor. The bedrooms have a mix of beds and bunks, bed linen is provided and all have en suite shower rooms. A two bedroom (4/5 person) cottage converted to a similar standard (graded VisitBritain 4*) is also available. The village of Scamblesby, at the heart of the Lincolnshire Wolds and on the Viking Way, has footpaths, bridle ways and meandering country lanes. The historic market towns of Louth and Horncastle are 10 minutes' drive, 1/2 hour to Lincoln, Boston and the coastal beaches. Cadwell Park racing circuit, Market Rasen racecourse and the Battle of Britain and Aviation Heritage centres are nearby. See website for activities in the area

DETAILS

- **Open** - All year, flexible accesss.
- **Number of beds** - 22 (27 including adjoining cottage).
- **Booking** - Booking advisable, 20% deposit, balance 1 month prior to visit.
- **Price per night** - From £20pp, family and group rates available. Whole barn hire Fri Sat Sun, 2 nights £350 per night, 3rd night at £270. Mon to Thurs, 2 nights £250 per night, 3 or 4 nights £220 per night. Whole barn hire £1500 per week.
- **Public Transport** - Trains: Lincoln, Grimsby. Coaches: Louth, Horncastle. Interconnect 6 (0845 234 3344) calls at Scamblesby and other villages in the Wolds.
- **Directions** - Scamblesby village is just off the A153 Horncastle to Louth road.

CONTACT: The Strawsons
Tel: 01507 343266
enquiry@brookhousefarm.com www.barnbreaks.co.uk
Watery Lane, Scamblesby, Nr Louth, Lincolnshire, LN11 9XL

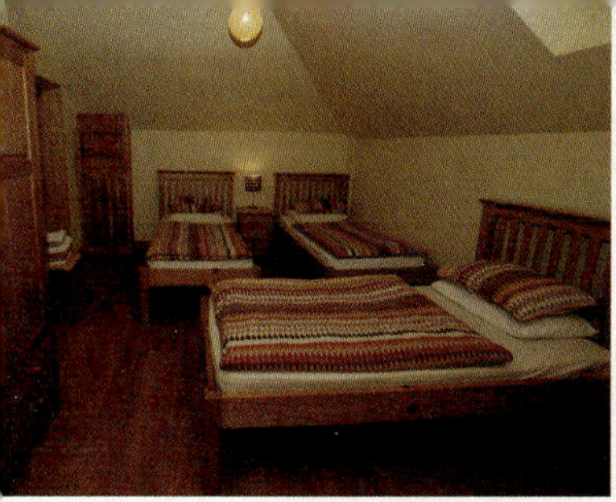
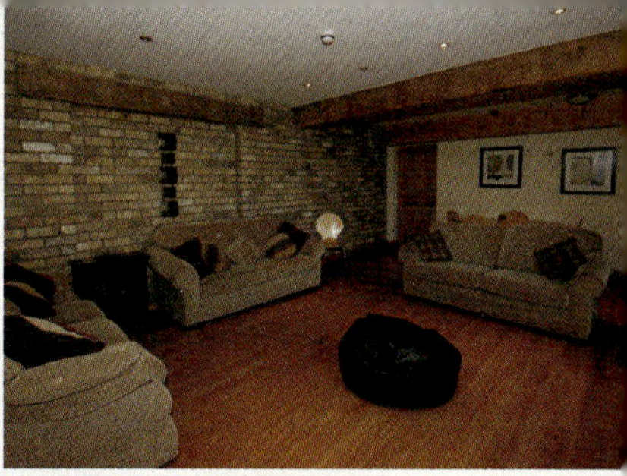
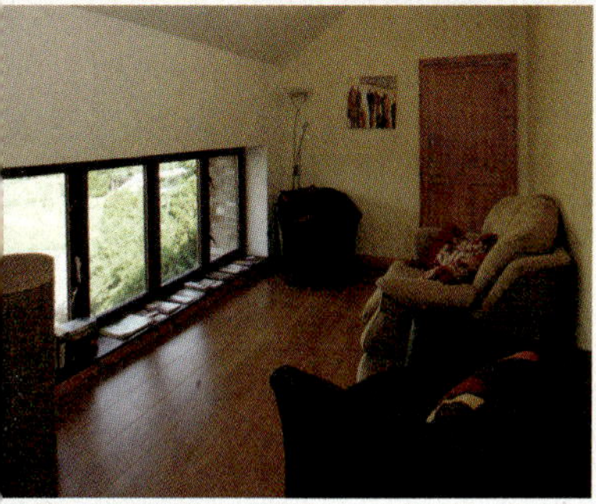
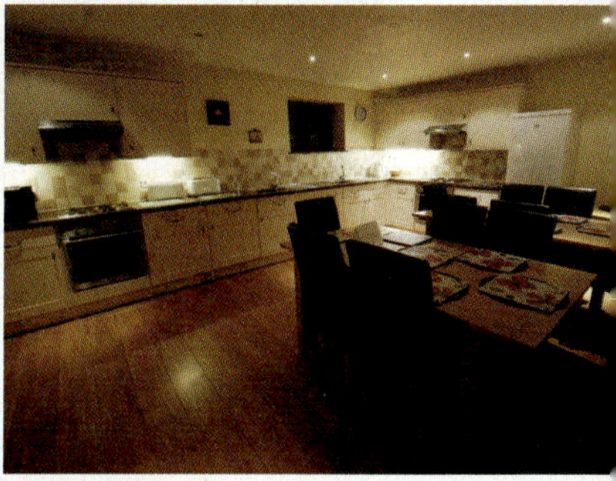
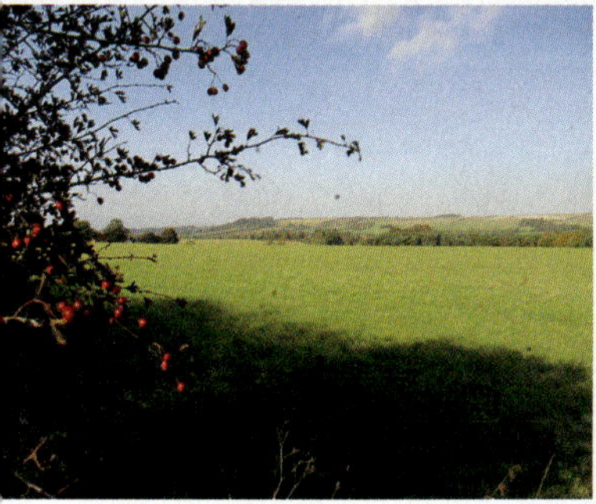
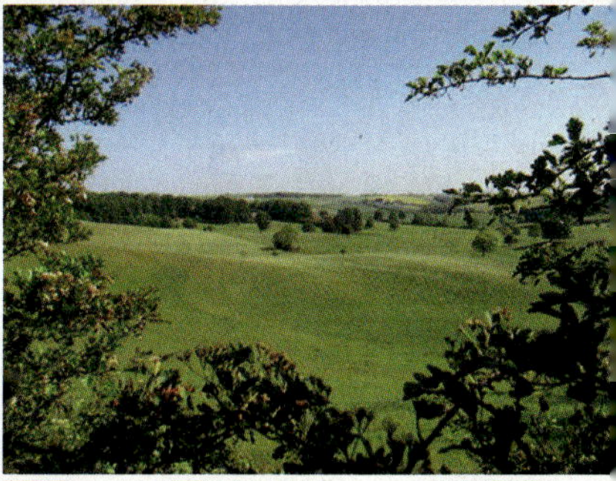
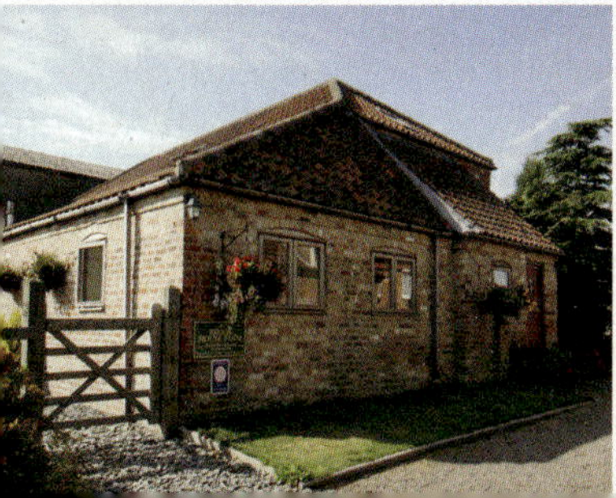
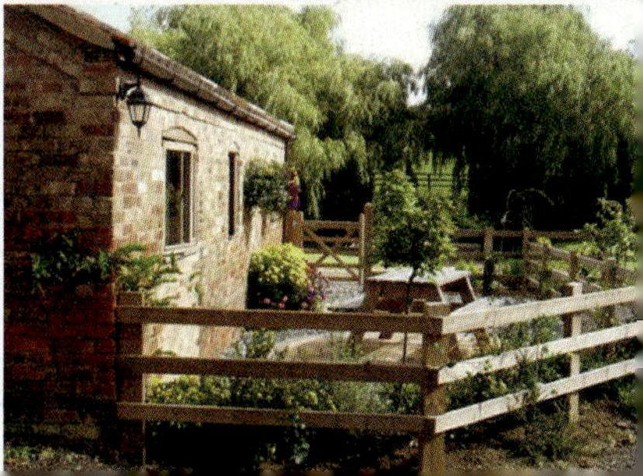

BRANCASTER ACTIVITY CENTRE (BAC)
ENGLAND

This Grade 2 listed flint cottage is located within the picturesque harbour of Brancaster Staithe on the North Norfolk Coast. Guests are never disappointed by the stunning sea views across the beautiful marshes. Brancaster Activity Centre offers group accommodation for up to 48, in 9 newly furbished dormitory bedrooms, of different sizes and with en suite facilities. Your group can be creative in the self-catering kitchen, or sample the local flavours in nearby pubs and café's. The upstairs 'snug' has a TV and wood burner and there is a garden with seating and BBQ. The perfect spot for activities such as sailing, walking, kite surfing and more; the Norfolk Coast Path runs by the door, as does the Coasthopper bus service and some of Norfolk's finest birdwatching reserves are only a stones' throw away.

DETAILS

- **Open** - All year by arrangement,
- **Number of beds** - 48
- **Booking** - Booking is essential. Call booking office on 0344 335 1296.
- **Price per night** - Half centre from £250 (Oct-Mar) and from £386 (Apr-Sep). Whole centre from £332 (Oct-Mar) and from £455 (Apr-Sep). Minimum of 2 night bookings. From 25 July to 29 August minimum of 7 night bookings. Bed linen hire £5 per single bed, £6 per double bed. Prices inc VAT.
- **Public Transport** - Train: King's Lynn 25 miles away. Pick up from station available for a small charge if sufficient demand, please enquire when making a booking. The coasthopper bus stop is 200 metres away.
- **Directions** - On the seaward side of the A149. Harbour Way is opposite the Northshore Sailing Shop. Centre is 200m on the left on "Harbour Way".

CONTACT:
Tel: 0344 3351296
group.accom@nationaltrust.org.uk. www.nationaltrust.org.uk/brancaster
Dial House, Harbour Way, Brancaster Staithe, Nr Kings Lynn, Norfolk PE31 8BW

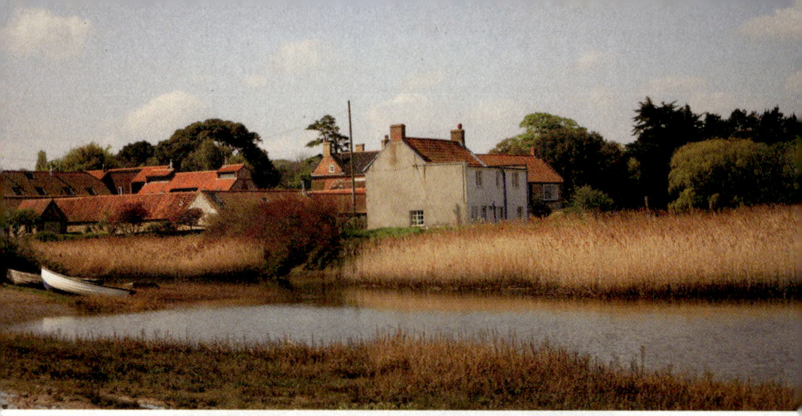

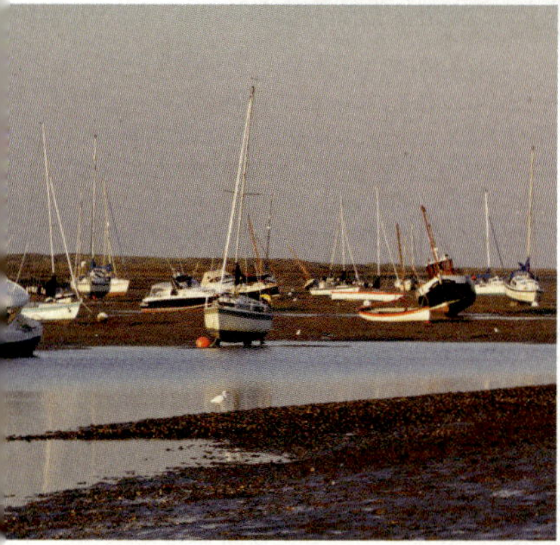

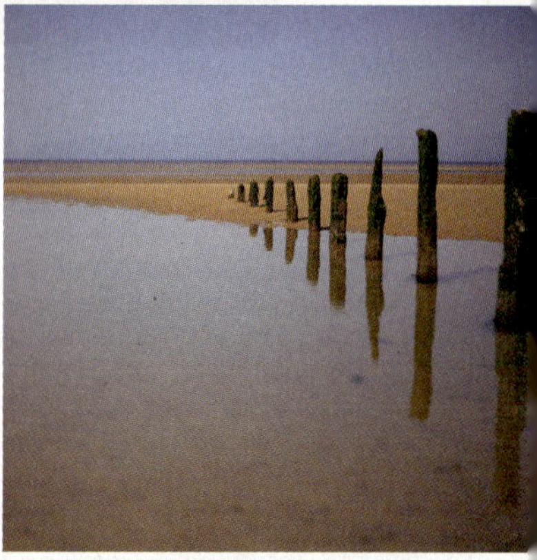

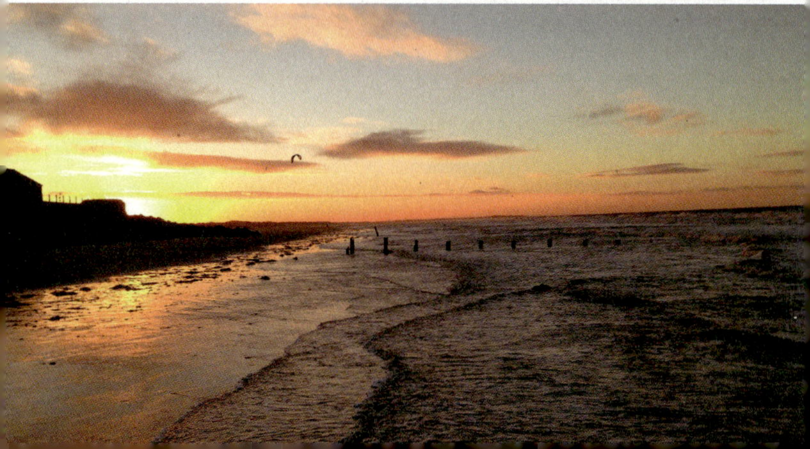

HUNSTANTON BACKPACKERS & YHA

ENGLAND

Greatly improved over the last 3 years, inc adding en suites, Hunstanton Backpackers is 3* VisitEngland approved. Providing an ideal affordable family break or activity getaway for walking, cycling, bird watching or fun on the beach. The nearby Norfolk Coast Path and Peddars Way are great for wildlife spotting, or you can take a boat trip to Seal Island. Accommodation is in bunkrooms of various sizes plus family rooms some en suite. Hire the property for sole use, for groups, friends reunions and family get-togethers. Facilities include self-catering kitchen, large lounge, conservatory dining area and an optional classroom/training area. Meals and drinks (including alcohol) can be provided (5* Food Hygiene). The garden has patio, benches & sea views. A five minute walk will take you to the sea front or town centre with a Sealife sanctuary, fantastic beaches and cliff top walks. A friendly, family welcome awaits you at Hunstanton Backpackers a great home-from-home on the east coast

DETAILS

- **Open** - All year (call if online booking not available). Reception 8-10am 5-9:30pm
- **Number of beds** - 47: 2x2, 1x3D inc WC, 2x4, 1x4 en suite, 1x4D(family) inc WC, 1x5/6, 2x6/8 en suite.
- **Booking** - Book online, by phone or email
- **Price per night** - Adults from £21.00 to £23.50. Enquire for discounts, family rooms and sole use. SCHOOL GROUPS full board packages available.
- **Public Transport** - Coast Hopper. Trains at Kings Lynn with bus to Hunstanton.
- **Directions** - Follow the coast road to Hunstanton, then signs for South Beach (Southend Rd). Turn right into Park Road, then first left, hostel is 20 yds on the left.

CONTACT: Neal or Alison Sanderson
Tel: 01485 532061 Mob: 07771 804831/07737 642828
enquiries@hunstantonhostel.co.uk www.yha.org.uk/hostel/hunstanton
15-17 Avenue Road, Hunstanton, Norfolk, PE36 5BW

DEEPDALE GRANARY[133]
GROUP HOSTEL
ENGLAND

A perfect base for groups to stay, explore and absorb the stunning North Norfolk coast. Deepdale Granary is a self-contained 17th century building sleeping 18 in four bedrooms with a fully fitted kitchen and dining/sitting room. Part of the award winning Deepdale Farm, right on the coast in the heart of an Area of Outstanding Natural Beauty. There are excellent pubs nearby, both traditional and chic, great restaurants and miles of unspoilt beaches and dunes.

The Norfolk coast is perfect for walking and cycling with miles of coast path and picturesque villages. Take time to discover our heritage sites including the Sandringham and Holkham estates or enjoy birdwatching in the tranquil beauty of the unique saltmarsh. The Granary is fully heated, has showers, a drying room and solar water heating. Dalegate Market onsite has shops, supermarket, and a brilliant café serving local food. Camping and tipis also available.

DETAILS

- **Open** - All year, all day. Collect key from Deepdale Information.
- **Number of beds** - 19: 2x6, 1x4, 1x3.
- **Booking** - Essential, 20% deposit, balance in advance. See website for details
- **Price per night** - From £150 per night, for up to 19 people.
- **Public Transport** - Trains / coaches at King's Lynn (25 miles) then excellent Coastal Hopper bus to Burnham Deepdale. Coastal Hopper service the coast from King's Lynn to Cromer, including Sandringham. Travelline 0870 608 2 608.
- **Directions** - GR 803443. On A149 coast road, halfway between Hunstanton and Wells-next-the-Sea. Beside Deepdale Garage & opposite Deepdale Church.

CONTACT:
Tel: 01485 210256
info@deepdalebackpackers.co.uk www.deepdalebackpackers.co.uk
Deepdale Information Centre, Burnham Deepdale, Norfolk, PE31 8DD

DEEPDALE BACKPACKERS

Escape to this Eco-friendly award-winning backpackers' hostel on the beautiful North Norfolk coast. Deepdale Backpackers offers private en suite rooms (double, twin, triple, quad and family), single sex and mixed dorms. Deepdale is a perfect base for walking and cycling with miles of coast path, the famous big skies and quaint fishing harbours. You will also be happy if you want adrenaline sport, great pubs and restaurants and miles of sandy beaches. A fully equipped farmhouse kitchen and cosy lounge with a TV and a wood burner for cooler nights, complement the lovely courtyard with barbeques for summer evenings.

Deepdale is an eco-friendly working farm with recycling, underfloor heating and solar water. Next door Dalegate Market has shops, a supermarket, and a café serving locally sourced food. Camping and tipis are also available. The hostel is now available as a whole unit perfect for a large family get together.

DETAILS

- **Open** - All day every day, collect key from Deepdale Information.
- **Number of beds** - 50: 5xdbl, 1twin, 1triple, 1quad, 2 family rms up to 6, + dorms
- **Booking** - Pre-booking recommended. Max group size 12, unless you hire the whole hostel which is avalable certain dates on request. - See website
- **Price per night** - From £15(£105 per week) dorm room. £30 twin/double room.
- **Public Transport** - Train / coaches at King's Lynn (25 Miles). Coast Hopper bus from King's Lynn to Cromer stops at Burnham Deepdale. Traveline 0870 6082608.
- **Directions** - GR 803443 On A149 coast road halfway between Hunstanton and Wells-next-the-Sea. Beside Dalegate Market, opposite Deepdale Church.

CONTACT:
Tel: 01485 210256
info@deepdalebackpackers.co.uk www.deepdalebackpackers.co.uk
Deepdale Information Centre, Burnham Deepdale, Norfolk, PE31 8DD

OLD RED LION

ENGLAND

Visitors to Castle Acre are entranced by the special atmosphere of this medieval walled town which lies within the outer bailey of an 11th century castle. Castle Acre is on the Peddars Way, an ancient track now a long distance path. The Old Red Lion, a former pub, is centrally situated and carries on the tradition of serving travellers who seek refreshment and repose. Guests can stay in private rooms or dormitories, where bedding and linen are provided free of charge. There are quiet areas (with wood burning stoves) for reading, meeting other guests and playing. There are two large areas: the flint and timber walled converted pub cellar, suitable for yoga and The Garden Room with kitchen and toilet adjacent, ideal for group use: celebrations, classes, courses, workshops and retreats. There is a ground floor room with double bed. Drying facilities. Local shops and pub. No smoking.

DETAILS

- **Open** - All year, all day access. Arrival times by arrangement.
- **Number of beds** - 24: 1x10, 1x8, 2x double, 2x twin
- **Booking** - Useful but not essential
- **Price per night** - Price includes self service, wholefood breakfast, use of fully equiped small kitchen exclusively for guests use; all day access, parking. For one night from £21 to £35
- **Public Transport** - Trains at King's Lynn & Downham Market. Buses from King's Lynn and Peterborough to Swaffham. Daily National Express coach between London Victoria & Swaffham. Norfolk Bus 0500 626116. Taxi from Swaffham £7.
- **Directions** - GR 818151. Castle Acre is 3.5 miles north of Swaffham (A47) on the A1065. The hostel is on left, 75yds down from Bailey Gate in village centre.

CONTACT: Alison Loughlin
Tel: 01760 755557
oldredlion@yahoo.co.uk www.oldredlion.org.uk
Old Red Lion, Bailey Street, Castle Acre, Norfolk, PE32 2AG

GLENORCHY CENTRE

The Glenorchy Centre is situated in the heart of the Derbyshire countryside on the edge of the Peak District National Park. Suitable for self-catering groups wishing to explore this attractive area. A few minutes' walk in any direction will find you in the rolling Derbyshire countryside. Within walking distance of the High Peak Trail for walking, pony trekking and cycling, and Black Rocks - great for bouldering and climbing. Nearby Cromford has Arkwright's mills and Cromford Canal to explore. The fully heated accommodation comprises 8 and 12 bed dormitories, one 4 bed and one 2 bed room, all with showers and toilets. Sheets and duvets provided, but not towels. There is a fitted kitchen with dining area and a large multi-purpose room with a large stage, ideal for recreation, conferences etc. There is a TV, DVD player, table tennis and a snooker table. Disabled access is possible to the main hall and dining area. All groups must include at least 4 adults. Graded as 3 star by Tourism England

DETAILS

- **Open** - Mid Feb to Early Dec, 24 hours
- **Number of beds** - 26: 1x12, 1x8, 1x4, 1x2
- **Booking** - Book with 25% deposit. Booking form on website or ring 01629 824323. WDURC, Coldwell Street, Wirksworth, Derbyshire, DE4 4FB
- **Price per night** - Mon 12am - Fri 12am £890; Fri 4pm - Sun 4pm £550; Sat 2pm - Sat 10am £1290. Smaller groups £16pp, minimum £350 over 2 nights. Incl. 9hrs heating per day, extra heating £5 per hour.
- **Public Transport** - Frequent local buses run to Belper and Matlock. Nearest trains at Cromford (2 miles).
- **Directions** - From the town centre go down past Red Lion pub then take next left.

CONTACT: The Secretary
Tel: 01629 824323
secretary@glenorchycentre.org.uk www.glenorchycentre.org.uk
Chapel Lane, Wirksworth, Derbyshire, DE4 4FF

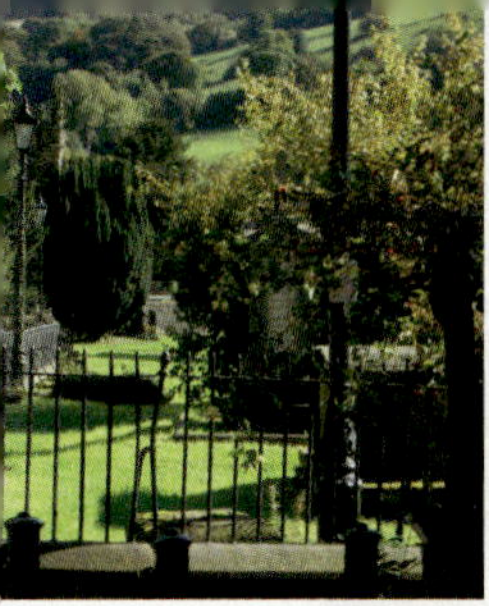
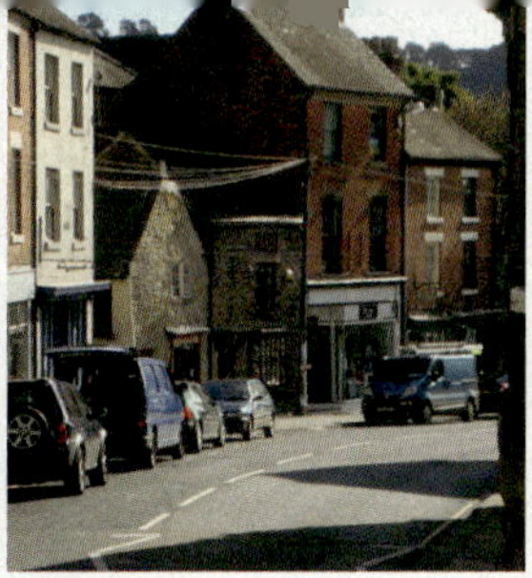
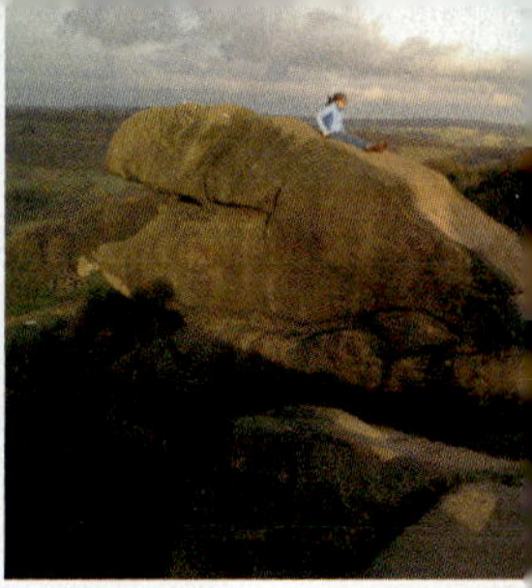
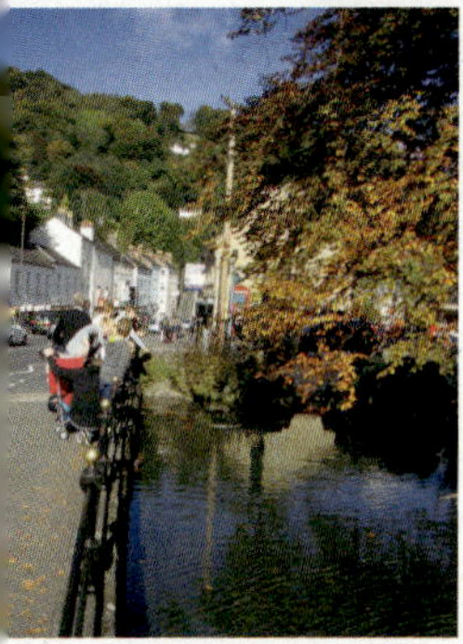
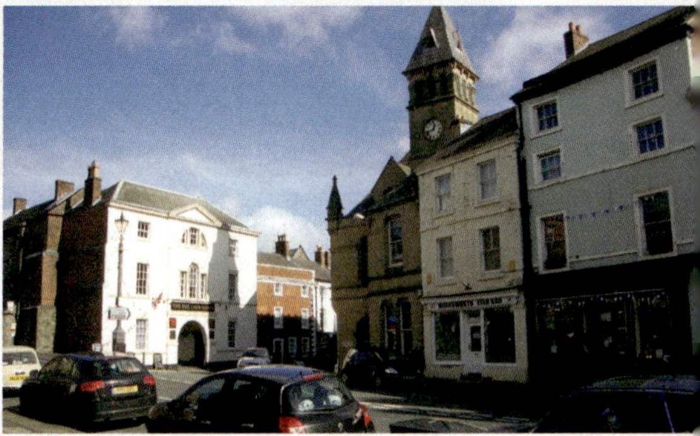
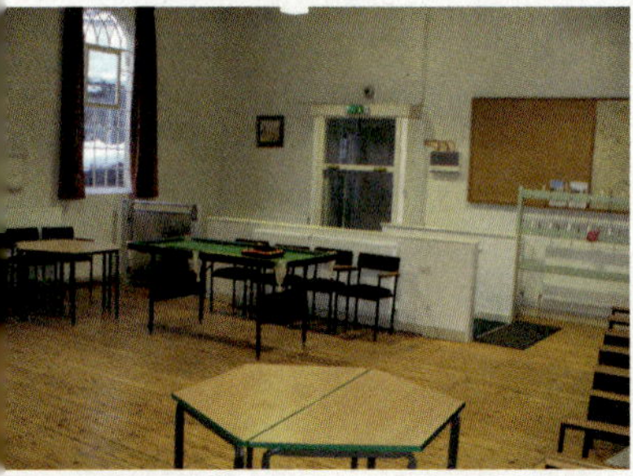
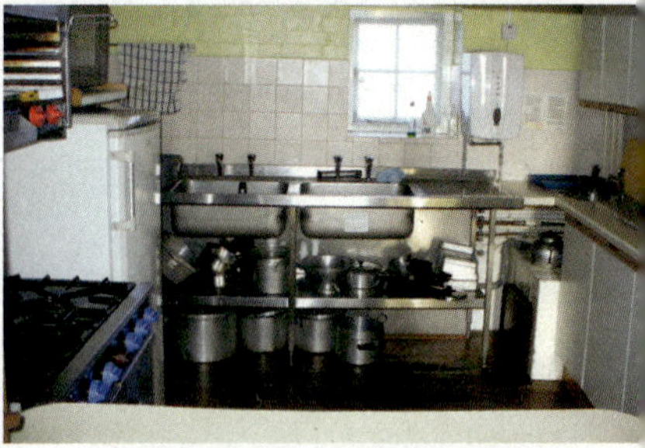
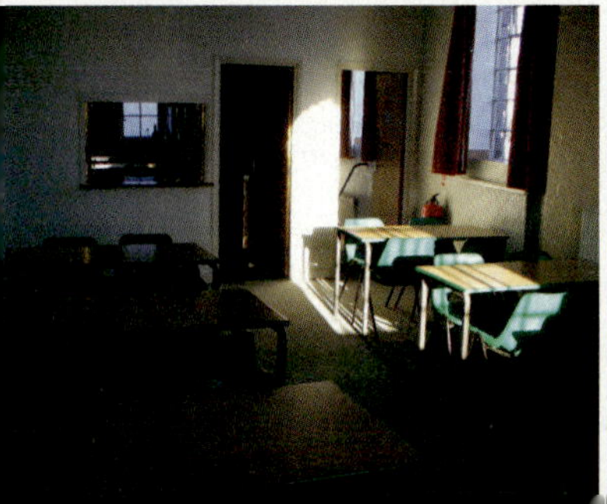
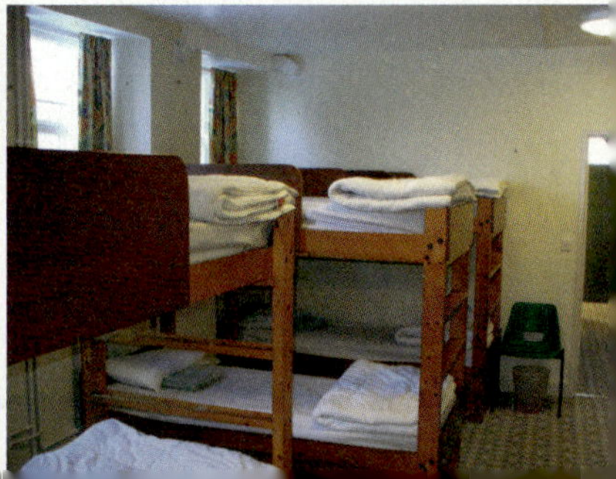

THE RECKONING HOUSE

ENGLAND

The Reckoning House camping barn has been renovated to a high standard including double glazing and insulation. It is situated on the edge of Lathkill Dale, 3 miles from Bakewell. Lathkill Dale is a nature reserve managed by English Nature to protect a variety of flora and fauna as well as some outstanding geological features. Horse riding, fishing, golf and cycle hire are all available locally. There are also many local walks including the Limestone Way.

It has a cooking area, 4 calor gas rings (gas supplied), a washing up sink with hot water, a toilet, wash basin, storage heaters in all rooms and shower inside the barn. Upstairs there are two separate rooms with bunkbeds.

DETAILS

- **Open** - All year, by arrangement
- **Number of beds** - 12
- **Booking** - Sole use bookings only, in advance (min 2 nights at weekends). £50 deposit, balance 4 weeks before arrival.
- **Price per night** - £15 per person. Sole use £95 per night.
- **Public Transport** - Train stations at Buxton (10 miles) and Matlock (13 miles). National Express drop at Bakewell. Local buses (enquiries 01332 292200) go to Bakewell from Monyash, Over Haddon, Matlock and Buxton.
- **Directions** - GR 184 666. Take the B5055 out of Bakewell towards Monyash. Continue for 3 miles. After passing Haddon Grove Farm holiday cottages (the second set of cottages on right), take the first turn left at the signpost to Haddon Grove. Bear left at the bottom of the lane. The camping barn is the first on the left in a half mile.

CONTACT: Rachel Rhodes
Tel: 01629 812416 / 07540839233
mandalecampsite@yahoo.co.uk www.mandalecampsite.co.uk
Mandale Farm, Haddon Grove, Bakewell, Derbyshire, DE45 1JF

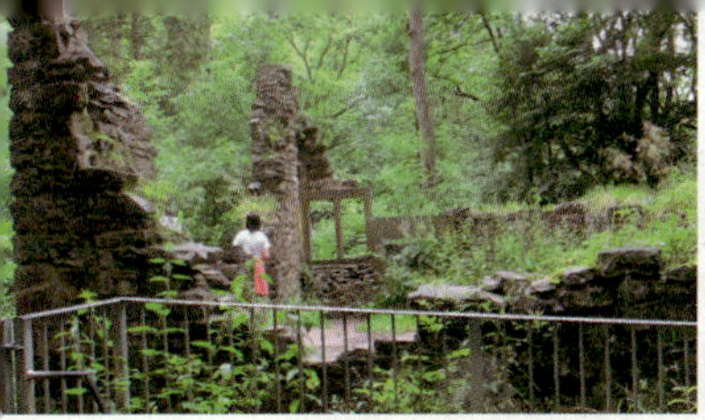
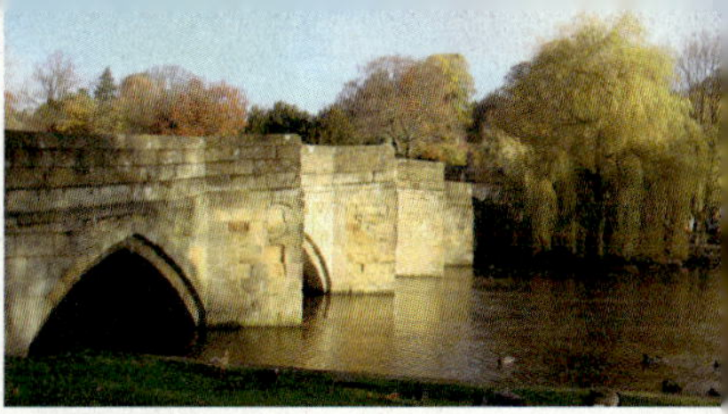
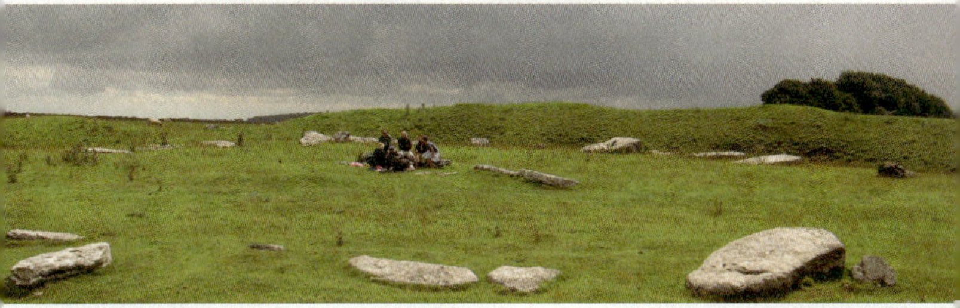
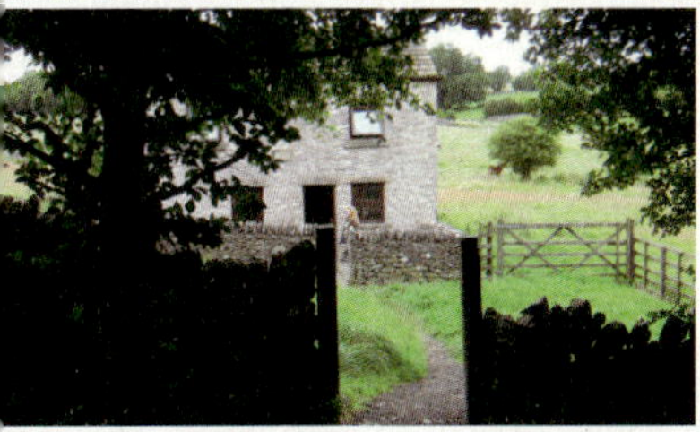
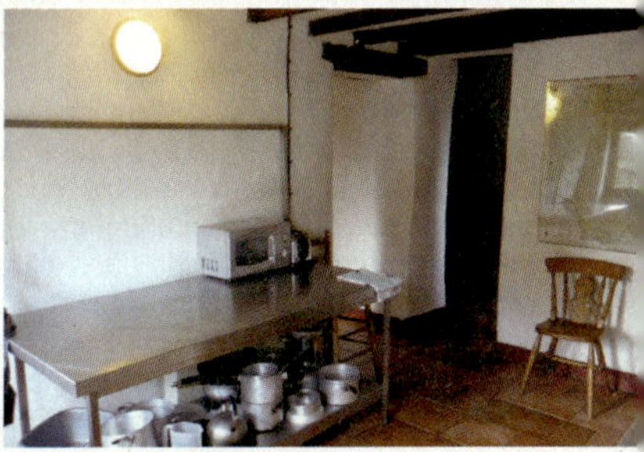
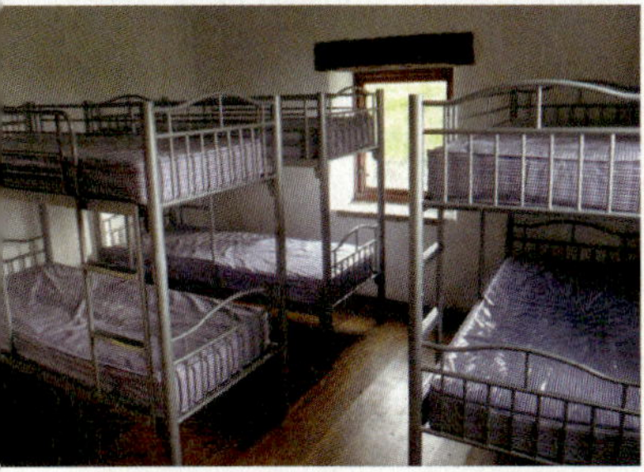
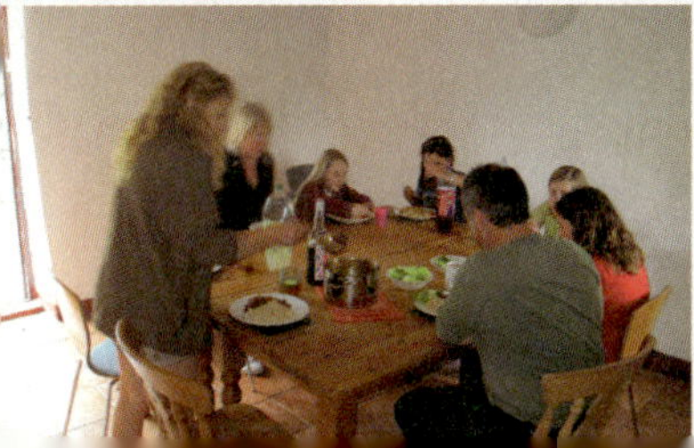
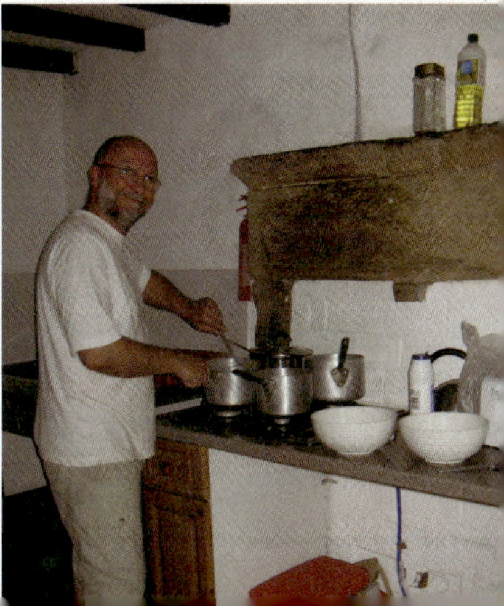

BARN FARM
BARNS AND CAMPSITE

ENGLAND

Barn Farm is in the village of Birchover with fine views over the Derwent valley. A few minutes' walk from the farm is Stanton Moor with Victorian stone carvings and the Nine Ladies stone circle. Robin Hood's Stride and other bouldering and climbing are an easy walk away. The Limestone Way passes by the village and there are two local pubs serving food. Barn Farm has four camping barns - Sabine Hay sleeps 15 in triple bunk beds, Hill Carr and Warren Carr sleep 12 in single beds, Stables Barn sleeps 6 in bunk beds. All the barns have fully fitted kitchens, TV, heating and some have private bathrooms and showers. The Gatehouse, a double bed unit with kitchen, bathroom and lounge/living area, is also available. Camping is available (no single sex groups). Caravan, motorhome and campervan pitches available with electric hook ups. Laundry facilities, games room, childrens' play area, shop, showers & toilets are on site. AA 5 star rated and VisitEngland 4 star rating.

DETAILS

- **Open** - 1st April - 31st October, enquire for opening hours.
- **Number of beds** - 47: 1x15, 1x12, 1x12, 1x6, 1x2 plus camping.
- **Booking** - deposits required: barns 50%, camping £10/tent/ngt all non refundable
- **Price per night** - Hill Carr £160, Sabine Hay £150, Warren Carr £240, Stables £100, Gatehouse £85, all per night (min.2 nights). Weekly rates available. Camping £8.50pppn (£5.50pppn D of E groups).
- **Public Transport** - The 172 bus runs from Bakewell to Matlock.
- **Directions** - From the A6 between Matlock and Bakewell take the B5056. Follow signs for Birchover, continue past the Druid Inn to farm sign at the top of the village.

CONTACT:
Tel: 01629 650245
gilberthh@msn.com   www.barnfarmcamping.com
Birchover, Matlock, Derbyshire, DE4 2BL

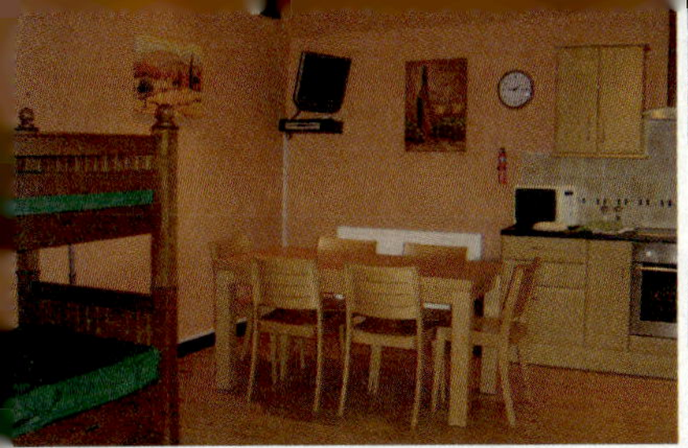
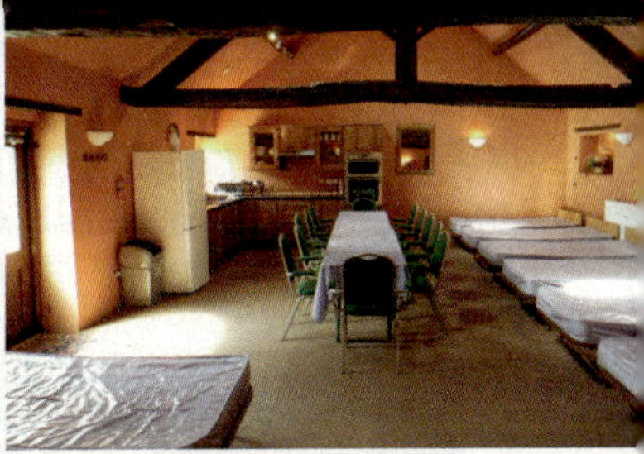
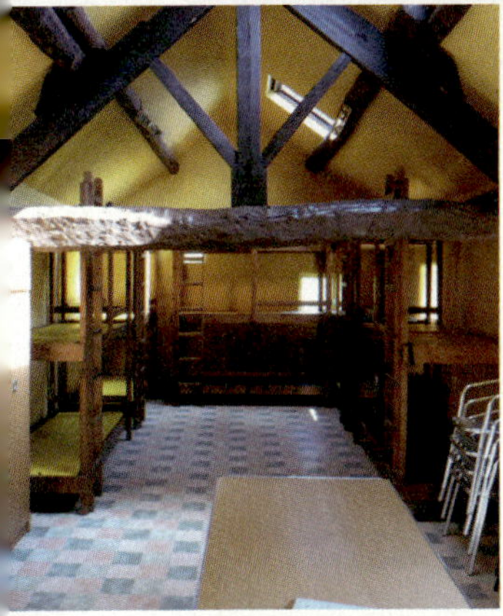
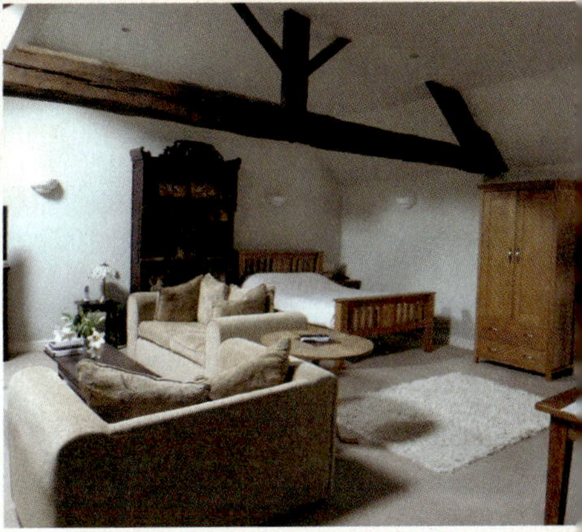
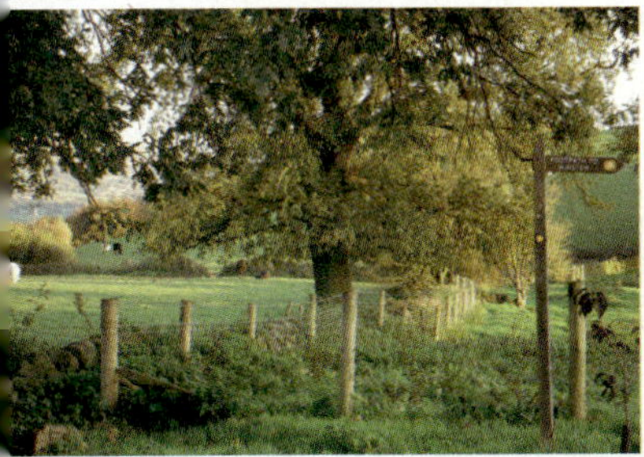
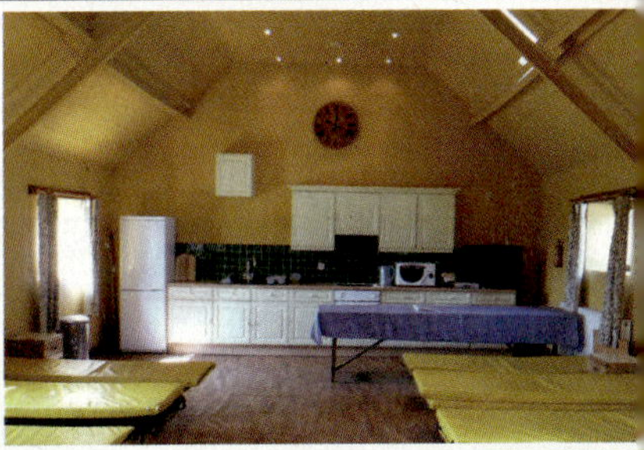
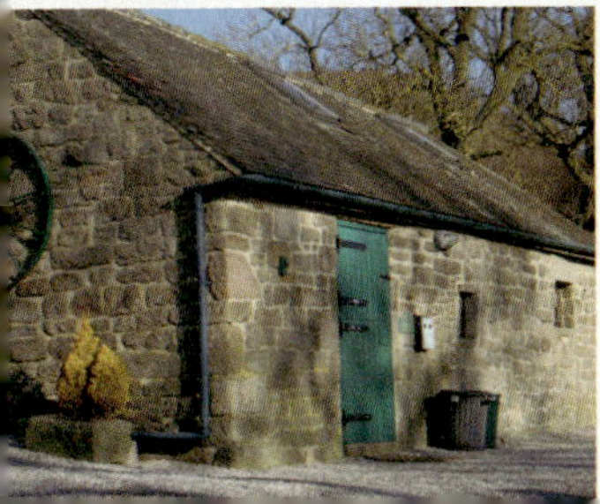
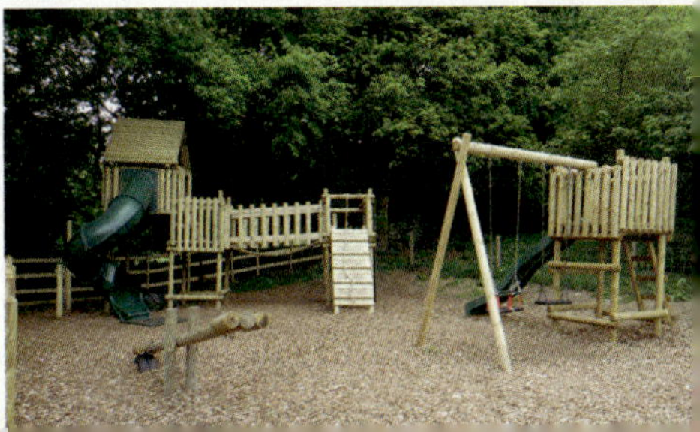

SHEEN BUNKHOUSE

Sheen Bunkhouse is a newly converted barn in a quiet corner of the Peak District, close to the beautiful Dove and Manifold valleys. Comprehensively equipped, it offers a large TV lounge, well-equipped self-catering facilities and two bunkrooms with wash basins. Toilets and showers are conveniently located for both rooms.

Passing close by the barn, the Manifold Valley Track, Tissington Trail and High Peak Trail provide easy access to beautiful countryside, ideal for families and cyclists. Dovedale, the Upper Dove Valley and the remote and mysterious moorlands around Flash and Longnor offer stunning scenery for walkers. Visit the markets and parks at Buxton (8 miles), Leek (10 miles) and Bakewell (12 miles) for a great day out. Other attractions include Alton Towers (20 mins by car) and the famous Opera House and show caves at Buxton.

DETAILS

- **Open** - All year, 24 hours access, reception 8am - 9pm
- **Number of beds** - 14: 1x8, 1x6
- **Booking** - Book by phone or email
- **Price per night** - From: adults £16, under 16s £11.
- **Public Transport** - Train station at Buxton. Daily bus operated by Bowers from Buxton to Hartington passes close to bunkhouse.
- **Directions** - On the B5054 between Hartington and Hulme End take the turning to Sheen (also signposted for 'Staffordshire Knott'). The bunkhouse is on the right 200yds after the pub.

CONTACT: Jean or Graham Belfield
Tel: 01298 84501, Fax: 01298 84501
grahambelfield@fsmail.net
Peakstones, Sheen, Derbyshire, SK17 0ES

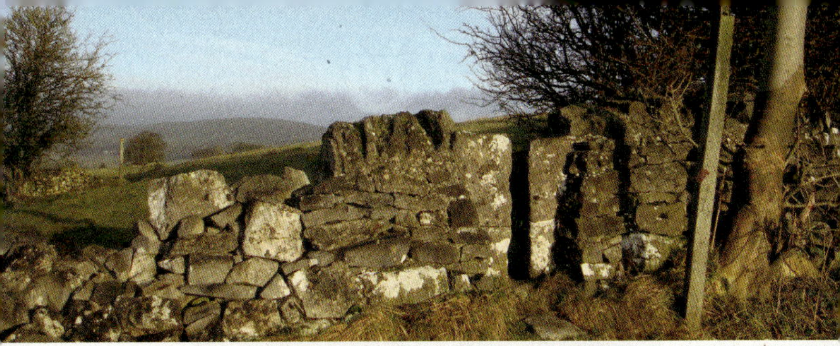

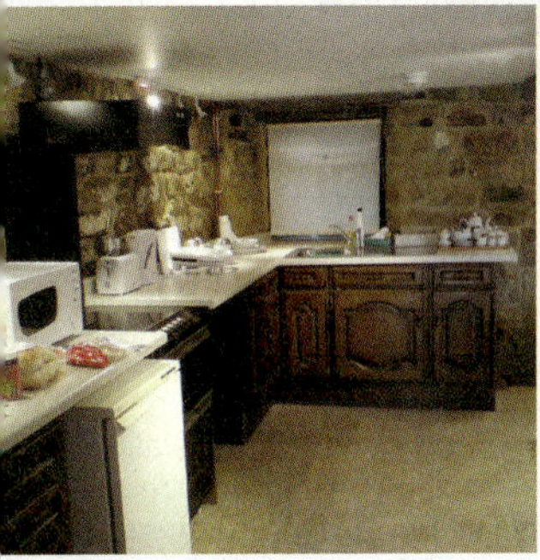

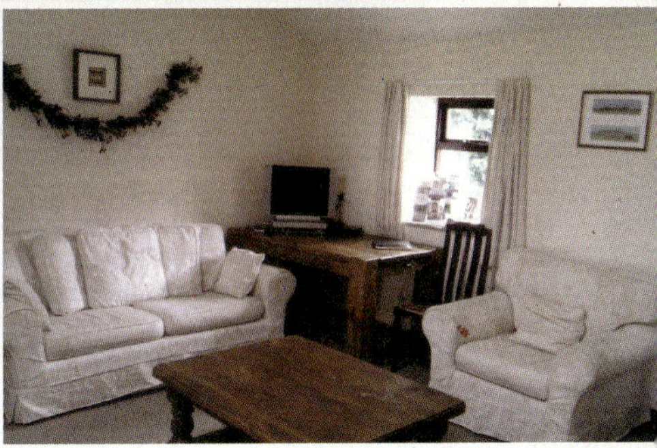

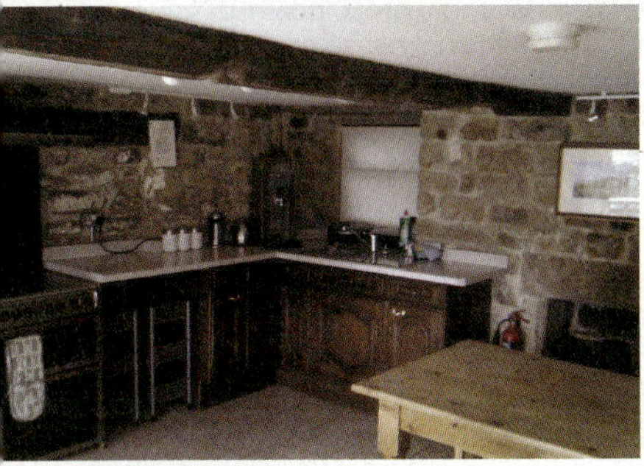

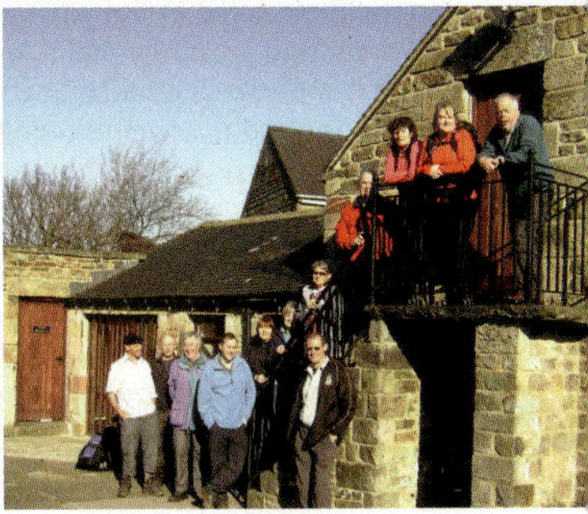

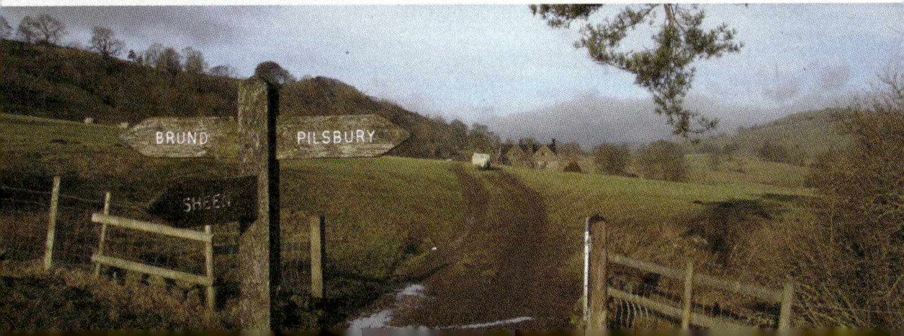
BRUND
PILSBURY
SHEEN

ILAM BUNKHOUSE

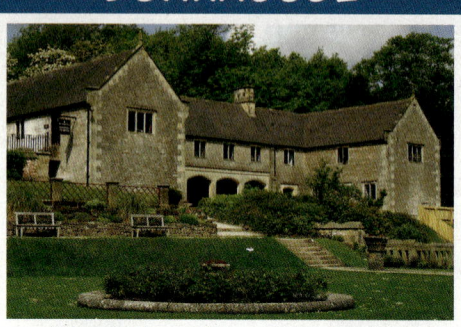

Ilam bunkhouse is located in an 18th century stable block which originally formed part of the Ilam Hall Estate. The estate is now managed by the National Trust and the bunkhouse sits within the grounds of Ilam Park. Ilam bunkhouse was refurbished in April 2012 and now provides high quality group accommodation for up to 16 people. There are 3 bedrooms with bunk beds, with each bunk provided with a locker, night light and plug socket, there is also a hand basin in each room. There is a sociable main living area comprising of a large dining table with benches, an open plan kitchen area and 2 large comfortable fitted sofas in the sitting room area. There are 3 individual toilet and shower rooms and an additional toilet room. Ilam bunkhouse is a fantastic base to explore the Peak District National Park, in particular the limestone hills and gorges, meandering rivers and beautiful woodland of the White Peak. There are lots of fantastic places for your group to explore nearby including Dovedale with it's famous stepping stones and Ilam Park with it's beautiful views, popular tea room and shop.

DETAILS

- **Open** - All year round,
- **Number of beds** - 16: in three rooms
- **Booking** - via peakdistrict@nationaltrust.org.uk or 01433 670368
- **Price per night** - Weekdays £160pn. Weekends £225pn.
- **Public Transport** - Trains at Uttoxeter (12 miles), Bus; Moorlands Connect service – bookable service stops in Ilam village 0300 111 8003.
- **Directions** - In Ilam follow signs for National Trust Ilam Park. Use main car park.

CONTACT: Lucy Chadburn
Tel: 01433 670368
peakdistrict@nationaltrust.org.uk   www.nationaltrust.org.uk
The Stableblock, Ilam Park, Ilam, nr Ashbourne, DE6 2AZ

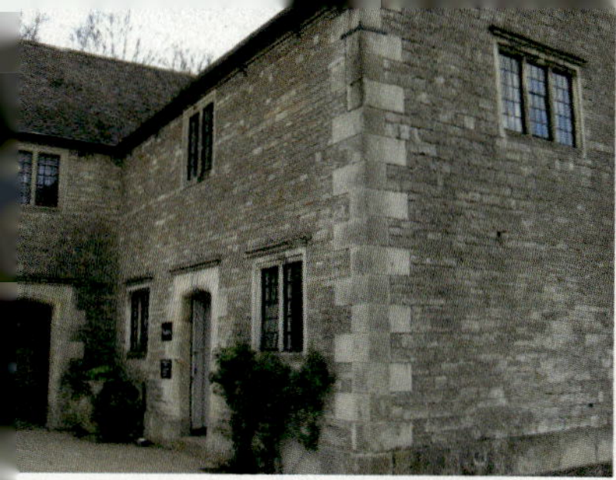
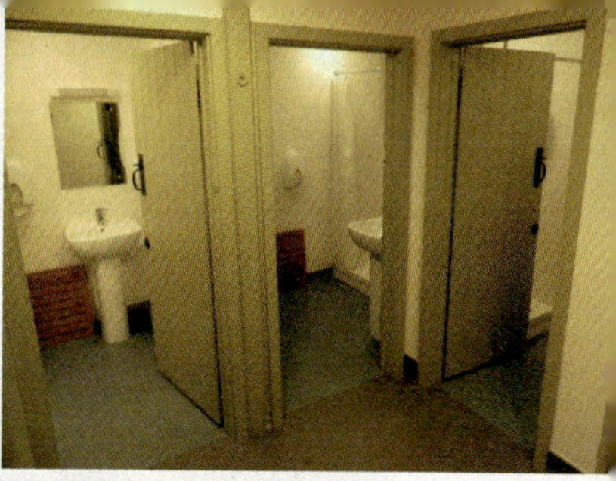
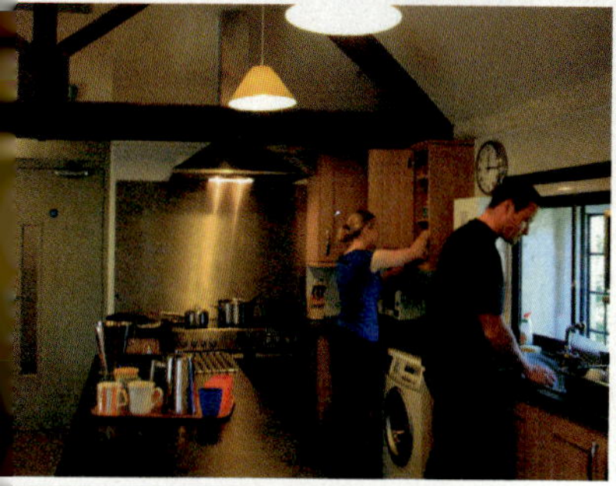
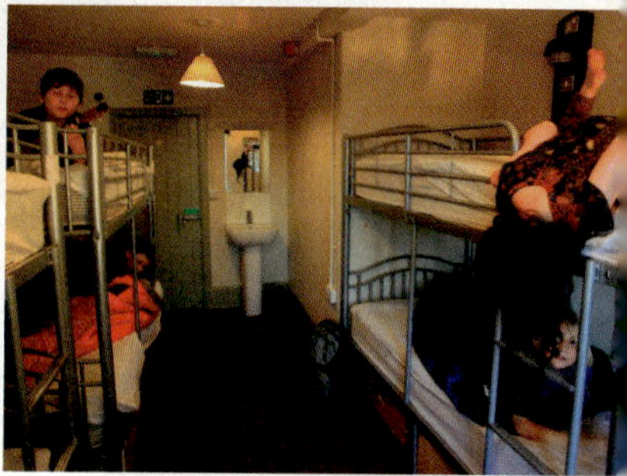
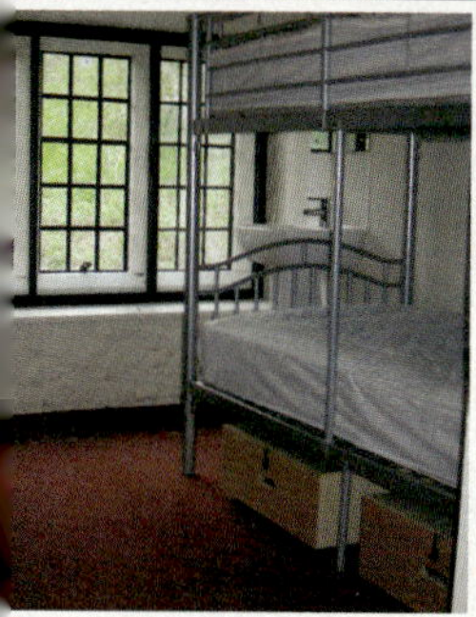
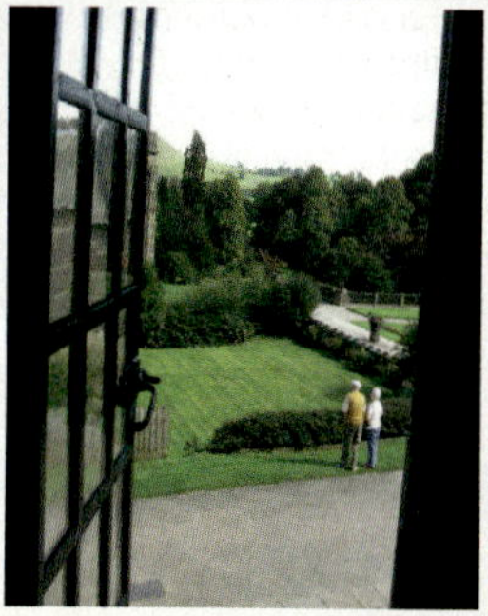
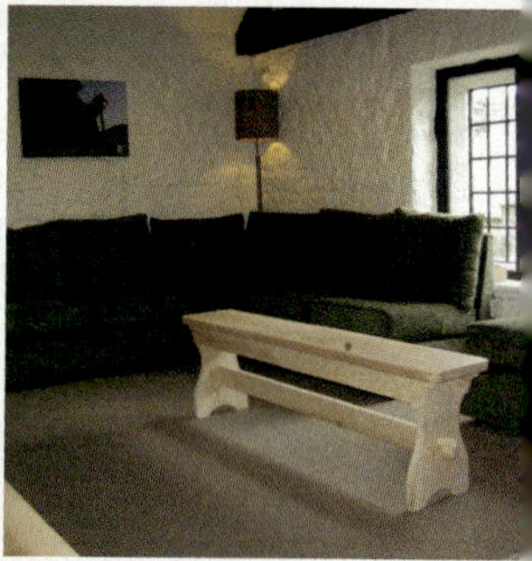
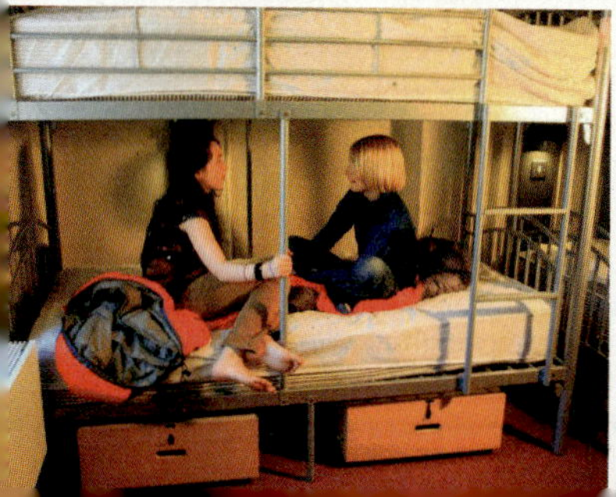
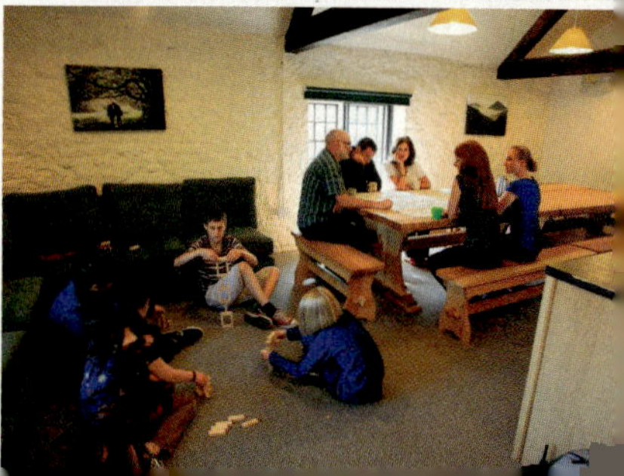

ST MICHAELS CENTRE

St Michaels Centre is at the heart of the bustling peak distinct village of Hathersage on the Hope Valley train line. It is an ideal base to explore the Derwent Valley reservoirs, the Gritstone Edges, Chatsworth estate and the caverns of Castleton, with limitless walking from the doorstep. Regular trains to local villages in the Hope Valley makes it possible to explore the area without a car. The centre provides high quality, warm, welcoming accommodation for large families or groups of around 20 or more. It can accommodate up to 38 people in bunk-bedded rooms with 4 extra beds available in an adjacent cottage. There is a self-catering kitchen (catering provided on request), a dining room and lounge area with TV/DVD and music, WiFi, a classroom, showers, toilets, drying room and a car park for 12 cars. Shops, pubs, cafés, rail station, bus route, tennis court and a fabulous open air heated swimming pool are all a few steps away. The centre may be able to arrange instruction and equipment for caving, climbing, rock hopping, abseiling, gorge walking and orienteering.

DETAILS

- **Open** - All year, 24 hours
- **Number of beds** - 38: 2x2, 1x4, 2x6, 1x8, 1x10. Plus 4 in adjacent cottage.
- **Booking** - Advanced booking available.
- **Price per night** - £20 per person with a minimum of £400 a night. Minimum of 2 night's hire. Activities: £250 per day (for maximum of 12 people).
- **Public Transport** - On the Hope Valley line with regular trains from Manchester and Sheffield. Buses daily to Sheffield, Hope, Castleton, Eyam, Bradwell, Bakewell.
- **Directions** - On the Main Road opposite Brookfield Manor and Catholic Church.

CONTACT: Bill Hanley
Tel: 01433 650309
joan.williams@nottscc.gov.uk http://www.nottinghamshire.gov.uk
Main Road, Hathersage, Derbyshire, S32 1BB

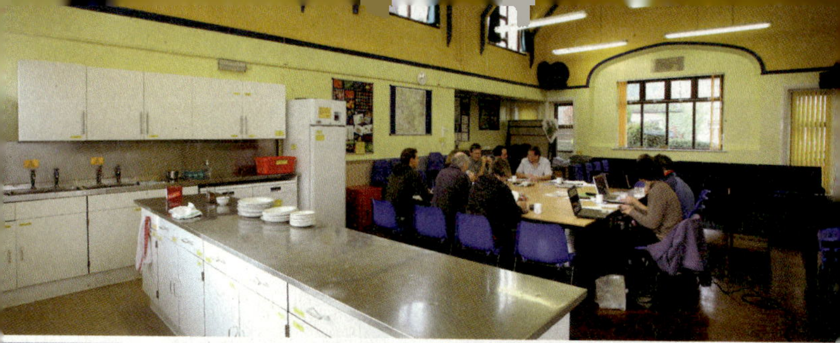
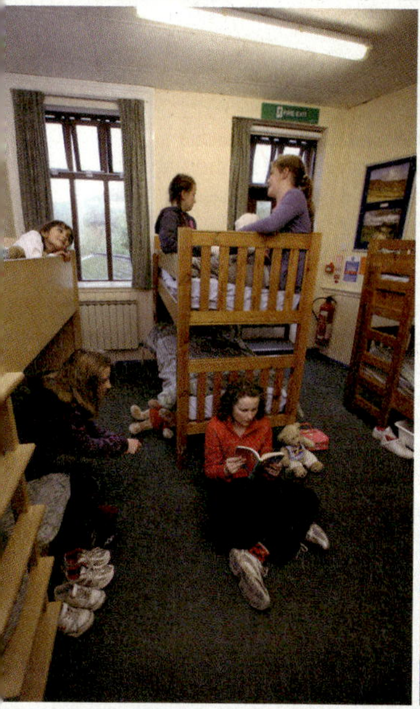
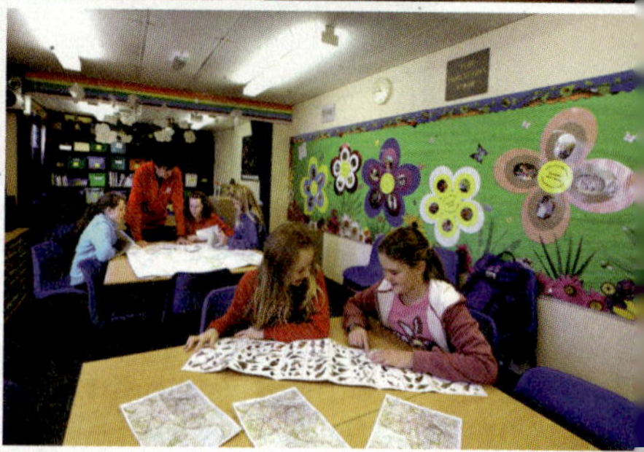
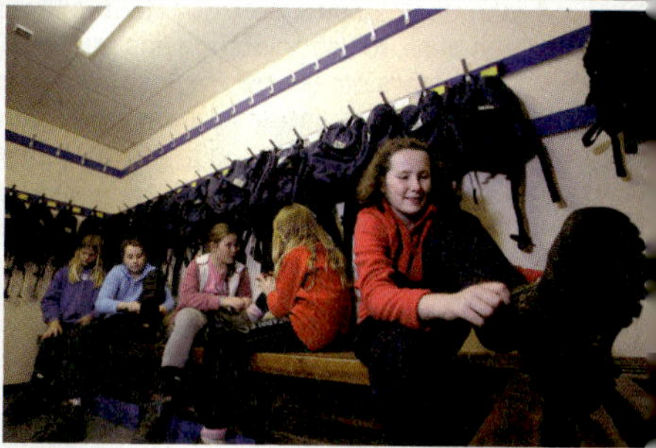
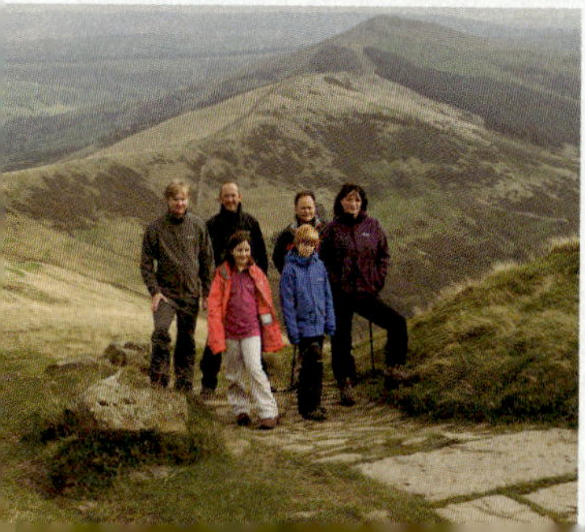
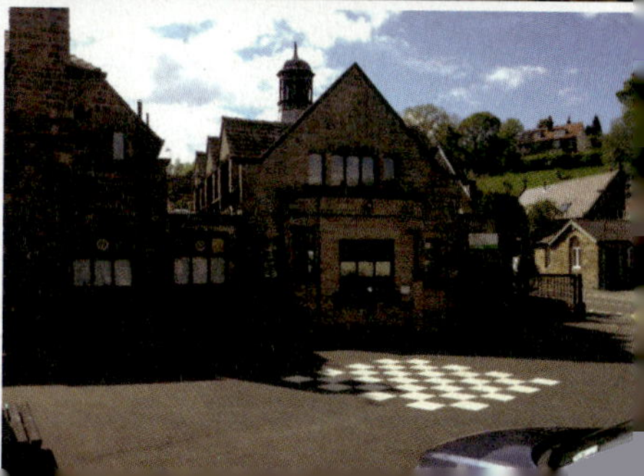

THORPE FARM BUNKHOUSES

ENGLAND

Thorpe Farm Bunkhouses are situated a mile northwest of Hathersage, on a family-run mixed dairy farm which makes its own ice cream.

The bunkhouses are 2 miles west of Stanage Edge. Other popular climbing and walking areas are nearby. Castleton is 6 miles up the Hope Valley and Eyam is 6 miles southwest. Each bunkhouse has dormitories with individual bunks each with mattress and pillow. There is some sleeping space in the sitting rooms and room for camping outside. The bunkhouses have heating, drying facilities, hot showers, toilets, electric / gas cooking, fridges, freezers, electric kettles, toasters etc. The Byre is all on one level with disabled facilities.

DETAILS

- **Open** - All year, no restrictions
- **Number of beds** - Old Shippon 32: 2x12, 2x4. Byre 14: 1x6, 1x4.living room 4. Old Stables 14: 1x8, 1x6. Pondside 14: 1x8, 1x6
- **Booking** - Essential for weekends.
- **Price per night** - See own website.
- **Public Transport** - Train station at Hathersage, 10 mins' walk from bunkhouse. Bus service 272 operates from Sheffield to Hathersage. Details phone Busline 01298 230980 or 01246 250450.
- **Directions** - GR 223 824. If walking from A6187/A625 in Hathersage turn right (just past the George Hotel) up Jaggers Lane, turn second right up Coggers Lane and fifth turning on left (signed Thorpe Farm). If driving follow the road from Hathersage towards Hope for ¾ mile, then turn right into private drive (signposted Thorpe Farm).

CONTACT: Jane Marsden
Tel: 01433 650659
jane@hope-valley.co.uk www.thorpe-bunk.co.uk
Thorpe Farm, Hathersage, Peak District, Via Sheffield, S32 1B

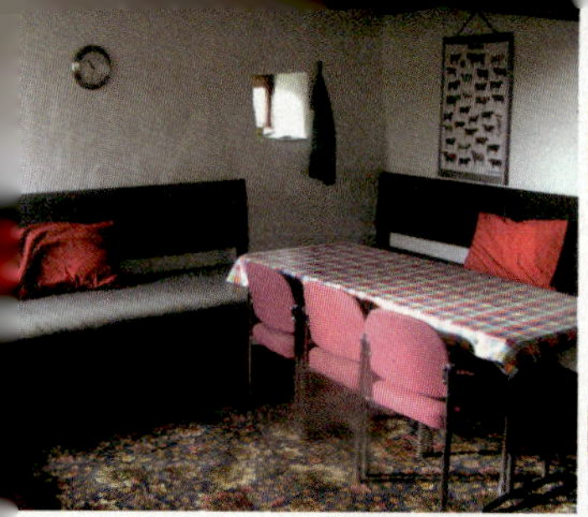
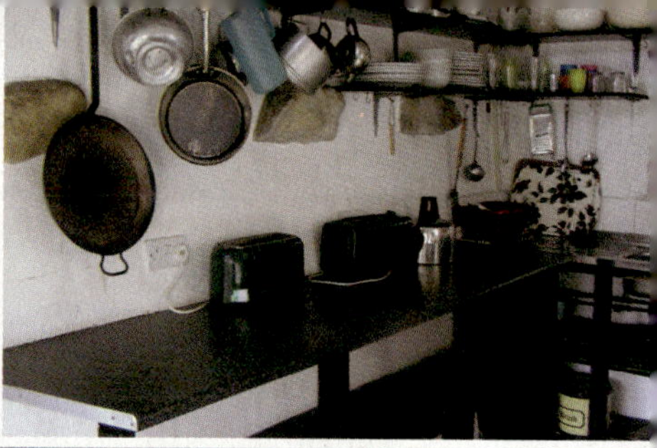
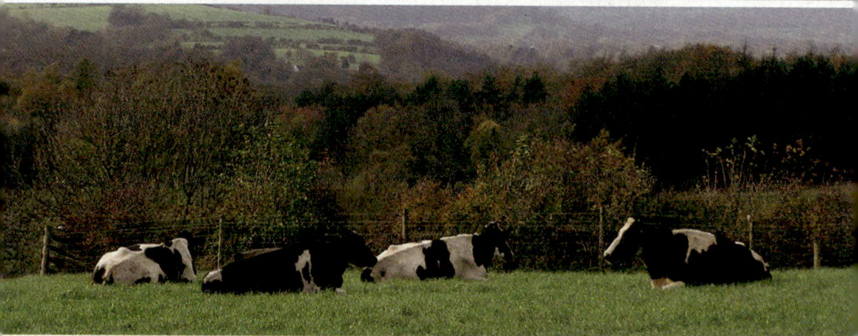
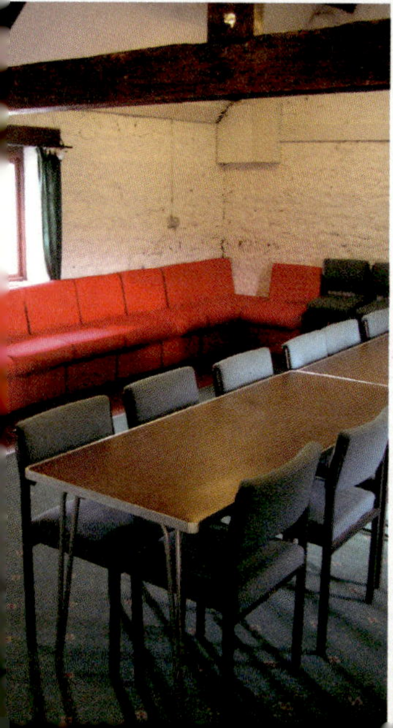
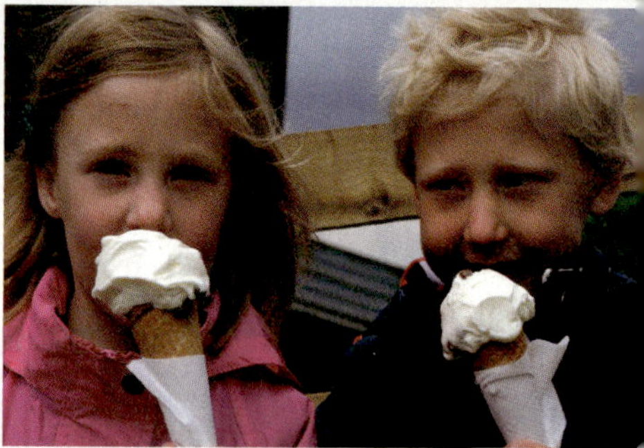
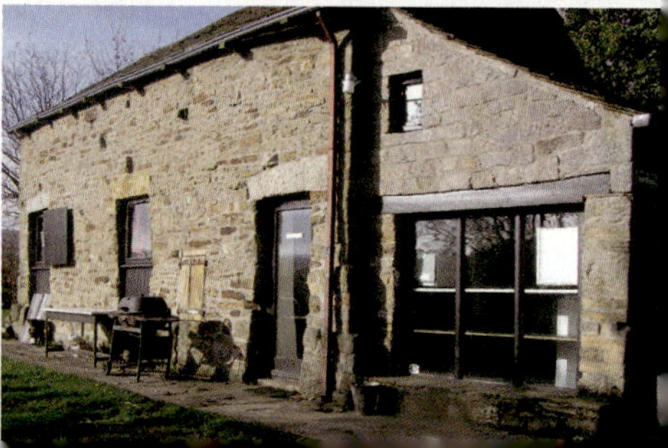

SHINING CLIFF HOSTEL

ENGLAND

With its own crags, streams, lakes and over 100-acres of mature woodland, the hidden Shining Cliff Hostel has nature on its doorstep. Completely refurbished in 2009, the hostel is ideal for groups wishing to enjoy time away in a peaceful woodland setting. The entrance porch, with space for hanging coats and boots, leads into the open plan kitchen, dining and lounge area. In the well equipped kitchen, there is a 6 ring gas hob, electric oven, microwave, fridge, freezer, dishwasher and water boiler. The dining area comfortably seats 20 people whilst the lounge provides seating and space to relax. Shining Cliff hostel offers a full range of activities, some are on-site such as bushcraft, abseiling, ecology and environmental art, while climbing, caving or canoeing can be enjoyed a little further afield. Activities must be booked in advance. The hostel is nestled within 100 acres of woodland and a ten minute walk, down a rough track, from the nearest parking area. Other paths lead through the woods to the A6 at Ambergate (20 mins walk). Ambergate has a food shop, pubs, buses to Derby and a train station with connections to Derby, Nottingham and London.

DETAILS

- **Open** - All Year,
- **Number of beds** - 20: 1 x 4, 2 x 6, 2 x 2
- **Booking** - Phone or email
- **Price per night** - £189.60 Apr - Oct, £157.20 Nov - Mar, minimum of 2 nights
- **Public Transport** - Ambergate rail station (1 mile). Transpeak bus on A6 (1 mile)
- **Directions** - See website for directions. Sat Navs NOT recommended.

CONTACT:
Tel: 01433 620377
enquiries@shiningcliff.org   www.shiningcliff.org
Jackass Lane, Alderwasley Belper, DE56 2RE

ROYAL OAK BUNKBARN

ENGLAND

Eat, drink, be merry and stay in a refurbished stone barn with a traditional award winning Peak District country pub on site. The Royal Oak serves fantastic pub grub and local cask ales (Winner 'Derbyshire Pub of the Year Awards' 2012 & 2010 and a close second 2011 & 2013). The Royal Oak has direct access to the High Peak and Tissington Trails which use disused railways to provide easy off road cycling. The area is also ideal for climbing and walking with stone circles and limestone gorges to explore. The bunk barn is perfect for any number from 1 to 34 (small and large groups welcome) wanting comfortable, clean, private bunk bed style rooms. The five separate bunk rooms all heated and lockable. All the bunk beds have comfortable mattresses, a pillow and fresh linen, just bring a duvet or sleeping bag. There is a small communal kitchen ideal for basic meals with fridge, oven and kettle and seating for 5/6 people. Separate ladies and gents toilets and hot showers are included in the simple per person tariff. Camp-site and holiday cottages (some sleeping large groups) available.

DETAILS

- **Open** - All year, all day
- **Number of beds** - 34: 3 x 8 (bunks), 1 x 6 (bunks), 1 x 4 (bunks)
- **Booking** - Booking in advance by phone or email
- **Price per night** - April to Sept £15pp, Oct to March £13pp.
- **Public Transport** - Nearest trains Buxton (8 miles). Local bus no.42 (Buxton to Ashbourne) drops off 15 minutes' walk away on A515
- **Directions** - From the A515 Buxton to Ashbourne road take road to Hurdlow oposite to B5055 road to Bakewell.

CONTACT: The Royal Oak
Tel: 01298 83288, Fax: 01298 83696
hello@peakpub.co.uk www.peakpub.co.uk
The Royal Oak, Hurdlow, Nr Buxton, SK17 9QJ

MOORSIDE FARM BUNKHOUSE

ENGLAND

Moorside Farm is a 300-year-old farmhouse set 1200 feet up in the beautiful Peak District National Park on the Derbyshire / Staffordshire border and approximately five miles from the historic town of Buxton. Sleeping accommodation is provided in two areas, one for 14 - this is alpine style with pine clad ceiling and a pine floor with bunk beds. The second area has 6 beds, also in bunks and is an ideal room for a small group or family. Downstairs there are showers, toilets and a large dining / general room. The farmhouse has full central heating and drying facilities are available. Provided at the bunkhouse is a three course breakfast, packed lunch and a substantial dinner in the evening, vegetarians are catered for. A small kitchen is available for making tea and coffee. Ample parking space is provided. All bookings have sole use of the accommodation.

DETAILS

- **Open** - All year, 24 hours
- **Number of beds** - 20: 1 x 14, 1 x 6
- **Booking** - Deposit required with minimum two weeks' notice.
- **Price per night** - £33.00 per person per night, includes bed, breakfast, packed lunch and evening meal. Bed and breakfast only £23.00 per person per night. Minimum booking 4 persons.
- **Public Transport** - Nearest train station Buxton. Take bus to Longnor or Travellers Rest. Bus enquiries 01332 292200.
- **Directions** - GR SK 055 670. Leave A53, Buxton to Leek road, at Travellers Rest, take 4th lane on left, down to T junction, take first left, Moorside Farm is first right entrance.

CONTACT: Charlie
Tel: 01298 83406
charliefutcher@aol.com www.moorsidefarm.com
Hollinsclough, Longnor, Buxton, Derbyshire, SK17 0RF

UPPER BOOTH
CAMPING BARN

153

ENGLAND

'We found it - the most beautiful site we've ever encountered'.

Upper Booth Camping Barn is located adjacent to a small camp-site alongside Crowden Clough on the National Trust's High Peak Estate. It is possible to hire the barn and additional pitches on the camp-site. There is space for cooking and tables for eating. Toilets, handbasins, washing up sinks and showers are shared with the camp-site.

Upper Booth camping barn is located on a working hill-farm. Walking and biking are available from the farm, the Pennine Way passes through the farmyard. An ideal base for outdoor enthusiasts.

DETAILS

- **Open** - March-November. Arrival between 3pm and 9pm. Departure before 10am. Not suitable for late night parties
- **Number of beds** - sleeping space for 12
- **Booking** - Pre-booking essential for weekends & bank holidays. Provisional booking held for 7 days. Confirmed if full payment is received within that time.
- **Price per night** - Exclusive use (up to 12 persons) from £90 per night plus vehicles. Individual spaces from £10 per person per night.
- **Public Transport** - Nearest station, Edale (Sheffield/Manchester line) approx 40 minutes' walk on footpaths to Upper Booth. Nearest bus stop Barber Booth (15 minutes' walk). Service 260 weekdays. 3 buses a day go to Upper Booth.
- **Directions** - GR103 853. Follow signs for Edale village, then for Barber Booth, immediately after river bridge turn right for Upper Booth.

CONTACT: Robert or Sarah
Tel: (01433) 670250
mail@helliwell.info   www.upperboothcamping.co.uk
Upper Booth Farm, Edale, Hope Valley, Derbyshire, S33 7ZJ

PINDALE FARM
OUTDOOR CENTRE

ENGLAND

A mile from Castleton in the heart of the Peak District. Pindale Farm comprises a farmhouse pre-dating 1340 and lead mine buildings from the 1850s, which have been completely rebuilt from near dereliction. The centre offers 5 different kinds of accommodation. The farmhouse offers traditional bed and (an AGA cooked) breakfast. The Barn has 6 independent self-catering units, 3 of these can accommodate people with certain physical disabilities. The Old Lead Mine Engine House is a self-catering unit sleeping 8. The Powder House, originally the mine's explosive store, is a small camping barn with basic facilities for up to 4 people. A camp-site, adjacent to the centre, has showers, hot water, and toilet facilities. All rooms have Freesat TV, WiFi is available in the barn and most of the camping areas (£2 a day). The ideal base for walking, climbing, caving, horse riding etc. Instruction is available if required. Well behaved pets welcome. Scouts, Cadets and DofE expeditions welcome, camping or in the bunkhouse.

DETAILS

- **Open** - All year (camping March-October), 24 hours
- **Number of beds** - 64 bunkbeds plus camping and B&B
- **Booking** - Early booking (deposit) is best.
- **Price per night** - Camping £7.50 pp (£4 for hook up). Barns £15 pp plus £1 electric tokens for cooker, shower and sockets. B&B with four poster bed and AGA breakfast enquire for prices.
- **Public Transport** - Train station in Hope. On local buses ask for Hope. Hope is 15 minutes' walk from the hostel. National Express Sheffield (taxi fare £15-£20).
- **Directions** - GR 163 825. From Hope follow cement works signs, turn off main road between church and Woodroffe Arms.

CONTACT: Alan Medhurst
Tel: 01433 620111, Fax: 01433 620729
pindalefarm@btconnect.com   www.pindalefarm.co.uk
Pindale Road, Hope, Hope Valley, Derbyshire, S33 6RN

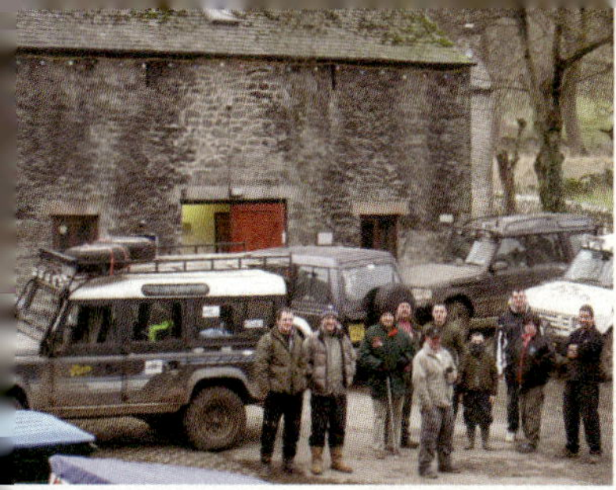
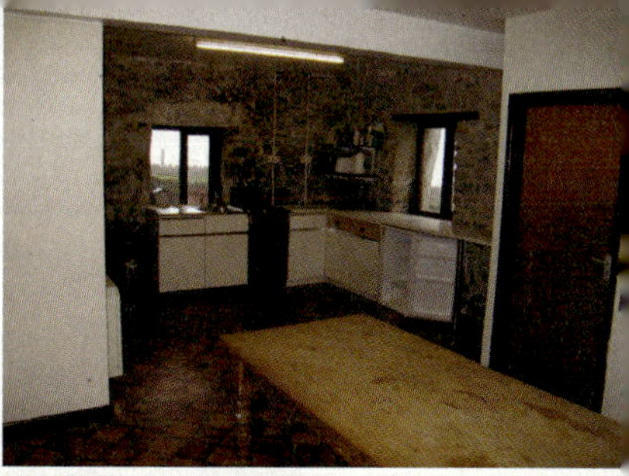
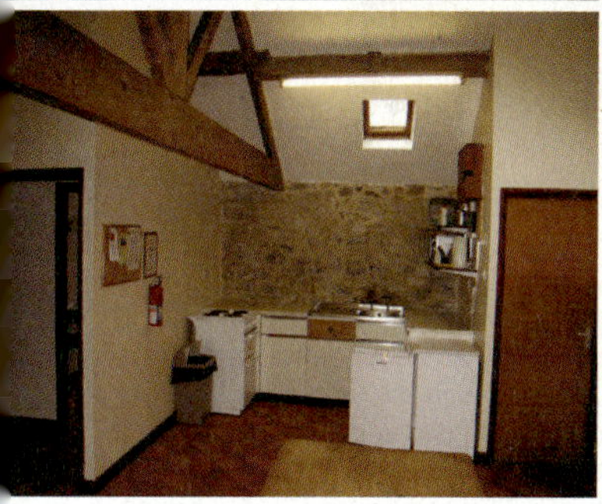
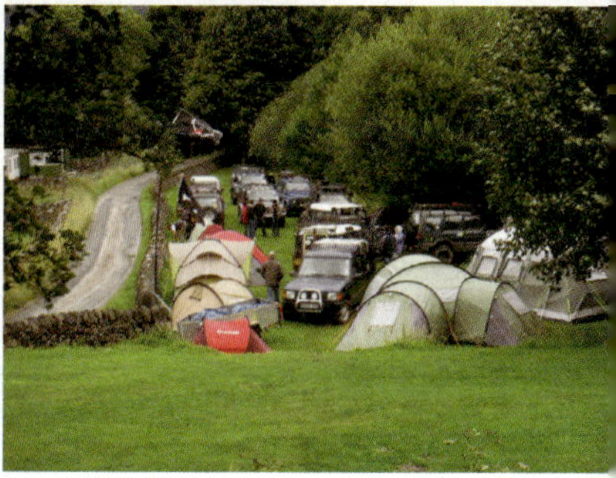
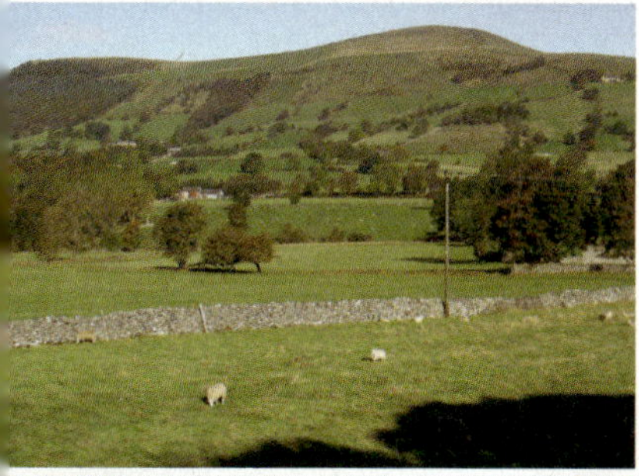
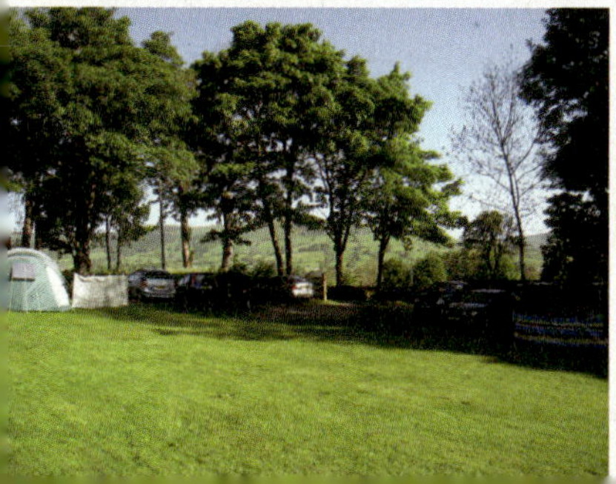
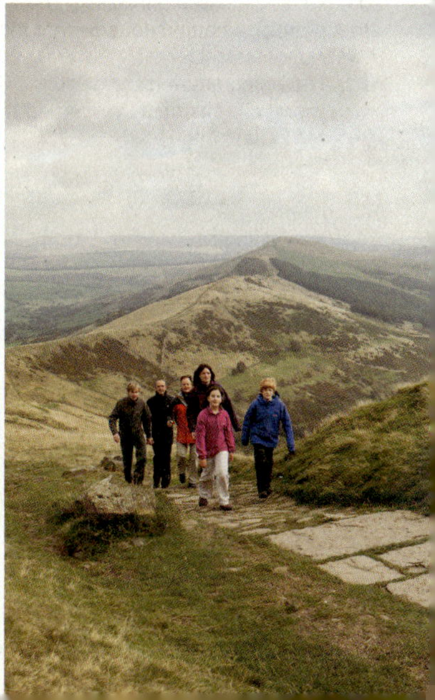

HOMESTEAD AND CHEESEHOUSE

These two bunkhouses are situated on a small mixed farm in the middle of Bamford, just 3 miles from Stanage Edge. The Derwent Dams are between 1.5 and 7 miles further up the valley. Castleton is 5 miles to the north, Chatsworth House and Park 10 miles to the southwest. Both bunkhouses have individual bunks each with mattress, fitted sheets and pillow (bring your own sleeping bags), gas central heating and drying facilities. Homestead has 22 beds in 3 rooms, and 2 bathrooms with 2 toilets and showers in each, a large dayroom with oak seating and a fully equipped kitchen with gas cooker. Cheesehouse is a self-contained bunkhouse with four bunks, ideal for a small family or group. It has a shower and toilet and is equipped with a kitchen having cooking rings, a microwave oven, toaster and kettle. The bunkhouses are 2 minutes' walk from a pub. Sorry, no dogs (working dogs on site).

DETAILS

- **Open** - All year, arrive after 2pm on day of arrival and leave by 11am on departure.
- **Number of beds** - Homestead 22: 1x10, 2x6. Cheesehouse 4: 1x4.
- **Booking** - Recommended for weekends.
- **Price per night** - From £15 per person. Sole use: Homestead £195, Cheesehouse £45. Minimum of 2 night booking for Homestead at weekends or phone for a quote for a single night fee.
- **Public Transport** - Nearest train station Bamford, 10 minutes' walk. Bus 274 & 275 operates Sundays Bamford to Sheffield or Castleton. Bus 272 Bamford to Sheffield and Castleton. Bus 241 Bamford to Bakewell.
- **Directions** - The farm is in the centre of Bamford on South View Lane (turn off A6013 at the 'Country Stores').

CONTACT: Helena Platts
Tel: 01433 651298
The Farm, Bamford, Hope Valley, S33 0BL

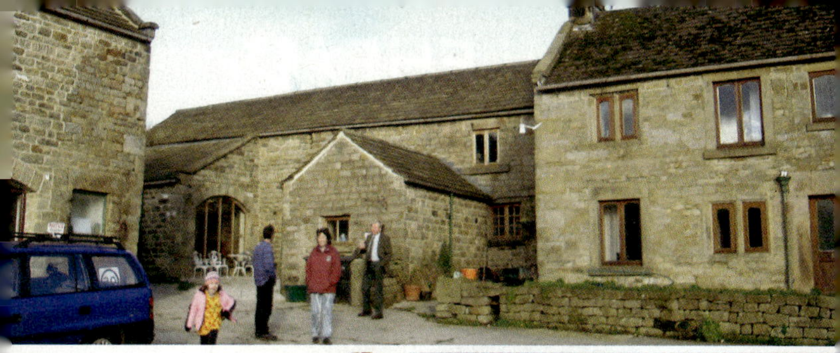

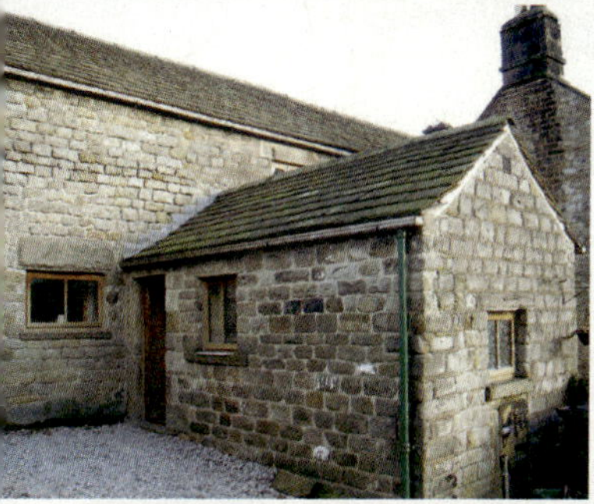

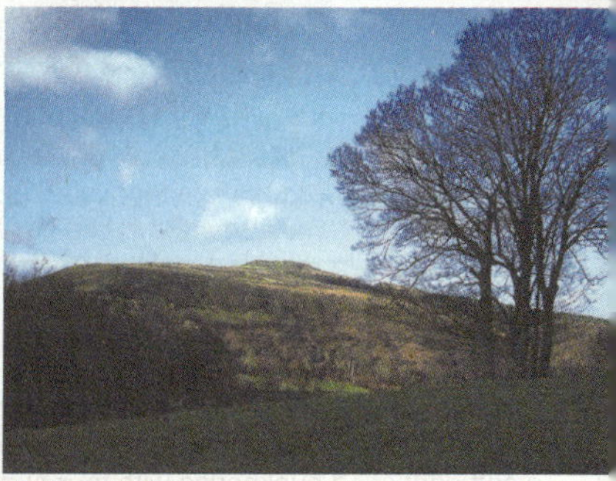

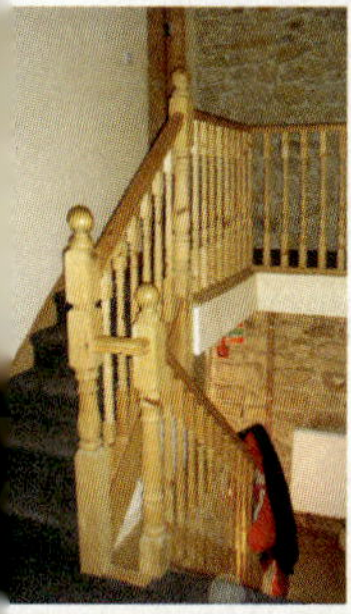

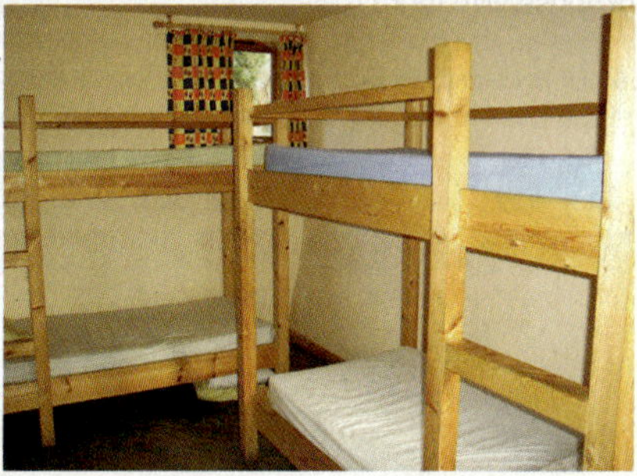

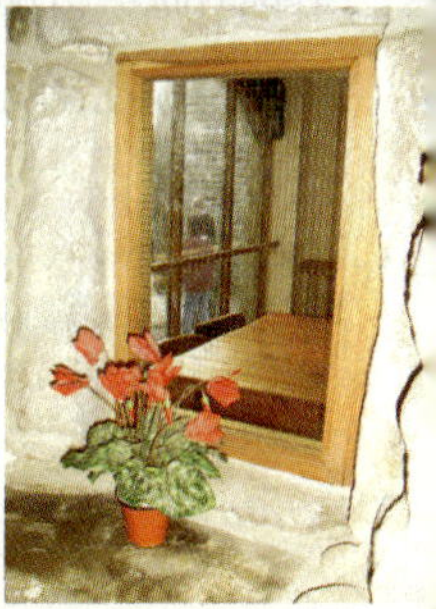

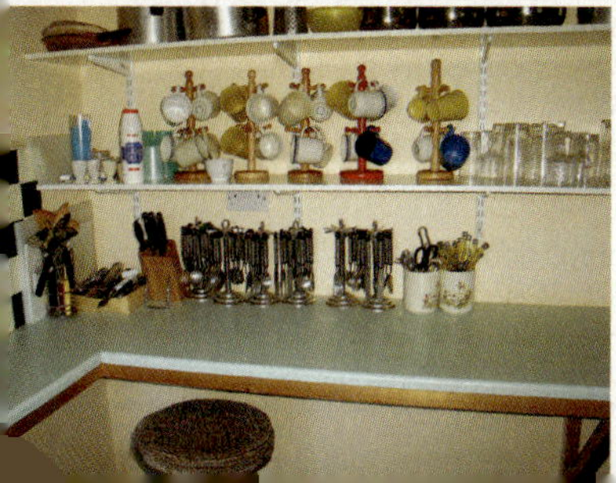

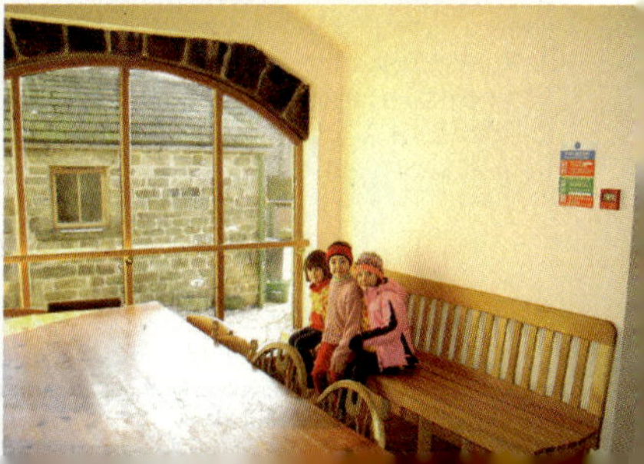

DALEHEAD BUNKHOUSE

Dalehead Bunkhouse is a renovated gritstone farmhouse on a working hill-farm at the remote head of Edale Valley. Providing basic but comfortable accommodation heated by log burner, there is a kitchen with fridge/freezer, a lounge, dining room and plenty of parking. Visitors must bring their own sleeping bags, pillows and towels. Edale is a very popular destination for walkers, climbers, mountain bikers, hang-gliders or for just enjoying the magnificent scenery. It lies between the gritstone of the peat-topped Kinder moors to the north and the cave-riddled limestone of the White Peak to the south. Despite its proximity to major cities and the straightforward rail service to Sheffield and Manchester, the Dark Peak remains unspoilt, with many places where it is possible to enjoy a sense of remoteness. Dogs are welcome on the ground floor of the bunkhouse for an extra charge of £15 per stay.

DETAILS

- **Open** - Open all year round, 24 hours
- **Number of beds** - 20: 1x6, 1x8, 1x6
- **Booking** - Telephone, email or complete enquiry form on our website. Contact postal address: National Trust, Dark Peak Area Office, Edale End, Edale Road, Hope Valley, Derbyshire, S33 6RF.
- **Price per night** - Weekdays (Mon-Thurs) £180 per night. Weekends (Fri-Sun) £250 per night. £250 refundable booking, damage and cleaning deposit.
- **Public Transport** - Trains at Edale (2 miles) to Sheffield and Manchester. Taxi service only available from Hope Station. Nearest bus station at Castleton (3 miles).
- **Directions** - SK101841 (OS map no. 110). At the western end of the dale 2 miles from Edale church.

CONTACT: Lucy Chadburn (Administrator)
Tel: 01433 670 368
peakdistrict@nationaltrust.org.uk www.nationaltrust.org.uk/darkpeak
Dalehead Bunkhouse, Upper Booth, Edale, Hope Valley, S33 7ZJ

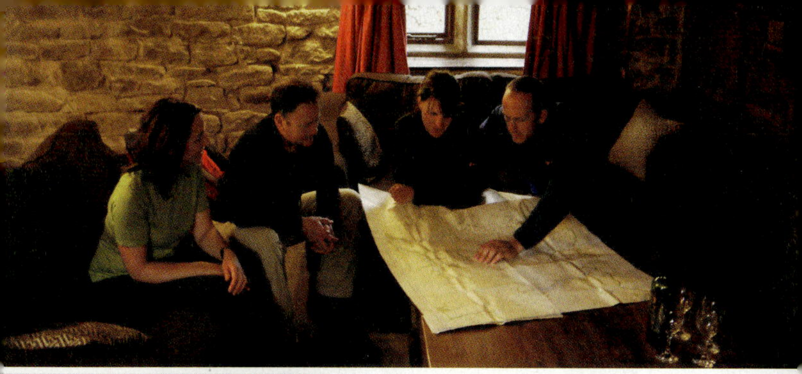

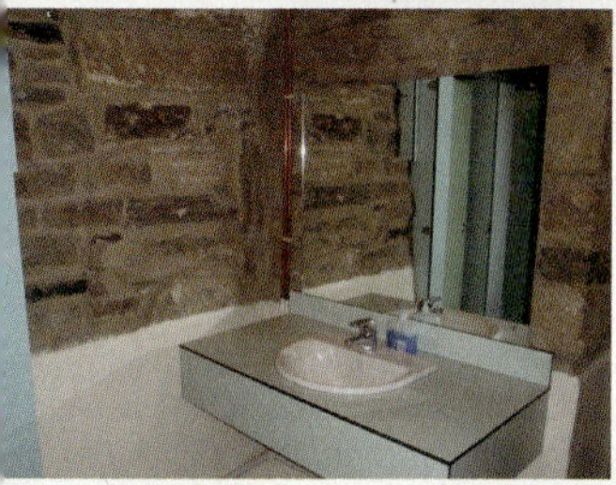

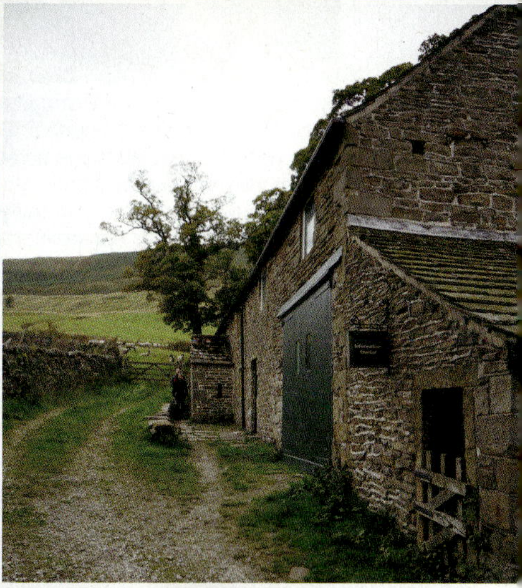

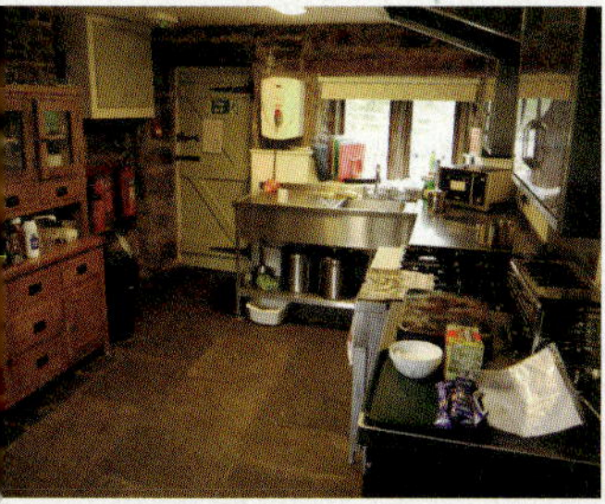

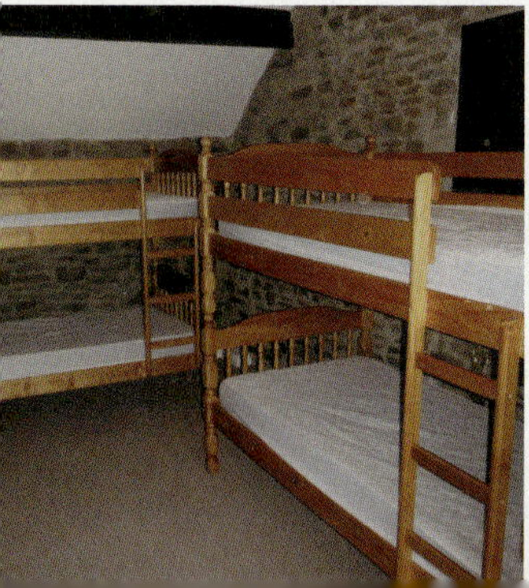

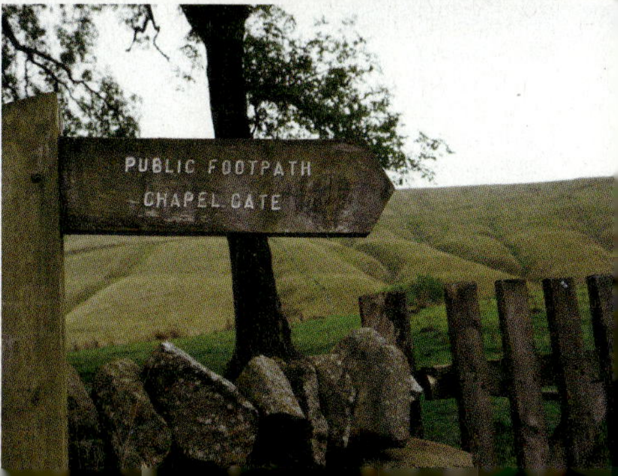
PUBLIC FOOTPATH
CHAPEL GATE

JOHN HUNT BASE
ENGLAND

The John Hunt Base, part of Hagg Farm Outdoor Education Centre, offers comfortable accommodation in a converted 19th century hill farm in the Upper Derwent Valley, with unparalleled views across the open moors of the Dark Peak. Walks from the door lead onto the high moors of Kinder and Bleaklow and around the Ladybower reservoirs and dams. The Hagg Farm descent cycle route passes close by and there is secure storage for mountain bikes. The Base has a lounge, TV/DVD, payphone, showers & toilets, drying room and kitchen, with good wheelchair access throughout. Dormitory accommodation consists of two rooms with bunks sleeping 6 and 8. In addition there are 2 rooms with 2 single beds in each. In the grounds are a wildlife garden, field, artificial climbing boulder, jacobs ladder, climbing tower and access to woodland. The site also lends itself to quiet pursuits such as art retreats. Groups have sole use during their stay, and all bedding is provided. Instructional support for various outdoor activities can be booked for a group of up to 12 people.

DETAILS

- **Open** - All year, 24 hours
- **Number of beds** - 18: 1 x 8, 1 x 6, 2 x 2
- **Booking** - Advance booking essential.
- **Price per night** - £252 per night, minimum 2 night stay, Instruction from £250 per day for a group of up to 12 people. Hire of boots & equipment £5 per person per day.
- **Public Transport** - Trains at Bamford (7 miles away) on the Hope Valley Line.
- **Directions** - From Ladybower Reservoir junction take A57 3 miles to west towards Glossop, look for sign to Hagg Farm on the right.

CONTACT:
Tel: 01433 651594, Fax: 01433 651525
haggfarm@nottscc.gov.uk www.nottinghamshire.gov.uk/haggfarm
Hagg Farm OEC, Snake Rd, Bamford, Hope Valley, S33 0BJ

Nottinghamshire County Council

FOUNDRY ADVENTURE CENTRE

The Foundry Activity centre has 2 units, Kinder; 31 beds and Howden; 21 beds, they can be combined to provide total 52 beds. With easy access to all parts of The Peak District National Park, the centre is an ideal location for outdoor activities and touring, welcoming a wide range of groups including schools, universities, corporate, clubs and large families. The spacious centre includes; comfortable lounges with a library, TV and wood burning stove, equipped kitchens and dining areas, four bathrooms and warm drying facilities. Bunks in rooms of 2 - 8 have optional bedding provision. There is parking for 20 plus vehicles with flat hard surfaced and grass areas for activities on site. Surrounding farmland and woodland can be accessed via an extensive network of footpaths. The centre is an AALA licensed provider and can also offer a wide range of adventure activities including abseiling, caving, climbing, hill walking, mountain biking & waters ports. These can be combined to create a range of team building and personal development courses.

DETAILS

- **Open** - All year, all day.
- **Number of beds** - 52
- **Booking** - Group bookings for minimum 15 people
- **Price per night** - From £17 per person per night
- **Public Transport** - Buses and trains via Hope Valley
- **Directions** - A623 (Chesterfield to Chapel en le frith), follow to Tideswell junction. Turn for Bradwell, take first right for Great Hucklow. On approaching the village, turn right at Queen Anne pub, then first right after 100m.

CONTACT: Libby King
Tel: 01298 873029
info@foundrymountain.co.uk   www.greatadventures.co.uk
The Old Playhouse, Great Hucklow, Derbyshire, SK17 8RF

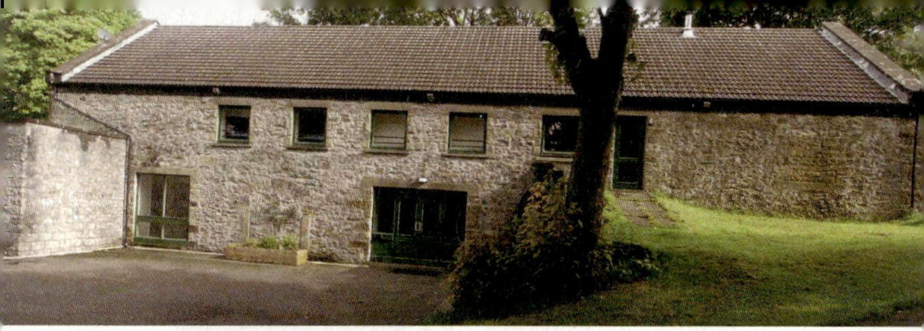
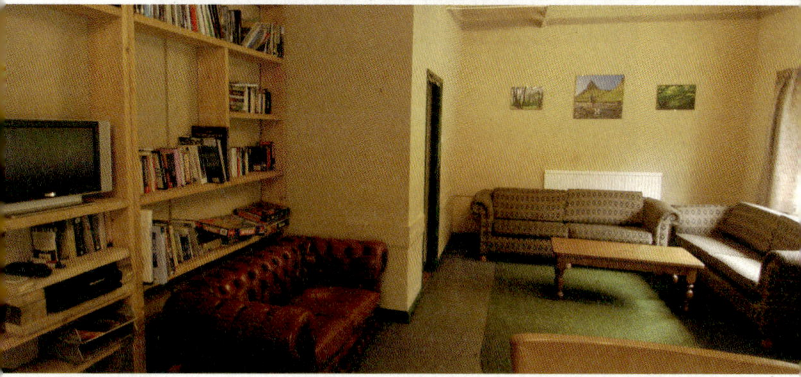
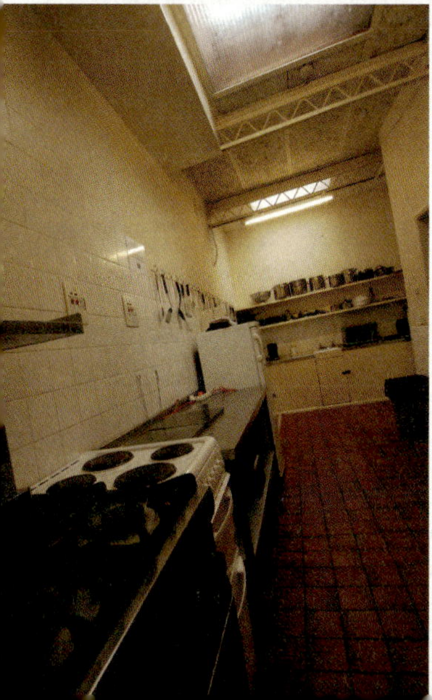
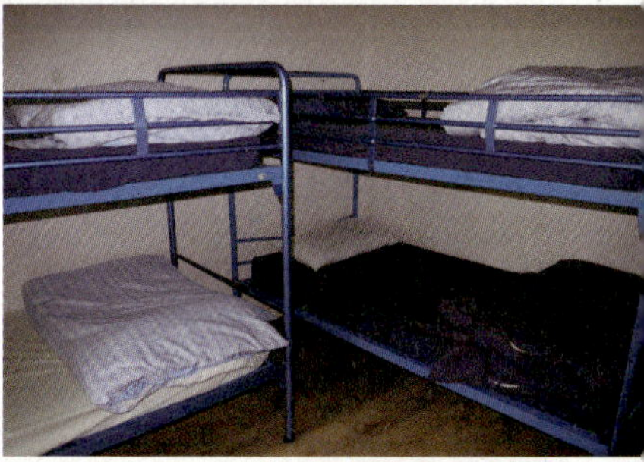
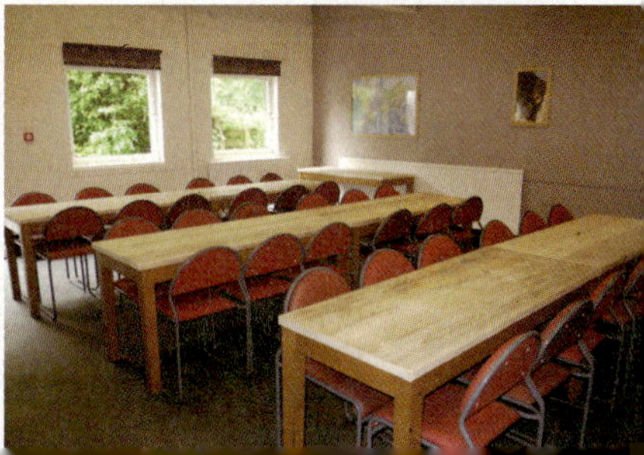

THE STABLES BUNKHOUSE

ENGLAND

The Stables Bunkhouse is a centrally heated barn on a working farm near the start of the Pennine Way, with easy access to Kinder Scout. The village of Edale is half a mile away, with a village store, two pubs serving food, a railway station and the Moorlands Information Centre. This is ideal walking country. It is a pleasant walk with stunning views over the Mam Tor ridge to Castleton, a pretty tourist village famous for its Christmas lights, with show caves and gift shops. Other places of interest include Buxton, Bakewell and Chatsworth House which are all within 40 minutes' drive. The bunkhouse sleeps 16 in 4 rooms, each with bunks sleeping four people. The bunks have a bottom sheet and pillow case, bring your own sleeping bag. There is a fully equipped kitchen, dining area, 3 newly refurbished showers, 2 toilets and drying facilities. Book sole use of the bunkhouse or book by the bed and share the barn with others. Weekends are reserved for groups until close to the visiting date, phone if you are unsure that your group is large enough. Plenty of car parking and dry secure cycle storage.

DETAILS

- **Open** - All year, all day. Arrive after 4pm depart before 10.30am.
- **Number of beds** - 16: 4x4
- **Booking** - Booking required with deposit, remainder to be paid 4 weeks in advance of stay. Weekends reserved for groups until 3 weeks prior to stay.
- **Price per night** - Sole use Monday to Thursday £180 per night, weekends (Friday to Sunday) £200 per night. See website or enquire for prices per bed or per room.
- **Public Transport** - Less than half a mile from Edale Train Station.
- **Directions** - Follow signs for Ollerbrook Booth from Edale or footpath from station.

CONTACT: Sheila
Tel: 01433 651471 or 01433 670235 Mob: 07971 865944
snakepassewe@gmail.com   www.edalecottagesandbunkhouse.co.uk
Ollerbrook Farm, Ollerbrook Booth, Edale, Hope Valley, Derbyshire, S33 7ZG

THE STABLES BUNKHOUSE

BUSHEY HEATH FARM

ENGLAND

Bushey Heath Farm is a family-run smallholding in the heart of the Peak District, central to all the popular visitor centres, but just off the beaten track. Offering a pre-booking group summer camp-site and bunkbarns for up to 28 people in three self contained units. The farm has been developed in an environmentally sensitive way with ground source heating, a wind turbine for electricity and rainwater harvesting for wc flushing, so visitors can experience practical sustainable ideas. The Hen House bunk barn has two bedrooms with bunks for 4 in each. The Little Barn has a large single bedroom with bunks for 6 people. Hadfield Barn sleeps 14 in two rooms of 6 and 8. All have luxury shower rooms and a combined fully equipped kitchen/diner open area. Sleeping bags/duvets required. Well behaved dogs accepted.

DETAILS

- **Open** - All year. Group only Camp-site May - October. Opening hours by arrangement
- **Number of beds** - 8: Hen House, 6: Little Barn, 14: Hadfield Barn.
- **Booking** - Camping always. Bunkhouse: early with deposit advisable.
- **Price per night** - Camping: £7. Bunkbarns: for sole use, Hen House: £160. Little Barn: £120. Hadfield Barn: £280. All per night.
- **Public Transport** - Nearest trains at Hope (4 miles). Nearest buses in Tideswell (2 miles). Bus numbers 65, 66, x67, 173, 177, 197, 202.
- **Directions** - GR SK 146 785. From Tideswell take Manchester Road past Star Pub and cross over A623, road stops at farm. Going west along A623, 1.5 miles past the Anchor Pub turn right at crossroads in 's' bends.

CONTACT: Rod or Lisa Baraona
Tel: 01298 873007 9am-8pm only
busheyheathfarm@gmail.com www.busheyheathfarm.com
Tideswell Moor, Tideswell, Buxton, Derbyshire, SK17 8JE

UNDERBANK
CAMPING BARN
ENGLAND

Located on Blaze Farm, a dairy farm, café, ice cream parlour and nature trail on the western edge of the Peak District National Park. Overlooking the Wildboarclough Valley and close to the well known viewpoint of Shuttlingsloe. The barn provides the perfect simple base for walking in this stunning landscape.

The sleeping area is on the first floor, with the living area, kitchen area with fridge, toilet and shower below. Bring your own sleeping bag, camping mattress and cooking equipment if you wish to self-cater. Blaze Farm has an ice-cream parlour and tea room for snacks or you can pre-order breakfast to set you up for the day.

DETAILS
- **Open** - All Year, arrive at 4pm leave at 10am (earlier arrivals by arrangement)
- **Number of beds** - 10
- **Booking** - Book via the YHA on 0800 0191 700 contact barn direct before arrival
- **Price per night** - From £8.50. Sole use of 10 bed barn: £85 per night. Electricity is metered, so please bring change.
- **Public Transport** - Train at Macclesfield (7 miles)
- **Directions** - 10 miles from Congleton and 7 miles from Buxton and Macclesfield. Travelling on the A54 from Congleton, Blaze Farm is the second farm access on the left hand side after the Rose and Crown pub. When travelling from Buxton, Blaze Farm is the second farm access on the right hand side after the turning for Wildboarclough.

CONTACT: Caroline & Marshall Waller
Tel: 01260 227 266
thesheeponthehill@gmail.com
Blaze Farm, Wildboarclough, Macclesfied, Cheshire, SK11 0BL

WANDERING DUCK
ENGLAND

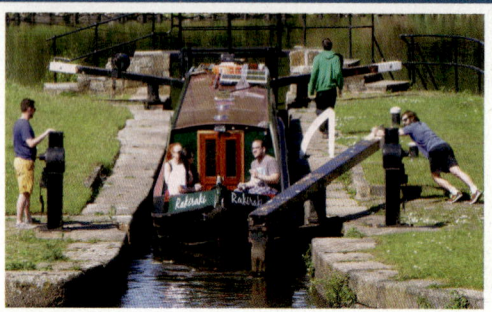

Wandering Duck is a unique hosted canal boat experience of 2 or 3 nights on board a 69ft narrowboat. It's like a floating backpacker's hostel. Trips take place around Manchester, Cheshire and Derbyshire. Come on your own and join a tour, or charter Wandering Duck for your own small group (max 10 people).

These experiences are very hands on and you'll be shown how to work the locks and encouraged to have a go at steering the 69ft boat. Choose between the 3 Night Canal Boat Adventure (Manchester to the Peak District) or the 2 Night Canal Boat Escape (Marple, Manchester to Congleton, Cheshire). Most meals are included in the price of the trip, as are hot drinks and home-made cake. On board you will find an on-board honesty bar, games, and an ipod dock. As well as many walking options, fishing gear is available free of charge or you can go for a paddle in the 3-man canoe (£6pp unlimited use).

DETAILS

- **Open** - March to October, 24 hrs
- **Number of beds** - 8: 2x4
- **Booking** - Website or phone
- **Price per night** - 2 night tour £145: 3 night tour £195: Charter the boat from £840 Tours include: accommodation on the boat, fully hosted experience, meals & cake.
- **Public Transport** - All trips are one-way and start and finish within walking distance of train stations.
- **Directions** - See website for details. Detailed directions sent with your booking confirmation.

CONTACT: Ruth
Tel: 07584 122614
duckmail@wanderingduck.co.uk www.wanderingduck.co.uk
Blackbrook House, Bugsworth Basin, Brookside, High Peak, SK23 7NE

HATTERS
ON HILTON STREET

ENGLAND

Hatters on Hilton Street brings new meaning to 'flash packing'! Your ideal choice for city centre accommodation in the heart of the bohemian Northern Quarter, with a combination of hotel quality en suite rooms with the social atmosphere of an international travellers' hostel. Catering for groups of all sizes and independent travellers, you can enjoy the benefits of WiFi, breakfast, en suite and standard rooms, large communal and outdoor areas, and enthusiastic, informative staff. Full board or half board options for groups of over 15. Convenient for all city centre attractions and transport links. Ask about discounts to Alton Towers, and about Man Utd and City football stadium tours. Lest we forget all that is FREE to do in Manchester...We are more than happy to help. Also a great base for day trips to the Peak District.

Come and enjoy our hospitality and explore all that Manchester has to offer!

DETAILS

- **Open** - All year, 24 hour reception. Check in 2pm, check out 11am
- **Number of beds** - 155; single, twin, double, triple, 4, 6, 8, and 12 bed rooms
- **Booking** - Booking not essential but recommended especially at weekends, with credit/debit card. Photo ID (eg. passport, driving license) required on check in. For group bookings please contact groups@hattersgroup.com
- **Price per night** - From £15.50 dorms, from £35 private rooms. All rooms include en suite, linen and breakfast. For group prices email groups@hattersgroup.com.
- **Public Transport** - Only 5 minutes' walk from Picadilly train and bus stations and Shudehill bus station, and 10 minutes' walk from Victoria train station.
- **Directions** - Please contact the hostel reception for details.

CONTACT: Reception
Tel: 0161 236 4414, Fax: 0161 236 5740
hilton@hattersgroup.com www.hattersgroup.com/#mcr
15 Hilton Street, Manchester, M1 1JJ

THE OLD SMITHY CAMPING BARN

The Old Smithy camping barn was at one time the village fire station. This "stone-tent" is situated in the village of Burwardsley, Cheshire, mid-way along the Sandstone Trail, one of the finest long distance walks in North West England. The barn is also on NCN route 45 Mercian Way.

The Old Smithy offers affordable country accommodation for up to 8 people. Ideal for families or groups of walkers, cyclists and others visiting this part of Cheshire or wanting to get closer to nature. There is an area for cooking & washing up, a toilet and an insulated sleeping platform. There is no electricity or hot water, nor beds, bring your own sleeping bag and roll mat. Lighting is via lanterns (candles and matches provided). You can pre-book or buy food and hot drinks at Burwardsley Post Office & Village Shop (5 min walk). The nearest pub is The Pheasant Inn. Also close by is the Candle workshop, Cheshire Fishery and the Ice Cream Farm. Bikes can be locked away overnight. Dogs welcome.

DETAILS

- **Open** - All year, 24 hours. Pre-arrange arrival times.
- **Number of beds** - 8: 1 x 8
- **Booking** - by phone or email. All bookings must be paid in full to be guaranteed.
- **Price per night** - £8 per person per night. Exclusive use £50 per night.
- **Public Transport** - The nearest train station is Chester (10 miles) with an hourly bus service to Tattenhall (2 miles).
- **Directions** - The Barn is on Burwardsley Road, close to the Post Office. Grid reference: 513 569 OS Landranger No.117

CONTACT: Rachel and Phillip
Tel: 01829 770359
rachel_hoarau@yahoo.co.uk
Burwardsley Post Office & Village Store, Harthill Road, Burwardsley, Cheshire CH3 9NU

HATTERS
ON NEWTON STREET
ENGLAND

Recently refurbished to its 100 year old splendour and winner of the Manchester Tourism Customer Care award; The Hatters has firmly established itself as the city's favourite funky hostel. Hatters' city centre location makes it the ideal spot to start exploring the north west of England.

Hatters caters for independent travellers and groups. It has a fully serviced kitchen with seating for groups of up to 50 and free all-day continental breakfast. Enjoy the FREE all-day coffee while using the FREE WiFi, or choose to socialise with other like-minded travellers and staff. We also offer full board or half board options for groups over 15 people. Let the knowledgeable and friendly staff guide you to the best that this great city has to offer, from live music and football to restaurants, shopping, museums, pubs and clubs.

DETAILS

- **Open** - All year, 24 hour reception. Check in 2pm, check out 11am
- **Number of beds** - 170. Private double/ single rooms. Dorm sizes include 18 bed, 10 bed, 6 bed and 4 bed.
- **Booking** - Booking recommended, with credit/debit card, especially at weekends. Photo ID is required at check in. Group bookings contact groups@hattersgroup.com.
- **Price per night** - From £12 for dorms and from £32 for private rooms. Overnight price includes linen and breakfast. Email for group prices.
- **Public Transport** - Easy walking distance from all public transport hubs: Picadilly Train Station 5mins, Picadilly Bus Station 5mins, Shudehill Bus Station 5mins, Victoria Train Station 10mins
- **Directions** - Please contact the hostel reception for directions.

CONTACT:
Tel: 0161 236 9500, Fax: 0161 236 5740
Manchester@hattersgroup.com www.hattersgroup.com
50 Newton Street, Manchester, M1 2EA

EMBASSIE
ENGLAND LIVERPOOL BACKPACKERS

The Embassie is a terraced house in an unspoilt Georgian square used in the filming of 'In the Name of the Father'. The house was built in 1820 and until 1986 it was the Consulate of Venezuela. Only 15 minutes' walk from the centre of Liverpool, known for its nightlife. A large student population ensures a lively scene, with late night bands and bars. The hostel has been refurbished and there are new kitchen facilities, a brand new shower suite and an all new games room and relax area with Sky Sports and HD television. Hostellers have a key to come and go, the hostel is clean, safe and staffed 24 hours. Bedding is provided (including sheets) and free coffee, tea, toast and jam are available 24 hours, eat as much as you want. International, or UK regional travellers only. Free Beatles guided tour every Thursday night at 8pm including free admission to the world famous Cavern Club (and free piece of Beatle memorabilia). The only tour given by a tour guide who saw the Beatles perform.

DETAILS

- **Open** - All year, 24 hr access.
- **Number of beds** - 50
- **Booking** - not essential for individuals. Groups over 6 should book (25% deposit).
- **Price per night** - £16 (Sunday to Thursday), £21 (Friday and Saturday).
- **Public Transport** - Liverpool has a train station and is served by National Express Coaches. A £3.50 taxi fare will bring you from the train or bus station to the hostel door, (good idea if you have a heavy rucksack).
- **Directions** - From the Anglican Cathedral (the third largest in the world) continue uphill along Canning Street away from the city centre. This will bring you into Falkner Square (15-20 mins). The hostel has a red door and is by a phone box.

CONTACT: Kevin
Tel: 0151 7071089
embassie@gmail.com   www.embassie.com
1 Falkner Square, Liverpool, L8 7NU

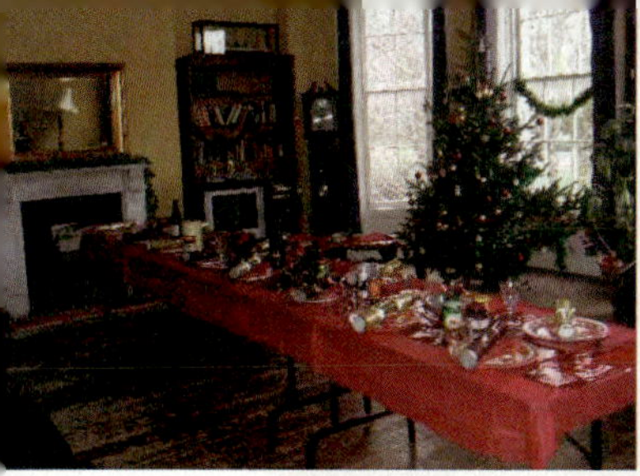
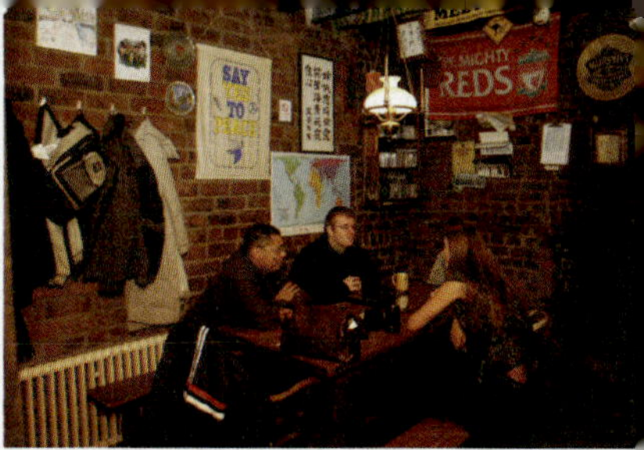
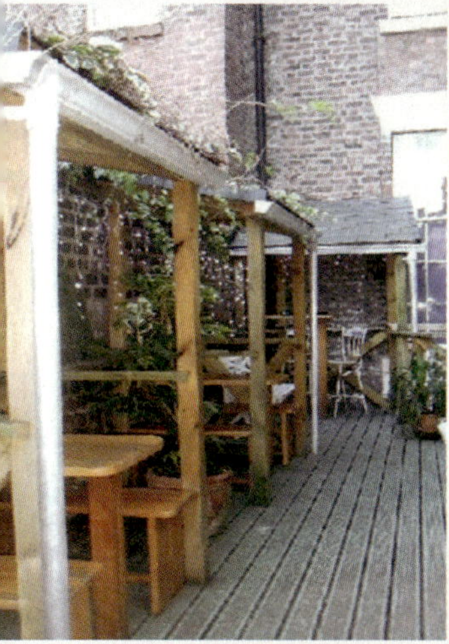
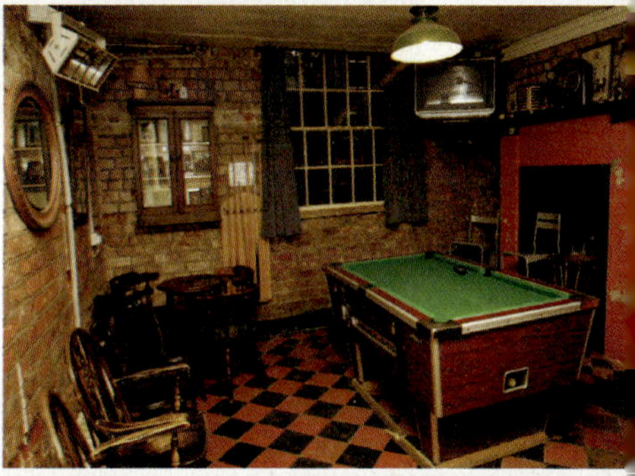
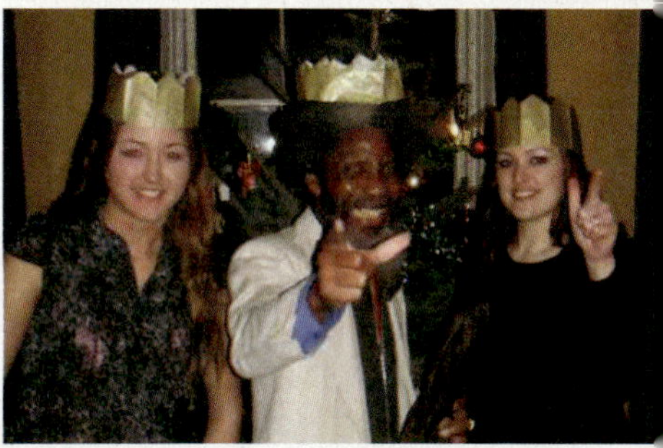
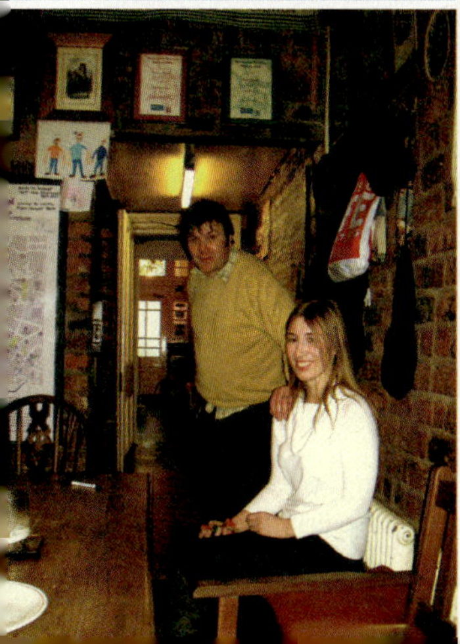
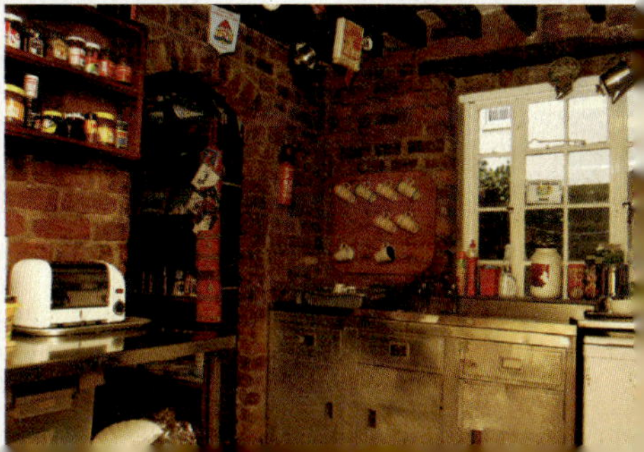

HATTERS LIVERPOOL

ENGLAND

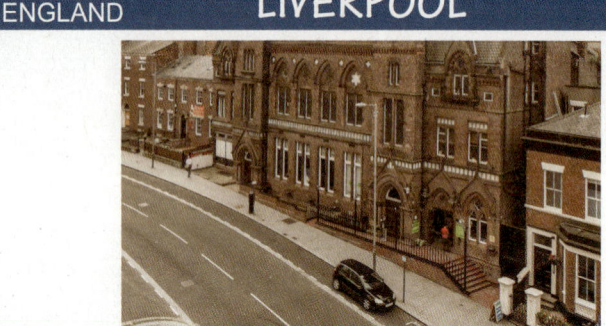

Your ideal choice for city central accommodation, Hatters Liverpool has combined hotel quality en suite rooms with the social atmosphere of an international travellers' hostel. Catering for groups of all sizes and independent travellers, you can enjoy the comforts of WiFi, continental breakfast, en suite rooms, large communal areas and enthusiastic, informative staff. We also offer full board or half board options for groups of over 15. Conveniently located for all city centre attractions and transport links, ask the reception staff about discounts to Alton Towers, Beatles tours, football stadium tours, Albert Docks, or many other FREE adventures....The perfect base for day trips to the historic city of Chester, Chester Zoo, or the majestic Lake District. Come and stay and enjoy what is making Liverpool one of the UK's top tourist destinations!.

Three star graded by Quality in Tourism.

DETAILS

- **Open** - All year, 24 hour reception. Check in after 2pm, check out 11am.
- **Number of beds** - 300 beds; single, double, twin, triple, 4, 6, 8 and 12 bed rooms.
- **Booking** - Booking not essential but recommended, especially at weekends. We require photo I.D (passport/drivers' licence) and credit/ debit card. For all group bookings please contact groups@hattersgroup.com
- **Price per night** - From £15.00 for dorms and from £39.00 for privates. Prices include en suite, linen and breakfast. Please email for group rates.
- **Public Transport** - Within walking distance of all public transport hubs. Liverpool Lime Street Station – 5mins, Northern Street Coach Station – 15mins
- **Directions** - Please contact the hostel reception for directions

CONTACT: Reception
Tel: 0151 709 5570, Fax: 0151 703 9283
liverpool@hattersgroup.com www.hattersgroup.com/#lpool
56-60 Mount Pleasant, Liverpool, L3 5SH

HEBDEN BRIDGE
HOSTEL

175

ENGLAND

Hebden Bridge Hostel (aka Mama Weirdigan's) is located in a former concert hall adjacent to a Grade II listed Baptist Chapel. The hostel provides accommodation in small dorms, private rooms and a 6-bed bunkroom, all en suite. Nestled into woodland only a short walk from the town centre, the hostel makes a good base for hiking, sight-seeing, shopping or experiencing Hebden Bridge's vibrant music and arts scene. Close to the Pennine Way, Calderdale Way, Hardcastle Crags, canal, river and popular cycle routes. 10am-5pm access is to the lobby only. No evening curfew but please respect other guests. Bed linen provided in dorms and private rooms. Bring sleeping bag and pillow for the bunkroom. Free internet, WiFi. Self-catering, vegetarian-only kitchen. Light breakfast & tea/coffee included.

DETAILS

- **Open** - Easter to November. Whole-hostel bookings possible in closed season. Check-in 5-8pm, check-out 10am.
- **Number of beds** - 33 : 6x4 (or 2), 1x3 (or 2), 1x6
- **Booking** - recommended but not essential (full payment on booking).
- **Price per night** - Bunk-room £14pp. Small dorm £20pp. Twin £55. Double £60. Private 4-bed room £75. Sole use available..
- **Public Transport** - 15 minutes' walk from Hebden Bridge train station (frequent, quick service to Leeds and Manchester). Buses from the station stop outside the Birchcliffe Centre (Dodd Naze Circular). Coach stations in Bradford and Leeds.
- **Directions** - From station follow road to T-junction, turn left (Burnley Rd), take next right (Keighley), right again (Birchcliffe Rd). Hostel is behind Birchcliffe Centre.

CONTACT: Em or Dave
Tel: 01422 843183
mama@hebdenbridgehostel.co.uk   www.hebdenbridgehostel.co.uk
The Birchcliffe Centre, Hebden Bridge, W Yorks, HX7 8DG

SCARBOROUGH YOUTH HOSTEL

Once a 17th century water mill, set on a quiet riverside, 1½ miles north of the town centre and 15 minutes' walk from Scalby Mills and the North Bay beach. A well equipped kitchen is available or guests can enjoy home cooked breakfast and evening meals in the dining room. Tasty packed lunches are also available. Scarborough Hostel provides quality low-cost accommodation for families, schools, groups and individuals who wish to enjoy, explore, or simply unwind on the beautiful North Yorkshire coast. With two long sandy beaches, miles of rugged coastline, and some of the largest areas of forest and moorland in the UK, Scarborough is a perfect base for activity breaks with excellent walking, cycling, surfing and sailing. There is plenty for those interested in birds, wildlife, history, geology and the seashore. The town regularly hosts quality live concerts and festivals, TT racing, surf competitions and theatre productions.

DETAILS

- **Open** - Open all year, 7.30 - 10.00 am and after 5pm
- **Number of beds** - 46: 5x6, 4x4.
- **Booking** - Please call directly on 01723 361176 or visit the YHA website and search for Scarborough
- **Price per night** - Beds from £13, rooms from £40, discounts for YHA members
- **Public Transport** - Bus or train to Scarborough, No 3 or 3A bus from York place to Sea Life Centre alight at Ivanhoe. Hostel is a 5 minute walk from Ivanhoe
- **Directions** - On A165 two miles north of town centre sharp left after the brick bridge (or make U-turn after the hostel and turn from the left). By foot: leave the Cleveland Way at the Helmsley sign, walk to Burniston road turn left down the hill to the hostel drive.

CONTACT: Robert Fletcher
Tel: 01723 361176
scarboroughhostel@gmail.com www.scarboroughhostel.com
The White House, Burniston Road, Scarborough, YO13 0DA

SAFESTAY
YORK

ENGLAND

Safestay York is a 4 star, city centre hostel situated on Micklegate, one of the oldest parts of York. This grand Grade 1 Georgian building was built in 1752 as a 'Town House' for the very wealthy John Bourchier of Benningbrough Hall. The hostel has many impressive features including a stone flagged entrance hall leading to a carved sweeping staircase. With its panelled rooms, vaulted cellar and fabulous Rococo ceiling depicting Shakespeare's head, the hostel holds a wealth of history and architecture. Entry to the rooms is by electronic key and secure lockers are provided. Guests travelling with laptops can take advantage of free WiFi in the spacious communal areas; these comprise a 24h reception, breakfast room, bar on the ground floor and games/computer room. There is also a free luggage store. Downstairs, there is a heated terrace and a well-equipped laundry room. The rooms & dormitories are all en suite (except one 4 bed dorm) and some have exquisite views. Safestay York offers a great stay with 24 hour access and staff to welcome you at any time of day.

DETAILS

- **Open** - All year, 24 hours
- **Number of beds** - 147: 1x12, 4x10, 6x8, 4x6, 3x4, 3x2,1x family(3),1x double.
- **Booking** - Credit card guarantees bed. Groups please enquire.
- **Price per night** - From £16pp. 10% plus discount for groups 10 or more
- **Public Transport** - 5 min walk from York rail and bus stations, close to Megabus.
- **Directions** - Car: Take A1036 into York. Continue past racecourse into Micklegate. We're 100m along on the left opposite the church. By rail or bus: turn right out of station for 300m. Take the first left through the medieval gate into Micklegate.

CONTACT: Reception
Tel: 01904 627720, Fax: 01904 361350
receptionyork@safestay.co.uk www.safestayyork.co.uk
Micklegate House, 88-90 Micklegate, York, YO1 6JX

YORK RACECOURSE CENTRE

ENGLAND

York Racecourse Centre is just a few minutes' drive from the centre of York, in one of the quietest parts of the city, overlooking the historical Knavesmire. The modern buildings provide quality budget accommodation for student & adult groups. The centre has 4 star hostel rating by the English Tourism Council. Free WiFi to all areas. The two-storey building contains 21 triple bed rooms with en suite toilets, that can be converted into four bed rooms by unfolding a bunk bed from the wall. The single storey annexe contains single, triple and 2 family rooms, each with wash basin. This building has separate toilet and shower facilities. There's a spacious dining room with cafeteria style seating up to 100 and a large lounge on the first floor of the main building suitable for conferences etc. A very large sports field adjoins the complex and the centre lies on the NCN Route 65 which gives traffic free access into the centre of town. B&B (full English breakfast), D,B&B and full board packages available. There is plenty of secure, ample free parking for coaches and cars and secure bike storage.

DETAILS

- **Open** - All year (except during race meetings), all day
- **Number of beds** - 133: 2x6, 21x4, 8x triple, 1x twin, 11 x single.
- **Booking** - Booking essential, by phone or email
- **Price per night** - B&B(Full English breakfast):1 night:£39.50pp, 2+nights £35pp. Based on twin occupancy. Towels included. Enquire for school group rates
- **Public Transport** - Trains: 20 min walk. City centre buses every 10 mins.
- **Directions** - Situated on the right hand side of the A1036 Tadcaster Road as you head towards York city centre, opposite the Fox & Roman pub.

CONTACT: Stuart or Fay
Tel: 01904 620 911 ext. 284, Fax: 01904 611 301
info@yorkracecoursecentre.co.uk www.yorkracecoursecentre.co.uk
York Racecourse Centre, York Racing Stables, York, YO24 1QG

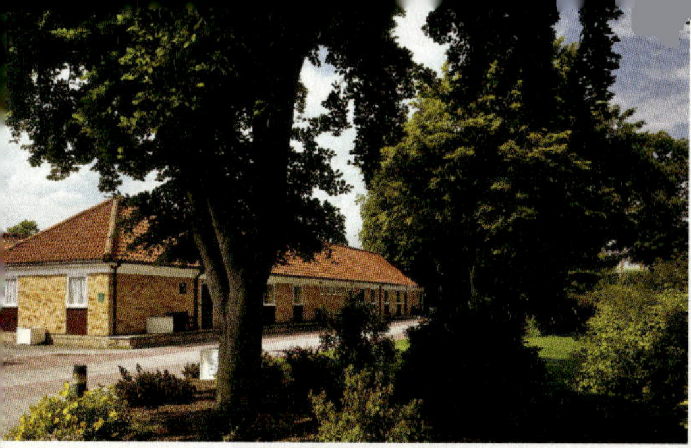
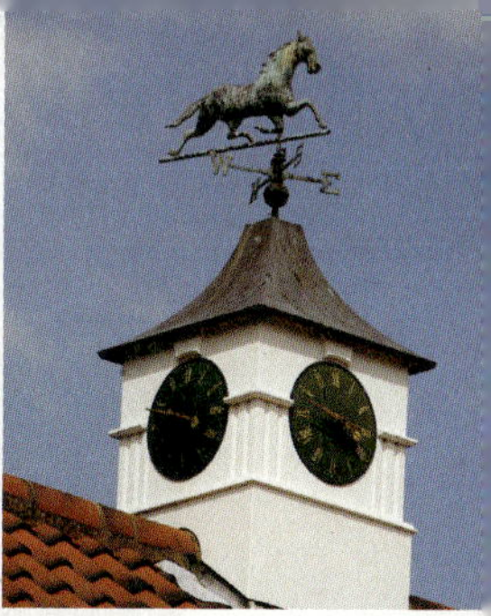
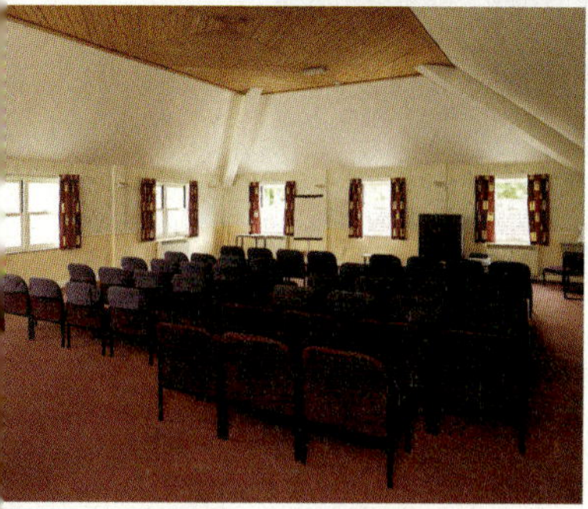
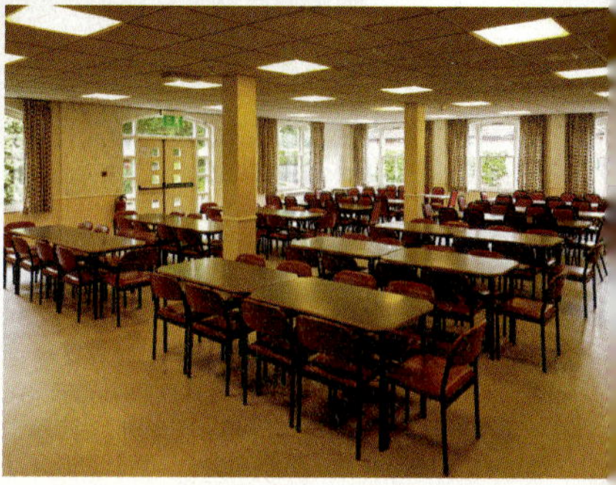
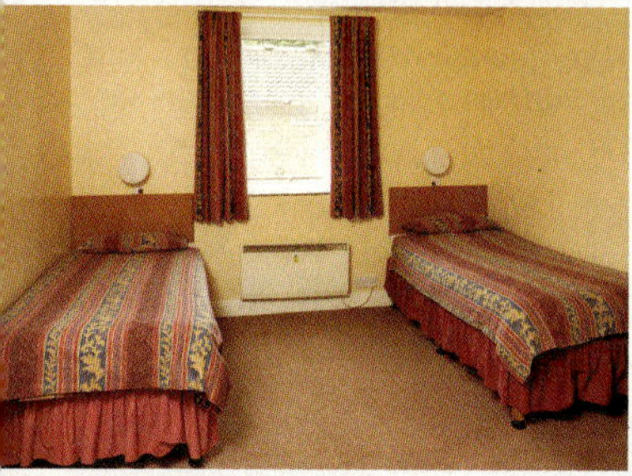
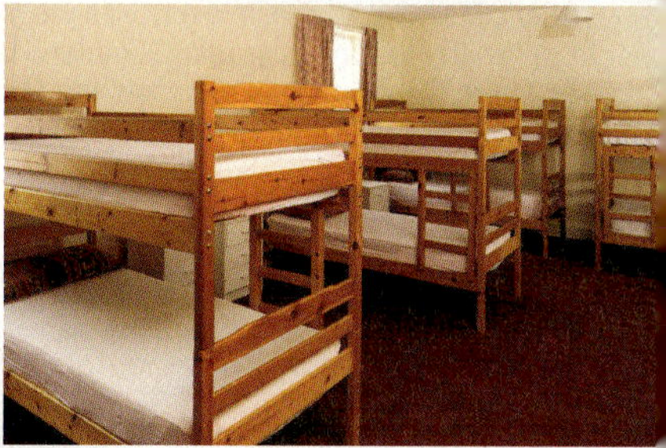
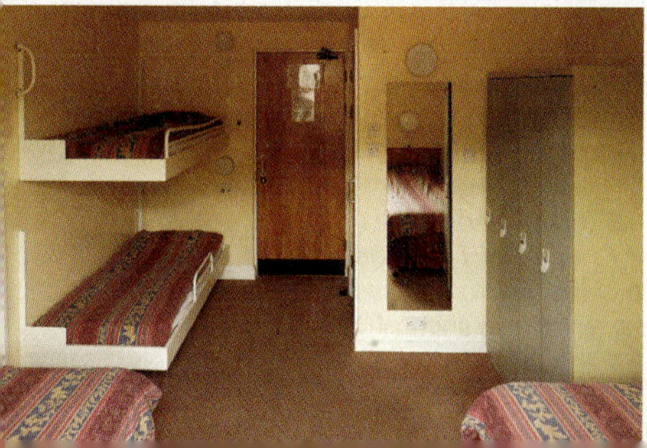
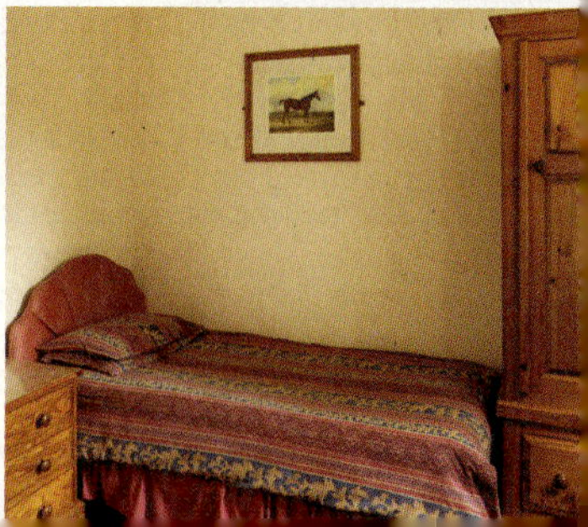

WHITBY BACKPACKERS
AT HARBOUR GRANGE

180 ENGLAND

Harbour Grange is Whitby's long established, friendly backpackers hostel. It is beautifully situated on the River Esk, in Whitby itself, and is only 5 minutes' walk from train and bus stations. The hostel is all on the ground floor and has good facilities for self-catering with a dining area and a separate lounge area, both big enough to seat 24 people. There are 5 dormitories and family rooms are available on request. The hostel is open all day but, so that everyone can have a chance of a good night's sleep, there is a curfew at 11.30 (quiet at midnight). The premises are non-smoking. Whitby is a beautiful little fishing town surrounded by beaches and moorland. Here you can find stunning views from cliff walks and visit lovely villages like Grosmont where steam trains run from Whitby to Pickering and Goathland where Heartbeat is filmed. Take a look at where Captain Cook lived and the Abbey that has stood as a landmark for 800 years.

DETAILS

- **Open** - 1st April - 31st Oct. Open all year for groups booked in advance, Hostel open in the day. Check in 5pm-9pm
- **Number of beds** - 24: 1x2, 2x4, 1x6, 1x8.
- **Booking** - Booking advised. Groups: 10% deposit, with the remaining to be paid 14 days before arrival. Payment in full for individuals when booked.
- **Price per night** - From £18 per person. Sole use £290 a night.
- **Public Transport** - Whitby has a train station and a bus station.
- **Directions** - From Whitby train and bus stations: cross the bridge and turn right. Follow the river. First right after the junction Church Street and Green Lane.

CONTACT: Birgitta Ward-Foxton
Tel: 01947 600817, Mobile 0777 9798611
backpackers@harbourgrange.co.uk www.whitbybackpackers.co.uk
Spital Bridge, Whitby, North Yorkshire, YO22 4EF

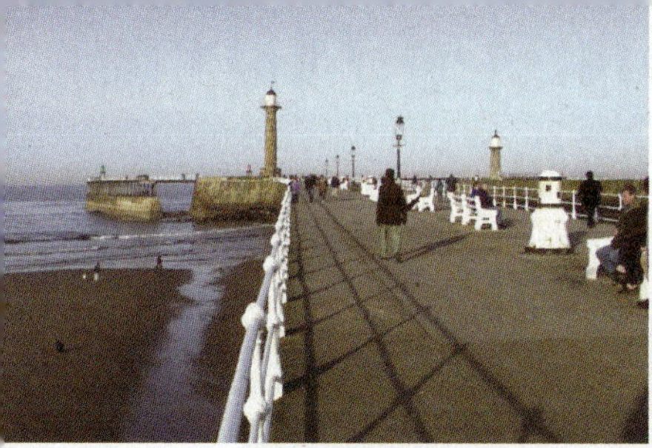
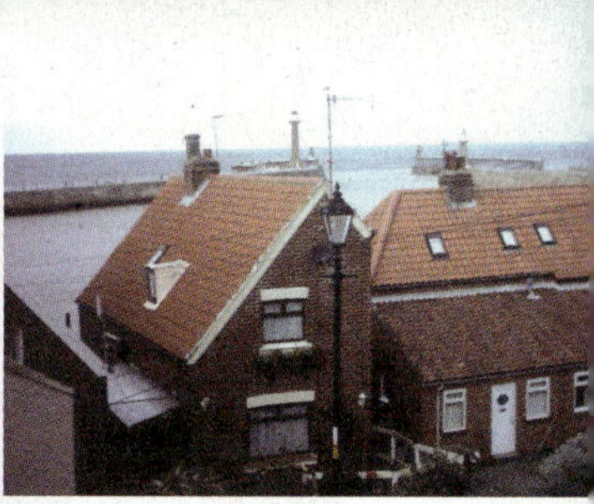
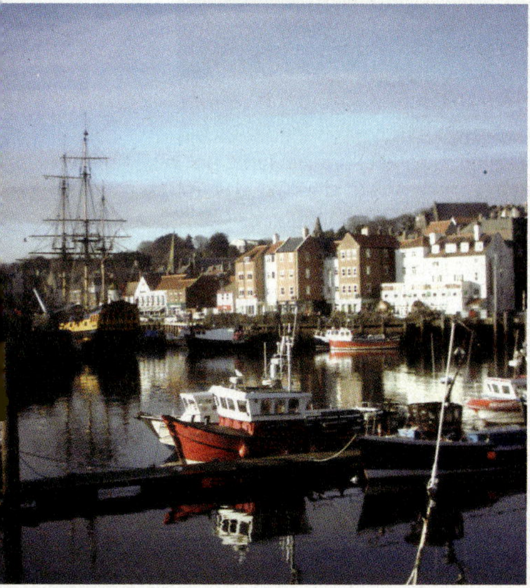
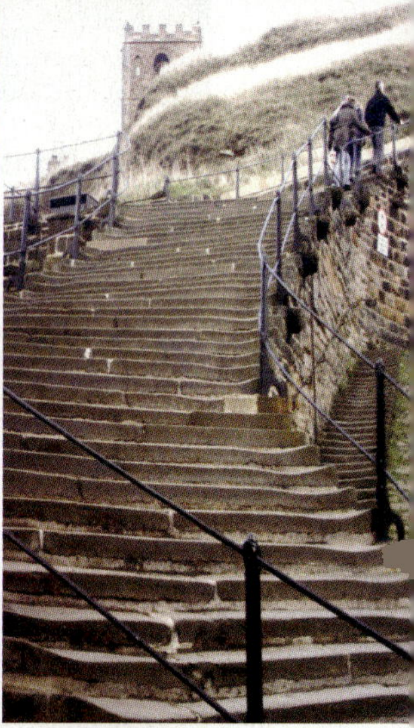
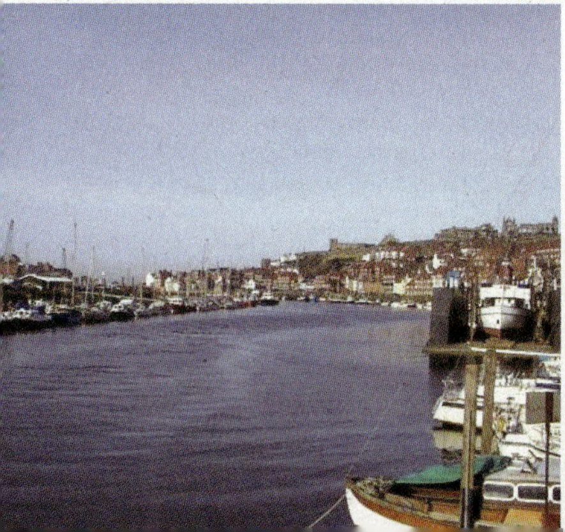
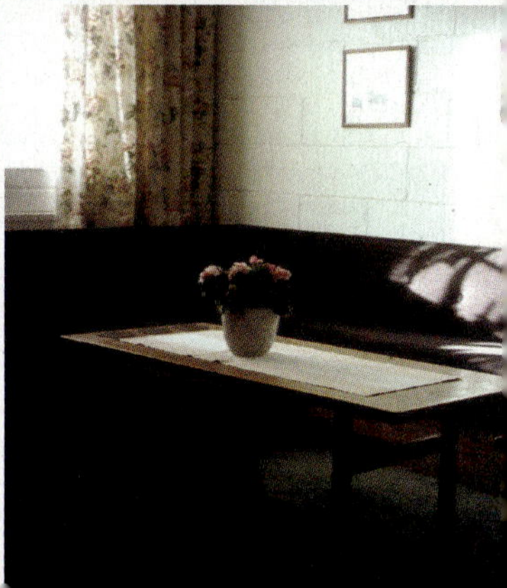

BANK HOUSE FARM HOSTEL

ENGLAND

A recent barn conversion (2011) on a working organic farm, set in beautiful Glaisdale in the North York Moors. The views are stunning and accommodation modern and excellent. Under-floor heating, drying room, 2 showers, 3 private toilets and one large dorm sleeping 11. Beds have sheet, pillow & slip. Large comfy kitchen/dining/living room with sofas. Picnic/BBQ area and garden with panoramic views. Some facilities for the disabled but steps are unavoidable. Bring sleeping bag/duvet, toiletries, towel and food. The farm's own organic beef & lamb is available for sale. Public footpaths/bridleways on the doorstep, Wainwright's Coast to Coast route 1m, Whitby & Jurassic coast 12 miles, Grosmont steam trains 3m, Esk Valley walk 3m. Sole use policy.

DETAILS

- **Open** - All year, 10am – 8pm for phone calls
- **Number of beds** - 1 x 11
- **Booking** - Booking preferred. Deposit required, balance 4 weeks before arrival.
- **Price per night** - Weekdays adults £20, children 6-16 £12. Weekends £400 for up to 10 persons (+£10/child or +£20/adult per night for over 10), Bank Hols: £600 (Fr, Sa, Su). Single night supplement: £5/adult, £3/child. 3-day weekend: Fri, Sat, Sun (not Bank Hol) £500 for up to 10 people (£50pppw/e)
- **Public Transport** - Glaisdale train station 3miles..'M&D Transport' minibus from Castleton to Whitby in Glaisdale village (2.5 miles). Nat. Express coaches at Whitby.
- **Directions** - From Glaisdale station go uphill through village and turn left at T junction 'Glaisdale Dale Only'. After 1 mile turn left by Witchpost Cottage. Pass New House Farm & Sheds then turn left over cattle grid. Follow farm track 1/3 mile to farmyard. Hostel is attached to farmhouse. Call at farmhouse for keys

CONTACT: Chris or Emma Padmore
Tel: 01947 897297
info@bankhousefarmhostel.co.uk www.bankhousefarmhostel.co.uk
Bank House Farm, Glaisdale, Whitby YO21 2QA

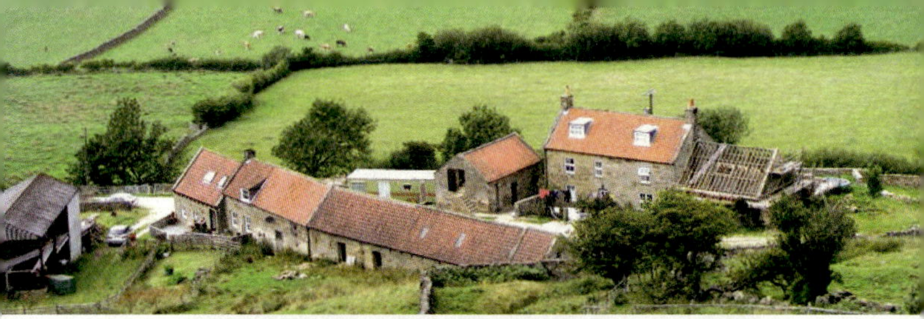
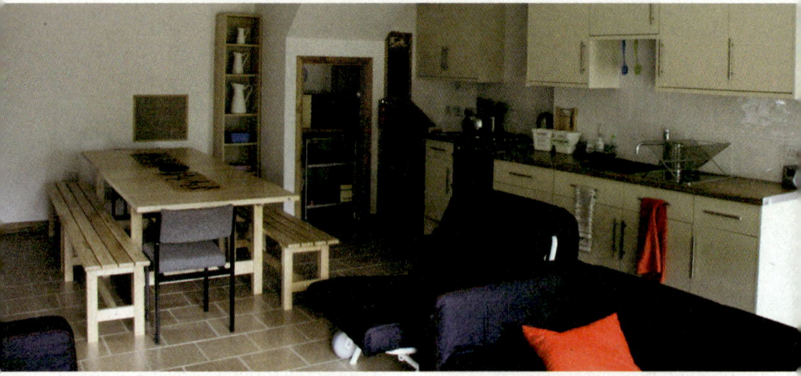
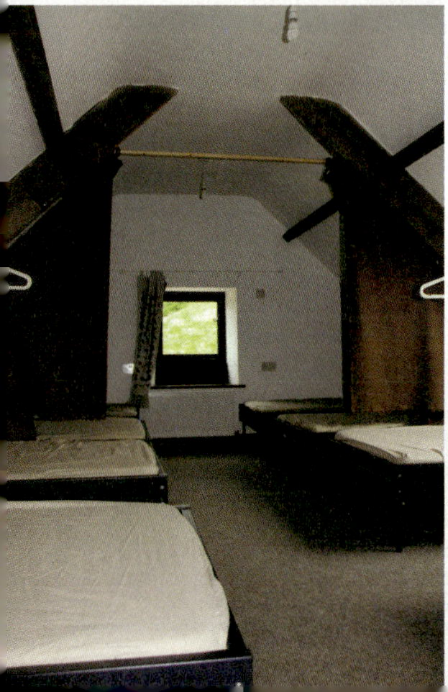
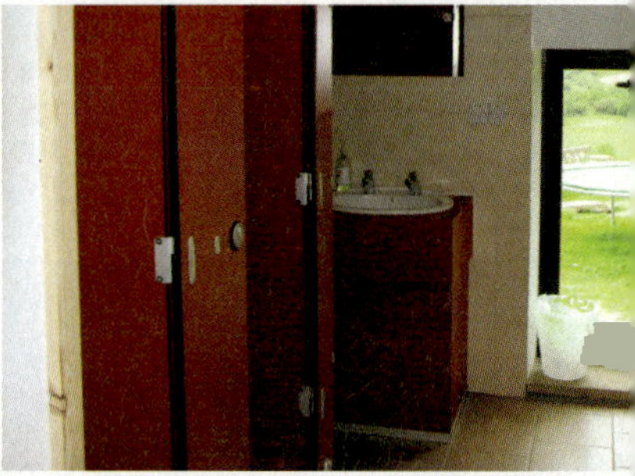
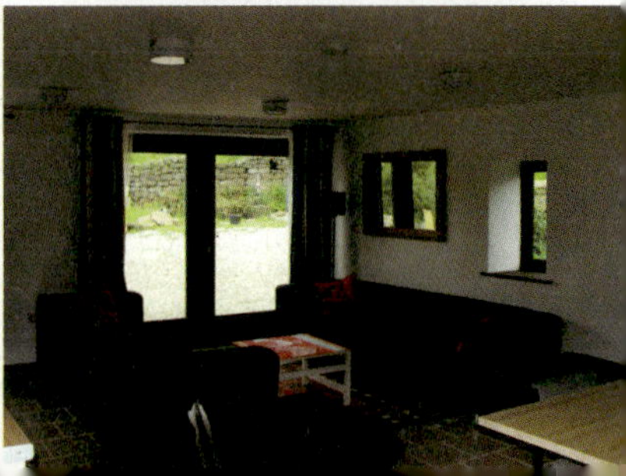

COTE GHYLL MILL

ENGLAND

NEWLY REFURBISHED BEDROOMS & SHOWER ROOMS OPENING JAN 2015. Situated in a beautiful and secluded valley in the North Yorkshire Moors National Park, this converted linen mill is a perfect location for those wishing to explore the whole of the Yorkshire Moors/Dales & Coast. Close to walking and cycling routes as well as orienteering at Cod Beck Reservoir, mountain bike routes, pony trekking, fishing & golf clubs. Osmotherley, offers pubs, a tea room and shops. The stream and woodlands in the mill grounds, provide an exciting exploring ground for children and adults. The Mill is bookable as a whole, by room (some en suite) or by bed. Great for educational groups, families, outdoor clubs and friends who wish to get together in a comfortable, great value venue. Fully catered or self-catering available using a well equipped kitchen. Other facilities include licensed bar and lounge, TV/games room, pool table, free WiFi, large garden, bike store, meeting rooms, laundry & drying room.

DETAILS

- **Open** - All Year, 7am -10am, 5pm-9pm
- **Number of beds** - 70 1x2 2x3 3x4 (2 en suite) 7x6 (all en suite)
- **Booking** - Advanced booking recommended – especially for groups
- **Price per night** - from £20.40 (per adult). Under14's from £14. Groups (over 16 people): adults £18.40 under 18s £12.50. For sole occupancy please contact the Mill
- **Public Transport** - Train to Northallerton, from the station the 80 or 89 bus (for Stokesley) stops in the centre of Osmotherley the hostel is a 10 min walk (1/4mile).
- **Directions** - From A19 or Northallerton A684 towards Osmotherley or Teeside into Osmotherley. At the T junction/village cross turn left. Cote Ghyll Mill is ¼ mile out of the village on the right, just after the Caravan and Camping Park

CONTACT: Reception
Tel: 01609 883425
mill@coteghyll.com   www.coteghyll.com
Osmotherley, Northallerton, North Yorkshire, DL6 3AH

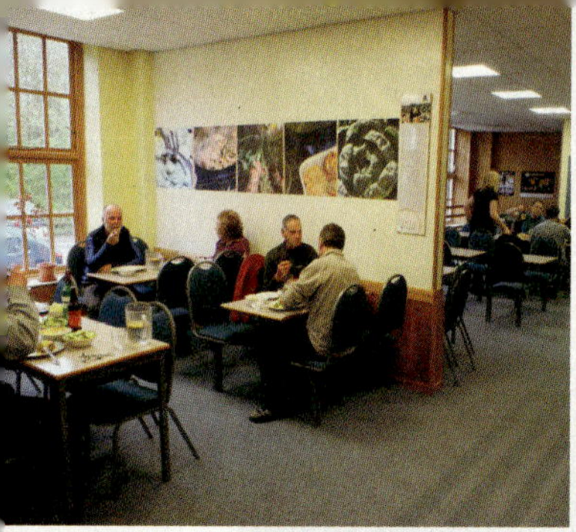
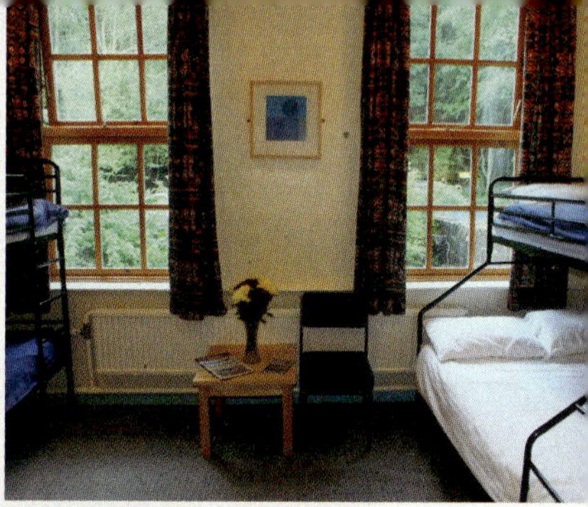
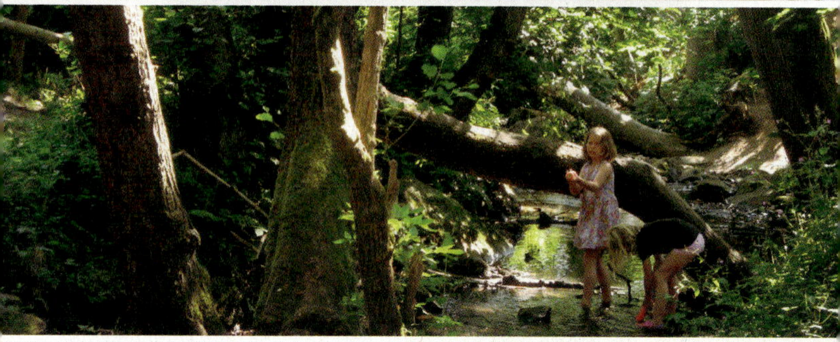
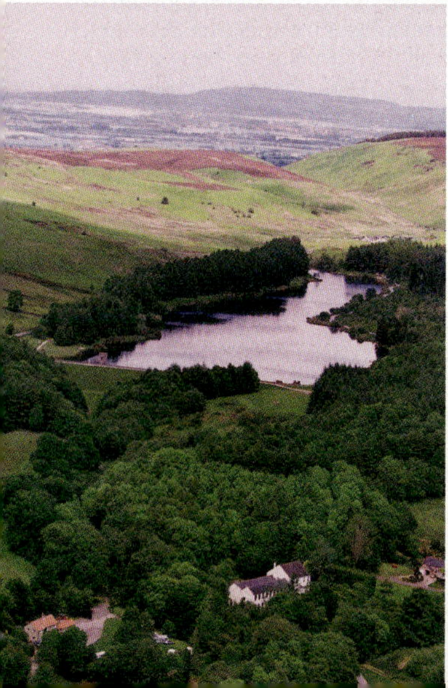
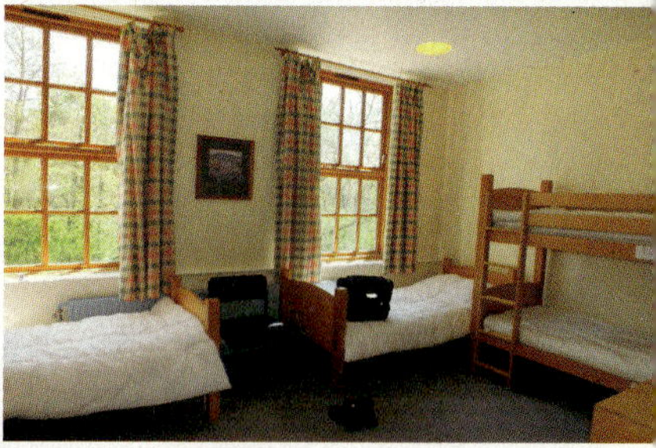
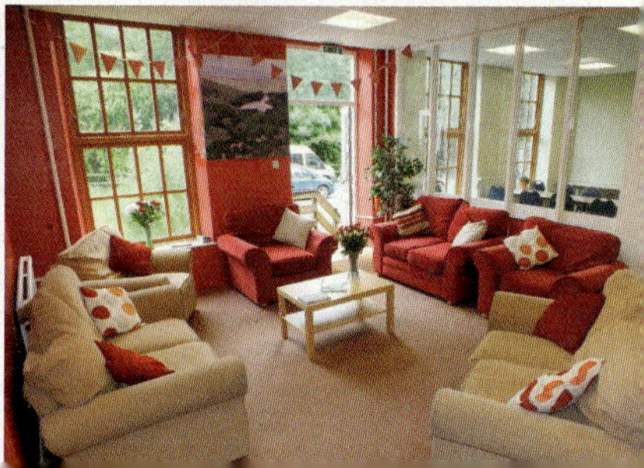

WEST END OUTDOOR CENTRE

ENGLAND

Situated in the Yorkshire Dales amidst stunning landscape overlooking Thruscross Reservoir in an AONB on the edge of the Dales National Park, this self-catering centre offers excellent facilities for up to 30 people in 9 bedrooms with bunk beds. The centre is fully centrally heated. Accommodation is in small dorms of 2 to 6 beds and the leaders' en suite accommodation has dining and lounge facilities. The main kitchen is well-equipped with a 4-oven Aga cooker, two fridges and a freezer, together with all the cooking utensils and equipment. There are 4 showers, 4 hand basins and 4 toilets. There are no extra charges for heating, lighting and hot water. Ideal for team building courses, schools, Scouts, Guides and family parties. Located only 12 miles from Harrogate and Skipton, 30 miles from the City of York. Managed by the owners for 20 years. All groups must be accompanied by an adult (25+). No stag or hen parties.

DETAILS

- **Open** - All year, flexible
- **Number of beds** - 30: 4x2, 3x4, 1x6, 1 x 4 en suite
- **Booking** - Advisable at weekends
- **Price per night** - Sole use only on Fri, Sat & bank holidays £325 per night (min stay 2 nights). Sole use Sun and midweek £210 per night (min stay 2 nights) or £300 for one night. £700 for 4 nights midweek. Sunday night, if staying for 2 other nights £150. Individuals and small groups £15pp if booking by large group is not expected.
- **Public Transport** -   Nearest train stations are at Harrogate and Skipton, both 12 miles from the hostel. Taxi fare from either station would be approximately £22.
- **Directions** - GR 146 575. Leave A59 at Blubberhouses, signed West End 2.5 miles. Do not turn off, centre is on left side.

CONTACT: Margaret and Hedley Verity
Tel: 01943 880207
m.verity@virgin.net www.westendoutdoorcentre.co.uk
West End, Summerbridge, Harrogate, HG3 4BA

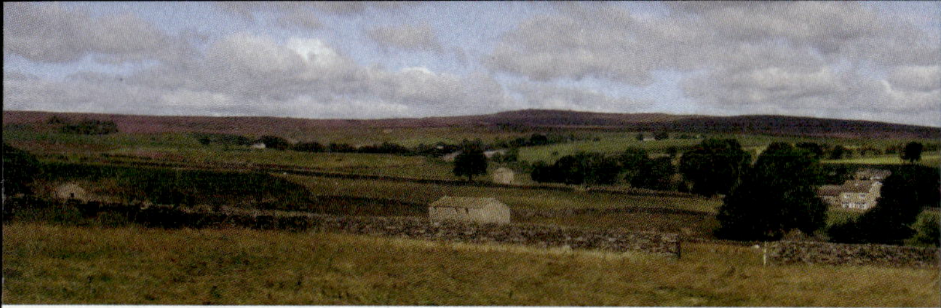
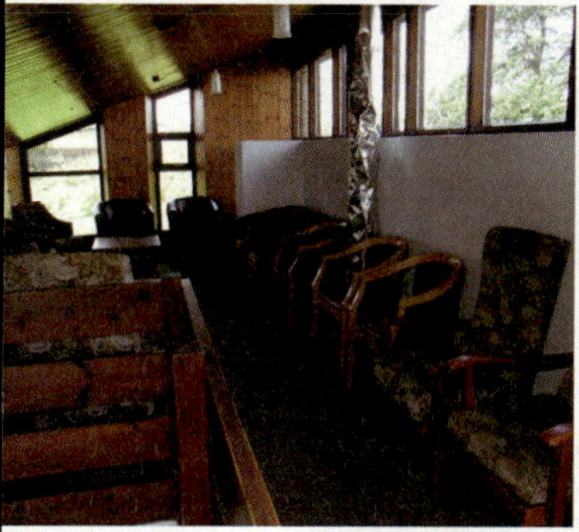
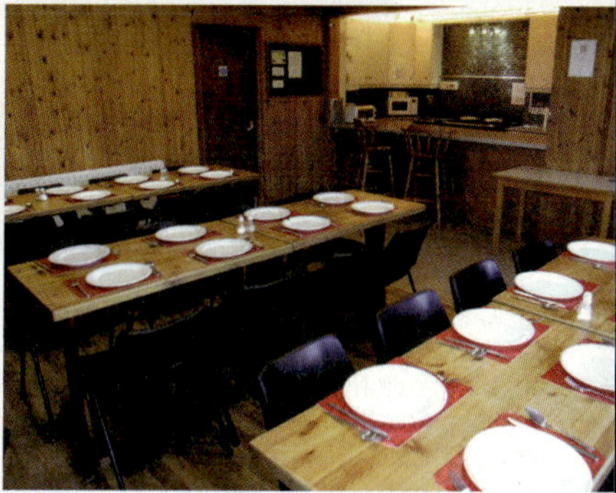
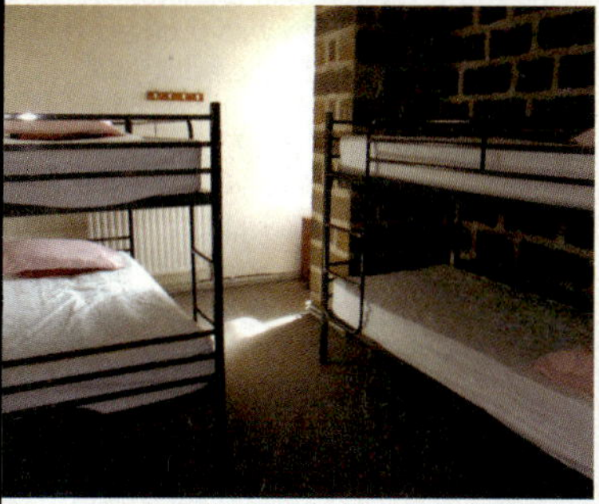
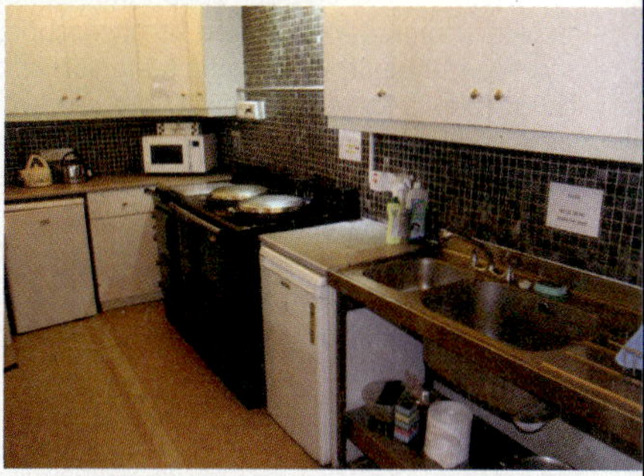
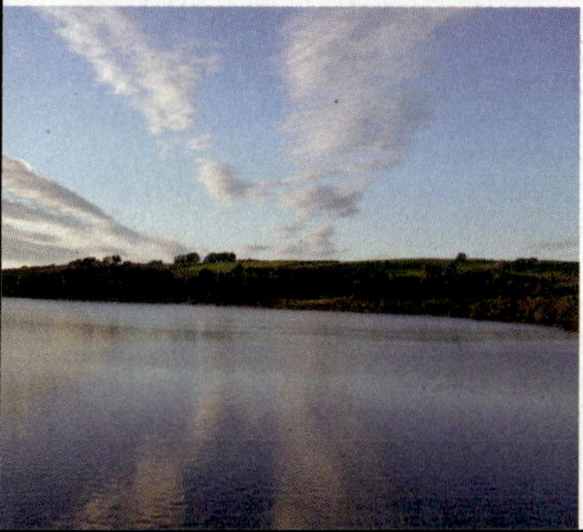
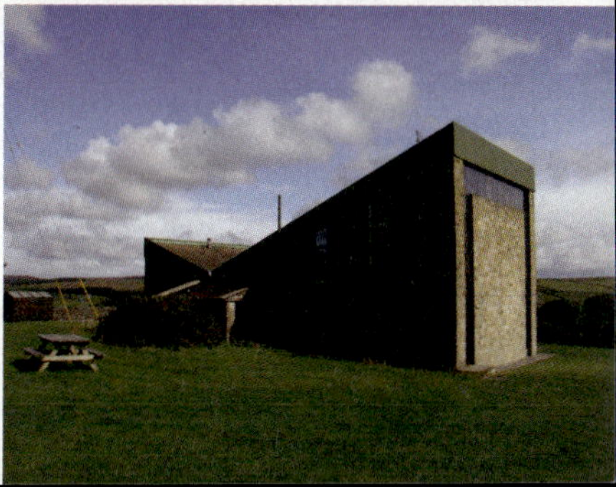

AIRTON BARN
FRIENDS MEETING HOUSE

ENGLAND

The recently renovated Airton Camping Barn offers overnight accommodation for up to 16 people. The barn is situated in the quiet village of Airton in central Malhamdale, on the Pennine Way and the Way of the Roses cycle route. It is an easy walk from Malham Cove, Gordale Scar and Janet's Foss. The Three Peaks and Bronte Country are a short drive away and the barn is in 1652 country where the first Quakers gathered. The Meeting House has been used by Quakers since the 1650s, and now offers a warm welcome to cyclists, walkers, mountaineers and family groups. There is a bunk room with 6 beds and two multi-purpose rooms for which airbeds can be provided. The enclosed flat garden is ideal for tents. There are two fully-fitted kitchens, two bathrooms and a separate toilet. Bedding can be provided on request, and there is a small store of basic non-perishable food supplies on site. Food can be ordered and collected from the village farm shop. Secure cycle storage available.

DETAILS

- **Open** - All year, friend residence on site.
- **Number of beds** - 6 bunk beds + 10 air mattresses. Camping in the garden
- **Booking** - Please contact the Friend in Residence. Prior booking recommended.
- **Price per night** - £17 per person, reductions for groups over 6.
- **Public Transport** - Trains at Skipton (11 miles) and Gargrave (7 miles by road, 4 miles by Pennine Way). Limited buses from Skipton (via Gargrave) and Malham.
- **Directions** - Coming into Airton from Gargrave take the first right. Barn is the fourth building on the right. Leave the Pennine Way at Airton Bridge, walk towards the village. Barn is first building on the left. Knock on the white door. GR SD 904592

CONTACT: Friend in Residence
Tel: 01729 830263
airtonbarn@gmail.com www.airtonbarn.org.uk
The Nook, Airton, Skipton, North Yorkshire, BD23 4AE

GRASSINGTON
BUNKBARN

ENGLAND

At almost 1000 feet, with spectacular views of Wharfedale, Grassington Bunkbarn offers comfortable accommodation for groups of up to 32 people in a magnificent location. The ground floor has 3 bunk rooms and a leader/disabled bedroom with private toilet/shower. On the upper floor there is a large dining area with open plan kitchen equipped for groups and a lounge/games area with Freeview TV, although you may be content with the dramatic views from the window! The barn has free WiFi and good mobile coverage. The ground floor has 3 bathrooms with 5 showers and 5 WCs along with a large drying room. The barn is heated by an environmentally sustainable wood pellet biomass boiler which fuels radiators in all the rooms and constant hot water. Outside there is a barbecue area, a large locked bike store and a large car park area. With walking, cycling, climbing, fishing, horse riding, archaeology, bird watching, geology, botany and even golf, the area has something for everyone.

DETAILS

- **Open** - From June 2014. Reception 9am - 5pm Mon - Fri, Sat Sun 10am - 2pm
- **Number of beds** - 34: 2 x 12, 1 x 6, 1 x 4
- **Booking** - 25% deposit, with balance 2 weeks before stay.
- **Price per night** - Weekends £900(2 nights). Bank holidays (Friday 3 pm to Monday 11am) £1100. Mon–Thurs £250 per night. 4 night stay £250 per night. 7 night stay from £1500. Individual beds: please ring for availability @ £20 per night
- **Public Transport** - Train to Skipton and then an hourly bus to Grassington. The bunk barn is about 1.25miles from the nearest bus stop.
- **Directions** - Take B6265 to Grassington, turn up Main St. through village to the Town Hall, then carry on up the hill (Moor Lane) for 1/2 mile bunk barn is on the left.

CONTACT: Paul or Janet Kent
Tel: 01756 753882, Fax: 01756 752865
enquiries@grassingtonbunkbarn.co.uk   www.grassingtonbunkbarn.co.uk
Spring Croft, Moor Lane, Grassington, BD23 5BD

WHARFESIDE HOUSE

In the centre of the village of Kettlewell in the Yorkshire Dales National Park, Wharfeside House is a perfect base for groups wanting to explore all that the Yorkshire Dales has to offer.

Ideal for D of E or other youth groups as well as groups of adults or families. The area attracts walkers, road cyclists, mountain bikers, bird watchers, painters, cavers, pot-holers, climbers, fishermen and women as well as those businesses who are keen to encourage team building but at economical prices.

Opened in 1969 by Huddersfield Wharfeside Youth Trust, Wharfeside house provides self-catering accommodation for sole-use groups of 15-30 people. Facilities include a well equipped, fully fitted kitchen with Aga stove and fridge freezer, shower facilities with separate male and female toilets, a large communal space, drying area and large indoor bike/equipment store. An onsite warden can provide daily support. There is onsite parking for up to 4 vehicles.

DETAILS

- **Open** - All year round including Christmas and New Year, 24 hours
- **Number of beds** - 30: 1x8, 1x8, 1x6, 1x4, 1x2, 1x2
- **Booking** - Please e-mail booking manager, Dorothy.
- **Price per night** - Adults from £16pp. Children from £12pp
- **Public Transport** - On a bus route from Skipton or Grassington
- **Directions** - Kettlewell is a village in Upper Wharfedale, North Yorkshire. It lies 6 miles (10 km) north of Grassington and 14.6 miles (23.5 km) north of Skipton.

CONTACT: Dorothy Bottom
Tel: 01484 530277
wharfesidehouse-kettlewell@hotmail.co.uk   www.wharfesidehouse.co.uk
Middle Lane, Kettlewell, Skipton, BD23 5QX

KETTLEWELL HOSTEL

191

ENGLAND

Newly owned and run by Saul and Floss Ward and part of the YHA Enterprise Scheme, Kettlewell Hostel is a great base for Yorkshire activity breaks.

The beautiful village of Kettlewell in Upper Wharfedale, north of Skipton was the location for the film Calendar Girls. It is surrounded by limestone pavements and lush green dales and is a haven for climbers and walkers and was on on the 2014 Tour de France route so there are simply amazing cycling routes whilst the hostel has secure cycle storage. Kettlewell Hostel is an old stone house with good access to the Embsay Steam Railway and Bolton Abbey, making it perfect for school trips. Self catering is available and the hostel also offers locally sourced, home cooked food, great breakfast, great packed lunch and delicious evening meals which will set you up for a day's walking or climbing and revive you when you get back! A wonderful place to stay on the Dales Way or just exploring the area. Kettlewell is family friendly, great for kids.

DETAILS

- **Open** - All Year. Reception times: 08.00 - 10.30 17.00 - 22.30
- **Number of beds** - 40
- **Booking** - Book online or by phone via the YHA.
- **Price per night** - Beds from £18
- **Public Transport** - Bus number 72 from Skipton train station.
- **Directions** - From Skipton travel north towards Grassington then follow signs to Kettlewell. In the village, cross two bridges then turn right in front of the Bluebell pub. At the T junction turn left. The hostel/Post Office is the second building on right.

CONTACT: Saul Ward
Tel: 0845 371 9025
saulward@hotmail.com www.yha.org.uk/hostel/kettlewell
Kettlewell, Skipton, North Yorkshire, BD23 5QU

WHITEFIELDS COTTAGE

ENGLAND

Situated in a Medieval deer park, Whitefields Cottage offers self-catering accommodation within Fountains Abbey and Studley Royal Estate. Cared for by the National Trust and awarded World Heritage Site status in 1986, the estate contains a beautiful water garden, Elizabethan mansion and a Cistercian abbey. Whitefields is a 19th century cottage on the edge of Studley Royal Deer Park, home to around 350 red, fallow and sika deer.

Whether you want to explore the water gardens and impressive abbey, or walk around the North York moors (1hr drive) or Yorkshire Dales, Whitefields is ideal. It offers groups of up to 16 people inexpensive but comfortable accommodation.

DETAILS

- **Open** - All year, except Christmas and New Year, no restrictions
- **Number of beds** - I6: 1x6, 1x8, 1x2.
- **Booking** - Bookings required 1 week in advance, non refundable deposit £60.
- **Price per night** - Mid week £140. Weekend (Fri/Sat) £180. Bookings of 7 nights or more charged at £140.00 night. £50 extra charge for 1 night stays at weekends
- **Public Transport** - Train station and National Express coaches at Harrogate (15 miles). Regular bus service between Harrogate and Ripon. Taxis Ripon to Whitefields £8 - Harrogate to Whitefields £20.
- **Directions** - From B6265 turn to Studley Roger. Drive through village, bear sharp right, before the National Trust sign, into deer park. Half a mile up main avenue turn right sign-posted 'estate vehicles only'. Turn right up the track at the end of this road, Whitefields is at top of track.

CONTACT: Andrew Moss
Tel: 01765 643172, Fax: 01765 601002
andrew.moss@nationaltrust.org.uk www.nationaltrust.org.uk/fountainsabbey
Fountains Abbey and Studley Royal Park, Fountains, Ripon, HG4 3DY

DALESBRIDGE

ENGLAND

Dalesbridge is located on the A65 at Austwick, on the edge of the Yorkshire Dales National Park, just five miles from both Ingleton and Settle. It is a comfortable venue for those visiting the Yorkshire Dales, whether you are a family, a group or an individual. The six bed units have a kitchen area with a cooker, fridge, washing up sink, shower and toilet. Crockery, cutlery and cooking pots are provided and there is a seating area in the middle of the room. The four bed units have a shower and toilet, small seating area with kettle, toaster, microwave, crockery and cutlery. These rooms are ideal for the smaller group not requiring full self-catering facilities. Utilising all the units provides group accommodation for up to 40. You will need to bring your own sleeping bag and pillow, alternatively bedding is available to hire. Dalesbridge has a great deal to offer: function bar, drying room, function catering, B&B and camp-site.

DETAILS

- **Open** - All year, reception open 9am - 5pm
- **Number of beds** - 40
- **Booking** - Advance booking with first night payment as deposit.
- **Price per night** - £13-£19 per person per night dependent on season, usually let by the unit. Check our website for your dates, or ring us on 015242 51021
- **Public Transport** - Settle railway station is 5 miles away and Clapham station 1.5 miles. There are infrequent buses but if you would like collection from either railway station please give us a call.
- **Directions** - GR 762 676. Dalesbridge is on the main A65. When travelling from Settle towards Ingleton it is situated on the left hand side between the two turnings into Austwick.

CONTACT: Jon
Tel: 015242 51021, Fax: 015242 20111
info@dalesbridge.co.uk www.dalesbridge.co.uk
Austwick, Nr Settle, LA2 8AZ

INGLETON YHA
GRETA TOWER

ENGLAND

A Victorian house in private grounds, Greta Tower is situated on the edge of the Yorkshire Dales, in the pretty village of Ingleton. Surrounded by magnificent countryside with caves, waterfalls and mountains, and dominated by Ingleborough the best known of Yorkshire's Three Peaks, the area is known for its walking routes, waterfall trail and has plenty to offer for walkers, climbers, mountain bikers and cavers. The Yorkshire Dales, Lake District, Forest of Bowland and Morecambe Bay coastline are all a short distance away. A great base for the Yorkshire Three Peaks Challenge. Whatever your agenda, you're sure of a relaxing stay at Ingleton. There's even an open-air swimming pool (summer only) and park next door, great for family breaks and school trips. This licensed hostel serves tasty meals. Offering dormitory-style rooms with bunk beds and shared bathroom facilities. 2 x private ensuite 5 bed rooms (includes one double bed) are now available. Exclusive hire available. Free parking.

DETAILS

- **Open** - Daily Mar to Oct. Sole use available in Winter. Reception 7-10am, 5-10pm.
- **Number of beds** - 66: 4x6, 8x4, 1x2, 2x4/5
- **Booking** - Recommended, essential for groups. By phone, e-mail or website.
- **Price per night** - Beds from £15, rooms from £30.
- **Public Transport** - The Leeds to Morecambe train stops at Clapham & Bentham. Ribblehead Station is the closest stop on the Settle-Carlisle line. All are approx. 10 mins drive to Ingleton. Bus services from Settle or Lancaster train stations.
- **Directions** - In centre of village, close to the outdoor pool and play area. Off the A65 Skipton to Kendal Road, 30 mins from Morcambe and 25 mins from Lancaster.

CONTACT: Manager
Tel: 015242 41444, Fax: 01524 451022
ingleton@yha.org.uk www.ingletonhostel.co.uk
Greta Tower, Sammy Lane, Ingleton, North Yorkshire, LA6 3EE

THE OLD SCHOOL BUNKHOUSE

195
ENGLAND

Situated 4.5 miles from Ingleton in Yorkshire Dales limestone country, between Ingleborough and Whernside with superb views of both, the bunkhouse makes an ideal base for sporting or nature holidays.

The area is well known for its scenery including the Three Peaks walk, (Ingleborough, Pen-y-ghent and Whernside), the Waterfalls walk and some of the best caves and potholes in the country including the famous Gaping Ghyll system and the White Scar show cave. This is a stone property, which has been converted from an old school, with much of the character remaining. It provides self-catering accommodation for up to 30 people and has a lounge, drying room, 4 shower rooms with hand basins and toilets, well equipped kitchen / dining room with industrial cooker, toasters, fridge, freezer, dishwasher, microwaves and payphone. No pets allowed. Nearest pub 100 yds.

DETAILS

- **Open** - All year, 24 hours
- **Number of beds** - 30 (5 x 6)
- **Booking** - Early booking advised for popular times. £150 deposit for 2 nights. 25% for 3 nights or over.
- **Price per night** - £280 per night (sole use) for up to 20 people with an extra £14 per person for groups over 20 people. Minimum of 2 nights at weekends.
- **Public Transport** - Ribblehead station 1 mile. No buses.
- **Directions** - 4.5 miles on the B6255 Ingleton to Hawes Road, just after Chapel-Le-Dale village on left hand side. 11 miles from Hawes on B6255.

CONTACT: Clare and Peter Fox
Tel: 01729 823835, Fax: 07801979945
pfox119@btinternet.com   www.oldschoolbunkhouse.co.uk
Chapel-le-Dale, Ingleton, Carnforth, Lancs, LA6 3AR

HARDRAW
OLD SCHOOL BUNKHOUSE
ENGLAND

Adjacent to the Pennine Way, on the edge of the picturesque village of Hardraw, The Old School Bunkhouse offers well-appointed and practical accommodation for individuals or groups of up to 26. The large school hall and enclosed grassed recreational area are used for communal activities. Off road parking, secure bike storage and bike wash area available. Hardraw has a camp-site, café, felt gallery and the Green Dragon Inn (folk music & Hardraw Force waterfall) whilst the small town of Hawes (shops, cafés, restaurants, pubs & the Wensleydale cheese factory) is a 1.5 mile walk across fields on a limestone slabbed footpath. Ideally situated, in stunning surroundings, for the many caves, bike and walking routes. Andy and Helen, qualified cave instructors, offer days out underground with discounts for bunkhouse guests. Outdoor activity badgework for guides, scouts and DofE. A great stopping point for individuals using the Pennine Way or groups wanting sole use for outdoor pursuits, educational visits and DofE.

DETAILS

- **Open** - All year, 24 hours
- **Number of beds** - 19 (26): 1x8, 1x9, (1x6, 1 x 3), 2x2 person tent spaces
- **Booking** - Advance booking preferred. 25% deposit for exclusive use, total fee payable for 1 night bookings but short notice bookings may be available.
- **Price per night** - £15 pppn (£12 under 12s), exclusive use £150-£275pn.
- **Public Transport** - Garsdale station 8 miles. Bus stop outside bunkhouse connects with Leeds-Carlisle services. Buses to Bedale and Leyburn from Hawes.
- **Directions** - Turn north off A684 approx. 1 mile west of Hawes and proceed for ½ mile. Hardraw Old School Bunkhouse is on the left as you enter the village.

CONTACT: Andy or Helen
Tel: 01969 666034 Mob: 07546894317
enquiries@hardrawoldschoolbunkhouse.co.uk www.hardrawoldschoolbunkhouse.co.uk
Schoolhouse, Hardraw, near Hawes, Wensleydale, North Yorkshire, DL8 3LZ

THE JONAS CENTRE

197

ENGLAND

At the heart of Wensleydale in the tranquil beauty of the Yorkshire Dales, The Jonas Centre is uniquely positioned to provide all that is needed for those seeking relaxation and to enjoy all that the area has to offer. An ideal centre for cycling, walking and sightseeing, with routes direct from the door. Activities can be arranged independently with local providers on or off site. Close to Redmire station on the Wensleydale Railway and near to Castle Bolton & Aysgarth Falls. Good pub for meals in Redmire village. 12 self-catering log cabins with bathroom, well equipped kitchen & TV sleep 5-7. Heated by night storage (additional heaters available). Freezer, coin operated washing machine & dryer are available. Meeting facilities and large kitchen available to groups. Linen and towels can be hired. Pets allowed (nightly charge). Children's playground, table tennis hut, ball games area, camp fire area as well as space just to relax in the peaceful surroundings. An ideal venue for conferences, training, teaching and fellowship as well as wedding receptions and family celebrations.

DETAILS

- **Open** - Open all year. Office open from 9am - 5pm Monday to Saturday
- **Number of beds** - 60
- **Booking** - Minimum 2 nights. The person making the booking must be over 18.
- **Price per night** - See website for special offers and group booking discounts.
- **Public Transport** - Train at Darlington & Northallerton (25 miles) local buses
- **Directions** - A684 westbound to Wensley, right toward Redmire. Entrance is on left after railway arch. A684 eastbound follow signs to & through Redmire entrance is directly ahead drive carefully down to reception, or park by top steps and walk.

CONTACT: Simon Eastwood
Tel: 01969 624900
stay@jonascentre.org www.jonascentre.org
The Jonas Centre, Redmire, Leyburn. North Yorkshire, DL8 4EW

DALES BIKE CENTRE

In the tiny village of Fremington in Swaledale, Yorkshire Dales surrounded by the best biking in Yorkshire in a stunning landscape, criss-crossed by ancient lanes, moorland tracks and roads, this is the perfect venue for cycling, mountain biking, trail running and walking. The 2014 Tour de France Yorkshire Grande Depart route goes right past the door. 14 bed, bunk accommodation, café, bike shop, hire, workshop and secure storage, bike wash, drying room and a wealth of knowledge about the Dales. 14 beds, in smart 2 and 4 bedded rooms, warmly decorated and with amazing views across the Swaledale. Bedding is provided, as well as a kitchenette with free tea and coffee. The café lounge can be used by guests, with magazines, free WiFi internet, internet radio and 24 hour cake access! A hearty breakfast is included. Evening meals are available in pubs and restaurants in Reeth, a five minute stroll away. On route for a Reeth stopover on Wainwright's famous Coast-to-Coast walk, the infamous Woodcocks off-road Coast-to-Coast mountain bike trip and the Yorkshire Dales Cycle Way.

DETAILS

- **Open** - All year, 24 hours
- **Number of beds** - 14: Old barn 1x4, 1x2; New barn 1x4, 2x2,
- **Booking** - Book by phone or email.
- **Price per night** - Bunk B&B £28, 2 or 4 sharing a room. Single occupancy £38.
- **Public Transport** - Trains Darlington (25 miles). Buses X26 & X27 every 15 mins from Darlington to Richmond. Bus 30 from Richmond to Reeth (7 per day till 6.15pm).
- **Directions** - 20 mins from A1M: from Richmond take A6108 then B6270 signed to Reeth. Once through Grinton, DBC is on left at end of a row of tall trees.

CONTACT:
Tel: 01748 884908
enquiries@dalesbikecentre.co.uk www.dalesbikecentre.co.uk
Parks Barn, Fremington, Richmond DL11 6AW

RICHMOND
CAMPING BARN

ENGLAND

East Applegarth Camping Barn, Richmond is converted from 3 former byres which are part of a listed, traditional dales, longhouse. It is situated at East Applegarth Farm, 3 miles west of the town of Richmond on the Coast to Coast walk. Grid ref NZ135017 OS Map 92. The farm borders the Yorkshire Dales National Park, with panoramic views over the lower valley of Swaledale and the River Swale. The barn is a great base for exploring the historic town of Richmond and The Yorkshire Dales National Park with all it has to offer. Sleeping accommodation is in two rooms on raised platforms with mattresses, pillows and lightweight sleeping bags. Heating and cooking facilities are available on a meter. Lighting is not metered and is included in the price. The shower is available on a separate meter. Cutlery, crockery and pans are provided.

DETAILS

- **Open** - 1st March to 30th November, access after 4pm and departure by 10.30am unless otherwise arranged.
- **Number of beds** - 12: 1 x 8, 1 x 4
- **Booking** - Book by phone or email
- **Price per night** - £9.00 per person. £108 sole use of barn.
- **Public Transport** - Nearest railway 15 miles away at Darlington. Bus service 3 miles away at Richmond. Local taxi service is available.
- **Directions** - On the A6108 in Richmond at the petrol station (Victoria Road) turn right into Hurgill Road. Continue for 3 miles. Farm entrance is on the left in a dip in the road 200 yds past the 2 radio masts on the right. The barn is at the end of the tarmac road ignoring the T-junction.

CONTACT: Mrs J Atkinson
Tel: 01748 822940
rebekah.atkinson@virgin.net
East Applegarth Farm, Westfields, Richmond, North Yorkshire DL10 4SD

FELL END BUNKHOUSE

Overlooking the unspoilt Howgill Fells, these two 18th century buildings provide comfortable bunkhouse accommodation for people wishing to explore this beautiful area. Perfect for mixed groups, DofE, families and people with special needs. Great for walking & cycling; canoeing & caving nearby; the Lake District is only 1 hour away. The Schoolhouse sleeps 8 in bunks in the central area with an extra bed in an adjoining room. There are two toilets, one shower and four wash basins and a fully equipped kitchen with a fridge, freezer, microwave and cooker. The living room has a multi-fuel stove, which also heats the radiators. Greenslack has a further 2 bunks and 1 single bed plus a bathroom for people with mobility problems. Get in touch if your group has fewer than 8 people but you require Greenslack for these facilities. Entry into both buildings is by a touch lock system. Dogs allowed under strict supervision. Fell End is owned by the Bendrigg Trust, a charity offering outdoor activities for disabled people.

DETAILS

- **Open** - All year,
- **Number of beds** - 14: 1x8, 1x5, 1x1.
- **Booking** - Completed booking form with 20% deposit to Bendrigg Trust, Old Hutton, Kendal, Cumbria, LA8 0NR. Payment by cheque or BACS
- **Price per night** - £11+VAT. Minimum booking: 6 for Schoolhouse, 8 for both buildings, 12 people if booking 1 night. (no charge under 5yrs))
- **Public Transport** - Trains at Kirkby Stephen (6 miles) on the Carlisle/Settle/Leeds line. Taxis more reliable than buses.
- **Directions** - Bunkhouse 6 miles NE of Sedbergh, just off A683. GR:723983

CONTACT: Lynne Irish
Tel: 01539 723766, Fax: 01539 722446
lynne@bendrigg.org.uk www.fellend-bunkhouse.org.uk
Ravenstonedale, Kirkby Stephen, Cumbria, CA17 4LN

BENTS
CAMPING BARN

ENGLAND

Bents Camping Barn was formerly a shepherds' cottage in the 1600s. There are 2 sleeping rooms on the first floor with bunk beds. On the ground floor there is a kitchen with cooking area, a dining area with tables and benches and a WC with washbasins. Other facilities include electric lighting and power points throughout (£1 coin meter), crockery, cutlery, toaster, fridge, microwave, 3 electric cooking rings, 2 electric kettles, 2 electric convector heaters and parking. You will need sleeping bags, walking boots and warm clothes. The barn is accessible from the Coast to Coast path and there is good fell walking in the Howgill Fells, Wild Boar Fell and Crosby Garrett Common. Smardale Gill Nature Reserve and Sunbiggin Tarn are nearby. The area is ideal for mountain biking and the Settle to Carlisle Railway is five miles away at Kirkby Stephen. There is a shop 2 miles away.

DETAILS

- **Open** - All year, all day
- **Number of beds** - 12 to 14: 1x10, 1x6
- **Booking** - Booking is essential for groups in advance with full payment. Individuals are advised to phone first.
- **Price per night** - £10 per person. Full barn £133 per night.
- **Public Transport** - Train station at Kirkby Stephen (5 miles). Local buses to village of Newbiggin-on-Lune.
- **Directions** - GR MY 708 065 OS map 91. From Junction 38 of the M6 take the A685 to Newbiggin-on-Lune. Take Great Asby Road on left then first right through tall gate. Follow tarmac road past Tower House and follow signs to Bents Farm up track.

CONTACT: Dorothy Ousby
Tel: Booking 017687 74301 Dorothy 01768 371760
www.bentscampingbarn.com
Newbiggin-on-Lune, Kirkby Stephen, Cumbria, CA17 4NX

LONGRIGG RESIDENTIAL CENTRE

ENGLAND

Longrigg Residential Centre, within walking distance of Sedbergh, only 10 miles from Kendal and less than 10 minutes from the M6, is an ideal location for exploring the Lakes and the Yorkshire Dales. Standing in its own grounds and overlooking the unspoilt splendour of the Howgill Fells the centre is perfect for mixed groups or families. Walking, cycling, canoeing and caving are nearby. Recently refurbished the centre has two six bed dorms in the main building and a larger separate building sleeps 20 in dorms of 2,4,6 and 8. There are ample shower and toilet facilities, a drying room and tumble drier. Sleeping bags and pillowcases are required. The large kitchen is equipped for group catering. The lounge has easy chairs and gives access to the patio area. A separate games room has pool table, TV and table football. The centre holds an Adventure Activity Licence and can offer instruction and equipment. Entry is by a touch lock system. The centre is owned by Action 4 Youth a registered Charity (No 1033626) and complies with relevant Health and Safety requirements.

DETAILS

- **Open** - All year, all day
- **Number of beds** - 32: 1x8, 3x6, 1x4, 1x2
- **Booking** - Book by phone or email
- **Price per night** - £16.00pp minimum of 10 people.
- **Public Transport** - Trains at Oxenholme on the West Coast Line.
- **Directions** - Longrigg Centre is located near the village of Sedbergh which lies on the edge of the Yorkshire Dales and is just 30 minutes from the Lake District. Easy access via M6 junction 37.

CONTACT: Rob Gregory
Tel: 01539 621161
longrigg.centre@kencomp.net www.longrigg.org.uk
Frostrow Lane, Sedbergh, Cumbria, LA10 5SW

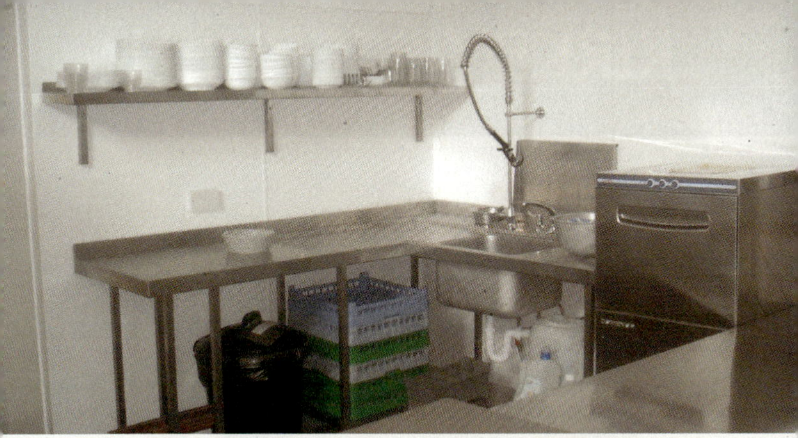
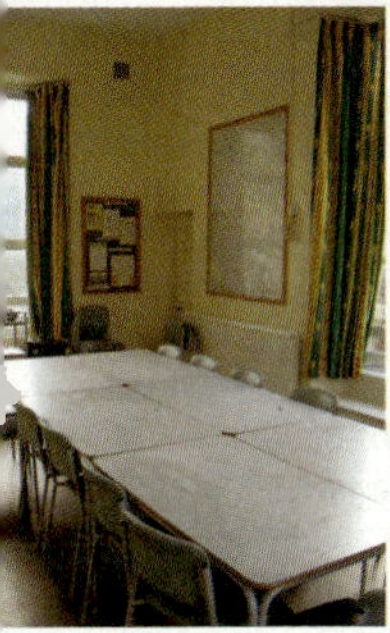
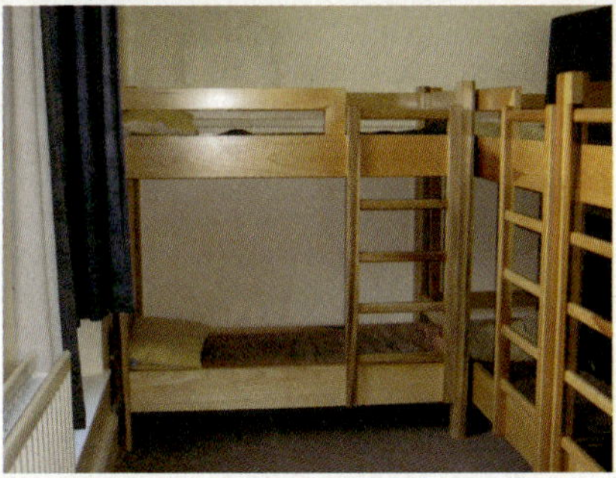
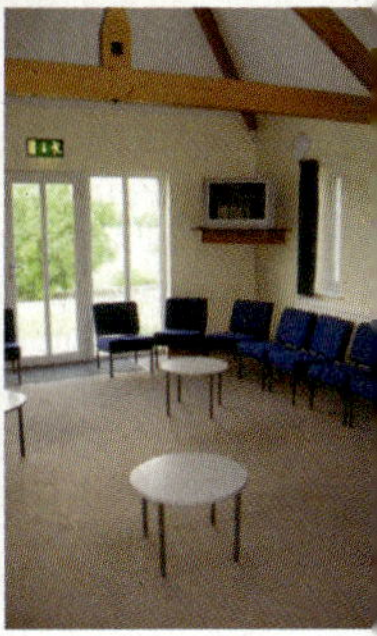
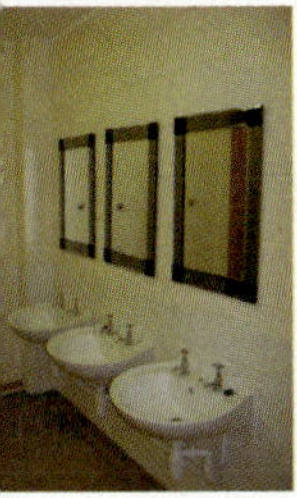
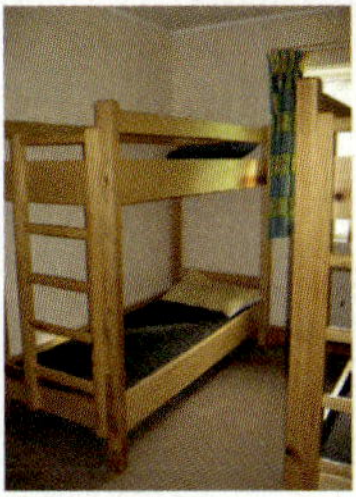
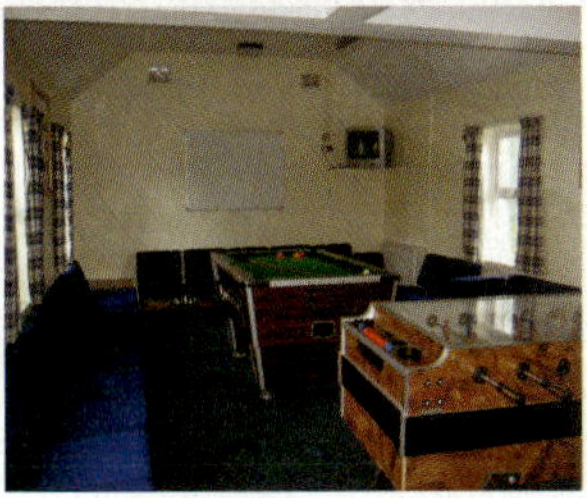
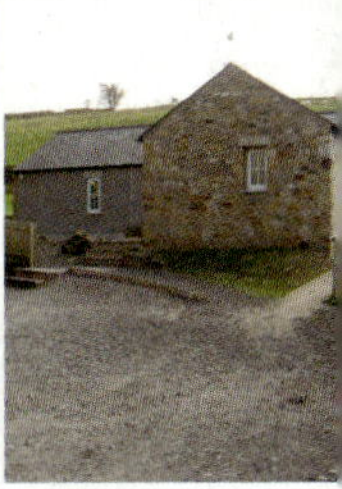
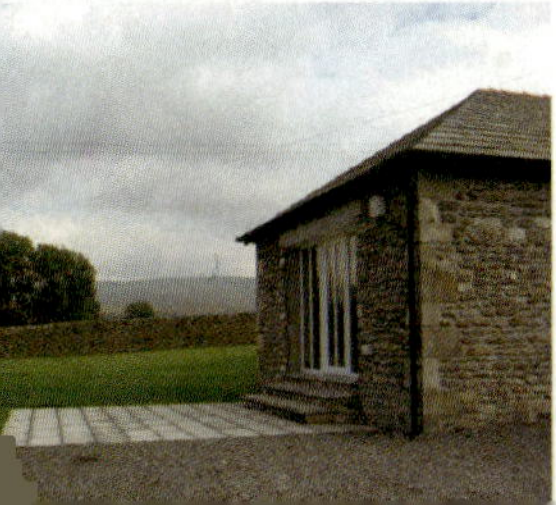
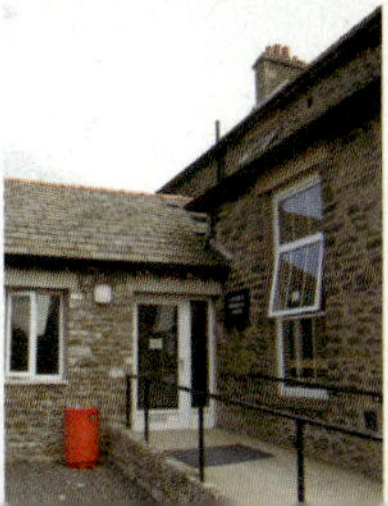
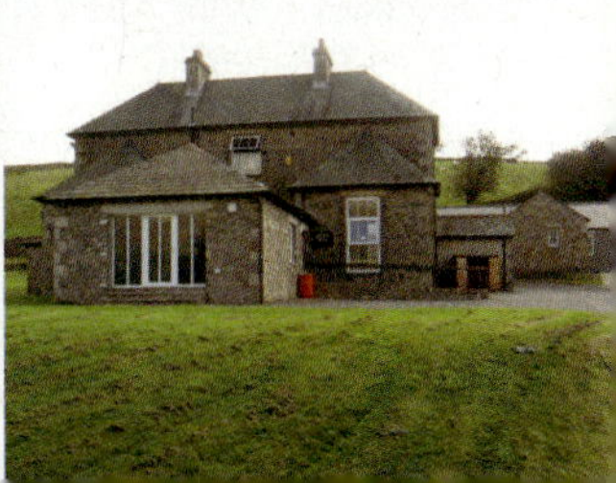

KIRKBY STEPHEN HOSTEL

ENGLAND

Kirkby Stephen Hostel, is a former YHA hostel converted from a Methodist Church and has been independent since 2010. The old chapel has a range of accommodation for individuals, families and groups amongst beautiful authentic features; stained glass windows, arches, oak panels and stone covings. The chapel houses a large dining room and kitchen, with a lounge/reading room in the gallery. The bedrooms and dormitories are in a building at the rear, with ample lavatories and showers, WiFi and a drying room. Kirkby Stephen is a pleasant market town in the upper Eden valley, situated 15 miles from Kendal, 15 miles from Hawes and on Wainwright's Coast to Coast path and the W2W cycle path. It enjoys easy access to Lady Anne's Walk, the Howgill Hills, the Dales National Park and the Lake District. The hostel stands prominently on the main street, with a range of restaurants, cafés, pubs, fish and chip shops and food shops on the doorstep. Paragliding is also available.

DETAILS

- **Open** - All year, please arrive after 5pm (or ring to arrange arrival)
- **Number of beds** - 38: 1x8, 3x6, 2x4, 1x2, 1x2 en suite
- **Booking** - Book by phone or email. Booking advised but not essential.
- **Price per night** - £20pp. Reductions for groups.
- **Public Transport** - One mile from Kirkby Stephen train station on the Leeds-Carlisle line. Regular buses from Penrith, Kendal and Appleby stop outside hostel.
- **Directions** - In the centre of town on main road. From M6 leave at junction 38 and follow signs towards Appleby.

CONTACT: Denise
Tel: 01768 371793 or 07812 558525
kirkbystephenhostel@btconnect.com   www.kirkbystephenhostel.co.uk
Market Street, Kirkby Stephen, Cumbria, CA17 4QQ

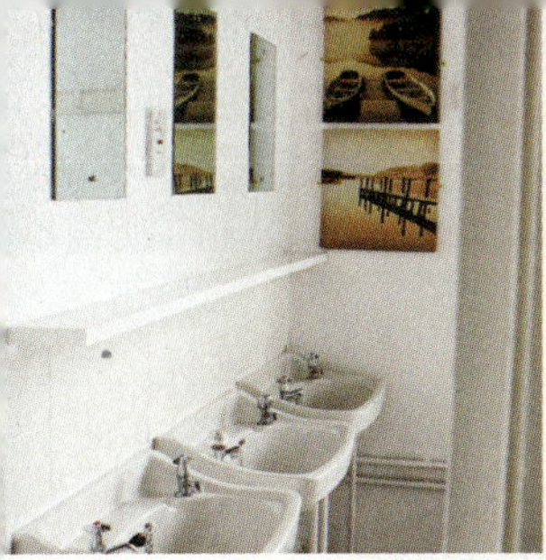
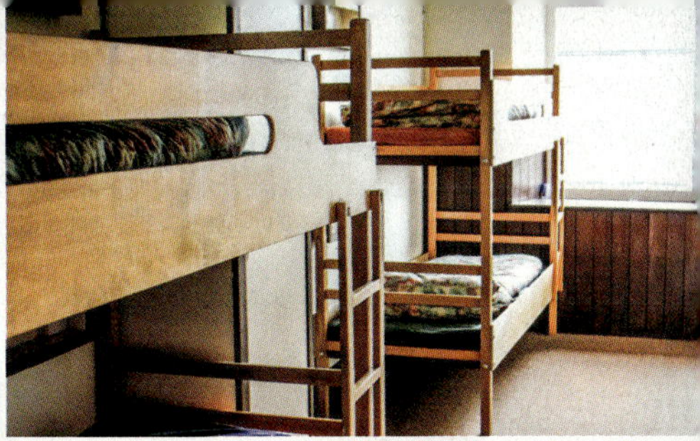
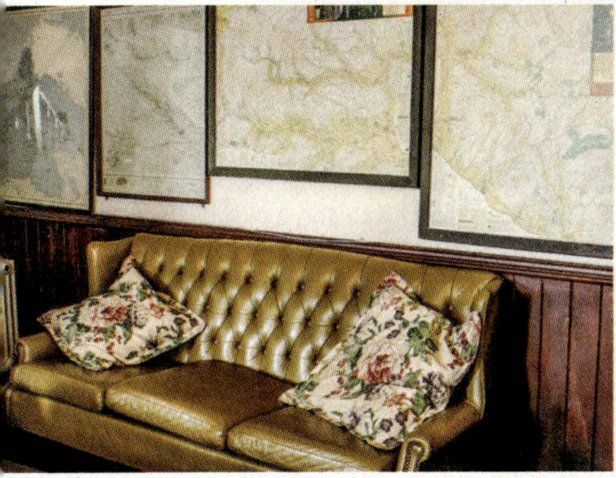
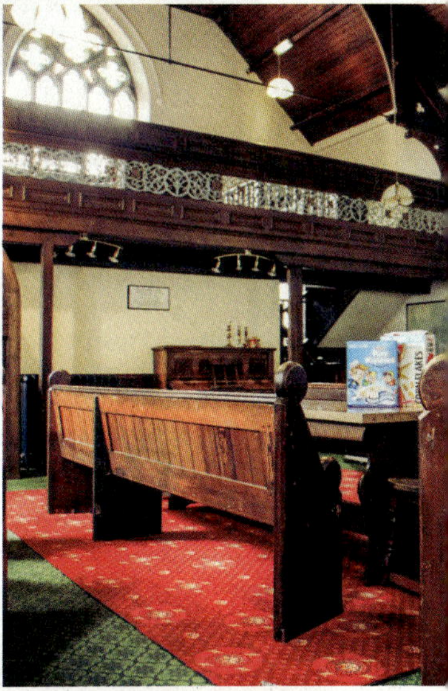
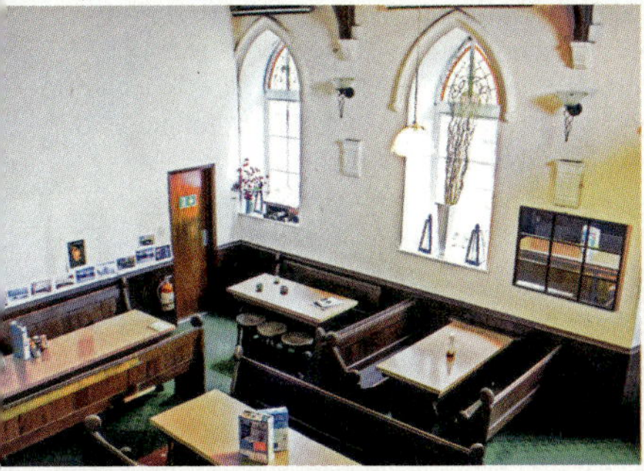
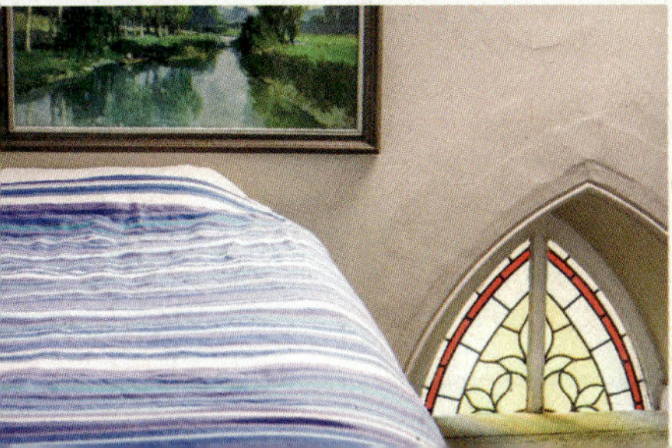
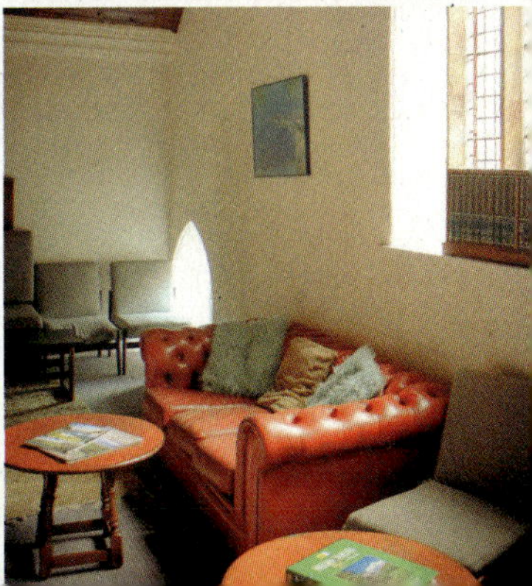

NEW ING LODGE

A friendly B&B/hostel situated in the Eden Valley, close to the Lake District, the Pennines and the Howgill Fells just minutes from the M6. This award winning hostel serves excellent home-made locally sourced meals and local ales, wines and ciders at the bar. Facilities include en suite rooms, secure bike storage, laundry facilities and kitchen. Planned for 2015 is a cinema and games room for use by groups. All heating and hot water is provided by a state of the art biomass boiler. Situated directly on Wainwright's Coast to Coast path, the Westmorland Way and the Miller's Way, New Ing is run by two brothers who are keen outdoor enthusiasts and can give advice on where to go and what to do whatever the weather. There is plenty of space outside with an acre of levelled and well kept field to the rear of the property and a walled front orchard. Sole hire available providing use of all 9 bedrooms, the bar, commercial kitchen, and the grounds from only £475 per night!

DETAILS

- **Open** - All year.
- **Number of beds** - 31:1x8,1x6,1x3, 2x2(twin), 3x2(dbl) 1x4 + camping
- **Booking** - Well in advance - deposit 50% via website or card payment by phone.
- **Price per night** - £17.50pp dorm with bedding, B&B (doubles, twins, singles and family room) from £25pp. Discounts available for larger groups and longer stays.
- **Public Transport** - Bus from Penrith or Kendal station. Pick-up from station is possible. No buses on Sunday.
- **Directions** - North end of Shap village, opposite the Bampton and Haweswater junction. 5th building on the left hand side if travelling from the North.

CONTACT: Scott or Jamie
Tel: 01931 716719
info@newinglodge.co.uk www.newinglodge.co.uk
New Ing Lodge, Shap, Penrith, Cumbria, CA10 3LX

EVENING MEALS
LAMB HOT POT
CHICKEN & BACON PIE
? BEAN VEGI CHILI

ALL HOME MADE
ORDERS TAKEN
BEFORE 18:30

GREENGILL BARN

ENGLAND

A converted traditional barn on the edge of Morland in Cumbria's rolling Eden Valley, close to the Lake District and handy for the M6. Great for weekend gatherings of family or friends. Bring your own food and drink. Central to the Lake District, the Pennines, the Howgills and the Borders, it accommodates 16 in 2 bunk rooms. Large fully equipped kitchen/dining room and a huge beamed recreation room with sofas, armchairs, pool table, library, dartboard and card table. Music system. A great space for a party. Night storage heating. 3 Mira Sports showers, 3 loos. Small camp-site and two self catering cottages next door. The Eden Valley is an idyllic cycling area with quiet rolling roads and wonderful views. Greengill Barn is on NCN route 71 and new Wiggo's Loop on C2C. Secure bike storage, ideal for road cyclists and mountain bikers. Good local walking, and easy access to lakes and fells. The local Mill Yard Café does pizzas on Friday nights, dinners on Saturday night, and full English breakfasts, coffees, lunches and take-aways. The Crown Inn opposite serves real ale.

DETAILS

- **Open** - All Year.
- **Number of beds** - 16: 2x8
- **Booking** - Exclusive group use only. Minimum 2 nights. 30% non-returnable deposit to confirm. Balance due a month before arrival. Payable online or by cheque.
- **Price per night** - £240 per night so £480 for 2 nights.(£15pppn for 16 people). Bunk sheet included. Own sleeping bags free or duvet, pillow, towel £5pp. Dogs £10.
- **Public Transport** - Nearest rail station and bus station in Penrith, 7 miles
- **Directions** - Last building in Morland on road to Great Strickland.

CONTACT: Freddy Markham
Tel: 01931 714244 Mob: 07831 428541
freddy@greengillholidays.co.uk www.greengillholidays.co.uk
Greengill Barn, Strickland Road, Morland, Penrith, Cumbria CA10 3AX

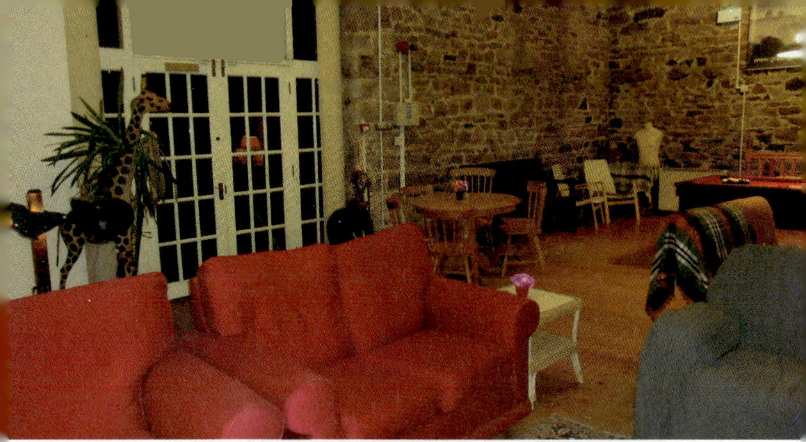

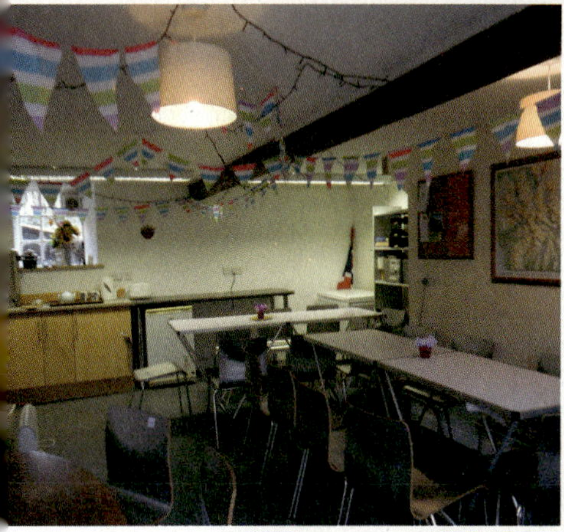

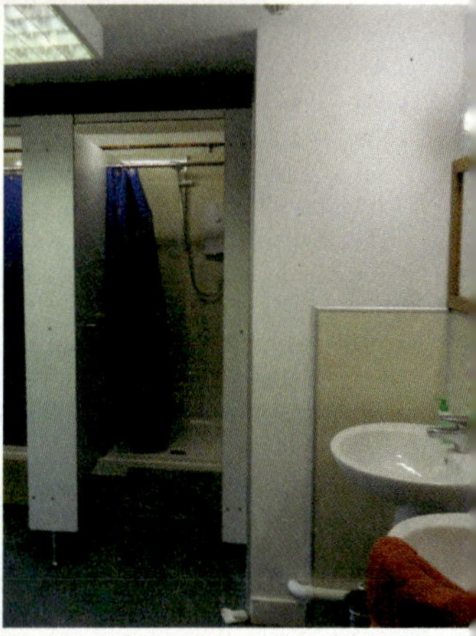

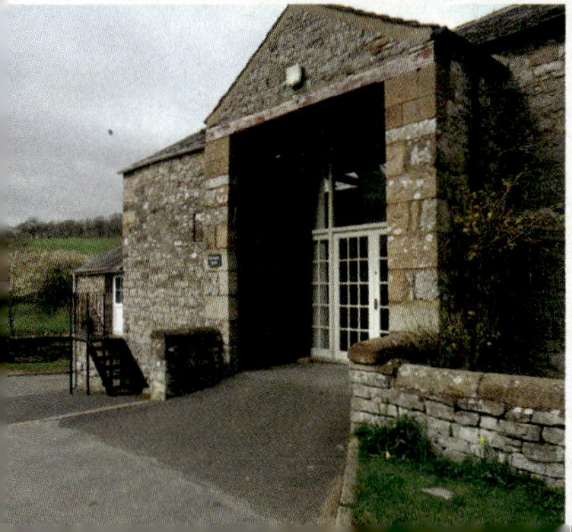

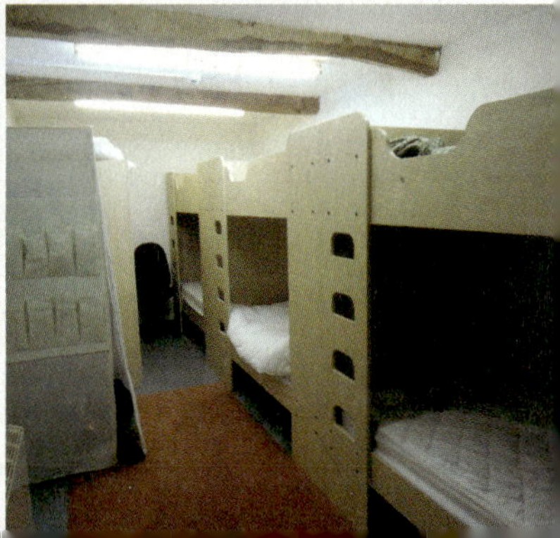

YEALAND OLD SCHOOL

Yealand Old School hostel is located in the middle of the village of Yealand Conyers, and is part of the Quaker Heritage of the village. The hostel is run on a not-for-profit basis by the adjacent Quaker meeting house. The hostel offers simple self-catering accommodation for all sorts of groups.

Facilites include a well equipped kitchen, which provides good dining space. The upstairs provides 3 good sized spaces used in various ways by different groups. One is a sizable hall, and another a comfortable sitting room.

Groups normally have sole occupancy of the building. The hostel is well located for walking, cycling, the RSPB reserve at Leighton Moss and is on NCN6. Camping in the adjacent field may be possible. Resident warden.

DETAILS

- **Open** - All year, unrestricted opening times
- **Number of beds** - 26: 1x4, 1x2, mattresses for 20+
- **Booking** - Contact warden for booking form.
- **Price per night** - £15/adult/night, £7.50 children 5 and over, min charge £100 for group Friday/Sat, £50 during week
- **Public Transport** - Carnforth station 3 miles, with a connection by local bus which stops outside the hostel.
- **Directions** - Exactly at the top of the hill on the main road through Yealand Conyers village, 5 mins from J35 M6

CONTACT: Sue Tyldesley
Tel: 01524 732336
yealandwarden@lancsquakers.org.uk www.lancsquakers.org.uk
Yealand Rd, Yealand Conyers, Carnforth, LA5 9SH

ARNSIDE
INDEPENDENT HOSTEL ENGLAND

Under new ownership since February 2014, This large Edwardian house above Morecambe Bay is perfectly situated and boasts great views of the Lake District mountains. Great budget accommodation for groups, individuals and family breaks especially if you love Lake District holidays but could do without the summer crowds. A good touring base for activity breaks in the Lake District and Yorkshire Dales. Great for walking: Take a guided walk across Morcombe Bay or round the coast and back over the Knott, just 2 hours but it seems like a whole walking holiday! Those looking for birdwatching holidays will enjoy the RSPB reserve, Leighton Moss and butterfly lovers shouldn't miss Arnside Knott.

Spend the evenings relaxing in the lounge, or choose from a large selection of games as well as pool or darts in the games room and enjoy good food in our licensed restaurant. Facilities: En suite rooms, games room, private parking, bar, double child bike trailer & child carrier back pack, film nights, outdoor seating, private garden, BBQ facilities, field study room/conference room hire.

DETAILS
- **Open** - All year except Christmas Day, reception: 07.30 - 10.00 17.30 - 22.30
- **Number of beds** - 72
- **Booking** - by phone or email
- **Price per night** - from £18.50
- **Public Transport** - 20 minute walk from Arnside Railway station
- **Directions** - M6 to J35 A6 Milnthorpe. B5282 to Arnside - follow main road through Arnside to YHA sign on right.

CONTACT: Martin
Tel: 01524 761781
enquiries@arnsidehostel.co.uk www.arnsideindependenthostel.co.uk
Oakfield Lodge, Redhills Rd, Arnside, Cumbria, LA5 0AT

FELL END CAMPING BARN

ENGLAND

Fell End is a traditional 18th century Lakeland stone barn, located within its own grass courtyard approximately ½ mile from Thornthwaite Farm. The farm is located in the quieter corner of the Lakes not far from Coniston, Grizedale and the Duddon Valley. It is surrounded by spectacular scenery, ideal for walkers, cyclists and wildlife enthusiasts. There are magnificent views, star-filled skies (a truly breathtaking sight) and the tranquil 'sound of silence'. Fell End Barn is lit by tea lights (provided) and heated by a woodburing stove. There is no electricity so you will need to bring your own cooking and lighting equipment and bedding with mat. There are 2 picnic tables, a wash basin and WC and an outside area for BBQs and camp fires (wood available). Thornthwaite Farm also has a range of 4 star holiday cottages and a fabulous new log cabin which are available for short stays as well as week breaks. Sleeping 2, 4 or 6 people these cottages come complete with everything you need.

DETAILS

- **Open** - All year, all day
- **Number of beds** - 12: 1x12
- **Booking** - Book online. Booking in advance is essential.
- **Price per night** - £10 per person.
- **Public Transport** - Trains: Foxfield (3 miles). Buses: Grizebeck (3 miles).
- **Directions** - Leave M6 at J36, follow the A590 towards Barrow. Near Greenodd Estuary take A5092 signed to Broughton-in Furness. Follow this road until you reach Grizebeck. Just before Grizebeck garage take lane on right signposted 'Woodland'. Follow for 2 miles then take lane on left signed 'Woodland Hall' and follow for 1 mile.

CONTACT: Booking Office or Jean Jackson
Tel: Booking Office 017687 74301, Farm 01229 716 340
info@lakelandcampingbarns.co.uk   www.lakedistrictcottages.co.uk
Thornthwaite Farm, Woodland, Broughton in Furness, Cumbria, LA20 6DF

DUDDON SANDS
HOSTEL

213

ENGLAND

The purpose built, self-catering Duddon Sands Hostel, overlooking the Duddon Estuary, stands in the grounds of The Ship. This cosy village inn built 1691 is known for its friendly atmosphere, good ales and ghost story, and has a beer garden with wonderful estuary and fell views, a brazier (for guests to use) and an all-weather barbecue hut which seats 16. The pub is open Thurs to Sun, with a fun quiz on the first Thursday each month, Sky Sports and a darts/pool room. It does not serve food, but nearby pubs do meals, and several excellent take-aways will deliver. All bedding provided (not towels) and a cot or cot sides are available. The hostel is easily accessible being on the Cumbrian Coastal Railway & the Cumbria Coastal Path. Extra B&B accommodation can be found nearby for larger parties if required. Celebrate an event, reunions, staff trips, a big birthday or just Friday again! Find Duddon Sands on Facebook for more photos or Tripadvisor for reviews.

DETAILS

- **Open** - All year, all day (phone to arrange arrival)
- **Number of beds** - 16 : 2x4, 1x8 + cot
- **Booking** - Essential, especially for large groups. A deposit required.
- **Price per night** - £17 per person. Special rates available for whole hostel sole use. No card facilities. Cash, cheque or BACS transfer only.
- **Public Transport** - Train: request stop at Kirkby. Bus: Take 7 or 7a (Barrow-in-Furness to Millom) get off at Moorland Stores Kirkby, follow signs for hostel & trains.
- **Directions** - At Moorland Stores crossroads on A595 in centre of Kirkby-in-Furness take turn for Sandside and Train Station. Hostel is at bottom of hill.

CONTACT: Tony
Tel: 07766527067
theship1691@googlemail.com   www.theship1691.co.uk
The Ship Inn, Askewgate Brow, Kirkby-in-Furness, Cumbria, LA17 7TE

ROOKHOW CENTRE

ENGLAND

Situated in the Rusland Valley, close to the heart of the Lake District, this small beautiful hostel has its own glorious woods where you can have a bonfire/BBQ or explore the woodland walks. Close to Coniston and Windermere and on the edge of the Grizedale Forest Park with its trails and sculptures, Rookhow is the perfect base for walking, orienteering, mountain biking, canoeing and all outdoor activities as well as quiet retreat, relaxation, study and artistic pursuits.

Converted from the stables of the nearby historic Quaker meeting house (available for conferences, seminars and group activities) the three sleeping areas can be rented as private or family rooms. Facilities: kitchen/dining area, cosy wood stove, picnic tables and BBQ. Private parking. WiFi by arrangement. Inn food 2/3 miles. Supermarkets 15mins or will deliver. Electric heating inc.

DETAILS

- **Open** - All year, all day
- **Number of beds** - 20: 1x9, 1x8, plus extra on bed settees. Also camping.
- **Booking** - Booking is essential (deposit).
- **Price per night** - From :- Adult £16.00, £8.00 for under 16s. Sole use from £190 (minimum) per night. Camping rate half the above. Duvet hire £5 pp.
- **Public Transport** - Trains at Grange-over-Sands and Ulverston. (11 miles, approx £25 by taxi). A seasonal bus service sometimes operates - check with the warden.
- **Directions** - GR 332896. From M6, Junction 36, follow A590, signs for Barrow. Leave A590 at Greenodd (A5092) junction and follow sign for Workington for ¼ mile. Take minor road to right signed Colton / Oxen Park. Continue through Oxen Park for 2 miles. Centre on left. From Ambleside: to Hawkshead, then to Grizedale. Continue beyond Grizedale for 3.5 miles (Satterthwaite - Ulverston Road). Centre on the right.

CONTACT: Warden
Tel: 01229 860231 Mob: 0794 350 8100
straughton@btinternet.com www.rookhowcentre.co.uk
Rusland Valley, nr Grizedale, Ulverston, Cumbria, South Lakeland, LA12 8LA

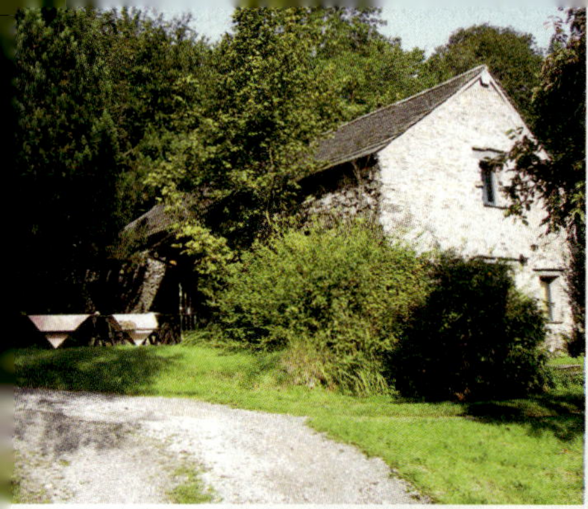

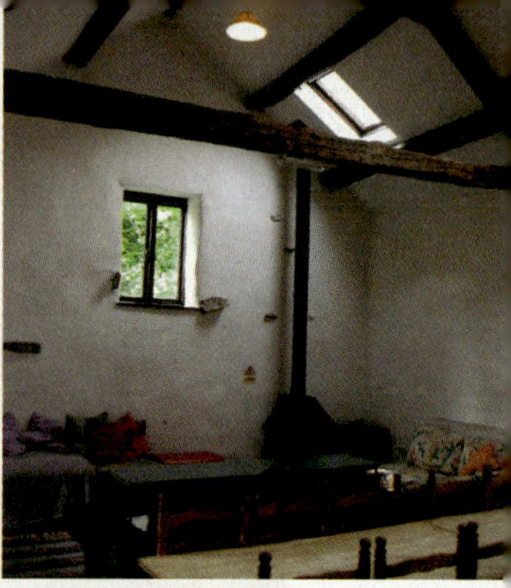

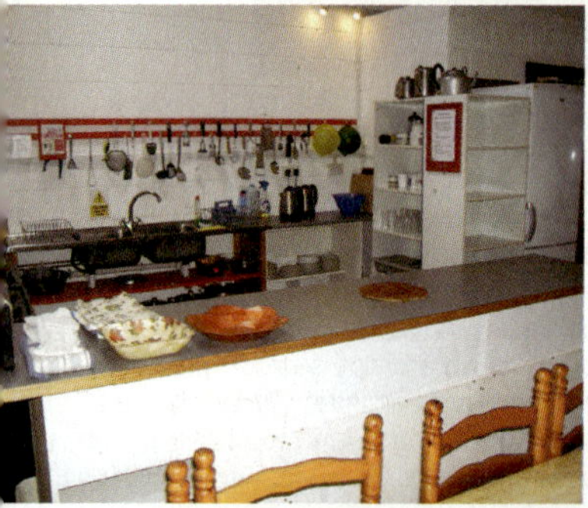

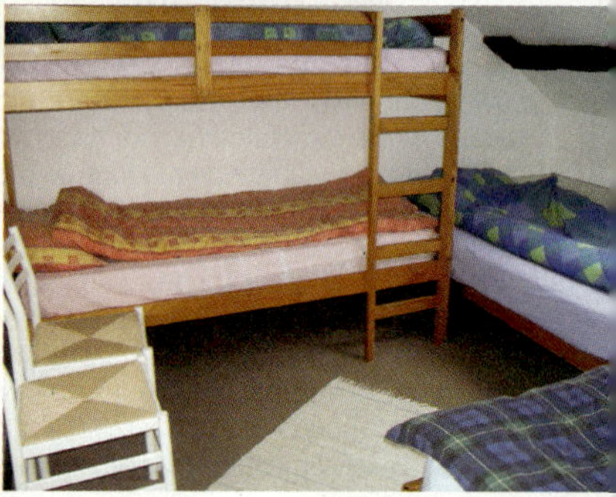

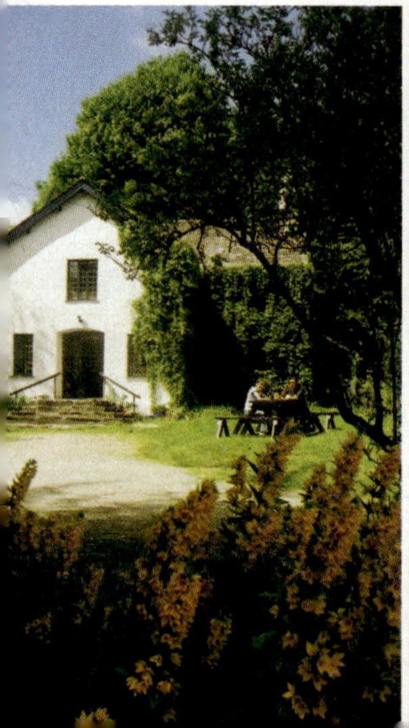

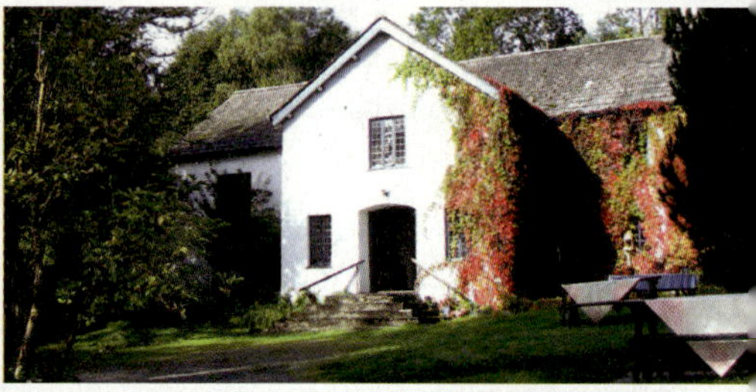

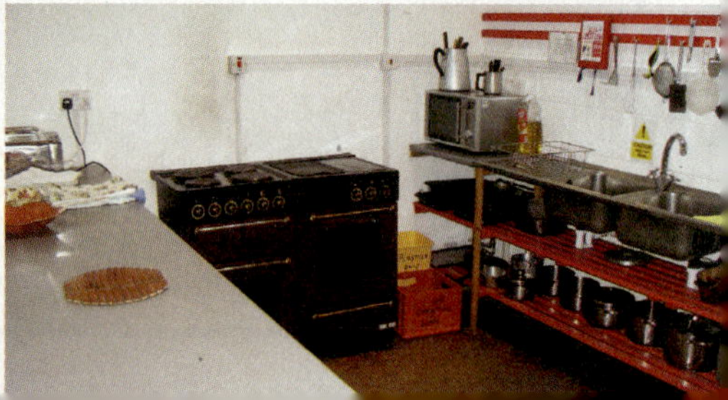

LOWICK SCHOOL BUNKHOUSE

ENGLAND

Lowick School Bunkhouse is based within the old Primary School at Lowick Green which is nestled between Coniston and Ulverston. The bunkhouse has 20 beds in 3 rooms plus a lounge/meeting room with wood-burning stove, kitchen/dining room, great views of the mountains, an outdoor area with campfire and more! River Deep Mountain High Activity Centre provides a wide variety of outdoor activities from gorge walking to mountain biking, kayaking to sailing and more. Visitors to the bunkhouse are required to book at least one activity although school/youth/college groups get an archery session included. Just 25 mins' drive from the M6 and only 4 miles from Coniston Water. It is less than a mile to 2 pubs – either a pleasant walk down a back lane to the Red Lion or down the main road to the Farmer's Arms.

DETAILS

- **Open** - March-September.
- **Number of beds** - 20: 2x8, 1x4
- **Booking** - An activity with River Deep Mountain High must also be booked to use this accommodation. Schools and youth/college groups can have a free archery activity included.
- **Price per night** - Adults £15pp, children up to 16 yrs £10pp, Whole bunkhouse available for £225pn weekends, £180pn mid week. £250 deposit required for groups.
- **Public Transport** - Buses from Windermere and Ulverston
- **Directions** - From the M6, jn36, follow the A590 to Greenodd. Turn right onto A5092 after 2.5 miles Lowick school is on the right after Esps Farm. If you get to Woodgate, you have missed it!

CONTACT: Emma Hoving
Tel: 01539528666
info@riverdeepmountainhigh.co.uk   snipurl.com/28752rs
Lowick Old School, Lowick Green, Ulverston LA12 8EB

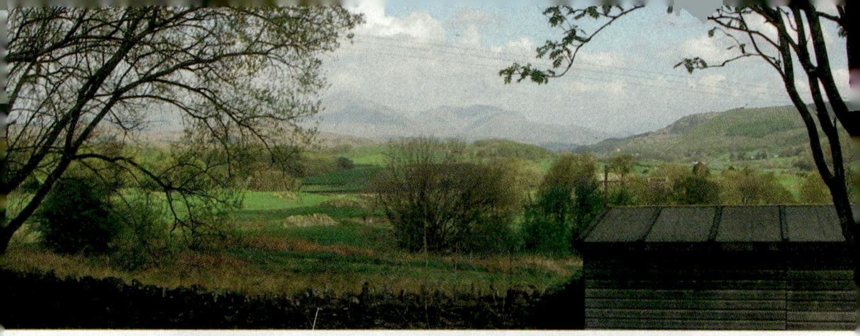

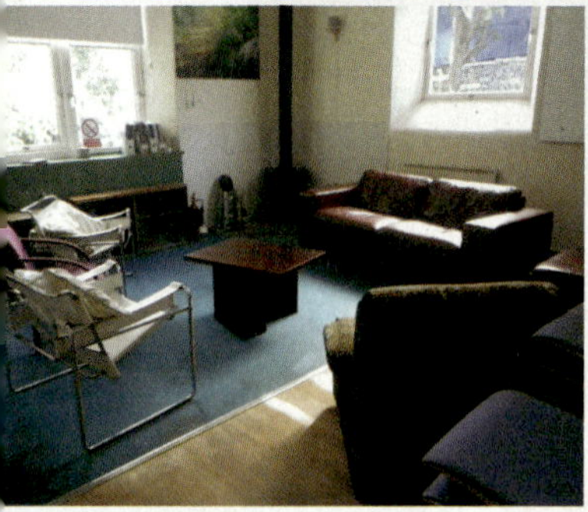

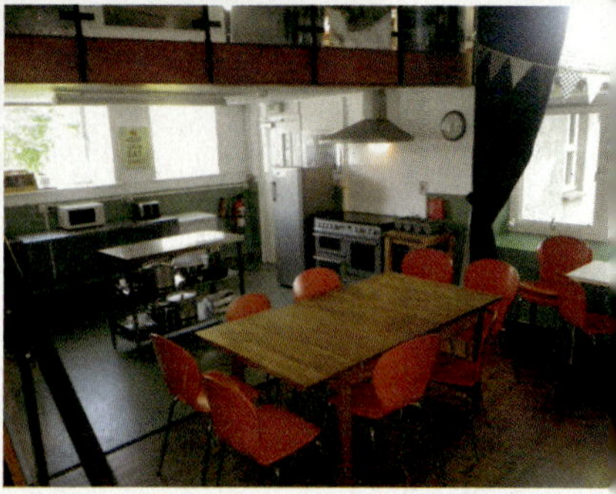

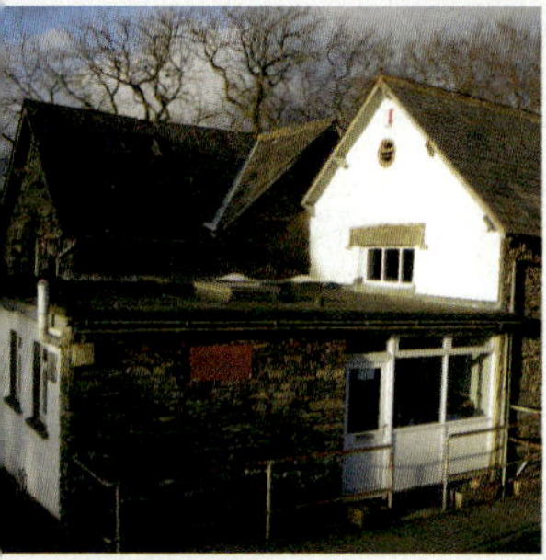

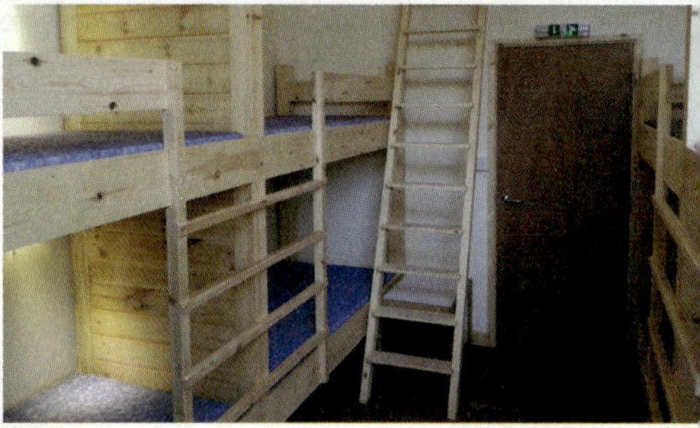

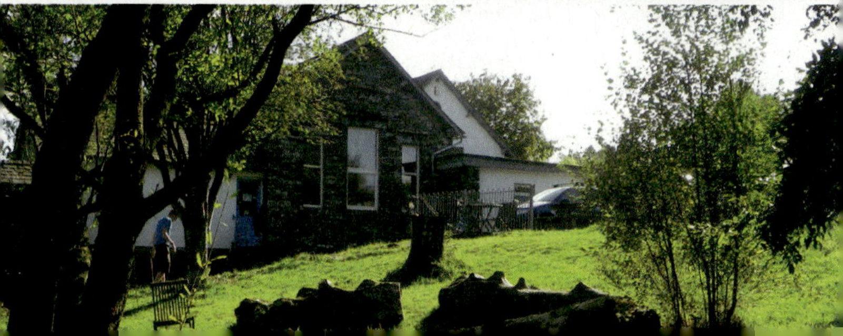

HIGH WRAY BASECAMP

ENGLAND

Situated in the heart of South Lakeland in secluded woodland, 4 miles from the village of Ambleside, High Wray Basecamp provides an ideal base for groups wishing to explore and take part in activities in the Lake District area. Local attractions include rambling, fell walking, climbing and water sports, with the Basecamp ranger being happy to assist with information on local walks and activities. The Longland Block has two separate fully centrally heated dormitories each sleeping 8, with a separate washing and living area/kitchen block. The comfortable living area is heated by a central wood burning stove and the kitchen has a commercial gas cooker, fridge freezer, microwave and utensils. The Acland block has two separate centrally heated dormitories sleeping 10 each, with toilet and shower room attached. The kitchen / lounge area is fitted with commercial gas cooker, fridges, microwave and utensils.

DETAILS

- **Open** - All year, 24 hours
- **Number of beds** - 16 + 22
- **Booking** - by email or phone
- **Price per night** - Longland £11.00pp (Mon-Thur), £14.00pp (Fri-Sun). Acland £11.50pp (Mon-Thur), £15.00pp (Fri-Sun).
- **Public Transport** - Nearest train station Windermere 8 miles. Local bus (505 'Coniston Rambler' Windermere - Hawkshead) stops 2 miles away at turning to Wray Castle (Cumbria travel-line 0870 6082608)
- **Directions** - GR: 373 995 Take A593 from Ambleside towards Coniston, bear left onto the B5286 signed Hawkshead, fork left for High Wray village, signed Wray Castle. Basecamp is ¼ mile up dirt road on the left at the end of High Wray village.

CONTACT: Philippa Barber
Tel: 015394 34633
Philippa.barber@nationaltrust.org.uk
High Wray, Ambleside, Cumbria, LA22 0JE

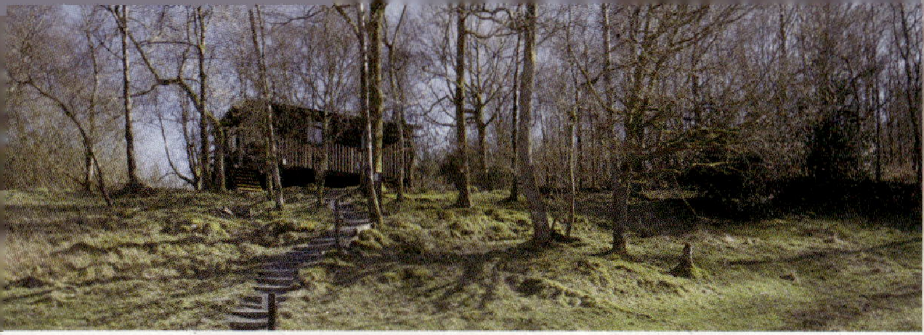

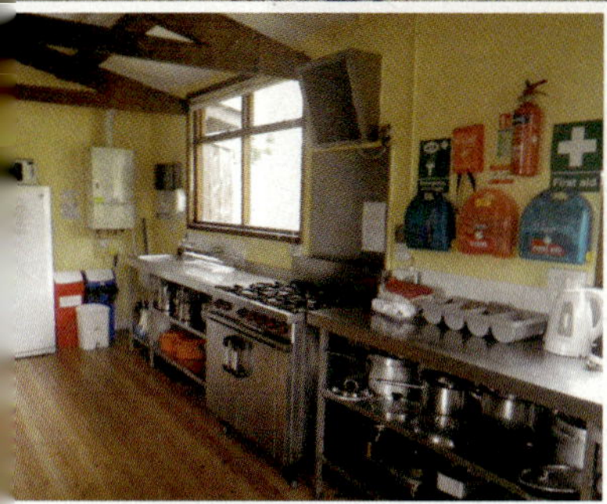

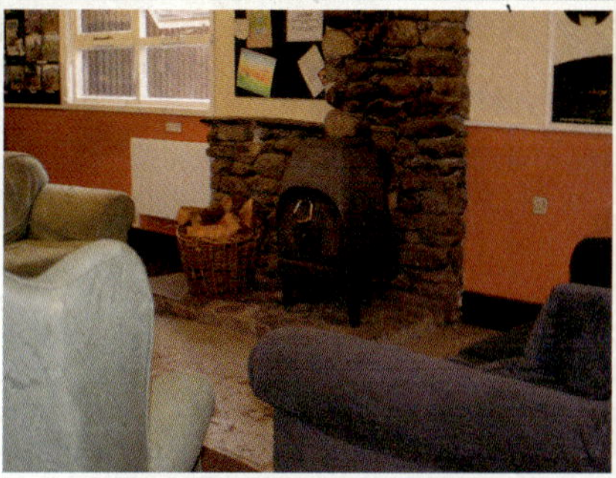

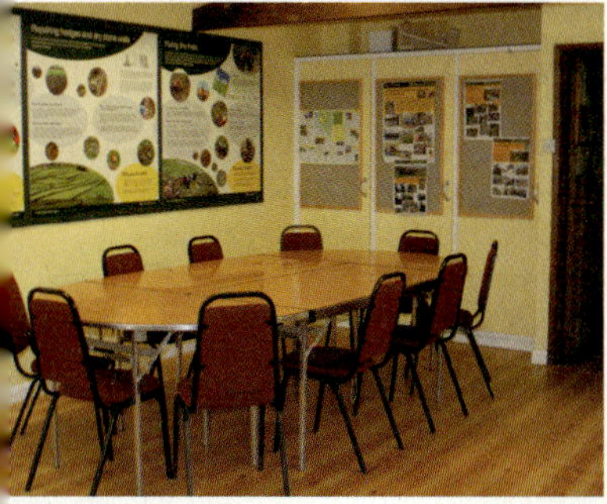

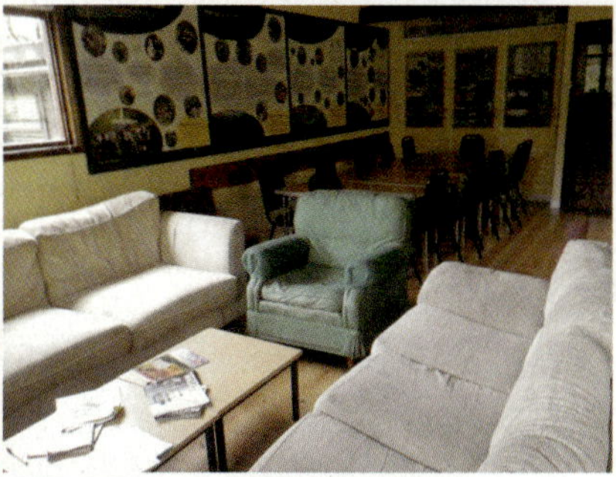

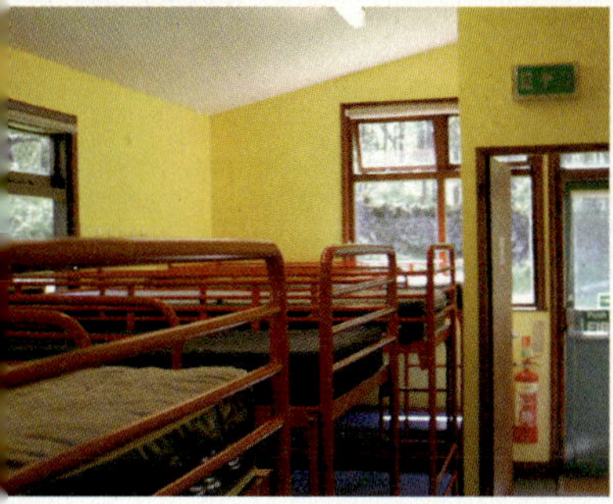

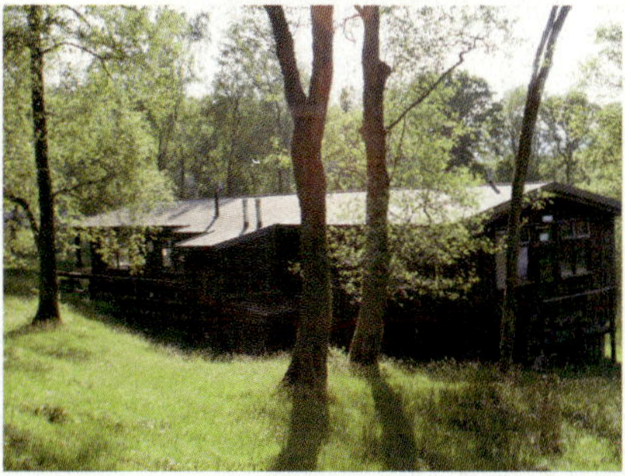

AMBLESIDE BACKPACKERS

ENGLAND

The English Lakes National Park is one of the most scenic areas of the UK made famous by the likes of Wordsworth and Beatrix Potter. Ambleside Backpackers has a great central location, ideal for fell and mountain walking, climbing, boating, scenic drives, cycle touring, mountain biking and outdoor activities. Fell walks from the front door with lakes nearby yet just 4 minutes' walk from the centre of Ambleside with its many outdoor equipment shops, cafes, restaurants and pubs. The hostel is a large, old lakeland house featuring a great lounge with comfy chairs, fire and piano, dining room & large well equipped, self-catering kitchen, drying room, laundry facilities and secure bike store. Free light breakfast, tea/coffee and internet access. With 52 beds Ambleside Backpackers can accommodate individuals, couples, groups, and families in rooms or dorms. Group and whole hostel bookings welcome. Sorry no stag, hen or drinking parties. Opening 27th March for 2015 season.

DETAILS

- **Open** - From 27th March 2015. Arive after 4.30pm and depart by 10.30am
- **Number of beds** - 52: 1x10, 1x8, 4x6, 2x4, 1x2
- **Booking** - recommended, essential for groups. See website for availability.
- **Price per night** - See website, reductions for three or more nights. All prices include light breakfast, tea, coffee, daytime and evening internet access.
- **Public Transport** - Windermere train station 4 miles then 555 bus to Ambleside.
- **Directions** - From Ambleside, Kelsick Rd bus stop: up hill to T junction turn right them immediately left into Old Lake Rd, hostel is 200m up on left. By road: A591 Windermere to Ambleside. At 2nd Hayes Garden Centre sign turn right into Old Lake Rd. hostel is 300m on right.

CONTACT: David
Tel: 015394 32340
bookings@amblesidebackpackers.com   www.amblesidebackpackers.co.uk
Ambleside BPs, Iveing Cottage, Old Lake Rd, Ambleside Cumbria, LA22 0DJ

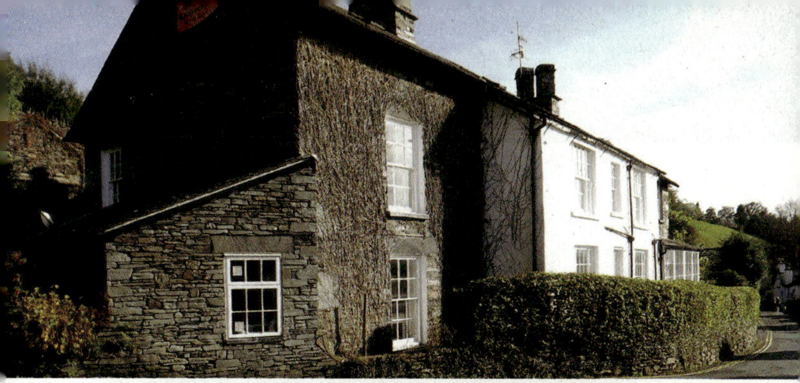

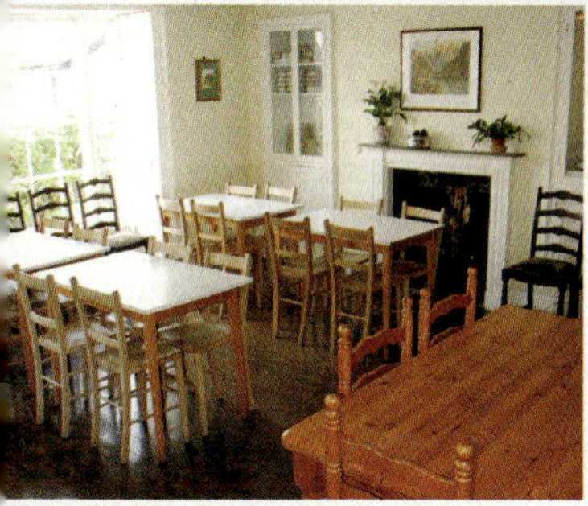

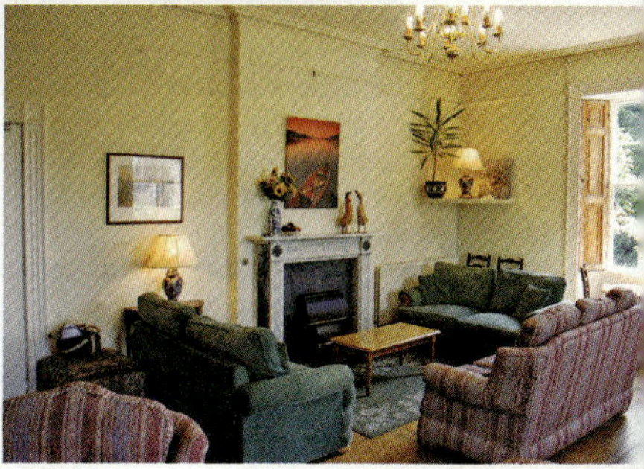

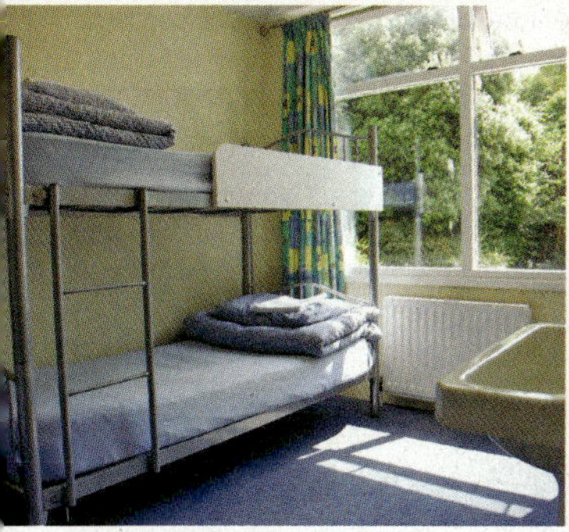

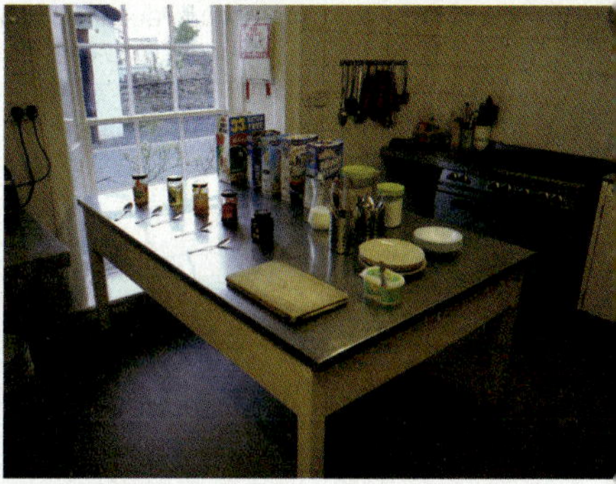

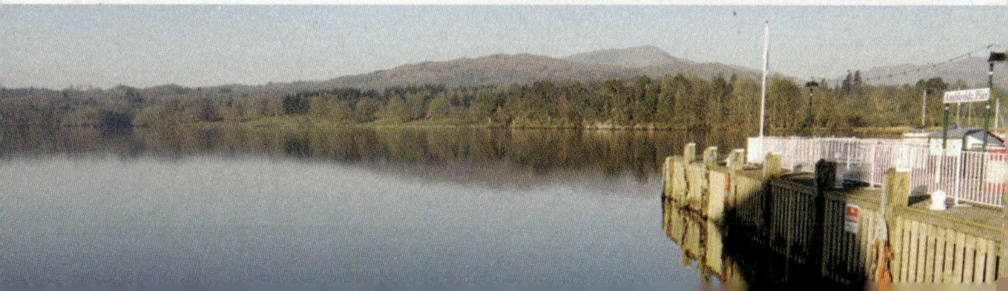

SHACKLETON LODGE

ENGLAND

This fantastic self-catered lodge is situated in a superb woodland setting at the heart of the Lake District. Located on the northern shore of Lake Windermere, 1 mile from the centre of Ambleside and 4 miles from Langdale, the combination of sweeping farmland, lake views, a backdrop of mountains and a comfortable, friendly environment ensure the best conditions for a memorable experience.

The bunkhouse features: a large communal room with 4 sofas, wide-screen TV/DVD (no reception, but great for DVDs/laptops/games consoles etc) and ample open space for games; segregated shower & toilet facilities; 9 bedrooms (there are facilities suitable for one wheelchair user). Bedding/pillows/towels are not provided. The well equipped kitchen/dining block with double-oven is another excellent communal room and also has a purpose built BBQ nearby. You may wish to bring tea towels/dish cloths, toilet rolls, soap etc. Shops and amenities can be found at Ambleside and Windermere

DETAILS

- **Open** - All year.
- **Number of beds** - 31 5x4, 2x2, 1x6, 1x1
- **Booking** - Book online, by email or by phone. £150 deposit to secure booking.
- **Price per night** - Always sole occupancy, ranging from £200 per night.
- **Public Transport** - Trains to Oxenholme, then change for Windermere (6 miles). 505 bus from Windermere train station to Clappersgate (Traveline 0870 608 2 608)
- **Directions** - Grid Ref: NY366027 1 mile from Ambleside on A593/B5286 to Hawkshead.

CONTACT: Rotha Satterthwaite
Tel: 015394 33942
admin@brathayexploration.org.uk   www.brathayexploration.org.uk/accommodation
Brathay Exploration Trust, Brathay Hall, Clappersgate, Ambleside, Cumbria, LA22 0HP

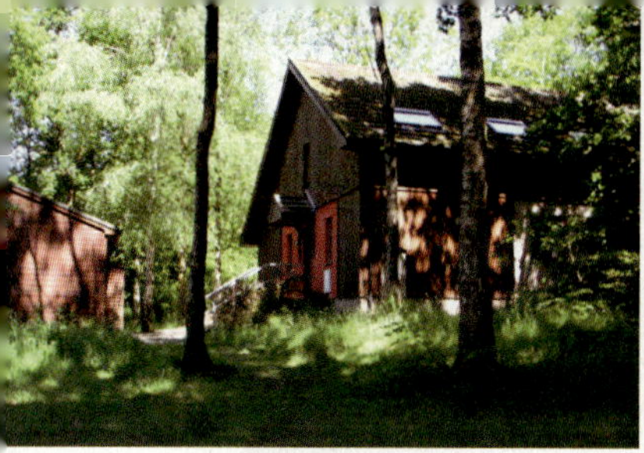
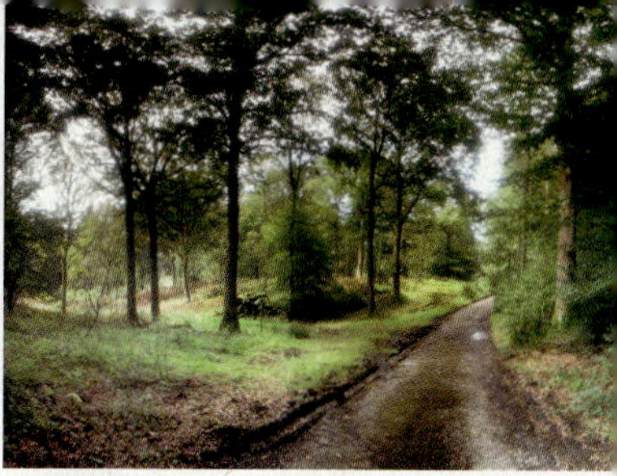
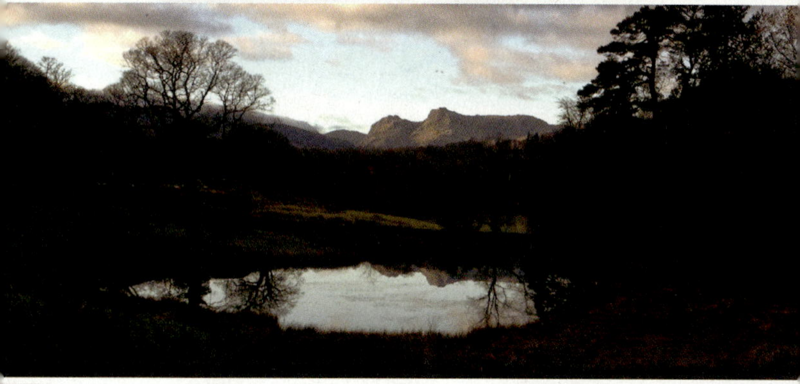
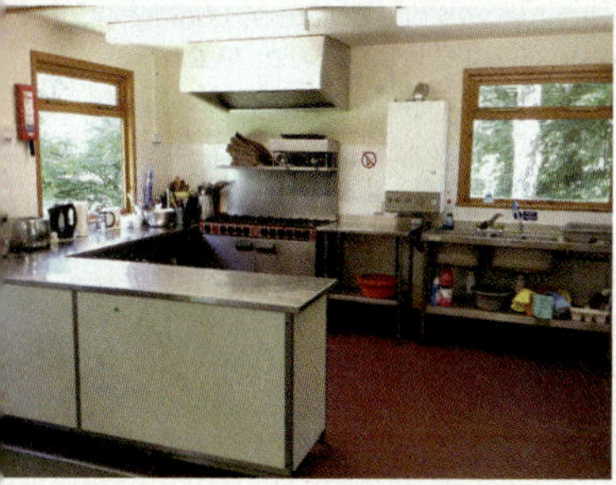
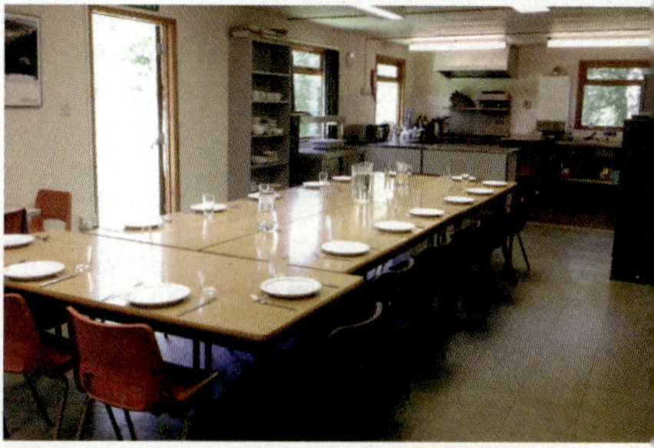
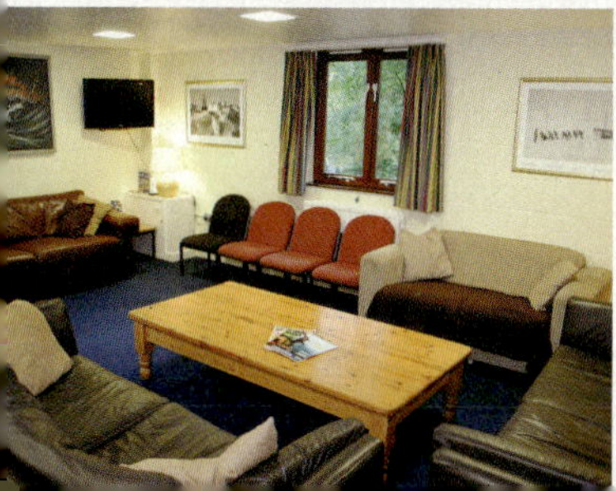
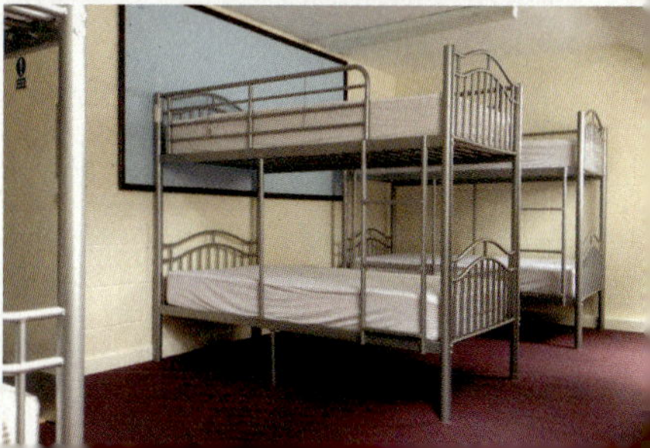

LAKE DISTRICT BACKPACKERS

ENGLAND

Situated in the heart of Windermere and central Lakeland, you will find this cosy, friendly hostel ideally situated for exploring the surrounding area. The owners can advise you on routes for walks and cycle rides and provide you with maps. Staff can also help to organise abseiling, canoeing, sailing, windsurfing, even caving! There is easy access to the lake and fells from our door and the hostel is adjacent to the main 555 bus route through Lakeland.

The hostel with its cosy dormitories provides you with every comfort but at a budget price. The hostel is right next to a number of pubs, restaurants and take-aways and only minutes away from the rail and bus stations. Lockers are available, Internet access with WiFi and Sky TV keep you in touch! A well equipped kitchen and comfortable common room make your stay one to remember.

DETAILS

- **Open** - All year, 24 hours with key code for front door.
- **Number of beds** - 20:- 1x6, 2 x4, 2 x double with single above.
- **Booking** - Essential, 24 hours in advance.
- **Price per night** - £15.50 dorms/ £18.00 private rooms. £2 discount per night for stays of 3+ nights. Includes self service continental breakfast and free tea/coffee.
- **Public Transport** - Windermere train station is 2 minutes' walk. National Express coach stop 2 minutes' walk.
- **Directions** - Turn left out of the station, walk to the information centre, the hostel is opposite, between Open Door Properties and the Lamp Lighter Bar, 2 minutes' walk from station.

CONTACT: Paul
Tel: 015394 46374, Fax: 01628 624339
info@lakedistrictbackpackers.co.uk   www.lakedistrictbackpackers.co.uk
High Street, Windermere, Cumbria, LA23 1AF

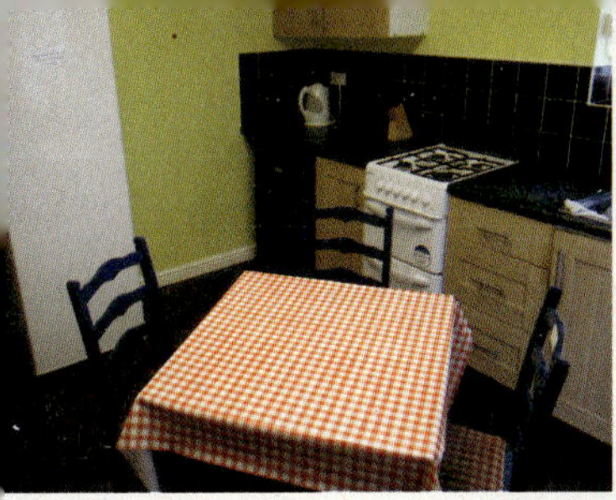
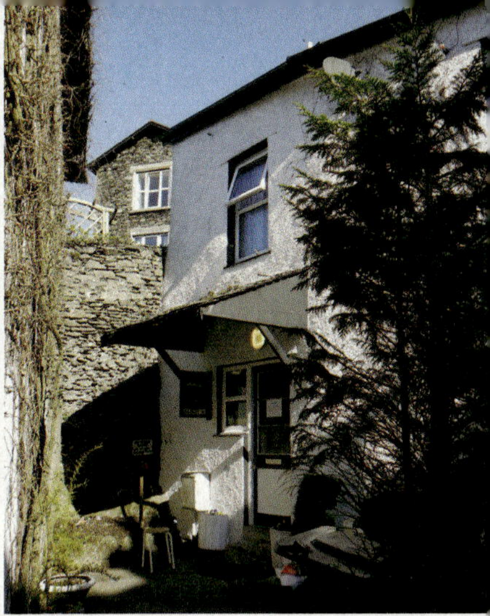
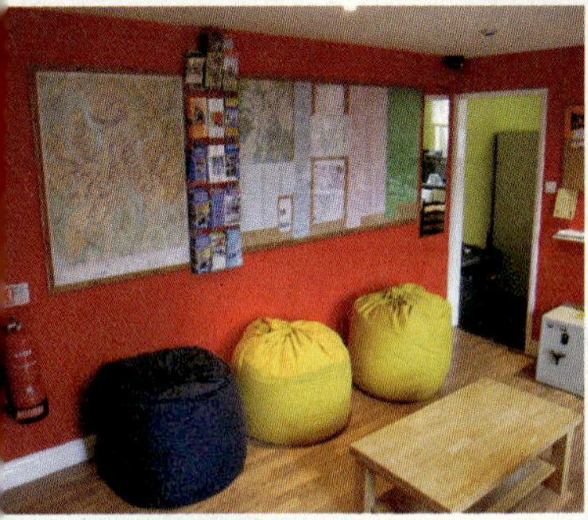
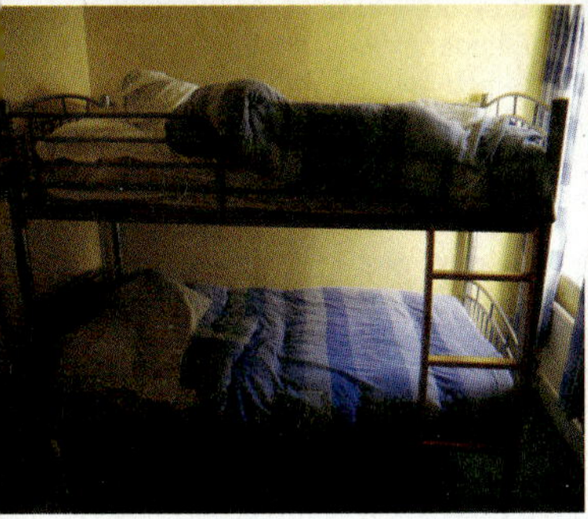
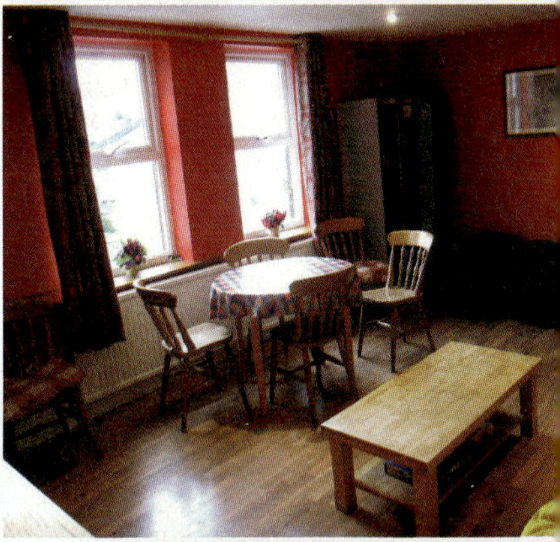
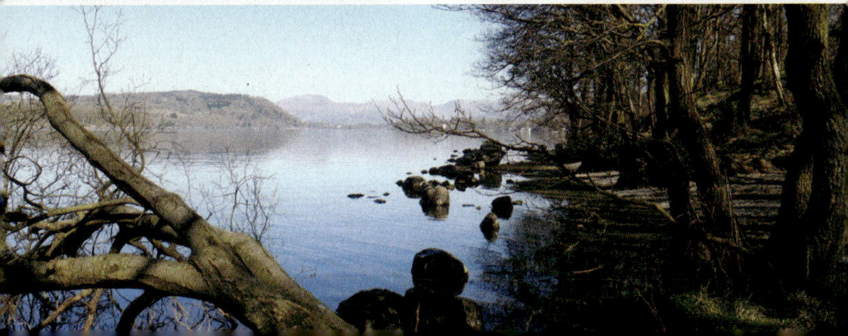

KENDAL HOSTEL

ENGLAND

Kendal Hostel is a Georgian town house in the historic market town of Kendal, next to the Brewery Arts Centre and only 200 yards to Kendal town centre. A family run, friendly hostel, home from home, with a comfortable lounge, well equipped kitchen, dining room, central heating, hot showers and drying room. The bedrooms are a range of sizes, two are en suite and all rooms have a wash basin. There is free WiFi and a good selection of local books. A Blue Badge guide lives on site and the hostel staff are always happy to pass on their excellent local knowledge. Kendal has many attractions to keep all the family entertained, including the castle ruins, Kendal Museum, Abbot Hall Art Gallery and more. A short drive/bus or train ride will take you to Lake Windermere and Bowness-on-Windermere for the Windermere Lake Cruises and the famous Beatrix Potter exhibition. The hostel is a great way to break a journey to and from Scotland as well as discovering this beautiful part of the country.

DETAILS

- **Open** - All year, 8am to 10am, 5pm to 8pm and by arrangement.
- **Number of beds** - 48:1x11,1x7(fam),1x6,1x4,1x4 (fam),1x3 (fam),1x3, 2x2. Family rooms can be used as dorms or doubles.
- **Booking** - Book by phone or email. Booking is preferable but not essential
- **Price per night** - £18.40 Sunday to Thursday, £20.40 Friday and Saturday.
- **Public Transport** - A555 National Express bus at Kendal train station. 2 minutes by taxi from Oxenholme railway station
- **Directions** - Jcn 36 A6 into Kendal 300 metres from parish church on LHS 5 minutes from bus station 10 minutes from train station.

CONTACT: Gary Muil
Tel: 01539 724066; Mob: 07795 198 197
kristina@kendalhostel.co.uk www.kendalhostel.co.uk
118-120 Highgate, Kendal, Cumbria, LA9 4HE

WYTHMOOR FARM
CAMPING BARN

227
ENGLAND

Wythmoor Camping Barn is on the Walney to Wear coast to coast cycle route and a few hundred metres from the Dales Way long distance footpath. It enjoys great views of the Howgill Fells and the distant mountains of the Central Lakes. Being only 4.5 miles from Kendal and less than 10 mins from the M6 this is an ideal location for exploring the Lake District and the Yorkshire Dales. The 19th century barn has hot water provided by solar panels (immersion heater backup), underfloor heating powered by ground source heat pump and mains electricity supplemented by wind turbine. The barn is generously sized for twelve people and includes facilities for wheelchair users, two separate heated shower rooms and a food preparation area with sinks and cooking slabs (bring your own camp-stove). Kettle and microwave are provided. Local taxis available for transport to Kendal and Sedburgh. Holmescales Farm Outdoor Centre is close by.

DETAILS

- **Open** - All year, all day
- **Number of beds** - 12: 1x12 (10 single beds, 1 double)
- **Booking** - Book online, by phone or email. Booking not always required
- **Price per night** - £10 per person.
- **Public Transport** - Oxenholme (6.5 miles) and Kendal (4.5 miles) have stations.
- **Directions** - Take Appleby Road (A685) from Kendal. After 2.5 miles turn right signed 'Docker' (single track). Opposite Docker Hall Farm, take left fork signed Lambrigg. Continue for 2 miles, barn is on left next to white farmhouse. From M6 Junction 37 take A684 towards Sedbergh; then direct left signed Lambrigg/Beck Foot. After 1.5 miles take left signed Lambrigg and Docker (single track). Barn is on right in half a mile next to white farmhouse. Sat Navs will direct you to a private drive.

CONTACT: Bruce Withington
Tel: Booking office 017687 74301
info@lakelandcampingbarns.co.uk www.lakelandcampingbarns.co.uk
Wythmoor Farm, Lambrigg, Kendal, LA8 0DH

RYDAL HALL
YOUTH CENTRE

ENGLAND

Refurbished recently, Rydal Hall Youth Centre is situated in the centre of Rydal Hall estate, sheltered on three sides by the Fairfield Horseshoe and offering access to the best of Lakeland's activities. Facilities inside provide accommodation for groups of up to 29. There are 2 dormitories sleeping 9 and 10 in each and 2 leader rooms each sleeping 4 and 6. A large common room can be used for dining or recreation. A drying room on the ground floor. A welcoming log burner provides additional warmth to the ample heating powered by our nearby water turbine. The kitchen is fully equipped for cooking. Guests need to bring sleeping bags, pillow cases and extra blankets during winter.

Rydal Hall also offers camping to groups and families and there is residential accommodation for up to 56 at the Hall in single, twin, double and family rooms with private facilities.

DETAILS

- **Open** - All year, 24 hours
- **Number of beds** - Dormitories 29: 1x10, 1x9, 1x6, 1x4.
- **Booking** - Required with deposit. No bookings by email please.
- **Price per night** - Peak season 1st April to 31st October £295.00. Off peak 1st November to 31st March £250. Late deals available please enquire.
- **Public Transport** - Trains at Windermere. National Express at Ambleside. Local Stagecoach service (555) from Lancaster to Keswick stops 200 yards from Hall.
- **Directions** - GR 366 064. Take the A561 from Ambleside to Grasmere, Rydal is reached after 2 miles. By the church turn right and go up lane for 200m.

CONTACT:
Tel: 01539 432050, Fax: 01539 434887
mail@rydalhall.org www.rydalhall.org
Rydal Hall, Ambleside, Cumbria, LA22 9LX

GREAT LANGDALE BUNKHOUSE

229 ENGLAND

Great Langdale Bunkhouse offers great value accommodation for groups, families and individuals. Situated amidst some of the finest mountain scenery in England with immediate access to world class mountain biking, road cycling, walking, fell running and climbing. The whole place is set up to explore the amazing mountains and ideal for those who love the outdoors.

The bunkhouse has 21 beds divided into 3 twin rooms, 1 room of 7 and 1 room of 8 (all bunk beds). It has gas central heating throughout with separate male and female shower and toilet facilities. There is a drying room and secure bike storage. There are no cooking or dining facilities. The Sticklebarn Tavern is located right next door and serves good value lunch and dinners. Sheet, pillow and pillowcase are provided, bring your own sleeping bag and towels. Well behaved dogs are allowed in the bunkhouse in a private room with owner.

DETAILS

- **Open** - All year, all day
- **Number of beds** - 21
- **Booking** - Booking is advised for weekends and groups, 50% deposit required.
- **Price per night** - From £15pppn
- **Public Transport** - Bus service 516 to Great Langdale from Ambleside, ask for New Dungeon Ghyll Hotel, walk 2 mins (timetable 01946 632222).
- **Directions** - From the A591 Windermere to Keswick road at Ambleside take the A593 turn to Coniston / Torver. After two miles take the B5343 to Great Langdale via Chapel Stile. The bunkhouse is adjacent to the Sticklebarn Tavern.

CONTACT:
Tel: 01539 437725
langdale.bunkhouse@gmail.com www.greatlangdalebunkhouse.co.uk
Great Langdale, LA22 9JU

THORNEY HOW
INDEPENDENT HOSTEL

Thorney How offers clean and comfortable holiday accommodation in Grasmere, the heart of the Lake District. Family-run and welcoming it provides bed and breakfast and self catering accommodation for individuals, families and groups. With the backdrop of magnificent fells, adjacent to the Coast to Coast path, local village amenities and lake, the tranquil location provides the perfect place from which to explore all the Lake District has to offer. The main house, a 350 year old gentlemen's farmhouse, is charming with well proportioned rooms and fabulous views, new for 2015 we have en suite accommodation either as a double room or a family room of 4. The newly refurbished bunkhouse overlooking the Easedale valley is ideal for smaller groups up to 16. Larger groups are automatically offered breakfasts and at least one evening meal as part of their booking price. Parking, electric car charging, bike hire, cycle store, drying room, licensed bar, café and spacious grounds complete the experience.

DETAILS

- **Open** - Open all year, closed 10.30am to 3.30pm – check in 3.30pm to 10.30pm
- **Number of beds** - 50: House 28. Bunkhouse 16. Separate unit 4/6 beds
- **Booking** - Booking online recommended, Or by phone/email. First night's fee, non-refundable, payment required to secure booking. No Pets,
- **Price per night** - House and bunkhouse beds from £18.50. Double en suite from £60.00 . 4 person rooms from £70.00. Large groups please contact hostel for prices.
- **Public Transport** - National Express coaches stop in Grasmere. Local bus 555 to / from Windermere & Keswick. Train station at Windermere.
- **Directions** - Grid ref: 332084. Half a mile NW of Grasmere Village.

CONTACT: Taylor Nuttall
Tel: 01539 435597, Fax: 01539435339
enquiries@thorneyhow.co.uk   www.thorneyhow.co.uk
Thorney How Off Helm Close & Easedale Road Grasmere Cumbria LA22 9QW

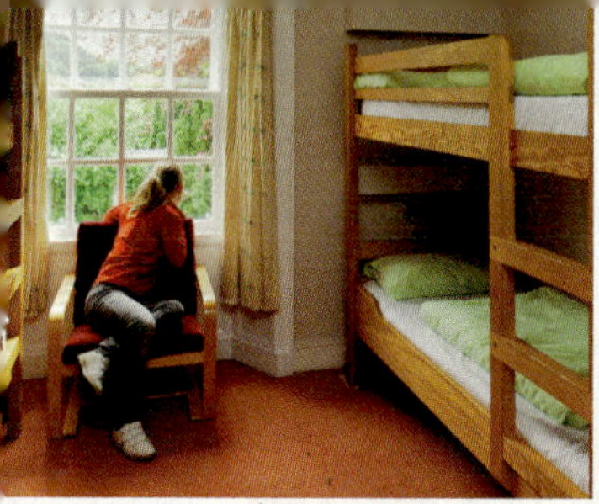
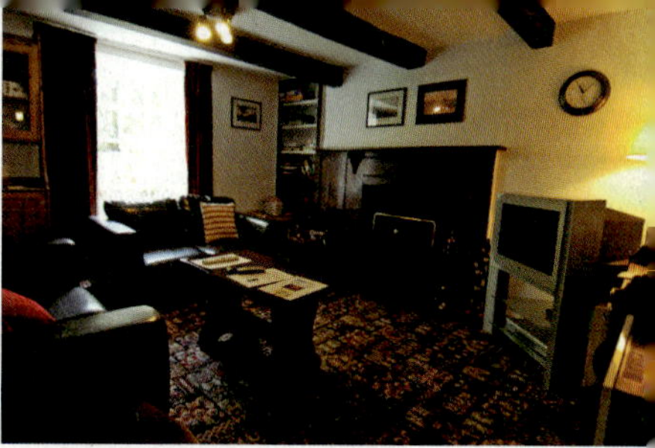
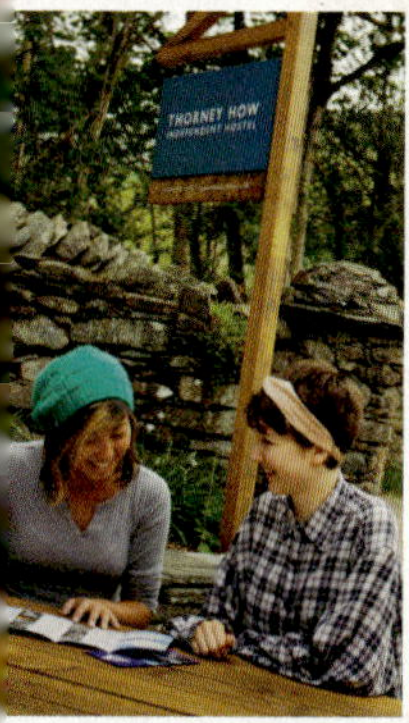
THORNEY HOW
INDEPENDENT HOSTEL
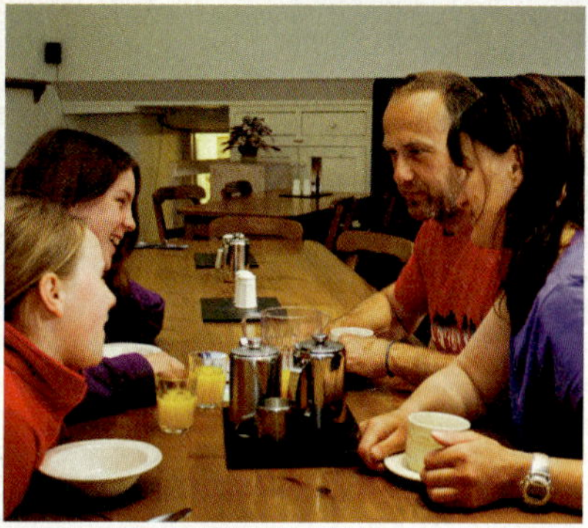
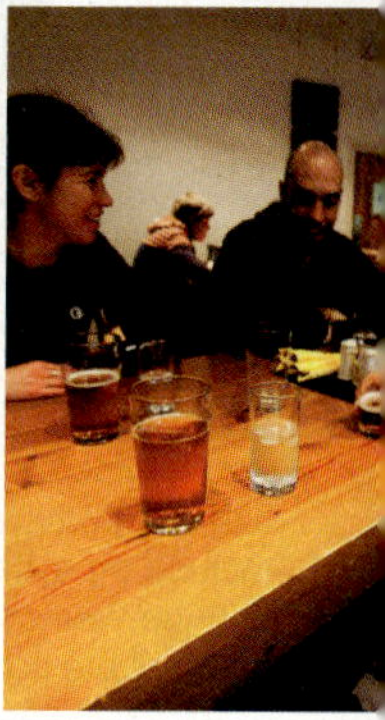
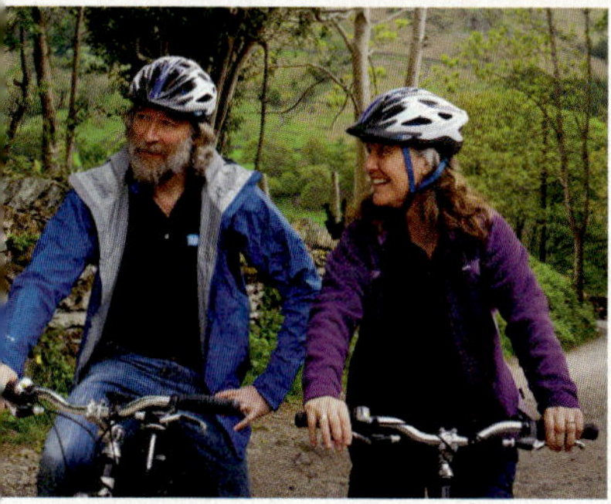
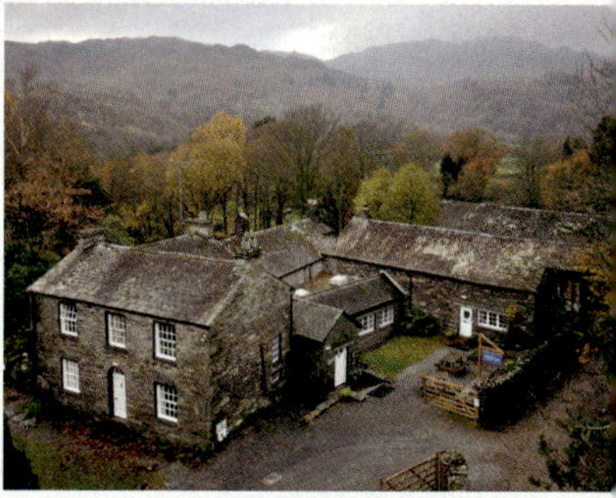
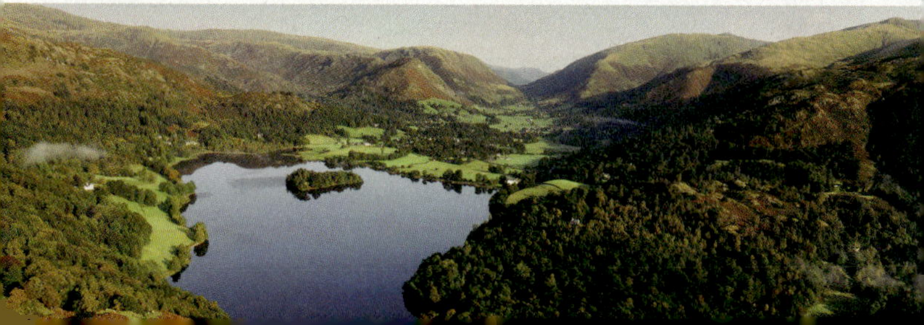

GRASMERE INDEPENDENT HOSTEL

ENGLAND

This small deluxe hostel is nestled in the heart of the Lake District National Park and a short stroll from the idyllic village of Grasmere. Grasmere Independent Hostel on Broadrayne Farm is a truly special place. The 4 star hostel is ideal for individuals, couples, families and groups. For parties requiring more space, 3 luxury cottages are available on the farm too. The hostel's extensive facilities include en suite bedrooms, 2 fully equipped self-catering kitchens, dining room, lounge, laundry area, secure bike storage, drying room, free WiFi and Internet PC, private parking, outside seating/BBQ area and even a sauna. An adjacent conference/studio room is available for an additional charge.

A stunning location midway between Windermere and Keswick makes Grasmere the perfect base for your holiday, whether you are on a quest for adventure, relaxation or celebration. Grasmere Independent Hostel has been praised by the Guardian, The Rough Guide and others.

DETAILS

- **Open** - All year, Reception open until 9pm. Keypad entry system.
- **Number of beds** - 24: 1x3, 1x4, 1x5, 2x6.
- **Booking** - Advisable.
- **Price per night** - From £20 pppn. Sole use from £475 per night.
- **Public Transport** - Trains at Windermere. 555 bus from Windermere or Keswick, ask for Traveller's Rest pub. National Express coach from London to Grasmere daily.
- **Directions** - GR 336 094 1.25 miles north of the village. Stay on the A591 right to our drive, 400m north of Traveller's Rest pub on the right hand side.

CONTACT: Dave Keighley
Tel: 015394 35055
dave@grasmerehostel.co.uk www.grasmerehostel.co.uk
Broadrayne Farm, Keswick Road, Grasmere, Cumbria, LA22 9RU

GRASMERE
Independent
HOSTEL
Tel: 015394 35055
www.grasmerehostel.co.uk

SHEPHERD'S CROOK BUNKHOUSE

234 — ENGLAND

Noran Bank Farm is situated near Lake Ullswater just through Patterdale in Cumbria. Only 5 minutes' walk away from the Coast to Coast route as well as The Westmorland Way which is a 95 mile walk along generally good paths beginning in the famous horse fair town of Appleby and ending at Arnside, all within the old County of Westmorland. Shepherd's Crook Bunkhouse is a barn conversion, converted to a very high standard and sleeps 8. Upstairs it has a two bedded room with en suite shower and a 6 bedded room. On the ground floor there is a fully equipped kitchen, seating area in which to relax, loo and wet room with 2 showers. Duvets, linen and towels are provided. DIY breakfast and packed lunches are available if pre-booked. A well behaved dog considered at owners discretion. "Shepherd's Crook" is very popular with overnight stays on the Coast to Coast route and with week-end breaks for walking and cycling enthusiasts. It is also a fantastic meeting place for family and friends get-togethers.

DETAILS

- **Open** - All year.
- **Number of beds** - 8: 1x6, 1x2
- **Booking** - Please book by phone or email.
- **Price per night** - £14pp(6 bed room), £19pp (double room) plus £5 for single occupancy. Sole use: £110 per night, D.I.Y breakfast £6, B&B in farmhouse £30pp. Dogs £4 per dog per night. Packed Lunch £5.
- **Public Transport** - Trains at Penrith (14 miles). Buses at Patterdale (half a mile).
- **Directions** - Take A592 from Patterdale south, farm is on right in half a mile.

CONTACT: Mrs Heather Jackson
Tel: 017684 82327 Mob: 07833 981504, Fax: 017684 82327
heathernoranbank@fsmail.net www.patterdale.org/Noranbank.htm
Noran Bank Farm, Patterdale, Penrith, Cumbria, CA11 0NR

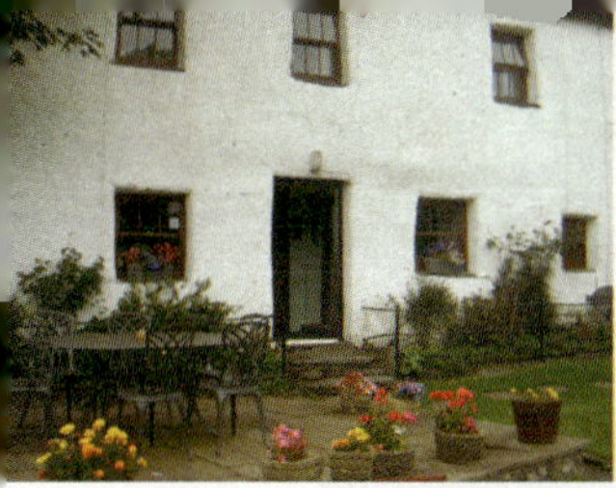
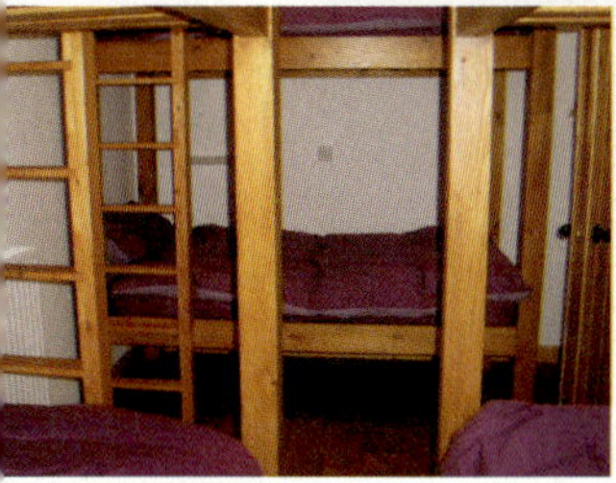
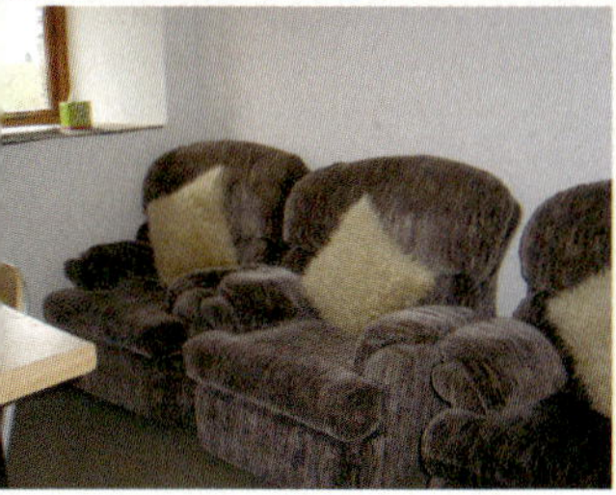
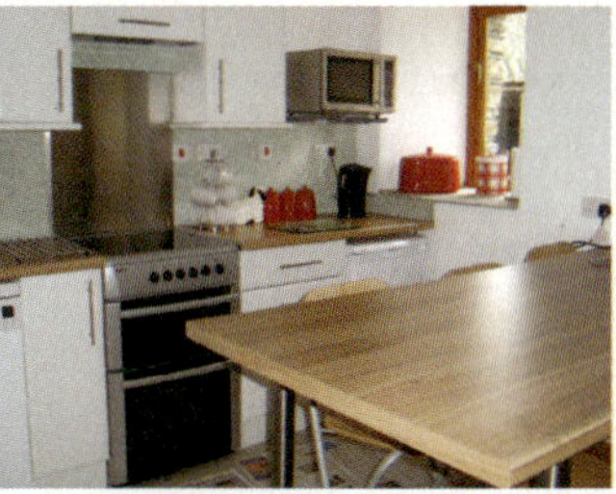
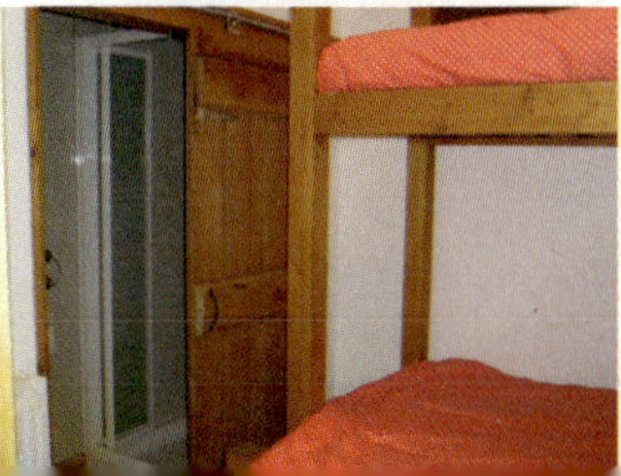
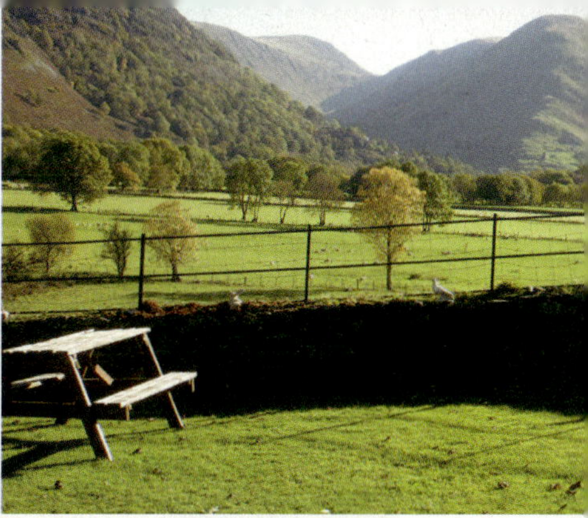
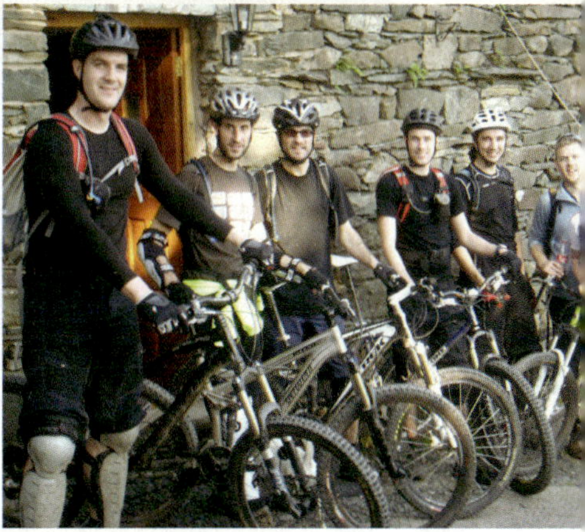
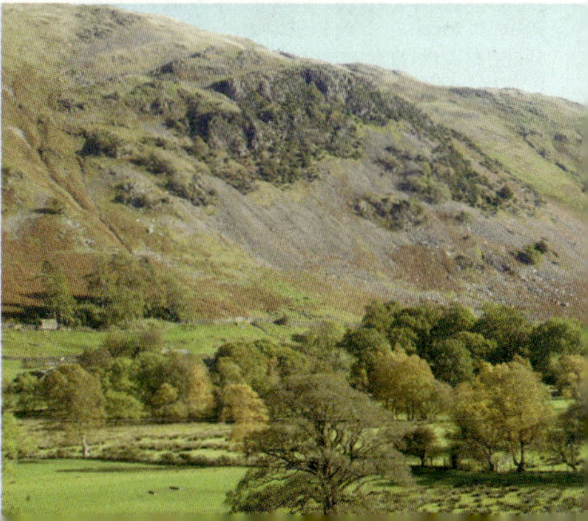

FISHER-GILL CAMPING BARN

ENGLAND

Situated in Thirlmere at the foot of the Helvellyn range of mountains, close to Sticks Pass and spectacular Fisher-gill waterfall, with numerous walks, hill and rock climbing from the barn, it's an ideal place for touring the Lake District being just off the A591 road, with local and national bus stops at the end of the lane. Accommodation consists of two rooms: a kitchen/diner with fridge, 4 ring calor gas stove, kettle, toaster, tables and chairs, and all pots, pans etc and a sleeping area consisting of 10 bunk beds with mattresses, pillows, blankets and duvets (sleeping bags/liners are required). Both rooms have a wood-burning stove with a daily allowance of wood included (extra is available from the farm). There's also a shower cubicle (metered), toilet, wash basin and a small seating area. Outside there is ample parking with a small patio area, tables and chairs. A pub serving meals is nearby (approx a quarter of a mile).

Keswick is 5 miles, Grasmere 7 miles. Open all year. Pets by arrangement. The barn is ideal for quite country retreats, not suitable for late night drinking parties.

DETAILS

- **Open** - All year, all day
- **Number of beds** - 10
- **Booking** - Advanced booking recommended.
- **Price per night** - £13pp. £130 sole occupancy.
- **Public Transport** - Local and national buses stop at the end of the lane on A591.
- **Directions** - Travelling on the A591 SE from Keswick, after about 5 miles take 1st lane on left after junction with B5322. Barn is after about 100m.

CONTACT: Mrs Jean Hodgson
Tel: 017687 73232 or 017687 74391
stybeckfarm@farming.co.uk   www.stybeckfarm.co.uk
Stybeck Farm, Thirlmere, Keswick, Cumbria CA12 4TN

ELTERWATER HOSTEL

ENGLAND

Elterwater Hostel (formerly YHA Elterwater) is located in the peaceful village of Elterwater, in the Langdale valley, 15 minutes' drive from Ambleside. The area has many walks for people of all abilities, from gentle riverside meanders to the challenge presented by the Langdale Pikes, Bowfell and Scafell. Banks, shops and other amenities are available nearby.

The area is also a favourite for both on and off-road cycling, rock climbing and many other outdoor activities. An ideal overnight stop on the Cumbria way.

The hostel is an ideal venue for individuals, families, outdoor groups, schools and college trips.

DETAILS

- **Open** - All year; (Nov-Feb Groups only), 7:30am to 11:30pm. Reception open 7:30 to 10:00 and 17:00 to 22:30
- **Number of beds** - 40: 6 x 2 beds, 1 x 4 beds, 4 x 6 beds
- **Booking** - Booking advisable all year round, via website or phone.
- **Price per night** - Beds from £18pppn. For exclusive hire please call. Low season discounts may be available.
- **Public Transport** - From Ambleside: Stagecoach-in-Cumbria route 516 towards Dungeon Ghyll
- **Directions** - from Ambleside take the A593. After 2 miles, turn right onto the B5343. After 2 miles go over cattle grid, then next left. Go through the village, the hostel is right.

CONTACT:
Tel: 015394 37245
enquiries@elterwaterhostel.co.uk   www.elterwaterhostel.co.uk
Elterwater YHA, Elterwater, Ambleside LA22 9HX

DERWENTWATER INDEPENDENT HOSTEL

ENGLAND

Family run and friendly, Derwentwater Independent Hostel is a Georgian mansion in 17 acres of grounds complete with its own waterfall. The glorious setting near the lake gives wonderful views of the surrounding mountains and is just 2 miles from Keswick. A great base for individuals, families, groups, family parties, reunions and conferences, the hostel has lounges, games rooms and free WiFi. It is licensed and offers a full meal service with a good reputation for home made food. Many of the spacious bedrooms have lovely original architecture. The grounds, which teem with wildlife, including red squirrels, have plenty of space for children to play, football goals, picnic tables and open water access for launching canoes & boats onto the lake. Borrowdale has something for everyone; walks along the lake shore, challenging mountains, water sports, mountain biking, climbing, gorge scrambling and tourist attractions. Friendly staff are happy to help you organise your days. The C2C route passes close by.

DETAILS

- **Open** - All year, 7am - 11pm
- **Number of beds** - 88: 1x4, 2x5, 3x6, 3x8, 1x10, 1x22
- **Booking** - Advance booking recommended - especially for groups
- **Price per night** - From £20 (adult), £15.50 (child). Family rooms from £68 (for 4). The smallest rooms are for 4 & 5 but please ask if you want a room for 2 or 3.
- **Public Transport** - Train to Penrith then X4 bus to Keswick. From Keswick take the launch to the jetty 100 metres from hostel or bus no 78 to hostel drive.
- **Directions** - Two miles south of Keswick on the B5289 Borrowdale road. Hostel entrance is directly off the main road, 150m after the turning to Watendlath.

CONTACT:
Tel: 017687 77246, Fax: 017687 77396
contact@derwentwater.org www.derwentwater.org
Barrow House, Borrowdale, Keswick, Cumbria, CA12 5UR

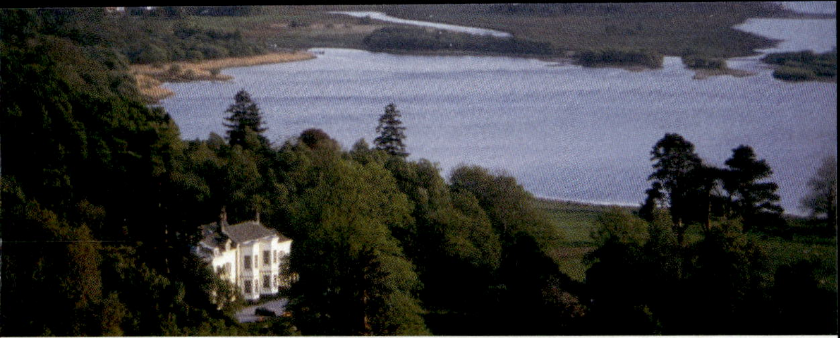
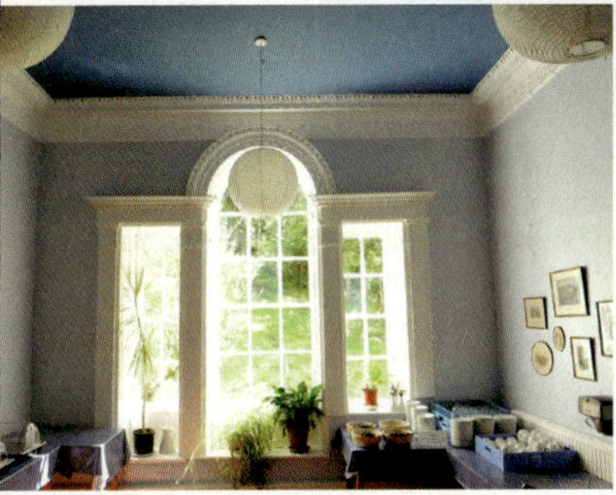
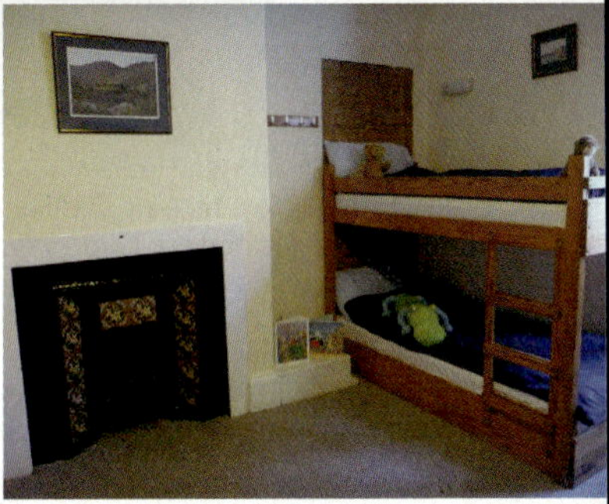
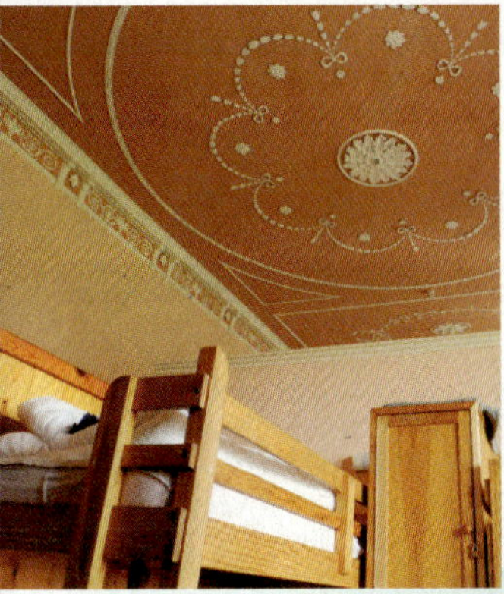
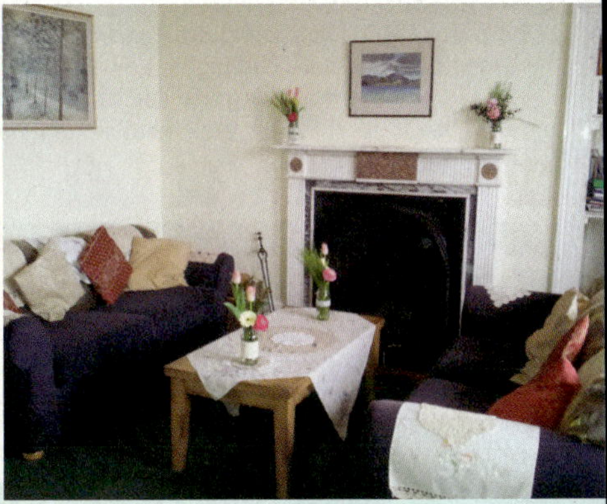
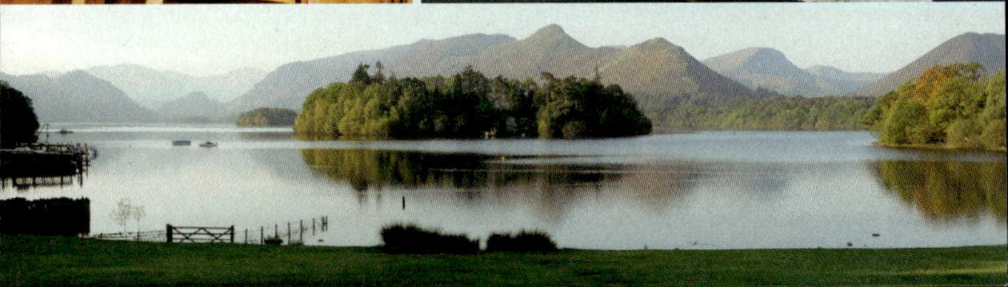

240 ST JOHN'S-IN-THE-VALE CAMPING BARN
ENGLAND

St John's-in-the-Vale Camping Barn is adapted from an 18th Century stable and hayloft, in an idyllic setting. Overlooking St John's Beck, the peaceful hill farm has stunning views to Blencathra, Helvellyn and Castle Rock.

The Barn has a sleeping area upstairs (mattress provided) with a sitting and dining area below. Separate toilet, shower and cooking area (bring your own stove, cooking and eating equipment) are within the building. A wood-burning stove provides a focal point and warmth!

There is a BBQ and seating area outside and, as there is no light pollution, this is magical on a star-filled night. Low Bridge End Farm has a tea garden - all home baking. To see more and book online go to:
www.lakelandcampingbarns.co.uk

DETAILS

- **Open** - All year, 24 hours
- **Number of beds** - 8 : 1x8
- **Booking** - Advised in advance. Credit card booking available on 017687 74301
- **Price per night** - £10 per person.
- **Public Transport** - Trains terminate at Windermere. From there take a 555 bus towards Keswick. Get off at Thirlmere Dam Road End (Smaithwaite). Climb over ladder stile and we are ½ mile north along a footpath.
- **Directions** - Leave M6 at junction 40. Take A66 towards Keswick for 14 miles. Turn left onto B5322 St Johns-in-the-Vale Road. 3 miles along the road on the right.

CONTACT: Graham or Sarah
Tel: 017687 79242 (Bookings 017687 74301)
info@campingbarn.com   www.campingbarn.com
Low Bridge End Farm, St John's-in-the-Vale, Keswick, CA12 4TS

MAGGS HOWE
CAMPING BARN

241

ENGLAND

Kentmere is a quiet, unspoilt valley within the Lake District National Park. It's a ramblers' paradise with woods, fields, lanes, a scattering of traditional lakeland farms and dwellings and of course the fells with their walks so favoured by Wainwright. The Lakeland to Lindisfarne long distance path passes this way as well as the mountain bikers' and horse riders' Coast to Coast. Kentmere offers plenty of activities which include biking, riding and fishing, but most of all quiet enjoyment. A pleasant day's visit can be found at the market town of Kendal and Lake Windermere which are only 20 minutes away. The converted barn has two sleeping areas, kitchen, two showers and toilets. All you need is your sleeping bag, mattresses are provided. Breakfasts and suppers are available next door at the B&B with notice.

DETAILS

- **Open** - All year, 24 hours
- **Number of beds** - 14: 1 x 6   1 x 8
- **Booking** - Recommended with 50% deposit for groups. Individuals can book but not essential
- **Price per night** - £12 per person or £120 sole use. Friday and Saturday night must be on a sole use booking at £120 per night or a surcharge of £60 added if only 1 night taken.
- **Public Transport** - Staveley 4 miles with train and bus service. Oxenholme train station is 10 miles. Kendal / Windermere National Express 8 miles.
- **Directions** - GR 462 041, MAP OS English Lakes South East. Green Quarter. Leave the A591 and come into Staveley, proceed to Kentmere for 4 miles, then take right fork to Green Quarter keeping right until you reach Maggs Howe.

CONTACT: Christine Hevey
Tel: 01539 821689
enquiry@maggshowe.co.uk   www.maggshowe.co.uk
Maggs Howe, Kentmere, Kendal, Cumbria, LA8 9JP

DENTON HOUSE

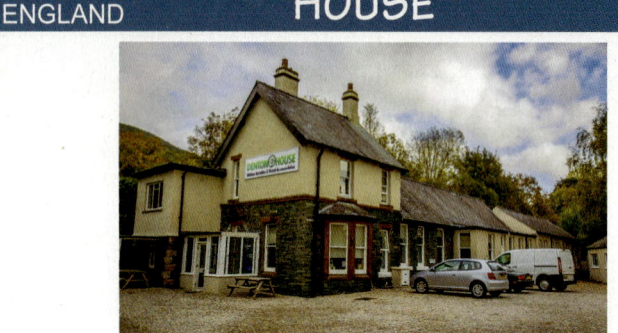

Denton House is a purpose built hostel and outdoor centre in the heart of the Lake District offering bunkhouse style accommodation designed for groups. There is plenty of hot water for showers, central heating throughout, a self-catering kitchen, a large dining room and solid bunk-beds. All linen provided. Breakfasts, packed lunches and evening meals are all available upon request.

The centre is also available for large groups looking for sole use. There is a car park for 40 cars and the outdoor centre provides traditional activities for groups seeking an adrenaline rush. Activities include Ghyll scrambling, climbing, abseiling, via ferrata and mountain challenge events. Storage for kayaks and bikes is available and there's access to the River Greta just across the road.

DETAILS

- **Open** - Open all year (including Christmas). Office hours 9.00am - 20.00pm everyday.
- **Number of beds** - 56: 1x4, 2x6, 1x8, 2x10, 1x12.
- **Booking** - Due to large number of school, youth and military groups, corporate team-builds and celebration weekends, early booking is advised. 25% deposit for groups with the balance due 28 days before arrival. No booking for groups undertaking activities elsewhere without prior arrangement
- **Price per night** - £17 midweek, £19 weekend. Sole use £900 (midweek) £999 (weekend). Breakfast £6. Pack Lunch £6. Dinner £10. Activities £30/half day.
- **Public Transport** - Nearest train station Penrith, buses hourly to Keswick.
- **Directions** - Go out of Keswick towards Windermere, keep the river on your left (approx 10 mins). Denton House is on the right after post sorting office.

CONTACT: Mark Johnson (Manager)
Tel: 017687 75351
keswickhostel@hotmail.co.uk www.dentonhouse-keswick.co.uk
Penrith Road, Keswick, Cumbria, CA12 4JW

THE WHITE HORSE INN [243]
BUNKHOUSE
ENGLAND

The White Horse Inn Bunkhouse has been converted from the stables of this traditional Lake District inn at the foot of Blencathra. The White Horse is a country pub with great pub food, open fires, local ales and a warm welcome. Four of the stables have been converted into bedrooms, two sleeping 6 people in bunks, one sleeping eight and one sleeping four. There is a basic kitchen with electric hob, microwave and a coin operated clothes dryer and a communal dining area seating 16-20 people. The toilet block has male and female toilets, basins and showers. Guests are welcome to socialise in the pub which is open from 11am to 11pm and has free WiFi, hot drinks and good beer. Food is served 12-2pm and 6-9pm on weekdays and all day on weekends. The White Horse is just outside the picturesque village of Threlkeld at the foot of the Blencathra and Sharp Edge, ideal for trekking, with paths to the mountains immediately from the beer garden. The Coast to Coast (C2C) route snakes past the front door of the inn which remains a popular stop for thirsty cyclists and walkers alike.

DETAILS

- **Open** - All year, all day access
- **Number of beds** - 24. 1 x 8, 2 x 6, 1 x 4
- **Booking** - Book by phone or email.
- **Price per night** - £10 pppn, 4 bunk room £40, 6 bunk room £60, 8 bunk £80, sole use £200. Pillow, sheet and duvet £5 for the stay. Enquire for Xmas/New Year prices
- **Public Transport** - From Penrith train station, 15 mins by taxi or catch the X5 or X4 bus from Penrith to Keswick and ask for Scales, stops outside pub on the A66.
- **Directions** - Just off A66 Penrith to Keswick road, 4m from Keswick (see signs).

CONTACT: Heather
Tel: 017687 79883
info@thewhitehorse-blencathra.co.uk www.thewhitehorse-blencathra.co.uk
The White Horse Inn, Scales, Nr Threlkeld, Keswick, CA12 4SY

SKIDDAW HOUSE
ENGLAND

At 1550 feet, Skiddaw House is the highest YHA affiliated hostel in Britain. A former shooting lodge and shepherd's bothy on the Cumbria Way, it is an ideal base for exploring the little used and quiet northern fells. This is a remote and isolated place in which to reflect on the wilderness, with no sign of the 21st century in any direction. With no electricity, phones, or TV to distract from the vista of a clear unpolluted starry night, this is simple accommodation with fires as the only heating. No noise pollution from traffic as the nearest road is 3½ miles away, yet only an hour or so's walk from civilisation. Low voltage electric lights provided by solar panels keep the quaint atmosphere of the hostel. Walkers and cyclists are advised to bring a map and torch. Campers welcome.

DETAILS

- **Open** - 1st March to 31st Oct, Open mornings until 10am and 5pm to 11pm
- **Number of beds** - 22 : 1 x 8, 2 x 5, 1 x 4
- **Booking** - Book for groups of 5 or more by email, text or phone (post is slow).
- **Price per night** - £18 (over 21), £13.50 (16-21), £9.50 (under 16).
YHA members £1.50 - £3 discount. Camping £9.50. Credit / debit cards not accepted.
- **Public Transport** - Nearest trains and National Express coaches at Penrith. From Penrith take X4 or X5 bus towards Keswick and Workington. Alight at the Horse and Farrier (Threlkeld). From Carlisle take 554 bus to Keswick (only 3 per day). Alight at Castle Inn (Bassenthwaite) and then walk 6 miles.
- **Directions** - No access for cars, nearest tarmac road 3½ miles. Vehicles can be left at Fell Car Park by Blencathra Centre above Threlkeld, at Lattrigg Car Park (end of Gale Rd near Applethwaite) or at Whitewater Dash Falls south of Bassenthwaite.

CONTACT: Martin or Marie
Tel: 07747 174293
skiddawhouse@yahoo.co.uk www.skiddawhouse.co.uk
Bassenthwaite, Keswick, Cumbria, CA12 4QX

CATBELLS
CAMPING BARN

245

ENGLAND

Catbells Camping Barn is part of a traditional set of farm buildings dating back to the 14th century. The barn is on the slopes of Catbells in the tranquil Newlands Valley, with magnificent views over the Lake District. The Cumberland Way passes through the farmyard. Keswick is only 4 miles away and both Borrowdale and Buttermere are within walking distance. The camping barn is on the ground floor and has sleeping accommodation for 10, with mattresses provided. Bring your own sleeping bags. The barn is heated with a multi-fuel stove (not suitable for cooking) and wood can be bought at the farm. In the adjacent building is a toilet and a cooking area suitable for a camping stove. Bring your own stove, cutlery, crockery and cooking utensils. It is possible to walk to a pub which serves food.

DETAILS

- **Open** - All year, , , 24 hours
- **Number of beds** - 10: 1x10
- **Booking** - Advisable, groups require deposit.
- **Price per night** - £10 per person.
- **Public Transport** - Trains at Penrith (20 miles). Regular buses (meet the trains) from Penrith to Keswick. Summer bus from Keswick to Buttermere stops ½ mile from barn. Summer ferry from Keswick to Hawes End (¾ mile from barn).
- **Directions** - GR 245211. Leave the M6 at Junction 40 and follow the A66 past Keswick. At Portinscale turn left, follow the Buttermere road for 3 miles. Turn sharp left at Stair, follow the sign for Skelgill, up the road for ½ mile and right into farmyard. Please follow these directions and not those from 'sat-nav'.

CONTACT: Mrs Grave
Tel: 017687 74301 or 0709 2031363
info@lakelandcampingbarns.co.uk www.lakelandcampingbarns.co.uk
Low Skelgill, Newlands, Keswick, Cumbria, CA12 5UE

HAWSE END CENTRE

ENGLAND

Hawse End Centre, at the head of the magnificent Borrowdale Valley and directly across Derwentwater from Keswick, has stunning views and access to lakeside, mountains and Keswick (via launch or lakeside walk). The house is a large, comfortable, country mansion, ideal for groups. It has a well equipped and spacious self-catering kitchen with a professional catering oven & hob, a large dining room, lounge, games room, classroom and extensive grounds leading down to the lake shore. The Cottage for individuals, families and groups has a basic self-catering kitchen, living room and a patio with picnic tables and views of the lake. Two yurts with stunning views and transparent domes for star gazing, are on a wooden platform close to the house. These felt and wood structures have electricity, tables and chairs (optional) and mats for sleeping. Picnic tables, a gas barbeque and water are also on the platform with toilets close by. A catering service can be made available by prior arrangement. Outdoor activities can all be booked in advance and are led by experienced and well qualified outdoor leaders.

DETAILS

- **Open** - All year.
- **Number of beds** - House 50: (9 rooms) Cottage 24: (6 rooms) Yurts: 24 (2x12)
- **Booking** - Please book by phone or email. Deposit required.
- **Price per night** - Price on application, subject to availability and season.
- **Public Transport** - Trains at Penrith (18 miles). Keswick Launch passenger ferry from Keswick to Hawse End. Service buses within walking distance in high season.
- **Directions** - 4 miles outside of Keswick.

CONTACT:
Tel: 01768 812280 , Fax: 01768 812290
cumbriaoutdoors.enquiries@cumbria.gov.uk
Hawse End Centre, Portinscale, Keswick, Cumbria, CA12 5UE

LOW GILLERTHWAITE FIELD CENTRE

ENGLAND

Towards the head of Ennerdale valley, one of the most beautiful, least spoilt and quietest valleys in the Lake District, at the foot of Pillar and Red Pike sits Low Gillerthwaite Field Centre. An ideal base for fell walking, classic rock climbs, bird and wildlife watching, mountain biking, orienteering, canoeing and environmental studies.

Originally a 15th century farmhouse, the centre has group self-catering facilities, drying room, a library of environmental books, a large barn for indoor activities (ideal for barn dances), a group lecture room and two lounges with log burning fires. Due to its remoteness the centre generates its own electricity via a hydroelectric scheme. Vehicle access is by forest track and a BT payphone is on site (most mobiles do not work here). Low Gillerthwaite is an ideal base for clubs, extended family groups, school and youth groups.

DETAILS

- **Open** - All year (except Christmas and Boxing Day), 24 hours
- **Number of beds** - 40: 2x4, 1x8, 1x10, 1x14
- **Booking** - See booking link. Always phone to check availability
- **Price per night** - From £11.00 per person (children and students), £14.50 (adults), camping is £5 per person.
- **Public Transport** - Whitehaven Station 12 miles. Buses to Ennerdale Bridge from Cleator Moor or Cockermouth (5 miles).
- **Directions** - GR NY 139 141. From Ennerdale Bridge take road east, via Croasdale, 3.5 miles to Ennerdale Forest. Continue on forest track 3 miles. Hostel is the first building below the RH road, 200m before the YHA.

CONTACT: Ellen or Walter
Tel: 01946 861229, Fax: 01900824718
Warden@lgfc.org.uk www.lgfc.org.uk
Ennerdale, Cleator, CA23 3AX

HIGH HOUSE

ENGLAND

High House in Seathwaite, at the head of the popular valley of Borrowdale, offers comfortable bunkhouse/hostel self-catering accommodation in a converted 16/17 century farmhouse set within its own grounds. It is popular with walking and climbing clubs and is regularly used by outdoor education and corporate groups. Early booking is advised, especially for weekends. The building is let to one group at a time. Two dorms are available each with toilet, washbasin and shower. There is a third dorm reserved for K Fellfarers members and on some occasions club members may use this room during your stay. There is a common room with stove, easy chairs, library and dining area, a recently upgraded kitchen and car parking. You will need to bring sleeping bags or duvets plus sheets, pillows, tea towels, firelighters and food. Basic food (eg. milk) is available from the café in Rosthwaite and the nearest supermarket is in Keswick. Eco friendly washing up liquid is provided to aid the septic tank.

DETAILS

- **Open** - All year, 24 hours
- **Number of beds** - 26: 1x18, 1x8
- **Booking** - Early booking essential. Clubs only. Min. 2 nights at weekends. £40pn deposit. Send to Briarcliffe, Carr Bank Rd, Carr Bank, Milnthorpe, Cumbria, LA7 7LE.
- **Price per night** - £145 irrespective of numbers. Midweek rates negotiable for multiple bookings. Including electricity and heating. £50 key deposit is required.
- **Public Transport** - The nearest train station is in Penrith 26 miles away. Buses run from Penrith to Keswick, and from Keswick to Seatoller (1 mile from High House).
- **Directions** - OS Grid Ref NY235119

CONTACT: Hugh Taylor
Tel: 01524 762 067
jhugh.taylor@btinternet.com   www.highhouse.talktalk.net/ff.htm
High House, Seathwaite, Borrowdale, Keswick.

CRAGG BARN
CAMPING BARN

249

ENGLAND

Cragg Barn Camping Barn is a traditional stone-built barn with stunning views of Buttermere fells. It has a kitchen and seating area with electric heater and socket on a meter, a sink and cold running water. There is a hot shower on a meter, a toilet and washbasin with hot and cold water. The sleeping area has 8 mattresses, bring your own sleeping bag. You need a stove and eating utensils if you wish to self-cater. Well behaved dogs welcome - sole occupancy only. Cragg Barn is a great base for walkers of all abilities. It is also ideal for climbing, mountain biking (bike storage in barn), fishing and wildlife/bird-watching. There are many local tourist attractions within a short drive. Cragg House Farm also has a holiday cottage sleeping two. Check the websites www.buttermerecottage.co.uk or www.lakelandcampingbarns.co.uk and book online.

DETAILS

- **Open** - All year, arrival from 4pm, late arrivals by arrangement
- **Number of beds** - 8: 1 x 8
- **Booking** - Booking essential at least 24 hrs in advance. Book online.
- **Price per night** - £10 per person.
- **Public Transport** - Train stations at Penrith / Workington. Bus links from Penrith station and Workington town centre to Keswick. Bus runs seasonally from Keswick.
- **Directions** - GR NY 173 171. From Keswick follow signs to Borrowdale, continue through Rosthwaite, Seatoller and over Honister Pass. Continue past Buttermere lake into Buttermere village. Keep on main road. Cragg House Farm is on the left on the brow of the hill before you get to NT car park. In icy conditions approach from Cockermouth town centre and continue through Lorton. Turn left to Buttermere following road signs. Cragg Farm is 1st on the right past the Buttermere village sign.

CONTACT: John and Vicki Temple
Tel: Camping Barn 017687 74301. Holiday Cottage 017687 70204
info@lakelandcampingbarns.co.uk www.buttermerecottage.co.uk
Cragg House Farm, Buttermere, Cockermouth, Cumbria, CA13 9XA

SWALLOW BARN
CAMPING BARN

ENGLAND

Lying in the picturesque Loweswater Valley, Swallow Barn is part of a traditional set of buildings dating back to 1670 on a working beef and sheep farm. The barn accommodates 18 people on mattresses in 4 sleeping areas.

There is a cooking and eating area with tables and chairs, 2 metered showers and a metered plug socket and 2 toilets. The barn is an excellent base for exploring the western fells with both high and low level walks and spectacular views, or you can enjoy the peace and tranquillity of the valley.

Fishing permits are available from the farm. The Coast to Coast cycle route is right on the doorstep. The Kirkstyle pub provides excellent food, just over a mile away and the market town of Cockermouth is only 8 miles. Check the website www.lakelandcampingbarns.co.uk and book online.

DETAILS

- **Open** - All year, all day
- **Number of beds** - 18: 1x9, 3x3
- **Booking** - Book online in advance, especially for school and bank holidays.
- **Price per night** - £10 per person.
- **Public Transport** - The nearest train station is Penrith with a bus to Cockermouth, then a taxi costing approximately £25.
- **Directions** - Leave the M6 at junct. 40 and follow the A66 to the Egremont turn off at Cockermouth. Follow the A5086, Egremont road for 6 miles. Turn left at Mockerkin and follow road to Loweswater. The farm is just past the Grange Hotel on the left.

CONTACT: Kath Leck
Tel: Booking office 017687 74301, Farm 01946 861465
info@lakelandcampingbarns.co.uk www.lakelandcampingbarns.co.uk
Waterend Farm, Loweswater, Cockermouth, Cumbria, CA13 0SU

FELLDYKE BUNKHOUSE

251

ENGLAND

Set in an idyllic location against the stunning backdrop of the Lake District mountains, which are 5 mins' walk away and located between Ennerdale and Loweswater, Felldyke bunkhouse is just 100m from the NCN route 71 (C2C) cycle route. Catering for groups of up to 23 in two bunk rooms, the accommodation includes a downstairs disabled access room for 3 people, ideal for leaders and teachers should a separate room be required. The upstairs room sleeps 20 and is sub-divided for privacy into sections of between four and six. Five high quality single shower rooms are provided and the bunkhouse is well equipped to cater for large groups. A comfortable lounge extension was completed in autumn 2013. Other facilities include: a kit drying cupboard, a range cooker, two dishwashers, plenty of fridge and freezer space, lots of food storage, large pans and sharp knives. This will hopefully keep your beer cold, your food hot and your fingers intact!

DETAILS

- **Open** - All year, all day
- **Number of beds** - 23
- **Booking** - By phone or email, terms and conditions can be found on the website.
- **Price per night** - Circa £500 per weekend, see website for tariff and deposits. Midweek, smaller groups welcome, plan on £15 per person per night.
- **Public Transport** - Local bus service runs within 10 minute walk, nearest train station in Whitehaven.
- **Directions** - From Cockermouth follow the A5086 for approx 6 miles past signs for Mockerkin. At Crossgates turn left. Go straight over staggered crossroads past Inglenook caravan park. Entering Felldyke turn immediately left into car park.

CONTACT: Phil and Rachel Gerrard
Tel: 01900 826698 or 07884 476708, Fax: 441900826698
felldyke.bunkhouse@gmail.com www.felldyke-bunkhouse.co.uk
Felldyke Bunkhouse, Felldyke, Lamplugh, Workington, Cumbria, CA14 4SH

TARN FLATT
CAMPING BARN

Tarn Flatt Camping Barn is a traditional sandstone barn on St Bees Head overlooking the Scottish coastline and the Isle of Man. It is on a working farm which also includes a lighthouse, RSPB bird reserve on 100 metre cliffs and access to Fleswick Bay - a secluded shingle cove. There is canoeing and fishing in the area and the rock climbing and boulders at the base of the cliff are superb. There are several local circular walks with panoramic views of the coast and the fells and there is easy access to the quieter western Lakeland fells and lakes. The award-winning historic Georgian town and harbour of Whitehaven is only 3 miles away and St Bees (the starting point of the Coast to Coast walk) is 2 miles via the coastal path. The barn has a raised wooden sleeping area on the ground floor. There is electric light, a cooking slab (please bring your own stove and utensils) and an open fire (wood available from the farm). Toilets, wash-basin and showers are in adjacent buildings. Meals are available by arrangement. Children welcome. Dogs are accepted in sole use only.

DETAILS

- **Open** - All year, 24 hours
- **Number of beds** - 12 bed spaces.
- **Booking** - Booking in advance is advised.
- **Price per night** - £10 per person.
- **Public Transport** - Trains at Whitehaven (4 miles) and St Bees (3 miles). Buses also at Whitehaven.
- **Directions** - GR 947 146. With Sandwith village green on right, pass row of houses and turn right, at phone box take private road for 1 mile.

CONTACT: Janice Telfer
Tel: Detail 01946 692162, Booking 017687 74301
stay@tarnflattfarm.co.uk www.tarnflattfarm.co.uk
Tarn Flatt Hall, Sandwith, Whitehaven, Cumbria, CA28 9UX

HUDSCALES
CAMPING BARN

253

ENGLAND

Hudscales Camping Barn is part of a group of traditional farm buildings, situated at 1000ft on the northern-most flank of the Lakeland Fells. It overlooks the villages of Caldbeck and Hesket Newmarket and is in an ideal position for exploring the northern fells. It is situated right on the Cumbria Way.

Sleeping accommodation is on the ground floor along with a separate cooking and eating area. You will need to bring sleeping bags and mats. If you wish to cook bring a camping stove and all utensils / crockery. There is a separate toilet and wash basin and a metered shower. A wood-burning stove is provided for added comfort (logs extra) and there is electric lighting plus metered power points, electric heaters are provided if required. There's also a games room with pool table and dart board.
Check the website www.lakelandcampingbarns.co.uk and book online.

DETAILS

- **Open** - All year, all day
- **Number of beds** - 12: 1x12
- **Booking** - Book online. Bookings preferred but not essential.
- **Price per night** - £10 per person.
- **Public Transport** - Penrith station 12 miles. Carlisle station 15 miles. No buses from Penrith. Limited service from Carlisle. Taxi fare from Carlisle approx £20.
- **Directions** - Leave M6 at J41 and take B5305 for Wigton. After approx 9 miles take left turn for Hesket Newmarket. Drive to top end of village and take left turn for Fellside. Hudscales Camping Barn is approx 1 mile on left up a lane.

CONTACT: Booking office / William or Judith
Tel: Booking office: 017687 74301/Farm: 016974 77199
wr.cowx@btconnect.com   www.lakelandcampingbarns.co.uk
Hudscales, Hesket Newmarket, Wigton, Cumbria, CA7 8JZ

WAYFARERS INDEPENDENT HOSTEL

ENGLAND

Wayfarers Independent Hostel is situated close to Penrith town centre, providing excellent value accommodation to those visiting Penrith, the Eden Valley and the North Lakes. Penrith is on the edge of the Lake District National Park, close to the M6 and on the West Coast Mainline with shops, pubs, restaurants and a cinema all within 5 minutes' walk of the hostel. The Coast to Coast cycle route passes 100m from the doorstep, secure indoor bike storage, a drying room, and cleaning and maintenance facilities make this an ideal place to stay after a hard day's ride. Newly refurbished in a comfortable, modern style, facilities include a lounge, full kitchen and dining facilities and an outside seating area for guests to enjoy. All bedrooms are en suite with made up beds (sheets & duvets), lockers, bedside lights, towels for hire and have free WiFi available. Individuals, small parties and groups of up to 18 are welcome.

DETAILS

- **Open** - All year, reception open 8am-11am, 4pm-9pm
- **Number of beds** - 16: 1x2, 1x6, 2x4.
- **Booking** - Recommended online, by phone or email.
- **Price per night** - From £22pp (dorm room bed). Sole use available from £320 pn. Family rates available Sun-Thurs from £55. Breakfast and packed lunches available.
- **Public Transport** - Trains and National Express to Penrith train station, 104 bus from Carlisle and X4-5 from Workington to Penrith bus station.
- **Directions** - M6 jcn 40 into Penrith along Ullswater Road. Past the station, bear left at first roundabout, straight over second heading down the hill past Booths and Morrisons. At bottom of the hill follow round to the left and take first turning on left.

CONTACT: Mark Rhodes
Tel: 01768 866011
guests@wayfarershostel.com   www.wayfarershostel.com
19 Brunswick Square, Penrith, Cumbria, CA11 7LR

HILLSIDE FARM
BUNKBARN

255

ENGLAND

A Georgian farmstead in a conservation area just steps away from Hadrian's Wall. Hillside Farm in the small village of Boustead Hill, near the Solway Coast AONB and RSPB nature reserve has stunning views over the Solway Firth marshes towards Scotland. Hadrian's Wall National Trail and Hadrian's Cycleway pass right by. Hillside farm is a working farm and the 4th generation of farmers welcome you to to the bunkbarn or the B&B rooms in the farmhouse. The bunkbarn in a converted stable block has cooking slabs, cutlery, crockery' a 2 ring gas stove, microwave and small electric oven. There are hot showers, towels and sleeping bags can be hired if required. The communal downstairs areas are heated but not the upstairs bunkroom. Shopping deliveries can be arranged via the farmhouse and with notice you can have breakfast or bacon sandwiches. Walking, cycling and family groups are most welcome.

DETAILS

- **Open** - All year, all day
- **Number of beds** - 12
- **Booking** - Book by phone or email.
- **Price per night** - £12 per person including shower. £4 full English breakfast, £2 bacon/sausage sandwiches.
- **Public Transport** - Trains at Carlisle. Bus: Stagecoach 93 (not Sundays or BH's). Ask to get off at Boustead Hill not Burgh-by-sands.
- **Directions** - From Jnct 44 of M6 take the western bypass sign posted Workington. Follow until you reach a roundabout signed to Burgh-by-Sands and Bowness on Solway. Follow to Burgh and continue for 2 miles. After crossing cattle grid on to Marsh Road take next left to Boustead Hill then 2nd left under arches into farmyard.

CONTACT: Mrs Sandra Rudd
Tel: 01228 576398, Fax: 441228576398
ruddshillside1@btinternet.com www.hadrianswalkbnb.co.uk
Hillside Farm, Boustead Hill, Burgh-by-Sands, Carlisle, Cumbria, CA5 6AA

CARLISLE CITY HOSTEL

Carlisle City Hostel is Carlisle's only independent hostel. Located on picturesque Abbey Street, the building is an old Georgian terrace that can accommodate up to 22 guests. There is a communal kitchen for you to prepare your own meals and communal lounge with TV, DVDs and book swap. Free tea, coffee and WiFi is available in communal areas. Secure bicycle and luggage storage is located in the large cellar. Come and explore this wonderful city and its surrounds. The staff look forward to welcoming you as their guest in their hostel and their city. On street parking is free from 6.30pm-8.30am during the week and all day Sunday. Nearest carpark: Devonshire Walk.

DETAILS

- **Open** - All year. Check in is between 3pm – 8pm ONLY (Sunday 4pm-8pm)
- **Number of beds** - 22: 1x8 1x6 1x4 1x4 (family/triple/double)
- **Booking** - by website with first night deposit. Cash only on arrival. Check before booking if you wish to arrive outside of check in times. Deposits are non-refundable
- **Price per night** - From £17 to £22 pp. Groups over 8 by pre-arrangement only.
- **Public Transport** - Carlisle City Hostel is located in the city centre of Carlisle. Bus station and train station are 5 minutes' walk from the front door of the hostel.
- **Directions** - From city centre: English Street bears left onto Castle Street, past cathedral, Left onto Paternoster Row which becomes Abbey Street. From M6 Jnc 43: follow signs for city centre. At Nando's traffic lights follow the road left. Get in the right hand lane and take a right through the old city walls. Turn left onto Victoria Viaduct then 2nd right -W Walls this becomes Annetwell Street. Turn right onto Castle Street Take the first right onto Paternoster Row which becomes Abbey Street.

CONTACT: Jonathan Quinlan
Tel: (+44) 01288545637 Mob:(+44) 07914720821
info@carlislecityhostel.com www.carlislecityhostel.com
36 Abbey Street, Carlisle, CA3 8TX

HAGGS BANK
BUNKHOUSE AND CAMP-SITE ENGLAND

Set in the stunning North Pennines Area of Outstanding Natural Beauty, often described as England's last wilderness, this location is ideal for anyone who loves the great outdoors - walkers, cyclists and mountain bikers . The 36 mile Isaac's Tea Trail walk passes through the site; directly on the C2C and with bicycle hire (including electric bikes) available nearby. The bunkhouse sleeps up to 24 in 3 bunkrooms of 4/5, 9 and 10 and includes a relaxing lounge, self-catering kitchen, modern shower room and large conservatory for chilling out in! Breakfast and evening meals can be provided for larger groups if pre-booked. Nestled between a special nature conservation area and the wildflower meadow, the campsite has been created with tiered pitches to enhance the infinite views across the Nent valley. Electric hook-ups for caravans and motorhomes are also available within the car park. The site has its own private supply of spring water, unique outdoor equipment washing area and secure bike and gear store. It has recently been awarded a Silver Green Tourism Award for commitment to sustainability.

DETAILS

- **Open** - All year, all day access
- **Number of beds** - 24 in 3 bunkrooms
- **Booking** - Contact by email or phone
- **Price per night** - £18pppn. Discount for sole use. Camping £8pppn. Motorhomes/caravans £20pn for up to 2 people
- **Public Transport** - On 889 / 888 bus routes operated by Wright Bros, Nenthead
- **Directions** - Directly on the A689 between Alston and Nenthead.

CONTACT: Danny Taylor
Tel: 07919 092403/ 01434 382486
info@haggsbank.com haggsbank.com
Haggs Bank Bunkhouse, Nentsbury, Alston, Cumbria, CA9 3LH

NINEBANKS

ENGLAND

4-star rated YHA Ninebanks is a recently renovated and extended 18th century cottage in a stunning rural location. It's a great place to stay, with high quality en suite bedrooms and a spacious multi-use dining room - and it has high environmental credentials! Situated in the beautiful county of Northumberland, within the North Pennines and close to the iconic Hadrian's Wall, it provides the perfect base from which to explore this spectacular part of the country. This family run hostel is part of the YHA network and is open to guests all year round. Book a bed, a room, or the whole hostel! Catering available for groups. You can be sure of a great welcome at YHA Ninebanks.

DETAILS

- **Open** - All year, open all day, reception from 5pm
- **Number of beds** - 28: 2x2/3, 2x4, 1x6, 1x8
- **Booking** - booking is recommended
- **Price per night** - beds from £10.00, rooms from £34, whole hostel from £200
- **Public Transport** - Buses are few and far between and get no closer than 1.5miles from the hostel. See the Wright's bus website for the current information. Trains: the nearest train stations are Haydon Bridge 11 miles and Hexham 15 miles (more trains stop at Hexham)
- **Directions** - From A686 take turning signposted Ouston, Ninebanks, Carrshield (left from Northumberland, right from Cumbria)- watch out for the blue and white YHA sign). Go down over the cattle grids turn right at the T junction, follow the road up the hill and the hostel and manager's cottage are the only buildings on the right side of the road.

CONTACT: Pauline Elliott
Tel: 01434 345288, Fax: 441434345414
pauline@ninebanks.com www.ninebanks.org.uk
Orchard House, Mohope, Hexham, Northumberland, NE47 8DQ

ALLENDALE BUNKHOUSE

ENGLAND

The Allendale Bunkhouse opened in October 2014, having been completely refurbished and thoroughly modernised. It sits on the market square in Allendale, overlooking the hustle and bustle of a small countryside town and the fells and river beyond. An oasis for walkers, cyclists, horse riders, families, groups of friends and youth & school groups alike. Allendale tea rooms, the Forge art gallery & café, a quirky gift shop, pharmacy, Allendale medical pratice and the library are all a stone's throw away. There is also bike hire (electric, mountain and hybrid bikes) and the C2C cycle trail runs close by. Art, heritage and music events run throuout the year across the valley. Book a bunk, a room, a floor (up to 18) or the whole bunkhouse for your group.

Downstairs is a large open plan area with a brand new fully equipped kitchen, dining area with seating for up to 34 and a lounge area with comfortable sofas to relax. Double french doors lead onto a BBQ, seating and patio area with steps into the large garden. (Garden to be landscaped in early 2015.)

DETAILS
- **Open** - All year, 8am-8pm
- **Number of beds** - 37: 2x6, 2x4, 1x7, 1x2, 1x3, 1x5
- **Booking** - via telephone or email. A deposit will be required.
- **Price per night** - From £14 - £30 per person per night.
- **Public Transport** - Nearest train stations: Hexham or Haydon Bridge. Buses available to Allendale Market Place. Pick up service can be arranged.
- **Directions** - on the market place in Allendale, 12 miles from Hexham.

CONTACT: Linda Beck
Tel: 01434618579
info@allendalebunkhouse.co.uk www.allendalebunkhouse.co.uk
Market Place, Allendale, Hexham, NE47 9BD

BARRINGTON BUNKHOUSE

Situated in the pleasant sleepy village of Rookhope in the stunning surroundings of Weardale. Next door is The Rookhope Inn for a welcome pint and substantial meals. The bunkhouse provides clean, comfortable accommodation with a self service continental breakfast ready for your day's activities. There are kettles, toasters and a microwave. Eggs are supplied as well as a microwave poacher. All welcome, especially cyclists on the Coast 2 Coast (C2C), walkers on the Pennine Journey, Weardale Way, and groups visiting the area. There are 12 bunk beds each with a personal reading light and an additional fold-up bed plus a fully fitted disabled wet-room with toilet, basin and shower and one able bodied shower and separate toilet. The large cast iron multi-fuel stove is used from October to March and oil-filled radiators provide extra warmth. There is a tumble dryer and a hair dryer is available on request. Visitors can also camp on the lawns - some camping equipment is available.

DETAILS

- **Open** - All year, all day
- **Number of beds** - 12 (+1): 1 x 12 plus 1 fold up bed
- **Booking** - Booking recommended, by phone or email. 50% non-refundable deposit for weekdays, and full payment in advance for weekends and bank holidays.
- **Price per night** - £22pp incl. continental breakfast. Camping £14 with breakfast, £10 without. Sole use rates negotiable depending on group size and time of year.
- **Public Transport** - Nearest train stations: Hexham 17 miles, Durham 25 miles, Bishop Auckland 23 miles. Buses to Crook, Durham and Bishop Auckland.
- **Directions** - Next door to Rookhope Inn in Rookhope.

CONTACT: Valerie Livingston
Tel: 01388 517656
barrington_bunkhouse@hotmail.co.uk www.barrington-bunkhouse-rookhope.com
Barrington Cottage, Rookhope, Weardale, Co. Durham, DL13 2BG

FELL HOUSE COTTAGE

ENGLAND

261

Fell House Cottage is situated on the fell over looking the village of Rookhope. Directly on the Coast 2 Coast cycle route this is a great base for cyclists, walkers and others alike. This 19th century cottage has been sympathetically rennovated to provide cosy bunkhouse accommodation. With the ability to sleep up to 8 people the cottage provides good clean accommodation with continental breakfast included. The property comprises an open dorm sleeping 6 people upstairs and the facility to sleep a further 2 down stairs. There is a small kitchen area downstairs, along with a shower and wc room. A drying room and secure bike storage is also available. All just a stone's throw away from the local pub.

With the option for additional onsite camping Fell House Cottage provides a great overnight stop for you and your party.

DETAILS

- **Open** - Open all year. All hours
- **Number of beds** - 8: 1x6, 1x2
- **Booking** - by phone.
- **Price per night** - £22pp incl. continental breakfast. Camping £14 with breakfast. Sole use rates negotiable depending on group size and time of year.
- **Public Transport** - Nearest train stations: Hexham 17 miles, Durham 25 miles, Bishop Auckland 23 miles. Buses to Crook, Durham and Bishop Auckland.
- **Directions** - From the front of Rookhope Inn turn right and walk up hill, Take first left and follow the track round to where it ends at Fell House. The Cottage is on the right.

CONTACT: Shayne Smith
Tel: 01388 517927
Bookings@fellhouse.co.uk Fellhousecottage.co.uk
Fell House Cottage, Fell house, Rookhope, Bishop Auckland, County Durham, DL13 2BD

GREENHEAD HOSTEL

ENGLAND

Greenhead Hostel is a converted Methodist Chapel in the village of Greenhead on Hadrian's Wall. It is ideal for those walking the Pennine Way or The Wall and is in a great location for those exploring the nearby Roman heritage sites. The church was built in 1886 to serve the village miners and gave its last service in 1972. It has been a YHA hostel since 1978.

Greenhead Hostel has a self-catering kitchen and guest lounge. There are 40 beds in four rooms of six beds and two rooms of eight beds. These can be booked as family rooms, by groups or by the bed for individuals. Above the hostel is a self contained flat with kitchen, lounge, two double rooms and a single room. Evening meals, breakfast and packed lunches are available. The hostel is operated by Greenhead Hotel (over the road) with a welcoming bar and restaurant. VisitEngland approved.

DETAILS

- **Open** - All year (groups only in winter, please enquire), hostel is open all day.
- **Number of beds** - 45: Hostel 40: 2x8, 2x6. Flat 5: 2dbl, 1 single.
- **Booking** - Book by phone or email.
- **Price per night** - Bunkhouse: adult: £15, under 18 £10. Flat £35pp. Reductions for large groups or full rooms. Sole use of hostel £400, £450 including flat.
- **Public Transport** - Trains: Haltwhistle 3 miles, Carlisle 19 miles, Newcastle 45 miles. Bus: May to Sept Stagecoach AD 122 from Newcastle to Bowness-on-Solway. Arriva 685 Carlisle-Newcastle passes Haltwhistle station and runs hourly all year.
- **Directions** - On the A69 between Carlise and Newcastle. Turn off at sign for Greenhead. Turn right at the T junction, the hostel is opposite the Greenhead Hotel.

CONTACT: Diane and family.
Tel: 01697 747411
daveandsuegreenhead@btconnect.com www.greenheadhotelandhostel.co.uk
Greenhead Hotel, Greenhead, Brampton, Cumbria, CA8 7HG

HERDING HILL FARM

263

ENGLAND

Located at the half way point of the Hadrian's Wall long distance path within the best section of the wall, Herding Hill Farm provides superb facilities for tents, motorhomes and caravans as well as providing glamping style heated wooden wigwams (some with hot tubs outside) and an accessible 6 berth holiday lodge. The newly converted bunkhouse sleeps 24 people in two centrally heated rooms, each with en suite facilities. One room accommodates 15 people and the other has 9 beds, these are linked by a lockable door and can be used as a shared facility. The bunkhouse has a comfortable lounge with sofas and TV, a dining area with communal kitchen facilities and private outside seating area with BBQ. The Hadrian's Wall Bus AD122 stops outside the farm and the Pennine Way and cycle routes 72 & 68 pass close by. Facilities include a drying room, secure bike storage, laundry room, and an eight person sauna that can be booked for private use. The on site take-away provides breakfasts, packed lunches, pizzas, and real ales. Dogs on campsite only.

DETAILS

- **Open** - All year.
- **Number of beds** - 24: 1x15, 1x9
- **Booking** - Can be booked or just turn up
- **Price per night** - From £15 per bed but group bookings obtain discount
- **Public Transport** - The Hadrian's Wall bus AD122 stops outside our gates.
- **Directions** - One mile south of Cawfields Quarry on Hadrian's Wall. Just outside Haltwhistle and sign posted from the B6318. Cyclists wanting to miss out the steep climb/descent to Haltwhistle, leave B6318 half a mile from Milecastle Inn crossroads.

CONTACT: Steve
Tel: 01434 320175
info@herdinghillfarm.co.uk   www.herdinghillfarm.co.uk
Shield Hill, Haltwhistle, Northumberland NE49 9NW

SLACK HOUSE FARM

ENGLAND

A working, organic dairy farm situated above Gilsland and the Irthing Valley. Slack House Farm overlooks Birdoswald Roman Fort on Hadrian's Wall, is on the NCN route 72 and only 0.5km from the Hadrian's Wall National Trail. The bunk and camping barn is adjacent to The Scypen licensed café and farm shop and the Birdoswald cheese dairy. Accommodation includes a camping loft (10 inflatable mattresses provided, bring a sleeping bag) and 5 bed bunkroom (bedding provided), with a 3 bed family room (+child's bed or travel cot) on the ground floor. Each room has its own shower, toilet, hot water, heated towel rail and electric lighting. Cooked breakfasts, farmhouse suppers and packed lunches can be provided. With wood-fired, under-floor heating on the ground floor and a laundry, drying room and separate sitting and eating area with wood pellet stove, this is a lovely cosy place to base your Hadrian's Wall stay.

DETAILS

- **Open** - All year. Check in from 17.00pm, check out by 10.00am.
- **Number of beds** - 18: 1x10, 1x5, 1x3 (family)
- **Booking** - Individuals: pre-booking advisable (credit card confirms bed). Sole use: booking essential with 50% deposit.
- **Price per night** - £8.50 camping loft, £15 bunkbed, under 5s free. For sole use of room: £50 per room, £40 family room.
- **Public Transport** - Carlisle-Newcastle train line 9km, bus 5km. AD122 bus (April-October) request stop 200m. (Kiln Hill junction).
- **Directions** - On B6318, GR NY670613, From A69, west take turning for Gilsland & Spadeadam. From east take right turn signed Greenhead. Follow Hadrian's Wall signs to Birdoswald. Do not turn left to the Fort but continue a further 200 metres.

CONTACT: Dianne Horn
Tel: 01697 747351
postmaster@slackhousefarm.plus.com www.slackhousefarm.co.uk
Slack House Farm, Gilsland Brampton, Cumbria, CA8 7DB

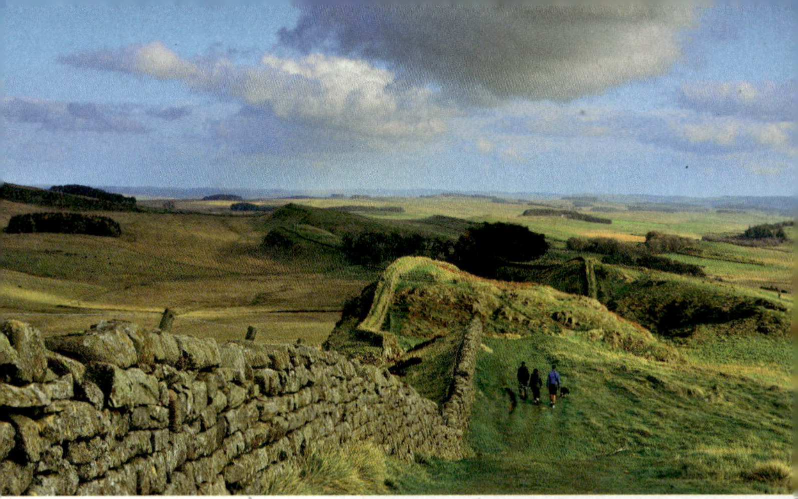

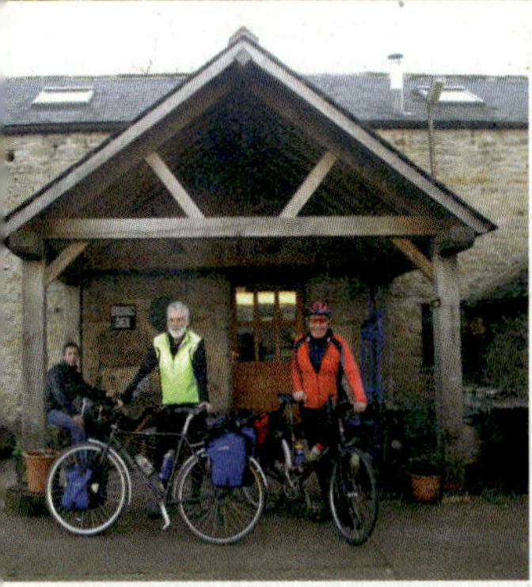

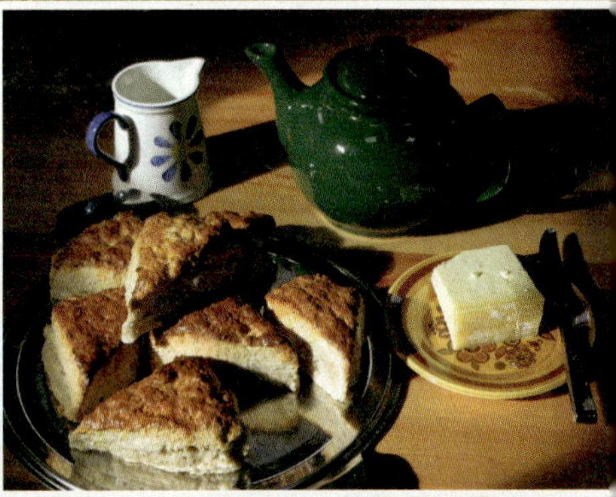

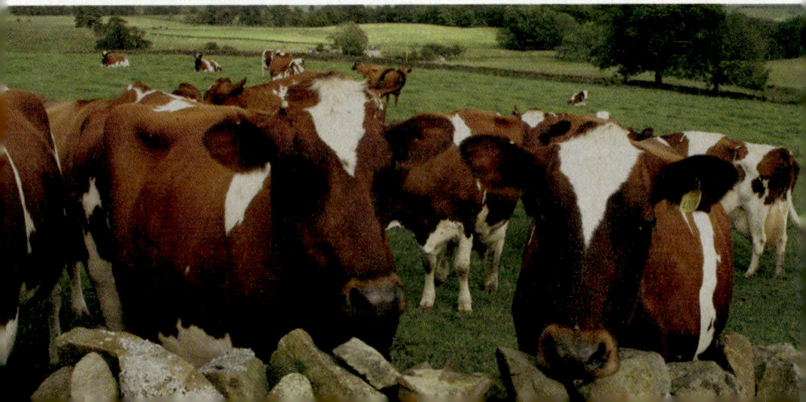

GIBBS HILL FARM HOSTEL

ENGLAND

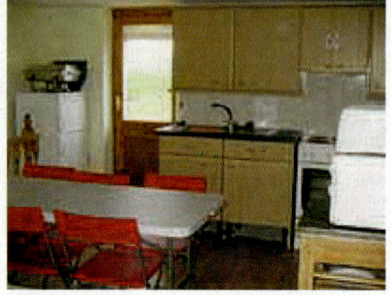

Gibbs Hill Farm Hostel is a new conversion of a barn on a traditional working hill farm near Once Brewed on Hadrian's Wall. The hostel is designed to reduce energy consumption and is centrally heated throughout. There are 3 bunkrooms, 2 shower rooms, 2 toilets, a well equipped kitchen, comfortable sitting and dining area and a large deck where you can enjoy the evening sun.

The hostel has a drying room, lockers, laundry facilities and safe cycle storage. Ideal for families who may take a whole room with private facilities. Study groups welcome. Situated near Hadrian's Wall it is an excellent base for exploring the Roman sites, Hadrian's Wall Trail and Northumberland National Park. Basic items of food may be purchased and evening meals can be ordered the day before. Continental breakfast £5, packed lunches £6.

DETAILS

- **Open** - All year, hours flexible but no check in after 9pm.
- **Number of beds** - 18: 3x6
- **Booking** - Advisable, groups require full payment 4 weeks before arrival.
- **Price per night** - £18 adult, £12 child (under 12), including bedding.
- **Public Transport** - Trains at Haltwhistle 6 miles. Regular bus service along A69 between Newcastle and Carlisle, and in summer the Hadrian's Wall Bus runs between Newcastle and Carlisle. Alight at Once Brewed Information Centre and walk north to farm. Last bus 5.30pm from Haltwhistle.
- **Directions** - From the A69, turn north at Bardon Mill, signed 'Once Brewed'. Follow the signs towards 'Housesteads'. At the B6318, turn right and then immediately left towards 'Steel Rigg'. Follow for 1 mile, turn right to 'Gibbs Hill'.

CONTACT: Valerie Gibson
Tel: 01434 344030, Fax: 01434 344030
val@gibbshillfarm.co.uk www.gibbshillfarm.co.uk
Gibbs Hill Farm, Bardon Mill, Nr Hexham, Northumberland, NE47 7AP

DEMESNE FARM BUNKHOUSE

267
ENGLAND

Demesne Farm Bunkhouse is a self-catering unit which was converted in 2004 from a barn on a working hill farm. The farm is situated on the Pennine Way, Route 68 cycle route, Reivers cycle route and is within 100 metres of the centre of the North Tyne village of Bellingham on the edge of the Northumberland National Park. The bunkhouse provides an ideal base for exploring Northumberland, Hadrian's Wall, Kielder Water and many climbing crags. It accommodates 15 and is perfect for smaller groups, individuals and families. The bedrooms are fitted with hand crafted oak man-sized bunk beds, high quality mattresses, pillows, curtains and cushion flooring and full bed linen. The communal living area with wood burning stove and fitted kitchen includes cooker, microwave, fridge, freezer, kettle, toaster, crockery, cutlery, cooking utensils, farmhouse tables, chairs and easy chairs. It has 2 bathrooms with hot showers, basins, toilets and under floor heating. In the courtyard there is ample parking, bike lock up, drying room and a gravelled area with picnic tables.

DETAILS

- **Open** - All year, flexible but no check in after 9pm
- **Number of beds** - 15: 1 x 8, 1 x 4, 1 x 3
- **Booking** - Please book in advance.
- **Price per night** - £18 per person, £15 under 18's (including linen).
- **Public Transport** - Trains at Hexham (17 miles), regular bus service from Hexham to Bellingham. Bellingham bus stop 100 metres from bunkhouse. By car: Newcastle 45 mins, Scottish Border 20 mins, Kielder Water 10 mins.
- **Directions** - 100 metres from centre of village, located next to Northern Garage.

CONTACT: Robert Telfer
Tel: 01434 220258 Mobile 07967 396345
stay@demesnefarmcampsite.co.uk www.demesnefarmcampsite.co.uk
Demesne Farm, Bellingham, Hexham, Northumberland, NE48 2BS

TARSET TOR BUNKHOUSE & BOTHIES

ENGLAND

Tarset Tor's striking timber eco-buildings integrate effortlessly into their natural surroundings deep in the Northumberland National Park, making the most of this remarkable location and providing the perfect base for outdoor adventures. The skies around Tarset Tor are now protected and are an International Dark Sky Reserve, making it the ideal spot from which to gaze at the stars. The stylish bunkhouse is a superb social space, offering comfortable, contemporary sleeping quarters together with shared cooking, eating, showering and lounge facilities. There is also a sauna and pool table. The incredibly versatile floorplan can be quickly adapted to create a welcoming venue for events, conferences and parties. The self-contained Bothy holiday homes enable guests to enjoy the peace and tranquility of Tarset Tor in a more private setting. A small number of campervan/camping pitches are also available.

DETAILS

- **Open** - Mid January - December, All day
- **Number of beds** - Bunkhouse: 16-20, Bothies: 6-8, 5 Campervan bays, 10 tents.
- **Booking** - Booking essential. Bothies OPEN July 2015.
- **Price per night** - Bunkhouse £200 to £384 p/n. Lowest rate: Sun-Thur. Astro tourist breaks: 4/5 bed rooms £60-£80 (Sun/Thurs). Bothy: £100-£192pn Lowest rate Sun-Thur. Campervans £20 (£15 wild). Tents £5 + £5 per person (U14s camp free).
- **Public Transport** - Nearest train station is Hexham 20 miles and a bus runs to Bellingham 3 miles. Pick ups and drop offs can be arranged.
- **Directions** - From A68 to Bellingham follow signs to Kielder Water. After 3 miles at Lanehead junction, look right to see Tarset Tor farmhouse. The bunkhouse and car park is just down the hill on the right.

CONTACT: Rob Cocker and Claire Briggs
Tel: 01434 240980
info@tarset-tor.co.uk www.tarset-tor.co.uk
Greystones Lanehead Tarset Hexham NE48 1NT

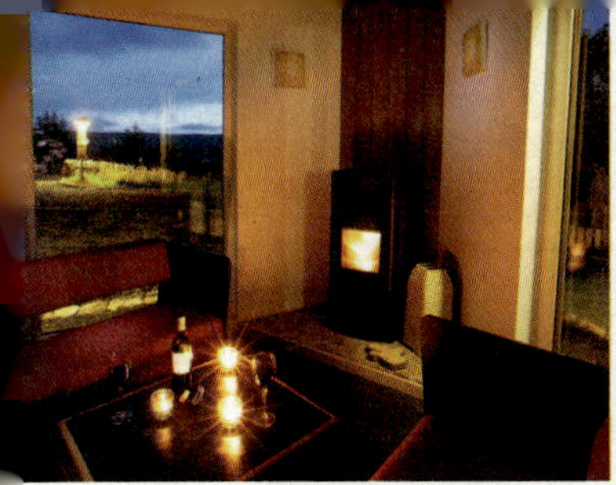

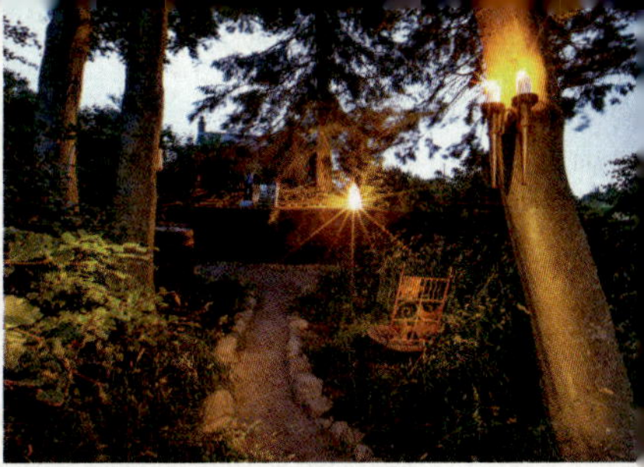

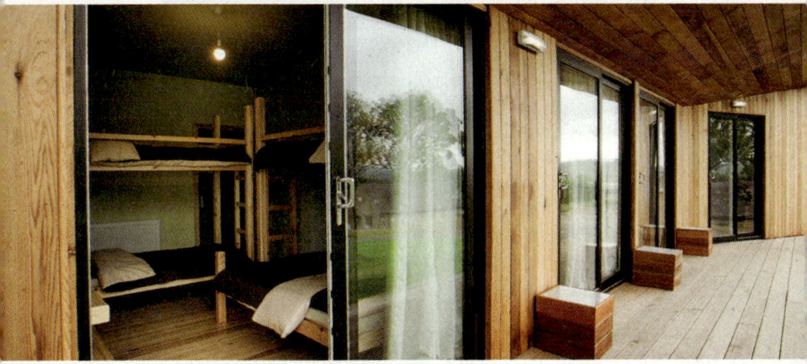

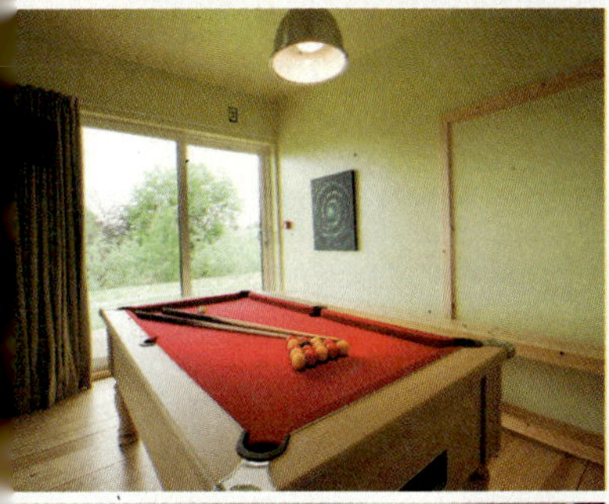

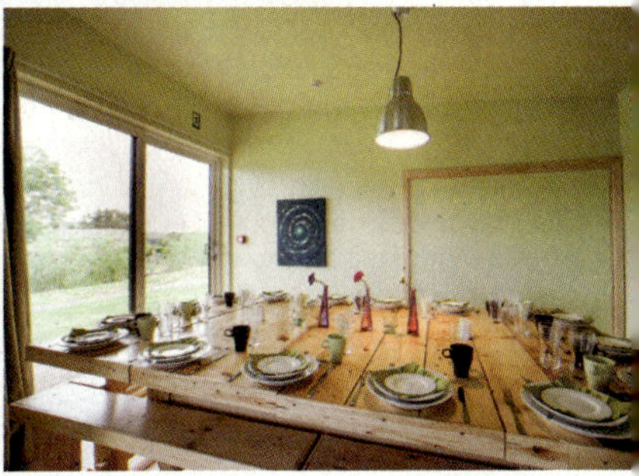

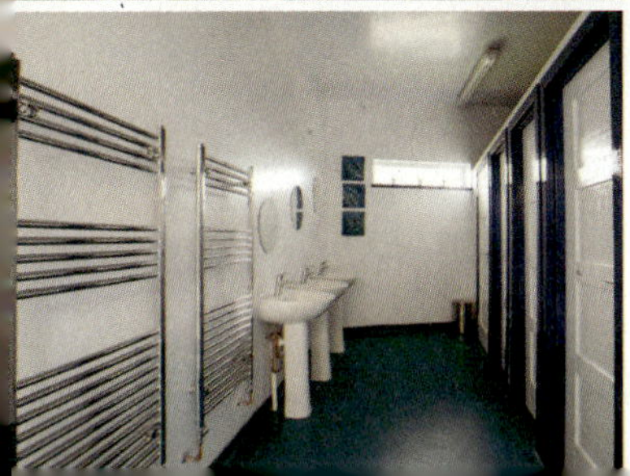

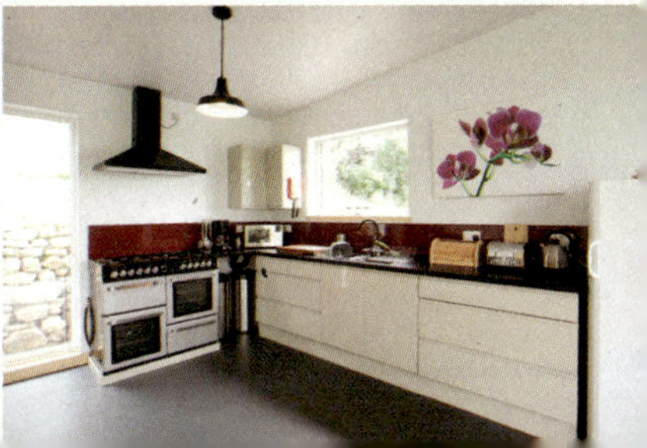

ALBATROSS BACKPACKERS IN!

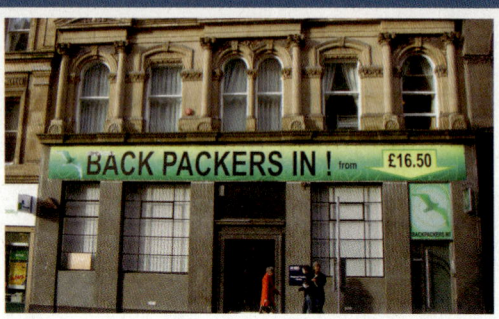

Fly high with the award winning "Albatross"! This clean and modern backpackers hostel is located in Newcastle's city centre. All in walking distance from sporting, musical and conference venues, art galleries, historical attractions, food markets and public transport facilities. We are open all year round. The Albatross – www.albatrossnewcastle.com - is primarily designed to provide affordable accommodation in the city centre for the international travellers, walkers, cyclists and bikers, exchange student groups, sports teams, choirs etc. We provide rooms from 12 bed to 2 beds and anything in between for as little as £16.50 and £22.50. The overnight price includes; linen, 24hr reception, fully fitted self-catering kitchen with free tea, coffee and toast, free WiFi access and computer terminals, pool table, satellite TV, outside sitting/ barbeque area, free baggage storage and laundry facilities. A young dedicated international team is looking forward to welcome you.

DETAILS

- **Open** - All year, 24 hours
- **Number of beds** - 177
- **Booking** - Recommended. Photo ID at check-in (passport or driving licence).
- **Price per night** - From £16.50pp (dorm) to £22.50pp (2 bed room)
- **Public Transport** - Five minutes' walk from central train, bus and metro stations.
- **Directions** - Central Station/Megabus drop off point: from main entrance, head right, take the first street on your left (Grainger St), you'll find us on your left 200m uphill. From National Express coach station: head down Scotswood Rd to Central Station. From Airport: take Metro to Central Station (20 mins travel). From port (ferry): buses travel between the port and Central Station and take 20 mins.

CONTACT: Reception
Tel: 0191 2331330, Fax: 0191 2603389
info@albatrossnewcastle.co.uk   www.albatrossnewcastle.com
51 Grainger Street, Newcastle upon Tyne, NE1 5JE

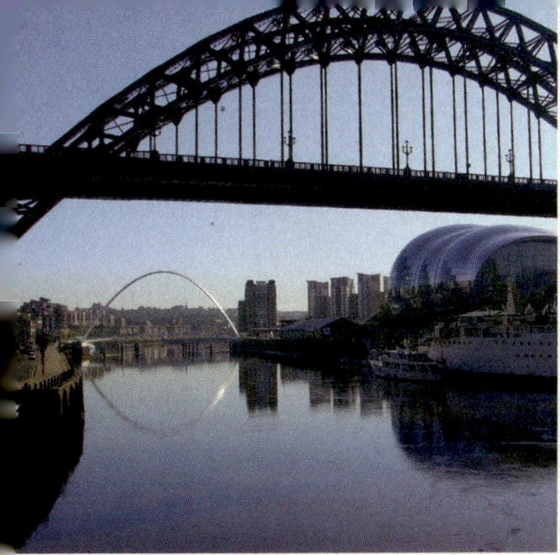

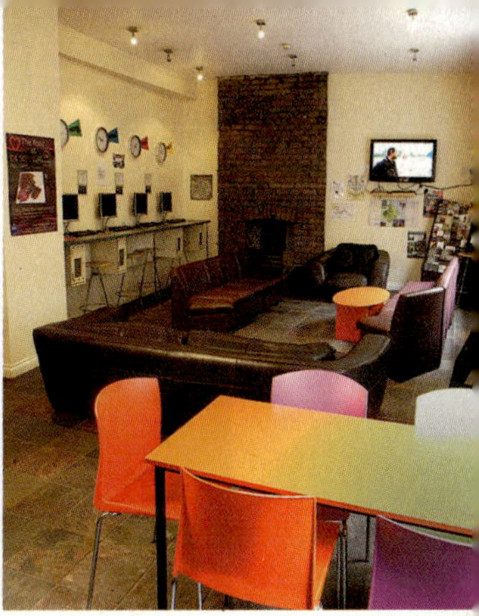

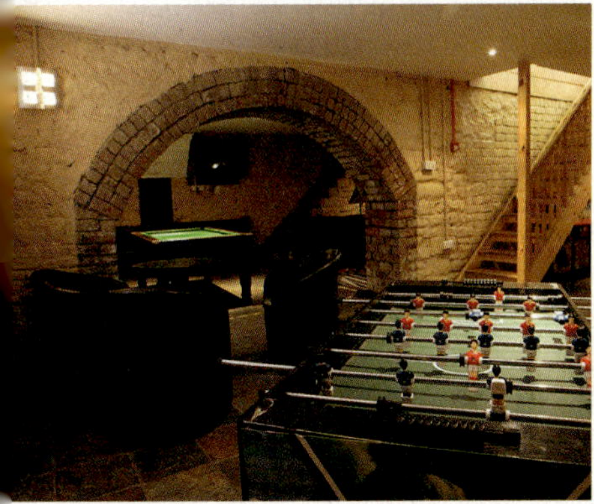

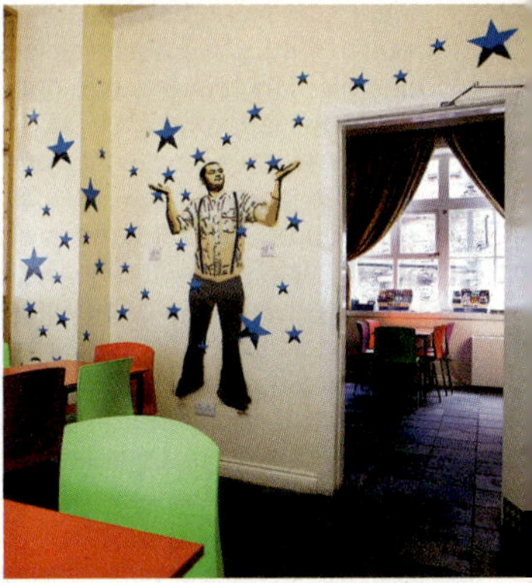

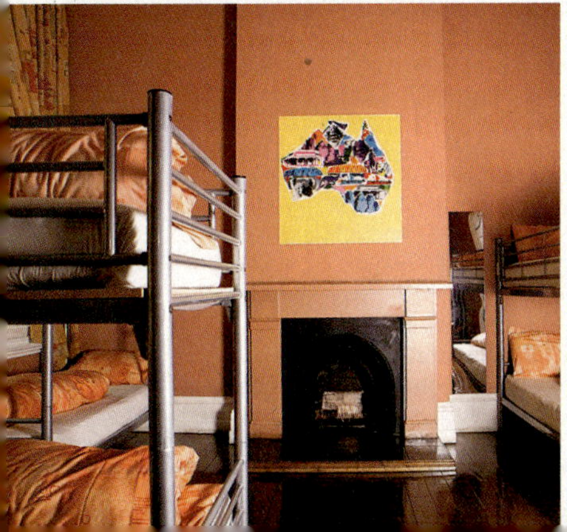

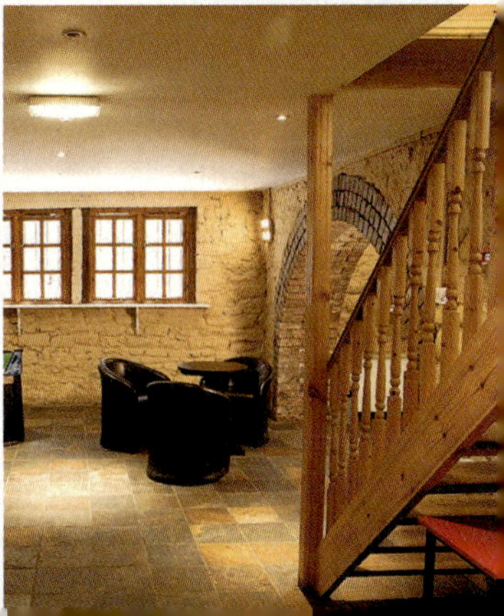

HOUGHTON NORTH
ENGLAND FARM ACCOMMODATION

Houghton North Farm, partly built with stones from Hadrian's Wall, has been in the Laws Family for five generations. It is situated in the beautiful Northumberland countryside right on the Heritage Trail and 15 miles from the start of the Hadrian's Wall Trail. Within the region walkers can enjoy marked woodland trails, rugged moorland & hills and some of the most beautiful deserted beaches in the UK. This newly built, spacious accommodation can take a group of up to 23 and is also ideal for individuals and families. A 4 Star Hostel with VisitBritain, the bunk style rooms (some en suite) are located around the central courtyard and include the use of a self-catering kitchen where a light breakfast is served. A well appointed TV lounge has a log fire and internet access and outside is a BBQ, secure cycle storage and parking. Long-term parking, baggage transfer and packed lunches are available on request. Within 10 minutes' walk are pubs, a restaurant and shops in Heddon-on-the-Wall.

DETAILS

- **Open** - All year (except Christmas and New Year). Arrive after 3pm depart by 10am
- **Number of beds** - 22: 1x5, 3x4, 1x3, 1x2
- **Booking** - Book with a non-refundable deposit of £10 per person per night
- **Price per night** - From £25 (adult), £15 (under 12) inc breakfast. Group discounts.
- **Public Transport** - Trains at Wylam (2 miles) and Newcastle (7 miles). The 685 Newcastle-Carlisle bus stops right outside the farm. Baggage transfer is available.
- **Directions** - From Newcastle take the Heddon turn off the A69 to the B6528. Farm is 1/4 mile outside of the village of Heddon. From Carlisle take Horsley junction and continue approx 3 miles beyond Horsley. Farm is on the left at the top of a hill.

CONTACT: Mrs Paula Laws
Tel: 01661 854364
wjlaws@btconnect.com   www.houghtonnorthfarm.co.uk
Houghton North Farm, Heddon-on-the-Wall, Northumberland, NE15 0EZ

TOMLINSON'S CAFE
AND BUNKHOUSE
ENGLAND
273

A former schoolhouse in the historic town of Rothbury overlooking the River Coquet, Tomlinson's is a one-stop shop for low-cost accommodation, wholesome homemade meals and cycle hire. Ideal for families, groups and independent travellers, there are five flexible rooms most with en suite showers. Guests can mix in the communal TV lounge, enjoy the views or a homemade meal in the café. Big windows give beautiful views over the River Coquet. The bunkhouse has laundry facilities, a wash down area for bikes and boots, secure bike storage and drying room. A 50 capacity function room for hire for celebrations and meetings. Rothbury is becoming the Northumberland National Park's cycling hub and the bunkhouse is just metres from a string of off-road cycle tracks and public footpaths. The bunkhouse has a fleet of mountain bikes available to hire and instructors to lead cycle groups of all ages. The Cheviot Hills and the Northumberland Coast are within a 30 minute drive and the area is awash with castles including Alnwick featured in the Harry Potter films.

DETAILS

- **Open** - All year, all day
- **Number of beds** - 21: 1x8, 1x7, 1x6
- **Booking** - Book by phone, online or email
- **Price per night** - From £20 per person, £400 for the whole bunkhouse.
- **Public Transport** - Trains at Morpeth (15 miles) and Alnmouth. Buses to Newcastle and Morpeth bus station run most days.
- **Directions** - Overlooking River Coquet, on the corner of Bridge Street and Haw Hill off the B6342 in Rothbury.

CONTACT: Jackie Sewell
Tel: 01669 621 979
info@tomlinsons-rothbury.co.uk www.tomlinsonsrothbury.co.uk
Bridge Street, Rothbury, Northumberland, NE65 7SF

ALNWICK YOUTH HOSTEL

ENGLAND

Once the town's Court House, today the accommodation offered by the Alnwick Youth Hostel is now somewhat less austere. Opened in 2011, this family friendly 4 star hostel is sure to meet the needs of every traveller, with a variety of en suite rooms, cosy lounge, games room and a bright and airy dining room.

The hostel's town centre location makes it ideal for a visit to historic Alnwick Castle, the medieval home of the Dukes of Northumberland, which had a starring role in the early Harry Potter films, as well as the neighbouring Alnwick Garden. A 15 minute car journey takes you to the beach with glorious views of Dunstanburgh and Bamburgh Castles and wildlife havens such as Holy Island and the Farne Isles. Only a short trip inland brings you to the stunning heather clad Cheviot Hills, Hadrian's Wall and Border Reiver country. Great for families, groups, cyclists and backpackers

DETAILS

- **Open** - All year, Reception open 08:00 to 10:00hrs and 16:00 to 21:00hrs
- **Number of beds** - 57: 1x1, 3x2, 1x3, 6x4,1x5, 3x6
- **Booking** - Booking advisable by phone or e-mail or book online via our website.
- **Price per night** - Adult dorm beds from £20, under 18 from £15. 2 bedded rooms from £45.00. Family 4 bedded rooms from £65.00
- **Public Transport** - Bus - X15 / X18 Newcastle - Alnwick train station - Alnmouth (4 miles) National Express 591/594 to Alnwick bus station.
- **Directions** - You will find the hostel opposite Alnwick library. A public car park is available at Roxboro Place, to the rear of the Job Centre.

CONTACT: Andrew Clarkson
Tel: 01665 660800, Fax: 01665 252800
info@alnwickyouthhostel.co.uk   www.alnwickyouthhostel.co.uk
34 - 38 Green Batt, Alnwick, Northumberland, NE66 1TU

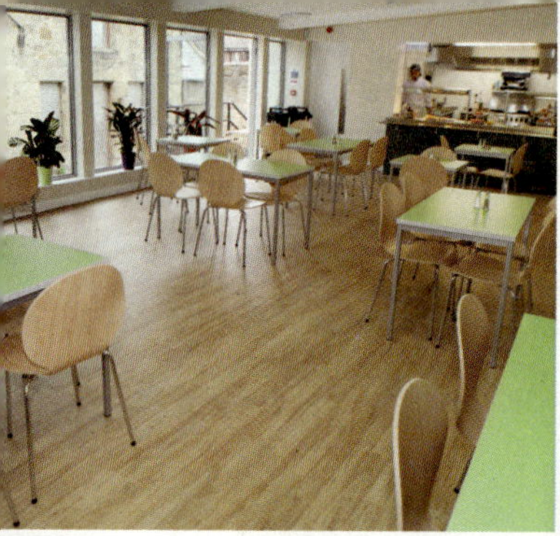

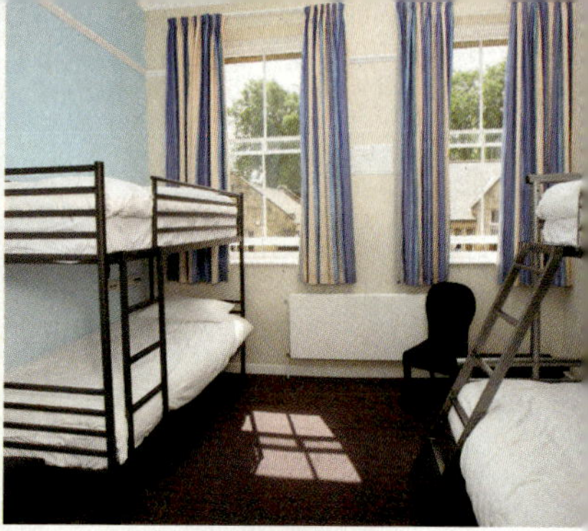

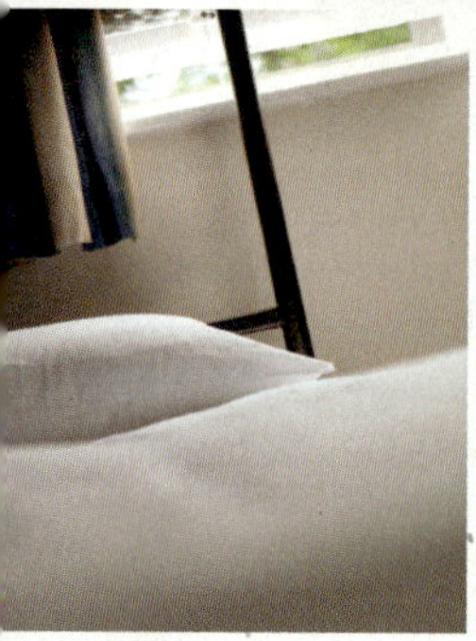

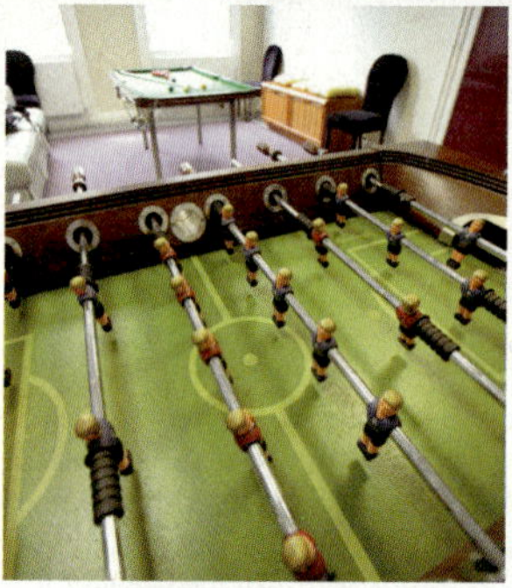

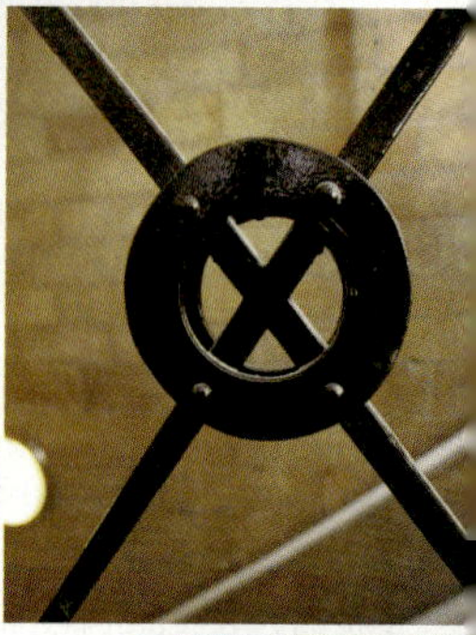

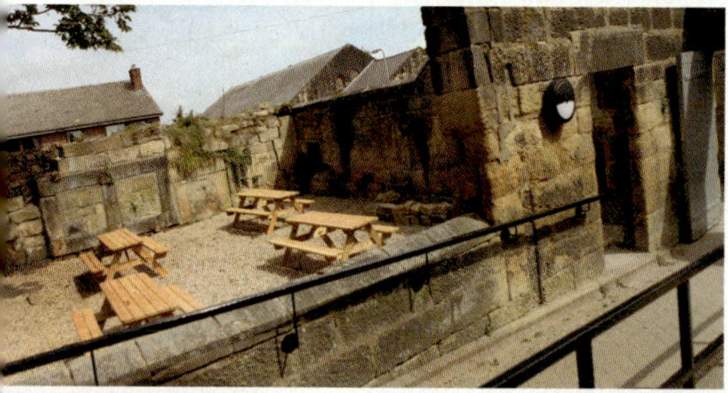

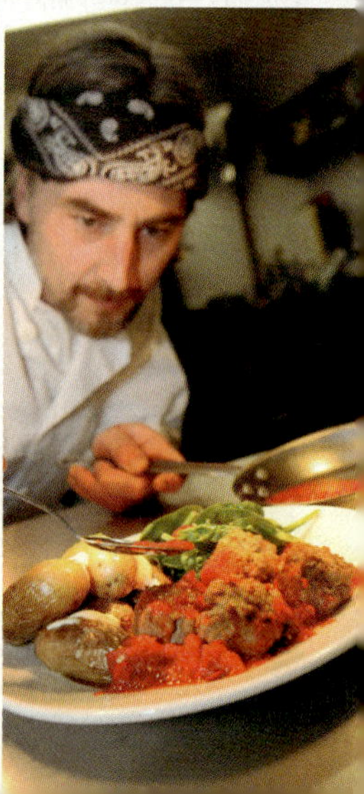

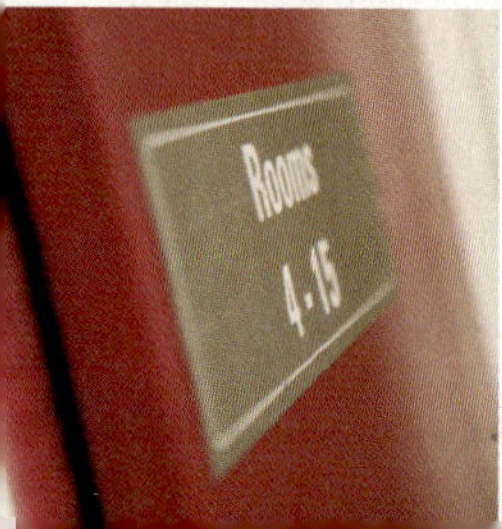
Rooms
4-15

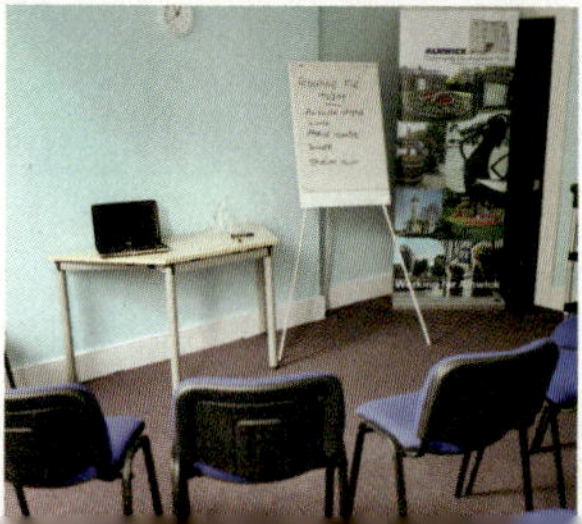

FOREST VIEW
WALKERS HOSTEL

Forest View is set in the hamlet of Byrness on the edge of Keilder Forest and Northumberland National Park. An ideal stopover on the A68 England to Scotland route. Byrness is the penultimate stop on the Pennine Way and at Forest View you can relax after a hard day's walking in the residents' bar/lounge.

The VisitBritain 4 star inn has walker friendly awards and offers quality furnished single, twin, double and triple rooms with clean modern en suite bathrooms. The Foresters' Bar & Restaurant serves quality home cooked meals & hand pulled local craft ales along with weekly guest ales. Forest View also has a well stocked shop and free to use laundry and drying facilities. Camping is also available. A recent national feedback survey rated Forest View at 99.5% for cleanliness, service and facilities.

DETAILS

- **Open** - All year, check in from 4pm - check out by 10.30 am.
- **Number of beds** - 14: 2 x single (private facilities), 2 x double (en suite), 1 x twin (en suite); 2 triple (en suite)
- **Booking** - Booking is recommended
- **Price per night** - Adults from £29 for bed and breakfast. Under 16s £19
- **Public Transport** - Nearest rail station Newcastle upon Tyne (40 miles) then National Express to lay-by 200yds from hostel.
- **Directions** - Forest View is just off the A68, 4 miles from the Scottish Border, 16 miles south of Jedburgh and 10 miles north of Otterburn.

CONTACT: Colin or Joyce
Tel: 01830 520425
joycetaylor1703@hotmail.co.uk   www.forestviewbyrness.co.uk
7 Otterburn Green, Byrness Village, Northumberland, NE19 1TS

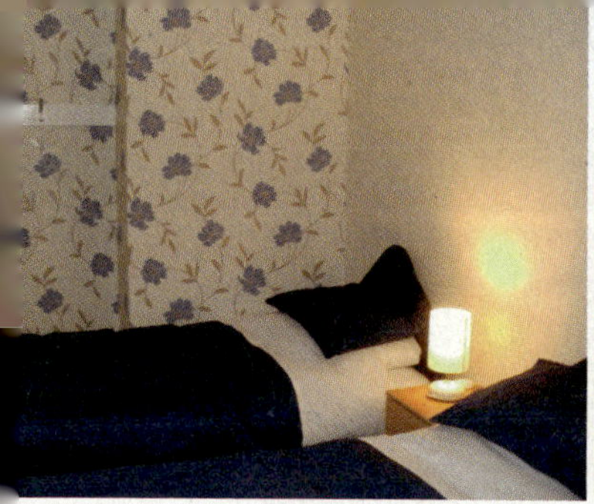
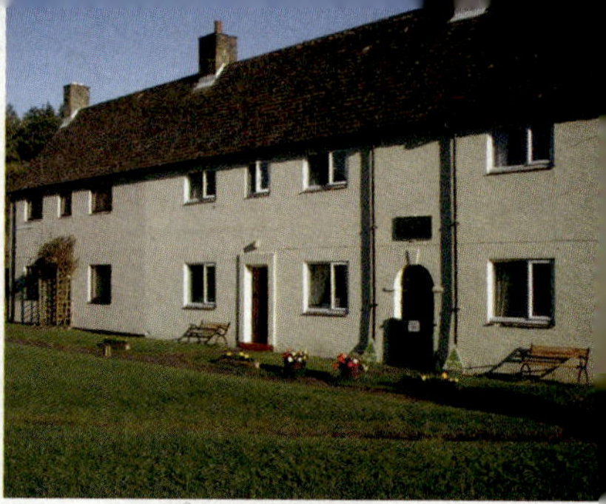
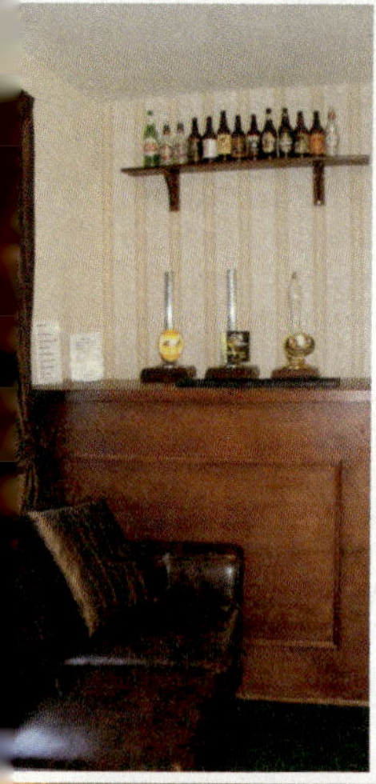
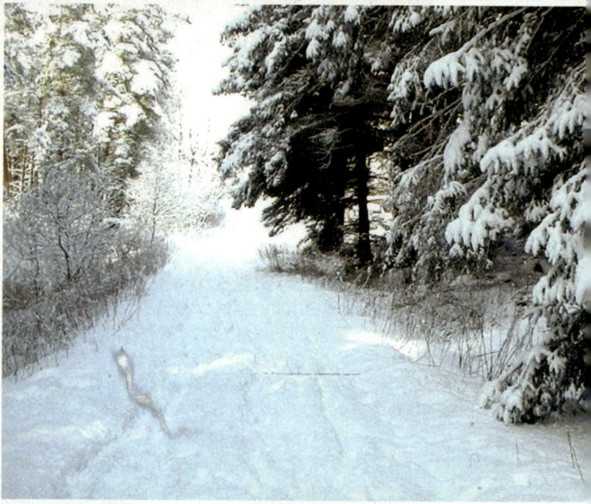
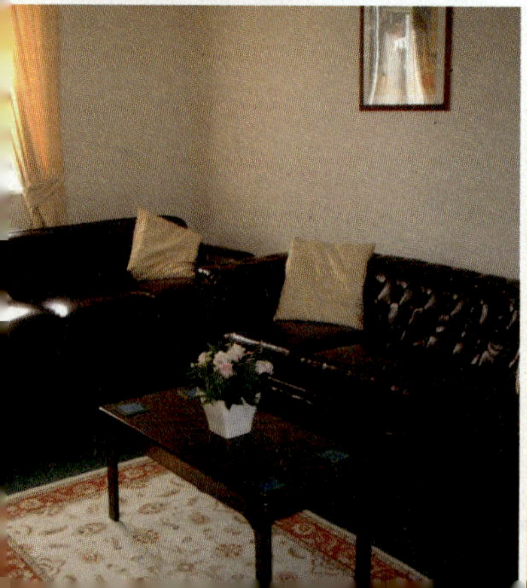
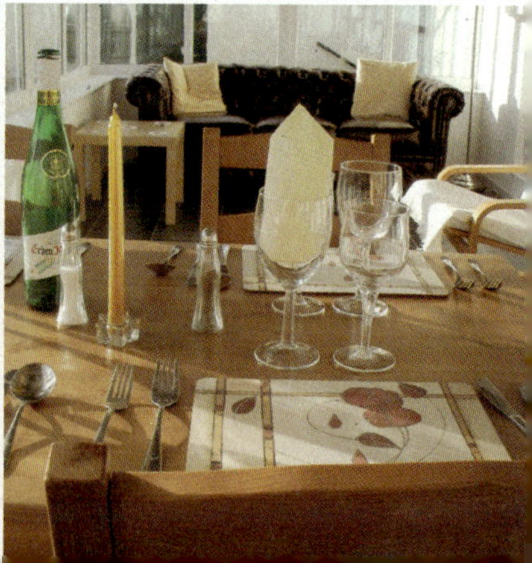

THE HIDES

ENGLAND

The Hides, located in Seahouses and run by Springhill Farm, are a fantastic affordable accommodation option. The Hides are perfect for groups, families or independent travellers. The accommodation is great value for money, comfortable, and very conveniently located. The Hides have a quiet and secluded location within Seahouses but also the convenience of being no more than a five minutes' walk from the village centre, harbour, shops, restaurants and bars. All five Hides can sleep up to 4 guests each with en suite facilities and the use of an on-site fully equipped kitchen and dining area, cycle store, drying room and laundry. Guests at The Hides are also welcome to use the children's play area and seasonal farm shop at Springhill Bunkhouse, just five minutes' walk away (see page 280). The Hides are available to book as a block or per hide per night (minimum occupancy charge of 2 adults/night).

DETAILS

- **Open** - All year, 9am - 6pm
- **Number of beds** - 20
- **Booking** - Online/phone; Min booking 2 nights. Deposit required when booking.
- **Price per night** - £19.50 adult, £14 under 14 (Under 1 free). Min charge 2 adults/night (£39). Christmas & New Year - £24/adult/night & £16/child/night min stay 3 nights. £5 pets/night. All 5 Hides £325/night. Sleeping bag & pillow hire £2.50/night
- **Public Transport** - Train station at Berwick upon Tweed. Buses run daily to Seahouses with the nearest bus stop being in North Sunderland which is the top end of Seahouses half a mile from Springhill.
- **Directions** - The Hides are on Main Street, Seahouses. From north or south follow B1340 to roundabout with large pub follow sign for riding centre to Main Street.

CONTACT: Miss Sarah Gregory
Tel: 01665721820
enquiries@springhill-farm.co.uk www.springhill-farm.co.uk
146 Main Street Seahouses Northumberland NE68 7UA

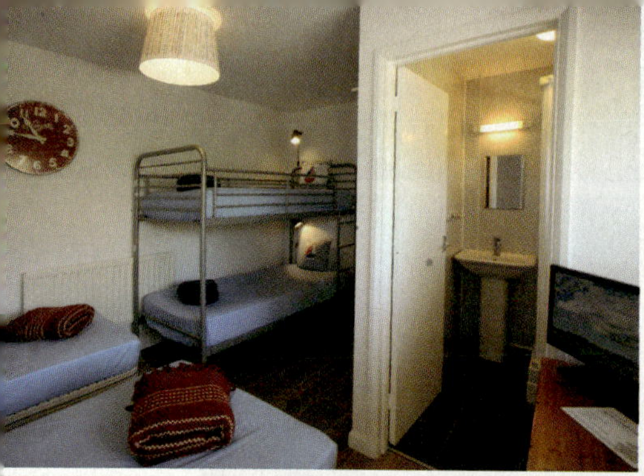
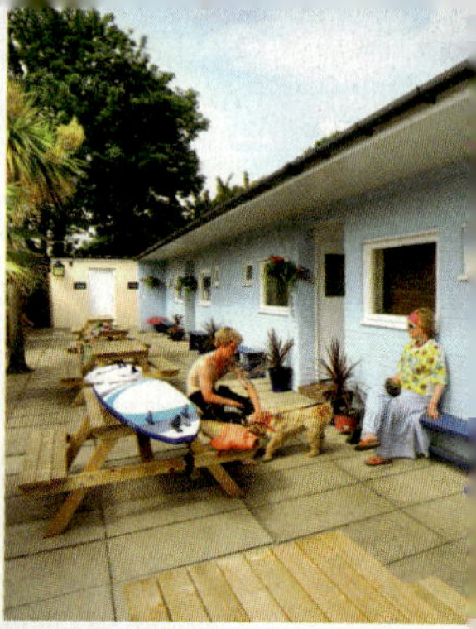
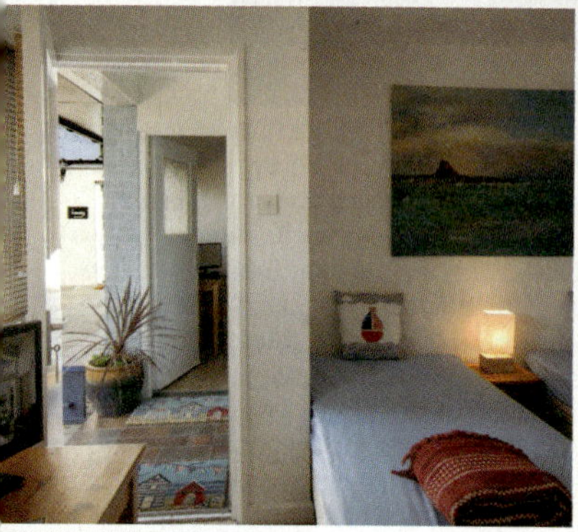
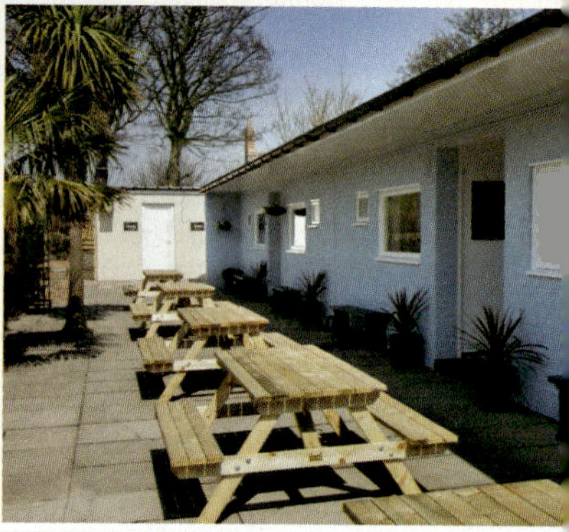
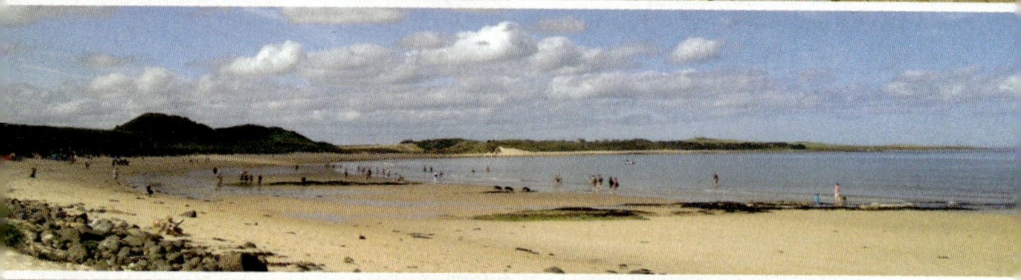
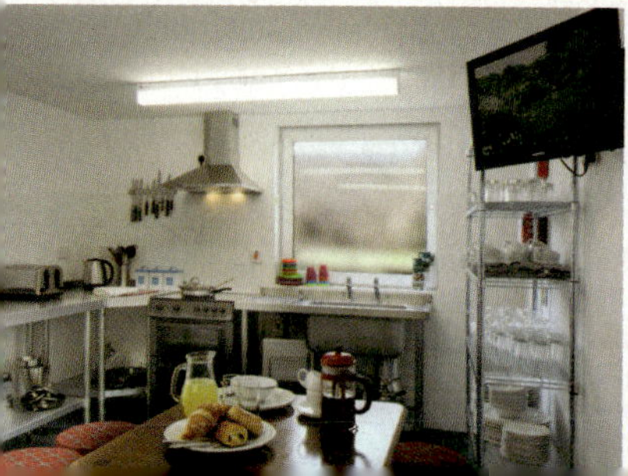
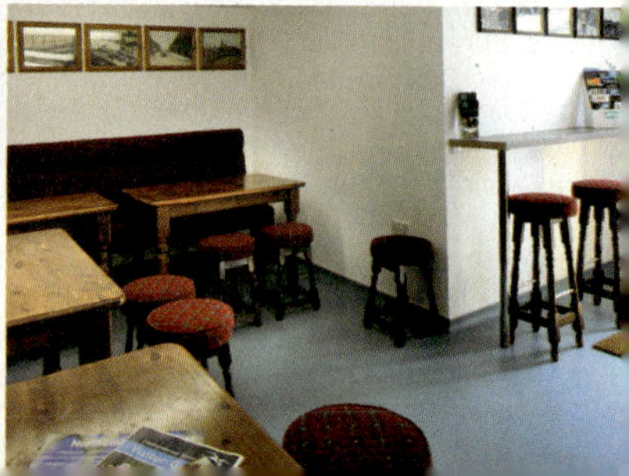

SPRINGHILL BUNKHOUSE

Springhill's Bunkhouse & Wigwams are ideal for groups, families or independent travellers looking for great value comfortable accommodation which can be booked as a whole or on a per bed/night basis. Superbly located on the Northumberland heritage coastline and AONB coastal path with stunning views towards the Farne Islands and Cheviot Hills, only 1 mile from Seahouses and 3 miles from Bamburgh. The Lookout Bunkhouse has 8 rooms of 4 beds with en suite shower rooms, fully equipped kitchen, dining and sitting area with TV/DVD, free WiFi, BBQ and outdoor seating. The five Wigwams sleep 5 on platform beds with mattresses, electric heating, lights, sockets, fridge, kettle and a separate loo block. The Wigwams have the use of a fully equipped kitchen and dining area with WiFi, TV/DVD and an outdoor seating area with BBQ's and fire pits. Cycle store, drying room and laundry onsite. Pets welcome. Springhill Farm also run "The Hides" just five minutes' walk away.

DETAILS

- **Open** - All year round, arrive 3pm-6pm, departure by 10am. Cleaning 12pm-4pm
- **Number of beds** - Bunkhouse 32: 8x4; Wigwams 25: 5x5
- **Booking** - Online, phone or email.
- **Price per night** - Bunkhouse £15 adult, £12 child (under 16). Wigwams £19.50 adult £14 child. Prices constant all year round.
- **Public Transport** - Closest railway stop with easy bus transfers is Berwick upon Tweed. Buses run daily to Seahouses with the nearest bus stop being in North Sunderland which is the top end of Seahouses half a mile from Springhill.
- **Directions** - Springhill Farm is 0.75miles from the coast road, which runs between Seahouses 1mile and Bamburgh 3.5miles. Alnwick is 15 miles and Berwick 25 miles

CONTACT: Sarah or Julie
Tel: 01665 721820, Fax: 07753856895
enquiries@springhill-farm.co.uk   www.springhill-farm.co.uk/bunkhouse
Springhill Farm, Seahouses, Northumberland NE68 7UR

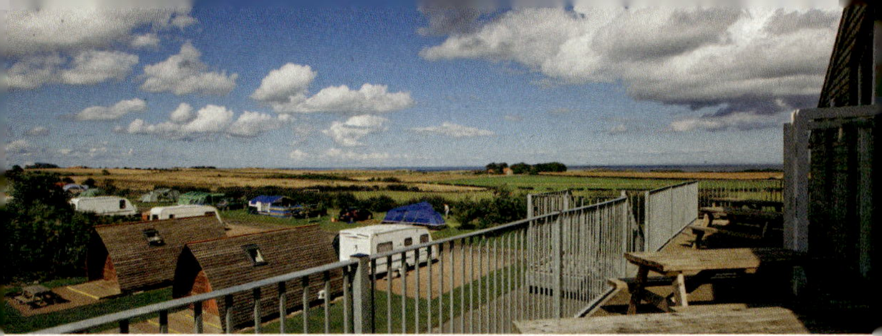
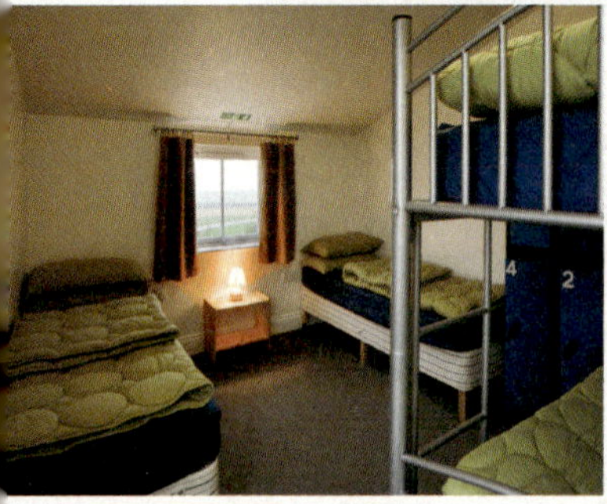
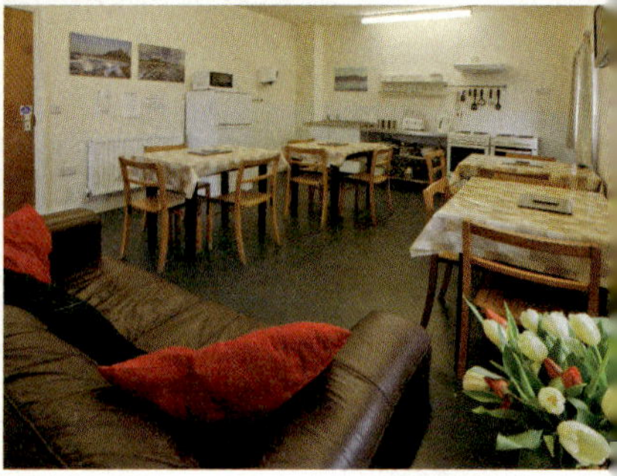
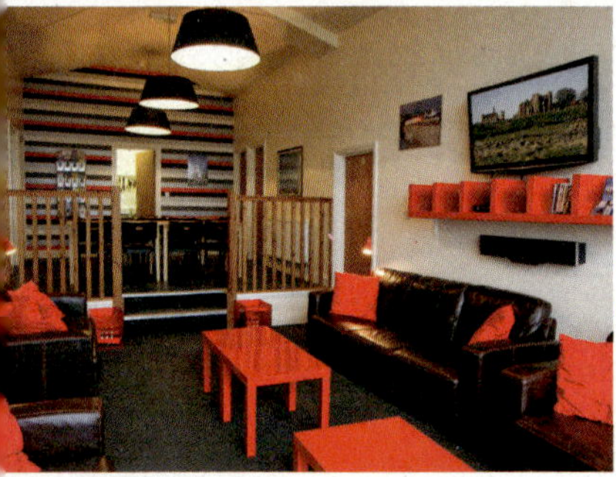
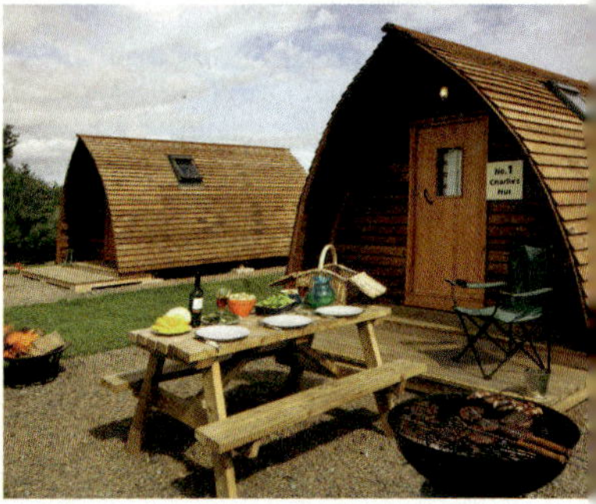
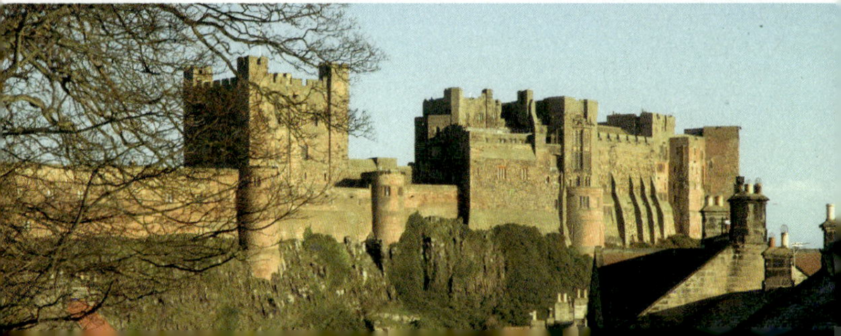

TACKROOM BUNKHOUSE

The Tackroom Bunkhouse is situated on a mixed working farm between the seaside villages of Beadnell and Seahouses, a stone's throw from beautiful sandy beaches on the spectacular Northumberland Coast. The area is ideal for walking, water sports, climbing, cycling, diving or just sightseeing.

Accommodating 12, the bunkhouse is ideal for smaller groups, individuals and couples. The two bedrooms are each fitted with 6 man-sized bunkbeds and a locker for each visitor. Sleeping bags are essential. The communal area has a mini kitchen with hob, microwave, fridge, toaster etc, a dining table to seat 12 and colour TV. All crockery, cutlery and cooking utensils are supplied but there is no oven. Adjoining the bunkhouse are male and female showers and toilets plus laundry room - shared with our small caravan and camping site. Also available is a lock-up and off road parking. The Tackroom Bunkhouse is heated. With regret, no dogs are allowed in the bunkhouse.

DETAILS

- **Open** - All year except Christmas and New Year, no check-in after 10pm.
- **Number of beds** - 12: 2 x 6.
- **Booking** - Recommended but not essential
- **Price per night** - £13 per person or £130 sole use.
- **Public Transport** - Train station at Berwick upon Tweed. There are intermittent local buses to Seahouses and Beadnell, passing ½ mile away from the hostel.
- **Directions** - From A1 take the B1340, follow road to Beadnell (signed Seahouses/Beadnell). Annstead farm is approx ½ mile past Beadnell on the left.

CONTACT: Sue Mellor
Tel: 01665 720387, Fax: 01665 721494
stay@annstead.co.uk www.annstead.co.uk
Annstead Farm, Beadnell, Northumberland, NE67 5BT

WOOLER
YOUTH HOSTEL

ENGLAND

Wooler Youth Hostel & Shepherd's Huts is set in its own spacious grounds on the edge of the town. It has newly refurbished en suite bedrooms & Shepherd's Hut sleeping cabins, a huge dining and common room, excellent drying facilities and a large self-catering kitchen, making it great for groups & families. There is also an excellent value restaurant, on site car parking and secure cycle storage.

Wooler has inns, grocery stores and specialist shops, and is an ideal base for exploring the Northumberland National Park, the Cheviot Hills (rich in archaeological sites), local castles and fine sandy beaches. For walkers there is the long distance St Cuthbert's Way and many day walks. For cyclists there's the Wooler cycle hub routes, Pennine Cycleway and many quiet lanes to explore. Nearby there are bridleways perfect for mountain-biking, some of the best bouldering in the UK, riding centres and even a gliding school. Bird watchers can take a boat trip to the Farne Islands and visit the Cheviot Hills.

DETAILS

- **Open** - April until end Oct (open for group bookings Nov to March), 7am-11pm
- **Number of beds** - 52: 3x2, 6x4,1x6,1x8. Shepherd's huts 3x2 & 1x3.
- **Booking** - Booking advised. Always call the hostel in advance of arriving.
- **Price per night** - From £15.50 adults, £12.20 children. Group booking discounts.
- **Public Transport** - Market Place, 400 yards from the hostel. Arriva Northumbria/Travelsure 464, Border Village 267 from Berwick. Travelsure 470/3 from Alnwick.
- **Directions** - From the Market Place at the bottom of the high street go up Cheviot Street past The Anchor pub. The hostel is 300 yards up the hill on the right.

CONTACT: Mick
Tel: 01668 281365
wooler@yha.org.uk   www.woolerhostel.co.uk
30 Cheviot Street, Wooler, Northumberland, NE71 6LW

BLUEBELL FARM
BUNKBARN

ENGLAND

Bluebell Farm caravan and camp-site is in the centre of the village, within walking distance of shops and pubs. It is ideally located for exploring Nothumberland's Heritage Coast Route, the Cheviot Hills National Park and the historic Scottish Borders. The bunkbarn sleeps 14, and there is also a wooden ark and five self-catering cottages. The bunkbarn has a family room for 6, an 8 bed dorm and a fully equipped self-catering kitchen. The Ark has a sleeping platform for 4 (but if you book for fewer you have sole use), fridge, microwave, toaster and kettle, with a patio area outside where you can cook on your own camping stove. All the beds are equipped with pillows and blankets and you can hire linen, duvets and towels or bring your own sleeping bag. Shared toilet block and bike store. Hot showers, electricity and gas included in the prices. Activities include golf, climbing, canoeing, diving, horse riding, fishing, cycling and walking. Dogs welcome by arrangement. Duke of Edinburgh groups welcome.

DETAILS

- **Open** - All year, check in by 9 pm, departure by 10 am.
- **Number of beds** - Bunkhouse 14 : 1 x 8, 1 x 6 Ark: 4
- **Booking** - Recommended throughout school holidays and for weekends.
- **Price per night** - Bunkbarn: £12.00, under 14s £6.00. Ark: £15.00, under 14's £7.50. Linen and towel hire £6.00 per person. Exclusive use available.
- **Public Transport** - Trains at Berwick upon Tweed. Buses from Berwick to Belford. National Express coaches stop in Belford. Local bus from Newcastle.
- **Directions** - From the A1 take B1342 into the village. Turn onto B6349 signposted for Wooler. Bluebell Farm is first main driveway on right, almost opposite the Co-op.

CONTACT: Phyl
Tel: 01668 213362
corillas@tiscali.co.uk www.bluebellfarmbelford.com
Bluebell Farm Caravan Park, Belford, Northumberland, NE70 7QE

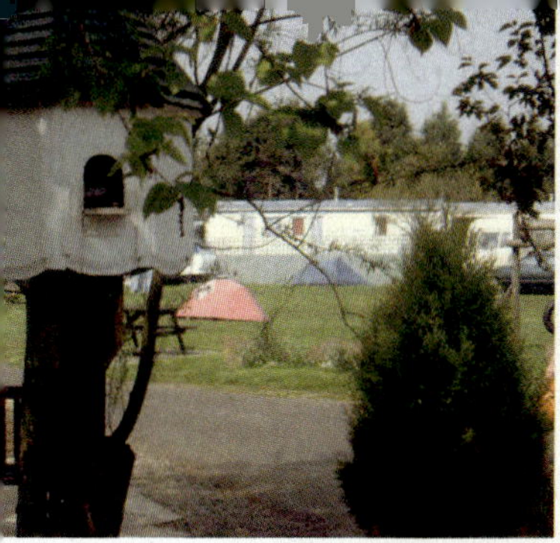

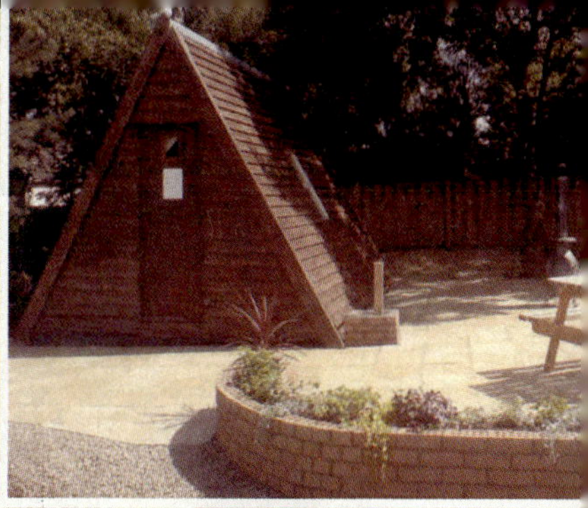

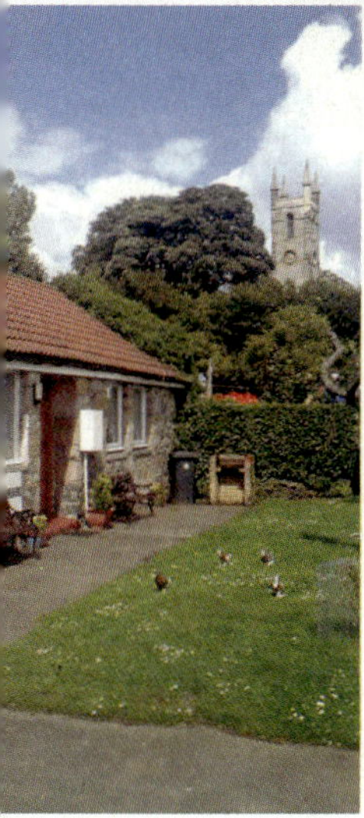

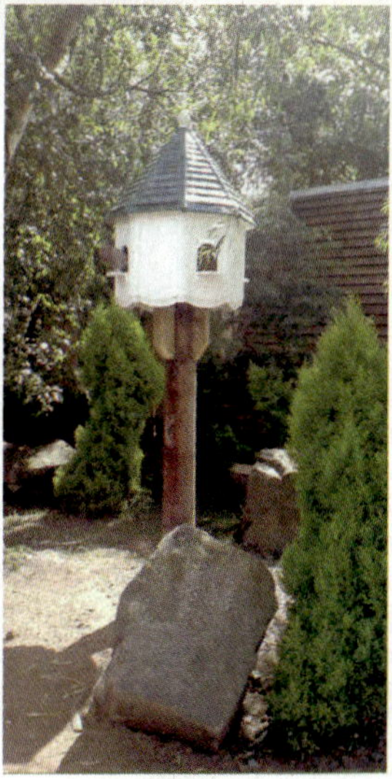

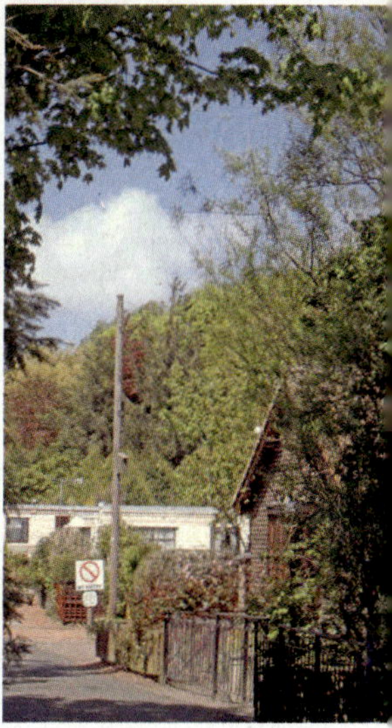

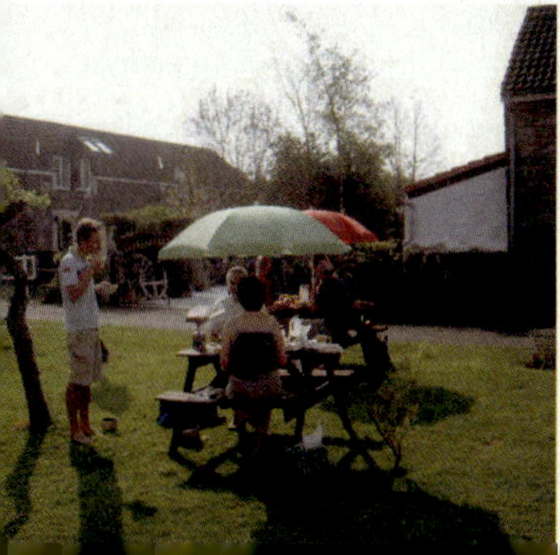

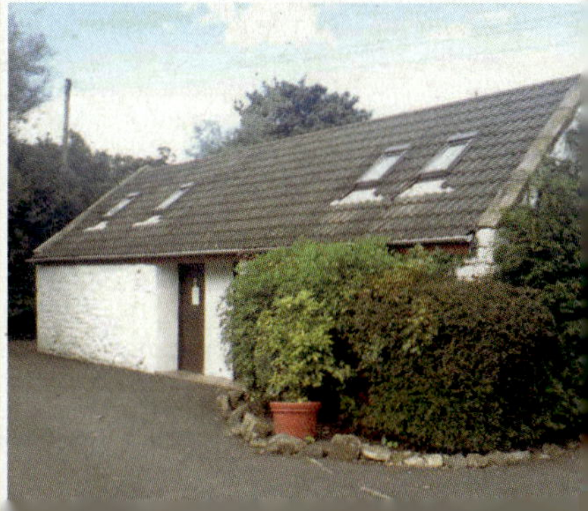

CHATTON PARK BUNKHOUSE

ENGLAND

Chatton Park Bunkhouse started life as a Smithy and has been converted into self-catering accommodation. It is situated on a mixed working farm which nestles around the River Till, half a mile from Chatton village.

Eight miles from the coast and five miles from the Cheviot Hills, Chatton Park is an ideal base for exploring Northumberland's vast empty beaches, heather clad hills & historic castles. Walking, water sports, climbing, fishing, golf and cycling are all available nearby. Accommodating 12, the bunkhouse is perfect for smaller groups, families & individuals. The 2 bedrooms are fitted with large custom made bunks and can be rented separately as secure units. Bedding can be provided at a small extra fee. The living area has a fully equipped kitchen & seating around the original blacksmith's fire. Wash & drying room with hot showers. Secure storage, ample parking. Room for 2 small tents. £10/dog/stay.

DETAILS

- **Open** - All year, flexible but no check in after 9pm
- **Number of beds** - 12: 2x6
- **Booking** - Booking recommended but not essential
- **Price per night** - £12 - £18 pp. Group bookings negotiable. Teenagers need to be accompanied by a responsible adult
- **Public Transport** - Nearest train station Berwick upon Tweed. Buses to Chatton from Alnwick / Berwick.
- **Directions** - From A1 take B6348 to Chatton. 4 miles at bottom of hill on right is Chatton Park Farm

CONTACT: Jane or Duncan
Tel: 01668 215247
ord@chattonpk.fsnet.co.uk www.chattonparkfarm.co.uk
Chatton Park Farm, Chatton, Alnwick, Northumberland, NE66 5RA

MAUGHOLD VENTURE CENTRE BUNKHOUSE
ENGLAND

Maughold Venture Centre Bunkhouse is built of Manx stone, overlooking farmland with views in the distance to the sea. It offers self-catering facilities with the option of purchasing meals from the neighbouring adventure centre if required (subject to availability). All bedrooms are en suite with full central heating.

Facilities include a basic but functional games room and kitchen. The local beach of Port e Vullen, 10 minutes' walk away, is popular with visitors and the bunkhouse is adjacent to the Venture Centre where you may arrange sessions of kayaking, abseiling, air rifle shooting, archery, gorge walking, dinghy sailing, power boating and team events. It has its own stop, Lewaigue Halt, on the Manx Electric Railway giving access to Douglas, Ramsay and to mountain walks and tranquil glens. Ideal for groups, families and individuals.

DETAILS

- **Open** - January - December, 24 hours
- **Number of beds** - 52: 2x2, 1x5, 4x8, 2x10
- **Booking** - Telephone reservation essential
- **Price per night** - £10-£15 per person
- **Public Transport** - No 3 bus or Manx Electric Railway from Douglas or Ramsey. Get off bus at Dreemskerry (5 minutes' walk); get off railway at Lewaigue Halt (nearby). Taxi from Ramsey £5. Taxi from Douglas £25.
- **Directions** - GR 469922. From Douglas take the A2 coast road. When the road begins to descend into Ramsey the Venture Centre is signposted on the right hand side. Follow the signs - it is the first building on the left.

CONTACT: Simon Read
Tel: 01624 814240
Contact@adventure-centre.co.uk www.adventure-centre.co.uk
The Venture Centre, Maughold, Isle of Man, IM7 1AW

South Wales

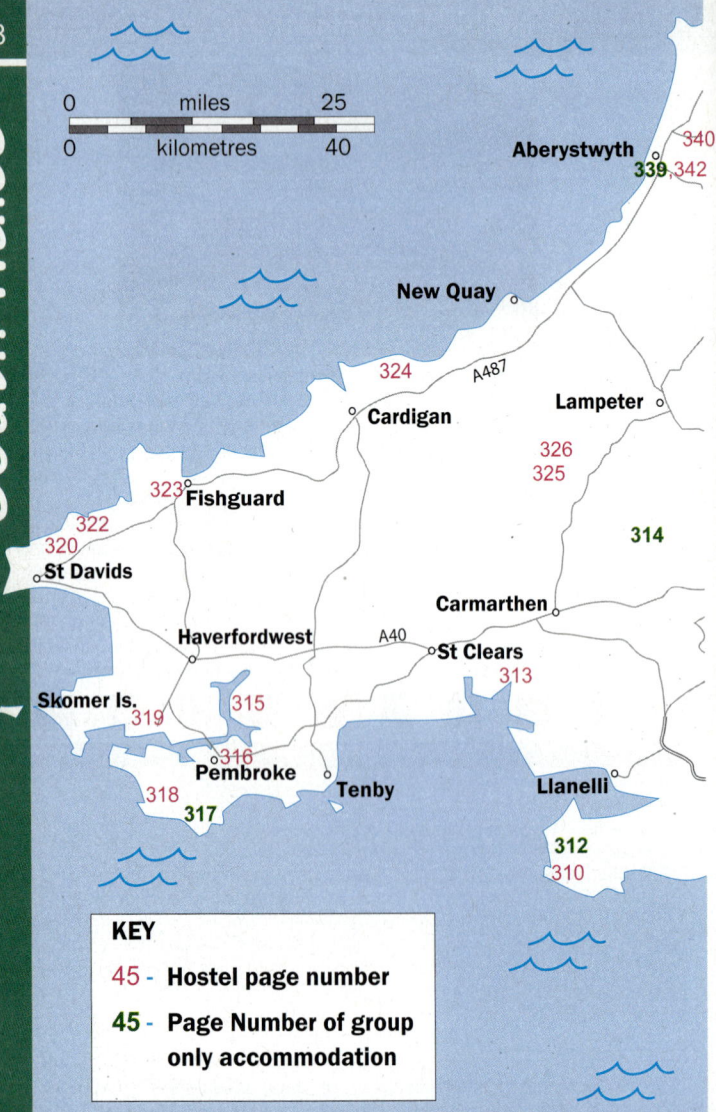

Map

Scale: 0–25 miles / 0–40 kilometres

Locations and page numbers:
- Aberystwyth — **339**, 340, 342
- New Quay
- Cardigan — 324
- Lampeter — 326, 325
- A487
- Fishguard — 323
- St Davids — 322, 320
- **314**
- Carmarthen
- Haverfordwest — A40 — St Clears — 313
- Skomer Is. — 319, 315
- Pembroke — 316, 318, **317**
- Tenby
- Llanelli — **312**, 310

KEY
- 45 - Hostel page number (red)
- **45** - Page Number of group only accommodation (green)

South Wales

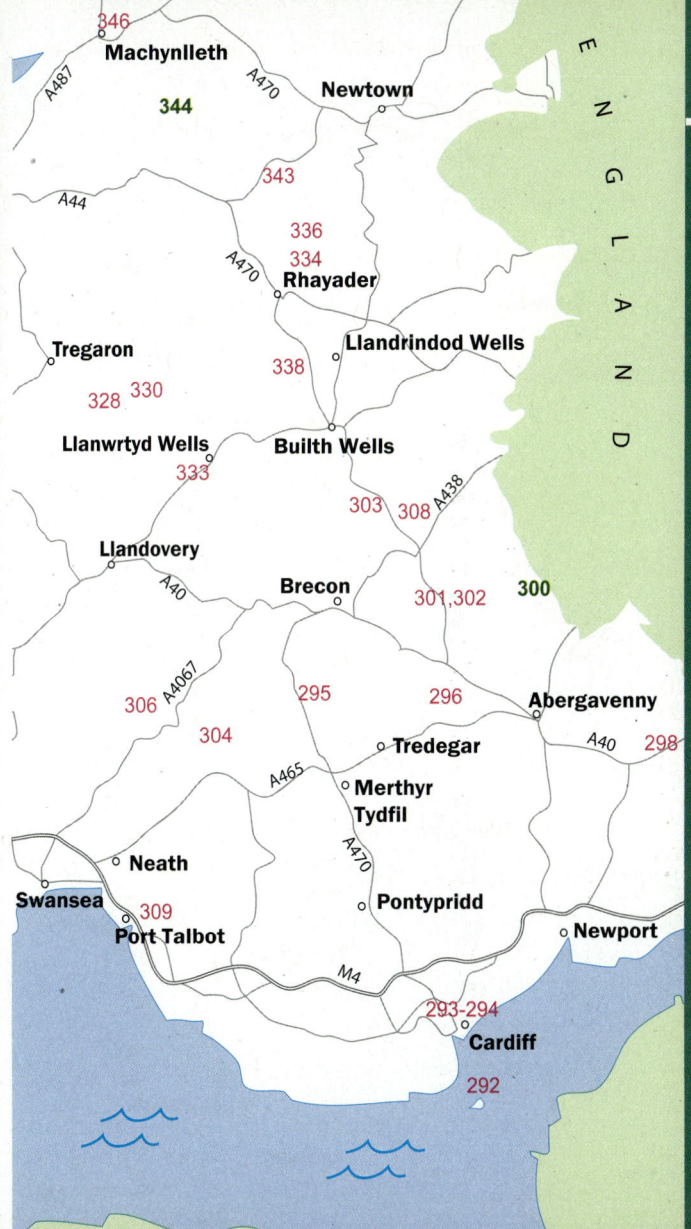

289

- 346 Machynlleth
- **344**
- Newtown
- 343
- 336
- 334
- Rhayader
- Tregaron
- Llandrindod Wells
- 338
- 328 330
- Llanwrtyd Wells
- Builth Wells
- 333
- 303 308
- Llandovery
- Brecon
- 301, 302
- **300**
- 306
- 295
- 296
- Abergavenny
- 304
- Tredegar
- 298
- Merthyr Tydfil
- Neath
- Swansea
- 309
- Pontypridd
- Port Talbot
- Newport
- 293-294
- Cardiff
- 292

ENGLAND

North Wales

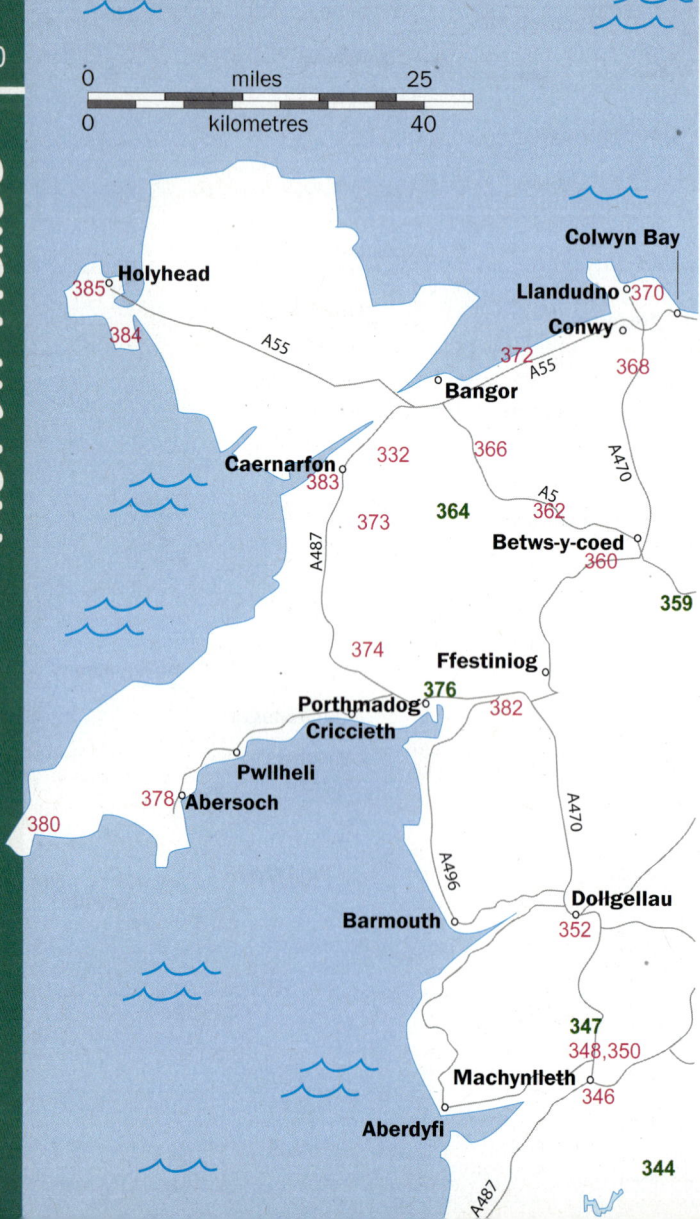

290

0 — miles — 25
0 — kilometres — 40

- Holyhead 385, 384
- Colwyn Bay
- Llandudno 370
- Conwy 372, 368
- A55
- Bangor
- Caernarfon 383
- 332
- 366
- 373
- 364
- A5 362
- Betws-y-coed 360
- A470
- 359
- 374
- Ffestiniog
- 376
- Porthmadog 382
- Criccieth
- Pwllheli
- 378 Abersoch
- 380
- A487
- A496
- Barmouth
- Dollgellau 352
- A470
- 347
- 348, 350
- Machynlleth 346
- Aberdyfi
- A487
- 344

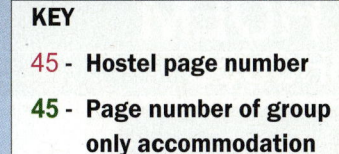

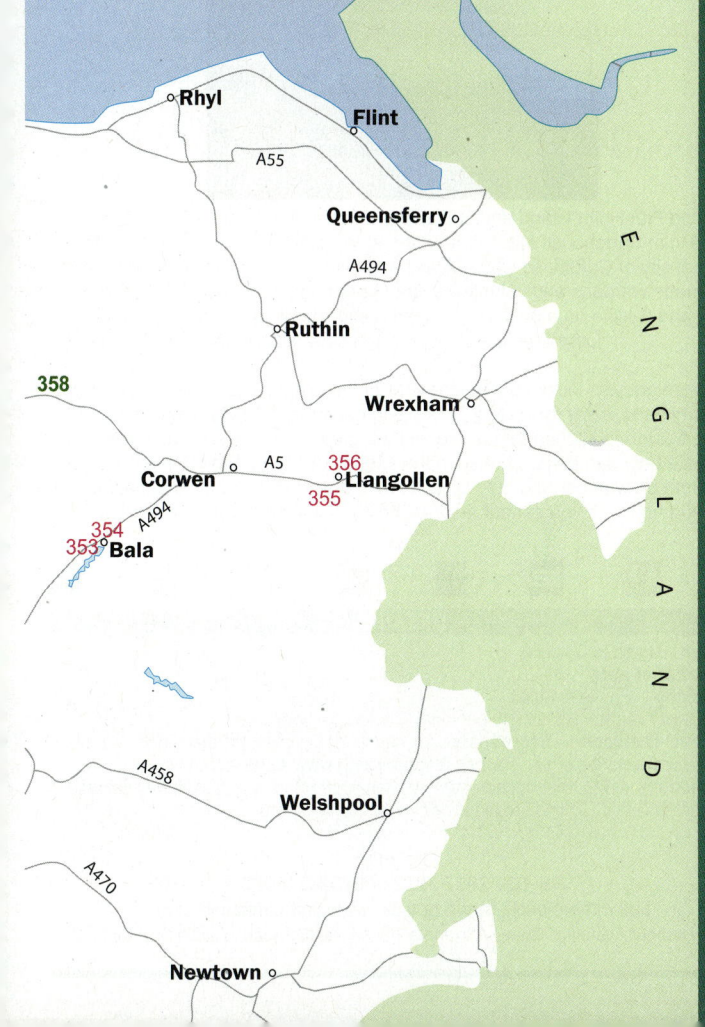

KEY

45 - Hostel page number

45 - Page number of group only accommodation

North Wales

- Rhyl
- Flint
- A55
- Queensferry
- A494
- Ruthin
- 358
- Wrexham
- Corwen — A5 — 356 Llangollen — 355
- 354 A494
- 353 Bala
- A458
- Welshpool
- A470
- Newtown

ENGLAND

FLAT HOLM FARMHOUSE

WALES

Travel to Flat Holm Island and stay in the most southerly hostel in Wales! The Flat Holm Farmhouse is located on the small island just five miles from the capital city of Cardiff, so why not visit and discover the magic of island life? Home to wardens and volunteers, stay here and experience the wealth of history and wildlife on a guided tour, take a shore walk and watch the sunset, or just sit back and relax in the cosy island pub.

An overnight visit includes a guided tour of the island. The mixed dormitories with bunkbeds, cater for up to 12 people in each room. Visitors have full use of the self-catering kitchen to prepare all their meals (snacks such as crisps and chocolate bars can be purchased in the island gift shop). Trips to the island are dependent on weather and may be cancelled due to strong winds, sometimes at short notice. If you cannot reschedule the ticket price will be refunded.

DETAILS

- **Open** - March to October,
- **Number of beds** - 24.
- **Booking** - Phone or email.
- **Price per night** - Hostel £19 per night. Contact for boat costs
- **Public Transport** - See websites for details of the boats to the island. Landing craft www.mwmarine.org or Fast rib (capacity x12) www.flatholmisland.com
- **Directions** - The boat departs from Weston-super-Mare and Cardiff Bay Barrage. Booking essential. To find out more visit www.mwmarine.org

CONTACT:
Tel: 029 2087 7912 or 07929365077
flatholmproject@cardiff.gov.uk   www.flatholmisland.com
Cardiff Harbour Authority, Queen Alexandra House, Cargo Road, Cardiff Bay, CF10 4LY

NOSDA STUDIO
HOSTEL

WALES

NosDa means "Good night" in Welsh and that is exactly what we promise. NosDa Studio Hostel is a hostel/hotel hybrid, a new concept of stylish budget accommodation. There's a choice of secure mixed and single sex dormitories and also a number of private rooms, each with their own pod style bathrooms, TVs and views of the Millennium Stadium. "NosDa is redefining the hostelling genre"- Lonely Planet. Uniquely situated along the banks of the river Taff, NosDa occupies a refurbished 19th century building with superb views of the iconic Millennium Stadium. Our lively bar has regular live music events, a selection of Welsh beers, ciders and spirits and the affordable menu lets you taste some delicious local produce. With the castle, stadium and train station all within sight, NosDa Studio Hostel is the most centrally located hostel with a view to die for and the facilities to match! \"like\" us on Facebook to keep up to date with latest events and offers.

DETAILS

- **Open** - All year, 24 hours
- **Number of beds** - 138: 3 x 4, 6 x 6, 1 x 7, 2 x 8, 1 x 10 + 60 beds in private rooms
- **Booking** - Essential for groups, advisable for individuals. Book online.
- **Price per night** - Dorms from £22.50. Private from £50. Private en suite from £65
- **Public Transport** - Train, coach and bus stations 5 minutes' walk from the hostel.
- **Directions** - By car: From the M4, take junction 32 and follow signs for city centre. Approaching the centre follow the road around the castle then straight ahead over the bridge crossing the River Taff. Take the next left into Lower Cathedral Road, then 1st left into Despenser Street. By foot from Cardiff Central Station turn left across the river and follow the embankment upstream, with the stadium opposite. Look ahead.

CONTACT: Reception
Tel: 029 2037 8866, Fax: 029 2038 8741
info@nosda.co.uk www.nosda.co.uk
53-59 Despenser Street, Riverside, Cardiff, CF11 6AG

RIVER HOUSE HOSTEL

This is an award-winning family run 4 star hostel in the heart of Cardiff, voted number 1 in the Hostelworld list of best hostels. Opened in 2007 to rave reviews, the brother and sister team have made sure this will be the best hostel experience you will come across on your travels. With fabulous views of the world famous Millennium Stadium and River Taff and with the central train and bus stations just 5 mins' walk away, what's stopping you?

Facilities include well equipped kitchen, cosy TV lounge, decked garden with barbecue, free lockers and free wireless broadband. Bikes, irons, and hairdryers available for hire. Linen, duvets and breakfast are included in the price and the beds are made up for you. Hostelworld awarded best Hostel in UK since 2008.

Treat yourself to a quality stay at budget prices.

DETAILS

- **Open** - All year, 24 hours.
- **Number of beds** - 50: 2 bed private rooms, 4 bed dorms and 6 bed dorms.
- **Booking** - Book by phone or online.
- **Price per night** - From £16pp. Private (twin) rooms from £36 for two people. All prices include breakfast.
- **Public Transport** - Cardiff Central coach and train stations, with regular services to UK cities and airports 5 minutes' walk away.
- **Directions** - From Central train station turn left and cross river on Tudor Street. Once over the river Fitzhamon Embankment is first turn on right.

CONTACT: Reception
Tel: 02920 399 810
info@riverhousebackpackers.com   www.riverhousebackpackers.com
59 Fitzhamon Embankment, Riverside, Cardiff, CF11 6AN

COED OWEN BUNKHOUSE

295

WALES

Holiday on an idyllic Welsh hill farm in the heart of the Brecon Beacons National Park. Coed Owen Bunkhouse provides fully equipped self-contained accommodation suitable for large or small groups and families who wish to spend some time exploring this beautiful area of South Wales. Walkers, cyclists, fishermen and all who enjoy the countryside are welcome at Coed Owen Farm.

With a newly renovated interior to sleep up to 25 and fitted with all modern conveniences, the bunkhouse is perfect for family celebrations, getaways, group visits and school trips. Spend some time exploring the beautiful outdoors found right on the doorstep. Coed Owen provides an easy gateway between the city and the Brecon Beacons. Enjoy walks, hiking, fishing, cycling and adventure activities, or simply relax in our warm, cosy bunkhouse with plenty of field space to play outdoor games and a BBQ area.

DETAILS

- **Open** - All Year round, 9am - 10pm
- **Number of beds** - 25: 2x6 bed dorm, 1x10 bed dorm, 1 double room and 1 single.
- **Booking** - Book by email or phone
- **Price per night** - From £20 pp which includes bed linen, tea and coffee. Minimum of two night stay at weekends.
- **Public Transport** - On route T4 in the area of Brecon, between the stops Storey Arms and Llwyn-on. Nearest railway station Merthyr Tydfil 10 minutes away. 1 hour from Cardiff International Airport
- **Directions** - On A470 between Brecon and Merthyr Tydfil at Nant Ddu.

CONTACT: Molly or Netty Rees
Tel: 07508544044   01685 722628
mollyrees_moo@hotmail.com   www.breconbeaconsbunkhouse.co.uk
Coed Owen Farm, Cwmtaff, Merthyr Tydfill, CF48 2HY

WERN WATKIN BUNKHOUSE

WALES

Wern Watkin Bunkhouse is located in the Brecon Beacons National Park, high up on Mynnedd Llangattock. It is also known as YHA Llangattock Mountain. There is direct access on foot to the mountainside and a flat mountain road to a National Cycle Route. The Bunkhouse is a converted stone barn with bunks for 30 people in 7, mainly en suite, bedrooms. The massive dining room and seating area opens out onto ancient woodlands. It has under-floor heating throughout, excellent drying facilities and ample hot water. The location is ideal for caving, rock climbing, canoeing, abseiling, orienteering, pony trekking and mountain biking. Outdoor pursuit training can be arranged from local qualified instructors. The bunkhouse is within easy walking distance of Llangattock cave complex (one of Europe's most elaborate cave systems) as well as climbing crags and open moorland. A short drive away are the rest of Brecon Beacons, the scenic Wye and Usk river valleys and a wealth of industrial heritage at the World Heritage site of Blaenavon. Catering can be provided for groups.

DETAILS

- **Open** - All year, all day.
- **Number of beds** - 30: 4x6, 1x4, 2x2. All rooms except one en suite
- **Booking** - Availability online. 20% deposit, balance three weeks in advance.
- **Price per night** - Sole use £450 week nights, £630 weekend nights. Smaller groups by negotiation £16pp week nights, £18.50 pp weekend.
- **Public Transport** - Trains Abergavenny (8miles). Nearest buses Crickhowell.
- **Directions** - Access can be either from Crickhowell or Brynmawr on small mountain roads. Detailed instructions will be sent with your booking.

CONTACT: Andrew Fryer
Tel: 01873 812307
enquiries@wernwatkin.co.uk www.wernwatkin.co.uk
Wern Watkin, Hillside, Llangattock, Crickhowell, NP8 1LG

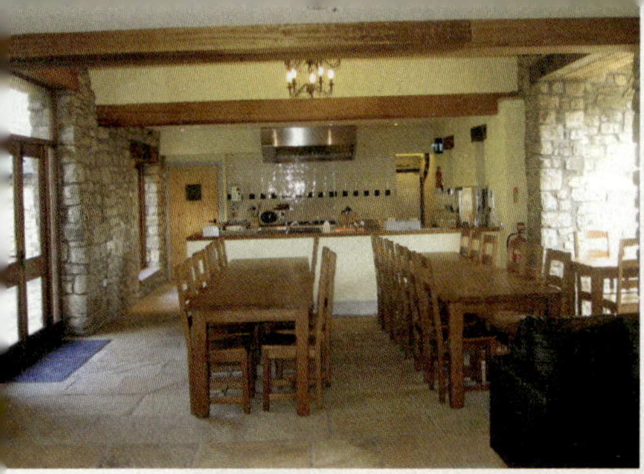
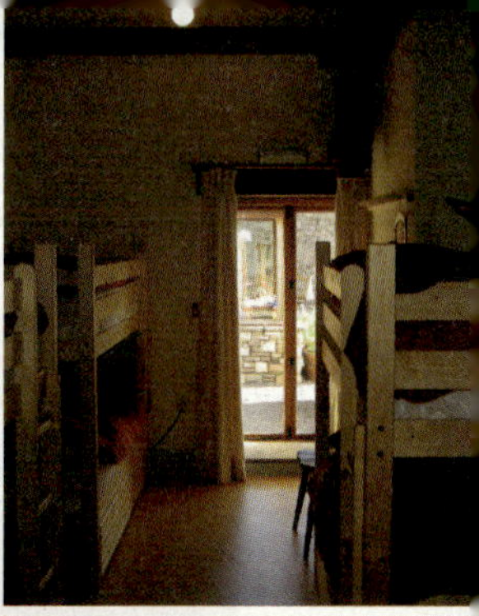
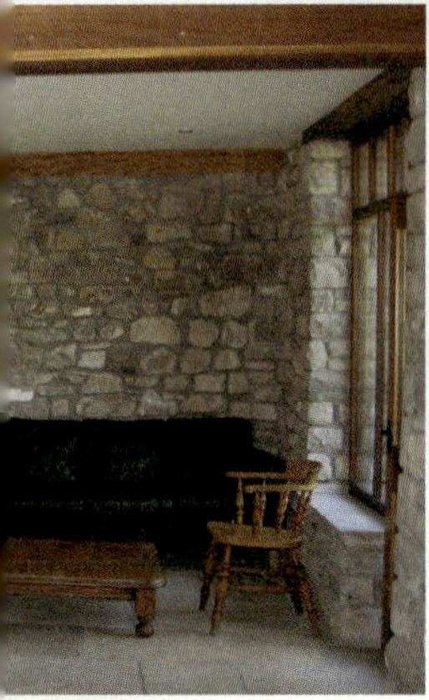
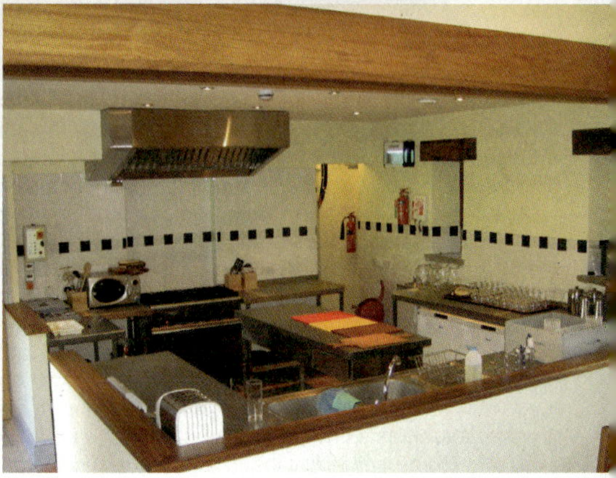
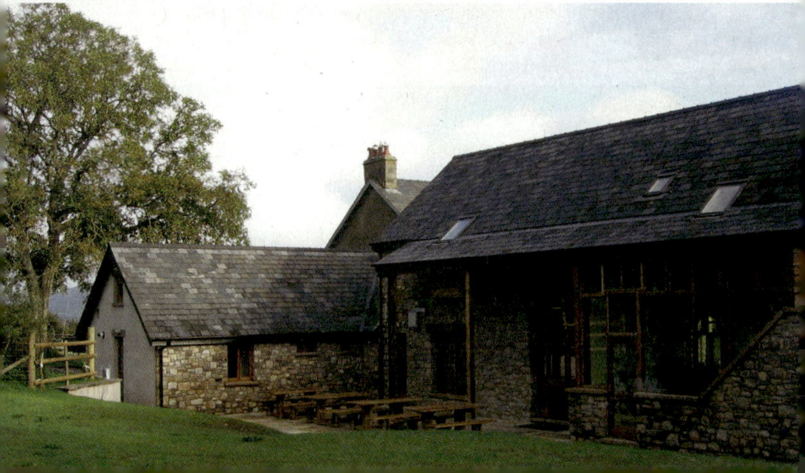

RICKYARD BUNKHOUSE

WALES

Rickyard Bunkhouse is set amidst idyllic countryside and well away from the hustle and bustle. Offa's Dyke footpath passes the entrance and it is within 25 mins of Wye Valley, Symonds Yat, and the Forest of Dean. Many outdoor pursuits can be enjoyed - canoeing, rafting, potholing, quad biking, rock climbing and paint balling to name but a few. The River Trothy borders the land; kingfishers and otters enjoy the peace and tranquillity of the Trothy valley. Buzzards circle high above, easily recognised by their distinctive call.
The Bunkhouse holds 20 easily, has an excellent, very well equipped kitchen, a separate dining/relaxing area with TV, and background heating. Sleeping accommodation is split into several areas. It is totally self-contained, and is ideal for reunions, groups and families. There is a large secure area for camping where children can safely play and ample parking with hard standing. Luggage transfer, breakfasts and packed lunches can be arranged. Bedding supplied, towels £1. Come and enjoy the tranquil surroundings (loud music or wild parties are not welcome). Exclusive use available, please enquire.

DETAILS

- **Open** - All year, all day.
- **Number of beds** - 20: + camping.
- **Booking** - Deposit required, no credit cards. Notice not always required.
- **Price per night** - £16.00pp. Prices include bedding, towels £1. Tents £5pp. Can be booked for sole use.
- **Public Transport** - Trains at Abergavenny (11m). Buses at Monmouth (3m).
- **Directions** - Next to the Hendre Farm House on the same side of the road.

CONTACT: Graham Edwards
Tel: 01600 740128
rickyardbunkhouse@googlemail.com www.rickyardbunkhouse.co.uk
Wonastow, Monmouth, NP25 4DJ

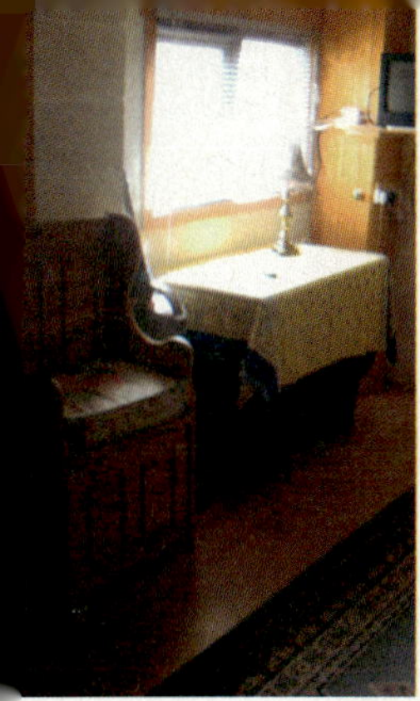

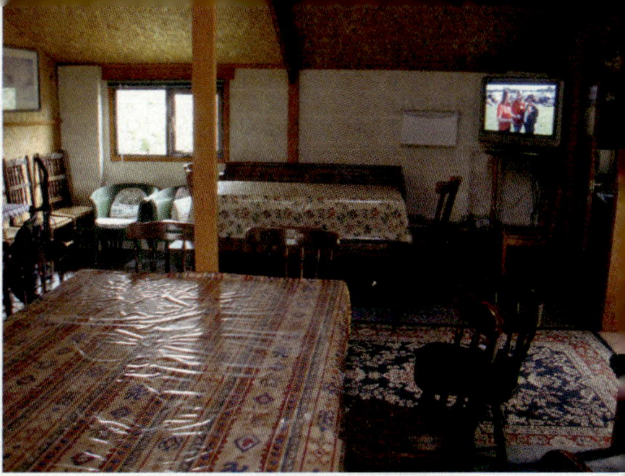

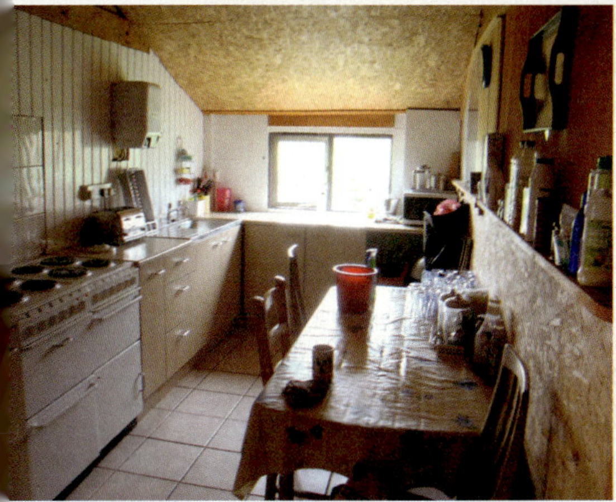

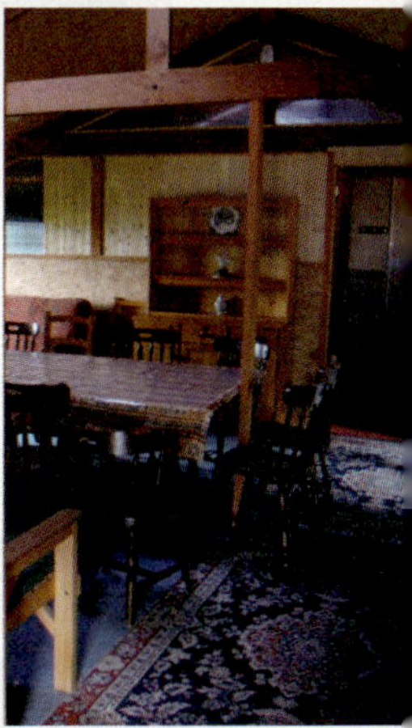

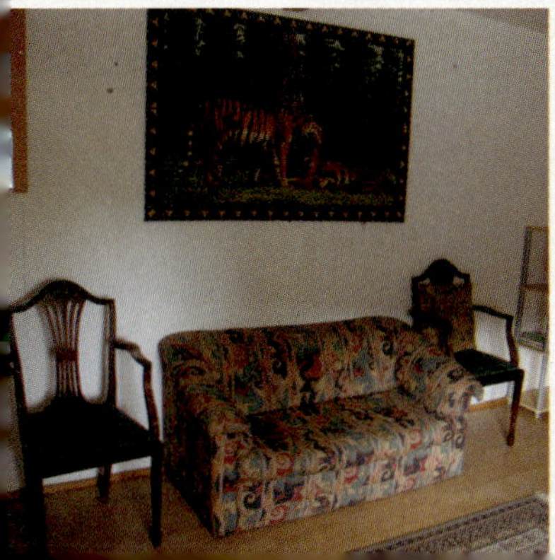

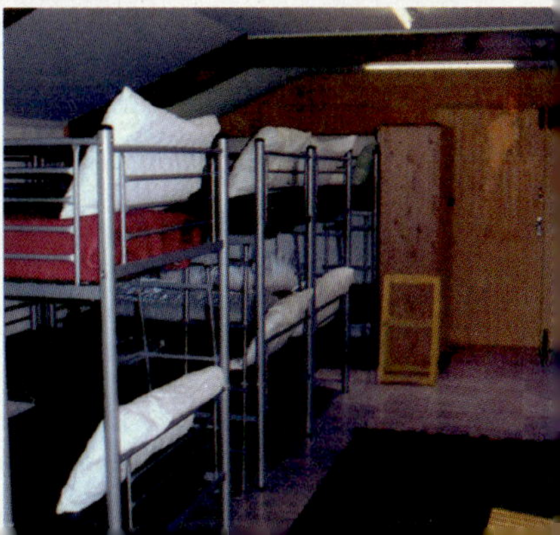

THE WAIN HOUSE

WALES

This old stone barn continues the tradition of 900 years when Llanthony Priory next door provided shelter and accommodation. Surrounded by the Black Mountains in the Brecon Beacons National Park, this spectacular setting is a superb base for walking, riding, pony trekking and other mountain activities.

Sixteen bunks are split into three separate areas for sleeping. There is a fully equipped kitchen, hot water for showers, heating throughout and a wood burning stove in the eating area. Small or large groups are welcome, but there is a minimum charge at weekends. Two pubs offer real ale and bar food.

Just 50 minutes from the M4 Severn Bridge and one hour from the M5/M50 junction, this must be one of the easiest bunkbarns to reach from the motorways - and yet you feel you are miles from anywhere.

DETAILS

- **Open** - All year, 24 hours, no restrictions
- **Number of beds** - 16: 1 x 8 ; 1 x 4 ; 1 x 6.
- **Booking** - Booking and deposit required.
- **Price per night** - £28 per person at weekends (2 nights) with a minimum charge of £280. Reduction for mid-week bookings.
- **Public Transport** - Abergavenny railway station 12 miles.
- **Directions** - GR SO 288 278 Map on website: Turn west off A465 Abergavenny to Hereford road at Llanvihangel Crucorney (5 miles' north of Abergavenny). Llanthony is 6 miles along country lane - follow signs to Priory. On cycle route 42.

CONTACT: Cordelia Passmore
Tel: 01873 890359
courtfarm@llanthony.co.uk   www.llanthonybunkbarn.co.uk
Court Farm, Llanthony, Abergavenny, Monmouthshire, NP7 7NN

DRAGONS BACK

WALES

The Dragons Back (formerly The Castle Inn) is a pub with B&B rooms, camping & 3 self contained bunkrooms, located at over 1000ft above sea level in an absolutely stunning location. All the bunkrooms are fully carpeted and centrally heated with en suite wet rooms. Book out the entire Bunkhouse from as little as £350 per night (£12.50pp). A new fully fitted dining/kitchen complete with WiFi and large screen TV, is located next to the bunkhouse so self-catering is an option, although meals are also available in the pub next door. The pub serves a range of local real ales and locally sourced ingredients for our home cooked food. There's a large log fire, fantastic beer garden, free WiFi in the bar, pool table & 50 inch TV. A great base for all sorts of outdoor activities, the bunkhouse has a drying room and secure bike storage and all the facilities you could wish for are on site. All groups welcomed including stag/hen parties.

DETAILS

- **Open** - All year. Arrive after 2pm, depart before 11 am
- **Number of beds** - 28 : 1x6, 1x10, 1x12
- **Booking** - Group bookings only. £100 non refundable booking deposit required. 28 days notice required for cancellation, otherwise full value of the booking (less deposit) will be charged.
- **Price per night** - £15pp, £20pp with breakfast. Minimum of 5 people required for 6 bunk room, 7 for 10 bunk room, or 9 for 12 bunk room. Book entire bunkhouse for £350, or £500 with breakfast.
- **Public Transport** - Railway station at Abergavenny, bus at Talgarth 3 miles away.
- **Directions** - Located on the A479 approx 3 miles South of Talgarth and 6 miles North of Crickhowell

CONTACT: Jill Deakin
Tel: 01874 711353, Fax: 01874711353
info@thedragonsback.co.uk www.thedragonsback.co.uk
The Dragons Back , Pengenffordd, LD3 0EP

BRECON BUNKHOUSE

WALES

Brecon Bunkhouse is a spacious, comfortable and clean bunkhouse in the Brecon Beacons offering fantastic value for money with a large self-catering kitchen, big dining room with plenty of tables and separate sitting room with a cosy wood-burner (logs provided). Brecon Bunkhouse is in a small valley in the Black Mountains, the eastern part of the National Park, and has fantastic mountain walks right from the front door. The area is ideal for horse riding and mountain bikes, with a white water canoe centre nearby. There is a riding centre on the farm and the bunkhouse has a drying room and storage/cleaning facilities for bikes and canoes. The adult-sized bunk-beds come with a freshly laundered sheet, pillow and pillow-case. Bring a sleeping bag/duvet, or hire a duvet with cover for £5 per stay. The friendly, helpful staff will give advice or leave you to get on with it as you chose. The market town of Talgarth, 4 miles away, has Walkers Welcome status and a variety of planned walks. Camping also available on the farm. Lovely pub 15 minutes' walk away.

DETAILS

- **Open** - All year round. All hours
- **Number of beds** - 28+3: 1x10,1x2,1x2,1x6,1x8. Plus extra 3 bed room available.
- **Booking** - 40% deposit required to book, balance due before arrival.
- **Price per night** - £15pp, £300 for exclusive use. £45 for extra 3 bed family room.
- **Public Transport** - Train station at Abergavenny. Taxi to bunkhouse costs £25-30 or phone bunkhouse to enquire about minibus transfer (advance notice needed).
- **Directions** - Travelling south from Talgarth on A479 take first left after Castle Inn. The Bunkhouse is on this lane after Trans Wales Trails banner at entrance to farm.

CONTACT: Paul and Emily Turner
Tel: 01874 711500
breconbunkhouse@gmail.com www.brecon-bunkhouse.co.uk
Brecon Bunkhouse, Cwmfforest Farm, Pengenfford, Talgarth, Brecon, LD3 0EU

TRERICKET MILL
RIVER CABIN & BUNKROOM WALES

River Cabin, a traditional stone building with eco credentials, is set in an old cider orchard overlooking the mill stream. It sleeps up to 4 in a cosy bunkroom with bunk beds & a double futon. There is a kitchen/lounge area, sunny dining porch, patio & private garden with picnic table, fire pit and BBQ. The price includes heating, hot water, showers & use of bike store. The small en suite bunkroom, on the back of the Mill overlooking the garden, is an ideal option for singles or 2 friends. It can be booked on a bed only or B&B basis. Includes use of guests lounge with complimentary tea & coffee facilities & fridge. From Easter - October a covered outdoor kitchen is available for simple cooking. There is also a small camp-site. Located on Wye Valley Walk and National Cycle Route 8 - fantastic exploration base for walkers and cyclists and anyone wishing to relax and explore this beautiful part of Mid Wales. Canoeing, pony trekking and riding, gliding, bike hire, rope and climbing centre all available locally.

DETAILS

- **Open** - All year, 24 hour access.
- **Number of beds** - 6 - 1 x 4, 1 x 2 en suite, plus 6 veggie B&B beds and camping.
- **Booking** - River Cabin (sleeps 4) - minimum booking 2 people for 2 nights. Bunkroom (sleeps 2) - singles welcome - no minimum stay.
- **Price per night** - Prices: From £18 per person per night.
- **Public Transport** - Train stations at Builth Wells (10 miles), Hereford (30 miles), Merthyr Tydfil (30 miles). Daily bus service - ask to be dropped at Trericket Mill. For travel information: www.traveline-cymru.info
- **Directions** - GR SO 112 414. Set back from the A470 Brecon to Builth Wells road between the villages of Llyswen and Erwood.

CONTACT: Alistair / Nicky Legge
Tel: 01982 560312
mail@trericket.co.uk www.trericket.co.uk
Erwood, Builth Wells, Powys, LD2 3TQ

CLYNGWYN BUNKHOUSE, B&B AND HUT

WALES

Clyngwyn Bunkhouse is situated in the Brecon Beacons, in the heart of waterfall country, very near to the caves and waterfalls of Ystradfellte and close to the famous Sgwd Yr Eira waterfalls. The terrain is ideal for mountain biking, gorge walking, canyoning, caving, abseiling, climbing, quad biking, photography and painting. Clyngwyn Bunkhouse is perfect for groups of friends or family. It sleeps up to 19 with camping available to larger groups, three double B&B rooms in the farm house and a romantic shepherd's hut in its own private meadow. There is a fully equipped kitchen, central heating, lounge with TV-DVD, dining room for 20, four acres of land for ball games and a large decked out polytunnel acting as a marquee, lockable storage and drying area. Relax in the evenings and enjoy the mountain views by a fire or BBQ. The villages of Ystradfellte and Pontneddfechan (2½ miles by mini bus taxi) have pubs with restaurants. Four star graded by Visit Wales. Dog friendly.

DETAILS

- **Open** - All year, all day
- **Number of beds** - Bunkhouse 19, B&B 6, Shepherd's Hut 2
- **Booking** - Booking essential. Only groups can book the bunkhouse at weekends. Credit/debit cards not accepted
- **Price per night** - Weekdays: sole use for up to 15 people £210, up to 19 people £265, £17pp for small groups. Weekends up to 15 people £240, or up to 19 £305. Small extra charge for bedding or bring your own. B&B in Farmhouse £28pp.
- **Public Transport** - Trains Neath or Merthyr (11 miles). Minibus can be arranged.
- **Directions** - From A465 leave at Glenneath drive through and take signs for Pontneddfechan. Then 2.5 miles up Ystradfellte road, turn right down small track.

CONTACT: Julie Hurst
Tel: 01639 722930
enquiries@bunkhouse-south-wales.co.uk   www.bunkhouse-south-wales.co.uk
Clyngwyn Farm, Ystradfellte Rd, Pontneddfechan, Powys, SA11 5US

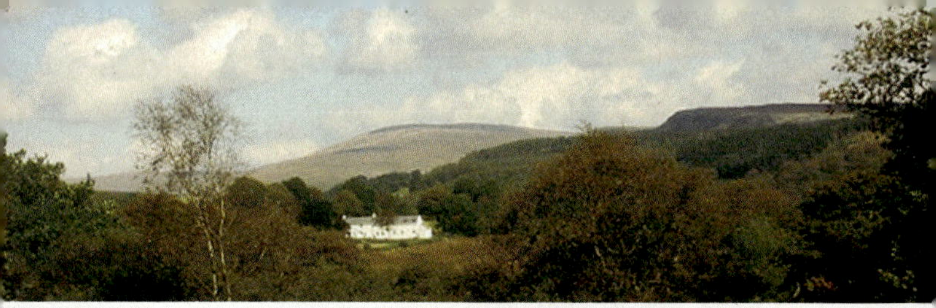
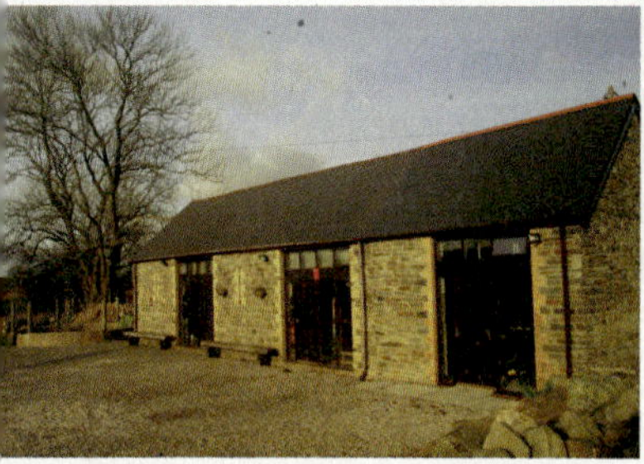
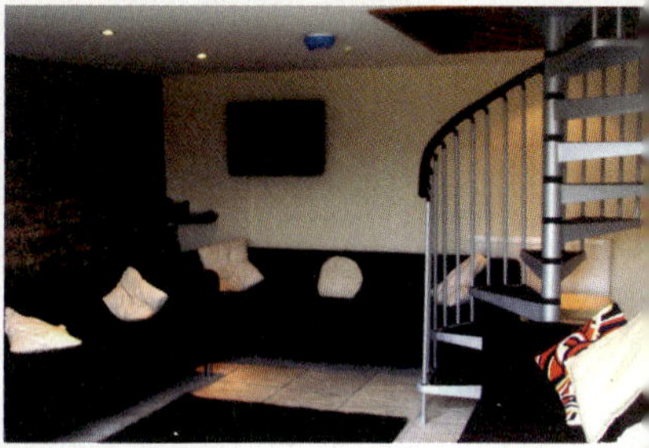
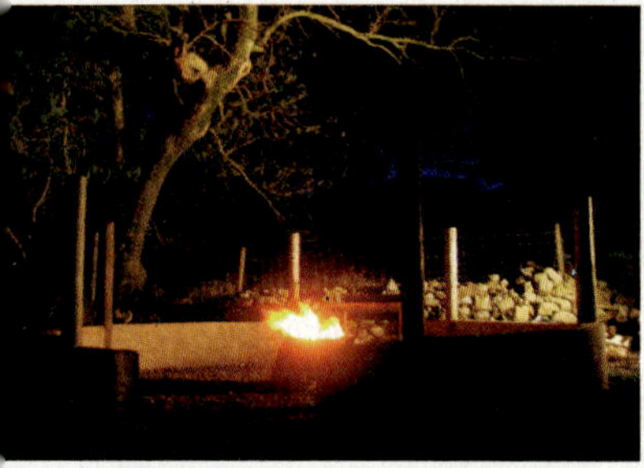
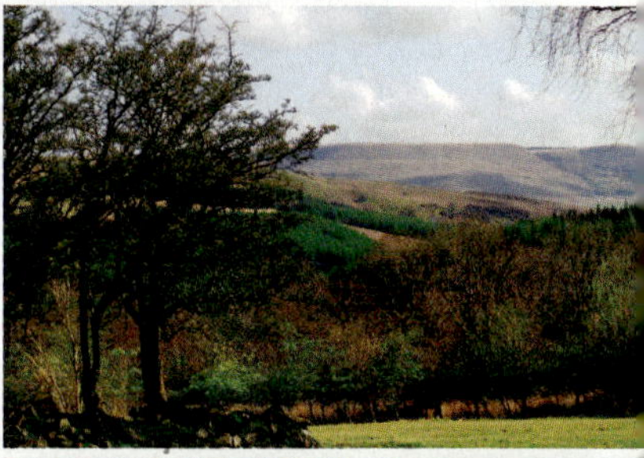
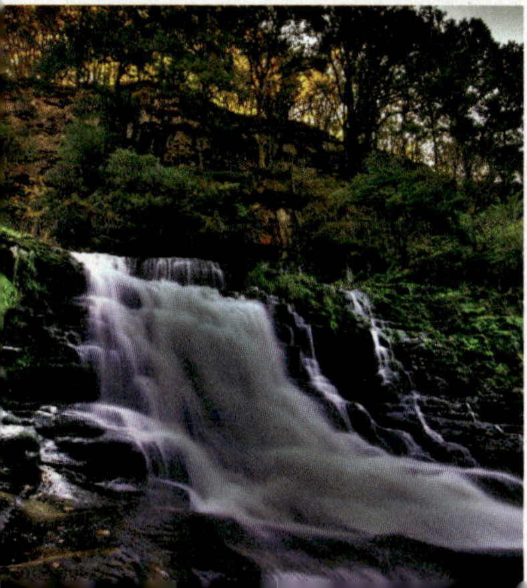
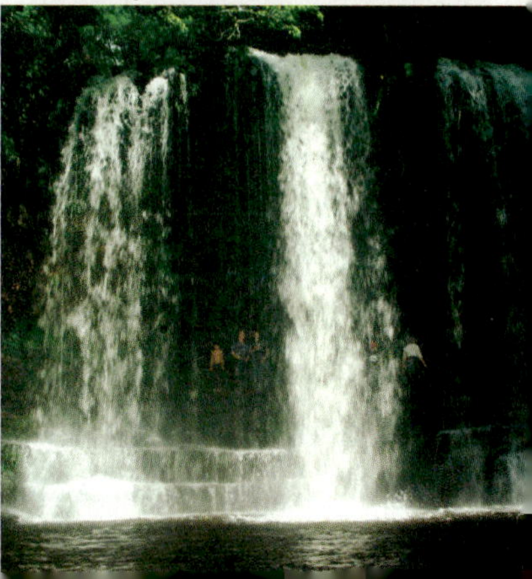

CRAIG Y NOS CASTLE

Craig Y Nos Castle is ideal for large groups, small groups and families. Situated between Brecon & Swansea, you can enjoy the mountain walks and reservoirs of the Brecon Beacons, or visit Gower's sandy bays. The Castle has en suite rooms for 64 people, a holiday cottage for 8 'The Farmhouse' and a self catering unit for 21 'The Nurses Block'. It also has good sized function rooms including a large conservatory for parties and meetings, a theatre seating 150, large dining room, cosy bar and further training rooms. There is a hot tub, a sports room and the gardens have great views of the adjoining county park. The Nurses Block is a self contained unit with a lounge and small self-catering kitchen. It has ten double/twin rooms, one single room, showers, loos and a disabled bathroom. There are adventure companies all around offering outdoor activities and you are welcome to join us for hearty meals and cosy evenings by the wood burning stove in the Castle's bar and restaurant.

DETAILS

- **Open** - 1st April to 31st October, 24 hours
- **Number of beds** - The Nurses Block: 21: 10 x 2, 1x1
- **Booking** - Call or email
- **Price per night** - Self catering groups from £10.75 per person (based on 5 night midweek stay for 10 in Nurses Block). Shorter stays and smaller groups pay more, larger groups pay less. B&B option also available. Please email or phone for a quote.
- **Public Transport** - Limited (Swansea/Brecon/Neath)
- **Directions** - Halfway between Swansea and Brecon at the foot of the Brecon Beacons. 17 miles from the Motorway at Swansea. 1/2 hour by car from train stations at Neath or Swansea

CONTACT: Reception
Tel: 01639 730725
info@craigynoscastle.com   www.groupaccommodationinwales.com
Craig Y Nos Castle, Brecon Road, Penycae, Powys, SA9 1GL

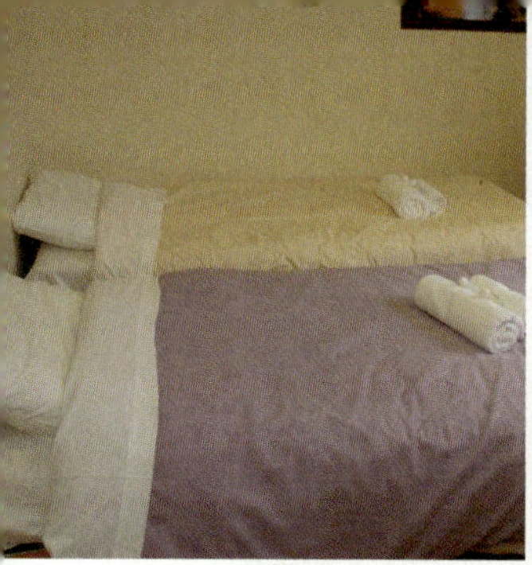
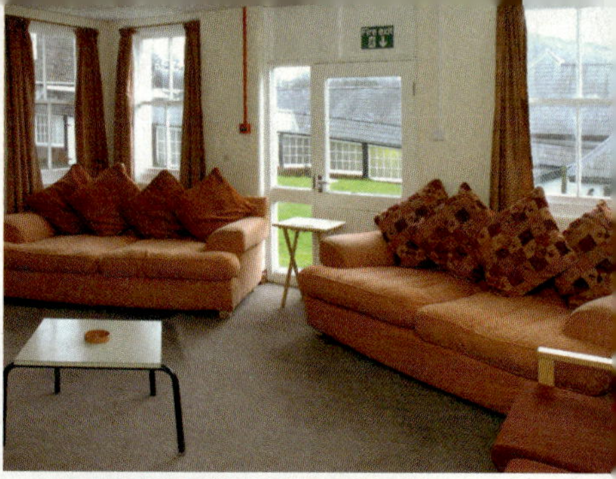
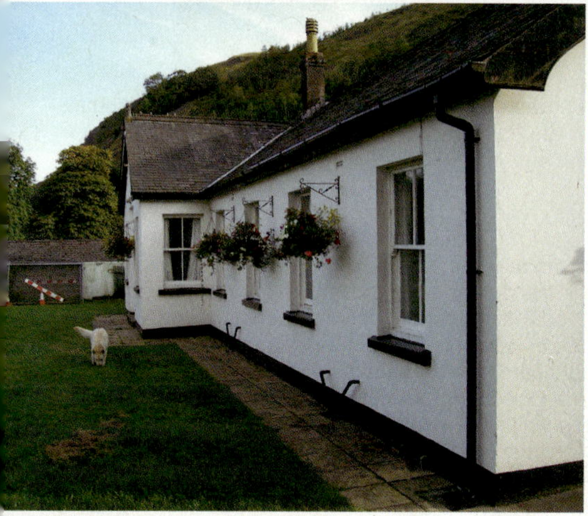
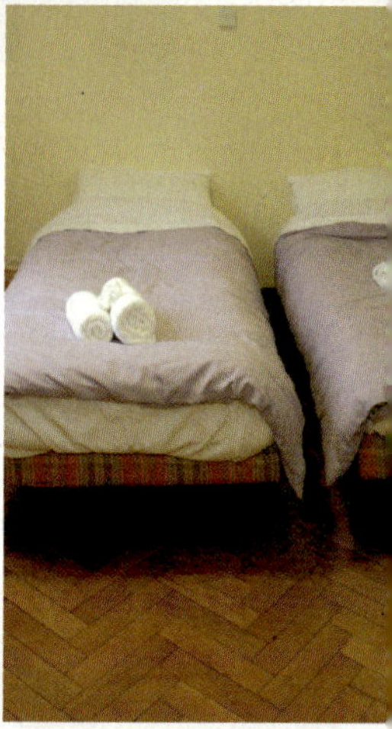
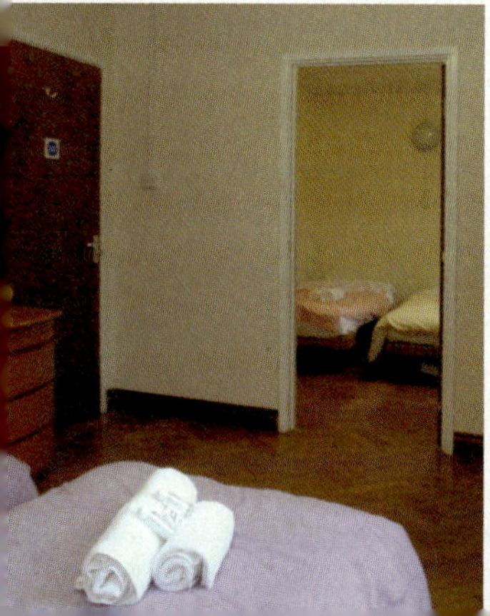
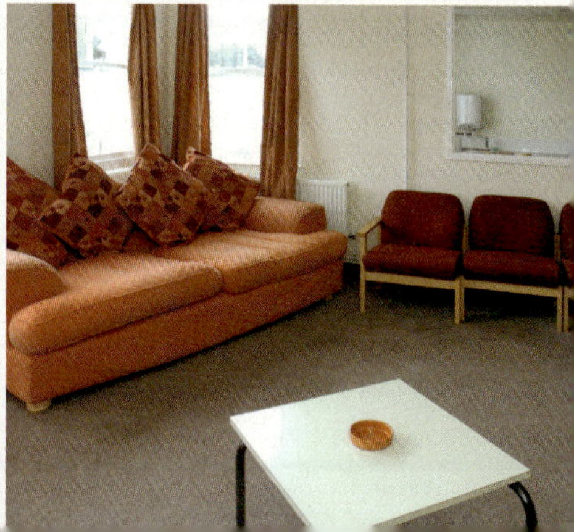

WOODLANDS BUNKHOUSE

Woodlands Bunkhouse, renovated in 2010, is a converted stable in the grounds of Woodlands Centre, a late Regency building, set in 10 acres of grounds. Overlooking the River Wye and with wonderful views of the Black Mountains.

Woodlands is within easy reach of the spectacular limestone area to the south. Nearby is the historic town of Hay on Wye, famous for its vast array of bookshops. With its modern facilities, the Bunkhouse provides comfortable accommodation for families and a variety of groups. With recent renovations increasing the capacity to 22, the ground floor has a well-equipped kitchen and dining room. There are 3 bedrooms on the ground floor, one with en suite facilities and six first floor bedrooms and shared bathroom facilities on both floors. Camping is also available in the grounds. The bunkhouse can arrange courses in outdoor activities which are individually designed to suit groups of all ages and abilities run by their fully qualified instructors.

DETAILS

- **Open** - All year, 24 hours.
- **Number of beds** - 22 in rooms of 1 to 6 plus camping in the grounds.
- **Booking** - Booking essential. Phone or email.
- **Price per night** - £16 pp + VAT. Reduction for children and large group bookings.
- **Public Transport** - Trains to Hereford. A local bus then runs from Hereford to Glasbury on Wye, service 39.
- **Directions** - On the B4350 just through the village of Glasbury accessed via the A438 Brecon road.

CONTACT: Annie Clipson
Tel: 01497 847272
annie.clipson@oxfordshireoutdoors.co.uk www.woodlandsoec.org
Glasbury on Wye, Powys, HR3 5LP

L & A
OUTDOOR CENTRE

WALES

L&A Outdoor Centre is a friendly family-run destination offering quality affordable accommodation and activities in the Swansea Bay area. Tailor-made for family holidays, the 6 and 8 bed two-storey self-catering cabins have upstairs bedrooms sleeping 2-3 in each room and downstairs, the toilet and shower, lounge with TV, fully equipped kitchen and dining area, all overlooking a tree-lined mountain stream. The bunkhouses, which sleep between 10 and 40, are clean and warm with access to self-catering. L&A facilities include a 10,000 sq.ft. activity hall, a large dining hall with professional catering, the Watering Hole bar/café, meeting rooms and over 50 acres of woodland and pasture with play area, open air swimming pool, campfire, pets corner, kennels, BBQs, bike wash and are dog friendly. For any number up to 250, L&A is the perfect base for conferences, training courses, summer camps and retreats. Activity Packages can be arranged. The area is ideal for mountain biking with Afan Aergoed and Glyncorrwg Trails just 10 mins. away and the Millennium and Liberty Stadia are within 30 mins.

DETAILS

- **Open** - All day.
- **Number of beds** - Cabin: 117: 6/8 bed units. Bunkhouse: 175:10,16,24,30,40 bed.
- **Booking** - Book or enquire by phone or email.
- **Price per night** - Bunkhouses: £12pp, £15 with bedding. Cabins: 6 bed £90 to £150, 8 bed £100 to £180, depending on length of stay. Groups please enquire.
- **Public Transport** - Nearest rail station is Port Talbot Parkway (two miles).
- **Directions** - One mile from Junction 40 of the M4

CONTACT: Nigel
Tel: 01639 885 509
info@landaoutdoorcentre.co.uk   www.landaoutdoorcentre.co.uk
Goytre, West Glamorgan SA13 2YP

RHOSSILI BUNKHOUSE

WALES

Situated at the end of the Gower Peninsula, in the UK's first Area of Outstanding Natural Beauty, Rhossili Bunkhouse is within easy walking distance of three glorious beaches, including Rhossili Bay (TripAdvisor: UK's #1 Beach 2014) and ideally located for a range of outdoor activities including walking, surfing, cycling, climbing and flying. The Gower Way starts nearby. This 4 star Visit Wales bunkhouse is great for groups of friends or families. It is run for the benefit of the community by Rhossili Bunkhouse Ltd on behalf of Rhossili Village Hall Trustees. Duvets and pillows provided. Bring single bed linen or sleeping bags. Central heating throughout. Self-catering in fully equipped kitchen. Lounge/dining room opens onto patio and garden. Games and books in lounge. Free WiFi. Secure store for bikes and boards, with drying room for coats and boots. Outside area for rinsing/drying wet suits. Card locks on all doors. Hall and meeting room for hire. Car park. No pets. No smoking.

DETAILS

- **Open** - All year except January. Check-in 4-9pm; check-out by 10:30am.
- **Number of beds** - 18: 1x4, 2x3, 4x2. 4 sofa-beds in lounge (Sole use).
- **Booking** - Advance booking recommended. Check our website for availability. Online form and virtual tour. Deposit 30%. Minimum booking: 2 people for 2 nights
- **Price per night** - Shared (small groups) £16-£19pp. Full (group of 18) £320. Sole (group of 22) £370.
- **Public Transport** - Regular buses (118) from Swansea stop outside. www.visitswanseabay.com/explorebybus www.traveline-cymru.info
- **Directions** - On the B4247 in Middleton, Rhossili. GR SS 421 878

CONTACT: Josephine Higgins
Tel: 01792 391509
bookings@rhossili.org www.rhossilibunkhouse.com
Rhossili Bunkhouse, Rhossili, Swansea, SA3 1PL

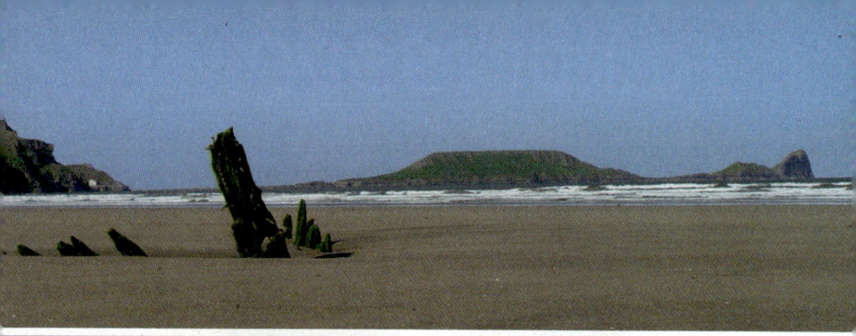

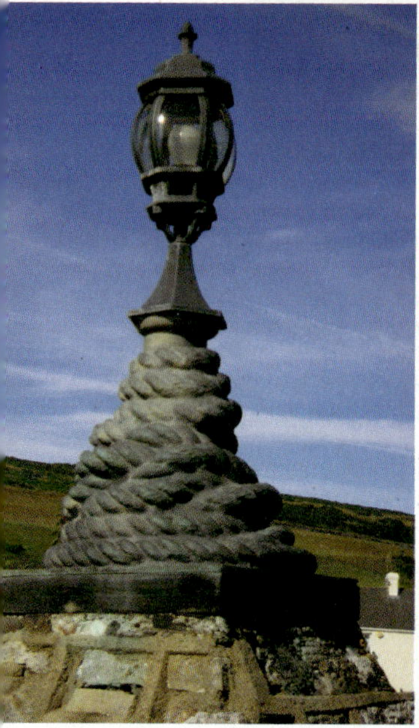

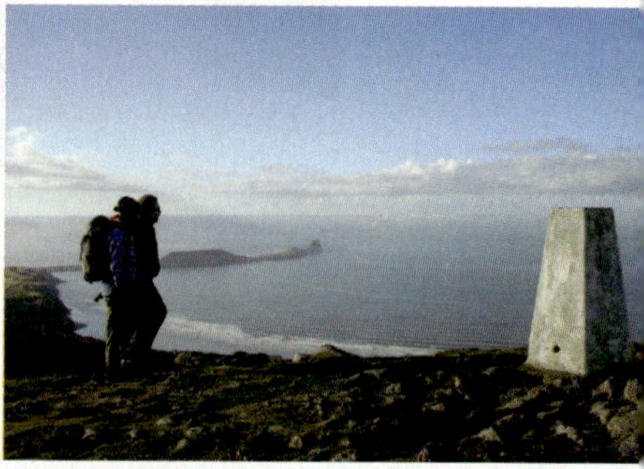

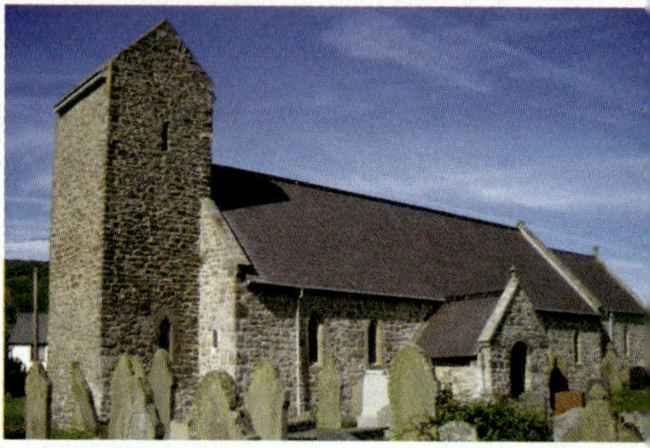

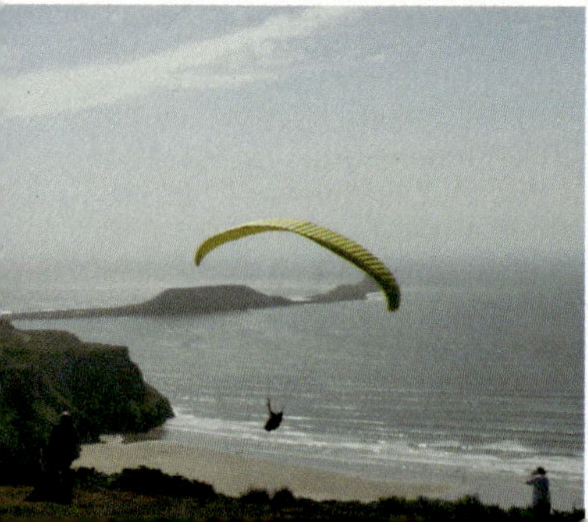

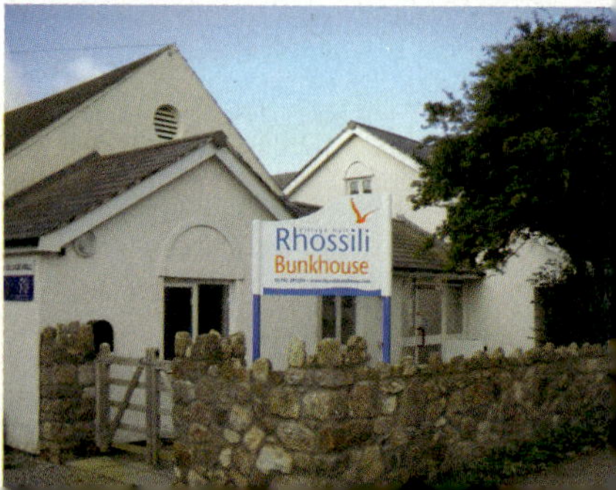
Rhossili
Bunkhouse

HARDINGSDOWN BUNKHOUSE

WALES

Hardingsdown Bunkhouse provides comfortable accommodation for families or groups in a tastefully restored stone barn on an organic farm. The Gower has National Nature reserves, outstanding coastal scenery, family beaches, castles and ancient monuments. Llangennith beach is one of the best surfing beaches in the south west, Mewslade Bay and Fall Bay are popular with climbers, while walkers and bikers can use the local network of footpaths and bridleways. The ground floor consists of a fully equipped kitchen, 2 shower/toilet rooms, a living room with 2 single sofa-beds and comfy chairs. Off the living room is a bedroom with a bunkbed sleeping 2 people. A spiral staircase leads upstairs where there are 3 bedrooms sleeping 5, 3 and 2 in bunks and single beds. There is a separate drying room and a lock-up for storing bikes, surfboards, canoes etc. Ample parking and a patio area that catches the evening sun. Shops and pubs are nearby.

DETAILS

- **Open** - All year, 24 hours.
- **Number of beds** - 14: 1x5, 1x3, 3x2
- **Booking** - Booking essential by phone or email and confirmed by 30% deposit.
- **Price per night** - SOLE USE £220pn (weekends, bank holidays and school holidays), £190pn (midweek). Weekly rates available. INDIVIDUALS Mid week, shared use, £18 per person.
- **Public Transport** - Regular bus (No116) from Swansea; 0870 6082608.
- **Directions** - Turn left off the B4295 ½ mile AFTER Burry Green (by bus shelter and post box). Follow lane 400m. End of tarmac road (and before rough track beyond) turn right into Lower Hardingsdown Farm. Bunkhouse is on left of farmyard.

CONTACT: Allison Tyrrell
Tel: 01792 386222
bunkhousegower@btconnect.com   www.bunkhousegower.co.uk
Lower Hardingsdown Farm, Llangennith, Gower, Swansea, SA3 1HT

PANTYRATHRO INTERNATIONAL HOSTEL

313
WALES

Llansteffan is a beautiful, quaint village set at the tip of the Towi River and Carmarthen Bay. The sandy beaches nestled below the castle offer swimming and relaxation. The virtually traffic free country lanes make this area ideal for cycling. For the walker we are on the Wales Coastal Path. Carmarthen, Wales' oldest city and ancestral home to Merlin of King Arthur's legends, offers most social and cultural activities. The Pantyrathro International Hostel provides dorm and double room accommodation and also 3 new en suite units of 6, 9 and 12 beds. Facilities include self-catering kitchen, dining area, TV lounge showers and free WiFi. Our two Mexican bars offer pool, darts, TV, weekly drink specials and food (eat-in or take-out). Horse riding and excursions for trekking, canoeing and surfing offered. Take a day trip, relax on the beaches or have a drink in our bars - something for everyone.

DETAILS

- **Open** - Febuary to January. 24 hours
- **Number of beds** - 50: 1 x 12, 1 x 9, 2 x 6, 4 x 4, 1 x 3
- **Booking** - Booking recommended. 50% deposit required in advance for groups.
- **Price per night** - £16pp dorm, Group discounts.
- **Public Transport** - Carmarthen has both coach and train stations serving South Wales, SW England and London. Local bus runs six times a day to Llansteffan. Ask driver to let you off at Pantyrathro.
- **Directions** - Pantyrathro is six miles from Carmarthen on the B4312, midway between Llangain and Llansteffan. Two miles from Llangain you will see the hostel signposted, turn right and follow signs to top of lane.

CONTACT: Ken Knuckles
Tel: 01267 241014
kenknuckles@hotmail.com   www.backpackershostelwales.com
Pantyrathro International Hostel, Llansteffan, Carmarthen, SA33 5AJ

GILFACH WEN BARN

WALES

Gilfach Wen Barn has been converted to provide competitively priced homely self-catering accommodation for individuals, extended families or groups on a working farm adjacent to Brechfa Forest. Graded as a 4 star bunkhouse it sleeps up to 32 in 7 bedrooms and has a large kitchen/dining room, lounge and drying room. There is a downstairs bedroom and shower room for disabled. The facilities are walker, cyclist and equestrian friendly. Adjacent to Brechfa Forest, the Cothi Valley and Llanllwni Mountain, Gilfach Wen Barn is a perfect venue for a holiday or weekend away – you need never leave the valley. The barn is WiFi enabled, fully equipped and Brechfa village with its shop and pub is within walking distance (1 mile). This is a stunningly beautiful area close to Brecon Beacons National Park, in the foothills of the Cambrian Mountains but only a short drive to Cefn Sidan Sands - an award winning 7 mile long beach. 360 degree virtual tour available on the barn's website.

DETAILS

- **Open** - Open all year, all day
- **Number of beds** - 32: 3x6, 1x5, 1x4,1x3,1x2 in 10 double beds and 12 singles.
- **Booking** - Advance booking required.
- **Price per night** - W/E Sole use £850. Mid week £350 per night. . Last minute and midweek special offers from £15 per person for individuals and small groups.
- **Public Transport** - Trains and coaches at Carmarthen. Daily bus from Carmarthen to Brechfa passes gate. Bus is a request stop service. You can ask to be dropped off and can catch the bus at the bottom of the drive.
- **Directions** - GR SN 513 292 On the B4310 between Horeb and Brechfa.

CONTACT: Jillie
Tel: 07780 476737
info@brechfa-bunkhouse.com   www.brechfa-bunkhouse.com
Gilfach Wen, Brechfa, Carmarthenshire, SA32 7QL

LAWRENNY
MILLENNIUM HOSTEL

WALES

Set in a picturesque village, surrounded by organic farmland and ancient oak woodland, this relaxed and friendly hostel is a great base for launching into everything Pembrokeshire has to offer. The hostel is warm, clean and comfortable, with modern facilities. There are 24 beds in 5 rooms, all of which can be reserved as family rooms. There's a large open plan kitchen and living room as well as a drying room, large car park and cycle shelter. Once a Victorian village school, the hostel is superbly placed for walking, boating, bird watching and kayaking, and is close to many top family attractions and the beautiful beaches of south Pembrokeshire. Groups are welcome and the whole hostel can be hired for holidays, training courses and events. WiFi is available. The adjoining village hall is available to rent. The hostel is run as a charitable trust and is a Friends of Nature hostel. The village has a community shop, pub and an award-winning tearoom.

DETAILS

- **Open** - All year. Arrange check in with warden/all day access.
- **Number of beds** - 24: 2 x 4, 1 x 8, 2 x double + bunks
- **Booking** - Online, email or telephone
- **Price per night** - Adults £16, children (4-17) £10. Double rooms £37 (couple), £50 (with children). Sole use of hostel £250 per night.
- **Public Transport** - Not easy! Coach/train to Kilgetty (8m). Get the 381 bus (Tenby to Pembroke Dock) and from Cresswell Quay it's a 2.5 mile walk to the hostel.
- **Directions** - From A40 St Clears to Haverfordwest road take A4075 signed Tenby and Oakwood. Just past the turning to Oakwood, turn right and follow signs to Lawrenny. Bear right in front of church and follow the car park signs.

CONTACT: Laura Lort-Phillips
Tel: 01646 651270
hostel@lawrennyvillage.co.uk www.lawrennyvillage.co.uk/hostel
Lawrenny Millennium Hostel, Lawrenny, Pembrokeshire, SA68 0PW

PEMBROKESHIRE ADVENTURE CENTRE

WALES

Set in the heart of Britain's only Coastal National Park, the Pembrokeshire Adventure Centre is the perfect place to begin exploring this captivating edge of Wales. The modern and comfortable bunkhouses overlook the stunning Cleddau Estuary and can sleep up to 80. Accommodation is in 4 blocks each with self-catering facilities, lounge area and 2/3 bathrooms. Guests have use of all on-site facilities including sports pitch, conference rooms and drying room. Bedding is included and we can provide catering for larger groups. At the Adventure Centre you can try an array of land and water based activities from coasteering to rock climbing! We welcome all ages from 8-80 on a tailor made adventure – families, experts and beginners, no-one is left out! We also provide programmes for schools, youth groups, team building and adventure training. Pembrokeshire's famous beaches like Barafundle Bay are under 30 minutes away. Alternatively try some local attractions like Oakwood or the Celtic Village at Castell Henllys! Feel free to ask staff any questions, they are happy to help! The centre is situated in Pembroke Dock with excellent rail, road and ferry links.

DETAILS

- **Open** - All year. All day
- **Number of beds** - 80: 2 houses of 6 x 4 beds; 2 blocks of 8 x 2 beds.
- **Booking** - Booking is essential.
- **Price per night** - From £15.60pp. Group discounts available.
- **Public Transport** - Pembroke Dock train station 1 mile, Irish ferry port 2 miles.
- **Directions** - From Pembroke head north on A4139, then onto A477. On A477 take 3rd right, just before the bridge. Turn right at roundabout, the Centre is after 1/2 mile.

CONTACT:
Tel: 01646 622013
adventure@princes-trust.org.uk   www.princes-trust.org.uk/adventure
Cleddau Reach, Pembroke Dock, Pembrokeshire, SA72 6UJ

STACKPOLE OUTDOOR LEARNING CENTRE

WALES

The 137-bed platinum eco-award-winning Stackpole Outdoor Learning Centre is in the heart of the Stackpole estate, and just a stone's throw from the banks of the Bosherston lakes. It's the perfect venue for large families, groups, team-building or private hire. The estate of countryside and coast includes a National Nature Reserve, ancient settlements, towering cliffs, wild woodlands and two stunning sandy beaches. The accommodation has been developed from a range of stone farm buildings. It comprises four large houses, three cottages and a manor house. Facilities include a theatre and bar. We provide adventurous activities such as coasteering, kayaking and surfing, whilst there are more than 30km of footpaths that criss-cross the estate.

DETAILS

- **Open** - All year, all day. Reception 9am - 6pm
- **Number of beds** - Swan House 13 bedrooms (sleeping 24 persons), Shearwater House 7 bedrooms (13 persons), Kestrel House 12 bedrooms (29 persons), Kingfisher 10 bedrooms (44 persons), Manor House 3 bedrooms (9 persons), 3 cottages 9 bedrooms (18 persons)
- **Booking** - Bookings are made through reception.
- **Price per night** - Minimum of two night's stay. Please contact bookings team for a quote. Prices range from £24 per person per night.
- **Public Transport** - Trains Pembroke (5 miles). Bus from Pembroke: Silcox 387 Coastal Cruiser.
- **Directions** - On the B4319 from Pembroke to Stackpole and Bosherton (various entry points onto estate).

CONTACT: Stackpole Reception
Tel: 01646 661425
stackpole.bookings@nationaltrust.org.uk www.nationaltrust.org.uk/stackpole-centre
The Old Home Farm Yard, Stackpole, nr Pembroke, Pembrokeshire, SA71 5DQ

BUNKHOUSE AT WARREN FARM

WALES

Beautiful big bell tents and warm & cosy bunkhouse right on the Pembrokeshire Coast Path with great views out to sea, close to fantastic climbing at Castlemartin Range, excellent surfing at Freshwater West & Broadhaven South and within striking distance of many of Pembrokeshire's beaches, countryside, wildlife, castles, river walks, charming pubs, film locations and other places of interest. The well-appointed 6m bell tents, which each sleep up to 8, are on secluded seasonal pitches with their own outside dining area, camp fire, fully equipped camp kitchen, and off grid shower & compost loo. The bunkhouse has purpose-built robust and good-sized bunkbeds for up to 12 adults all year round, complete with wet room and toilets. The bunkhouse has no cooking facilities but BBQ & firepit are available to hire. Pedestrianised, step-free & dog- friendly site with plenty of parking, grassy lawns and enclosed picnic courtyard. All mattresses are orthopedic & hypo-allergenic, so you'll get a good night's sleep even after the most energetic day. Please note: this is a remote rural location with no mobile signal, there's usually WiFi in the farmhouse.

DETAILS

- **Open** - All year. Flexible check in
- **Number of beds** - 1 x 12, plus camping
- **Booking** - Via Website. Bunk house sole use only. Camping also available.
- **Price per night** - Bunkhouse £153 (up to 12) Bell tent £101/week and £117/we.
- **Public Transport** - Train & Ferry Pembroke. Bus route: 387/388 Coastal Cruiser
- **Directions** - Take the B4319 from Pembroke and follow red-edged signs to Castlemartin Range. Then turn right through Merrion, Warren Farm is on the right.

CONTACT: Jane, Hannah or Chris
Tel:
hverrall@email.com   www.warrenfarmwarren.com
Warren Farm, Warren, near Castlemartin, SA71 5HS

UPPER NEESTON
LODGES

319

WALES

Environmentally sensitive barn conversions on a small family run sheep farm, close to the Milford Haven Waterway in the Pembrokeshire Coast National Park. Ideal for divers, climbers, walkers or for family and friends having a get-together. The four independent units, all have access to garden/patio, laundry/drying room, wash-down area, secure storage and ample parking. THE COWSHED BUNKHOUSE- single storey with disabled access. Large sitting room and kitchen/dining area, and two bedrooms each with en suite shower rooms. THE BARN BUNKHOUSE has an upstairs sitting room and kitchen/dining area whilst the two downstairs bedrooms have en suite shower rooms. THE GRANERY LODGE also has an upstairs sitting room/kitchen. The ground floor bedroom sleeps up to 3 people and has an en suite shower room. The DAIRY LODGE is single story with bathroom, 2 single beds and diner kitchen. All units have fully fitted kitchens, fridge freezers, microwave, toaster, crockery, TV, CD player and wood burning stove. Graded 5 Star bunkhouse by Visit Wales.

DETAILS

- **Open** - All year, check in from 4pm. Check out before 10.30am.
- **Number of beds** - Cowshed 10 1x6,1x4. Barn 8 1x6,1x2, Granary 1x3. Dairy 1x3
- **Booking** - Provisional booking taken by phone/email and confirmed by deposit.
- **Price per night** - £16pp (inc linen). Exclusive use: min 6 Barn, 8 Cowshed. Min 2 nights at weekends (3 nights bank hols). Smaller groups / individuals by agreement.
- **Public Transport** - Puffin coastal shuttle passes farm www.traveline-cymru.org.uk
- **Directions** - Follow A4076 through Milford Haven to roundabout by Docks. Take first exit (signed Hakin). Follow for 2 miles, look for first farm on left (next to layby).

CONTACT: Sean or Mandy Tilling
Tel: 01646 690750
mail@upperneeston.co.uk www.upperneeston.co.uk
Upper Neeston Farm, Dale Road, Herbrandston, Milford Haven, SA73 3RY

CAERHAFOD LODGE

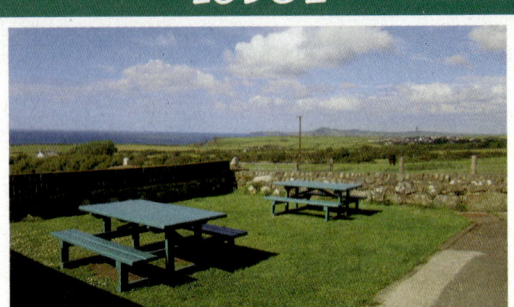

WALES

Ideally situated between the famous cathedral city of St Davids and the Irish ferry port of Fishguard, the Lodge overlooks the spectacular Pembrokeshire coastline. Within walking distance of the well known Sloop Inn at Porthgain and the internationally renowned Coastal Path. An ideal stopover for cyclists with The Celtic Trail cycle route passing the bottom of the drive. The Lodge is a great base for all outdoor activities: boat trips around Ramsey Island, coasteering, kayaking, surfing or just lazing on the beach. The lodge sleeps 23 in 5 separate rooms, all en suite with great showers. There is a modern fully equipped kitchen/diner with sea view patio & picnic tables with a panoramic view from the Preseli mountains to Strumble Head and the North Bishop with glorious sunsets over the Irish sea. There is also a sitting room for cosy evenings, on-site washing/drying room and secure storage area. Dogs welcome by prior arrangement. Smoking outdoors. Visit Wales graded 4 star.

DETAILS

- **Open** - All year, check in from 4pm, check out 10.30 am. All day access.
- **Number of beds** - 23: 3x4 : 1x5 : 1x6.
- **Booking** - Advised in high season. 50% deposit.
- **Price per night** - Adult £18. Under 16 £14.00. Group rates available.
- **Public Transport** - Trains at Fishguard (9m) and Haverfordwest (17m). Fishguard/Rosslare ferry. National Express: Haverfordwest. 413 Bus: St Davids-Fishguard 50yds from Lodge. Seasonal coastal shuttle service for walkers.
- **Directions** - GR Landranger 157, SM 827 317. A40 from Haverfordwest, left at Letterston (B4331) to Mathry. Left onto A487 to St Davids, right in Croesgoch for Llanrhian, at crossroads right for Trefin. Lodge is on right after ½ mile.

CONTACT: Carolyn Rees
Tel: 01348 837859
Caerhafod@aol.com www.caerhafod.co.uk
Llanrhian, St Davids, Haverfordwest, Pembrokeshire, SA62 5BD

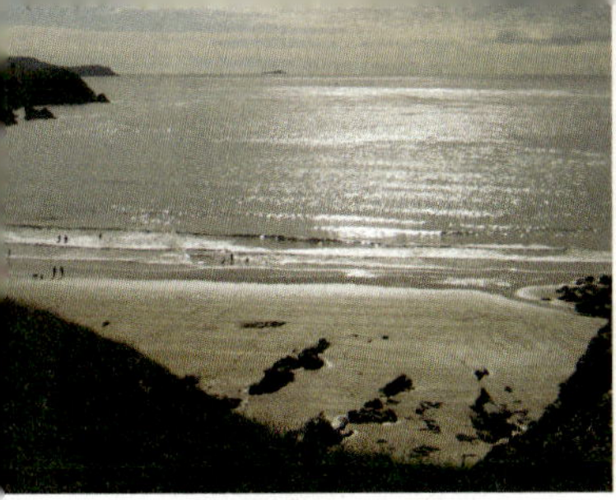

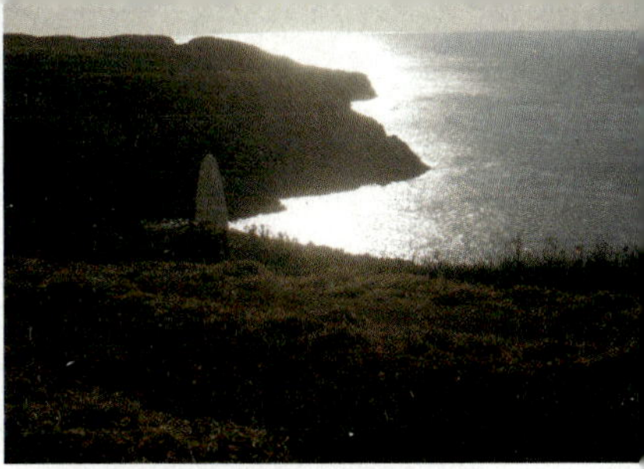

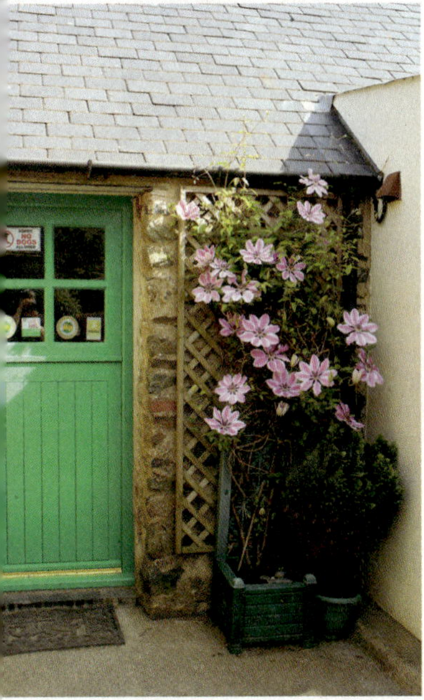
NO DOGS

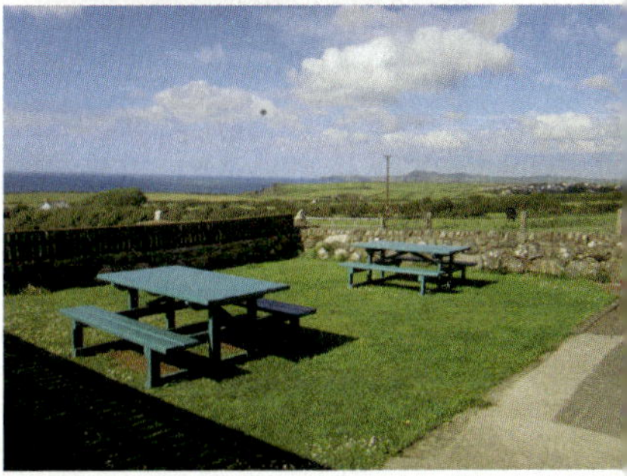

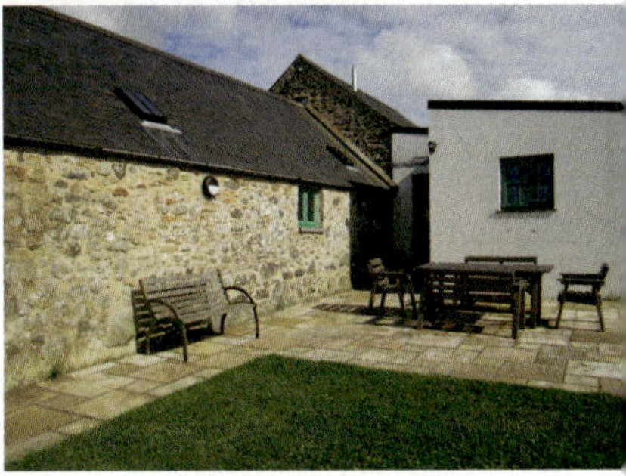

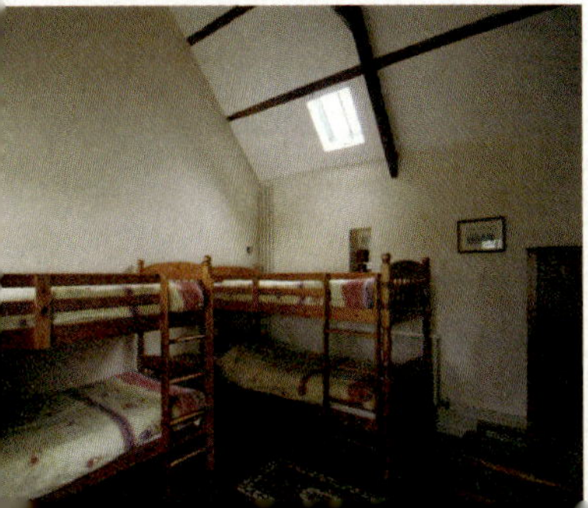

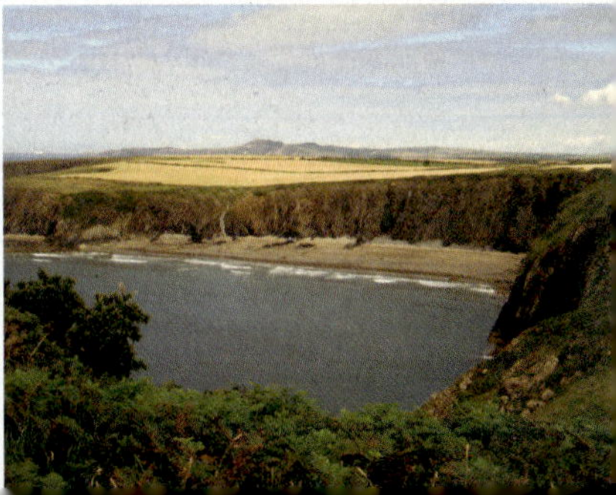

OLD SCHOOL HOSTEL
FORMERLY YHA TREFIN
WALES

Escape to this wonderful, wild and rugged corner of the Pembrokeshire Coast National Park. Stay in Trefin, an attractive village with a pub and cafe, just a quarter of a mile from the world famous coast path. The cathedral city of St Davids and popular family and surfers' beach of Whitesands Bay are only 20 minutes away by car. Other stunning wild beaches and small harbour villages are close by and can be visited as part of a day's circular walk. This friendly characterful 4 star hostel offers comfortable accommodation at prices that are hard to beat. There are singles, twins, doubles, family rooms and dorms and most have en suite solar showers. Organic breakfast and packed lunches are available and there is free internet and WiFi. Affiliated to Friends of Nature, this hostel is powered by renewable energy, offers 'eco' and 'longer stay' discounts and plants a tree for every booking. Create a forest for the future-come and stay

DETAILS

- **Open** - March-October, Check in from 5pm. All day access once checked in.
- **Number of beds** - 19 beds in singles, 24 beds utilising doubles, in 7 rooms.
- **Booking** - Advance booking recommended
- **Price per night** - Dorms from £13, private rooms from £15 per person, singles from £18, family rooms from £38. Exclusive use of hostel from £225 per night.
- **Public Transport** - Train to Fishguard & Goodwick station then bus 413 to Trefin or train/National Express coach to Haverfordwest then 2 x buses. See www.traveline-cymru.info.
- **Directions** - Heading west on the A40 turn left onto the B4331 at Letterston then left onto the A487 towards St Davids. After 2.5 miles turn right just after the Square and Compass pub for Trefin.

CONTACT: Sue or Chris
Tel: 01348 831800
oldschoolhostel@btconnect.com   www.theoldschoolhostel.co.uk
Ffordd-yr-Afon, Trefin, Haverfordwest, Pembrokeshire, SA62 5AU

HAMILTON BACKPACKERS

323

WALES

Hamilton Backpackers Lodge is an excellent overnight stop on the stunning Pembrokeshire Coast Path. It is also an ideal overnight stay five minutes from the ferries to Rosslare in Ireland. Pembrokeshire has a wealth of natural beauty and local history and many beautiful secluded beaches. The Backpackers Lodge is a very comfortable and friendly hostel with small dormitories and a double room, all centrally heated. There is a dining room and TV lounge. The garden at the back of the hostel has a hammock, barbecue and picnic tables. Free tea, coffee and light breakfast are provided. There is parking close by and the hostel is in the centre of town near to a number of pubs serving good meals. There is no curfew. Smoking is permitted only in the garden patio. To find out more see website.

DETAILS

- **Open** - All year, 10 am to 10 pm
- **Number of beds** - 9: 1 x 4, 1 x 3 and 1 x 2.
- **Booking** - Booking advised to confirm beds. 50% deposit required from groups.
- **Price per night** - £18 to 20 pp in dorms, £24pp in double en suite.
- **Public Transport** - Fishguard ferry port has a train station and ferries to Rosslare in Ireland. The port is 1 mile from the hostel (approx taxi fare £7). National Express coaches call at Haverfordwest (15 miles). For local buses in Pembrokeshire phone Richard Bros 01239 613756.
- **Directions** - From Haverfordwest (A40) to Fishguard Square (A487), across roundabout then take first right by tourist office, 50 yds on left. From Cardigan A487 (North Wales Road) up hill and first left. From harbour 1 mile to Fishguard Square, left, first right, 50 yards on left.

CONTACT: Steve Roberts
Tel: 01348 874797 / 07813 687570
hamiltonbackpackers@yahoo.co.uk www.hamiltonbackpackers.co.uk
23 Hamilton Street, Fishguard, Pembrokeshire, SA65 9HL

PIGGERY POKE
4 STAR HOSTEL

WALES

Piggery Poke is a 16 bed, 4 star hostel on the public footpath that loops from the Ceredigion Coast Path between Mwnt and Aberporth. Local cycle routes link the road at the top of the entrance drive to long distance cycle routes Lôn Teifi (within 4 miles) and the Celtic Trail (see Sustrans Route 82).

Piggery Poke is a new conversion of an old building and has 3 dormitories sleeping up to 8, 5 and 3, each with en suite facilities. The dining room seats 16 at one sitting. There is a drying room on the ground floor and wireless broadband is available by arrangement. There is a large garden area with sea views and barbeque and there is a secure cycle store. Courtesy collection and delivery service is usually available from points within 15 miles along the coast for walkers or cyclists and/or their cycles/luggage. Ample parking is provided.

DETAILS

- **Open** - All year round. 4pm to 10pm and 7.30am to 10am
- **Number of beds** - 16: 1 x 8, 1 x 5, 1 x 3
- **Booking** - Book by phone or via website.
- **Price per night** - £21 per person.
- **Public Transport** - Trains at Aberystwyth and Carmarthen. From Aberystwyth station take the X50bus to Blaenannerch or 550 bus to Felinwynt, via Aberporth. From Carmarthen station take the 460 or 461 bus to Cardigan (Finch Square) then change to the 550 bus to Aberystwyth via Aberporth, alighting at Felinwynt.
- **Directions** - Piggery Poke hostel is part of Cardigan Coastal Cottages, at Ffrwdwenith Isaf, Felinwynt, half-way between Mwnt and Aberporth, 4 miles along the coast north of Cardigan. Lat: 52.13108, Long: -4.58939. Map X222837, Y251268.

CONTACT: Paul or Angela
Tel: 01239 811777
hostel@piggerypoke.co.uk   www.piggerypoke.co.uk
Ffrwdwenith Isaf, Felinwynt, Cardigan, SA43 1RW

SHAGGY SHEEP

WALES

This budget bunkhouse is nestled in the Teifi valley, perfect for exploring the local area.

Bedding is included and facilities include a self catering kitchen and a lounge, with terraced garden and BBQ area.

Twenty Five minutes' drive will take you to the stunning Ceredigion coastline.

There are many village pubs and restaurants within walking distance.

Shaggy Sheep are experts in organising adventure activity holidays ideal for hen & stag weekends, corporate team building, youth groups, couples and families. Look at our website or get in touch to find out more.

DETAILS

- **Open** - Jan-Dec, 24hrs
- **Number of beds** - 22 (5x4, 1x2)
- **Booking** - Essential: by email or through the website
- **Price per night** - email with numbers and stay length for a quote
- **Public Transport** - Nearest Train Station Carmarthen (18 miles). Bookable bus 01239801601 to Llandysul.
- **Directions** - Take A484 from Carmarthen to Saron. Turn right at Rhos. Through Pentrecwrt to Llandysul, turn right at Half Moon pub, see us on the left or follow Sat Nav to SA44 4AJ.

CONTACT: Chris
Tel: 01559 363911
bookings@shaggysheepwales.co.uk   www.shaggysheepwales.co.uk
Old Commerce House, Pontwelly, Llandysul, Carmarthen SA44 4AJ

THE LONG BARN

WALES

The Long Barn is a traditional stone barn providing comfortable and warm bunkhouse accommodation. It is situated on a working organic farm in beautiful countryside with views over the Teifi Valley. The stunning Ceredigion Coast and the Cambrian Mountains are both an easy drive away and the busy small town of Llandysul (1.5 miles) has all essential supplies.

The barn's location is ideal for exploring, studying or simply admiring the Welsh countryside. Activities enjoyed by guests in the surrounding area include fishing, swimming, climbing, abseiling, canoeing, farm walks and cycling.

The barn is open all year, having adequate heating with lovely warm log fires, roof insulation and double glazing throughout

DETAILS

- **Open** - All year, all day.
- **Number of beds** - 40.
- **Booking** - Essential, deposit required
- **Price per night** - £15pp . Discount for groups and mid week bookings.
- **Public Transport** - Trains and National Express at Carmarthen (16 miles). Local bus service at Landysul (1.5 miles) details/booking 0871 2002233 www.bwcabus.info
- **Directions** - OS map 146, GR 437 417. In Llandysul, at the top of the main street, take right hand lane. Turn sharp right down hill. After 100 yds turn sharp left. Another ½ mile turn first right. Continue for 1 mile and Long Barn is on your right.

CONTACT: Tom or Eva
Tel: 01559 363200 Mob 07733 026874 , Fax: 01559 363200
cowcher@thelongbarn.co.uk www.thelongbarn.co.uk
Penrhiw, Capel Dewi, Llandysul, Ceredigion, SA44 4PG

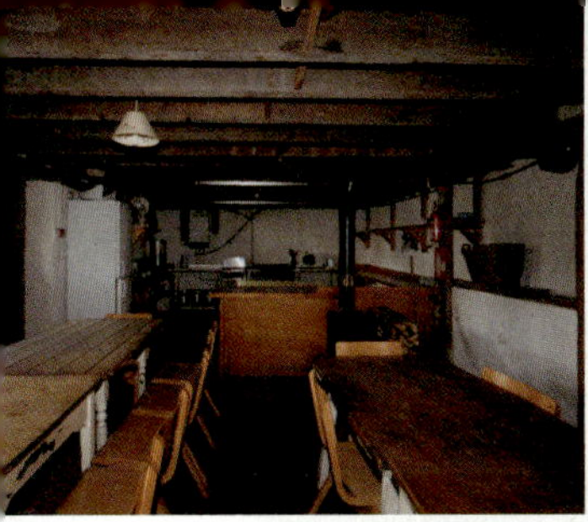
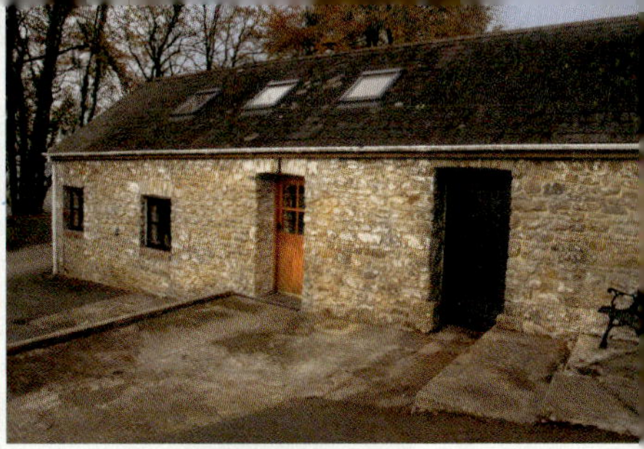
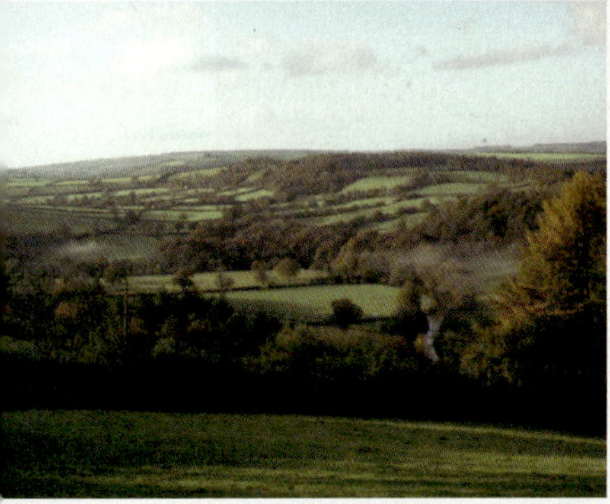
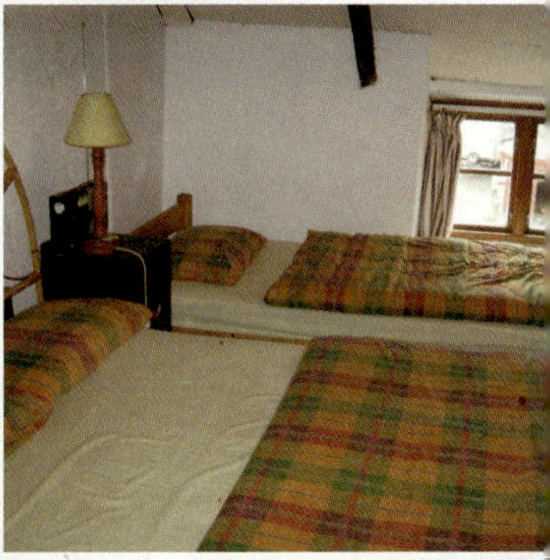
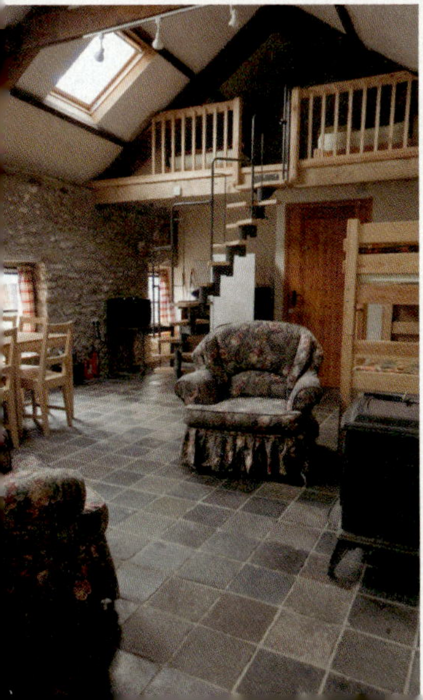
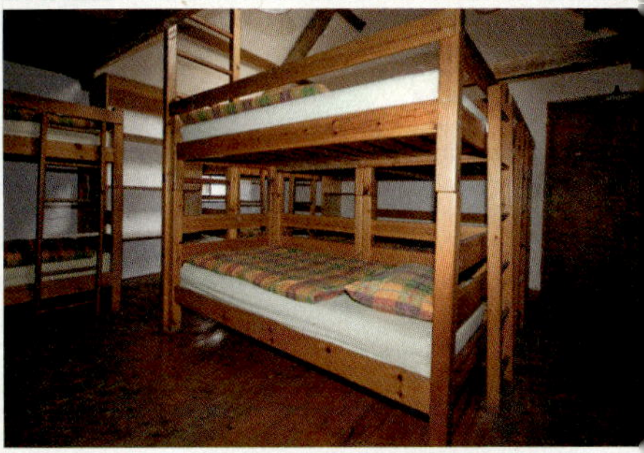
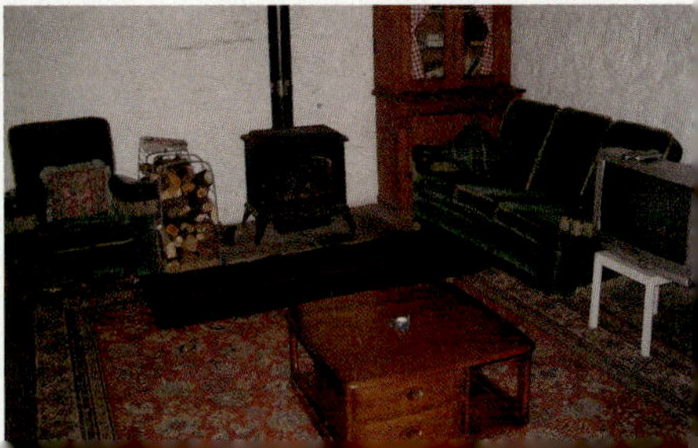

TY'N CORNEL
TYNCORNEL HOSTEL

WALES

Ty'n Cornel Hostel is an isolated former farmhouse in the hills, with a cosy open fire. Favoured by walkers, cyclists, bird watchers and lovers of solitude it is in the beautiful Doethie valley on the Cambrian Way long distance footpath.

There are comfortable wooden bunk beds and good self-catering facilities. Camping is also available. You can enjoy the wild open moorlands of the Elenydd uplands. Other attractions include the Cors Caron National Nature Reserve, the Red Kite Centre and museum in Tregaron, Teifi Pools, Llyn Brianne reservoir, Dolaucothi Roman gold mines, Strata Florida Abbey and National Trust Llanerchaeron.

DETAILS

- **Open** - All year, 24 hours. Reception 5pm -11pm, 7am -10am.
- **Number of beds** - 16: 2x8.
- **Booking** - Booking advisable; essential mid November to mid March. Book online at www.yha.org.uk, ring YHA booking office on 0800 0191700 or ring hostel managers on 01980 629259.
- **Price per night** - £12 per adult, £9 (under 18s). Block bookings negotiable.
- **Public Transport** - Trains: Aberystwyth 28m, Llanwrtyd Wells 16m, Cynghordy 12m. Coach: X40 (Cardiff – Aberystwyth) Lampeter 15m. Bus: 585 (Lampeter – Tregaron) Llanddewi-Brefi 7m.
- **Directions** - Road from Llanddewi-Brefi, near Tregaron: follow hostel signs SE 7m (last mile track). Bridle path S up Doethie valley on the Cambrian Way (Llandovery 15 m) or byway 2m NW from Soar y Mynydd chapel.

CONTACT: YHA booking office
Tel: 0800 0191700 or 01980 629259 , Fax: 0870 7706081
tyncornel@yha.org.uk www.elenydd-hostels.co.uk
Llanddewi Brefi, Tregaron, Ceredigion, SY25 6PH

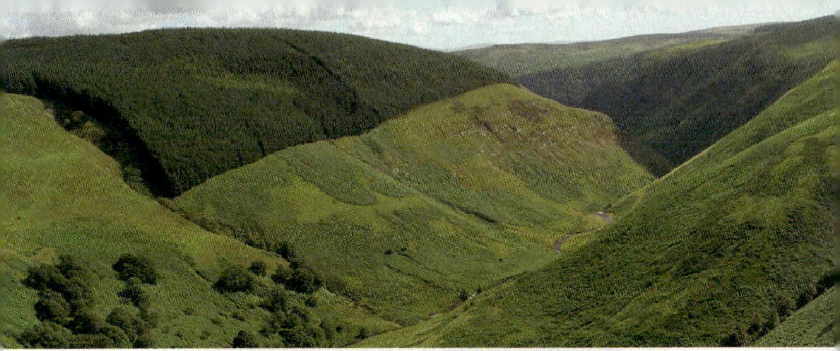
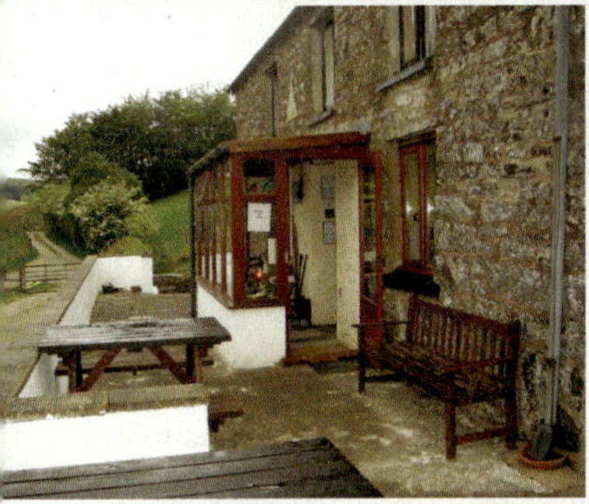
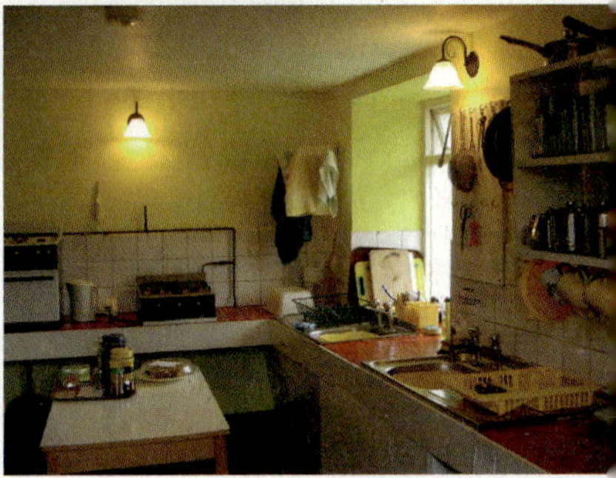
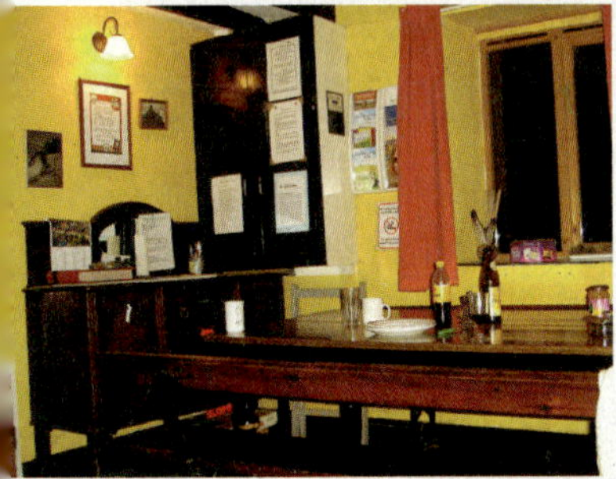
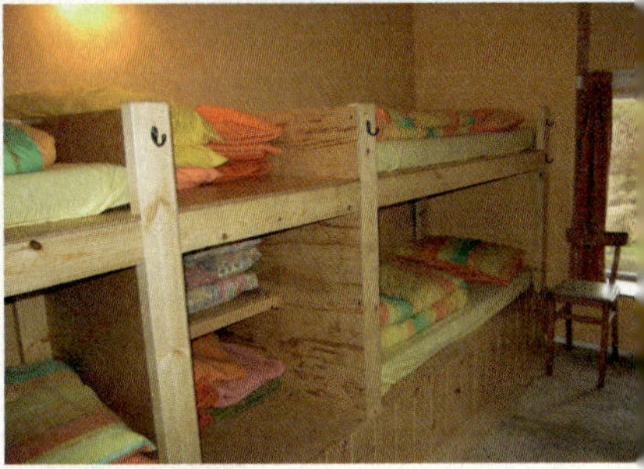
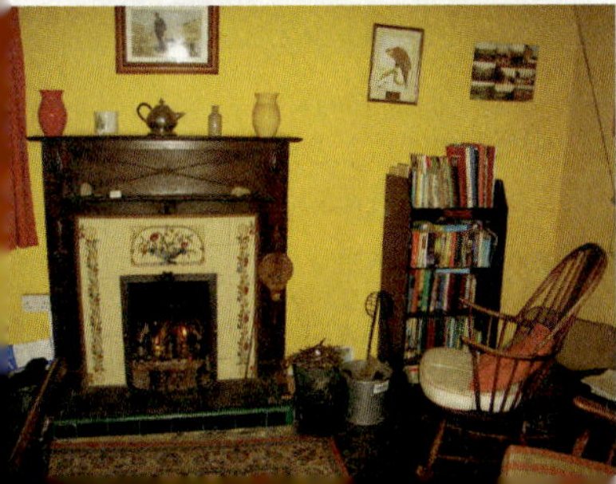
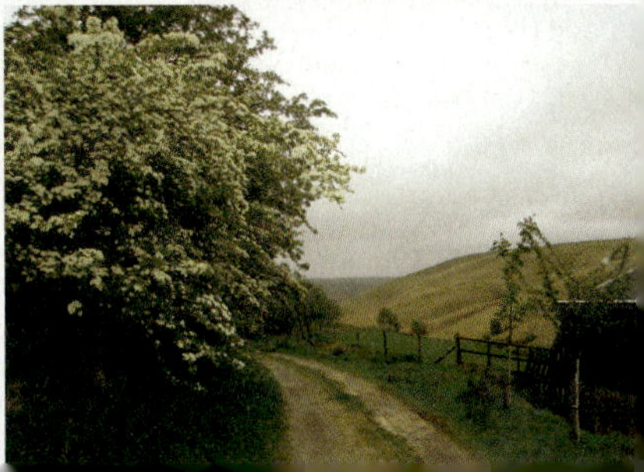

DOLGOCH HOSTEL

WALES

Come and experience the peace of this unique location in the remote Tywi valley. A stay in this 17th century farmhouse will take you into an era before electricity, with a log burner for heat. Dolgoch is a traditional simple hostel owned by the Elenydd Wilderness Trust. It has hot showers, a self catering kitchen/dining room and 20 beds in 3 dormitories and has been refurbished to include new toilets and showers and less able accommodation. Private rooms are also available and the access track has been upgraded. The Lôn Las Cymru (Welsh National Cycle Route) and the Cambrian Way pass nearby and there are many other mountain tracks to explore on foot, by mountain bike or pony. The hostel is ideal for bird-watchers and lovers of solitude and is close to an old drovers' track which leads over the scenic Cambrian mountains for 5 miles to the equally remote and simple Ty'n Cornel Hostel. Why not stay a night in each hostel and follow in the treads of the old drovers?

DETAILS

- **Open** - All year, 24 hours. Reception 5pm -11pm, 8am -10am.
- **Number of beds** - 20: (in 3 rooms). Private rooms available.
- **Booking** - Booking information on yha.org.uk or from Gillian Keen
- **Price per night** - £12 per adult, £9 (under 18). Campers £6.
- **Public Transport** - Train to Aberystwyth, Carmarthen or Llanwrtyd Wells. Bus X40: Cardiff/Carmarthen to Lampeter/Aberystwyth, Bus 585: Lampeter/Aberystwyth to Tregaron. Postbus 287: Llandovery to Rhandirmwyn.
- **Directions** - SN 806 562. You can walk to Dolgoch over the hills from Tregaron or take the winding Abergwesyn mountain road. The hostel is ¾ mile south of the bridge, along an unsurfaced track.

CONTACT: YHA Booking Office or Gillian Keen
Tel: 01440730226
dolgoch@yha.org.uk   www.elenydd-hostels.co.uk
Dolgoch, Tregaron, Ceredigion, SY25 6NR

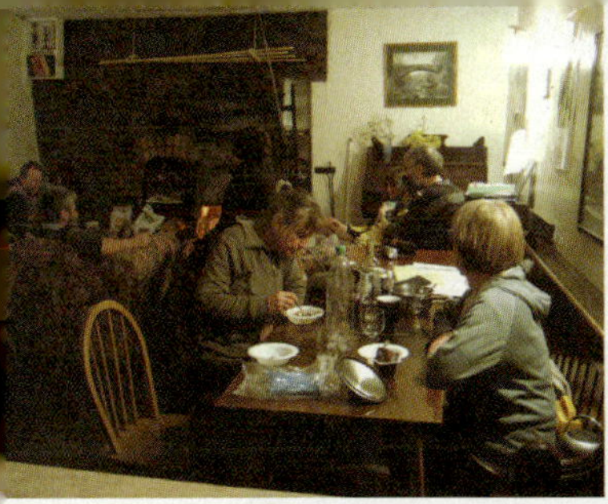

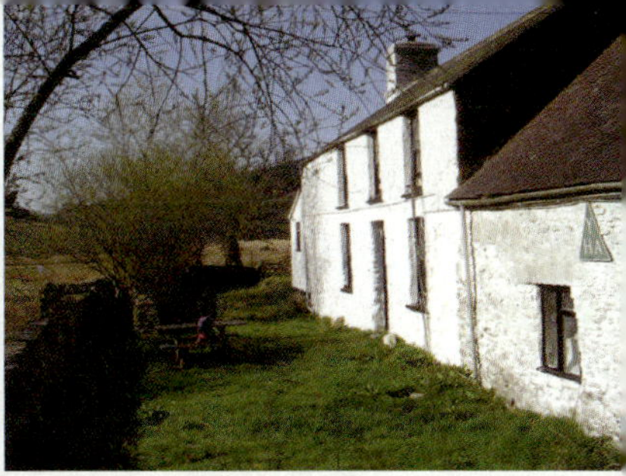

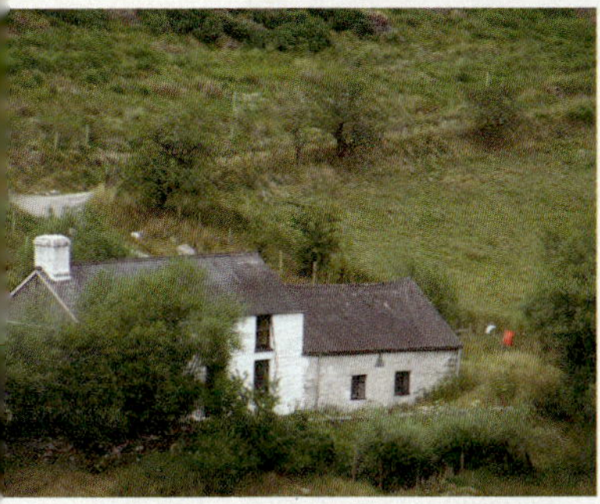

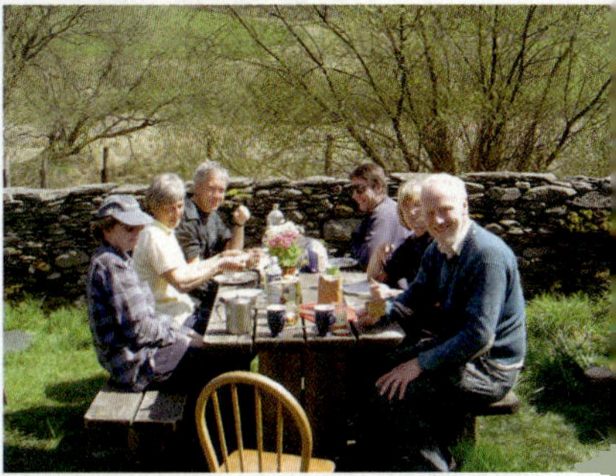

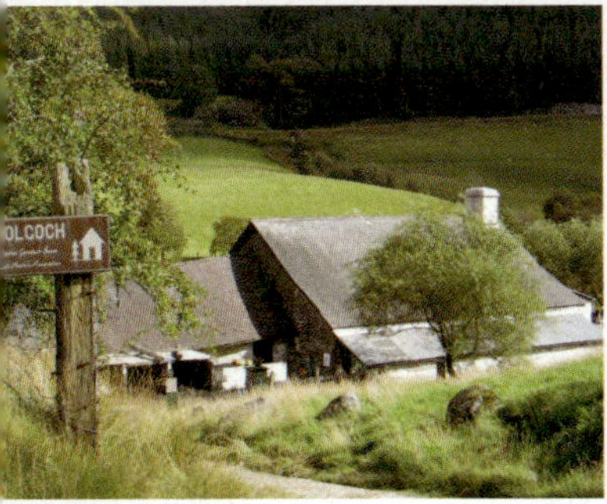
OLCOCH

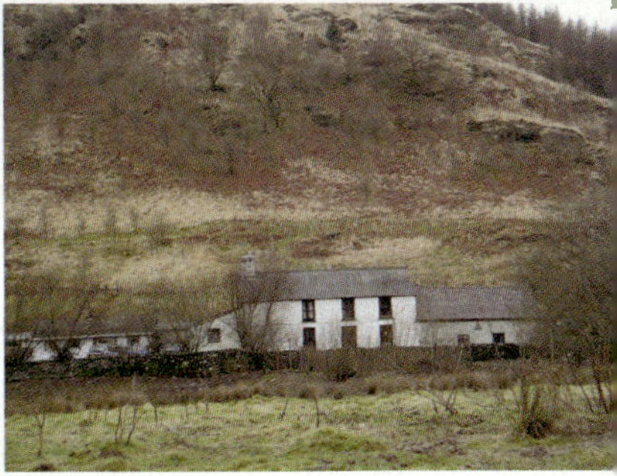

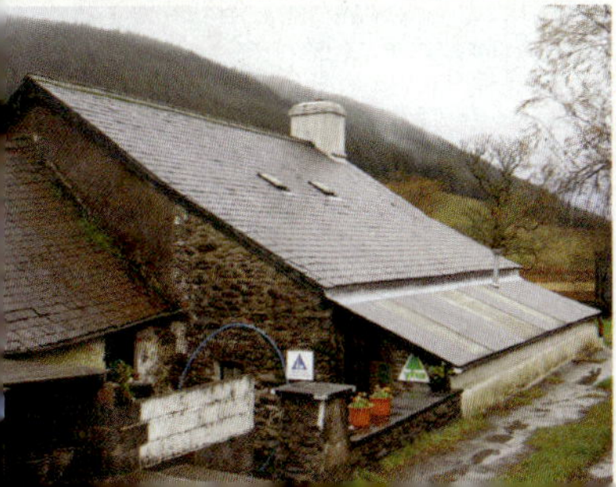

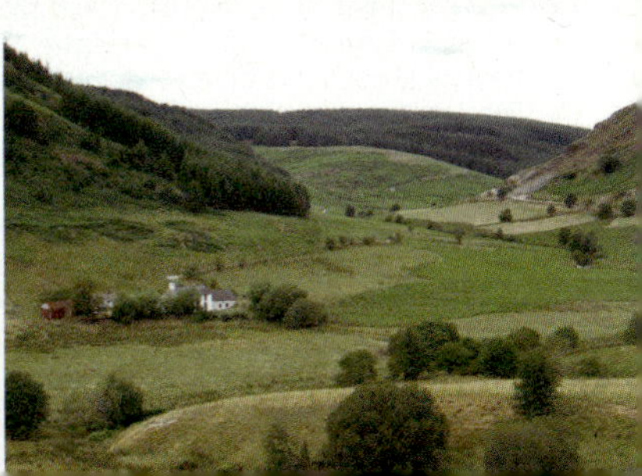

ARETE OUTDOOR CENTRE

The Arete Outdoor Centre in Snowdonia National Park, offers excellent access to the stunning coastline, meandering rivers, awesome mountains and large lakes of North Wales and Anglesey. With comfortable, affordable, bunkhouse style accommodation and catered (3 course meal + soup) or self-catering options, this is a great base for groups of friends or family. The area is passionate about its language, music and history and is rich with magnificent castles, steam railways, heritage and festivals, so theres plenty to do. The team are happy to help with advice on how best to spend your stay and a range of exciting outdoor activities are available through the centre's well qualified and experienced staff. Large well equipped kitchens are available as are several social rooms for down-time the games room having pool and table tennis tables. Large storage for bikes, kayaks and surfboards and a cloakroom with individual space for outdoor kit. Linen can be hired, Parking is available both on-site and on the road outside. For local eating out the Glyntwrog Inn is just 200m away.

DETAILS

- **Open** - All year, all day
- **Number of beds** - 72 in 13 rooms can be split into two blocks of 25 and 20 beds
- **Booking** - Min 4 people for accommodation via email or phone 01286 672136.
- **Price per night** - Catered £30pp, self-catering £15 pp. Sole use deals available.
- **Public Transport** - Airport: Anglesey. Trains: Llanfairpwll or Bangor. Coaches: Caernafon. Local buses from Bangor and Caernarfon. Pickup from Bangor possible,
- **Directions** - Sat navs use LL55 4AP. From A55 At jct 11 follow signs to Llanberis and then Llanrug. Turn left just before the Glyntwrog pub the centre is 200m on right.

CONTACT:
Tel: 01286 672136
info@aretecentre.co.uk www.aretecentre.co.uk
Arete Outdoor Education Centre, Llanrug, Caernarfon, Gwynedd, LL55 4AP

STONECROFT LODGE

WALES

Stonecroft Lodge self-catering guest house is situated in Llanwrtyd Wells, 'the smallest town in Britain'. Surrounded by the green fields, mountains and glorious countryside of mid Wales, Llanwrtyd is in renowned Red Kite country and is a great centre for mountain biking, walking, pony trekking, etc. The town hosts many annual events such as the Man v Horse Marathon, World Bog Snorkelling Championships and the mid-Wales Beer Festival.

The hostel offers a warm welcome and a comfortable stay. It is Wales Tourist Board Star Graded and has private and shared rooms with fully made-up beds. There is a fully equipped kitchen, a lounge with TV and video, free laundry and drying facilities, central heating, a large riverside garden and ample parking. The hostel adjoins our Good Beer Guide pub, Stonecroft Inn (where great food is available), and is truly your 'home away from home', offering the best of everything for your stay.

DETAILS

- **Open** - All year, all day - phone on arrival
- **Number of beds** - 27: 1 x 1 : 3 x 4 : 1 x 6 : 4 x (dbl + 1 sgl)
- **Booking** - Welcome, 50% deposit.
- **Price per night** - £16. Discounts for 3+ nights. Phone for exclusive-use rates.
- **Public Transport** - Llanwrtyd Wells station on the Heart of Wales line is a few minutes' walk from the hostel.
- **Directions** - GR 878 468. From Llanwrtyd town centre (A483) take Dolecoed Road towards Abergwesyn. Hostel is 100 yds on left. Check in at Stonecroft Inn.

CONTACT: Jane Brown
Tel: 01591 610327, Fax: 01591 610304
party@stonecroft.co.uk www.stonecroft.co.uk
Dolecoed Road, Llanwrtyd Wells, Powys, LD5 4RA

BEILI NEUADD BUNKHOUSE

WALES

Beili Neuadd Bunkhouse is a converted 18th century stone barn beautifully positioned in quiet, secluded countryside with delightful views, its own paddocks, stream, pools and woodland. The centrally heated barn sleeps 16 in 3 en suite bunkrooms and includes a fully equipped kitchen/dining room and drying room. The bunks have full sized mattresses, bed linen is included and towels can be hired. Accommodation is also available in an adjacent chalet, there is B&B in the main house and space to camp in the paddock. The paddock has picnic tables and a BBQ and there is ample parking in the yard. The barn is 2.5 miles from the small market town of Rhayader - the gateway to the Elan Valley reservoirs, 'the Lakeland of Wales'. A wide range of activities are possible including cycling, mountain biking, fishing, pony trekking, canoeing, bird watching and walking. Perfect for celebrations and get togethers.

DETAILS

- **Open** - All year, all day access.
- **Number of beds** - 16: 2x6,1x4. Chalet: 1 double, 2 singles. B&B 3 double rooms
- **Booking** - Booking preferred (with deposit).
- **Price per night** - Bunkhouse: £18 per person, 4 bed room £70, 6 bed room £100, sole occupancy £260. Chalet £20pp or £80 full occupancy (4/5 people). B&B £50pp.
- **Public Transport** - Nearest trains at Llandrindod Wells -12 miles. Some buses from Rhayader. Taxi from Rhayader about £4. Assistance with transport available.
- **Directions** - OS Explorer 200/OS147 GR 994698. Take the A44 east bound from Rhayader town centre (clock). After 0.4 miles turn left on unclassified road signposted Abbey Cwm-hir with Beili Neuadd sign. Take 1st left after 1.5 miles. Beili Neuadd is 2nd farm on right after 0.4 miles.

CONTACT: David and Alison Parker
Tel: 01597 810211
info@beilineuadd.co.uk www.beilineuadd.co.uk
Beili Neuadd, Rhayader, Powys, LD6 5NS

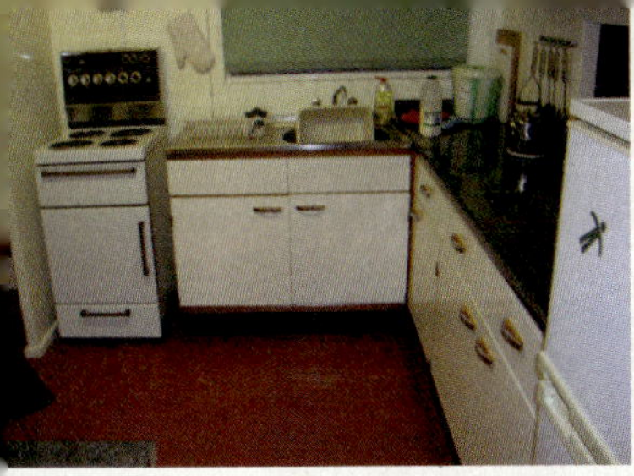
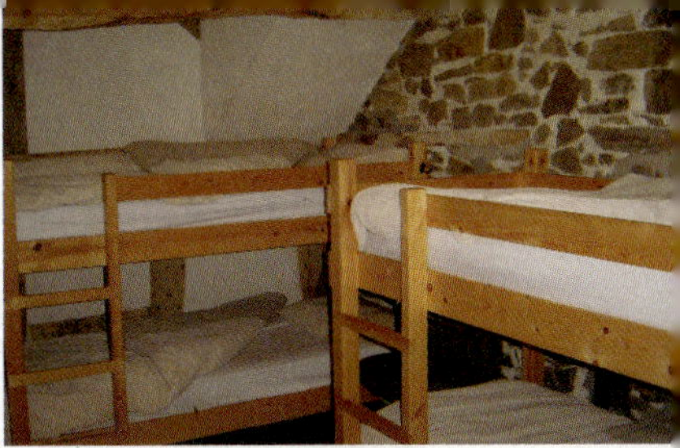
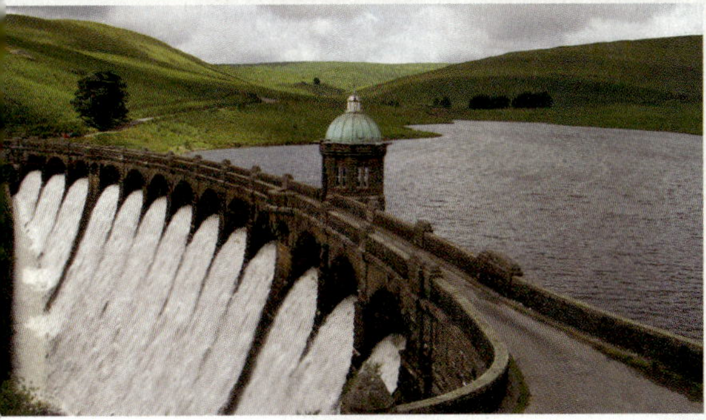
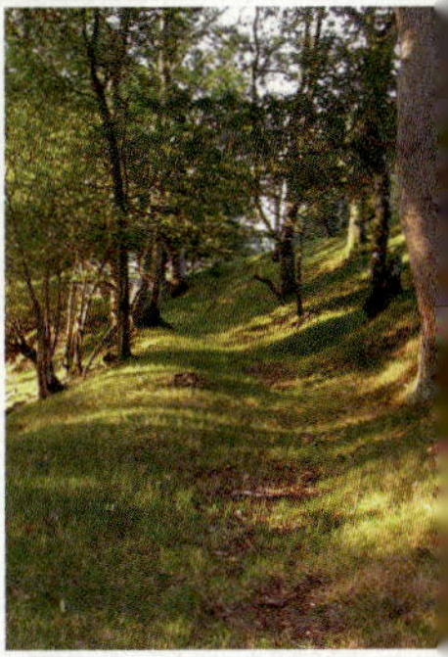
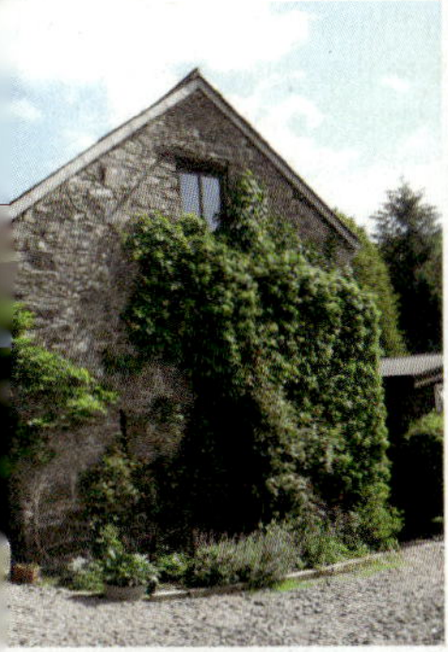
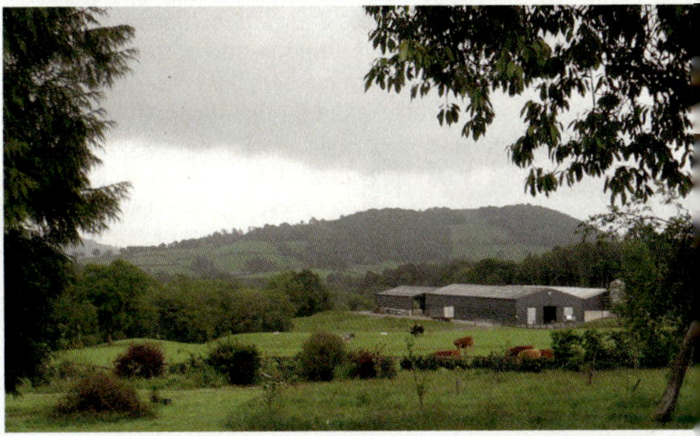
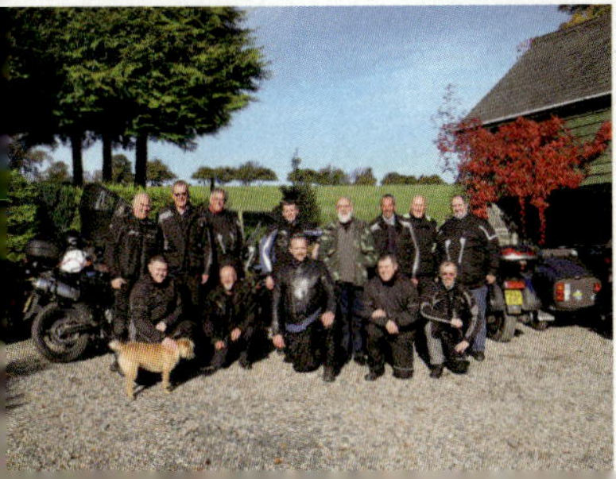
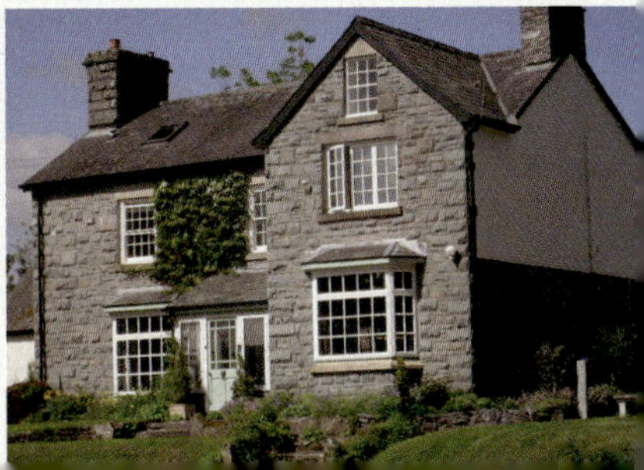

MID WALES BUNKHOUSE

Mid Wales Bunkhouse, offers affordable, warm and comfortable accommodation for individuals or groups. Set in outstanding hill country, convenient for the Elan Valley, Wye Valley, Trans Cambrian Trail, Glyndwrs Way and Cycle Routes 8 and 81. There are lots of circular walks and rides from the door and with the Cambrian mountains just to the west the whole area is ideal for walking, mountain biking, cycling, horse riding, bird watching, fishing and trekking. Grazing for horses available by arrangement. Fully equipped kitchen for self-catering or meals available if arranged in advance. Outside there is a covered veranda and garden with barbeque and pizza oven. Access to the River Marteg where otters and many bird species have been spotted. Covered cycle storage. An ideal base for DofE, scout groups etc. Camping and tipi hire also available.

DETAILS

- **Open** - All year, 24 hours. Arrivals after 3pm (advise if after 7pm), depart by 11am.
- **Number of beds** - 20
- **Booking** - Booking online, by email or phone with deposit, and full payment 8 weeks before arrival. If arriving at short notice please phone to check availability.
- **Price per night** - £15pp, £70 for private 6-bed room. Sole use of dormitory area (sleeps 14) £170 per night, sole use of entire bunkhouse (20 people) £220 per night
- **Public Transport** - Trains at Llandrindod Wells/Newtown. NE coach to Llanidloes. Buses from Llandrindod to Rhayader and limited service to St. Harmon and Pant Y Dwr. We can collect from Llandrindod, Llanidloes or Newtown by arrangement.
- **Directions** - From Rhayader take A44/A470 towards Llangurig then B4518 towards St Harmon. At the Mid Wales Inn turn right, After a mile turn right, Bunkhouse on right in half a mile. SatNav use is not advised. GR SN998750.

CONTACT: John or Steph
Tel: 01597 870081
enquiries@bunkhousemidwales.co.uk www.bunkhousemidwales.co.uk
Woodhouse Farm, St Harmon, Rhayader, LD6 5LY

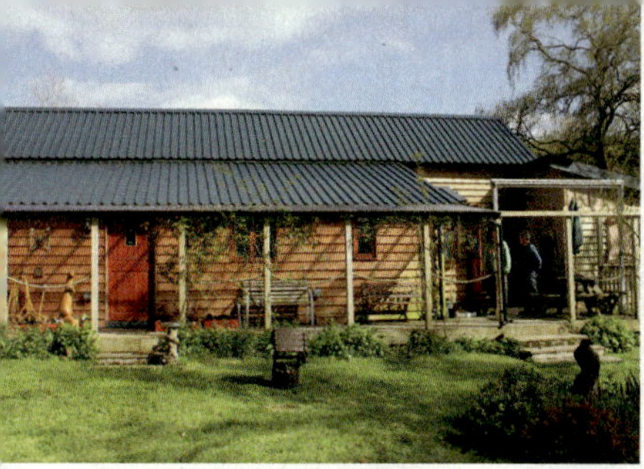
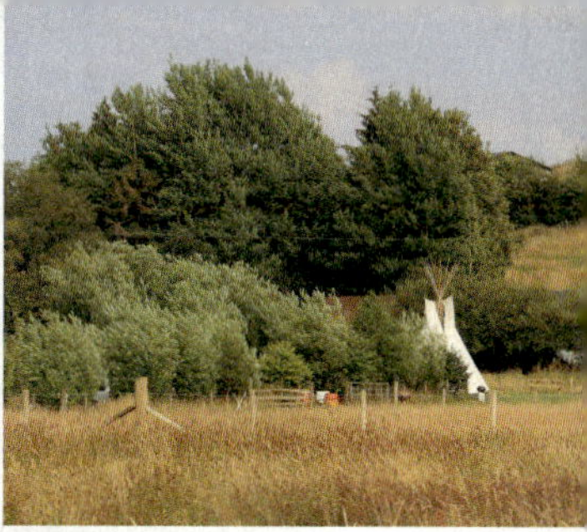
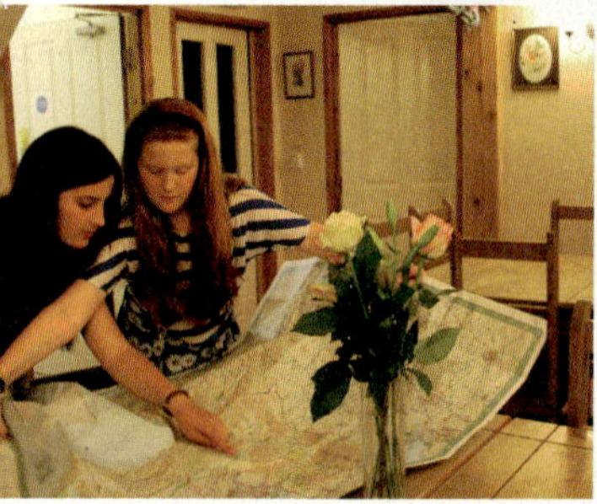
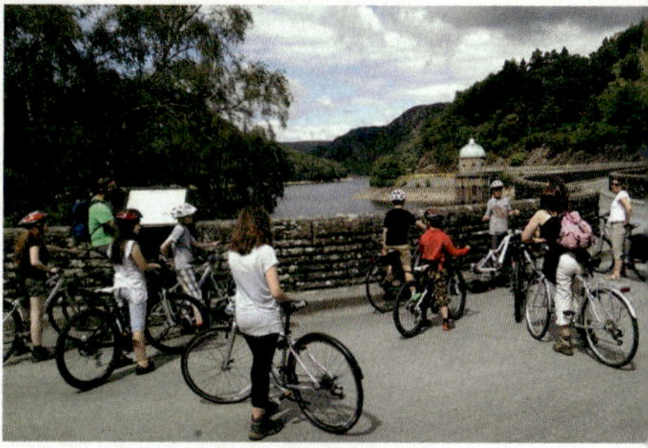
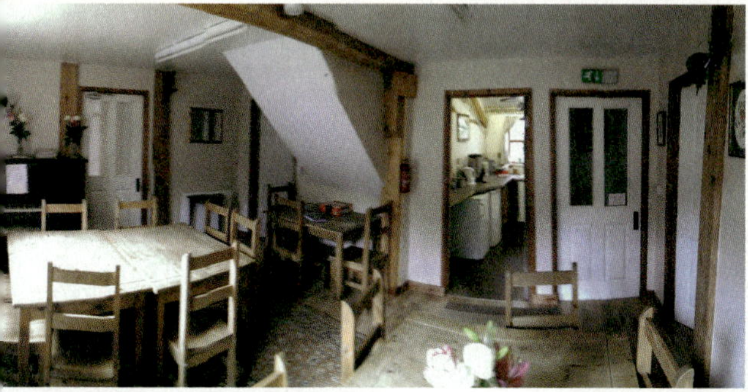
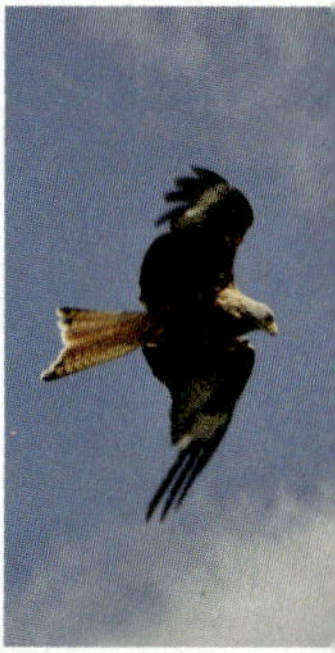
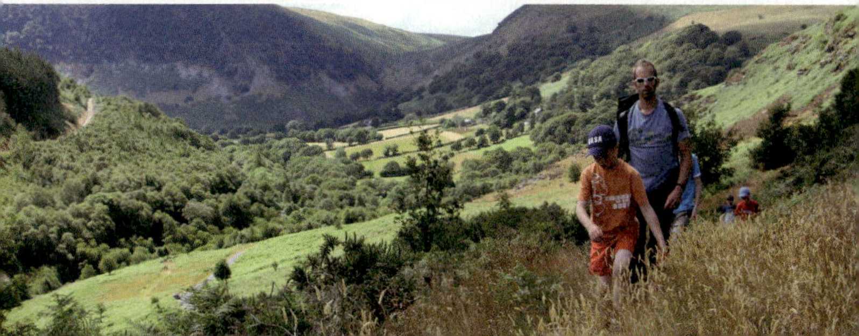

NEW INN BUNKHOUSE

WALES

Stay at the 16th century New Inn on the River Wye and discover the forgotten countryside of mid Wales. The New Inn has a bunkhouse ideal for parties of walkers and cyclists as well as double, twin and family B&B rooms. The bunkhouse has its own entrance and a large lobby which can be used for boots and waterproofs. Secure storage is available for cycles and motor-cycles. The bunkhouse is self-contained with toilets and showers.

There are no self-catering facilities but the Inn specialises in serving imaginative home-cooked locally grown food. A Welsh breakfast of home-made sausages and dry cured bacon is available for £5.50 Explore the surrounding countryside, inhabited by Red Kites, or relax in the secluded beer garden. There is plenty of parking and a large function room for parties

DETAILS

- **Open** - All year, all day. Pub closed 3pm - 5pm some days.
- **Number of beds** - Bunkhouse 10: 1x6, 1x4; B&B 11: family rooms, double & twin
- **Booking** - Book by phone or email.
- **Price per night** -   £12 pp (Bunkhouse), £60 sole use of 6 bed room, £40 sole use of 4 bed room. Breakfast £5.50pp. En suite B&B in Inn £60 double/twin. Family rooms also available from £80.
- **Public Transport** - Trains at Llandrindod Wells (5 miless). Infrequent bus service.
- **Directions** - Newbridge-on-Wye is on the A470 between Builth Wells and Rhayader. Travelling north on the A470 take a right turn in Newbridge and the New Inn is on the right.

CONTACT: Debbie and Dave
Tel: 01597 860211
dave@pigsfolly.orangehome.co.uk www.pigsfolly.co.uk/bunkhouse.htm
New Inn, Newbridge-on-Wye, Llandrindod Wells, Powys, LD1 6HY

BRYNCARNEDD
COUNTRY COTTAGES

WALES

Brycarnedd operate a selection of self catering cottages located just outside the popular seaside town of Aberystwyth. The cottages are unique and have between 2-6 bedrooms. They are all are fully equipped as self catering properties. Storage available on site for bicycles.

We welcome small or large groups, for short or long stays. We are happy to accept pets. We can also provide cots and highchairs on request. Most of our cottages have utility rooms, and for those who don't we have installed a small laundry area on site. All of our properties have parking, and some also have free Wi-Fi.

Aberystwyth is a small University town nestled in the heart of Cardigan Bay. Its diverse shops and friendly atmosphere appeal to people of all ages.

There is something for everyone on your holiday away.

DETAILS

- **Open** - All year, 8am-10pm
- **Number of beds** - 115: in 19 houses sleeping 2-20 in small rooms
- **Booking** - Deposit of £200 on booking, full payment 4 weeks prior to arrival
- **Price per night** - From £17.50 per person per night
- **Public Transport** - Railway station at Aberystwyth. Summer buses run to Clarach.
- **Directions** - Please call for detailed directions which will also be provided in the full confirmation.

CONTACT: Nerys Evans
Tel: 01970612444, Fax: 07970617435
info@aberholidaycottages.com www.aberholidaycottages.com
Clarach Road, Aberystwyth, Ceredigion, SY23 3DG

PLAS DOLAU
COUNTRY HOUSE HOSTEL

WALES

Plas Dolau is set in 25 acres of quiet countryside just 3 miles from the popular coastal town of Aberystwyth. Ideal for exploring West Wales, walking, cycling, riding, fishing and golf etc. The holiday centre includes a warm country mansion (WTB 4 star hostel) with mainly dormitory style accommodation and an adjoining Scandinavian style farmhouse (WTB 3 star guest house).

Plas Dolau includes meeting rooms, dining rooms, games room, outdoor areas and walks. The centre can accommodate groups of up to 45 people. Various options for accommodation, provision of food, cooking facilities, etc are available. Ideally suited for youth groups, field courses, retreats, house parties and many other groups or individuals. WiFi available to all from the guest house. Please feel free to phone to discuss your requirements.

DETAILS

- **Open** - All year, 24 hours
- **Number of beds** - 45: + cots etc. Plus 16 in farmhouse.
- **Booking** - Recommended.
- **Price per night** - From £20 (including basic breakfast) to £35 (private room, en suite with full breakfast). From £650 per night for the whole mansion.
- **Public Transport** - Nearest train station is in Aberystwyth. Taxi from the station will cost around £5. National Express coaches and local buses (525 and 526) will set down at the end of the hostel drive.
- **Directions** - GR 623 813, OS map 135. On the A44, 3 miles from Aberystwyth, 1 mile from Llanbadarn railway bridge, 0.6 miles from turning to Bow Street. Sign on roadside says 'Y Gelli', B+B. Reception in 'Y Gelli'.

CONTACT: Pat Twigg
Tel: 01970 617834
enquiry@plasdolau.co.uk www.plasdolau.co.uk
Lovesgrove, Aberystwyth, Ceredigion, SY23 3HP

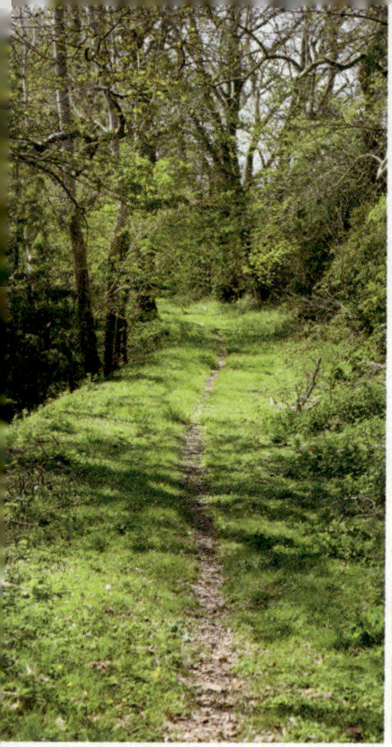
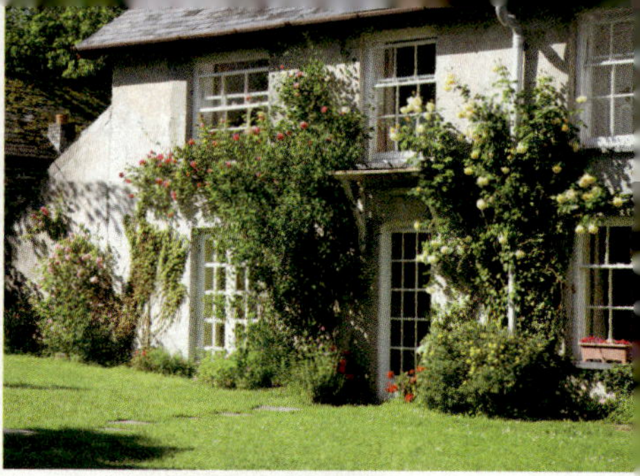
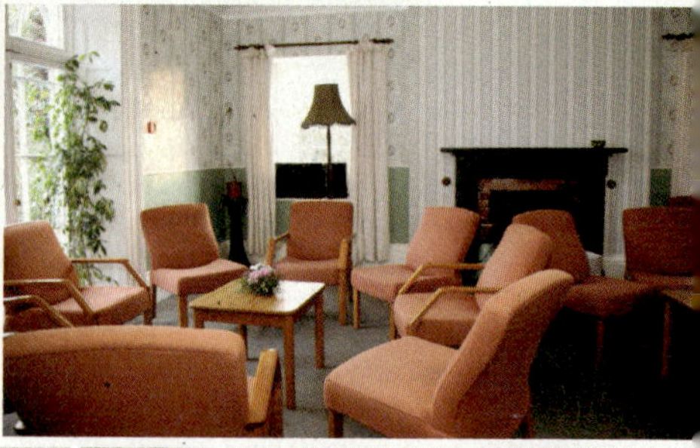
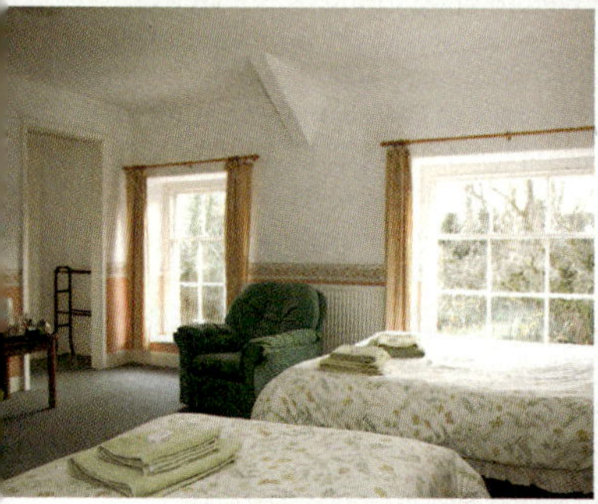
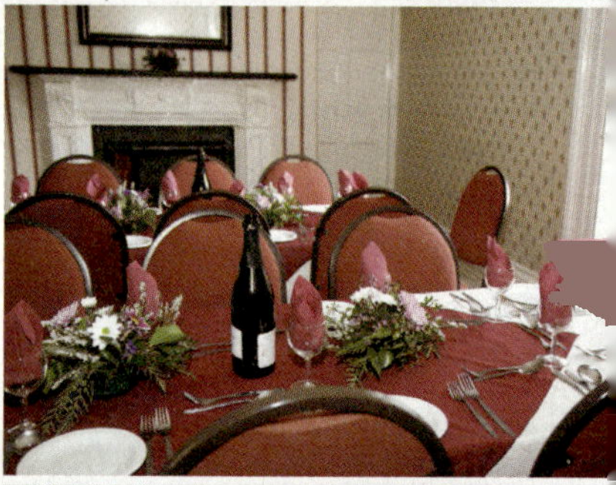
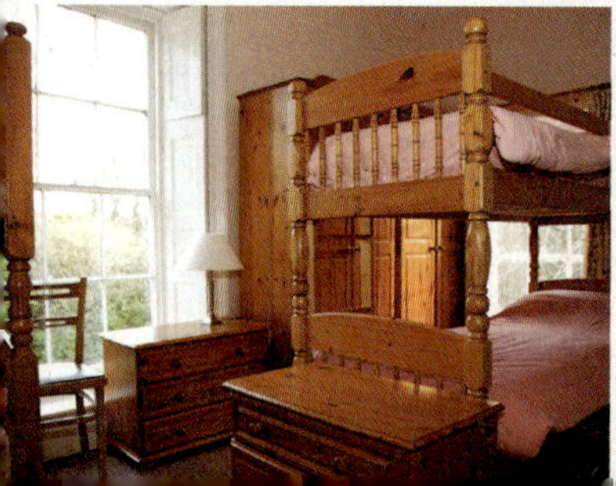
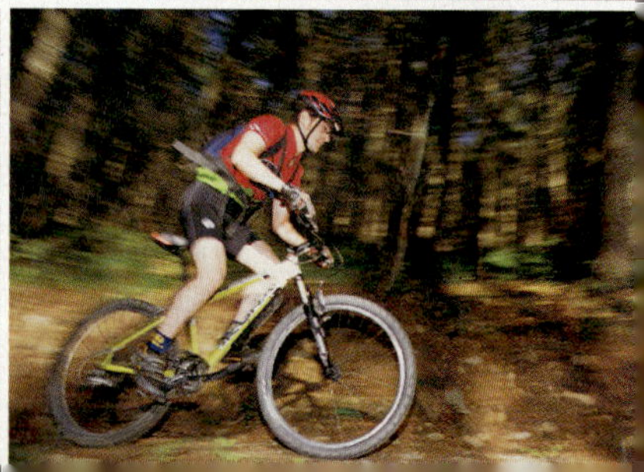

MAES-Y-MOR

WALES

Maes-y-Mor offers superior accommodation at a budget price. Ideally situated near the town centre, around the corner from the beach and 5 mins' walk to train and bus stations. Accommodation at the hostel is room-only. There is a large kitchen/diner with fridge-freezer, hob oven, microwave and toaster enabling guests to prepare their own food. Bedrooms have TV, tea/coffee making facilities and beds of a superior quality to ensure a good night's sleep. Free WiFi internet and towels are provided. Themed in Welsh history pictures. There is a car parking area at rear and secure shed for bikes. A new self catering 4 star house is also available for hire. Aberystwyth is an ideal base for exploring Wales. Visit Devil's Bridge with its dramatic waterfalls, the Vale of Rheidol narrow gauge railway, the National Library of Wales, the castle and the harbour. Aberystwyth is a university town with plenty of night life. Personal and helpful service. Croeso Cymraeg Cynnes i bawb / A warm Welsh welcome to all!

DETAILS

- **Open** - All year, 8am to 10pm.
- **Number of beds** - 20: 8 x 2, 1 x 4 (en suite).
- **Booking** - Booking advisable.
- **Price per night** - Twin and double rooms from £48.00. Single room from £30.00. Discount for larger groups.
- **Public Transport** - Bus and train stations are within approximately 400 mts.
- **Directions** - From bus and train stations follow Terrace Road in a straight line towards beach. Turn right at Tourist Board Shop, then Maes-y-Mor is about 30 mts along, next to the cinema.

CONTACT: Gordon or Mererid
Tel: 01970 639270 or 07966 502715, Fax: 01970 623621
maesymor@hotmail.co.uk www.maesymor.co.uk
25 Bath Street, Aberystwyth, Ceredigion, SY23 2NN

PLASNEWYDD BUNKHOUSE

WALES

Set in the beautiful mid-Wales countryside on the Glyndwrs Way the bunkhouse is an ideal location for exploring or unwinding. Built to the highest standards, with 4 star tourist board rating, it provides high quality accommodation for groups or individuals. It can also be booked for conferences and seminars. There is a well equipped kitchen and a large communal area with fabulous elevated views over the mid-Wales countryside. The bunk beds are large with comfortable mattresses. Pillows and pillowcases are included, sheets and duvets can be hired for £3 per set. Attractions close by include sailing, golf course, outdoor pursuit centre, shooting range, motorbike school and the picturesque market town of LLanidloes (0.5 mile) with many places to eat and drink. You will need to bring your own soap and towels. Boots and dirty footwear must be kept in the drying room so please bring footwear for indoors. Taxis for walkers and cyclists to / from routes available.

DETAILS

- **Open** - All year, 24 hours. Arrival and departure times by arrangement.
- **Number of beds** - 27 in 2 dormitories and 1 family room.
- **Booking** - Booking is required (with non-refundable deposit) by phone, email or booking form on plasnewyddbunkhouse.co.uk.
- **Price per night** - Sole use £403 per night. Individuals £20 pp.
- **Public Transport** - Caersws train station (7 miles), Llanidloes bus station (0.5 mile). Pick ups can be arranged from these points if required.
- **Directions** - From Llanidloes take the Gorn Road and Plasnewydd is signposted on the left hand side after about half a mile.

CONTACT: Susan
Tel: 01686 412431 or 07977 508 648 / 07975 913049 , Fax: 447975913049
susanvaughan67@aol.co.uk www.plasnewyddbunkhouse.co.uk
Gorn Rd, Llanidloes, Powys, SY18 6LA

OLD WEATHER STATION

WALES

This comfortable bunkhouse is located on the edge of the Hafren Forest, close to Plumlimon, in a quiet rural location between Llanidloes and Machynlleth in the Cambrian Mountains. The centre provides an ideal base for walking, running, cycling (both on and off road), kayaking, wildlife watching, family groups and parties. The surroundings are breath-taking, with mountain, forest, streams and lakes on the doorstep. Watersports are available on Llyn Clywedog and there are many excellent local rivers for kayaking / canoeing.

The bunkhouse has full central heating and a wood burner in the lounge. The full equipped catering kitchen looks out onto the forest and slopes of Plumlumon. The bunkhouse is equipped with flat screen TV / DVD player and 2 toilet / shower areas [6 showers in total].

Family friendly, disabled access, well behaved pets by arrangement. Adventure activities available through local outdoor centre.

DETAILS

- **Open** - All year,
- **Number of beds** - 28: 1x3, 3x4, 1x5, 1x 8
- **Booking** - Essential. Sole use only
- **Price per night** - From £16 per person per night
- **Public Transport** - Nearest station Caersws, nearest buses Llanidloes.
- **Directions** - 8 miles from Llanidloes / 12 miles from Machynlleth

CONTACT: Adrian Roberts / Matt Jones
Tel: 01686 430372, Fax: 01298 873028
theoldweatherstation@gmail.com www.theoldweatherstation.co.uk
Staylittle, nr Llanidloes, Powys, SY19 7DB

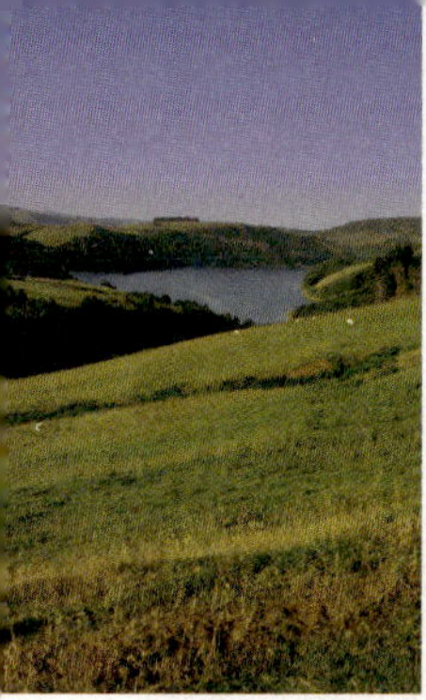
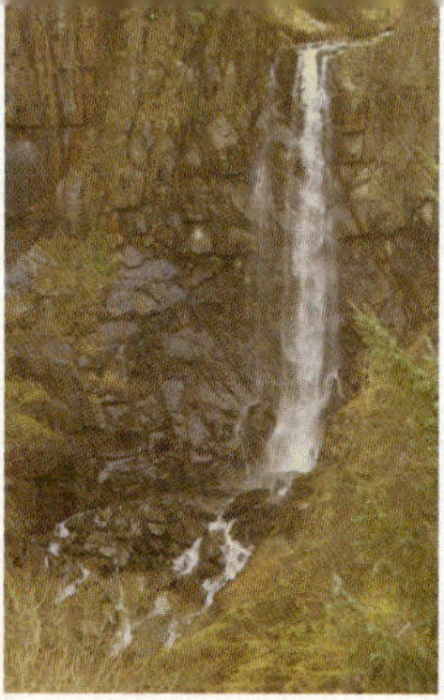
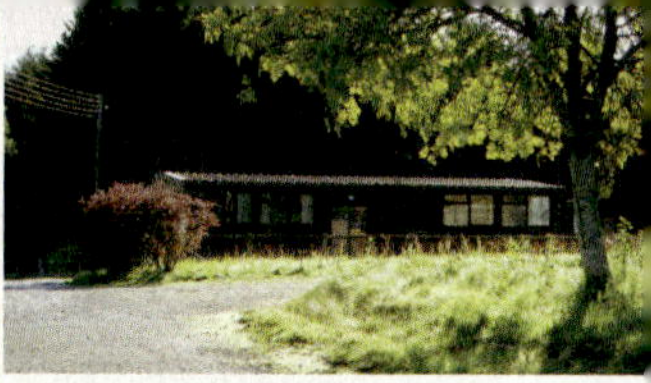
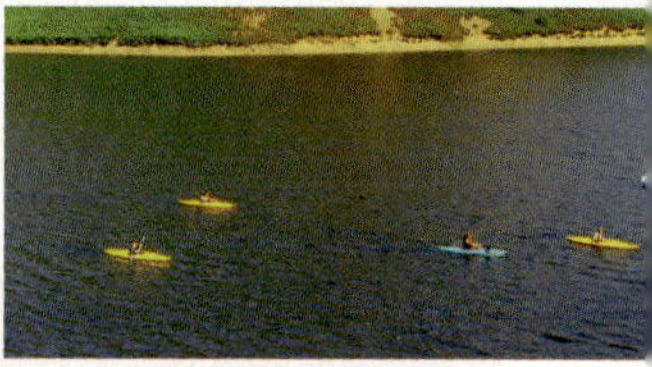
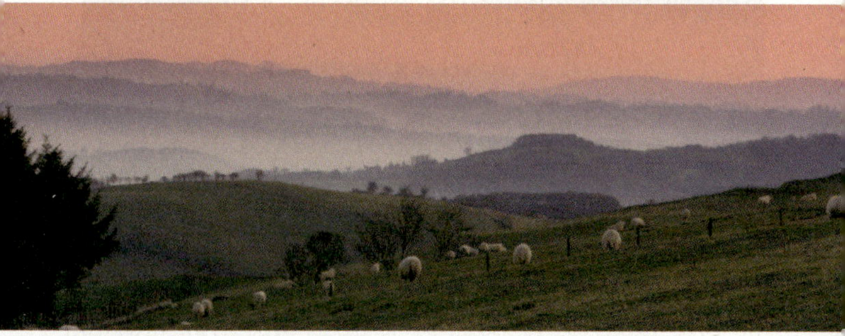
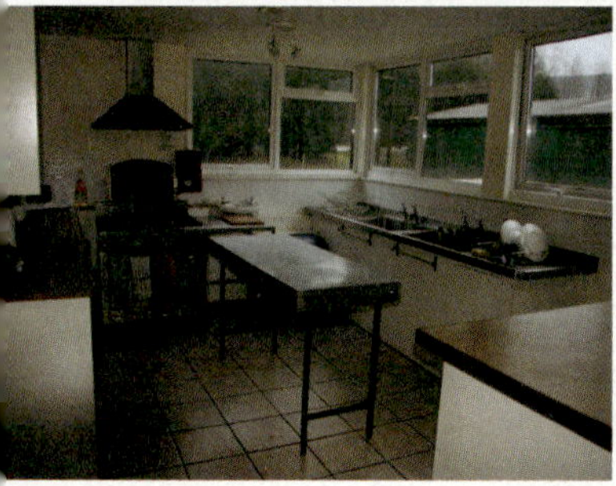
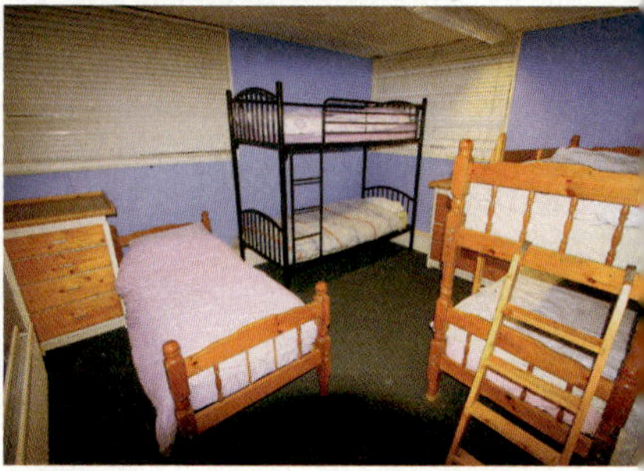
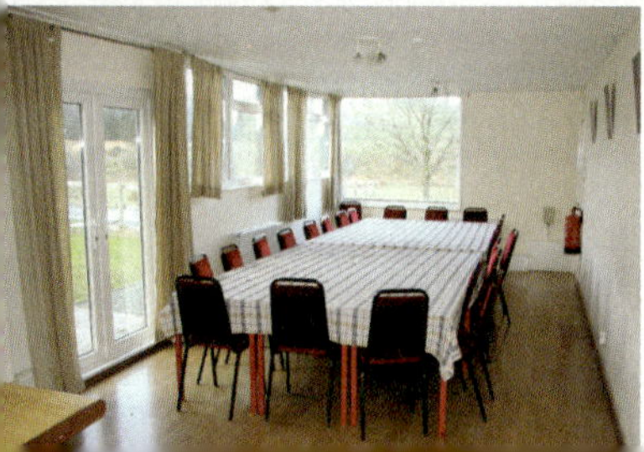
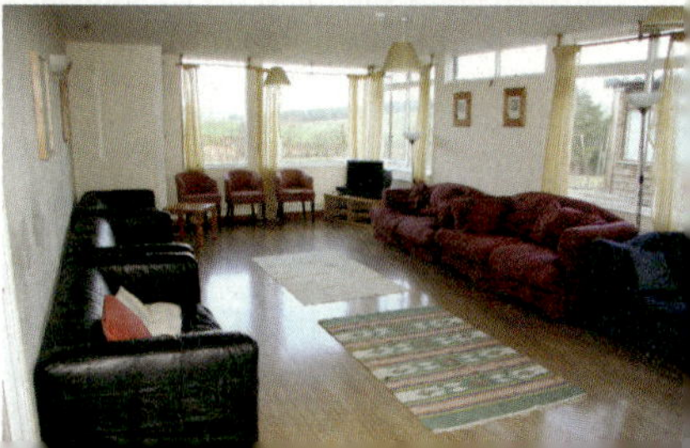

TOAD HALL

WALES

Toad Hall is a privately owned family hostel in mid Wales, close to Snowdonia and in the beautiful Dovey Estuary. The estuary is a UNESCO biosphere including the Yns Hir RSPB reserve and the long sandy beaches of Aberdovey. The influential Centre for Alternative Technology is 2 miles away. Toad Hall is very close to the railway station in the historical town of Machynlleth. The town has a livley feel with a busy Wednesday market, and many residents with a progressive and alternative slant. Cader Idris mountain is 6 miles away. Toad Hall has 4 private bedrooms, a self-catering kitchen, a large games room (available until 9pm), a flat garden for bike/canoe storage and camping, and a workshop for bike repairs. Please phone to arrange use of these facilities. Under 18s and well behaved dogs welcome with prior agreement. Guests are not accepted without bookings. Email is a good way to book since the phone is not always manned. There may also be periods when the hostel is unavailable.

DETAILS

- **Open** - Phone to find out if open, 9am-9pm. Please vacate rooms from 12 till 3pm for cleaning. No arrivals after 11pm.
- **Number of beds** - 10: 1x4 (family), 1x2 (twin), 1x2 (dbl), 1x2
- **Booking** - Advance booking necessary - phone on the day if necessary. Payment in advance or a deposit of 1 night's fee.
- **Price per night** - £16 pp + £2 per stay for bedding. Reductions for groups.
- **Public Transport** - 200m to train station (services to the Midlands, North Wales and Aberystwyth). 100m to Lloyds coaches depot and local bus stop
- **Directions** - Down a private lane directly opposite the turning to the train station.

CONTACT: Eva
Tel: 01654 700597 Mob: 07807 849216 or 07866 362507
willcoyn@hotmail.com
Toad Hall, Doll St, Machynlleth, Powys, SY20 8BH

TY'N Y BERTH
MOUNTAIN CENTRE

347

WALES

Ty'n y Berth is a former school at the foot of Cadair Idris on the southern edge of the Snowdonia National Park. Surrounded by mountains, valleys and crystal clear rivers, yet only 12 miles from the coast, it's a great location for outdoor activities and family holidays. The spacious accommodation sleeps up to 46. The main room is divided into dining and lounge areas. There is a commercial kitchen, recently renovated, with large oven, hob and microwave, plenty of toilets & showers, drying room, pay phone, lockable storage for boats & bikes and parking for 10 cars. Corris is within walking distance and has two pubs: the Slaters Arms, which does bar meals, and the Braich Goch Inn, which regularly has live music. Courses are also available in climbing, mountain walking, abseiling, gorge scrambling, mine exploration, ropes courses, orienteering, and team building. Accommodation for a further 36 is available at the Bryn Coedwig Centre (also run by Wide Horizons), four miles from Ty'n Y Berth in the village of Aberllefenni.

DETAILS

- **Open** - All year, all day
- **Number of beds** - 46: 2x8, 4x6, 1x3, 1x2, 2x1
- **Booking** - Book by phone/fax or email.
- **Price per night** - £260.00 - £325.00 + VAT on a self catering, sole use basis.
- **Public Transport** - Trains run from London to Machynlleth with a change at Birmingham New Street.
- **Directions** - On entering Corris Uchaf from north on A487 you will enter a 30 mph speed limit. Ty'n y Berth is the old school on the right, just inside the 30mph signs.

CONTACT: Jane or Dave
Tel: 01654 761678, Fax: 0872 115 3187
info@corris-bunkhouse.co.uk www.corris-bunkhouse.co.uk
Corris Uchaf, Machynlleth, Powys, SY20 9RH

BRAICH GOCH
BUNKHOUSE & INN

WALES

The Braich Goch is a 16th century coaching inn situated 3 miles from Cadair Idris. There are stunning views of the Dulas Valley and Dyfi Forest. The Braich has been specifically set up with outdoor enthusiasts in mind. Facilities include drying room, secure bike storage and large well equipped self-catering kitchen. There are 6 bedrooms, 4 en suite and a further two bathrooms. WiFi. See a 360 degree virtual tour on our website. The location is ideal for walking, mountain biking, cycling, climbing and canoeing at all levels as well as bird watching or simply chilling out. The Cli-machx Trail & Dyfi Forest mountain bike trails are on the doorstep. The Braich is also a pub with pool table, darts and other games to keep you entertained in the evening! In the area are King Arthur's Labyrinth and Corris Craft Centre, Centre for Alternative Technology, Coed-y-Brenin Forest Park, Nant yr Arian and the coast.

Wales Tourist Board 4 stars. Walkers & Cyclists Welcome Awards.

DETAILS

- **Open** - All year, all hours by arrangement
- **Number of beds** - 26: 5 x 4, 1 x 6
- **Booking** - Essential for groups. 20% deposit, balance 4 weeks before arrival.
- **Price per night** - £17.50pp
- **Public Transport** - Nearest train station to Corris is Machynlleth. Bus stop outside the 'Braich Goch' Inn. Taxis can be hired from Machynlleth.
- **Directions** - GR 754 075 On A487 between Machynlleth and Dolgellau at Corris turning. 2.5 miles north of Centre for Alternative Technology.

CONTACT: Ann or Andy
Tel: 01654 761229 Mobile: 07881 626734
AnnBottrill@aol.com www.braichgoch.co.uk
Corris, Machynlleth, Powys, SY20 9RD

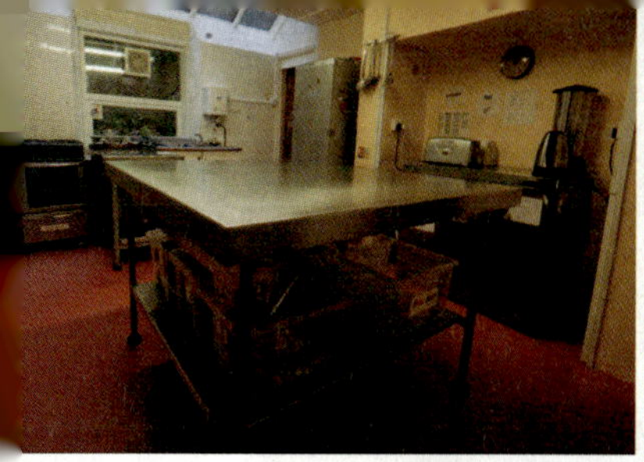

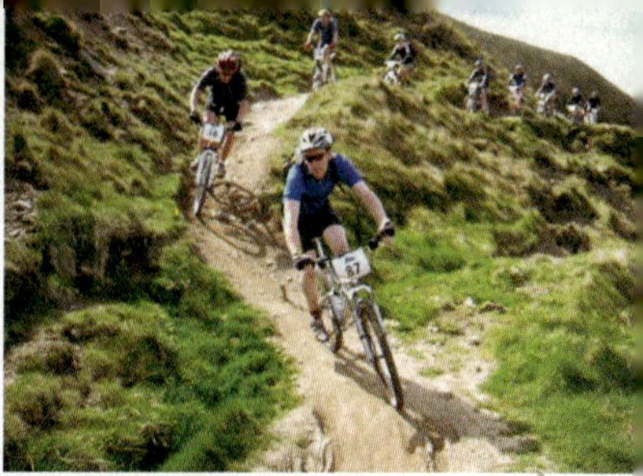

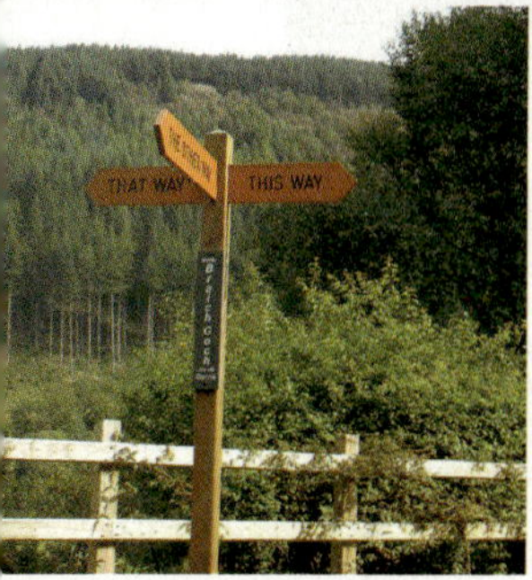
THAT WAY
THIS WAY

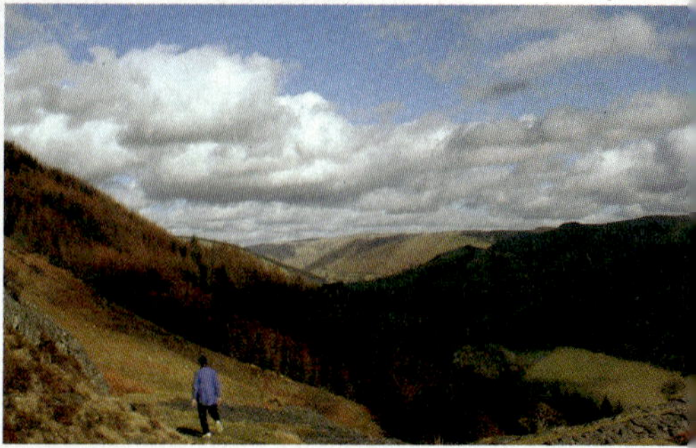

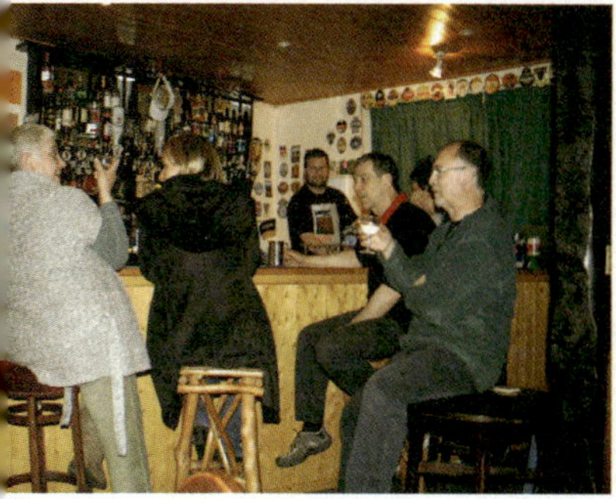

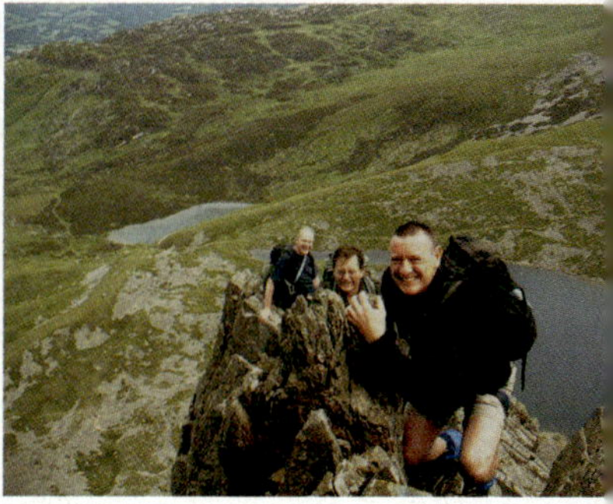

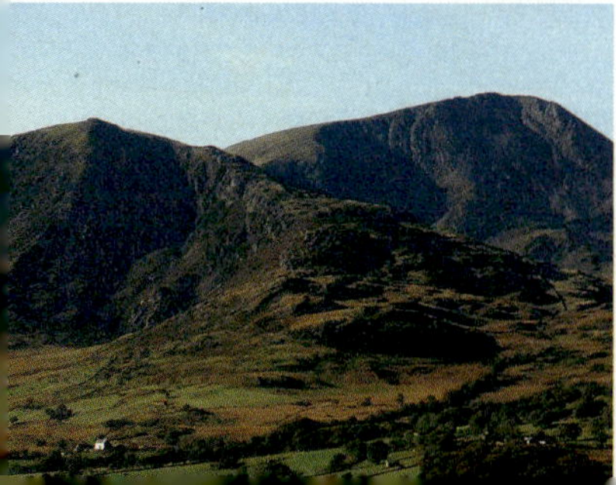

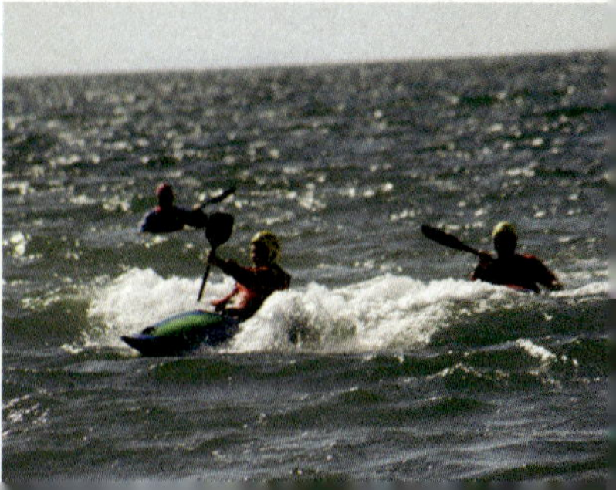

CORRIS HOSTEL

WALES

Perfect for group activity and family gatherings, Corris Hostel offers a very special atmosphere that disengages the stresses of the outside world. The award winning hostel is renowned as a spiritual haven with its caring, easy going atmosphere, friendly staff, meditation areas, cosy wood fires and collection of inspiring books, games and artefacts.

Outdoors the terraced landscaped gardens provide a serene, inspirational environment for even the largest groups. An added bonus are the barbecue and camp fire areas. Nestled in the foothills of Cadair Idris, the hostel enjoys splendid views over the Dyfi Valley in the Snowdonia National Park. Down river are the Dyfi Biosphere nature reserves and miles of golden beaches at Aberdyfi, while the lofty Cadair Idris nestles in the next valley. Close by is the Centre for Alternative Technology and a range of environmental activities.

DETAILS

- **Open** - All year, all day access.
- **Number of beds** - 42/44
- **Booking** - Phone to check.
- **Price per night** - Adult £16 child £13, Breakfast £4.25. Private rooms extra.
- **Public Transport** - Transport: Buses 30, T2, 34 and X28 pass Machynlleth train station on the Cambrian Coast line with connection to Aberystwyth and Birmingham.
- **Directions** - GR 753 080. We are in the mountain village of Corris 6 miles north of Machynlleth. At Braich Goch turn off A487 into Corris. At Slaters Arms pub turn left, hostel is 150m uphill just beyond a small private car park. Guests can park in the private car park.

CONTACT: Michael or Debbie or Kevin
Tel: 01654 761686, Fax: 447429344132
mail@corrishostel.co.uk   www.corrishostel.co.uk
Old School, Corris, Machynlleth, Powys, SY20 9TQ

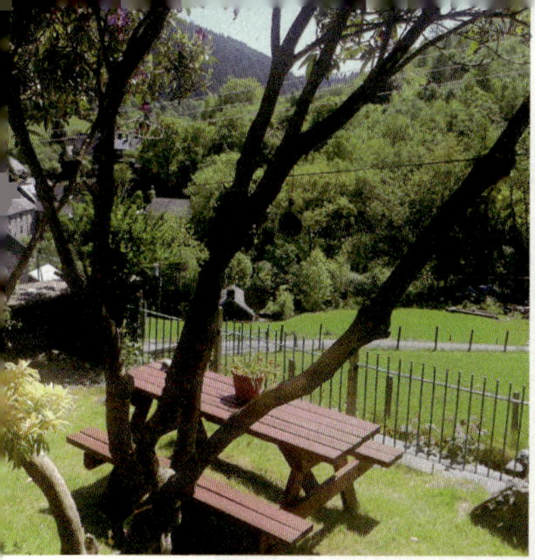
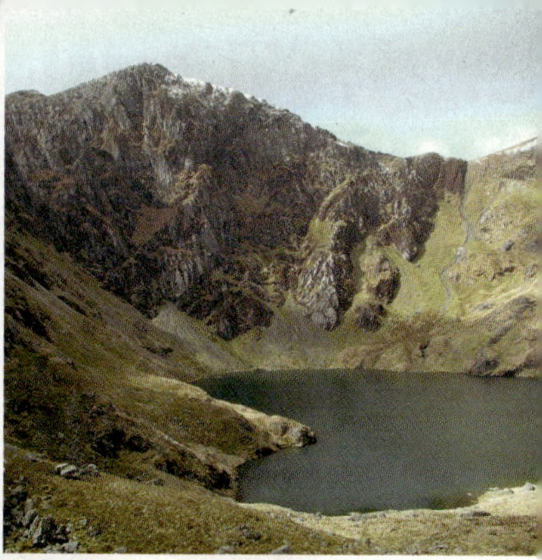
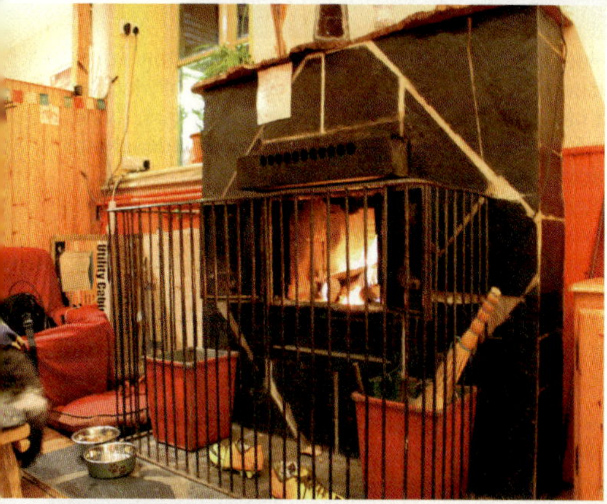
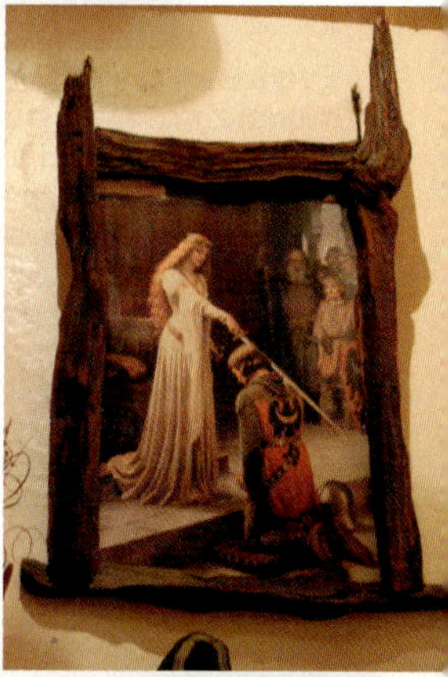
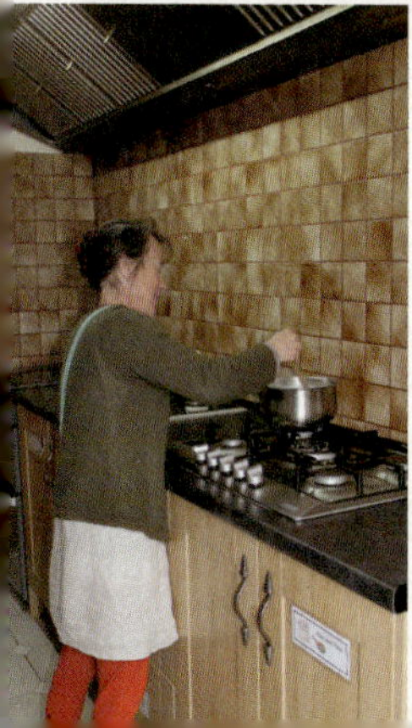
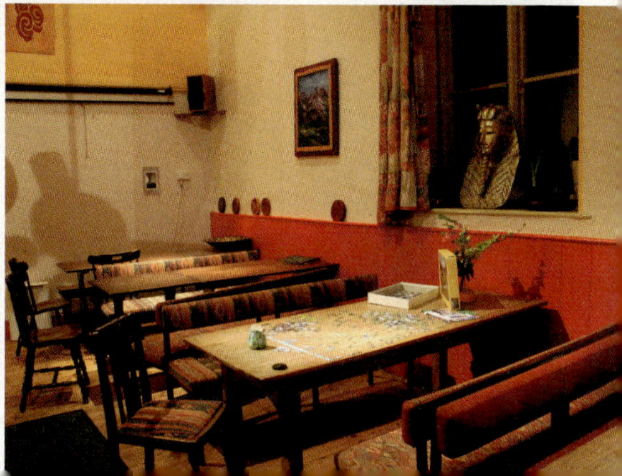

HYB BUNKHOUSE
DOLGELLAU

WALES

HyB Bunkhouse is on Heol y Bont (Bridge St) in the old market town of Dolgellau, mid Wales, nestling at the foot of Cader Idris. It is centrally located above Medi gift shop, and has free parking at rear, for up to four cars. Near pubs, shops and restaurants, HyB Bunkhouse backs onto the Mawddach trail and the Marian fields, near the river Wnion. It is 10 minutes' drive to Coed y Brenin mountain biking centre. This quirky listed building has original features such as oak floors, beams and panelling and consists of four bunk rooms, sleeping 16 in total. Each room has a mini-kitchen for basic self-catering with fridge, hob, toaster and kettle. One room is en suite, and there are also two other modern bathrooms. Bring your own bedding. HyB has wireless internet connection. Limited bedding sets are also available to rent on request @ £5 per set... Strictly no stag parties...

DETAILS

- **Open** - Closed Xmas and New Year , book before 4.30 pm, key pad entry code allocated for arrival
- **Number of beds** - 16: 4 x4.
- **Booking** - Please phone or email before 4.30pm.
- **Price per night** - £20 per person
- **Public Transport** - Buses stop at Eldon square (1 minute walk) and link with train stations at Machynlleth and Barmouth for connections to Midlands and London.
- **Directions** - HyB is above Medi - the last shop before the main bridge on the one way system out of Eldon square. By car turn into Y Marian car park and take a sharp left behind the public loos into HyB car park through the double wooden gates.

CONTACT: Nia
Tel: 01341 421755, Fax: 01341421755
post@medi-gifts.com   www.medi-gifts.com
2-3 Heol y Bont (Bridge St), Dolgellau, Gwynedd, LL40 1AU

BALA BUNKHOUSE

353

WALES

The bunkhouse is a converted 200-year-old Welsh stone building, set back from the road in over an acre of picturesque grounds with private parking.

Modernised to provide accommodation for outdoor activity groups, it is light, airy and comfortable with storage heating. There is a large lounge/dining area and bunk rooms for 2, 4 and 8 plus annexe for 6. Separate ladies' and gentlemen's toilets have washing areas and hot showers. Fully equipped self-catering kitchen. Also there is a self-contained bunkroom sleeping 6, with small kitchenette, shower and toilet/washing area, which is ideal for smaller groups and families. Sheets, pillows & pillowcases are provided - bring a sleeping bag.

There is a splendid view of the Berwyn Hills; together with the Aran and Arenig hills they provide superb walking. Bala Lake and the National White Water Centre are brilliant for water sports. Good pubs, restaurants and shops in Bala.

DETAILS

- **Open** - All year, no restrictions
- **Number of beds** - 26 : 1x2, 1x4, 1x6, 1x8, 1x6 self-contained
- **Booking** - Book if possible, ring or write with 20% deposit. Weekends are busy.
- **Price per night** - Single night £16 pp, two or more nights £15 pp per night.
- **Public Transport** - Trains at Wrexham (30 miles). National Express at Corwen (10 miles). Local buses call at Bala (1.6 miles from hostel). Call hostel for a taxi.
- **Directions** - GR 950 372. From England take M6, M54, A5 through Llangollen then A494 for Bala. We are on the A494 1.5 miles before Bala.

CONTACT: Guy and Jane Williams
Tel: 01678 520738, Fax: 01678 520738
thehappyunion@btinternet.com   www.balabunkhouse.co.uk
Tomen Y Castell, Llanfor, Bala, Gwynedd, LL23 7HD

BALA BACKPACKERS

WALES

For outdoor adventures within the Snowdonia National Park, Bala Backpackers offers good value hostel-style self-catering accommodation. Accommodation includes; 30+comfy SINGLE BEDS, 3 private TWIN ROOMS and 3 new EN SUITES, The 19th century character buildings are located in a quiet, sunny, chapel square, in the bustling market town of Bala, Mid North Wales. It is clean, safe and nice for the price with a careful, old, arty, homely atmosphere, with hints of luxury, now called "Posh-Packing!". 4-Star showers, bedrooms, wet-room, dining facilities & guest kitchen. Catering is available. Bala boasts a five-mile-long lake, a white-water river for raft rides, and nestles beneath three 900 metre peaks. The lakeside, river and leisure pursuits are 5 mins' walk away. Plan your activities or just soak up the atmosphere by day or evening in town.

DETAILS

- **Open** - All year by arrangement, 8.30-20.30. Front door lock 00.30 – 6.00am
- **Number of beds** - 45: 2x3, 3x4, 3x5 + 3 twin rooms + 3 en suites
- **Booking** - On-line or by phone or email.
- **Price per night** - 1 night £21, 2 nights £39, 3 nights £49, weekly £89. Twin room: £49 or en suites from £59 . Double holiday-let: £220/4 nights. Hostel sheet-bag hire £3/week or bring sheets & pillowcase.
- **Public Transport** - Trains: Wrexham (30 miles) or Barmouth (30miles). Bus no 94 every 2 hours daily from Wrexham and Barmouth.
- **Directions** - GR 926 358. Bala is on A494. Turn in the middle of Bala High Street, opposite the White Lion Royal Hotel, down Tegid Street to see HOSTEL Sign. Unload outside Hostel, but park round corner, in FREE overnight pay & display.

CONTACT: Stella Welch
Tel: 01678 521700
info@Bala-Backpackers.co.uk www.Bala-Backpackers.co.uk
32 Tegid Street, Bala, LL23 7EL

NANTYR
OUTDOOR EDUCATION CENTRE WALES

Nantyr OEC has excellent bunk house facilities with 22 beds, toilets and showers, fully equipped self-catering kitchen and dining area, activity room/lounge including TV/DVD, drying room & a small camping area with fire pit and separate toilets and showers. The centre is situated above the beautiful Ceiriog valley, 3 miles from Glyn Ceiriog and 6 miles from Llangollen and the River Dee. Located at the foot of the Berwyn Mountains, it is ideally positioned to utilise the local area's many wonderful outdoor locations and resources. Nantyr is committed to providing high quality, challenging outdoor educational opportunities for all, in a safe and enjoyable learning environment. The centre is licensed to provide a wide variety of outdoor activities including: hill walking and rock climbing, kayaking, canoeing, gorge scrambling, improvised rafting, bushcraft and mountain biking (all activities are at an extra cost).

DETAILS

- **Open** - All Year. All Day
- **Number of beds** - 22 - 1x10, 1x8, 2x2
- **Booking** - Booking essential by email or phone
- **Price per night** - £160 sole use of centre. Small groups please contact for rates.
- **Public Transport** - Public transport to Glyn Ceiriog (3.5 miles) but not to Nantyr
- **Directions** - Sat-Nav directions are inaccurate please use the following: B4500 from Chirk to Glyn Ceiriog; at Glyn Ceriog roundabout, go straight on, signposted Llanarmon DC. After approx 0.2 miles take the right hand fork in the road signposted Nantyr. After 3 miles, the road begins to slope down hill. Nantyr OEC is at the bottom of the hill, on the right hand side, opposite a phone box and a Chapel.

CONTACT: Paul Lawrence-Wyatt
Tel: 01691 712833
nantyr@wrexham.gov.uk www.nantyr.co.uk
Nantyr Outdoor Education Centre, Nantyr,nr Glyn Ceiriog,Wrexham LL207DL

LLANGOLLEN HOSTEL

WALES

Llangollen Hostel offers clean and comfortable twin and double rooms, en suite family rooms, private four-bed and six-bed en suite rooms, and a great value six-bed dorm. There is a fully-fitted kitchen and all prices include a complimentary breakfast. You can enjoy your meals in the dining room, then relax in the spacious lounge by the log fire. We have a book exchange, free WiFi, plenty of games, laundry facilities, a drying room, and bicycle/canoe storage. Perfect location for walking, climbing, canoeing and mountain biking in the Vale of Llangollen. Families will love visiting the steam railway, horse drawn canal boats and Pontcysyllte Aqueduct - a World Heritage Site. The town offers a great choice of restaurants/pubs and is home to a fringe music and arts festival and the International Eisteddfod. Llandegla, Chester, Wrexham and Offa's Dyke Path are all nearby. You are assured of a happy and comfortable stay, freedom to come and go as you please, and above all, a warm welcome.

DETAILS

- **Open** - All year, all day.
- **Number of beds** - 32.
- **Booking** - Internet, email or phone.
- **Price per night** - From £18pp dorm. £20pp for a private 3,4,5 or 6 bed room. £45 Twin/Double or £50 en suite. Family of 4 £60, £10 per extra child. Inc light breakfast.
- **Public Transport** - Daily National Express from London. Trains Ruabon (5 miles). Buses all day.
- **Directions** - From the A5 heading west, the hostel is located 50 yards past the main set of traffic lights on the right. Parking is at the rear of the hostel on Market Street – at the main traffic lights, turn right then first left.

CONTACT: Arlo Dennis
Tel: 01978 861773, Mob: 07783 401894, Fax: 01978861773
info@llangollenhostel.co.uk   www.llangollenhostel.co.uk
Berwyn Street, Llangollen, LL20 8NB

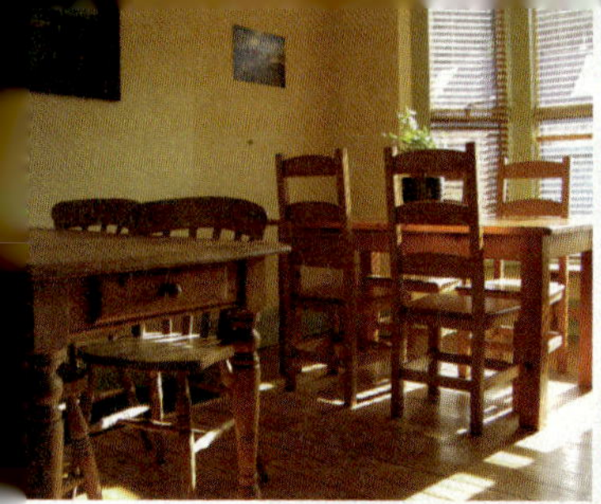

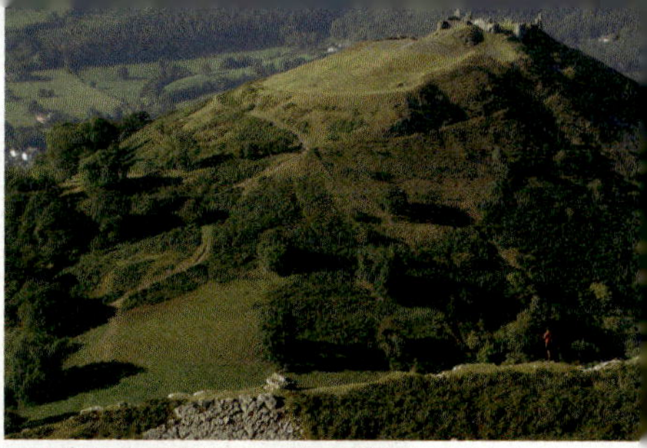

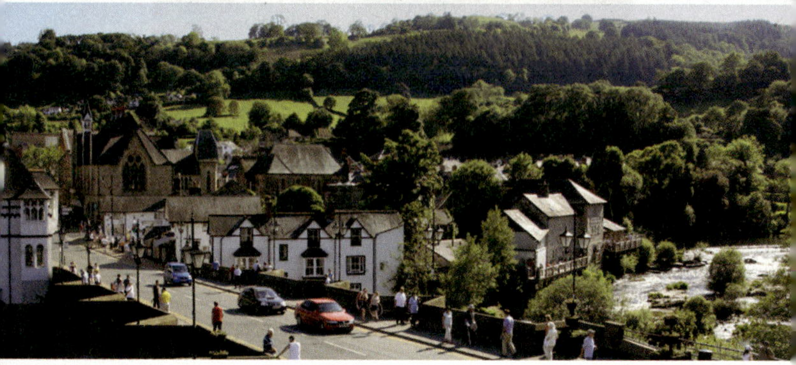

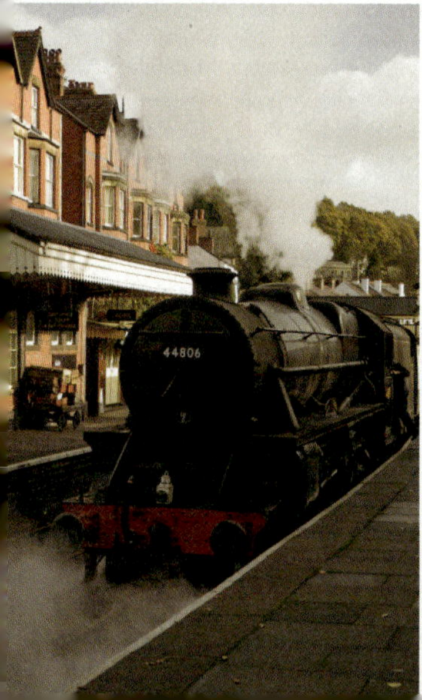
44806

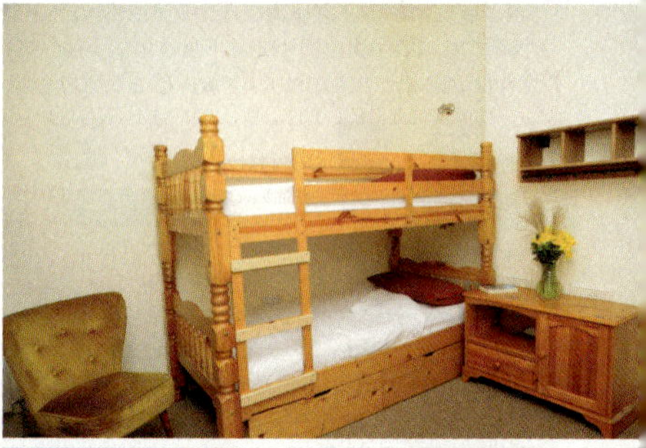

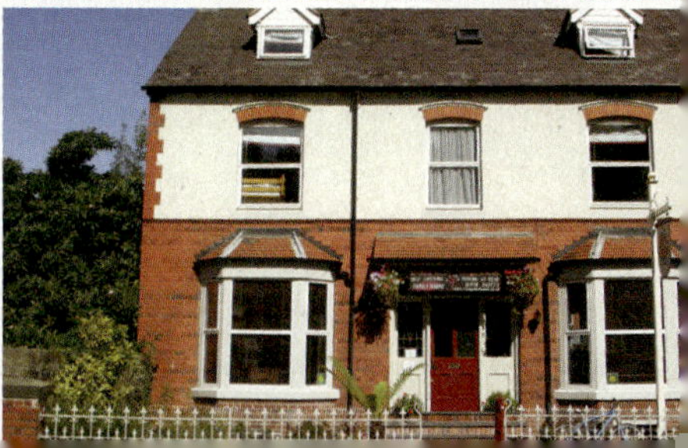

TYDDYN BYCHAN

WALES

Tyddyn Bychan is an 18th century traditional Welsh farmhouse and barns set in private grounds and surrounded on all sides by farmland. Situated in an excellent central location, for mountain biking, road cycling, canoeing, walking, climbing, fishing and numerous watersports including whitewater rafting.

The main bunkhouse sleeps 19 in two en suite rooms. All the bunks are handmade and of a very high standard. The smaller bunkhouse sleeps 9 in two en suite rooms and has its own kitchen, conservatory and lounge.

All bedding is included. Delicious homemade food is available if booked in advance. The bunkhouses are ideal for self-catering with very well equipped kitchen/dining rooms. There is a large parking area well away from the road.

DETAILS

- **Open** - All year, all day.
- **Number of beds** - 28: 1x10; 1x9; 1x6; 1x3
- **Booking** - Booking is essential
- **Price per night** - £14 pp including bedding.
- **Public Transport** - Nearest train station is at Betws-y-Coed. Nearest National Express service at Llandudno. Phone 01492 575412 for details.
- **Directions** - GR 931 504. Turn off A5 at Cerrigydrudion. Take B4501 out of village for Llyn Brenig, take the turning on left for Cefn Brith. After about 2 miles you will see a phone box on left, chapel on right and the road widens for a layby. The gate for Tyddyn is on the left directly opposite junction on the right.

CONTACT: Lynda
Tel: 01490 420680 Mob: 07523 995741
lynda@tyddynbychan.co.uk www.tyddynbychan.co.uk
Cefn Brith, Cerrigydrudion, Conwy, LL21 9TS

HENDRE ISAF
BASECAMP

359

WALES

This converted Grade II listed stone farm building offers the perfect base for enjoying the Snowdonia National Park. In a rural setting on the 8,000 hectares Ysbyty Estate it has easy access to the A5 and is only six miles from Betws-y-Coed. The 400 year old building offers group accommodation with lots of character, substantial dining and social space and a large private car park. The large enclosed garden at the rear of the bunkhouse has picnic benches and a barbecue area. There is excellent access to outdoor activities in the surrounding area including walks from the door of the bunkhouse so you can forget your car for a few days. Local attractions include the Tree Top Adventure Course at Betws-y-Coed, Zip World at Penrhyn Quarry, Bethesda, Zip World and Bounce Below at Llechwedd Slate Caverns, Blaenau Ffestiniog, the Plas y Brenin National Mountain Centre at Capel Curig, shops, leisure centre, swimming pool at Llanrwst and the seaside resort of Llandudno. No pets.

DETAILS

- **Open** - All year, 24 hours
- **Number of beds** - 18: 2 x dormitories + 1x1 single bedroom.
- **Booking** - Early booking recommended (March to October is very busy).
- **Price per night** - Short breaks: 2 nights from £495. 7 nights from £1,295
- **Public Transport** - Trains at Betws-y-Coed (6 miles), Llandudno Junction (20 miles) and Llanrwst (10 miles); National Express bus station at Llandudno. Some local buses to Betws-y-Coed, but we advise bringing your own transport.
- **Directions** - Situated 6 miles SE of Betws-y-Coed near the junction of the A5 and the B4407 (signposted Ysbyty Ifan and Ffestiniog). GR855511 (OS sheet 116).

CONTACT: National Trust Cottages Group Accommodation Team
Tel: 0844 3351287, Fax: 01690 713301
group.accom@nationaltrust.org.uk www.nationaltrustcottages.co.uk/group-accommodation
Hendre Isaf Bunkhouse, Pentrefoelas Road, Betws-y-Coed, LL24 0HP

LLEDR HOUSE

WALES

Lledr House is nestled in the heart of Snowdonia National Park. A former YHA, this newly refurbished hostel is delightfully situated in its own woodlands in the beautiful Lledr Valley just outside the picturesque village of Dolwyddelan. Guests come back year after year, having delighted in the huge improvements, including luxury memory foam mattresses, modern bathrooms, well equipped kitchen, free WiFi and an extended car park also suitable for motorbikes. Whether you are a lone traveller, large family, DofE, college or a group of friends, Lledr House offers clean, cheap, comfortable accommodation. All bedding is provided in private single, twin and family rooms plus one nine-bed dorm. There is also a luxury self-contained cedar log cabin, sleeping 5, in the grounds. Enjoy the riverside garden, patio and BBQ area. Woodland walks and cycle trails surround the hostel. Views of Moel Siabod and surrounded by forest. Pub and Spar shop within walking distance. Betws-y-Coed, stunning Llyn Elsi and Tree Tops High Rope course just 4 miles away.

DETAILS

- **Open** - All year (except Christmas week), check in from 5pm till 10.30pm.
- **Number of beds** - 31: 1x9, 2x4,1x6, 3x2, 2x1.
- **Booking** - Book by phone/email with credit card. First night's deposit for groups.
- **Price per night** - £18pp. Sole use £450, Bank Holidays & New Year extra.
- **Public Transport** - Pont-y-Pant station on the Conwy Valley Line is ¾ mile away.
- **Directions** - On the A5 from Llangollen to Bangor turn left just before Betws-y-Coed onto the A470 (signed Dolgellau). The hostel is 4 miles on right side of road. Walking from Pont-y-Pant station, turn left and left again after stone road bridge.

CONTACT: Brian or Melanie Quilter
Tel: 01690 750202 Mobile: 07915 397705 or 07915 397660
Lledrhouse@aol.com   www.ukyh.com
Pont-y-Pant, Dolwyddelan, North Wales, LL25 0DQ

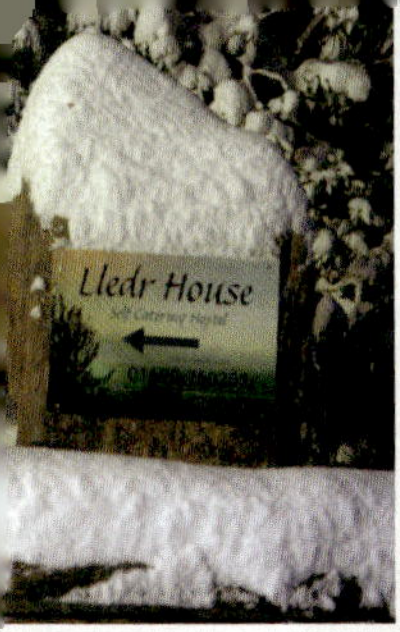
Lledr House

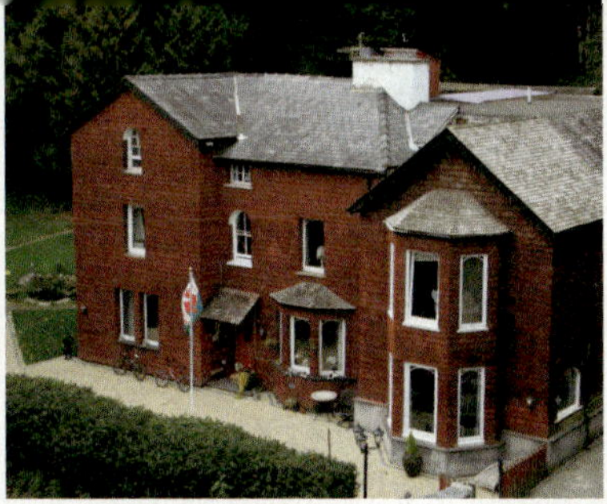

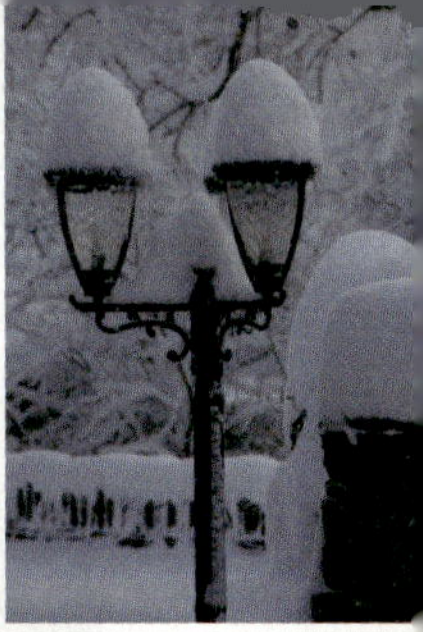

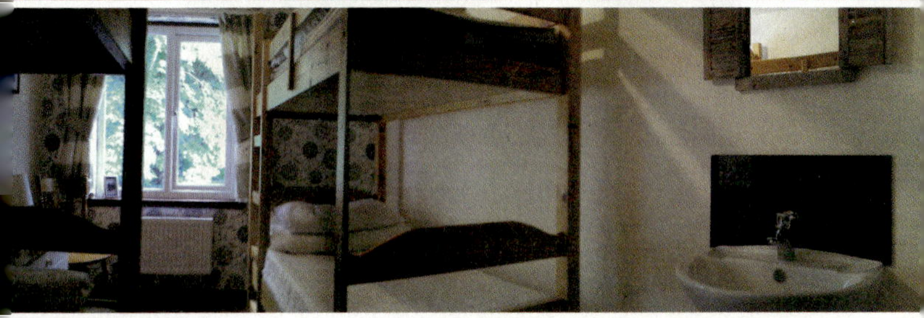

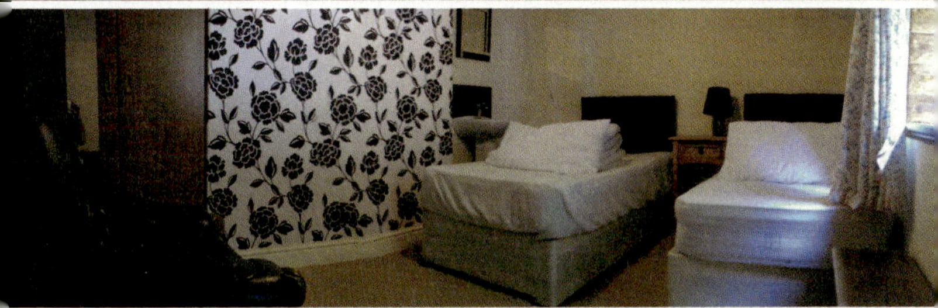

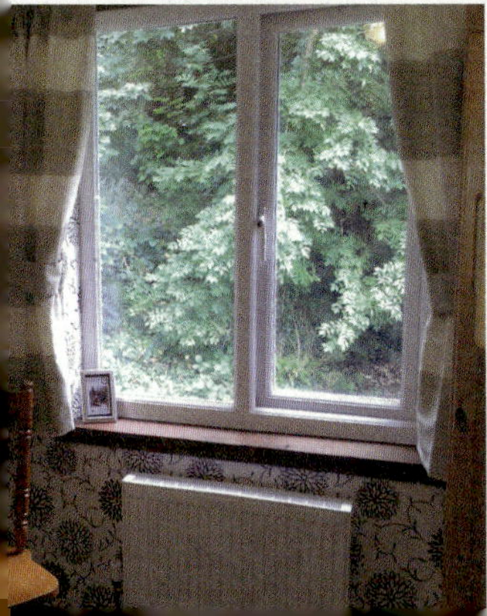

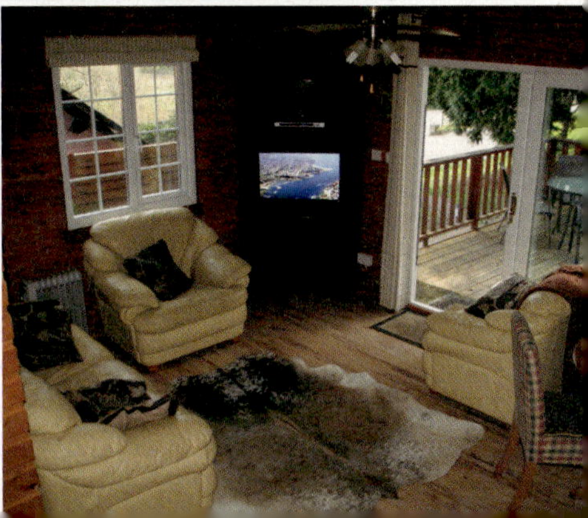

PLAS CURIG HOSTEL

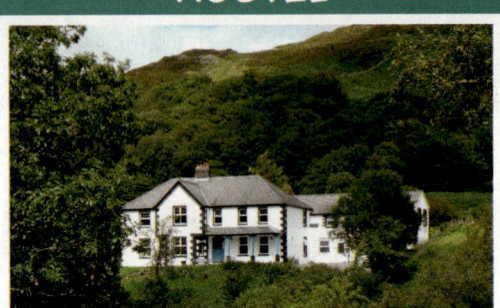

WALES

This five star hostel has been stylishly refurbished since its previous existence as Capel Curig YHA and provides luxurious comfort in stunning surroundings. With views of Snowdon, the hostel is in the village of Capel Curig, the heart of Snowdonia National Park, and only 10 mins' drive from the Snowdon Horseshoe path. Plas Curig is the only five star hostel in Wales and welcomes individuals, couples, families and groups. The dorm rooms sleep from 4 to 8 people in bunks and family rooms, doubles and twins are also available. Each bunk has a comfy mattress, curtains for privacy, light, socket and is ready made with hypo-allergenic bedding. There is well equipped self-catering kitchen and dining facilities to sit 40 people. The TV room, lobby, lounge and library have free WiFi and there are private shower rooms with WC and basins. There is a drying room, outside storage for bikes/canoes and car parking. Well behaved dogs welcome in private rooms. Pubs and cafés close by. Snowdonia has it all!.

DETAILS

- **Open** - All year, 5-10pm for check-ins.
- **Number of beds** - 59: 1x8, 2x6, 4x4, 1x 4/5, 2x 3/4, 2x 2/3, 1xDouble, 1xTwin
- **Booking** - Book online with card.
- **Price per night** - Dorms from £22.50. Family rooms from £90 per room. Doubles & twins from £50 per room. Dogs £5. Exclusive hire of hostel from £1000 per night.
- **Public Transport** - Trains at Betws-y-Coed (5 miles). Buses: Snowdon Sherpa 97A Portmadog to Betws-y-coed, S2 Pen-y-Pass to Betws-y-Coed and S6 from Bethesda (with connections to Bangor) all run past the hostel.
- **Directions** - On the A5 in the centre of Capel Curig village.

CONTACT:
Tel: 01690 720 225, Fax: 441690720225
info@snowdoniahostel.co.uk www.snowdoniahostel.co.uk
Plas Curig, Capel Curig, Betws-y-Coed, North Wales, LL24 0EL

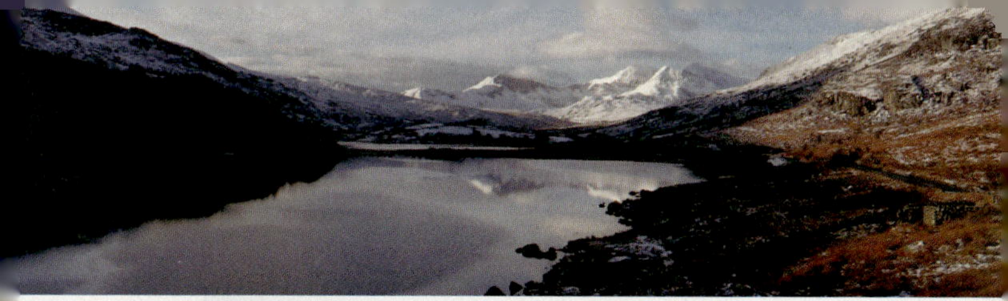

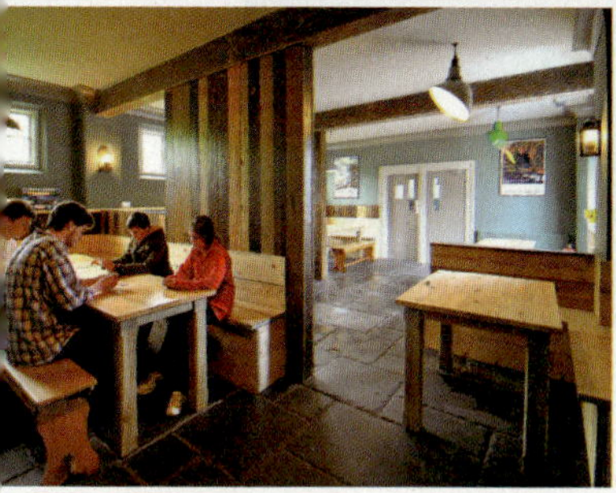

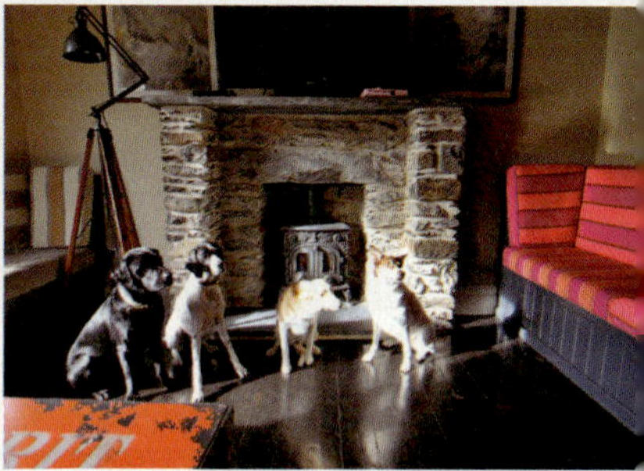

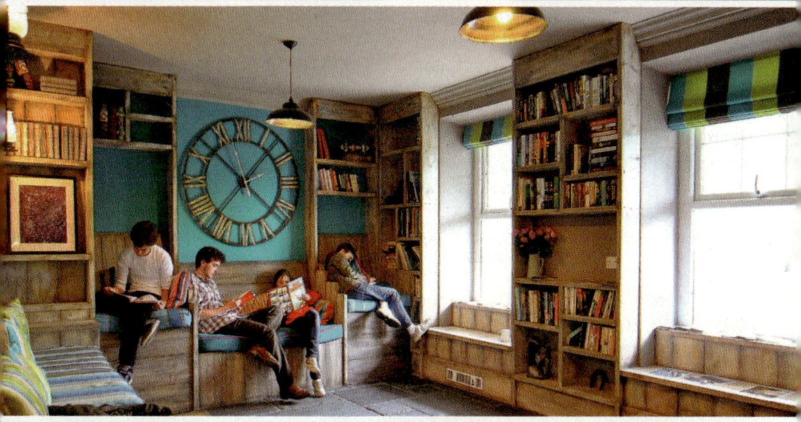

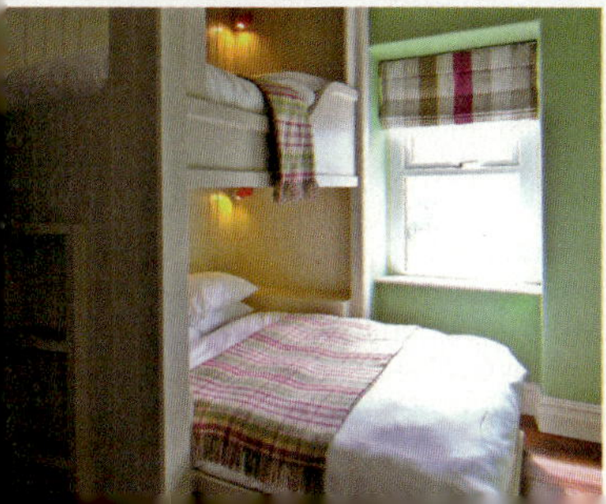

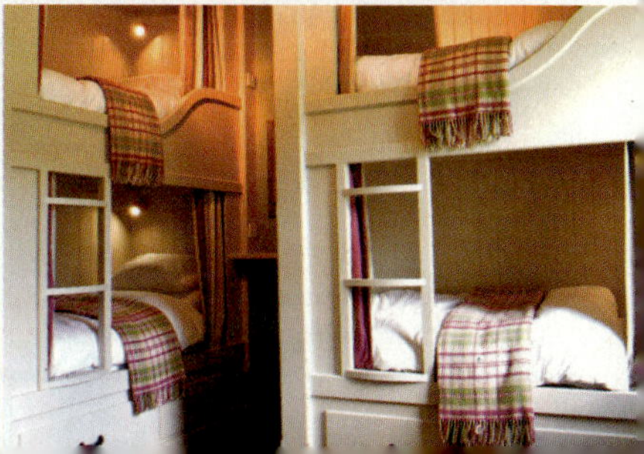

SNOWDON HOUSE BUNKHOUSE

WALES

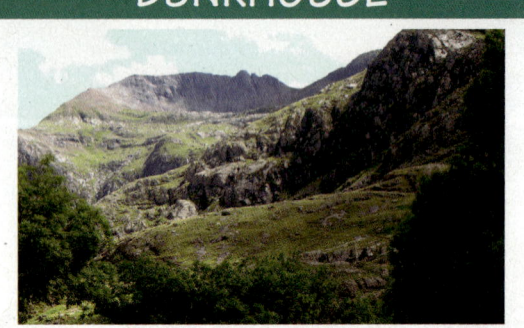

Snowdon Bunkhouse is the longest established bunkhouse in the National Park, dating from 1959 and is the closest to Snowdon. Situated amidst magnificent scenery, a short walk from historic Nant Peris and the Vaynol Arms Public House, it is close to famous routes for walkers, mountain bikers and climbers of all abilities. You can do Tryfan, Adam and Eve, Brisley Ridge, the Cantilever Stone and Castle of the Winds and arrive just 200m from the Bunkhouse on the public footpath. The Miners Track, the Snowdon Horseshoe, the Llanberis Path and route of the Fifteen Peaks are only minutes away. Llechog Buttress, directly opposite the bunkhouse, is great for scrambling and you can boulder at the Gromlech up to E8. Nearby Vivian Quarry has a diving centre or canoe on local rivers. Snowdon Bunkhouse sleeps 14 people on two alpine sleeping platforms. Each one has 3 kingsize mattresses and guests bring their own sleeping bags. There is a separate kitchen/dining area & outdoor BBQ area. A recent upgrade included central heating, double-glazing and new shower block. Campsite also available. Plenty of parking. No stag parties.

DETAILS

- **Open** - All year, all day
- **Number of beds** - 14: 1x14 two alpine sleeping platforms
- **Booking** - Book by phone or email.
- **Price per night** - £12pp. Sole use for two night weekend £295, three night weekend £350. Full bunkhouse mid-week for only £60.
- **Public Transport** - Snowdon Sherpa bus stops right outside.
- **Directions** - On the A4086 from Caernarfon, 1 mile after Nant Peris.

CONTACT: Jim & Anne Cumberton
Tel: 01286 650152
info@snowdonhouse.co.uk www.snowdonhouse.co.uk/home.html
Snowdon House, Nant Peris, Caernarfon, Gwynedd LL55 4UL

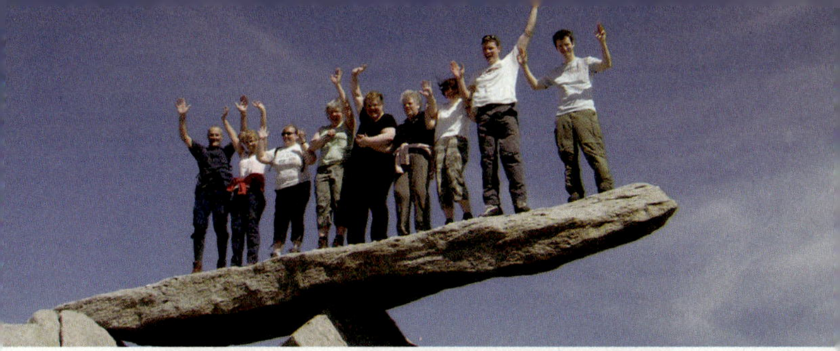
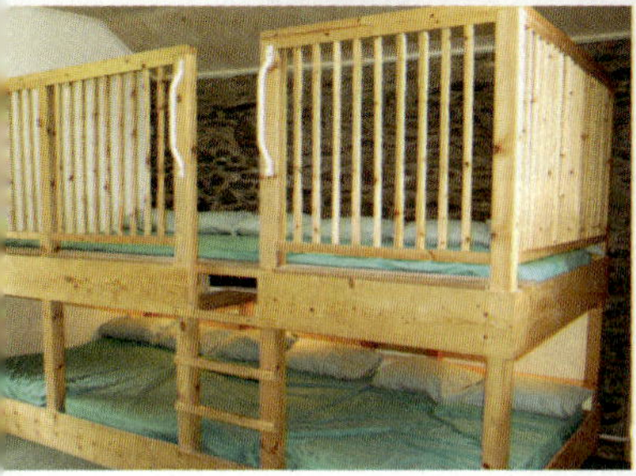
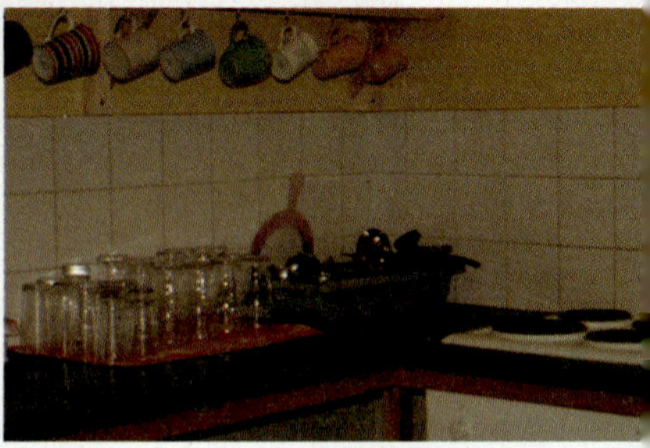
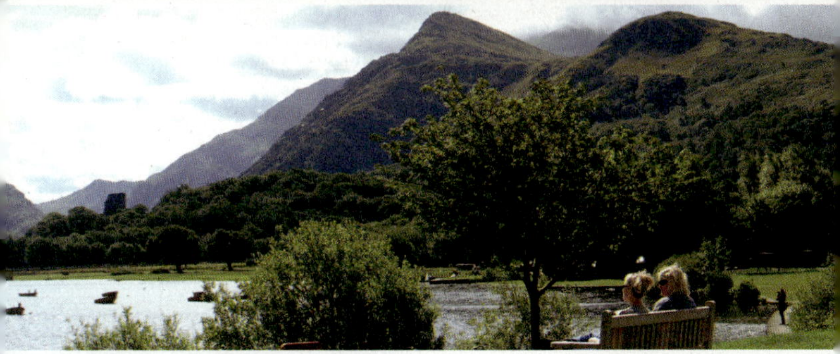
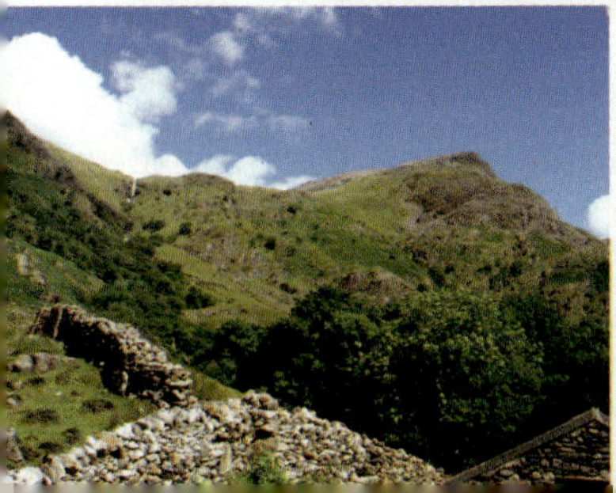
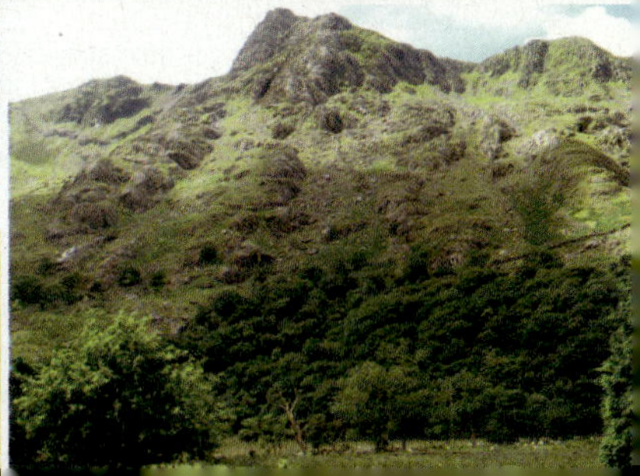

CABAN CYSGU
GERLAN BUNKHOUSE

WALES

Caban Cysgu offers comfortable, purpose-built accommodation at the foot of the Carneddau in the Welsh-speaking village of Gerlan. A warm welcome is guaranteed at this community run bunkhouse. An ideal location for walking in Snowdonia, providing an great base for the 'Fourteen 3000ft Peaks' long-distance challenge. For the adrenalin junky, it's just a 5 minute drive to Zip World; the longest and fastest zip line in Europe "The Nearest Thing to Flying"!! Brilliantly located for mountain biking with plenty of off road trails nearby. And for road cyclists the bunkhouse is ideal for exploring Snowdonia, whilst for leisurely rides the hostel is within a mile of Sustrans route 'Lôn Las Ogwen'.

Rock-climbing at Idwal is close at hand, as well as Ysgolion Duon for the dedicated winter climbers. The nearby Afon Ogwen provides a popular venue for canoeists. For more leisurely pursuits, try visiting Coed Meurig, Penrhyn Castle or the Greenwood Centre. Shops, pubs and cafés in Bethesda are within walking distance.

DETAILS

- **Open** - All year, all day
- **Number of beds** - 16 : 1x5, 1x2, 1x1, 1x8
- **Booking** - Not essential, but recommended (with 20% non-returnable deposit).
- **Price per night** - From £13 - £15.50
- **Public Transport** - Bangor train station is 6 miles. Catch a bus from Bangor bus station to Gerlan (66), or Bethesda (fare £1.40). Taxi from Bangor approx. £10.
- **Directions** - GR 632665. A5 southbound, turn left in Bethesda centre just before Spar. Bear right, up hill over 2 cross-roads. Hostel is 300m at the old school on left.

CONTACT: Dewi Emyln, Manager
Tel: 01248 605573 Mob: 07784760838
dewi@cabancysgu-gerlan.co.uk www.cabancysgu-gerlan.co.uk
Ffordd Gerlan, Gerlan, Bethesda, Bangor, LL5 3TL

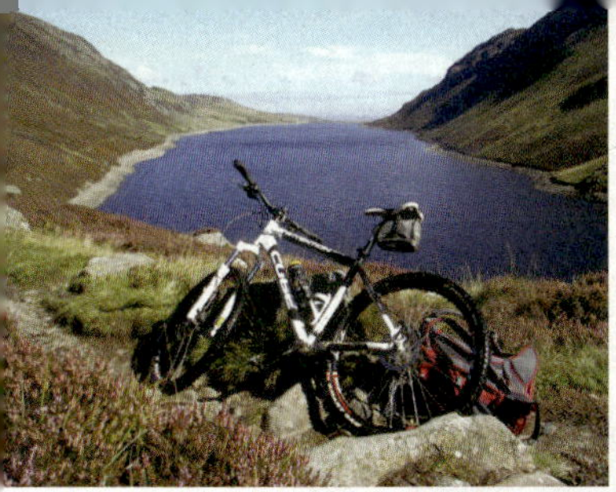
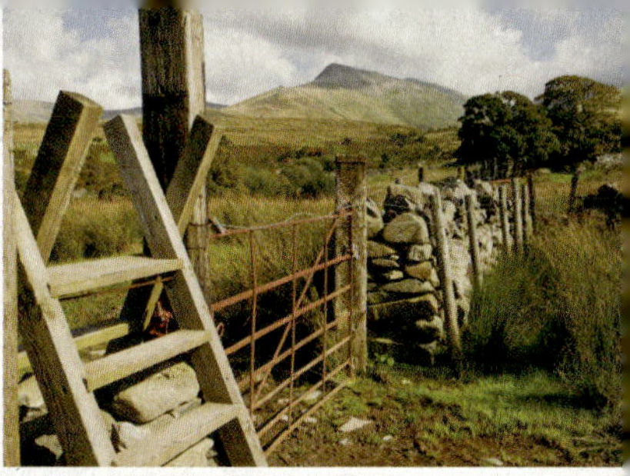
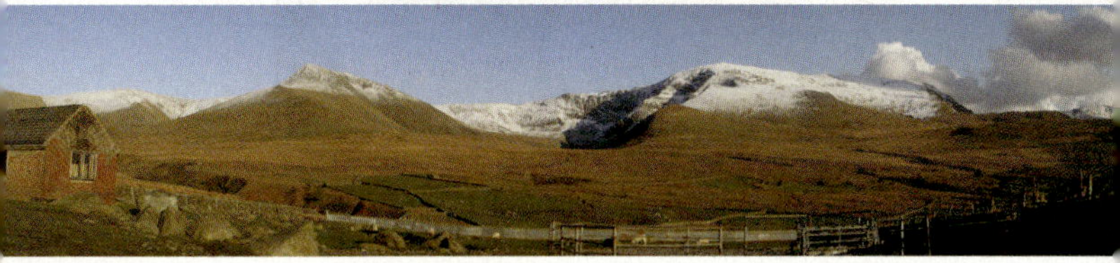
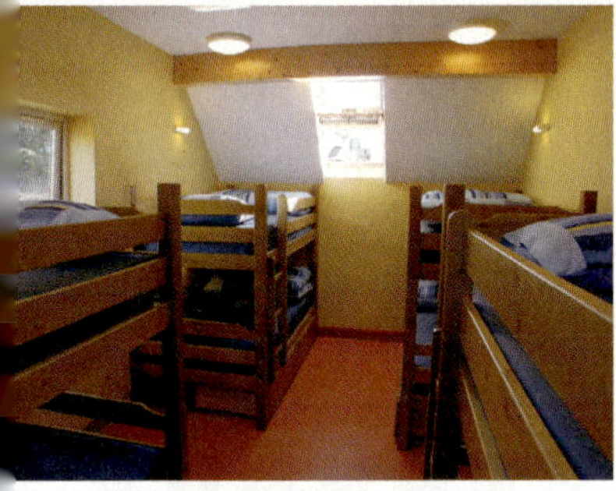
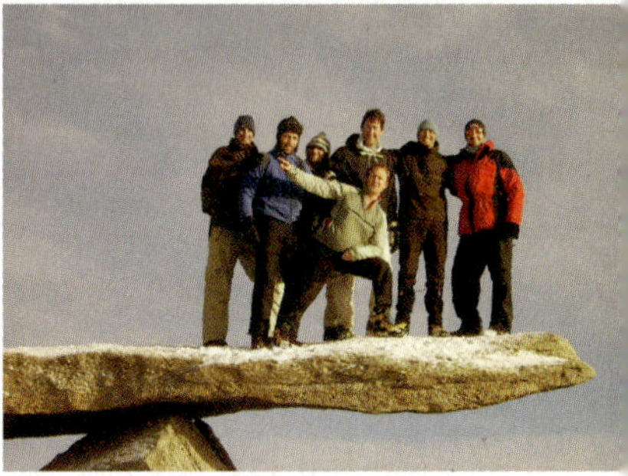
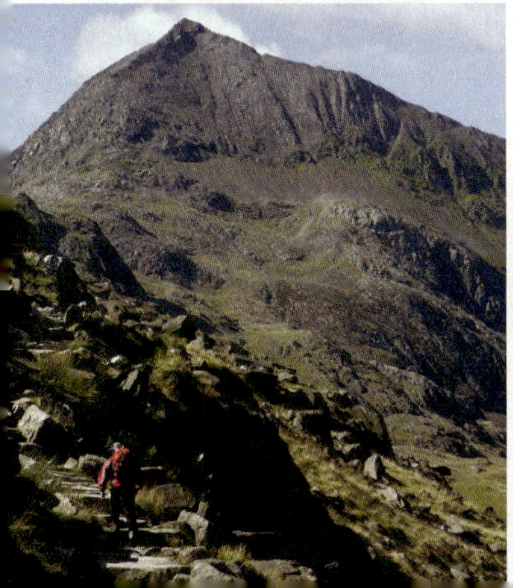
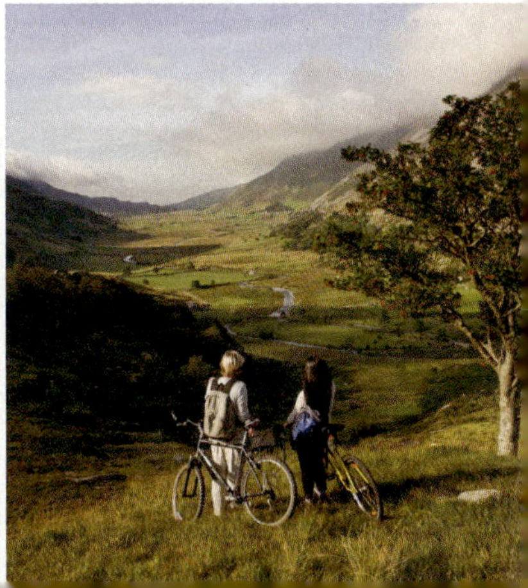

CONWY VALLEY BACKPACKERS BARN

WALES

Conwy Valley Backpackers is situated on a peaceful working farm with organic status in the heart of the beautiful Conwy Valley, with excellent access to Snowdonia. Centrally heated with fully equipped self-catering kitchen, log fires, hot showers and a fire alarm system. There are three separate dorms sleeping 4, 6 and 10, two of which have their own toilet facility. Secure bike/canoe storage, grazing for horses and tourist information are available.

Beside the barn is a small stream and guests may picnic and BBQ on the river bank. An ideal space for restoration, relaxation and retreat. Bring a sleeping bag or hire bed linen (£3). Continental breakfast (£3.50), packed lunch (£5) and buffet suppers (£10) are available by arrangement. Local activities range from fishing and hiking to white water rafting and mountain biking and there are some great pubs and eating places within walking distance.

Groups are welcome. No dogs.

DETAILS

- **Open** - All year, all day
- **Number of beds** - 20: 1 x 4; 1 x 6; 1 x 10.
- **Booking** - Not essential but recommended
- **Price per night** - From £20pp. Sole use from £250. £3pp bed linen hire.
- **Public Transport** - Train stations and coaches at Llandudno Junction and Conwy. Local bus 19 or 19a runs every 20 minutes from Conwy and Llandudno Junction, ask driver to drop you at Pyllau Gloewon farm gate.
- **Directions** - GR 769 697. Six miles south of Conwy on the B5106, look for Backpackers sign just before entering Tal-y-Bont.

CONTACT: Claudia or Helen
Tel: 01492 660504
claudia.bryan@btconnect.com   www.conwyvalleybarn.com
Pyllau Gloewon Farm, Tal-y-Bont, Conwy, Gwynedd, LL32 8YX

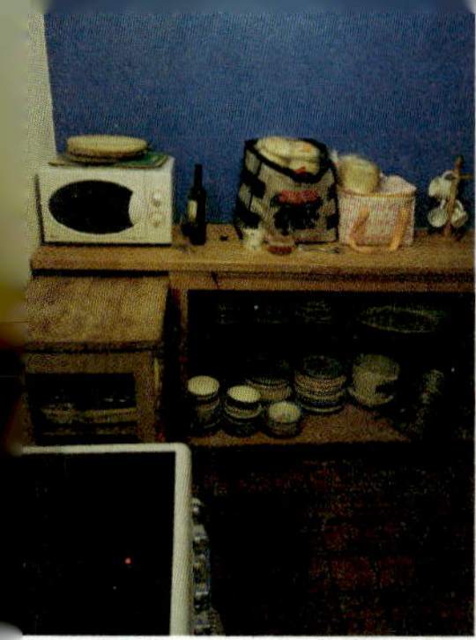

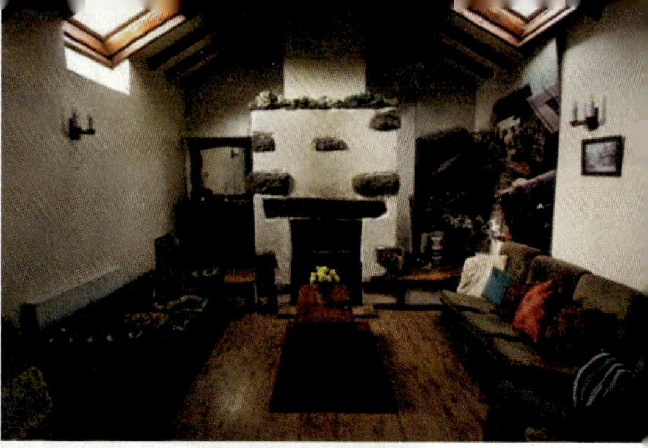

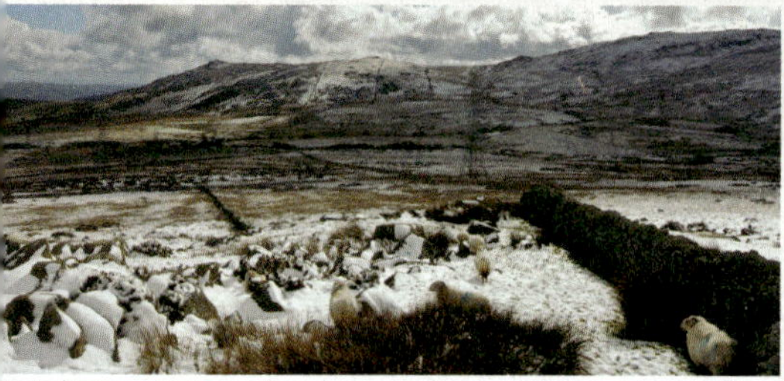

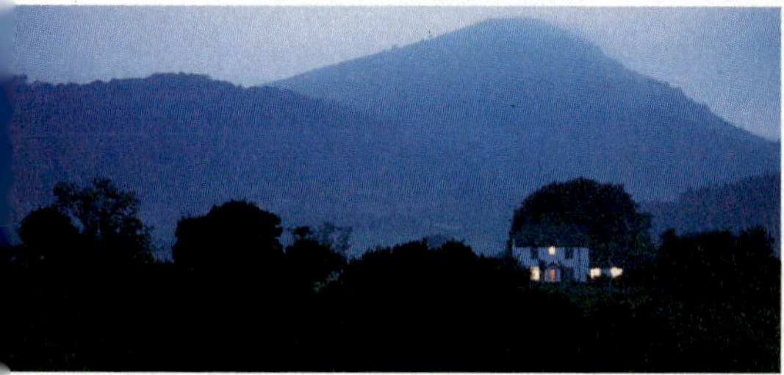

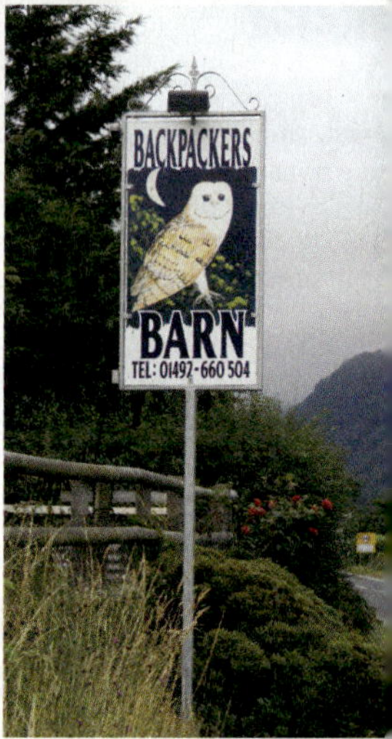
BACKPACKERS
BARN
TEL: 01492-660 504

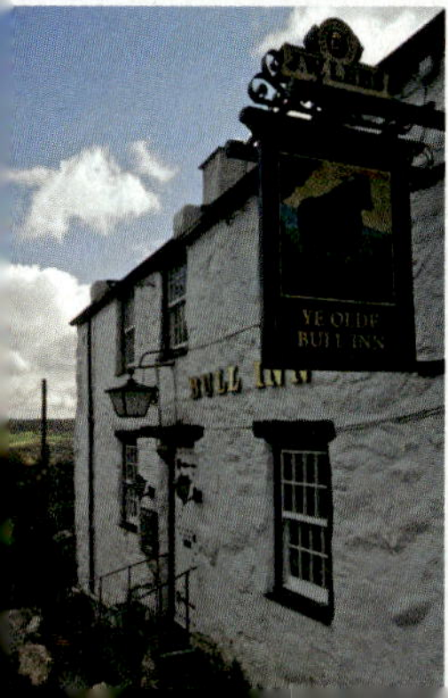
YE OLDE
BULL INN
BULL INN

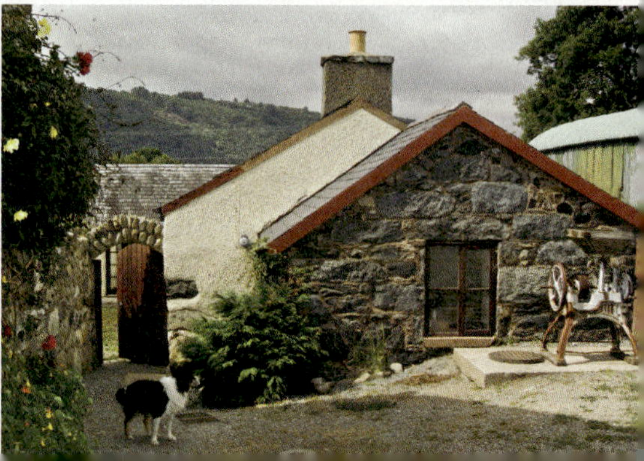

LLANDUDNO HOSTEL

WALES

James and Melissa would like to invite you to their charming Victorian 4 star boutique hostel. We are a friendly hostel where individuals, families and groups (including schools) are welcome all year. Some of the guests' comments: "friendliest hostel we've ever stayed in", "Wow isn't it clean", "these bathrooms are fabulous, as good as any hotel". Come and try us, we love to meet new people and look forward to getting to know you.

Set in the heart of the Victorian seaside resort town of Llandudno, an ideal place to shop or explore the many and varied local attractions. Excellent blue flag beaches, dry slope skiing, toboggan run, ten pin bowling, bronze age copper mine, traditional pier and many museums, fishing trips, etc. Llandudno is within easy travelling distance of Snowdon, Bodnant Gardens and local castles. We are able to book local attractions for groups and secure some discounts.

DETAILS

- **Open** - All year. (telephone in winter prior to arrival). All day.
- **Number of beds** - 46: 2x8, 2x6, 4x2, 1x4, 1 x family.
- **Booking** - Essential April to July.
- **Price per night** - From £18 per person, £48 per private twin room, £54 per private twin en suite. Group and family rates on request. Special offers autumn /winter.
- **Public Transport** - Trains at Llandudno. Turn right as you exit station, cross road, turn left down Vaughan Street (towards the beach), left into Charlton Street.
- **Directions** - From the A55 take A470 and follow signs to Llandudno town centre, straight through all roundabouts, after Asda turn 3rd left into Vaughan Street (signed train station), then 1st right into Charlton Street. Hostel is No 14.

CONTACT: James
Tel: 01492 877430, Fax: 01492 863100
info@llandudnohostel.co.uk www.llandudnohostel.co.uk
14 Charlton Street, Llandudno, LL30 2AA

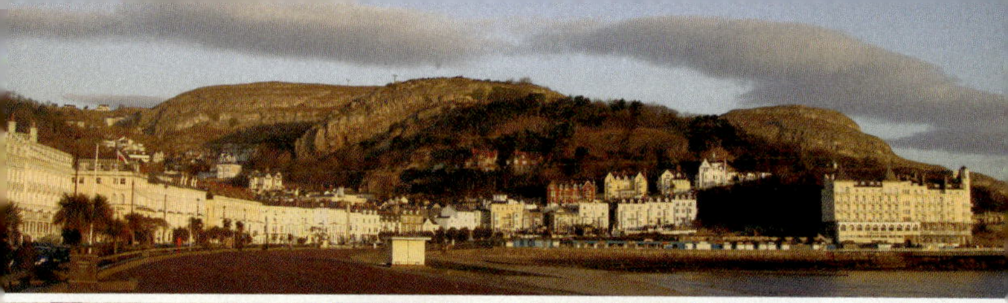
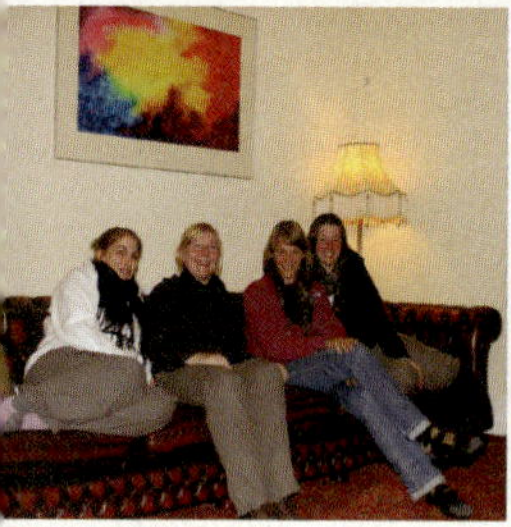
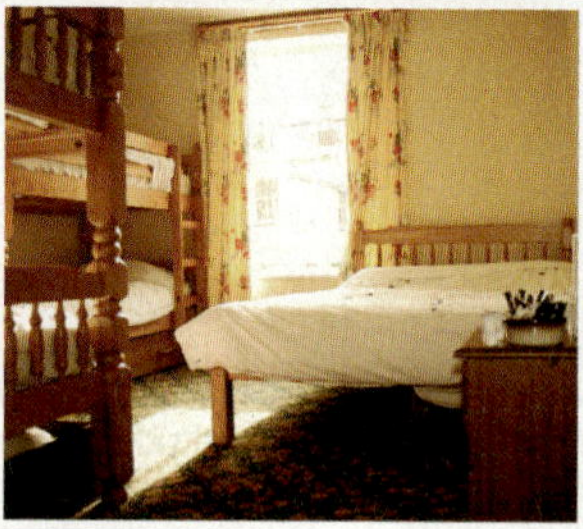
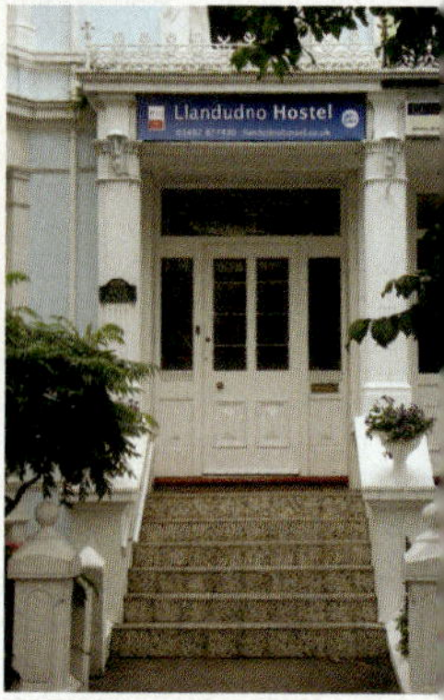
Llandudno Hostel
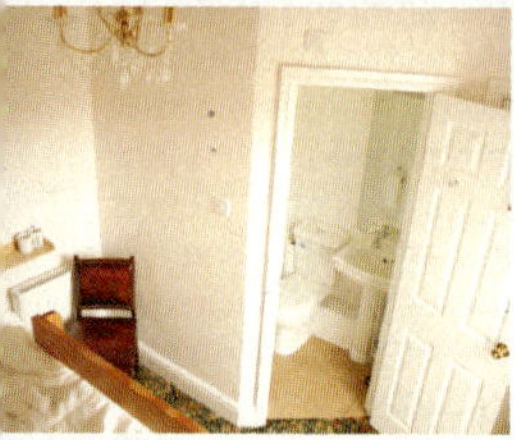
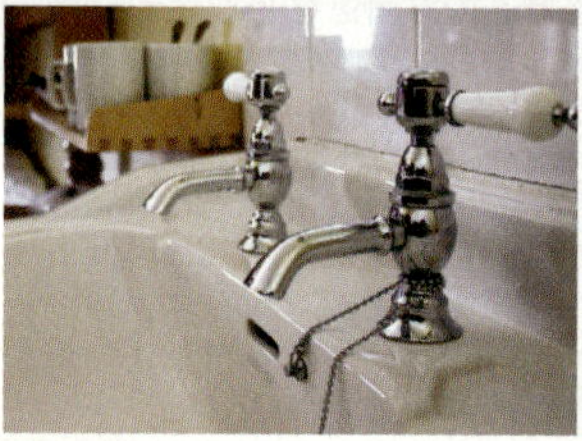
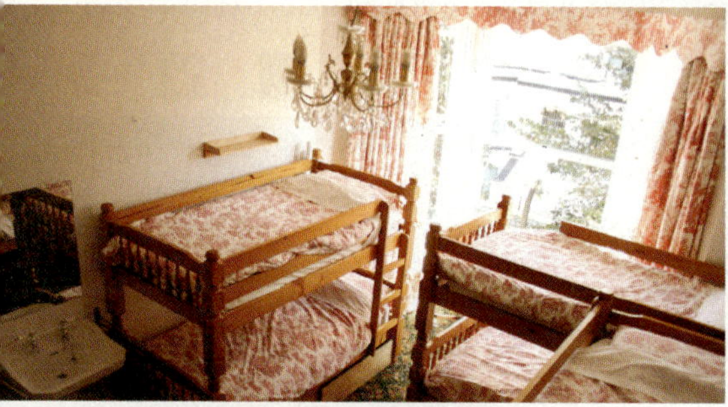
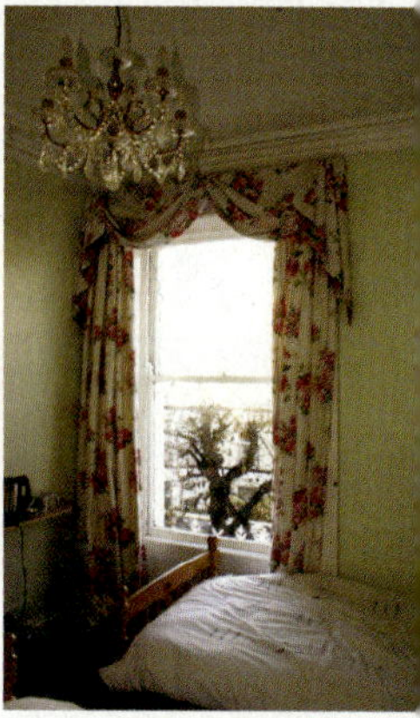
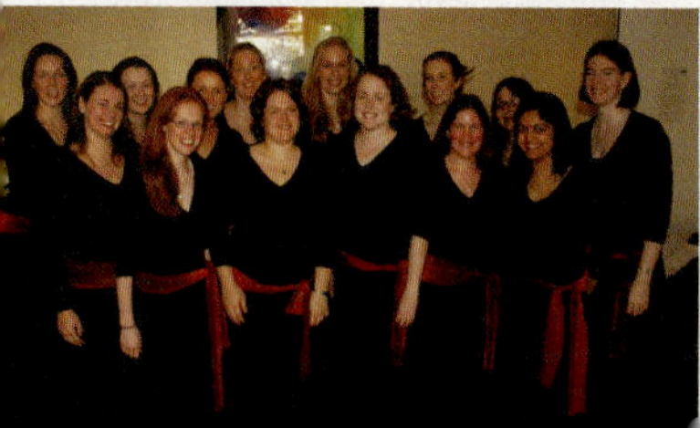
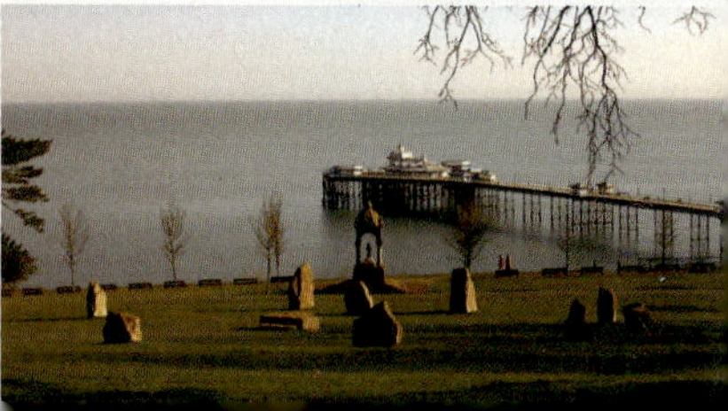

PLATT'S FARM BUNKHOUSE

WALES

Platt's Farm Campsite and Bunkhouse is situated within a range of Victorian farm buildings dating back to 1858, in the charming village of Llanfairfechan. Ideally situated close to the A55, the Bunkhouse sits at the start/end of the 14 Welsh 3000 peaks walks in the Snowdonia National Park, within a 10 minute walk to the Wales coastal path and on the No.5 cycle route. There is a large bedroom to sleep 10 people in bunk beds. The kitchen is equipped with a four ring cooker, microwave, kettle, fridge/freezer, toaster, TV, table to seat 10 and electric wood burner. Heating is by electric storage heaters and all heating and lighting is included in the price. Pans, crockery, cutlery, sheets and pillowcases are provided. Please bring your own sleeping bags/duvets. Ample off road parking and adjacent covered area for BBQs. 11 camping pitches with covered picnic areas also available. Shops, pubs and cafés are within 5 minutes' walk.

DETAILS

- **Open** - All Year, check out before 11am, check in after 2pm
- **Number of beds** - 10
- **Booking** - Deposit required. Non refundable balance is payable 2 weeks before arrival. Most major credit or debit cards and PayPal accepted.
- **Price per night** - £12.50 per person per night. Exclusive use £120 per night.
- **Public Transport** - By train to Llanfairfechan station. Bus from Llandudno or Bangor stops right by the entrance. National cycle route No 5 passes the entrance
- **Directions** - A55 westbound Exit 15, remain on this road. The entrance to Platt's Farm is a sharp turn on the right just after the traffic lights and bus stop. A55 eastbound Exit 14 follow the road over the A55 then turn left on to Aber Road.

CONTACT: Sam Davies
Tel: 0(44)1248680105
sam@plattsfarm.com www.plattsfarm.com
Platts Farm Bunkhouse, Aber Road, Llanfairfechan, Conwy, LL33 0HL

PENTRE BACH
BUNKHOUSE

373

WALES

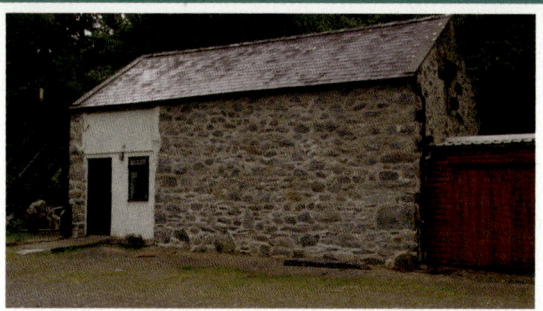

Pentre Bach Bunkhouse provides dog friendly alpine style accommodation, outdoor activities and a campsite. The Bunkhouse is heated with electric radiators and has two floors. The ground floor has tables with benches and a cooking area with gas burners, microwaves, fridge and freezer. Upstairs are alpine sleeping platforms with mattresses for 16. Drying room and toilets with washing facilities and showers, shared with the campsite, are just across the yard. Based between Waunfawr and Betws Garmon, Pentre Bach is surrounded by the superb scenery of Moel Eilio and Mynydd Mawr and has views towards Mount Snowdon. There are great walks from the bunkhouse or take a short car journey to the Nantlle ridge and the main footpaths up Snowdon. Bach Ventures provides guided walks, kayaking, climbing, gorge-scrambling and coasteering. Large or small groups and individuals all welcome. Local pub is CAMRA Pub of the year in the area. Great beer and good food.

DETAILS

- **Open** - All year. Enquiries 9am-10pm. Arrival from 4pm until late.
- **Number of beds** - 16: 1x16.
- **Booking** - One night's deposit required with balance payable before arrival. Short notice bookings accepted by phone or email with deposit/balance payable on arrival.
- **Price per night** - £11.50 per person (inc gas / electric / showers). Sole use bookings negotiable according to group size.
- **Public Transport** - Train station at Bangor. S4 bus from Caernarfon to Beddgelert stops at the bottom of the drive on request.
- **Directions** - GR 531 579. At Pentre Bach just south of Waunfawr on the Caernarfon to Beddgelert road (A4085). Look for Camping Barn sign.

CONTACT: Karen Neil
Tel: 01286 650643(5-10pm) or 07798733939(9-5pm)
info@bachventures.co.uk   www.bachventures.co.uk
Pentre Bach, Waunfawr, Caernarfon, Gwynedd, LL54 7AJ

CWM PENNANT
HOSTEL & TRAINING CENTRE
WALES

Cwm Pennant Hostel is a 56 bed independent hostel offering relaxed accommodation for individuals, families and groups. It also offers adventure activities for groups provided by Outdoor UK Ltd. The hostel is set within stunning grounds in the Snowdonia National Park and has fantastic views of the Cwm Pennant valley and Moel Hebog. It is 5 miles from Porthmadog. Cwm Pennant Hostel has a lounge, drying room, games/training room and self-catering kitchen. Home cooked food is available on request. Guests have access to complimentary tea and coffee. A range of additional facilities are available including a power washer for mountain bikes, on-site parking and secure storage for bikes, kayaks and canoes. The area is ideal for hill walking, rock climbing and canoeing.

DETAILS

- **Open** - Open to advance bookings February to December, 7:30-12; 4.30-10
- **Number of beds** - 56: 4 x 4, 1 x 6, 1 x 8, 1 x 10, 1 x 16.
- **Booking** - Advance booking recommended, a non-refundable deposit is required.
- **Price per night** - £17.50 (adult), £15 (under 18). B&B £21.50 (adult) and £18 (under 18). Full-board £35 (adult) and £29 (under 18). £1,500 whole building weekend hire.
- **Public Transport** - Porthmadog train station is 5 miles away. Take the number 1 bus towards Caernarfon and get off at the Cwm Pennant turning on the A487. From here follow the brown hostel signs - one-mile walk to the hostel.
- **Directions** - From Porthmadog take the A487 towards Caernarfon. Take second turning on the right after passing through Penmorfa village and follow the brown hostel signs.

CONTACT:
Tel: 01766 530888 or 01706 877320
info@cwmpennanthostel.com www.cwmpennanthostel.com
Golan, Garndolbenmaen, Gwynedd, LL51 9AQ

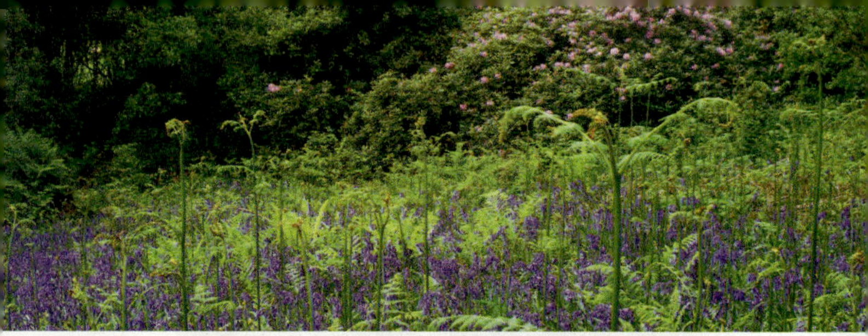

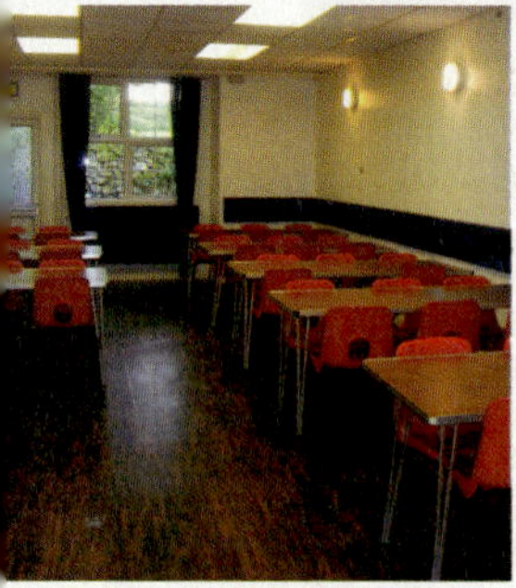

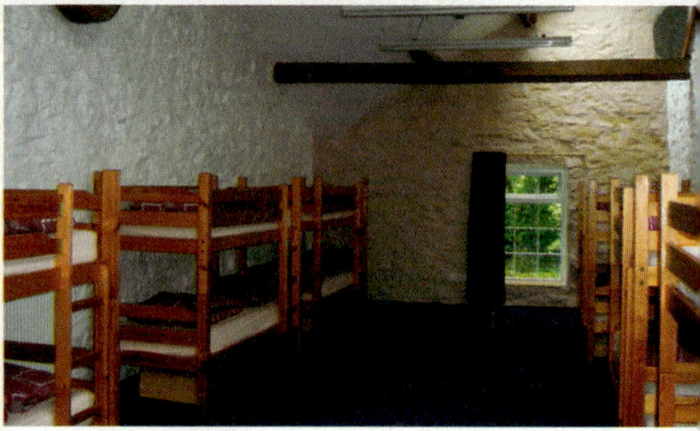

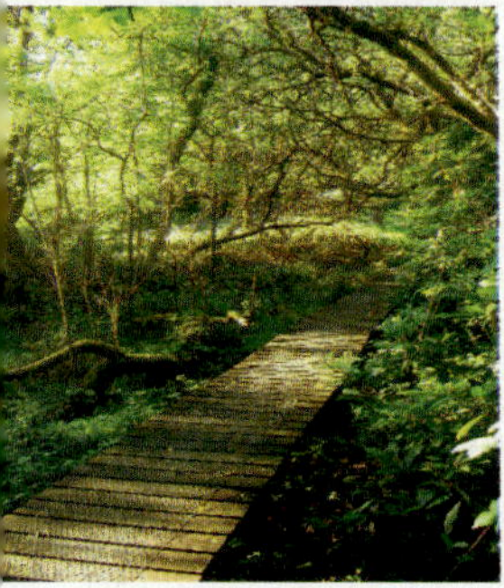

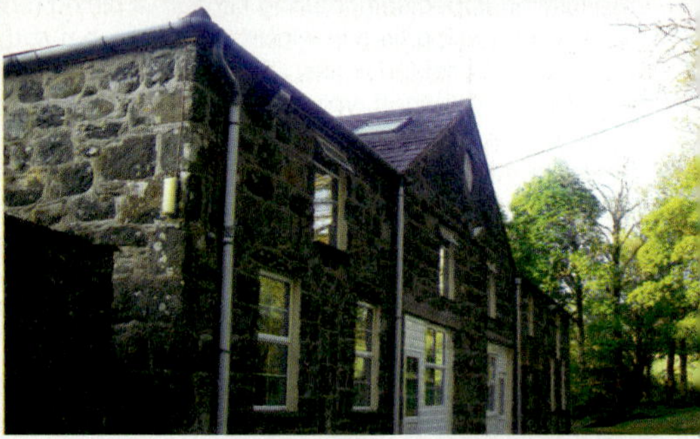

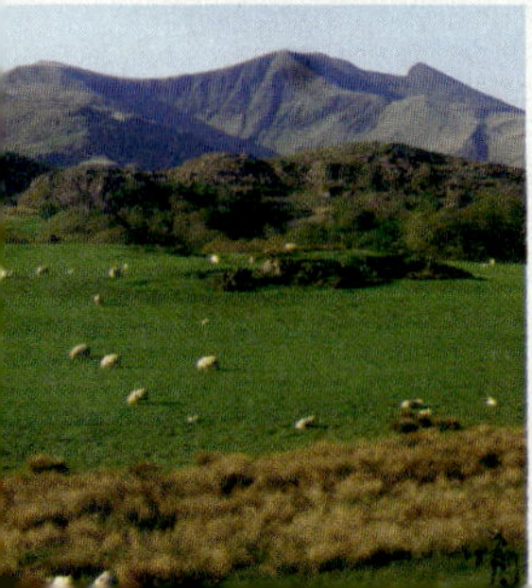

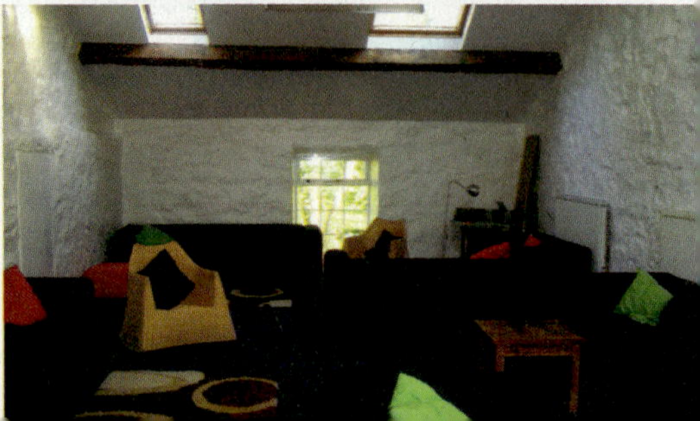

SNOWDON LODGE
GROUP HOSTEL

WALES

Stay in the birthplace of Lawrence of Arabia! Snowdon Lodge hostel provides comfortable self-catering style group accommodation in a large grade 2 listed character building. The property is located in the picturesque village of Tremadog. Snowdon Lodge is perfect for a family reunion or simply as a base for a group of friends to explore this beautiful part of Snowdonia and the nearby Lleyn Peninsula. The hostel has 10 rooms of different sizes (twins, doubles and small dormitories). Bathroom and shower facilities are shared. There is a large fully equipped self-catering kitchen, a dining room seating 38, 2 lounge/TV rooms with real log fires in winter, a drying room and a private car park leading to extensive woodland walks. Snowdon Lodge is ideally positioned just 6 miles from Mount Snowdon, yet only 2 miles from beautiful beaches such as Black Rock Sands. The famous Italianate village of Portmeirion is also only 4 miles away. Within a mile are the Ffestiniog and Welsh Highland railways and the famous Tremadog rocks for climbers. Sorry, no stag or hen parties.

DETAILS

- **Open** - January – December, all day access.
- **Number of beds** - 35: 2 x 6 (family), 1 x 5, 1 x 6 , 3 x twin, 3 x double
- **Booking** - Essential.
- **Price per night** - Sole use £550 per night. Minimum 2 nights, bank holidays minimum 3 nights. Longer stays could attract discounted prices, please ask.
- **Public Transport** - Half mile from Porthmadog train station and 250 yards from National Express coach stop.
- **Directions** - Half a mile from Porthmadog on Caernarfon road (A487).

CONTACT: Carl or Anja
Tel: 01766 515354
info@snowdonlodge.co.uk   www.snowdonlodge.co.uk
Lawrence House, Tremadog, Nr Porthmadog, Gwynedd, Snowdonia, LL49 9PS

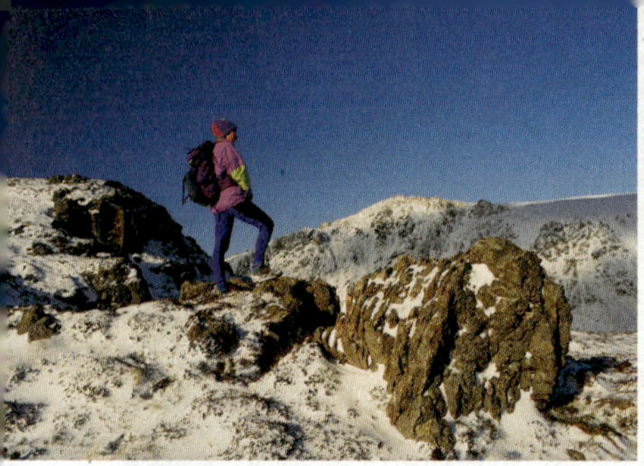

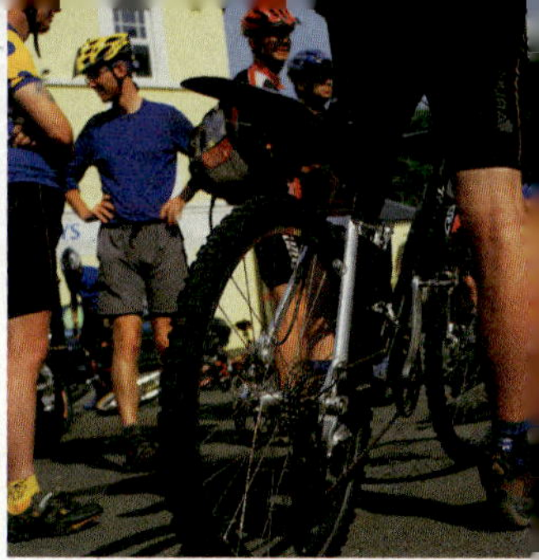

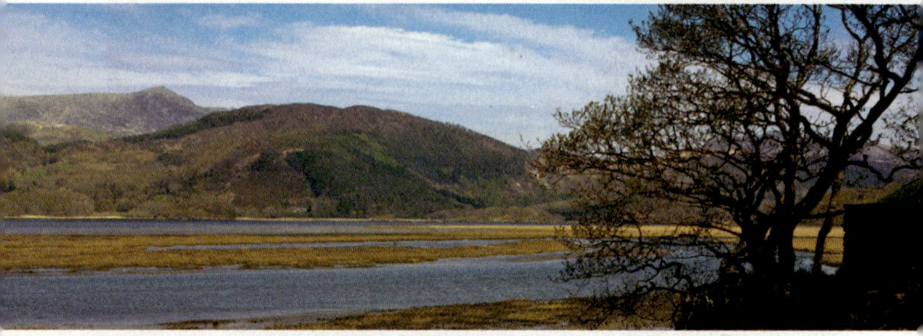

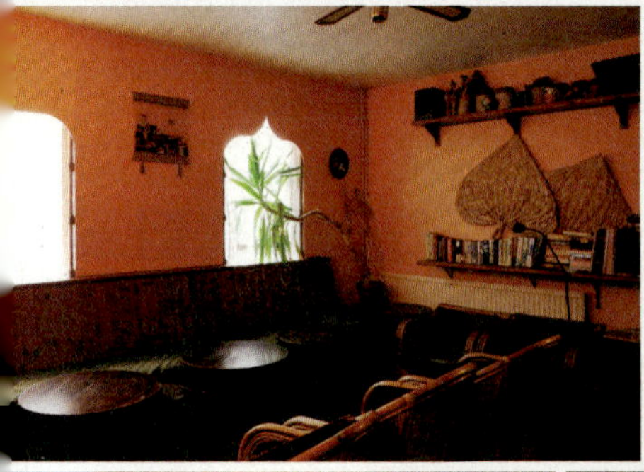

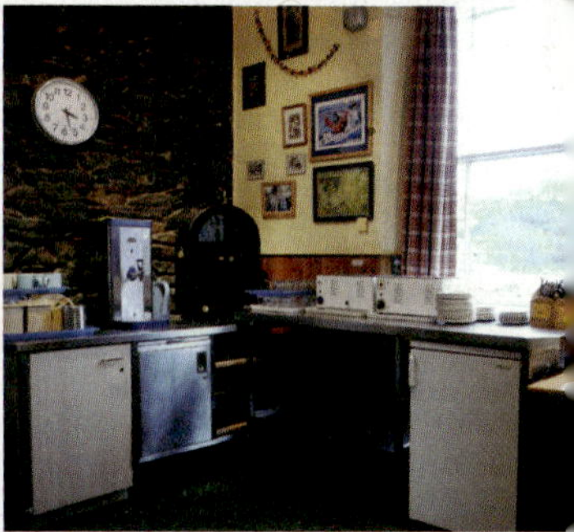

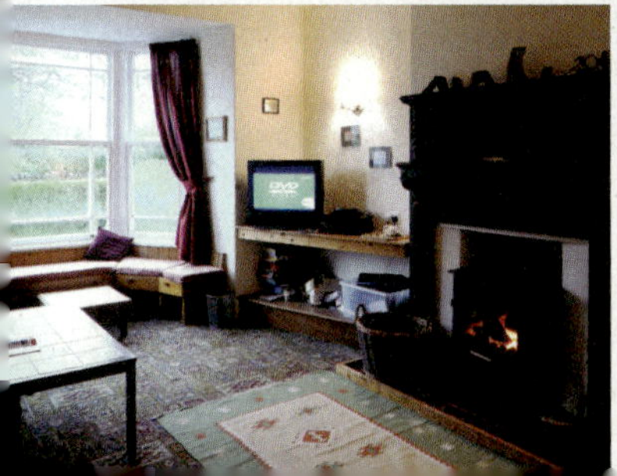

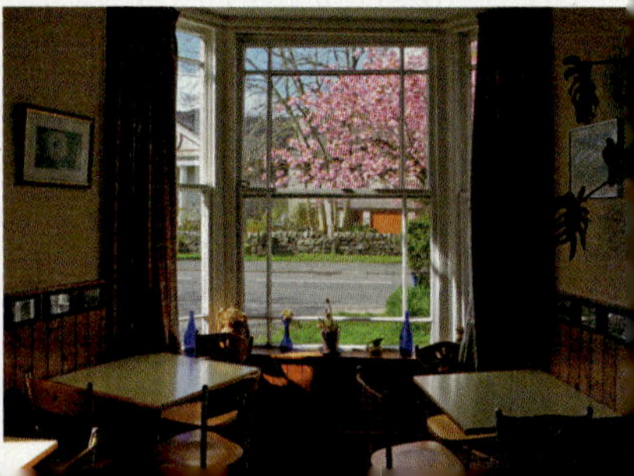

ABERSOCH
SGUBOR UNNOS

WALES

Croeso/Welcome! Sgubor Unnos provides luxury bunkhouse accommodation on a Welsh speaking, traditionally run, family farm in the village of Llangian, one mile from Abersoch. Abersoch is famous for its watersports and there are great surfing beaches at Hell's Mouth and Porth Ceiriad. Centrally located, the bunkhouse is the ideal base for outdoor activities including walking the newly opened Llyn Coast Path, surfing, cycling, golf, fishing and sailing. A few miles from Llangian, at the tip of the Peninsula lies Bardsey Island where 20,000 saints are buried! Why not pay them a visit? Trips around the island for its wildlife and heritage can be arranged. The modern bunkhouse offers three bedrooms ideal for individuals or groups. There is a fully equipped kitchen/lounge, disabled facilities, covered BBQ area, secure storage and private parking. There is a traditional village shop and phone box 500m away. For details on area see website. Photos taken by Tony Jones www.llynlight.co.uk

DETAILS

- **Open** - All year, all day
- **Number of beds** - 14: 2 x 4 : 1 x 6
- **Booking** - Not essential but recommended.
- **Price per night** - £18 (adult), £8 (under 10 years), including a light breakfast and bed linen. Discount for more than 2 nights.
- **Public Transport** - Nearest train station is Pwllheli (7 miles). Good local bus and taxi service to Llangian. Public transport details on website.
- **Directions** - GR 296 288 On entering Abersoch from Pwllheli, take the right hand turning up the hill signed to Llangian (follow brown signs). On left on leaving village.

CONTACT: Phil or Meinir
Tel: 01758 713527
enquiries@tanrallt.com www.tanrallt.com
Fferm Tanrallt Farm, Llangian, Abersoch, Gwynedd, LL53 7LN

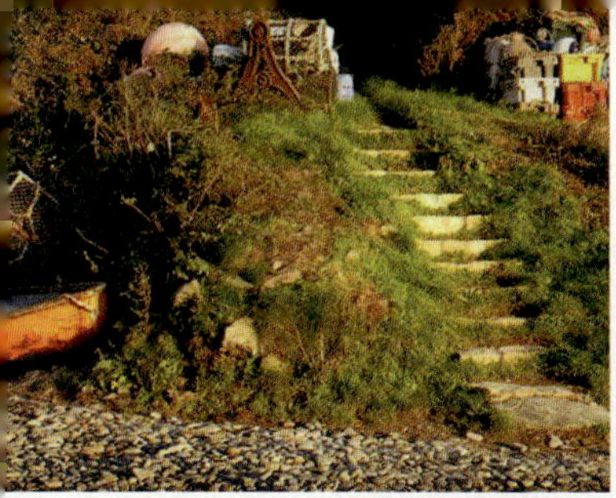
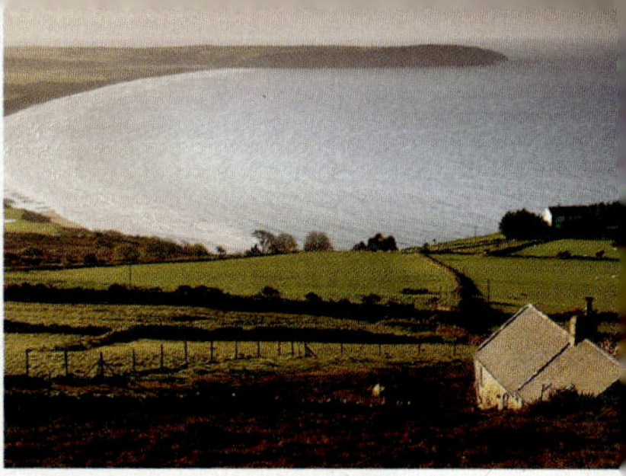
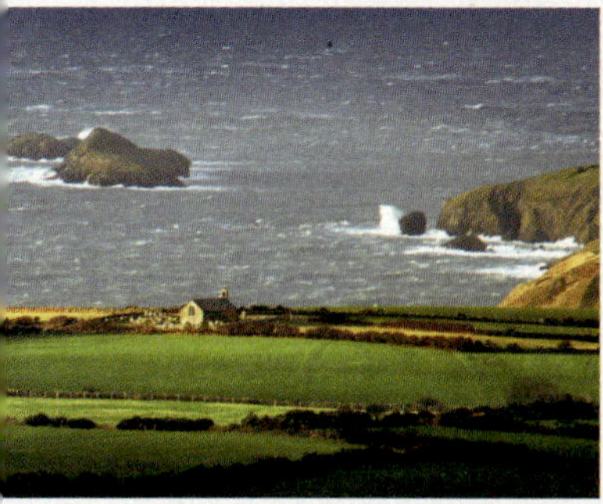
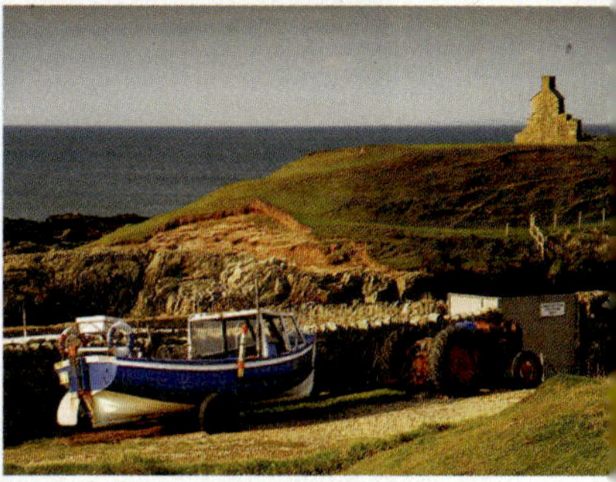
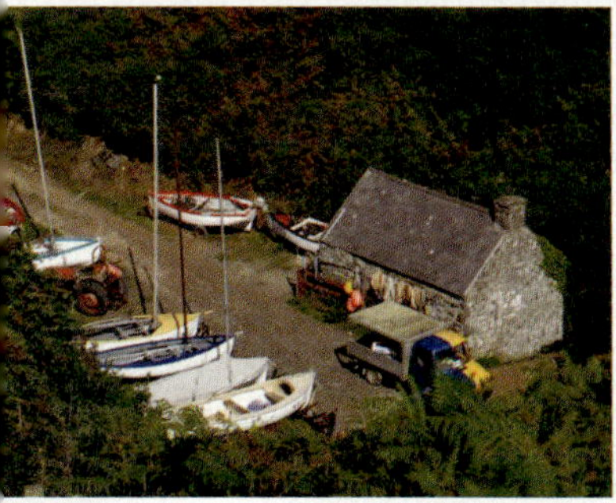
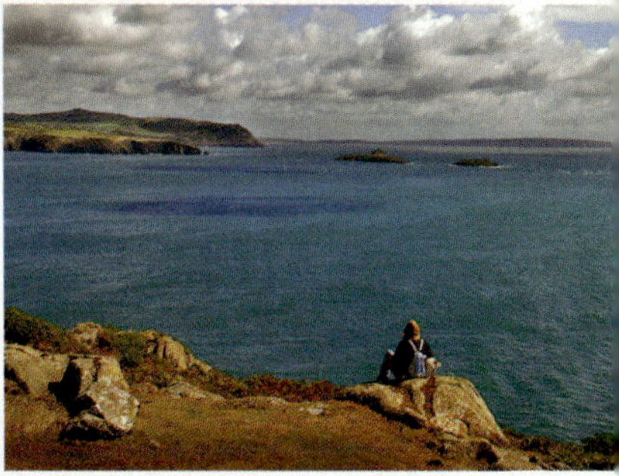
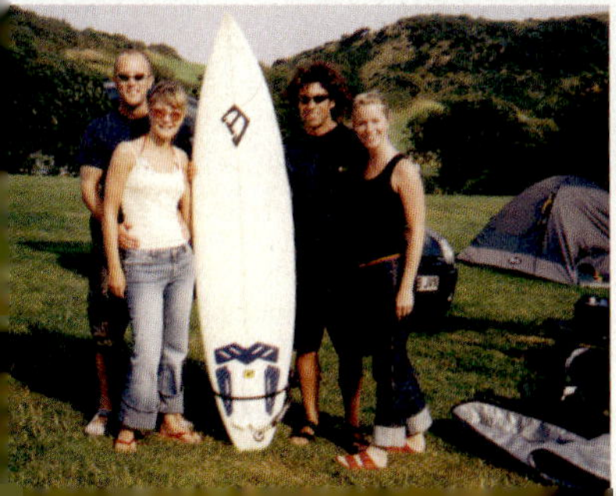
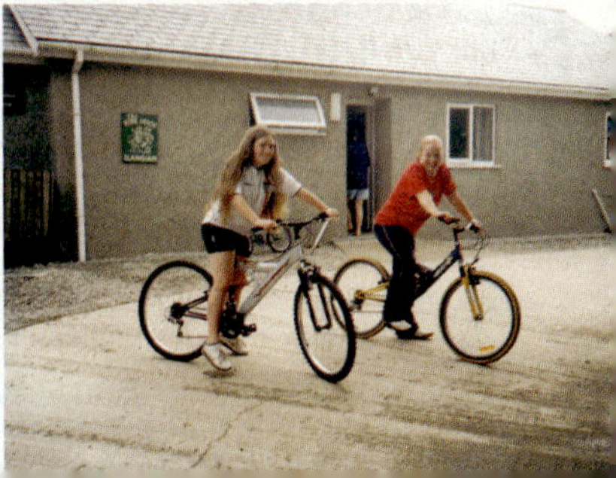

ABERDARON FARM BUNKHOUSE

WALES

Aberdaron Farm Bunkhouse is two miles from Aberdaron village with its white-painted fishermen's houses, sandy beach and water's edge church. The Bunkhouse has underfloor central heating and 3 bunk rooms sleeping 8, 4 (en suite) and 3 (en suite) in a bunk and camp bed. There is a large social room with dining tables, chairs, beanbags, TV, Nintendo Wii and board games. The small basic kitchen has a hob, microwave, George Foreman cooking machine, kettle and toaster. A self service breakfast of cereal, bread, tea and coffee is provided. Bring sleeping bags or hire duvet and pillow for £3. There is a drying room with washing machine & tumble dryer and toilet & shower blocks. Whistling Sands is only 1.5 miles away and Bardsey Island (Ynys Enlli) lies across The Sound two miles off the tip of the Llyn Peninsula. The Island has been a place of pilgrimage since early Christianity and a boat from Aberdaron to Bardsey is a great place to see the seals. Pets allowed (with notice). Bike hire available. Holiday cottages and camping are also available on the farm.

DETAILS

- **Open** - All year, all day (arrive after 4pm and leave by 11am)
- **Number of beds** - 15: 1x8, 1x4 (en suite), 1x3 (en suite)
- **Booking** - Deposit of 50% paid by credit or debit card, remainder to be paid 4 weeks prior to arrival. Booking held for 5 days without deposit.
- **Price per night** - £16pp, £18 pp (en suite) inc breakfast. Enquire for sole use of room or bunkhouse and family room prices. Minimum of 3 days on bank holidays.
- **Public Transport** - Arriva bus17, Pwllheli to Aberdaron, runs 6 times a day.
- **Directions** - Follow signs for Anelog, the first one is just after entering Aberdaron.

CONTACT: Gillian Jones
Tel: 01758 760345 Mob: 0779 414 7195
enquiries@aberdaronfarmholidays.co.uk www.aberdaronfarmholidays.co.uk
Y Gweithdy, Anelog, Aberdaron, Pwllheli, LL53 8BT

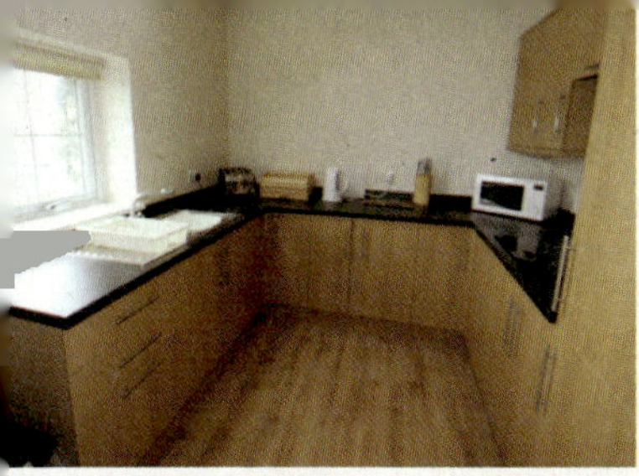
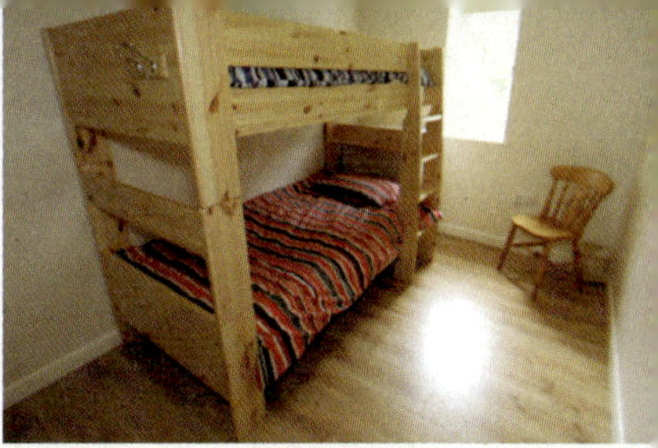
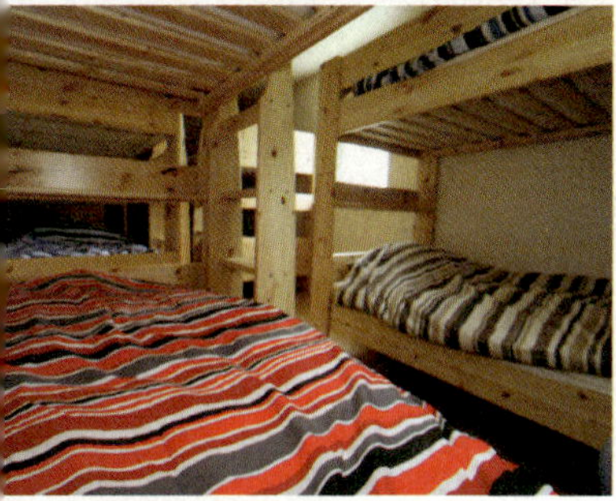
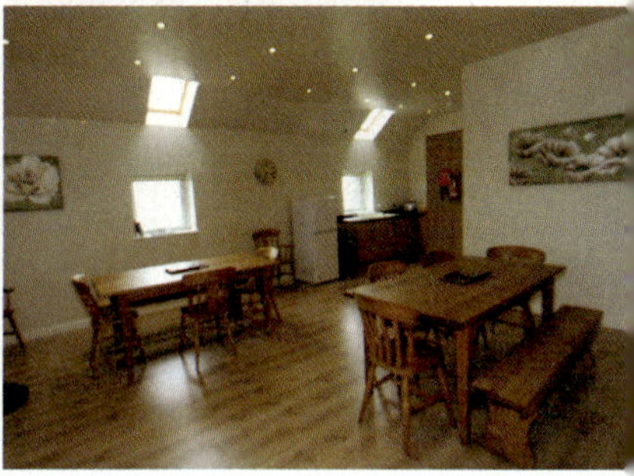
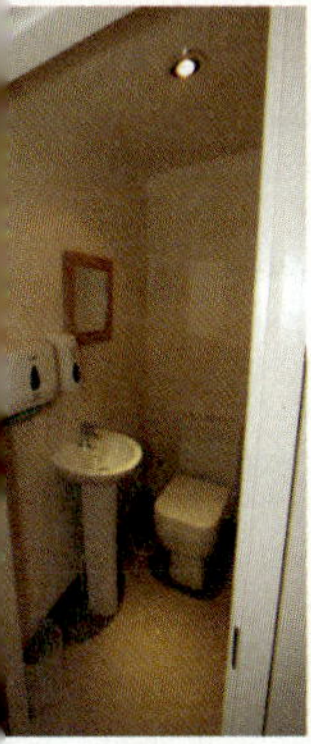
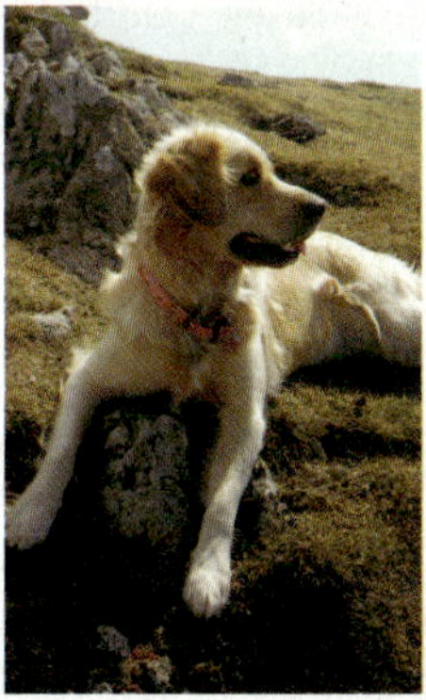
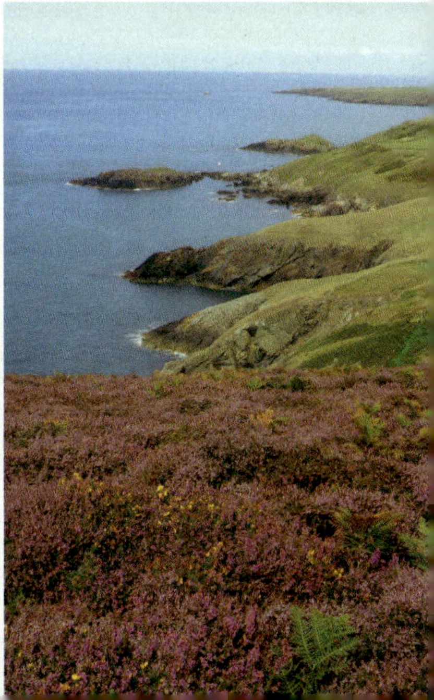
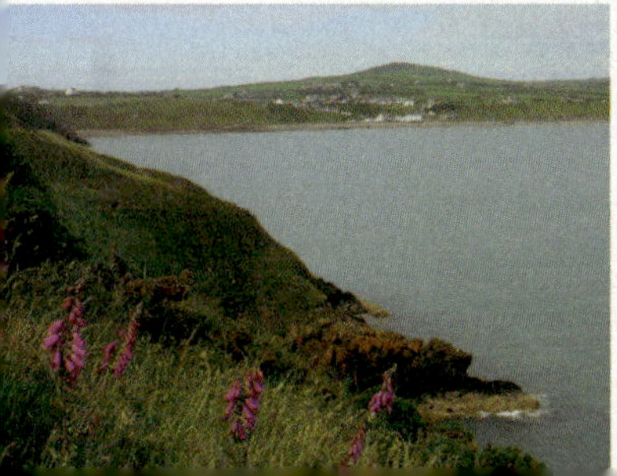

MAENTWROG BUNKHOUSE

WALES

Maentwrog bunkhouse is a newly renovated 200 year old cowshed situated on a working beef and sheep farm.

It has a fully equipped kitchen, underfloor heating, TV/DVD player, BBQ area, laundry facilities, power washer and lockup available for bikes.

Local activities range from hill walking (Moelwyn and Cnicht are 10 minutes away), white water rafting, Coed y Brenin cycling centre, Blaenau Ffestiniog down hill cycle track, RopeWorks, canyoning, Ffestiniog narrow gauge railway and several beautiful beaches are all within 15 to 20 minutes' drive as well as the Welsh costal path passing at the end of the lane.

Please contact direct for any other information

DETAILS

- **Open** - All Year.
- **Number of beds** - 4
- **Booking** - booking essential
- **Price per night** - £18 pppn bring sleeping bags or hire bed linen @£3 pp
- **Public Transport** - Public bus to bottom of lane 400m walk
Arriva Wales train to Penrhyndeudraeth
- **Directions** - Turn into Maentwrog village then follow the A496 towards Harlech for 1 mile with lay-by on right, take immediate left up small lane for 400m, first farmhouse on right

CONTACT: Mrs Eurliw M Jones
Tel: 01766590231
emj2@hotmail.co.uk www.bunkhousesnowdonia.com
Felen Rhyd Fach, Maentwrog, Blaenau Ffestiniog, Gwynedd, LL41 4HY Wales

TOTTERS

383

WALES

Totters is situated in the heart of the historic castle town of Caernarfon. Sheltered by the castle town wall, it is only 30 metres from the shores of the Menai Straits and enjoys some fantastic sunsets. The town not only offers the visitor a huge selection of pubs and restaurants to choose from, but also acts as the perfect base for trips into the Snowdonia National Park. There is very good public transport in and out of the National Park. The hostel is a 200-year-old, five floored town house, which is fully heated and with all the comforts of home. Facilities include a common room with TV and games, book exchange, dining room and a secure left luggage facility. There are five bedrooms which sleep either 4 or 6 and can be arranged as mixed or single sex dorms and the Penthouse room, a huge double en suite room with views over the Straits, this can be a double or a family room. Across the road there is a self-catering town house which sleeps 6. See website for more details of all our accommodation.

DETAILS

- **Open** - All year, all day access. Book in by 10pm.
- **Number of beds** - 28 : 3 x 6, 2 x4, 1 x 2 (en suite), 1x2 (twin)
- **Booking** - Booking is essential for groups in June, July, August and September.
- **Price per night** - £18.50pp in a dorm. £50 for a double/twin en suite. £44 for a twin. Discounts for groups.
- **Public Transport** - Bangor train station is 9 miles from the hostel. Catch a bus from outside the station to Caernarfon. National Express coaches drop off in Caernarfon 200m from the hostel.
- **Directions** - Coming by road: follow signs for town centre, turn right 200m after the big Celtic Royal hotel, keep going and Totters is the last house on the left.

CONTACT: Bob/Henryette
Tel: 01286 672963 Mob: 07979 830470
totters.hostel@googlemail.com www.totters.co.uk
Plas Porth Yr Aur, 2 High Street, Caernarfon, Gwynedd, LL55 1RN

ANGLESEY OUTDOOR CENTRE

WALES

Anglesey Outdoor Centre is an ideal base for groups, individuals or families to explore and enjoy the outdoor playground and mild climate of Anglesey. The island has opportunities for both adrenalin adventures and gentle relaxation. From coasteering, sea kayaking, climbing, and windsurfing to beach activities, gentle walks and bird watching. The centre is just a mile from Porthdafarach Beach and the Anglesey Coastal Path and only 2km from the start of Sustrans Cycle Route 8 to Cardiff. The Centre has four self contained areas each with their own self-catering and bathroom facilities. These can be hired individually or together to provide options for all group sizes and budgets. There are dorms, private and family rooms. Bedding is provided or you can use your own sleeping bags in the Gogarth dorms. Full catering is also available and there is an on-site bar/bistro, The Paddlers Return. Yurts and 2 Cabans also available to hire. 14 acres of grounds. Cycle & gear store, ample parking, drying room and WiFi.

DETAILS

- **Open** - All year, 24 hour access
- **Number of beds** - 68; Main Centre 33:1x7,4x5,1x4,1x2. Maris Annexe 10:5x2; Ty Pen Annexe 8:1x4,2x2. Gogarth Dorms 16:1x7,1x7,1x2. Some extra beds available.
- **Booking** - Not essential but recommended
- **Price per night** - From £9pp (Gogarth Dorms) to £18pp (en suite twin in Main Centre). Sole use prices available for all Centre or each annexe. Please get in touch.
- **Public Transport** - 2km from trains and ferry at Holyhead. Regular buses ½ mile.
- **Directions** - Arriving at the last roundabout on the A55, take the third exit toward Trearddur Bay. Immediately take the first left turning onto Porthdafarch Rd. Follow for approx 1.5miles. Signed on left hand side for Anglesey Outdoors & Paddlers Return.

CONTACT: Penny Hurndall
Tel: 01407 769351
angleseyoutdoors@gmail.com   www.angleseyoutdoors.com
Porthdafarch Road, Holyhead, Anglesey, LL65 2LP

OUTDOOR ALTERNATIVE

WALES

Wonderfully situated at the south end of Holy Island, Anglesey, in a 7 acre Area of Outstanding Natural Beauty, and 300m from a beach. The centre is an excellent base for so much in the outdoors and is immediately adjacent to the Anglesey Coastal Path - good walking on a varied and accessible coast. All around there are prehistoric remains, spectacular geology, a wide range of habitats and species of marine life and plants, and excellent bird watching opportunities. For kayakers there are classic sea tours, overfalls, playwaves, surf and rockhopping. Climbers have Gogarth nearby and Rhoscolyn offering all grades in an attractive setting. Divers can beach launch for wrecks and fish.

The Centre has two self-contained units and camping with toilets and showers. Careful energy use is encouraged, with composting and recycling. Nearby Holyhead has rail links and ferries to Ireland. Walking distance to pub.

DETAILS

- **Open** - All year, 24 hour access
- **Number of beds** - 20: 2x2, 1x4, 2x6. 16: 1x3, 2x4, 1x5.
- **Booking** - Essential
- **Price per night** - £340 for exclusive use, £19.50 per person.
- **Public Transport** - Trains at Holyhead (10km) (London direct 4.5 hrs) or Valley (5km). National Express at Valley (6km). Bus 23/25 Holyhead - Rhoscolyn (1km) or 4/44 Holyhead - Four Mile Bridge (3km). Ferry: Holyhead - Dublin or Dun Laoghaire.
- **Directions** - GR SH 278 752. From A5 traffic lights at Y Fali/Valley take B4545 Trearddur. After 2km at Four Mile Bridge fork left at sign to Rhoscolyn 2miles. After 2km sharp left at camping symbols. After 800m fork right at large white gatepost.

CONTACT: Jacqui Short
Tel: 01407 860469
enquiries@outdooralternative.co.uk www.outdooralternative.co.uk/
Cerrig-yr-Adar, Rhoscolyn, Holyhead, Anglesey, LL65 2NQ

South Scotland

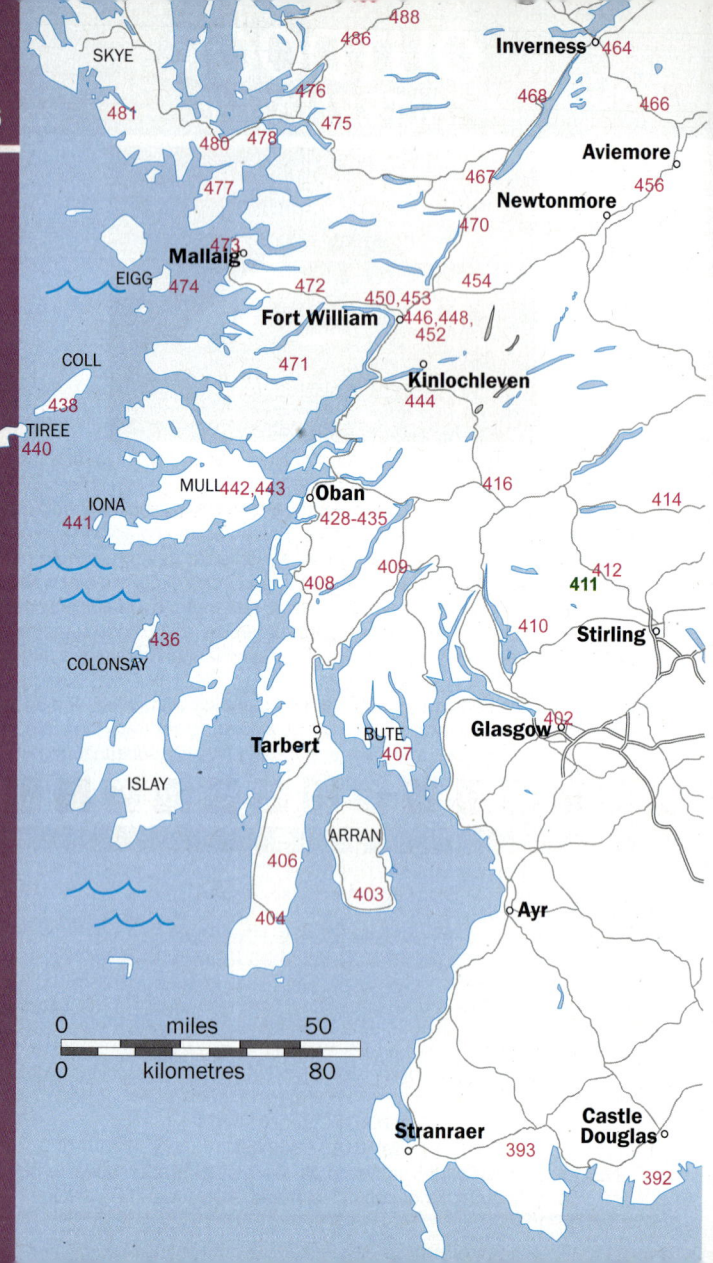

386

South Scotland

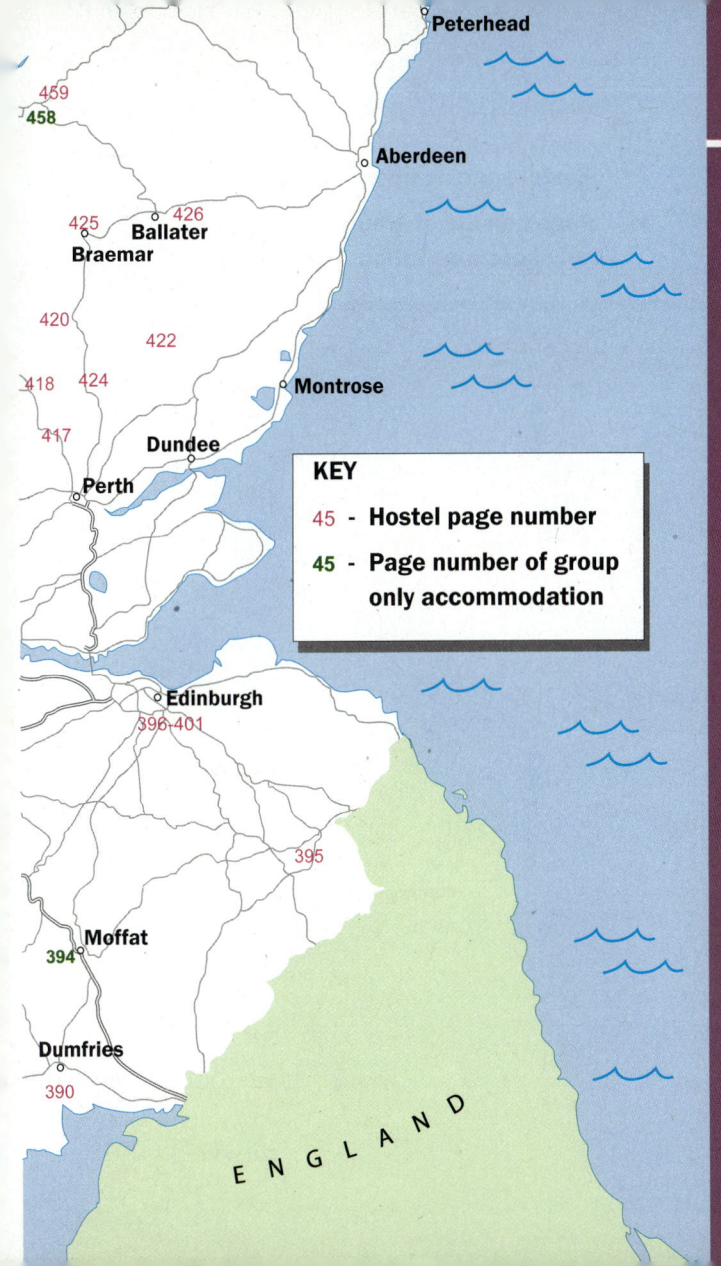

Peterhead

459
458

Aberdeen

425   426
Ballater
Braemar

420
    422

418   424

417
Dundee
Perth

Montrose

KEY

45   -   Hostel page number

45   -   Page number of group only accommodation

Edinburgh
396-401

395

Moffat
394

Dumfries
390

ENGLAND

North Scotland

388

KEY

45 - **Hostel page number** (red)

45 - **Page number of group only accommodation** (green)

Scale: 0–50 miles / 0–80 kilometres

- Durness 499
- Stornoway 484, 485 (LEWIS)
- 492
- Ullapool 491
- 490
- HARRIS 483
- Gairloch
- 489
- 488
- 486
- Portree (SKYE) 481
- 476
- 480 478 475
- 468
- NORTH UIST
- 477
- 467
- 470
- SOUTH UIST
- BARRA 482
- Mallaig 473
- 474
- 472 450, 453 454
- EIGG
- Fort William 446, 452, 448
- 471
- COLL 438
- Kinlochleven 444

North Scotland

ORKNEY
- 510
- 509
- 505
- 500, 501
- Stromness
- Kirkwall
- 506, 508
- 502
- 504

Thurso
John O'Groats

- 511
- 512
- Lerwick

SHETLAND

- 498
- 497
- Helmsdale
- 496
- 495

- Fraserburgh
- 494
- 460
- 461
- 462
- Peterhead
- 493
- Inverness
- 464
- 466
- 459
- **458**
- Aviemore
- 456
- Aberdeen
- Newtonmore
- 425
- 426
- Ballater
- Braemar
- 420
- 422
- Pitlochry 418
- 424
- Montrose

389

MARTHROWN OF MABIE BUNKHOUSE

SCOTLAND

Marthrown is set in the heart of Mabie Forest, about 6 miles south of Dumfries. It has a traditional sauna, a wood burning spring water hot tub, a large BBQ, garden areas and plenty of room for groups. The forest has newly developed mountain bike routes, ranging in length and difficulty. Bike hire is available nearby and there is access to the 7Stanes mountain bike trails. Although we are a self-catering hostel meals are available to order. Marthrown is suitable for all age groups. Facilities include secure dry store for bikes and equipment and a large dining area suitable for meetings. For something a little different why not try staying in the Roundhouse or Yurt? Are you looking for a completely different type of Scottish wedding venue to tie the knot? The Bunkhouse, Round house and Yurt are also available for forest and outdoor weddings. For more info see website.

DETAILS

- **Open** - All year, 24 hours - late arrival by arrangement
- **Number of beds** - 26: 1x8:1x7:1x6:1x5 + Roundhouse, Yurt, Tipi and camping.
- **Booking** - Telephone a few days in advance.
- **Price per night** - £16 to £19.50.
- **Public Transport** - From Dumfries (White Sands) take the Stagecoach bus service 372 to Mabie Forest. It is best to arrive in daylight. 1.5 mile walk from road.
- **Directions** - From Dumfries take A710 (west) to Mabie Forest passing through the village of Islesteps. Turn right signposted Mabie Forest and Mabie House Hotel. Follow tarmac road over speed bumps to the end of the Hotel and Forest Rangers Office, through courtyard and onto forest track, Marthown is signposted and is exactly one mile into the forest.

CONTACT: Mike or Pam Hazlehurst
Tel: 01387 247900, Fax: 01387 255611
pamhazlehurst@hotmail.com www.marthrownofmabie.com
Mabie Forest, Dumfries, DG2 8HB

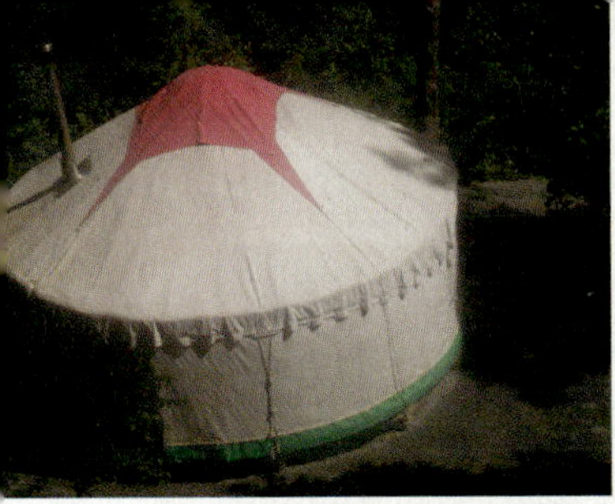
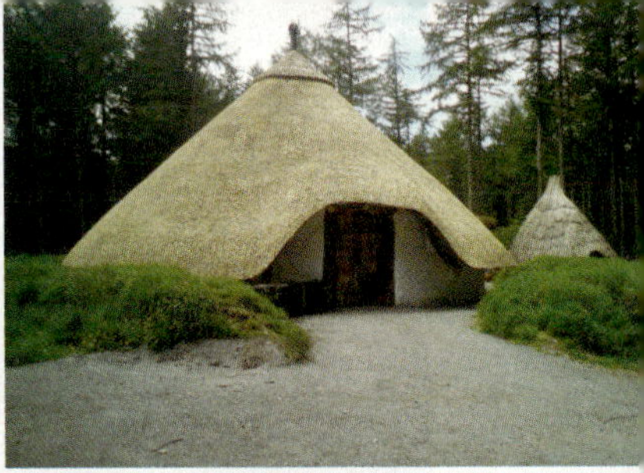
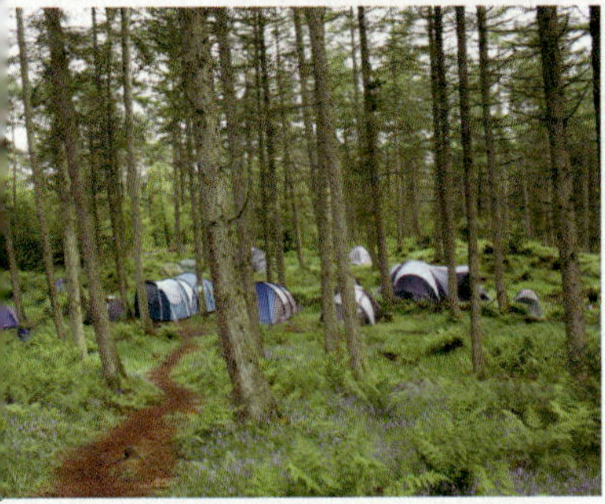
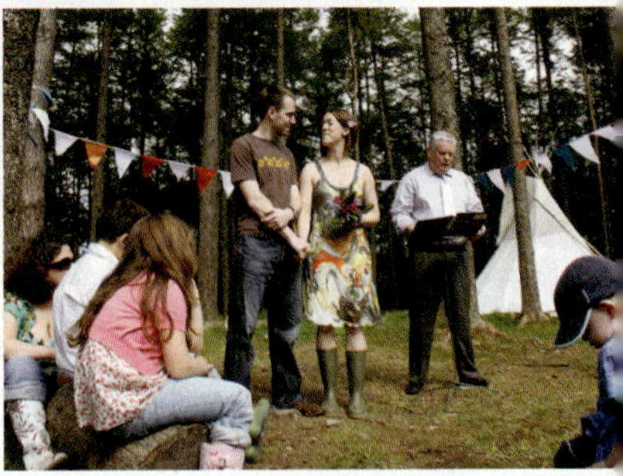
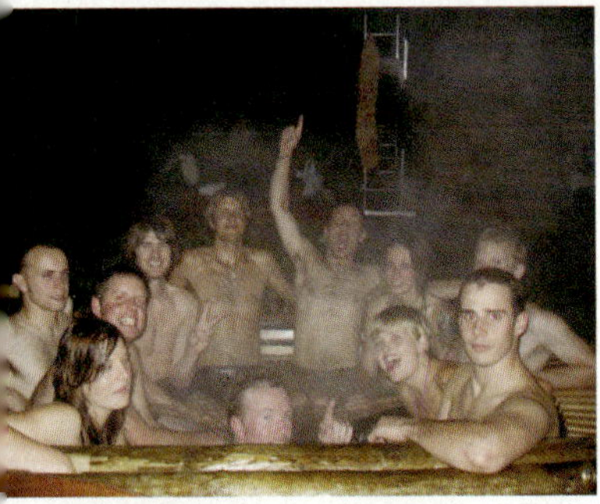
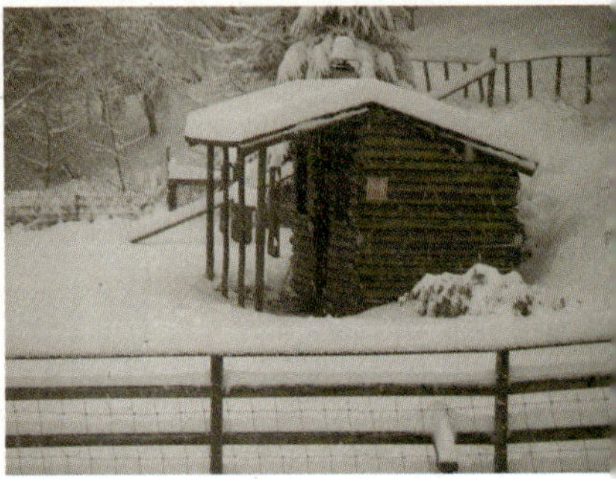
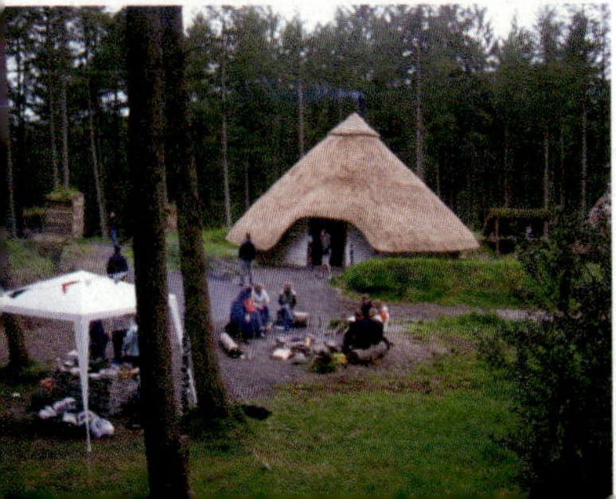
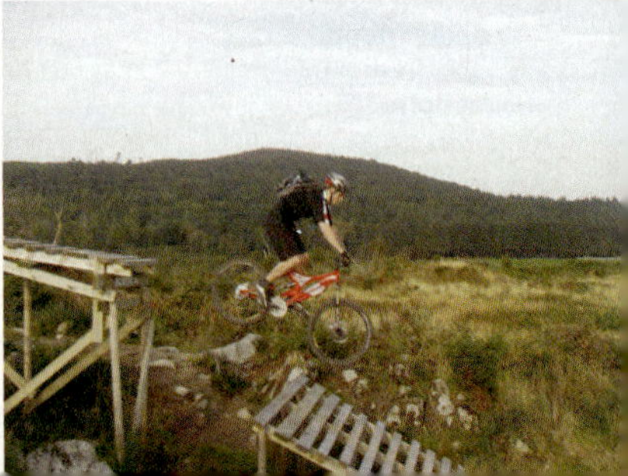

CASTLE CREAVIE
HAY BARN

SCOTLAND

Castle Creavie Haybarn has recently been converted to a comfortable family friendly Independent Hostel sleeping 4. Quietly set on a working farm it is surrounded by spectacularly beautiful Galloway countryside. Hugely spacious open plan design, oak floors, with 4 comfortable beds, dining area, wood burning stove, separate kitchen with basic cooking facilities, fridge, washroom and W.C. Also available on site are: hot showers, washing/drying facilities, bike wash and safe store, farmhouse breakfast (pre booked) £7.50 pp. Ideal base for walkers and cyclists with 7Stanes and NCN Route 7 (3 miles away). Guests are welcome to enjoy the farm footpaths and observe the daily life on this working sheep farm. Available seasonally: fresh baked bread, cakes and honey, home reared pork and lamb, sausage, bacon and fresh farm eggs. Castle Creavie is named after two Iron Age forts, and is 4 miles from the popular harbour town of Kirkcudbright which has a good range of pubs, cafés, and restaurants. Galloway is famed for its many castles, abbeys, first class walks and long sandy beaches.

DETAILS
- **Open** - All year, all day.
- **Number of beds** - 4: 1x4.
- **Booking** - Book by phone and online. Deposit required by post or PayPal.
- **Price per night** - £15pp with beds made up.
- **Public Transport** - 4 miles from Kirkcudbright citylink services.
- **Directions** - From the A75 take the A711 to Kirkcudbright. In the town centre turn left at the Royal Hotel onto the B727 (Gelston), pass the cemetery and at the next road junction go straight on (Auchencairn / Dundrennan). Follow for approx 4 miles.

CONTACT: Charlie and Elaine Wannop
Tel: 01557 500238, Fax: 01557 500238
elaine@castlecreavie.co.uk www.castlecreavie.co.uk
Castle Creavie, Kirkcudbright, Dumfries and Galloway, DG6 4QE

GALLOWAY YURTS

SCOTLAND

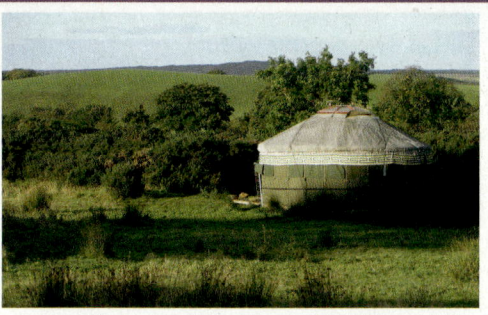

Low Threave Steading is a sustainable small holding set in the beautiful Machars, on the edge of the World Heritage Dark Skies Park. Ideal to explore Dumfries and Galloway or as a stop off on the way to Cairn Ryan and Northern Ireland. The traditional Mongolian Yurt is family friendly with made up beds, cooking facilities and heated by a log stove. Solar power provides lighting and charging facilities and there is a fire pit (firewood available), wash room and dry composting toilets. A Bell Tent sleeping four is available with advance notice, bring your own beds, bedding and cooking equipment. This part of Scotland is host to the 7Stanes world class mountain biking routes as well as quiet roads for on-road cycling. There are quiet unspoiled beaches within 10 miles ideal for fishing, caving and barbeques and miles of footpaths through the Galloway Forest, Britain's largest area of forested land. Home baked bread, jam, organic vegetables/salad and eggs are available seasonally. Bring a torch.

DETAILS
- **Open** - All year, arrive after 1pm and leave by 11am.
- **Number of beds** - Yurt 5 : (4x1) or (1xdbl + 3x1); Bell Tent 4.
- **Booking** - Please book by phone or email, deposit required by post.
- **Price per night** - Yurt: sole use only £40- £60. Bell Tent: £25. Discounts for more than two nights
- **Public Transport** - X75 city link service or 500 to Newton Stewart 5 miles, train to Barrhill 17 miles or Dumfries 55 miles.
- **Directions** - Take A75 to Stranraer, when you reach Newton Stewart stay on A75 and turn left at the next small cross roads. Follow road for 5 miles, take track on the left after the farm Mid Threave. They are through the gate and at the end of the track.

CONTACT: Alison Roberts
Tel: 01671 830368 Mob: 07787556161
yurtinthewoods@hotmail.co.uk
Low Threave, Kirkcowan, Newton Stewart, DG8 0BU

WELL ROAD CENTRE
SCOTLAND GROUP ACCOMMODATION

The Well Road Centre is a large Victorian house set in its own grounds in the charming spa town of Moffat. The centre is ideal for youth groups, adult groups, conferences, residential workshops, sports events, multiple family gatherings and outdoor activity clubs. All rooms are fully carpeted and centrally heated. The Centre has two spacious meeting rooms, a large bright self-catering kitchen fully equipped for 65, a games hall for indoor sports, a table tennis room and a snooker room. There are 13 bedrooms of various sizes, two of them with en suite facilities. Two separate toilet/shower areas for mixed groups. Bring your own sleeping bags or duvets. Ample parking for cars, minibuses and equipment trailers and the nearby park can be used for sports activities. Moffat is in the Southern Uplands, an hour from Edinburgh and Glasgow. An ideal area for golfers, bird watchers, walkers and cyclists, it is central to the "7Stanes" mountain bike venues. All groups have sole use.

DETAILS

- **Open** - All year, all day
- **Number of beds** - 70: in 13 rooms (2 en suite).
- **Booking** - Check availability and send £100 deposit to secure booking.
- **Price per night** - From £750 for two nights for up to 30 people. £25 per person for 31 people or more.
- **Public Transport** - Trains at Lockerbie (16m). Citylink bus to Glasgow/Edinburgh.
- **Directions** - From A74 take Moffat turning and enter the High Street (town square). Turning to the right around the shops on the south side of the square, follow Holm St to the T-junction. Turn left into Burnside, following up and right into Well Rd.

CONTACT: Ben Larmour
Tel: 01683 221040
Ben8363@aol.com www.wellroadcentre.co.uk
Well Road Centre, Well Road, Moffat, DG10 9BT

KIRK YETHOLM
FRIENDS OF NATURE HOUSE SCOTLAND

395

Kirk Yetholm Friends of Nature House, nestling below the picturesque village green, is a former village school that has been offering hostel style accommodation for over 70 years. Located at the start / end of the Pennine Way it is a classic stop and is also ideal for those doing the St. Cuthbert's Way and for cyclists on the Borderloop Cycle Route or Sustrans Route 84. A great base for local day hikes, particularly suited to individuals, families and small groups. Recently upgraded, the house offers a friendly and peaceful retreat after a day exploring the stunning countryside and local heritage. There is a comfortable lounge, a well equipped kitchen, seating for 18 in the dining area and secure bike storage. Evening meals and breakfast are available in adjacent Border Hotel. Well stocked village shop and other eateries 10 min's walk away. FoN is one of Europe's oldest environmental groups with 600K members and 800 houses across Europe.

Under 16's should be accompanied by an adult sharing the same dorm.

DETAILS

- **Open** - All year (Nov-Feb incl. groups only), Access; 5pm-11pm, check out 10am
- **Number of beds** - 22: 1x7, 1x5, 1x4, 2x2 (twin), 1x2 (bunk)
- **Booking** - Book via website, email or phone. Verbal bookings held until 6pm daily.
- **Price per night** - From £17, under 18's from £14. Discounts for IFN and SYHA/HI.
- **Public Transport** - Kelso to Kirk Yetholm approx every 2hrs. Stops within 100m of building. Connections onwards from Kelso to all parts of country and to rail station
- **Directions** - OS Grid Ref: NT 826 282. Geo-Coord: 55.533378 -2.277233. 7 miles from Kelso on Pennine Way. Located 100m below the village green at Kirk Yetholm.

CONTACT: Manager
Tel: 01573 420639
kirkyetholm@thefriendsofnature.org.uk www.thefriendsofnature.org.uk
Friends of Nature House, Waukford, Kirk Yetholm, Kelso, Roxburghshire, TD5 8PG

SMARTCITYHOSTELS
EDINBURGH
SCOTLAND

Smart City Hostels redefines the hostel experience. As Edinburgh's premier 5 star hostel, SmartCityHostels is in the heart of the city, just off the Royal Mile in the old town, providing private rooms as well as dorms – all en suite.

Bar 50 is the hostel's lively, licensed bar and kitchen serving locally sourced food and drinks at a great price from 8am til late. You'll find pool tables, comfy couches and wide screen TVs in Bar 50 and an outdoor heated terraced area too. Free WiFi throughout the building, reception is 24 hours with no curfew, and there are free locker facilities to make your stay as comfortable as possible.

All of Edinburgh's lively night scene and famed attractions are on the doorstep. A perfect base for groups, big or small, and individuals, to explore all the city has to offer.

DETAILS

- **Open** - All year, 24 hours
- **Number of beds** - 617
- **Booking** - Not essential, but recommended in summer
- **Price per night** - From £12 per person per night. Group rates available on request.
- **Public Transport** - Airport transfer and Waverley train station 5 minutes' walk; St Andrews Bus Station 5-10 minutes' walk.
- **Directions** - From Waverley Bridge turn left into Market Street, then turn right into Jeffrey Street. At first set of traffic lights at the Royal Mile turn right. Blackfriars Street is first left and Smart City Hostels is on your right.

CONTACT: Reservations
Tel: 0131 516 7996 , Fax: 0131 524 1988
info@smartcityhostels.com www.smartcityhostels.com
50 Blackfriars Street, Edinburgh, EH1 1NE

HIGH STREET HOSTEL

SCOTLAND

The High Street Hostel has become a hugely popular destination for world travellers since opening in 1985 and is one of Europe's best regarded and most atmospheric hostels.

Located just off the historic Royal Mile in a 400 year old building it is the perfect base for exploring all the city's attractions – and of course its wonderful nightlife.

Providing excellence in location, ambience and facilities, the hostel is highly recommended by more than ten of the world's top backpacker travel guides.

DETAILS

- **Open** - All year, 24 hours.
- **Number of beds** - 156.
- **Booking** - Booking in advance not always crucial, 1 night's payment for booking.
- **Price per night** - From £14 per person. ID required for check in.
- **Public Transport** - Only a 5/10 minute walk from Edinburgh bus station or Waverley train station. Taxis cost between £3-£5 from each. The airport bus also stops outside the train station on the last stop so it is very easy to get to the hostel.
- **Directions** - From the bus station (St Andrews Square) turn left onto Princes Street then first right onto Northbridge. At top turn left onto the High Street on the Royal Mile and hostel is on Blackfriars St. on right. From railway station main exit turn left onto Waverley Bridge then right at the mini rounbdaout and straight ahead up the Mound, at the junction go left, then at cross roads left again going down the Royal Mile. Cross at the traffic lights at Northbridge and Blackfriars St is second on the right. From airport take bus 100 to last stop, Waverley Bridge and follow as above.

CONTACT: Reception
Tel: 0131 557 3984
highstreet@scotlandstophostels.com   www.scotlandstophostels.com
Blackfriars Street, Edinburgh, EH1 1NE

HAGGIS HOSTELS

SCOTLAND

Occupying a recently renovated building dating from 1862, Haggis Hostels is situated in the heart of Edinburgh just 50 metres from Princes Street. The hostel offers self-catering facilities and fully equipped rooms with privacy curtains, reading lights and international sockets so there is no need for travel adaptors. There is adjustable heating in every room. The communal kitchen is of a high specification and features two of every appliance – ideal for groups of up to 34. Being so centralised in the Scottish capital, Haggis Hostels has everything on its doorstep whether you're heading to the theatre, concert hall, pub or club. There is something for everyone. Their staff will help you plan your day's excursion in and around Edinburgh and provide you with all the information you need to make your stay as enjoyable as possible. The hostel offers free breakfast, high speed WiFi internet access, luxury bedding and towels, a laundry service, secure storage and a communal kitchen with dining area.

DETAILS

- **Open** - All Year, 24 hour reception.
- **Number of beds** - 34.
- **Booking** - Online on our website, phone or email.
- **Price per night** - Standard mixed room - from £18. Female or male only room from £22. Family room from £80.00. Breakfast and taxes included in all prices.
- **Public Transport** - Buses to St Andrew Square bus station. Air link shuttle service to Edinburghs Waverley train station direct from Edinburgh Airport. Trains to Edinburgh's Waverley train station. Tram service to St Andrew's Square.
- **Directions** - At the east end of Princes Street, follow the road round to the left, and you will find us on the right.

CONTACT:
Tel: 0131 557 0036, Fax: 01315570036
info@haggishostels.co.uk www.haggishostels.co.uk
Haggis Hostels 5/3 West Register Street, EH2 2AA

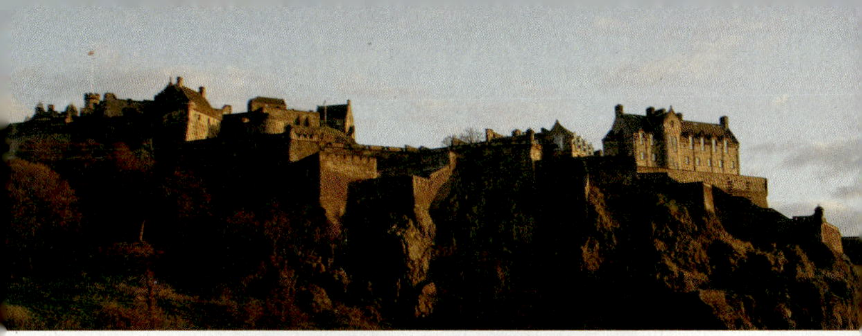

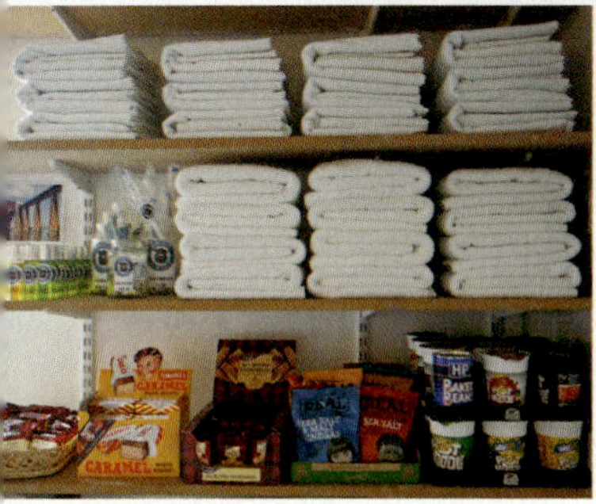
CARAMEL

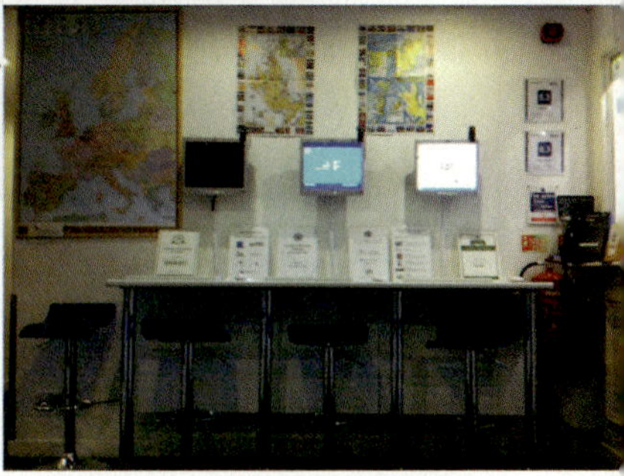

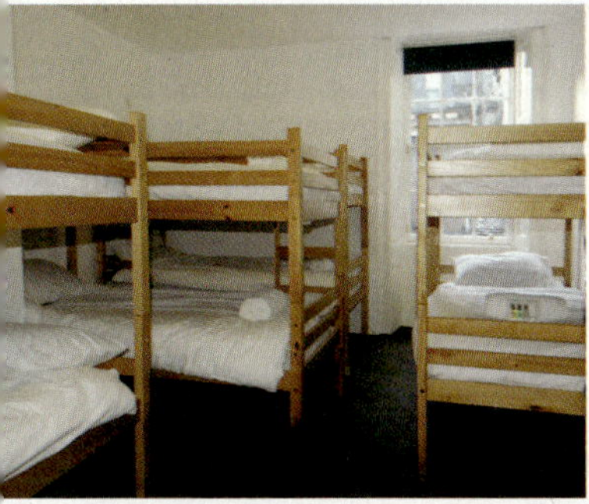

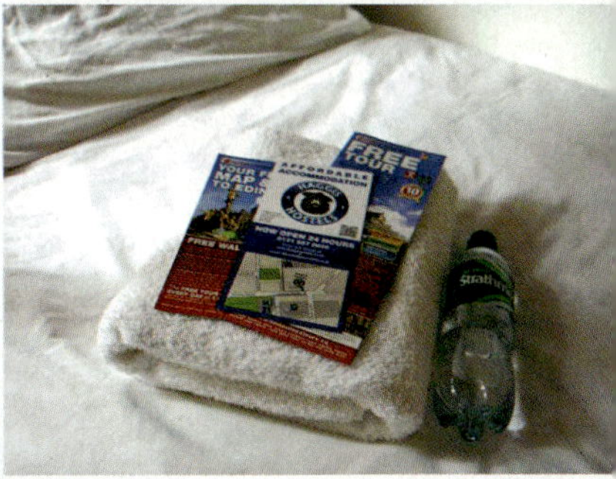
FREE TOUR

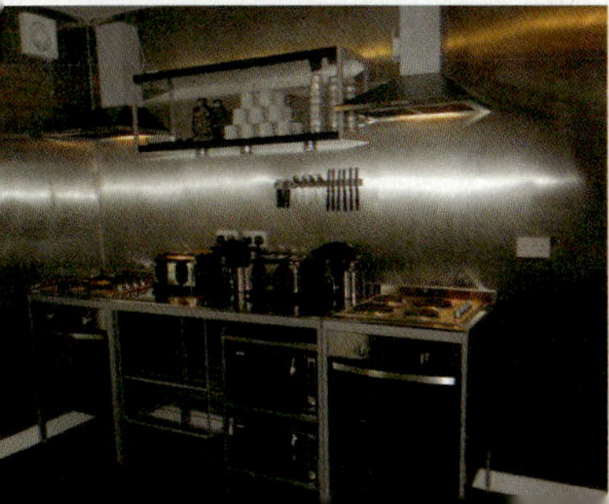

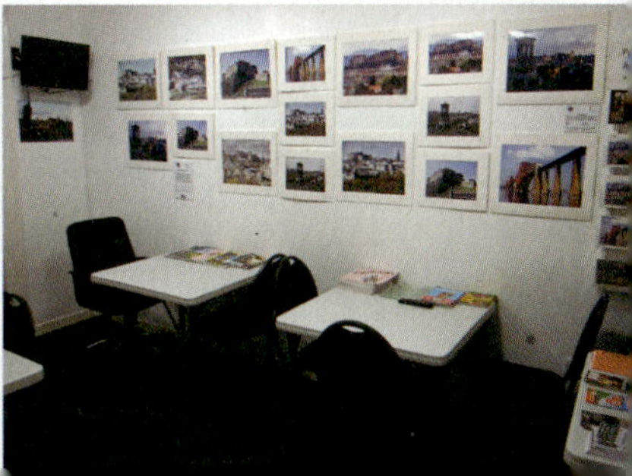

ROYAL MILE BACKPACKERS

SCOTLAND

Royal Mile Backpackers is a small and lively hostel with its own special character! Perfectly located on the Royal Mile, the most famous street in Edinburgh, Royal Mile Backpackers is the ideal place to stay for the independent traveller.

Our comfortable beds and cosy common areas will make you feel at home and our friendly staff are always on hand to help you make the most of your time in Edinburgh.

DETAILS

- **Open** - All year, all day. Reception 7am – 3am (24hrs during August)
- **Number of beds** - 48
- **Booking** - Booking not always essential, 1st night's payment required for booking.
- **Price per night** - From £14 per person. ID required for check in.
- **Public Transport** - Only a 5/10 minute walk from both Edinburgh bus station and Waverley train station. A taxi costs between £3-£5 from each. The airport bus also stops out side the train station on the last stop so is very easy to get to the hostel.
- **Directions** - From main bus station turn left onto Princes Street then take first right onto Northbridge. At top turn left onto the High St. on the Royal Mile. From train station take the Princes Street exit (up Waverley Steps), at top go right then right again up Northbridge, then left at cross roads, hostel's on the left above the Oxfam shop. From airport take bus no.100 to city centre, get off at Waverley Bridge.

Walk away from Princes St. towards the roundabout, go over roundabout onto Cockburn Street. At the top of Cockburn Street turn left onto the High St. on the Royal Mile. Cross traffic lights at Northbridge and hostel is on left above Oxfam.

CONTACT: Receptionist
Tel: 0131 557 6120
royalmile@scotlandstophostels.com www.scotlandstophostels.com
105 High Street, Edinburgh, EH1 1SG

CASTLE ROCK
HOSTEL

401

SCOTLAND

In a wonderful location, facing south with a sunny aspect and panoramic views over the city, Castle Rock Hostel is just steps away from the city centre with the historic Royal Mile, the busy pubs and late-late nightlife of the Grassmarket and Cowgate and of course the Castle. Most of the rooms have no traffic noise, there are loads of great facilities, 24 hour reception and no curfew.

With its beautiful and dramatic skyline Edinburgh is truly one of the world's great cities. The cobbled streets of the Old Town lead past mysterious gothic buildings up to the magnificent castle. Below the castle's rocky pinnacle lies the New Town's 200 year old Georgian splendour.

DETAILS

- **Open** - All year, 24 hours.
- **Number of beds** - 302
- **Booking** - Booking not always essential. First night's payment needed to book.
- **Price per night** - From £14 per person. ID required for check in.
- **Public Transport** - 5/10 minute walk from Edinburgh bus stn and Waverley train stn. (taxis £3-£5). Airport bus goes to train station so it's easy to get to the hostel.
- **Directions** - 10 minutes' walk from Waverley train station – turn left out of the station and continue to small roundabout. Cross over and continue up Cockburn Street to the top. Turn right onto the Royal Mile and follow uphill towards the Castle. Take the left fork at the Hub (church) and the hostel is situated 200 yards on the left side of Johnston Terrace next to two red telephone boxes. By Car – follow signs for city centre towards the Castle turning onto Royal Mile uphill towards the castle then left fork at the Hub on to Johnston Terrace.

CONTACT: Receptionist
Tel: 0131 225 9666
castlerock@scotlandstophostels.com www.scotlandstophostels.com
15 Johnston Terrace, Edinburgh, EH1 2PW

EURO HOSTEL
GLASGOW

SCOTLAND

A smarter alternative to a hotel in the city, with a prime location, five mins' walk from Glasgow Central Station, friendly staff, lively bar and clean comfortable private/shared en suite rooms. Perfect for clubbing, shopping, discovering the city's cultural heritage, vibrant nightlife and live music scene, visiting family, coast to coast cycle rides, sporting events or a good sleep to break a long journey. The hostel's stylish bar "Mint & Lime" provides an all you can eat buffet breakfast and bar meals (12–9pm). It is the perfect place to sit back and relax with other guests, with teas, coffees and a sky sports screen also available. An ideal pre-club venue. Our 24 hour reception will help you with discounted sightseeing tickets, free nightclub tickets, room upgrades and discounted car parking. The hostel offers a self-catering kitchen, dining area and laundry. Group dinners and half board packages can be arranged. FREE WiFi and internet kiosks throughout. Five mins' drive from the new Hydro, SECC and Clyde auditorium. Five mins' walk to the arches, 02 academy & Hamden.

DETAILS

- **Open** - All year, early check-in/late check-outs no problem
- **Number of beds** - 364: single, doubles, twins, 4, 8 and 14 person all en suite
- **Booking** - Book online with 10% deposit, Full balance within 28 days for groups.
- **Price per night** - From £10 B&B pp en suite. Discount available online at www.euro-hostels.co.uk. Ask about our group discounts.
- **Public Transport** - Central Railway Station 2 mins, Queen Street Railway Station 7 mins, Buchanan Bus Station 10 mins, Glasgow Airport 8 miles.
- **Directions** - The hostel is on the corner of Jamaica Street and Clyde Street.

CONTACT: Reception
Tel: 0141 222 2828, Fax: 0141 222 2829
glasgow@euro-hostels.co.uk www.euro-hostels.co.uk
318 Clyde Street, Glasgow, G1 4NR

KILMORY LODGE
BUNKHOUSE

403

SCOTLAND

Kilmory Lodge Bunkhouse provides ideal group accommodation in a tranquil, rural setting. The Isle of Arran is one of the most accessible Scottish islands, only one hour by ferry from the mainland. It offers the visitor hill-walking, mountaineering, golf, fishing, cycling, pony trekking and a bewildering choice of extreme sports. The bunkhouse is affordable, modern, comfortable and able to sleep up to 23. All the bed linen is supplied, so there's no need to bring anything except your towels and food! There is a great, contemporary kitchen with all you'll need. Attached to the bunkhouse is the village hall which can provide extra rooms and an auditorium at extra cost. Ideal for educational groups, weddings, music workshop groups, clubs or any group needing extra facilities. Kilmory Lodge welcomes your family, club, group, school or any combination of these except stag parties! Also adjoining the Bunkhouse is the 1934 Club (Social Club) which is open at the weekend. Phone or email with your queries. Registered Scottish Charity SC028200.

DETAILS

- **Open** - All year, 24 hours
- **Number of beds** - 23: 2 x 8, 1 x 4 (en suite) 1 x 3 (en suite)
- **Booking** - Book ahead, 40% deposit. £150 security deposit on arrival.
- **Price per night** - £16 per person for groups of 15+. £21 pp for smaller groups.
- **Public Transport** - Buses stop on demand directly outside the Hall and Bunkhouse. These buses meet all the ferries that arrive and depart from the main ferry terminal at Brodick.
- **Directions** - Bunkhouse attached to Kilmory Public Hall located in village centre.

CONTACT: Jean Clark
Tel: 01770 870345
kilmory.hall@btinternet.com   www.kilmoryhall.com
Kilmory, Isle of Arran, KA27 8PQ

CAMPBELTOWN BACKPACKERS

SCOTLAND

The Campbeltown Backpackers is housed in the newly refurbished Old Schoolhouse, a Grade B listed building. Offering easy access to the facilities of Campbeltown including swimming pool, gym, the "wee toon" cinema and Springbank distillery tours, it is a good final stop along the Kintyre Way which gives walkers spectacular views of the surrounding islands. The area also enjoys very good wind surfing, surfing, mountain bike routes and other major cycle trails as well as golf, horse riding along beaches or forest trails, and geocaching from the Network Centre in Carradale. Kintyre is full of cultural and historical interest being the place where St Columba came ashore from Northern Ireland bringing Christianity to Scotland. Robert the Bruce spent time in Kintyre on his way to Rathlin, whilst the beach at Saddell was the location for Paul McCartney and Wings' video for "Mull of Kintyre". For wildlife lovers the Kintyre Peninsula is a great place to see otters. seals and even golden eagles as well as red, roe and sika deer.

DETAILS

- **Open** - All Year, out by 10.30am on day of departure.
- **Number of beds** - 16 1x6, 1x10
- **Booking** - By email, only phone if you require a booking within 4 days
- **Price per night** - £18 per person
- **Public Transport** - 5 buses a day from Glasgow (926). Passenger and cycle ferry links to Northern Ireland and Troon. The islands of Gigha, Islay, Jura and Arran are all served by ferries. Two flights per day to and from Glasgow International Airport
- **Directions** - Adjacent to the Heritage Centre on the B842 towards Machrihanish

CONTACT: Alan
Tel: 01586 551188
info@campbeltownbackpackers.co.uk   www.campbeltownbackpackers.co.uk
Kintyre Amenity Trust, Big Kiln, Campbeltown, Argyll, PA28 6JF

WELCOME
Campbeltown BACKPACKERS
Tel: 01586 551188

IFFERDALE FARM BUNKHOUSE

SCOTLAND

A warm welcome awaits you at Ifferdale, a working family farm set deep in the countryside at the head of Saddell Glen. The farm buildings have been renovated to provide a bunkhouse and three self-catering cottages with a district heating system and lots of hot water. The farm is managed sustainably producing beef and lamb, and is surrounded by ancient forests buzzing with wildlife. There is a fantastic beach at Saddell and activities available in Kintyre include golf, sailing, walking, surfing, fishing, stargazing or simply mucking about on the beaches and enjoying quality Scottish fayre. Campbeltown has a leisure centre with swimming pool and other rainy-day activities. The Bunkhouse sleeps 8 and shares its kitchen and dining accommodation with The Bothy which sleeps 2-3. The other two cottages are ideal for couples or families. Towels and linen are provided. Eggs, beef and lamb produced by the farm are available and evening meals and packed lunches can be ordered in advance.

DETAILS

- **Open** - All year round,
- **Number of beds** - 17: 8: Bunkhouse, 2-3: Bothy, 2-4: Hayloft, 2: Loosebox
- **Booking** - Full payment to secure. Deposit taken for longer group bookings.
- **Price per night** - From £24 per person in bunkhouse. Hayloft £80 per night, min of 2 nights. £420 a week. Loose box £60 per night, weekly rate available.
- **Public Transport** - West Coast Motors Cambeltown to Carradale Bus stops in Saddell (2 miles away), Buses connect Cambeltown to Glasgow
- **Directions** - On the B842 10 miles north of Campbeltown, North of Saddell take turning west signed Ifferdale Farm. Follow lane 1.5m to farm.

CONTACT: Monica Gemmill
Tel: 01583 431666
ifferdale@gmail.com Ifferdalefarm.co.uk
Ifferdale Farm, Saddell By Campbeltown, PA28 6QZ

BUTE
BACKPACKERS HOSTEL SCOTLAND

Bute Backpackers, a friendly independent hostel with panoramic views of Rothesay seafront, has 40 beds with a mixture of single, twin, double and family rooms. The main house has a sea front sun lounge with woodburner and open fire. The self-catering kitchen is equipped to the highest standard and there is a large seafront dining room with catering facilities. Some of the rooms are en suite and there are separate male and female showers and toilets on each level. There is also a separate self-contained cottage dorm with its own fully equipped kitchen and bathroom. Other facilities include Sky TV, internet, WiFi access, drying room and laundry. There is a private car park for twelve cars and secure bike racks. There are regular live music sessions which includes open mic for any budding musos to join the fun. VisitScotland rated as 4 star.

DETAILS

- **Open** - All year, 24hr access, no curfew. Reception 10am - 10pm.
- **Number of beds** - 40: Main House 32 in 14 rooms; Cottage 8.
- **Booking** - Deposit only required for group bookings.
- **Price per night** - From £20 per person.
- **Public Transport** - Take train to Wemyes Bay Station and Ferry Port (40 mins from Glasgow Central). Then ferry to Rothesay, Isle of Bute. Hostel 900m from ferry or take a taxi (taxi rank adjacent to port) which costs approximately £2.50.
- **Directions** - Turn right as you leave ferry and walk straight ahead for 200m past the discovery centre and putting green. Continue straight ahead for another 250m and Bute Backpackers is on your left. By car turn right on to main road. Continue for 300m to the mini roundabout. Head straight on for a further 300m and the hostel and access to the private car park is adjacent to the main road on your left.

CONTACT: Reception
Tel: 01700 501876
butebackpackers@hotmail.com www.butebackpackers.co.uk
The Pier View, 36 Argyle Street, Rothesay, Isle of Bute, PA20 0AX

TORRAN BAY HOSTEL

SCOTLAND

With 16 en suite rooms and great views of Loch Awe, Torran Bay Hostel is the perfect base for a fantastic Highlands holiday. Free fishing from Torran Farm land is included, or why not venture out on the loch? Boat and canoe launching is available along with a large parking area. Boat hire can be arranged through the hostel. Just 30 miles from Oban, 13 miles from Lochgilphead and close to the Crinnan canal, Torran Bay is located at the south end of Loch Awe which is 25 miles long. Excellent for fishing for brown trout, pike, arctic char, perch and roach or just a day relaxing on the loch with TBFL boat hire. Other activities include Walking, on Torran Farm land and beyond, hiking, cycling, bird watching and golf. The hostel can accomodate up to 40 guests, with rooms arranged in different combinations, has two well equipped kitchens for self-catering and the local Indian/Chinese takeaway delivers to the hostel. Prices inlude continental breakfast and all rooms have TV, DVD and WiFi

DETAILS

- **Open** - All year round. All day
- **Number of beds** - 38:10 x 2, or double, 2 x double and single, 1 x 4 , 2 x 3
- **Booking** - booking 4 rooms or more, full payment required 14 days before arrival
- **Price per night** - from £45 to £72 per room. inc continental breakfast and parking. Group bookings welcome. Please note. prices per room not per person.
- **Public Transport** - Buses Lochgilphead to Ford, Monday, Wednesday and Saturday
- **Directions** - From Glasgow take A82 to Tarbet then take the A83 to Lochgilphead, Lochgilphead to Kilmartin A816. 1 mile past Kilmartin follow signs to Ford B840. From Ford take Dalavich road for 1 mile. Hostel on the right.

CONTACT: Joachim or Sheila Brolly
Tel: 01546 810 133 or 01546 810 270
torranbayhostel@mail.com www.torran-bay.co.uk
Torran Farm, Ford,Lochgilphead. PA31 8RH

INVERARAY HOSTEL

SCOTLAND

Inveraray Hostel is a purpose-built wooden building in extensive grounds. An excellent self-catering kitchen, plus dining and sitting areas, provide a friendly ambience where the staff encourage guests to interact. Small 2 or 4 bed dorms make the hostel equally suitable for solo travellers, couples, families and small groups. Bed linen is provided and towels are available for hire. A large car park, bike shed and drying room are available.

Inveraray is a small planned town in the southern Highlands of Scotland with a range of shops, restaurants, 2 pubs and a cash machine. Attractions include a magnificent C18th castle set in wooded grounds and gardens, and a jail where you can experience the lifestyle of former inmates! There are local forest walks and a modest climb to a viewpoint with a fantastic view down the loch. From Inveraray you can drive to access points for several Munros and the famous "Cobbler". Well-located for cyclists, walkers, motor bikers and those touring Scotland by car.

DETAILS
- **Open** - March to October. Sole-use October to March. Reception 5pm-9pm
- **Number of beds** - 28: 4 x 4, 6 x 2, all bunk beds
- **Booking** - On website. Larger groups and families book by email.
- **Price per night** - From £17pp. Families please enquire. Breakfast £3.50 May-Sept.
- **Public Transport** - Bus 926 or 976 from Glasgow (about 6 per day, 7 days). Bus 976 from Oban (3 per day, 7 days). Bus 926 from Campbeltown.
- **Directions** - From A83 at Inveraray take A819, hostel 200m on left.

CONTACT: Manager
Tel: 01499 302 454
enquiry@inverarayhostel.co.uk www.inverarayhostel.co.uk
Dalmally Road, Inveraray, Argyll, PA32 8XD

BALMAHA
SCOTLAND BUNKHOUSE / HOSTEL

Set on the banks of Loch Lomond on the West Highland Way, Balmaha Bunkhouse offers quality assured accommodation for up to 14 at an affordable price. Continental breakfast, bedding, WiFi, tea and coffee are included and there is a self-catering kitchen. The bunkhouse is ideal for hen, stag and family get togethers, corporate away-days, meetings, conferences or as a base to explore the wider area. There is a private self-catering chalet called The Roost sleeping 4 people in a double bed and one set of bunks and Bed & Breakfast in the main house with en suite rooms and breathtaking views over the loch. The accommodation is situated on the shores of Loch Lomond, just 5 minutes paddling to the first of the islands (Inchcailloch), from where you can explore other islands with ancient graveyards with the burial place of Rob Roy`s cousin and scenic landscapes. Kayaks and canadian canoes can be hired on site. Friendly dogs welcome, please visit our website for details. Welcome to the romantic, adventurous and beautiful experience of Loch Lomond.

DETAILS

- **Open** - All year subject to availability. Arrive 2pm-7pm leave before 10am
- **Number of beds** - Bunkhouse 14: 1x6,1x4 (family),1x2 (double/twin),1x2 (twin); The Roost 4: 1x4; B&B: 1xDbl, 1x2(bunks)
- **Booking** - phone or email for availability. Book in writing. Nov-Feb Groups 6+ only.
- **Price per night** - £20pp. Sole use of bunkhouse £280. Chalet £80. Dog (in bunkhouse only) £5, B&B £35. No credit/debit cards.
- **Public Transport** - Train from Glasgow Queen Street to Balloch then 309 Bus.
- **Directions** - Opposite the bay and the telephone box. Bus stop 100m from hostel

CONTACT: Jock and Gwen Cousin
Tel: 01360 870 218 Mob: 07921 293285
jock@balmahahouse.co.uk www.balmahahouse.co.uk
Balmaha, Loch Lomond, Stirlingshire, G63 0JQ

TROSSACHS TRYST

SCOTLAND

411

Now whole house groups only. Trossachs Tryst has been purpose-built on its own 8 acre site, set amidst beautiful scenery (on Sustrans route 7c) just outside the bustling tourist town of Callander. This Visit Scotland 4 star hostel provices quality, comfortable accomodation, finished to a very high standard and has won accolades in many guide books and websites.

The rooms are all en suite and are either 8, 6 or 4 bedded. The 4 bed family rooms can be used as twin rooms on request. There is a spacious dining/common room, well equipped kitchen, and drying room. The Hostel has a large comfortably furnished sitting room with great views to the surrounding hills. There is an on-site cycling centre. Other activities available locally include hill walking, pony trekking, Go-ape, Segway treks, canoe hire/instruction, fishing and sailing.

DETAILS

- **Open** - All year (Sept to June, whole hostel bookings only),   Reception 8am - 9pm
- **Number of beds** - 30
- **Booking** - Groups must book with deposit.
- **Price per night** - From £17 including linen and free tea/coffee. 2 night minimum with discounts for 4 nights or longer.
- **Public Transport** - Nearest train station is at Stirling (15 miles). Nearest Citylink coach stop is at Callander (1.5 miles). Pick up from Callander can usually be arranged.
- **Directions** - GR 606 072. The hostel is situated one mile up Invertrossachs Rd from its junction with the A81 (Glasgow Rd) in Callander.

CONTACT: Mark or Janet
Tel: 01877 331200
info@scottish-hostel.com www.trossachstryst.com
Invertrossachs Road, Callander, Perthshire, FK17 8HW

CALLANDER HOSTEL

SCOTLAND

Situated within the village of Callander at the start of the Loch Lomond and Trossachs National Park, Callander Hostel is a great location for tourists and outdoor enthusiasts alike. With outstanding views over Ben Ledi this Visit Scotland 5 star Hostel has recently been refurbished to a high standard. The comfortable beds, en suite rooms and fully equipped self-catering kitchen will ensure that you have all you need for the perfect retreat. The bunk beds have a utility board with reading lights, plug sockets and USB charging facilities. The hostel has a bright, spacious lounge with comfy sofas, WiFi and a wood burning stove. The gardens have a childrens play area, BBQ pods and seating to enjoy the stunning views. Callander is known as the Gateway to the Highlands and has walking and cycling routes, golf, fishing, sailing, horse riding and canoeing. Callander Hostel is an inspiration from the Callander Youth Project. The hostels website www.callanderhostel.co.uk will be available soon

DETAILS

- **Open** - Open all year, all day
- **Number of beds** - 26: 2 x 8, 1 x 6, 2 x twin/double
- **Booking** - Debit/credit card secures booking
- **Price per night** - £18.50 per person in dorm, £60 per twin/double en suite room.
- **Public Transport** - There is a bus from Stirling to Callander. Easy walk from bus stop to the hostel. Exit the bus at Ancaster Square, turn left and walk down the street to the "Golf Shop", then turn left on to Bridgend.
- **Directions** - From A84 in Callander turn onto Bridgend and cross the bridge. Callander Hostel is on the right hand side just over the bridge.

CONTACT: Reception
Tel: 01877 331465
bookings@callanderhostel.co.uk   www.callanderyouthproject.co.uk
6 Bridgend, Callander, FK17 8AH

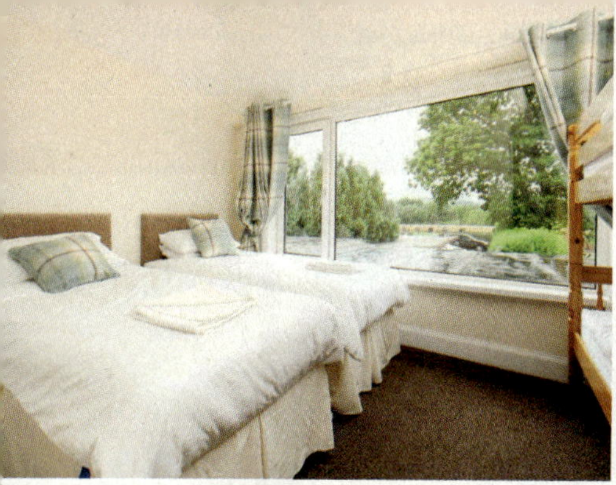
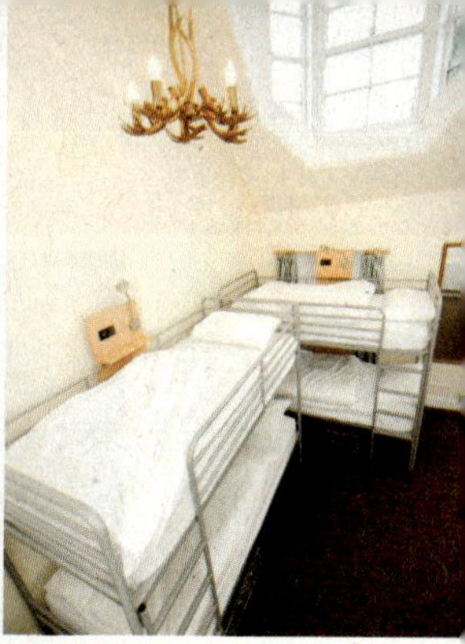
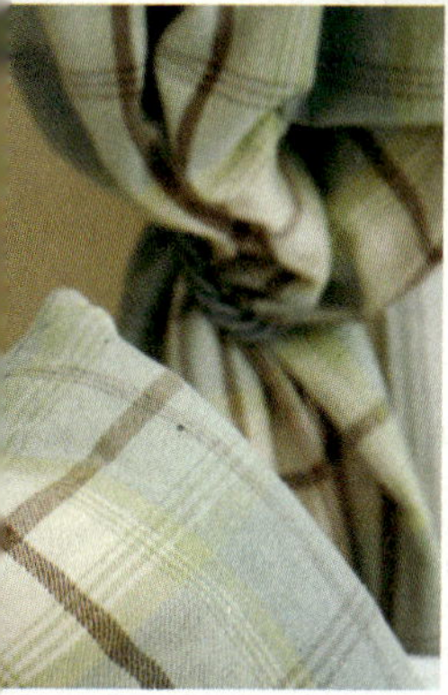
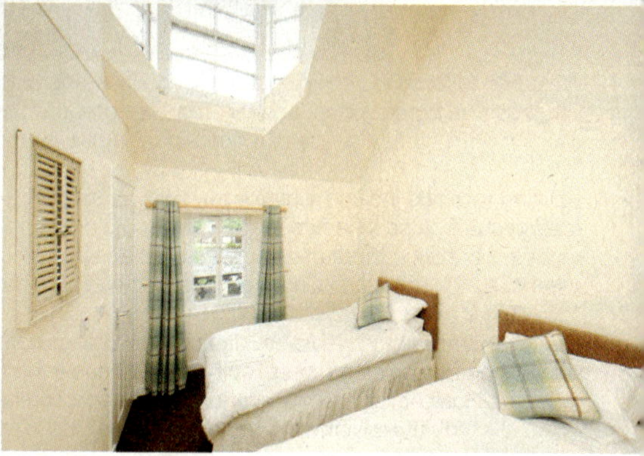
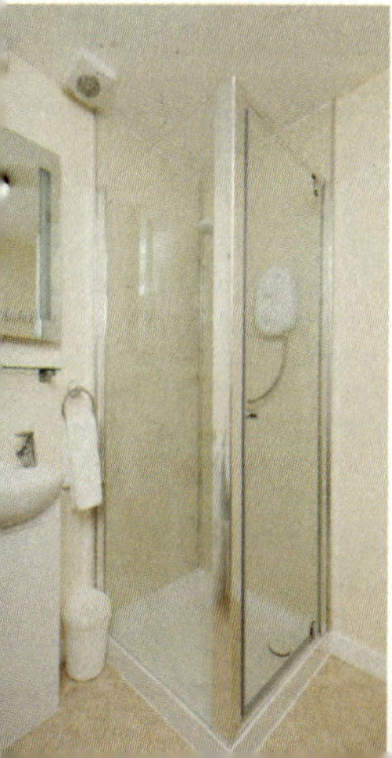
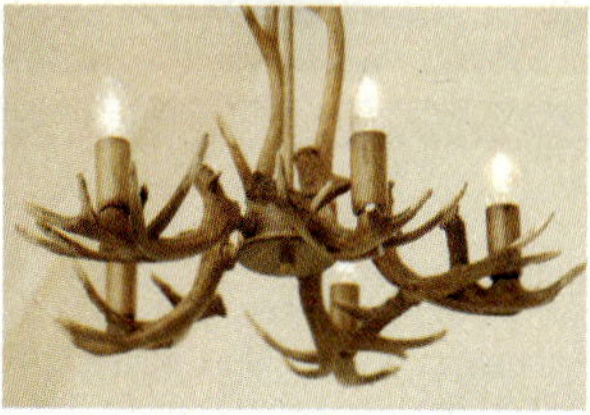
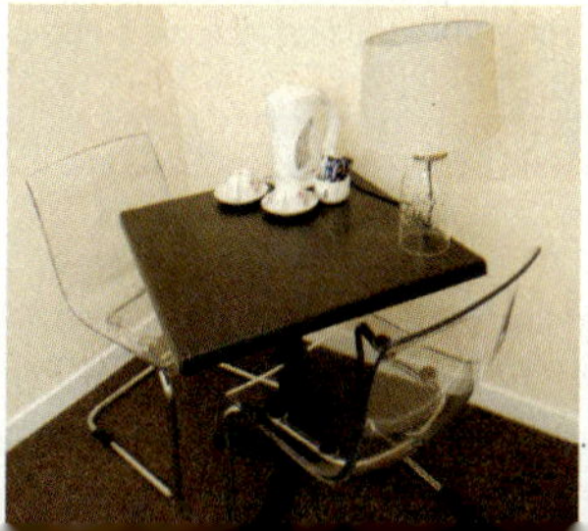
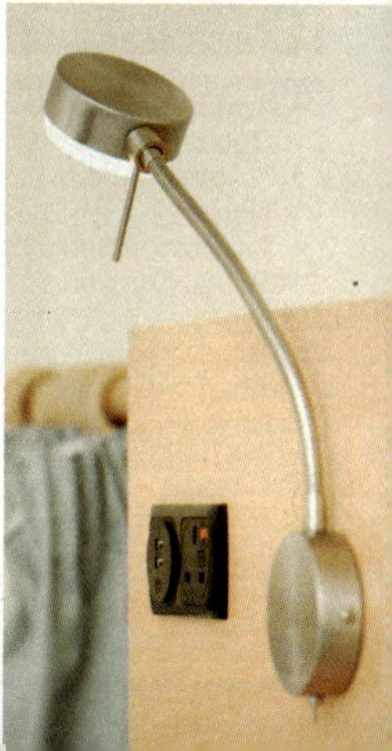

COMRIE CROFT

SCOTLAND

Welcome to Scotland's Hiking and Mountain Biking Hostel. 4* hostel, camping with fires and nordic katas, and the Tea Garden Cafe combine with NEW hiking and mountain-biking trails.

Biking facilities include a bike park, swoopy single-track and family-friendly valley routes. Also bike hire for all ages and a workshop should you need any repairs. For hiking there are four way-marked trails on site and a new link path to the village, glens and mountains beyond.

Just over an hour's drive from Edinburgh or Glasgow, the Croft is great for any kind of getaway on wheels or legs. You can even get married there! Comrie Croft holds a 'Gold' award in the Green Tourism Business Scheme. Guests arriving without a car get a 10% discount.

DETAILS

- **Open** - All year. All day
- **Number of beds** - 56 + 46 + 14 (3 units)
- **Booking** - Recommended
- **Price per night** - From £16 adults, £8 U16, U5 free.
- **Public Transport** - Train stations: Dunblane, Stirling, or Perth. Our own bus stop is served by no. 15 from Perth (approx. every hour). Summer only Citylink service to Oban and Fort William. Ring of Breadalbane hop-on hop-off service from Easter to October (see breadalbane.org)
- **Directions** - Signposted from A85 between Crieff (5miles) and Comrie (2miles).

CONTACT:
Tel: 01764 670140
info@comriecroft.com www.comriecroft.com
Comrie Croft, By Crieff/Comrie, Perthshire, PH7 4JZ

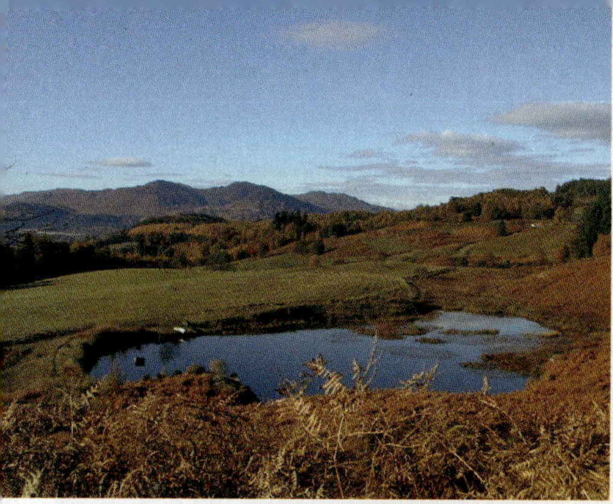
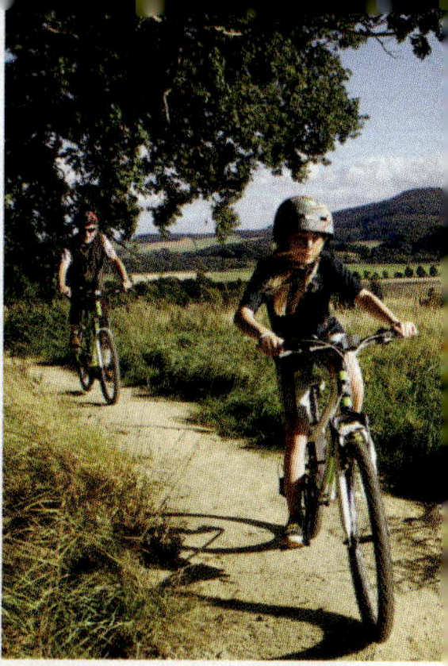
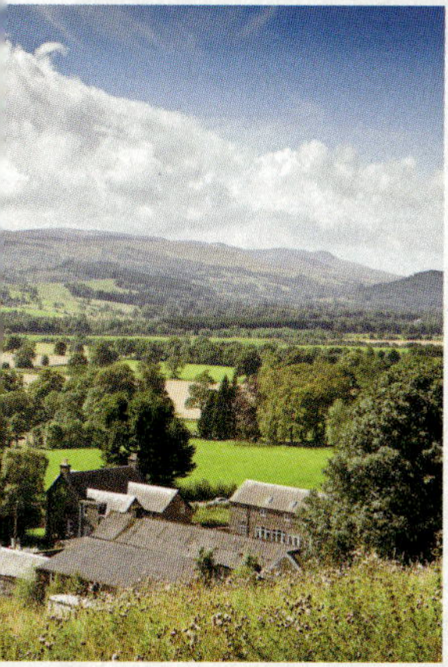
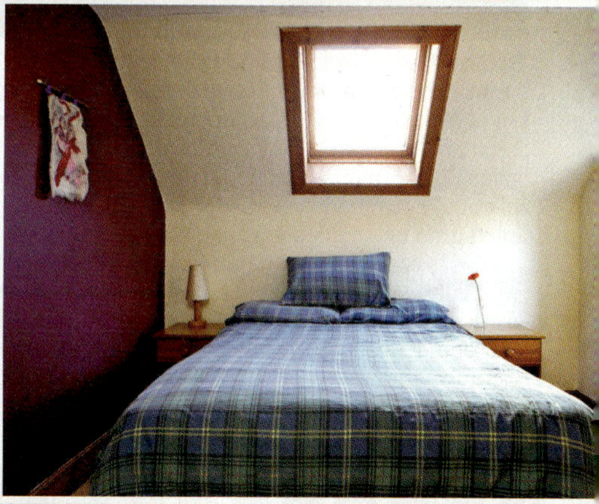
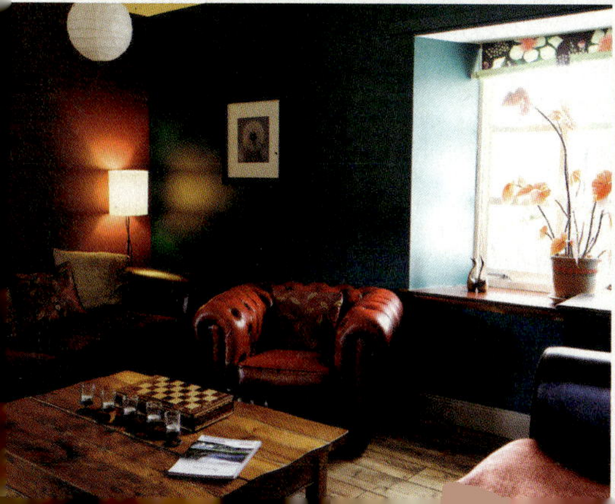
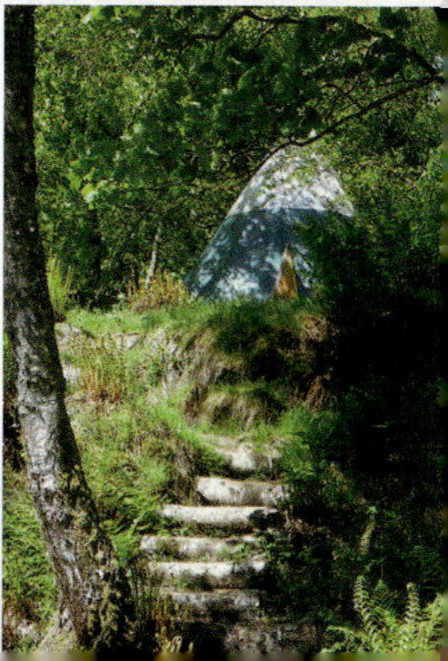

BY THE WAY
HOSTEL AND CAMPSITE
SCOTLAND

By The Way Hostel and Campsite can be found in the Loch Lomond National Park halfway between Arrochar's peaks and the grandeur of Glencoe. The site is aimed primarily at outdoor enthusiasts and with great walking (the West Highland Way passes by the hostel), climbing, and white water rafting, there is lots to be enthusiastic about (Munro-baggers can find 50 Munros within 20 miles). Accommodation options range from camping (with an indoor cooking/dining area and campers' drying room), basic trekker huts/cabins (own cooking utensils required) and a purpose built four star hostel with twin and double rooms as well as dormitory accommodation, great self-catering facilities and drying room. For more comfort still there's a three bedroom chalet and two bedroom chalet. By The Way is in Tyndrum with the village pub, shops, café and Tourist Information Centre nearby. The Glasgow to Fort William road is 250m from the site (far from the madding traffic noise) and both the Glasgow Oban and Glasgow Fort William trains stop in Tyndrum.

DETAILS

- **Open** - All year. Camping from April to end September. 8am - 10am & 2pm - 8pm
- **Number of beds** - 26 in hostel; 36 in huts; 50 camping.
- **Booking** - Always phone in advance. Deposit (Visa/Access) guarantees bed.
- **Price per night** - Hostel dorms from £18pp. Huts vary in price. Camping £8pp
- **Public Transport** - Intercity coach and rail service pick-up points in Tyndrum to Edinburgh, Glasgow, Fort William and Oban. Sleeper service to London.
- **Directions** - GR NN 327 302. Travelling on A82 follow sign in village for Tyndrum Lower Station. Hostel is immediately before station.

CONTACT: Kirsty Burnett
Tel: 01838 400333
info@TyndrumByTheWay.com   www.TyndrumByTheWay.com
Lower Station Road, Tyndrum, FK20 8RY

WESTER CAPUTH STEADING

SCOTLAND

Wester Caputh Steading Hostel can be found in the peaceful village of Caputh, 4 miles east of Dunkeld on the River Tay. Located in central Perthshire, it is just over an hour's travel from Edinburgh and Glasgow. Dunkeld is delightful, centred around a medieval square and Cathedral. There are excellent cycling routes nearby, and beautiful woodland and river walks. The River Tay offers some of the best rafting, canoeing and fishing in the country, the wildlife in the area is plentiful and there are five castles and four distilleries within an hour's drive. The Hostel has five bunk bedrooms and there is a large comfortable living area with wood-burning stove and a kitchen equipped for all your cooking needs. Outside is a paved patio and a large grassy area to the rear with picnic benches and charcoal BBQ.

DETAILS

- **Open** - Closed mid-week during the winter months, check-in from 4pm
- **Number of beds** - 16: 3x2, 1x4, 1x6
- **Booking** - Booking advisable
- **Price per night** - from £18 for all beds used, babies in cot free.
- **Public Transport** - Train station at Birnam (5 miles). Hourly Stagecoach bus from Perth (Mill St), ask for Caputh Village. Infrequent buses from Dunkeld. Local taxis.
- **Directions** - From north: From A9 take A923 to Dunkeld. After Dunkeld bridge turn right onto A984 to Caputh (4.5 miles). After church on right turn right (B9099) then 1st right at foot of hill. A few hundred yards on right (long white building). From south: From A9 take B9099 through Luncarty and Murthly. Cross river into Caputh. Turn left at foot of hill (signed Dunkeld). A few hundred yards on right (long white building).

CONTACT: Lesley Sibbald
Tel: 07977 904198 , Fax: +44 (0) 7977 904198
info@westercaputh.co.uk www.westercaputh.co.uk
Manse Road, Caputh, By Dunkeld, Perthshire, PH1 4JH

PITLOCHRY BACKPACKERS HOTEL
SCOTLAND

Located right in the centre of beautiful Pitlochry, this friendly and comfortable hostel is an old Victorian hotel literally bursting with character and providing dorms and private rooms (with en suite). Comfy beds come with fitted sheets, duvets and 2 fluffy pillows and private rooms have fresh towels included. If you are visiting Pitlochry to enjoy the vast array of outdoor activities or simply want to get away from it all and relax, the hostel has everything you need to ensure you make the most of your time in this beautiful Perthshire town. Overlooking the street below, the bright spacious lounge has comfy sofas and as much free tea, coffee and hot chocolate as you can drink. It also has free WiFi, loads of local information, some games and musical instruments and a free pool table. A separate Movie Lounge has comfy sofas and loads of films to chose from. A great place to meet like minded people and although you might think you're only staying one night, you'll end up staying three or four - it's that kind of place!

DETAILS

- **Open** - March to November, 7.30am-1pm & 5pm-10pm (please check at reception as times may vary).
- **Number of beds** - 79.
- **Booking** - Booking in advance not always essential, first night's payment required.
- **Price per night** - From £15pp for dorms. Private rooms from £20 pp
- **Public Transport** - Buses stop on Atholl Road and the hostel is only 1min walk. The train station exits onto Atholl Road also, only 5 mins' walk.
- **Directions** - Take the A924 Atholl road from the A9 the hostel is on the right if coming from the south and left if coming from the north as customer carpark behind the building is accessed from Birnham Place (just past/before the hostel).

CONTACT: Receptionist
Tel: 01796 470044
info@pitlochrybackpackershotel.com www.pitlochrybackpackershotel.com
134 Atholl Road, Pitlochry, PH16 5AB

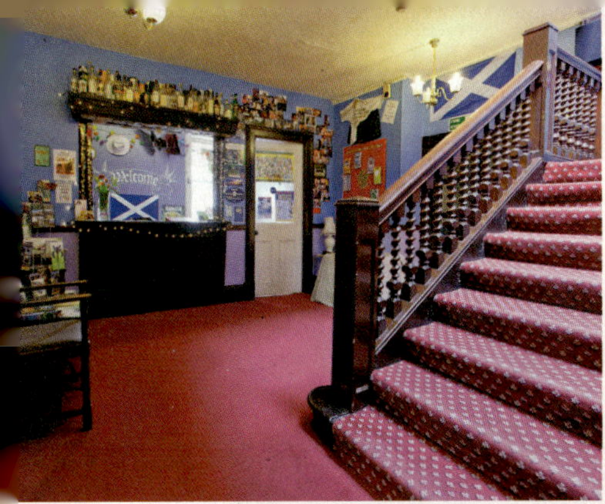
Welcome
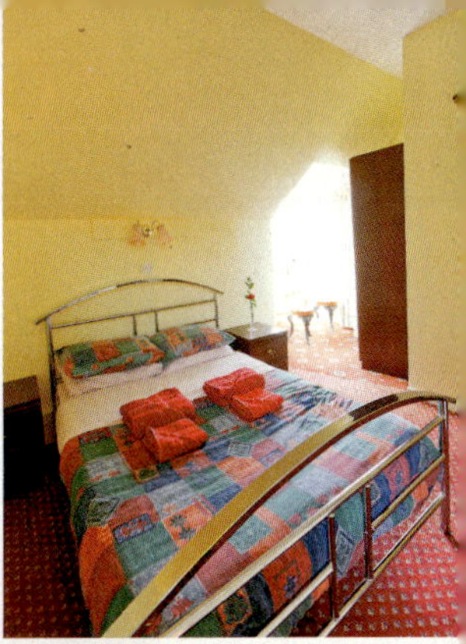
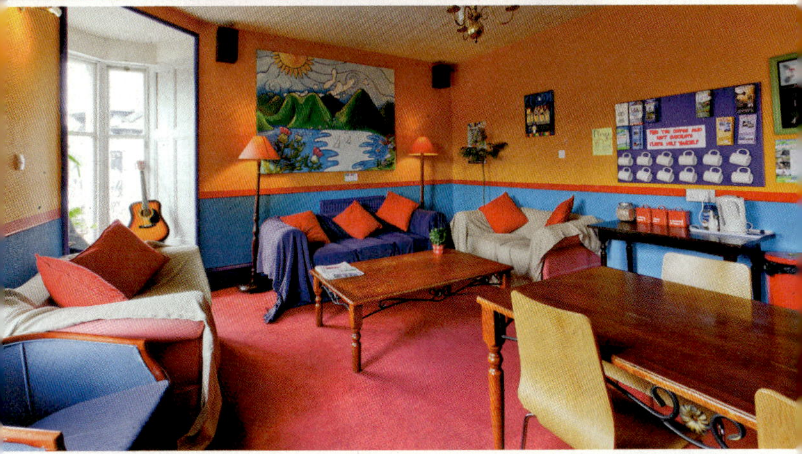
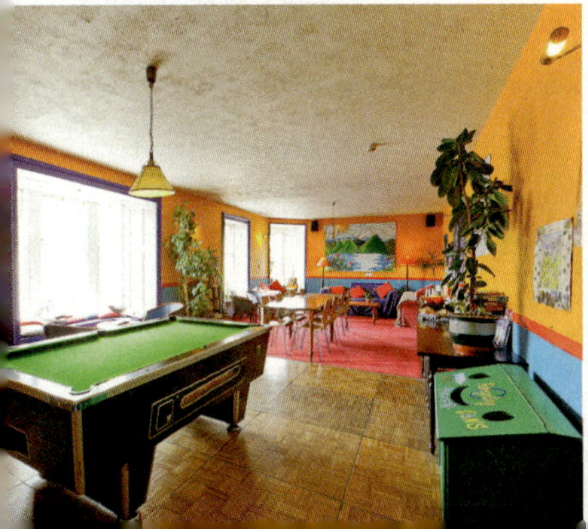
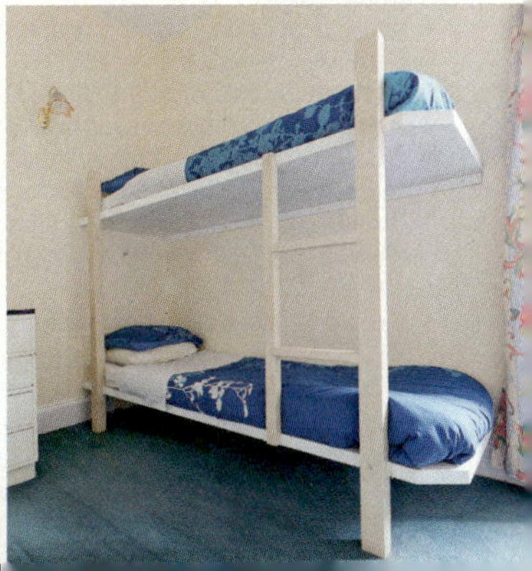

GULABIN LODGE

SCOTLAND

Gulabin Lodge is beautifully situated in the heart of Glenshee at the foot of Beinn Gulabin and is the nearest accommodation to the Glenshee Ski Slopes. The lodge offers excellent accommodation for individuals, families and groups, has under-floor heating throughout and two cosy lounges with log fires for those colder months. All rooms have been tastefully decorated with some rooms having mezzanine platforms which are ideal for families. Based on site at the lodge there are many activities available for all ages and abilities including a Ski School and equipment hire facility for the winter months. The lodge is an ideal base for schools groups and for activities such as climbing, walking or mountain biking. Mountain bike hire and guided trips are also available. Meals can be provided for groups and also transport to and from airports and rail stations. Registered 4 Star VisitScotland Activity Accommodation provider. AALA Registered L9768/R1801.

DETAILS

- **Open** - All year, 24 hours
- **Number of beds** - 37: 9 rooms available.
- **Booking** - Booking advisable.
- **Price per night** - From £20pp self catering. Family rooms, twins, 4 person and 6 person rooms. Full board available. Sole use available.
- **Public Transport** - Train and bus stations at Pitlochry (22 miles), Blairgowrie (20 miles), Glasgow (100 miles), Edinburgh (70 miles). Post bus calls half a mile away.
- **Directions** - Gulabin Lodge is on the A93 road at Spittal of Glenshee - 20 miles north of Blairgowrie and 19 miles south of Braemar. Transport can be arranged.

CONTACT: Darren and Tereza
Tel: 01250 885255 Mobile: 07799 847014
info@gulabinlodge.co.uk www.gulabinoutdoors.co.uk
Spittal of Glenshee, By Blairgowrie, PH10 7QE

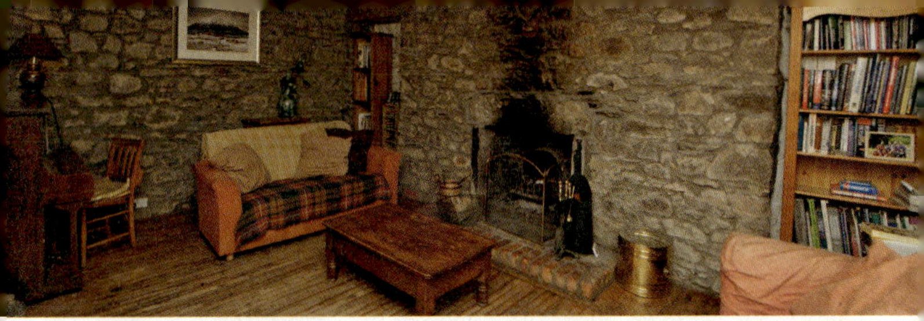
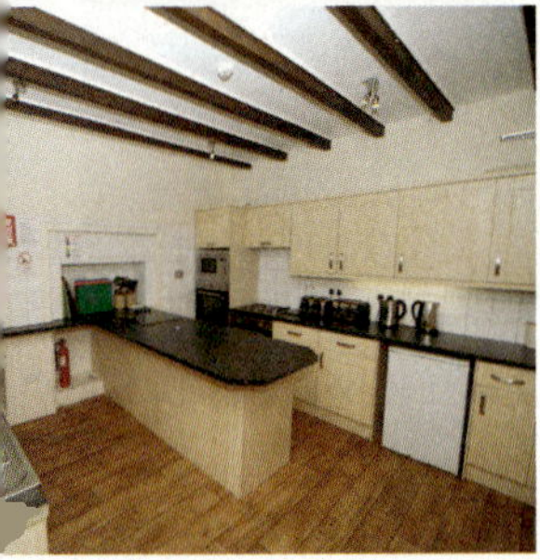
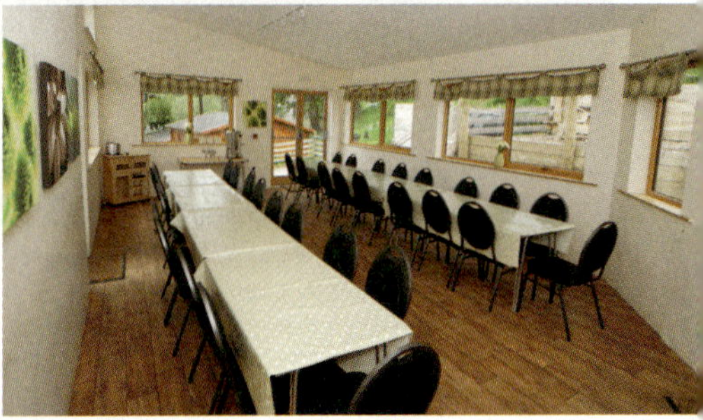
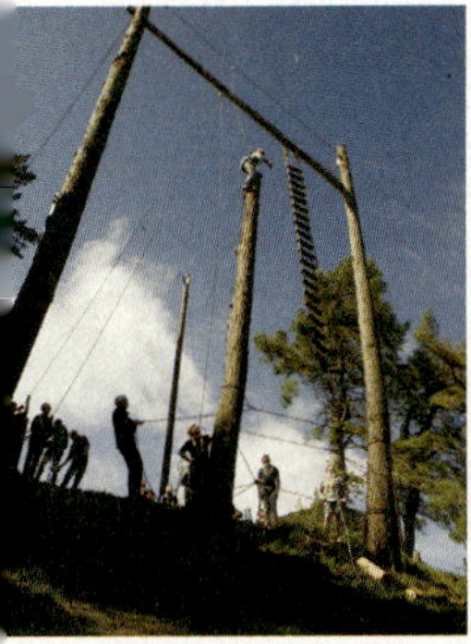
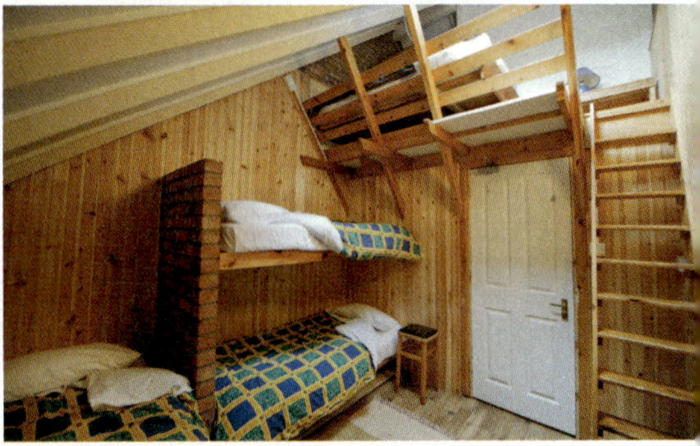
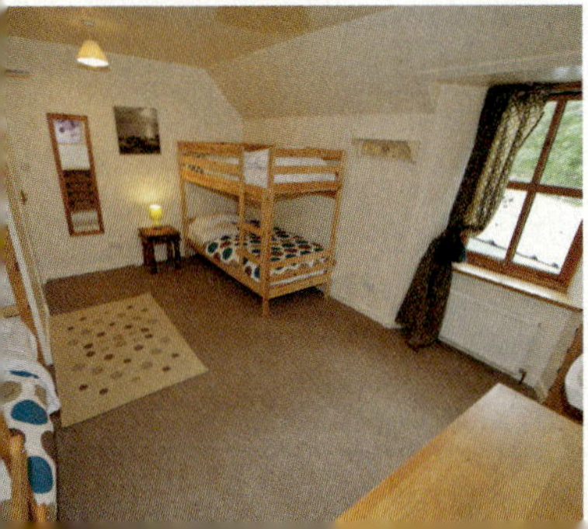
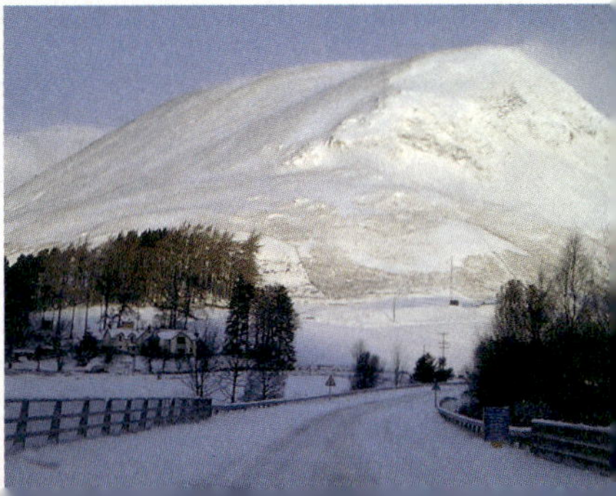

PROSEN HOSTEL
SCOTLAND

Glenprosen is the most intimate of the Angus Glens on the southernmost edge of the Cairngorms National Park. Two Munros, the Mayar and Driesh link Glenprosen to the Cairngorms plateau. The Minister's Path leads over to Glen Clova, whilst a new footbridge and path along the prettiest stretch of the river Prosen connect to Glenisla and the Cateran Trail in Perthshire. Prosen Hostel was recently converted from an old school to provide accommodation for those using the upgraded East Cairngorms footpath network. Converted to the latest and greenest specification, the living room has a wood burning stove, internet connection, and raised area for admiring the view (and red squirrels) through the school's huge windows. A drying room and laundry facilities complete the cosy welcome. It sleeps a total of 18 in 4 bunkrooms, sleeping 4, 4 and 6 and a family room sleeping 4. The nearby village hall is available to rent for ceilidhs, music sessions, parties and celebrations. STB 4 star.

DETAILS

- **Open** - All year, all day
- **Number of beds** - 18:1x6, 3x4
- **Booking** - Book by phone or email.
- **Price per night** - £17 - £20 per person. Minimum periods apply for Christmas and New year.
- **Public Transport** - Trains Dundee; buses Kirriemuir (regular to Dundee and Forfar)
- **Directions** - From Kirriemuir follow B955 signed to Prosen, Clova and Cairngorms National Park. At Dykehead fork left. Carry on for 7 miles until public road ends at telephone kiosk. Turn acute right and follow tarmac 200m uphill to hostel.

CONTACT: Hector or Robert
Tel: 01575 540238/302
sih@prosenhostel.co.uk www.prosenhostel.co.uk
Prosen Hostel, Balnaboth, Kirriemuir, Angus, DD8 4SA

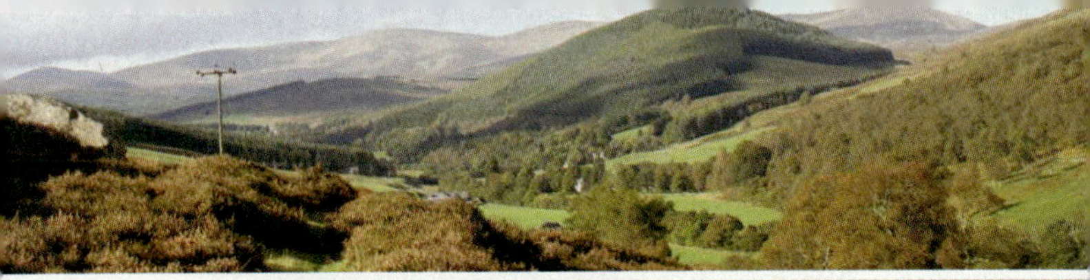
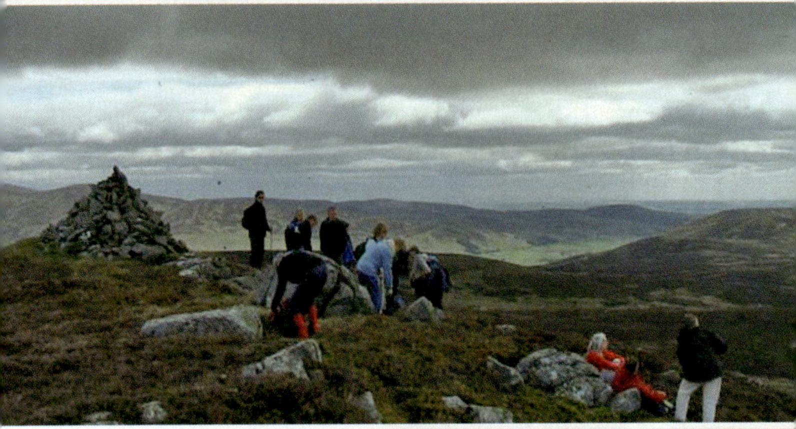
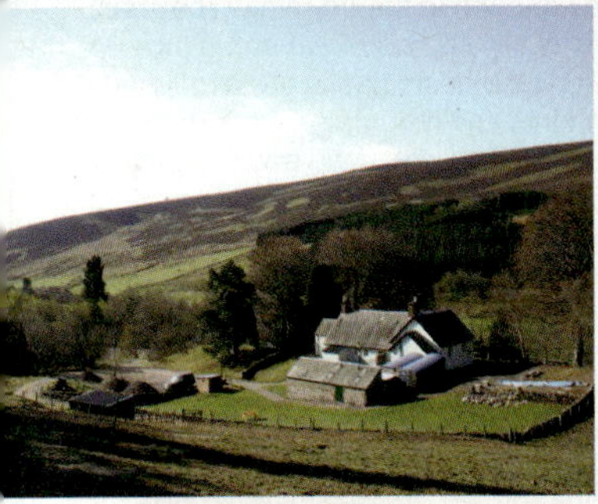
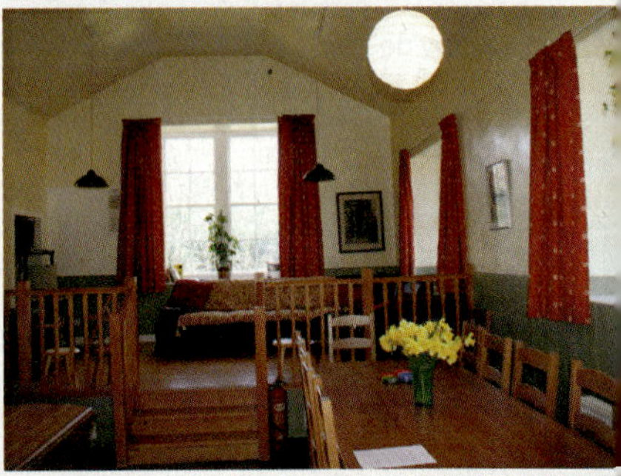
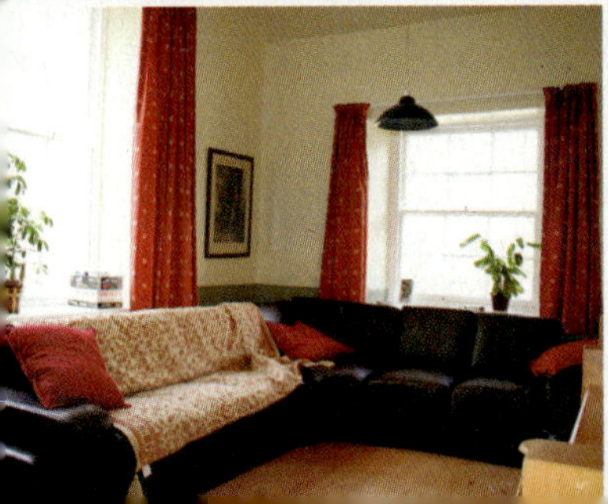
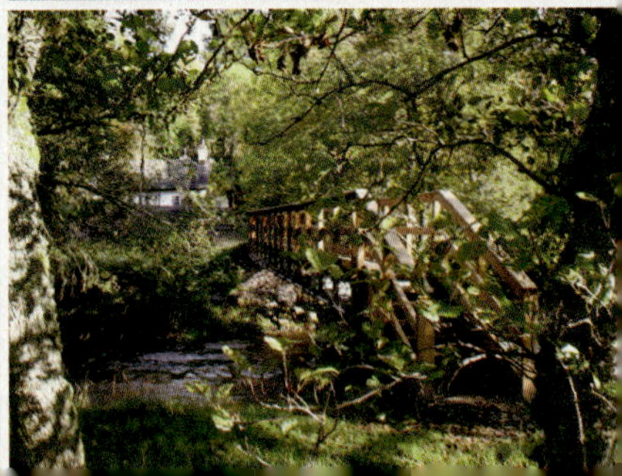

ECOCAMP GLENSHEE

SCOTLAND

Ecocamp Glenshee provides all-year glamping in 6 heated 5 bed wooden pods. An off-grid 10 bed yurt with wood-burning stove and two shepherd's huts, sleeping 2 (off-grid) and 4. There are also 2 seasonal bell tents sleeping 2 and 6 both off-grid. There is communal space in the traditional bothy with wood burning stove. The bothy has fridge/freezer, cutlery, crockery, hot water and a safe area for a camping stove; bring your own stove. The toilet and shower block is heated and cosy all year round. Bring your own sleeping bag or hire one. The Calvin family bring tea/coffee to your pod in the morning. They can also provide home cooked breakfasts from locally sourced food and a pick-up/drop-off service to the Cateran Trail and to local hostelries in the evenings.

The area offers great cycling for both roadies and mountain bikers (family and challenging), canoeing and fishing, skiing (in winter) and an abundance of stunning walking for all abilities including the Cateran Trail. The area offers some of the best Geocaching in Britain, we are located on the Haggis Highway. Equipment drying and secure bike storage/cleaning available.

DETAILS

- **Open** - All year, owners live on site.
- **Number of beds** - 54: 6 pods sleeping 4/5, 10 bed yurt & 2 shepherd's huts
- **Booking** - Book online, by phone or email.
- **Price per night** - Pods from £45 per night. Yurt from £110 per night
- **Public Transport** - Buses from Perth and Dundee to Blairgowrie. Local buses from Blairgowrie, stop a mile away. Collection from Blairgowrie with advance notice.
- **Directions** - Signed posted off A93 6 miles north of Bridge of Cally.

CONTACT: Simon or Fiona
Tel: 01250 882284 Mob: 07881 620890
info@ecocampglenshee.co.uk www.ecocampglenshee.co.uk
Blacklunans, by Blairgowrie, PH10 7LA

BRAEMAR LODGE
BUNKHOUSE

425

SCOTLAND

Surrounded by the beauty of Deeside, Braemar Lodge Hotel and Bunkhouse is in a quiet setting only a two minute walk from the village itself. Braemar Lodge Hotel was formerly a Victorian shooting lodge and is set in extensive grounds two minutes from the centre of Braemar in the heart of Royal Deeside.

The great value Bunkhouse provides comfortable accommodation for up to 12 people within the hotel grounds. The bunkhouse is equipped with two shower rooms, one of which is suitable for wheelchair access. The bunkhouse also has good drying and laundry facilities, excellent for damp clothes and ski boots. A generous fully equipped kitchen is available for all your self-catering needs. Guests are also welcome to use the hotel's excellent dining facilities if a rest from self-catering is required. All bed linen and towels are supplied for the duration of your stay.

DETAILS

- **Open** - All year, all day
- **Number of beds** - 12: 3x4
- **Booking** - Book by phone or email
- **Price per night** - From £15 per person
- **Public Transport** - Aberdeen airport 59 miles. Railway stations at Perth (50 miles) and Aberdeen. Buses to Braemar from Aberdeen where the bus and rail station are side by side. Two minute walk to hotel from Braemar village bus stop.
- **Directions** - The hotel is situated on the A93 on the left if you are arriving from the south. Two minutes' walk from the village centre.

CONTACT: Reception
Tel: 01339 741627, Fax: 01339 741627
mail@braemarlodge.co.uk www.braemarlodge.co.uk
6 Glenshee Rd, Braemar, Aberdeenshire, AB35 5YQ

HABITAT @ BALLATER

SCOTLAND

Set in the village of Ballater with a range of shops, pubs and restaurants, this is a stunning, purpose built hostel ideal for families, groups and independent travellers. Within the Cairngorms National Park it is a great position for enjoying a variety of outdoor activities.

All rooms are en suite, ranging from 8 bed dorms to 4 bed rooms suitable for families and a twin/single room. The hostel is fully accessible for wheelchair users. Bedding is included. There's a large kitchen /dining / lounge area with wood burning stove. There is an excellent drying and laundry room and secure storage for bikes.

Ballater is an ideal location for exploring the eastern Cairngorms, Royal Deeside and Aberdeenshire.

Habitat@Ballater is a VisitScotland five star hostel.

DETAILS

- **Open** - All year, (closed mid November-Xmas), all day
- **Number of beds** - 25: 1x 8, 1x6, 3x family rooms (2-4) 1x single/twin
- **Booking** - Book by phone, email or online.
- **Price per night** - Bunkrooms from £20 per person per night. Private rooms from £24 per person per night.
- **Public Transport** - From Aberdeen bus station (phone 01224 212266).
- **Directions** - On A93 just west of bridge over river in centre of Ballater.

CONTACT: Claudia Leith
Tel: 013397 53752
info@habitat-at-ballater.com www.habitat-at-ballater.com
Bridge Square, Ballater, Aberdeenshire, AB35 5QJ

HABITAT
ballater

BACKPACKERS PLUS
OBAN
SCOTLAND

Backpackers Plus has become many people's favourite hostel thanks to its friendly atmosphere, excellent facilities and beautiful seaside town setting. There's an enormous self-catering kitchen, a pool table and other games and lots of information from the knowledgeable staff about Oban and Argyll. A great little minibus is available for transfers and famous custom made tours. Oban is a town with spectacular views across to the islands - the view at dusk from McCaig's Tower can provide an amazing sunset. The bustle of fishing boats, ferries, yachts and seabirds make the waterfront a lovely place to be. Ferries leave Oban to the many beautiful Scottish Isles. Ancient standing stones, medieval castles, hairy coos and whisky distilleries are all in the area. The best fish and chips in Scotland are within 200 metres.

DETAILS

- **Open** - All year. Reception 7am-10.30pm, occasionally closed in middle of the day.
- **Number of beds** - 50-60 dorm beds, family, double, twin rooms, some en suite.
- **Booking** - Booking is strongly recommended but not essential – deposit equivalent to first night's accommodation to be paid in full to confirm the booking.
- **Price per night** - From £14.90 pp, private rooms from £17.90 pp.
- **Public Transport** - Close to Oban train station and Citylink buses.
- **Directions** - From A85 turn left at the Kings Knoll Hotel onto Deanery Brae. Follow the road sharp right onto Breadalbane Street. Backpackers Plus is at the bottom of the street on the right, with a big 'Backpackers' sign. By bus or train - walk along the waterfront through town, keeping sea on left. Continue straight up George Street, past cinema on the right, then the Taj Mahal restaurant. Hostel is straight ahead on the left, in the church building.

CONTACT: Receptionist
Tel: 01631 567189
info@backpackersplus.com www.backpackersplus.com
The Old Church, Breadalbane Street, Oban, Argyll PA34 5PH

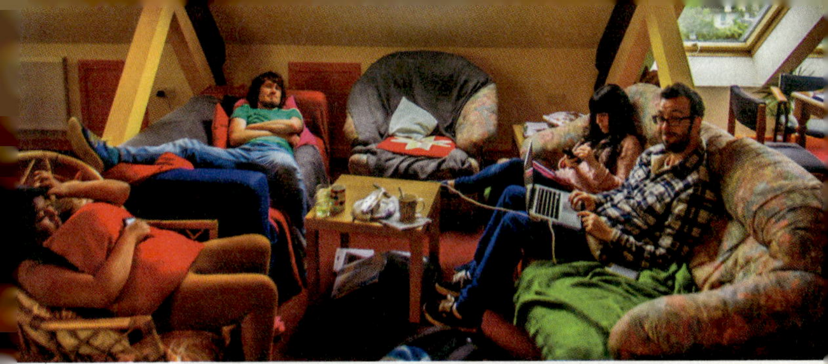
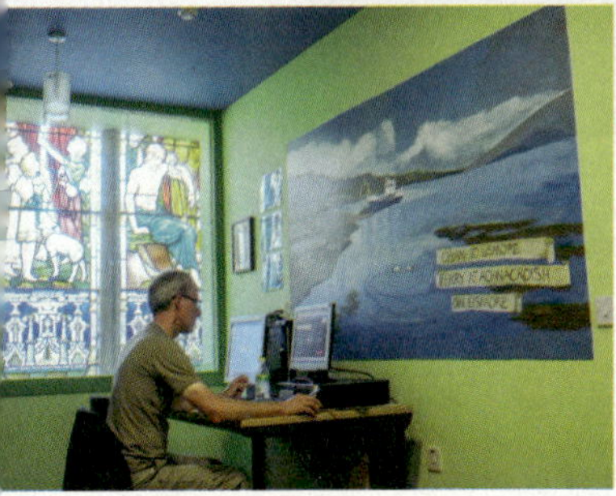
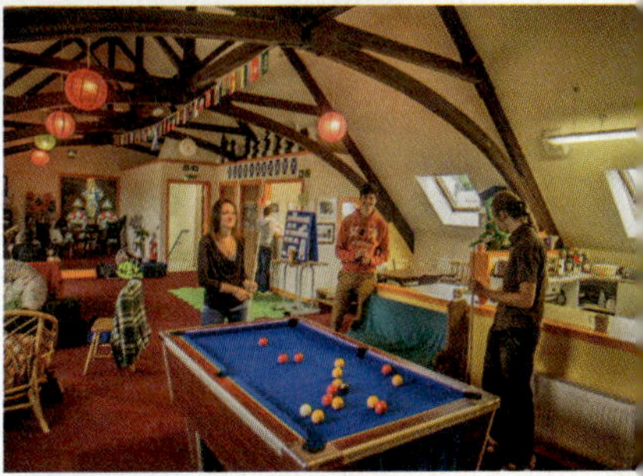
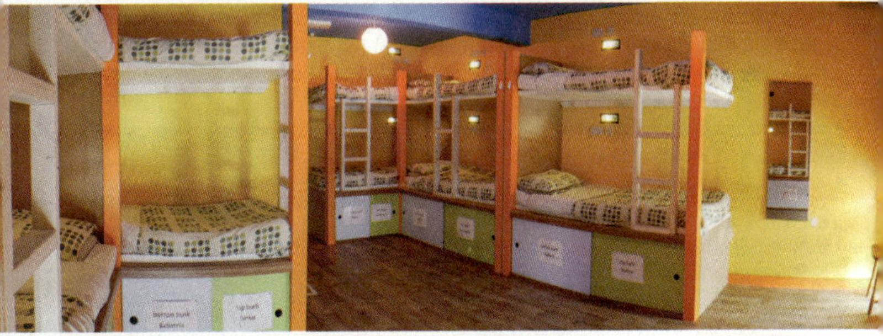
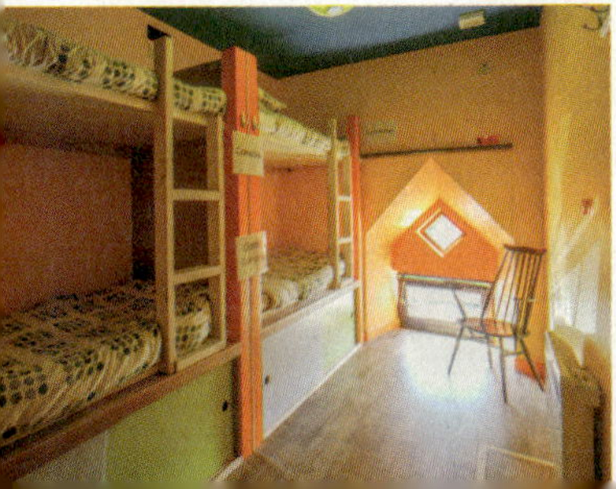
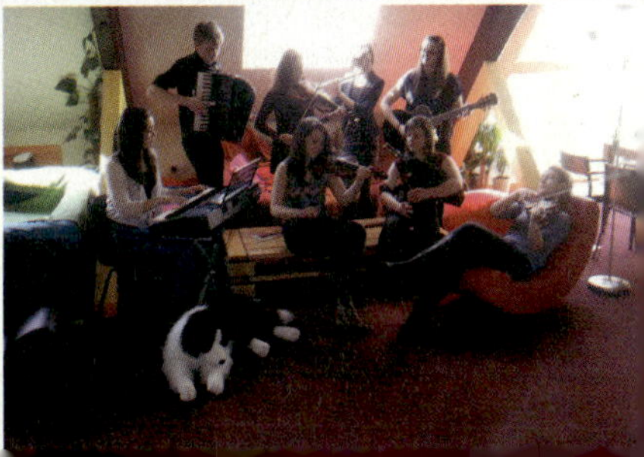

JEREMY INGLIS
OBAN HOSTEL

SCOTLAND

Excellent value, warm and friendly hostel accommodation in Oban, Argyll. The Jeremy Inglis Hostel has been operating for more than 30 years and in that time has built up an excellent reputation for quality and value.

The hostel is centrally situated just off Argyll Square, Oban and is the closest hostel to all transport connections. Ferries to the Islands leave 300 metres away, trains and buses 200 metres. Three large supermarkets are close by. Cosy twin, double, single and family rooms (no bunk beds) give some privacy.

Prices include linen and towels as well as a continental breakfast with muesli, cereals and toast, vegemite and home-made jams; raspberry, damson and marmalade etc. There is a large, modern and well equipped kitchen with free tea, coffee and WiFi.

DETAILS

- **Open** - All year, no curfew, 24hr access with key.
- **Number of beds** - 37
- **Booking** - Booking preferred. Deposit in certain circumstances.
- **Price per night** - Special dorm rate from £13.00. Double or twin from £15pp and singles from £17pp (depending on availability and season).
- **Public Transport** - Nearest train and Citylink drop off 150 metres from hostel. Ferries to islands 300 metres. For ferry enquiries phone 01631 566688.
- **Directions** - The hostel is in Airds Crescent, one of the streets off Argyll Square. The hostel is on the second floor, pink door.

CONTACT: Jeremy or Katrin
Tel: 01631 565065, Fax: 01631 565933
jeremyinglis@mctavishs.freeserve.co.uk www.jeremyinglishostel.co.uk
21 Airds Crescent, Oban, Argyll, PA34 5SJ

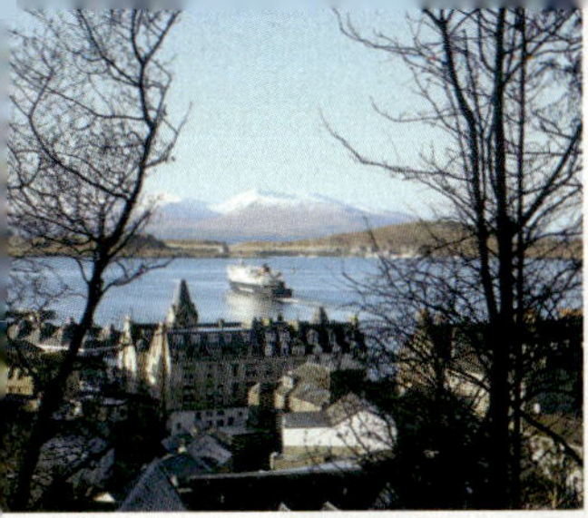
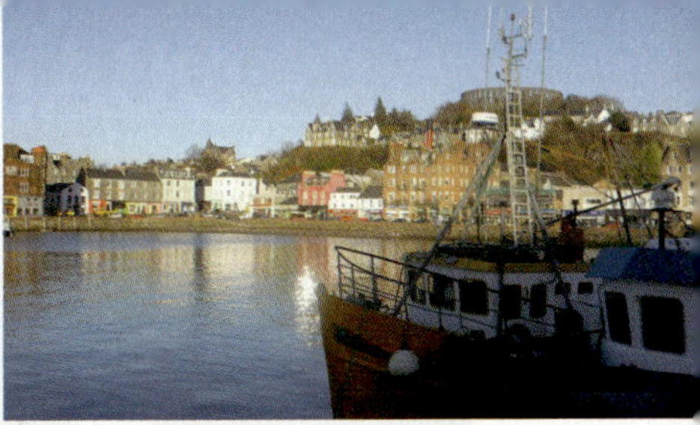
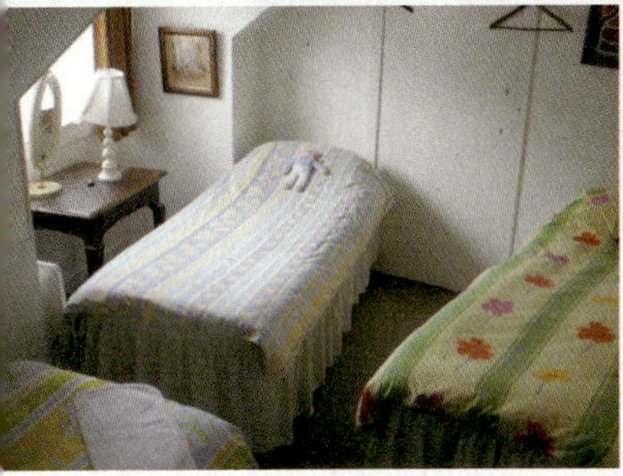
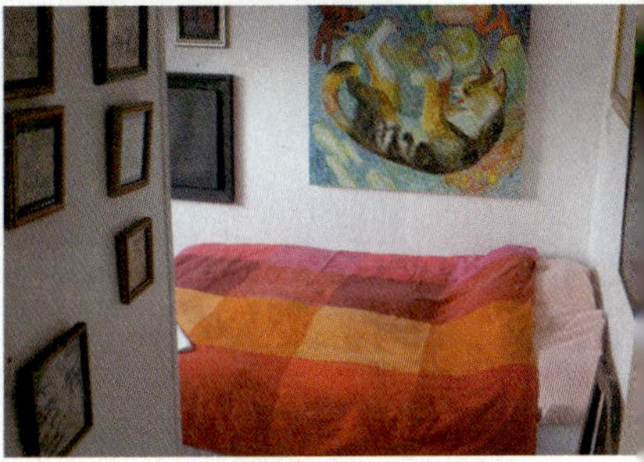
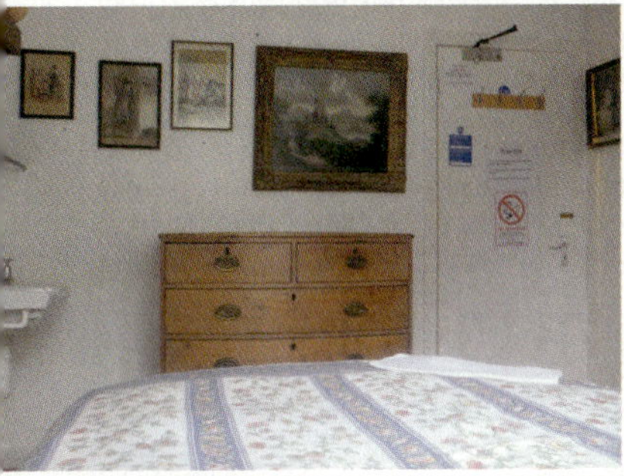
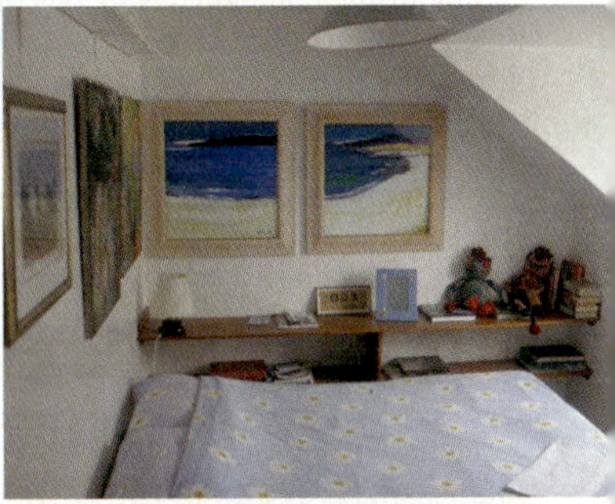
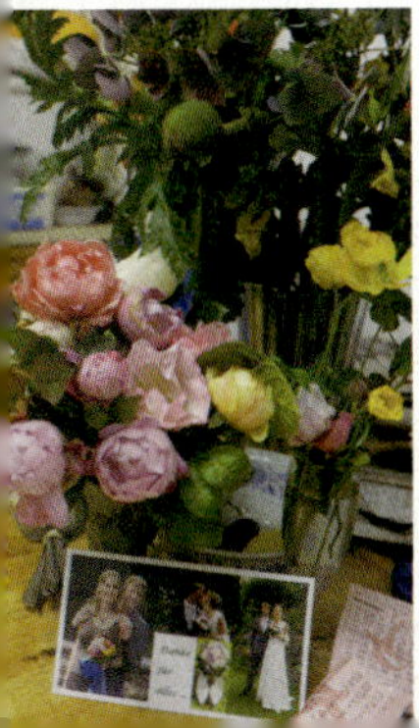
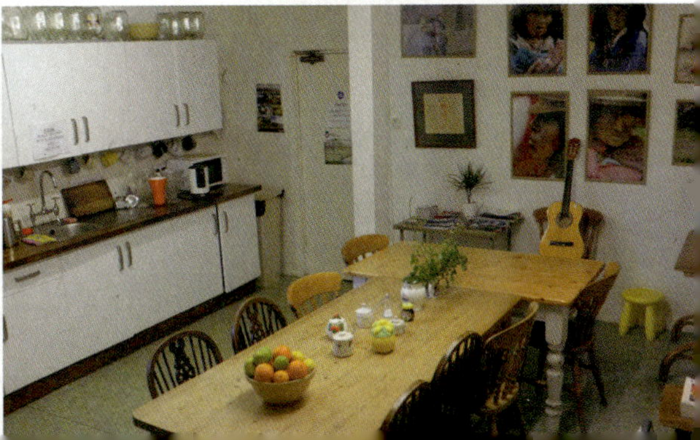

OBAN BACKPACKERS

SCOTLAND

Whether you're passing through Oban on the way to the Islands, or staying for a couple of days and exploring historic and beautiful Argyll, the original Oban Backpackers is a great place to stay, meet like minded people and probably end up staying longer than planned. Situated in the heart of the town Oban Backpackers is perfectly located to enable you to experience all Oban has to offer without burning a hole in your wallet. Completely refurbished in May 2013 the hostel offers dormitory accommodation with wide, comfortable, bunks, made up with fitted sheets, duvets and pillows. Powerful showers with loads of hot water add to the comfort and if required, towels can be hired from reception. The fully equipped kitchen has everything you will need to cook up your favourite meals and there is plenty of storage and fridge space available. The big cosy lounge with a real fire, pool table, free hot drinks, WiFi, musical instruments, games and book swap makes it a great place to stay and unwind.

DETAILS

- **Open** - March - November, all day
- **Number of beds** - 54: 1x12, 1x10, 1x8, 1x6
- **Booking** - Online or by phone, first night's fee as deposit
- **Price per night** - From £15. Whole hostel bookings-email for quote
- **Public Transport** - 10 minute walk to Oban train station and Citylink buses
- **Directions** - From A85 turn left onto Deanery Brae take the sharp right onto Breadalbane Street. Oban Backpackers is on the left. From bus and train - walk along the waterfront keeping sea on left. Continue straight up George Street, bare right to Bredalbane Street. The hostel is on the right.

CONTACT: Reception
Tel: 01631 562 107
info@obanbackpackers.com   www.obanbackpackers.com
Breadalbane Street, Oban, PA34 5NZ

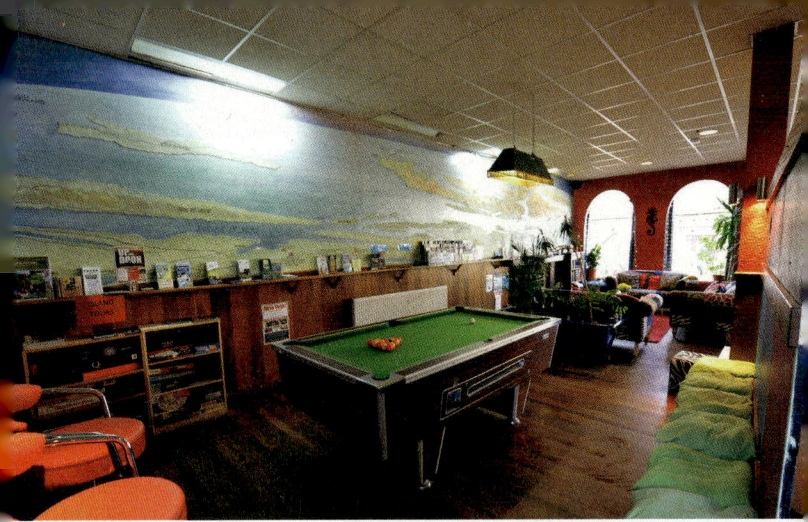

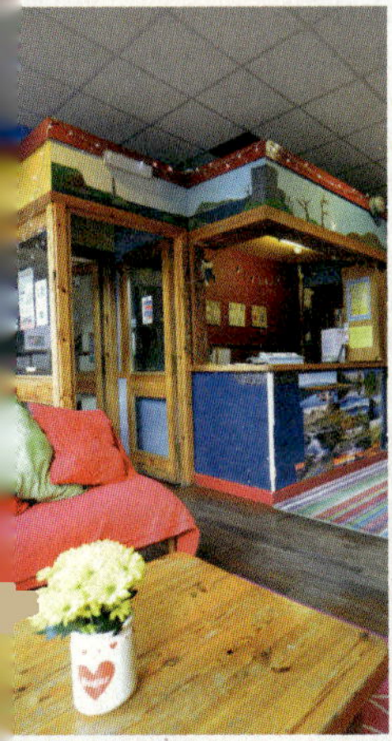

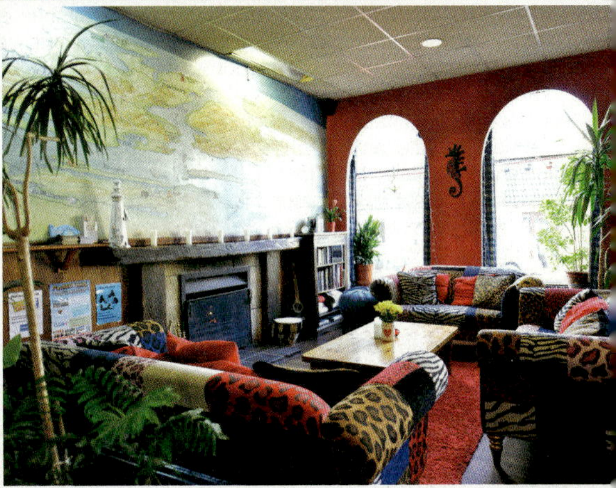

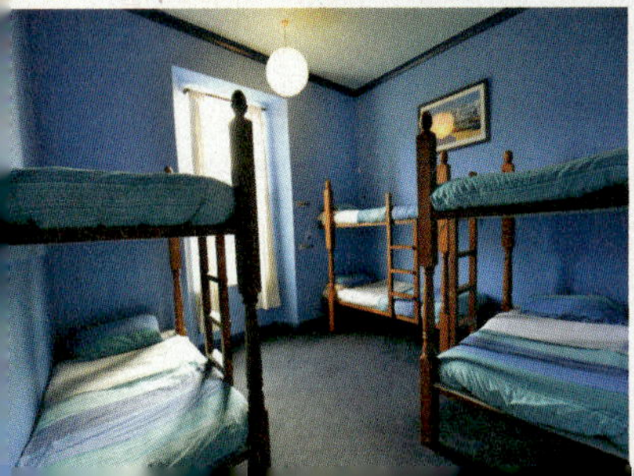

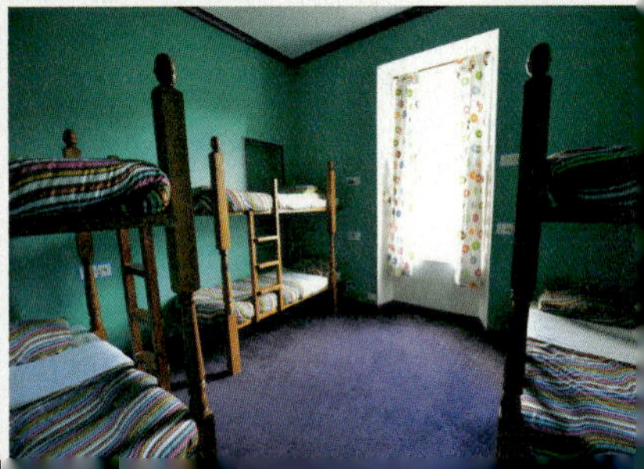

CORRAN HOUSE

SCOTLAND

Corran House is part of a Victorian terrace with magnificent seascapes across the bay to the Isle of Kerrera and the hills of Mull. There is a warm welcome for visitors and reasonably priced accommodation for singles, couples, families and groups. The house has a large self-catering kitchen, spacious TV lounge, comfortable, commodious, well appointed guest rooms and 4 bed dormitories with generous size beds. Most rooms have en suite facilities. Corran House is well situated for exploring Argyll and visiting the inner Hebrides. It is only a short walk along the sea front to the bus, train and ferry terminals. Downstairs is Markie Dans bar with patio and spectacular views. The pub offers great highland hospitality, tasty meals, live entertainment, widescreen TV, pool table and a late licence all year round to enable the discerning drinker to sample the best range of malt whiskies on the west coast. Pony trekking trips available with prior booking.

DETAILS

- **Open** - All year. Reception 10am-9pm. Check in after 3pm.
- **Number of beds** - 62 in total - 26 bunks- 5x4 1x6. Plus guest rooms: 16
- **Booking** - Advisable. Credit card secures bed. Early/late arrival with notice.
- **Price per night** - Bunk rooms £17 standard/£19 en suite. Guest rooms from £22pp. Out of season rates available
- **Public Transport** - Oban train, bus and ferry terminals are 900m from the house.
- **Directions** - Corran House overlooks Oban Bay to the west of the town centre. From the Tourist Information and all the Oban transport terminals, with the sea on your left, walk along George Street past the Columba Hotel into Corran Esplanade. Follow the seafront for 300m. Corran House is on your right above Markie Dans Bar.

CONTACT:
Tel: 01631 566040, Fax: 01631 566854
enquiries@corranhouseoban.co.uk www.corranhouseoban.co.uk
1 Victoria Crescent, Corran Esplanade, Oban, Argyll, PA34 5PN

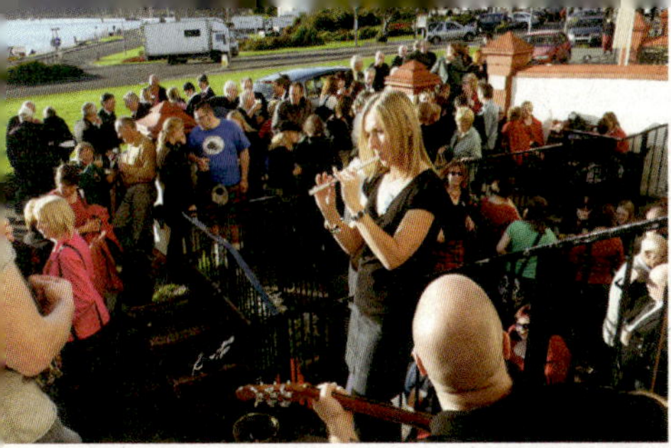
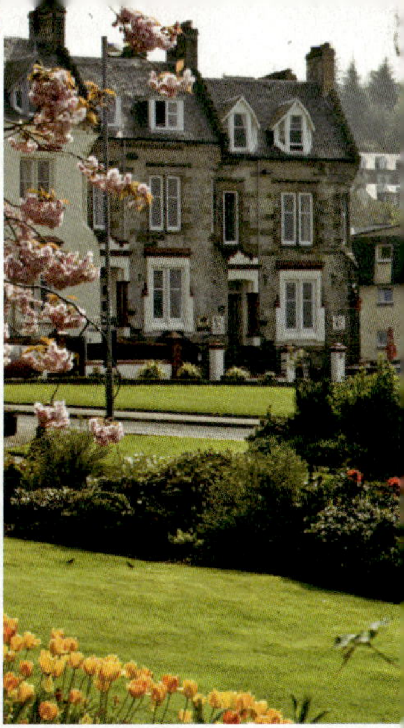
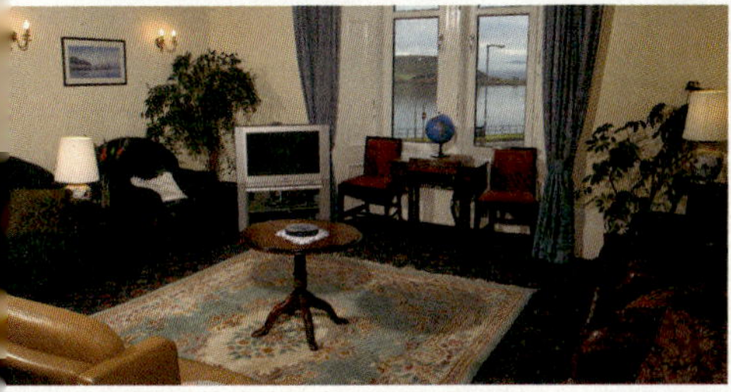
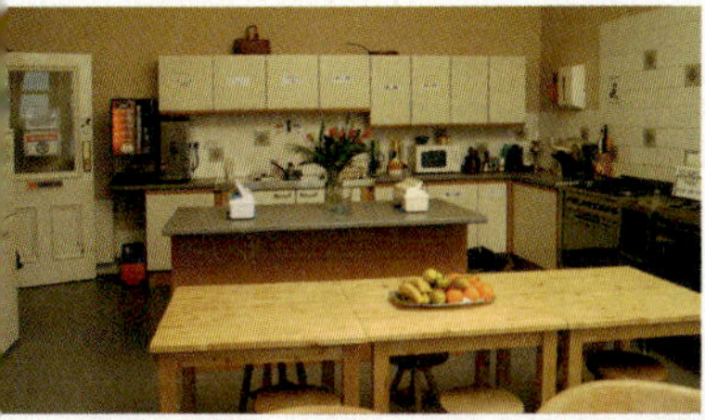
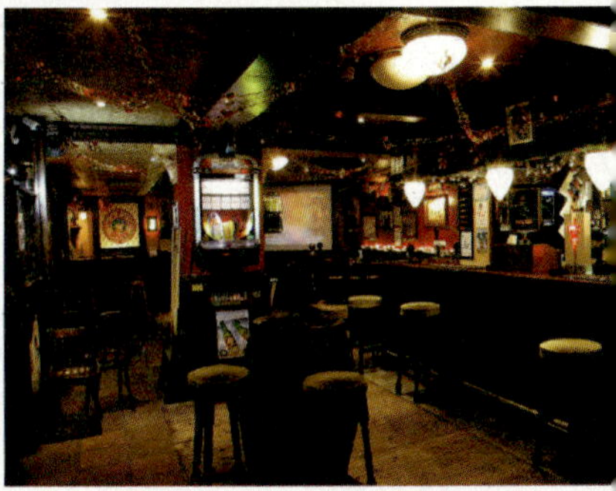
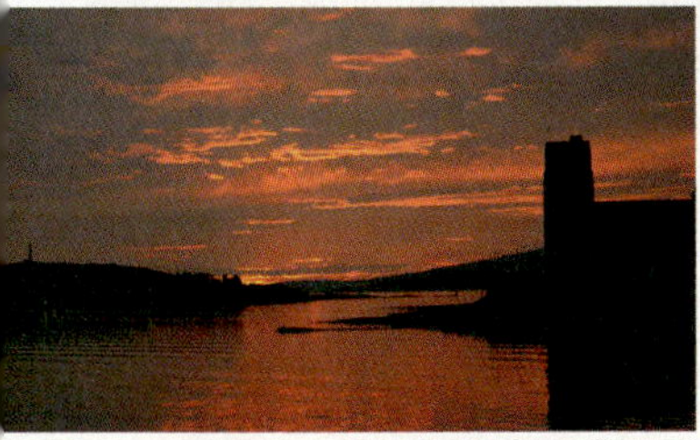
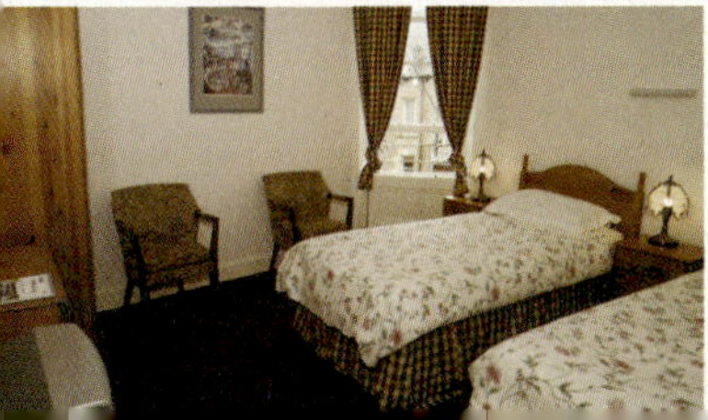
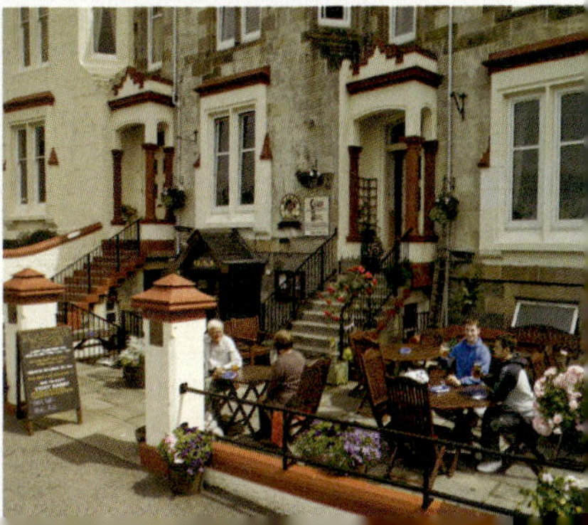

COLONSAY BACKPACKERS LODGE
SCOTLAND

Colonsay Backpackers Lodge is located on a peaceful and idyllic Inner Hebridean island to the south of Mull which boasts magnificent sandy beaches, ancient forests and beautiful lochs. The place is teeming with wildlife which includes dolphins, seals, otters and many rare species of bird. There are ancient standing stones and a 14th century priory with exceptional carved Celtic tombstones. The famous Colonsay House gardens and café are open to visitors to enjoy twice a week. The pub, café, shop and village hall, where there are regular Ceilidhs, are all within three miles. Fresh lobster, crab and langoustines can be bought from fishing boats in the harbour and don't forget the best oysters in the world are grown on Colonsay. The lodge is a refurbished former gamekeeper's house with bothies. Centrally heated, it has 2 twin, 3 twin bunk and 2 three bedded rooms. It has a very large dining/cooking/sitting area and a separate sitting room with a log fire. Bed linen provided.

DETAILS

- **Open** - All year, 24 hours
- **Number of beds** - 16: 5 x 2; 2 x 3
- **Booking** - Required 24 hours in advance.
- **Price per night** - £25pp twin, £19.50pp bothy
- **Public Transport** - Train and coach to Oban. Caledonian MacBrayne ferry to Colonsay takes 2.5 hours. Flights Hebridean Air from Connel
- **Directions** - Ferry departs Oban 6 times per week April to October, Sun, Mon, Wed, Thurs, Fri, Sat (rest of year Mon, Wed, Fri, Sat). Flights Tues, Thurs from Connel Airport, nr Oban. Transport from the harbour can be arranged if required.

CONTACT: The Manager
Tel: 01951 200312
cottages@colonsayestate.co.uk   www.colonsayestate.co.uk
Colonsay Estate Cottages, Isle of Colonsay, Argyll, PA61 7YP

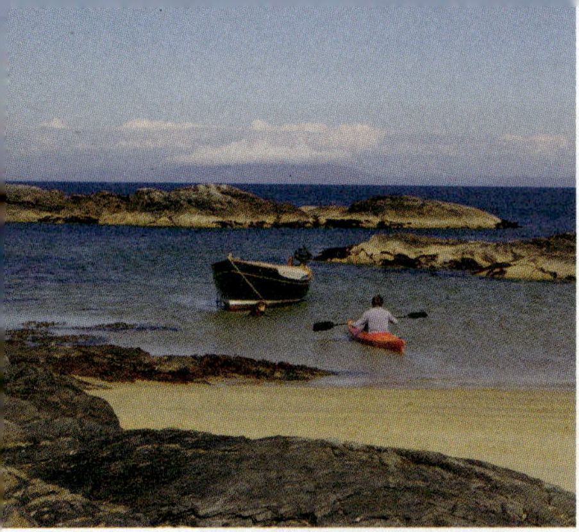

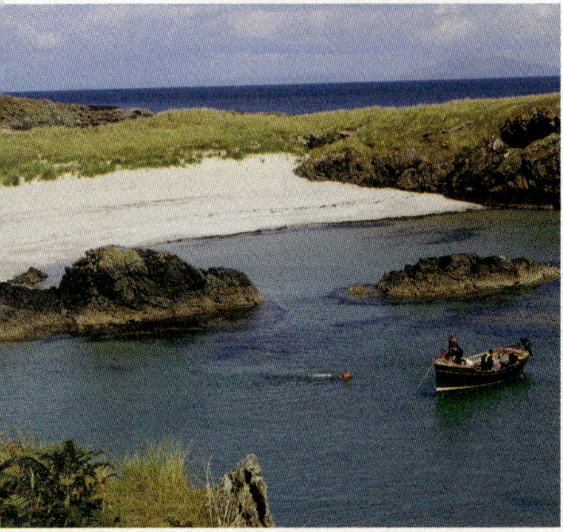

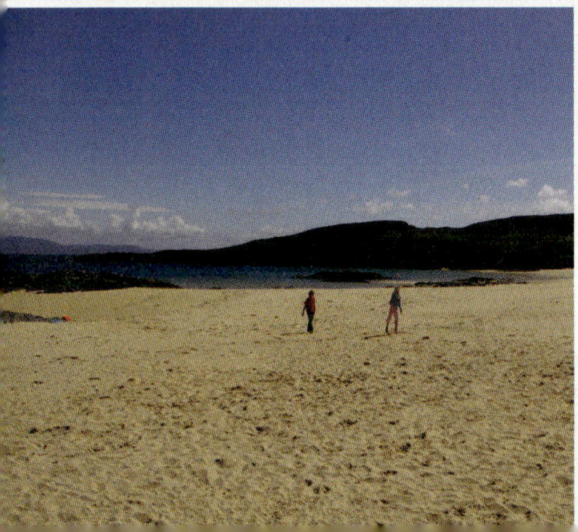

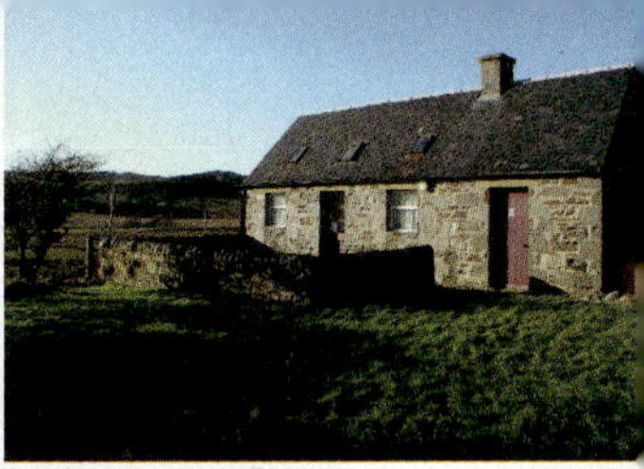

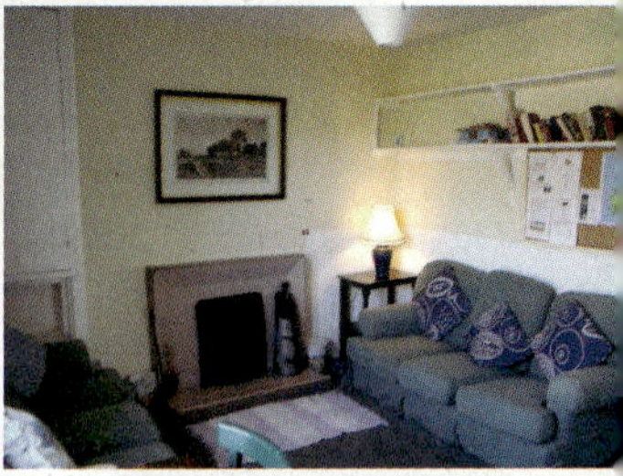

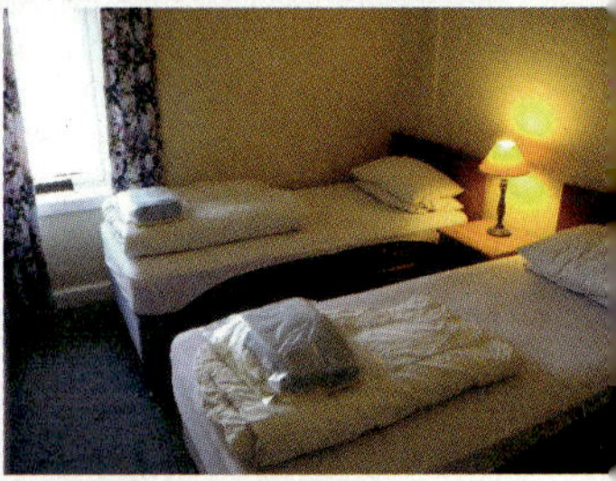

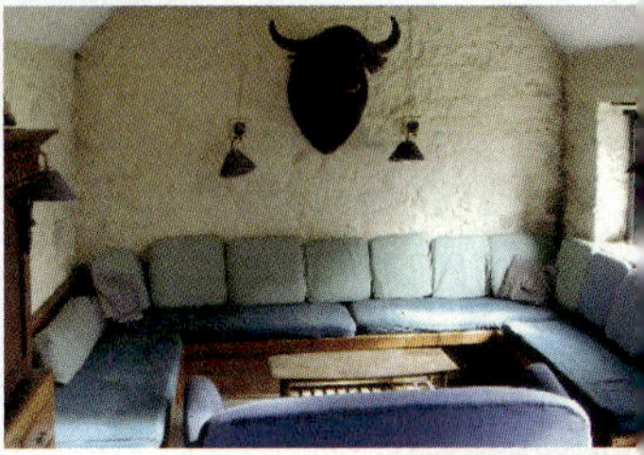

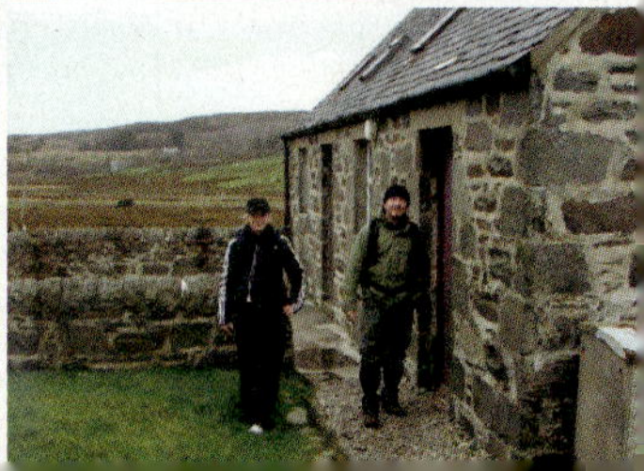

COLL BUNKHOUSE

SCOTLAND

Coll Bunkhouse provides five star hostel accommodation in the Inner Hebrides. The beautiful Isle of Coll offers so much, whether you are into walking, stargazing, wildlife-spotting, diving, cycling, sailing or kayaking, you can do all of this and more. The bunkhouse is small and cosy, with 16 beds in two dorms of 6 and one family room for 4 (can also be booked as a twin), ideal for small groups or independent travellers. The building is brand new, with a fully equipped kitchen and modern facilities throughout. Whether you're looking for an island adventure or a quiet place to relax, a warm welcome awaits!

DETAILS

- **Open** - All year, 24 hours
- **Number of beds** - 16: 2x6, 1x4
- **Booking** - Not always essential but highly recommended. Full payment is required at time of booking, or a deposit for a group booking.
- **Price per night** - £21pp (dorm). Private rooms £80 (quad), £65 (triple), £50 (twin). Discounts for group bookings (exclusive use) of two nights or more from 5% to 50%.
- **Public Transport** - Ferry from Oban takes 2.40 hours. Sailings every day in summer and five times a week in winter. Flights from Oban four times a week. Bikes are free on the ferry and can be booked onto trains to Oban. Free car parks in Oban.
- **Directions** - Coll Bunkhouse is situated in the centre of the village of Arinagour, very close to the local shop and the hotel/bar. From the ferry walk along Main Street continuing onto Shore Street. The bunkhouse is on your left hand side, next door to An Cridhe, the new community centre. From the airport take the road to Arinagour and the bunkhouse will be on your right hand side as you enter the village.

CONTACT: George
Tel: 01879 230217, Fax: 441879230000
info@collbunkhouse.co.uk   www.collbunkhouse.com
Arinagour, Isle of Coll, Argyll, PA78 6SY

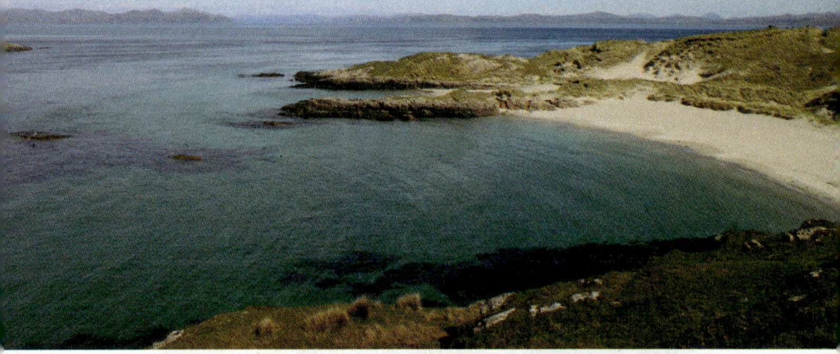
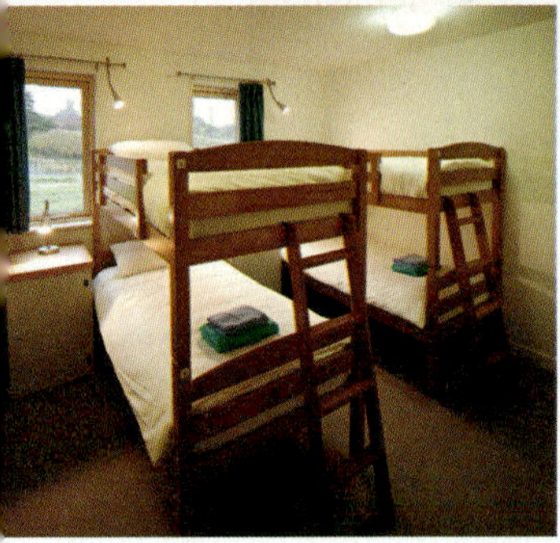
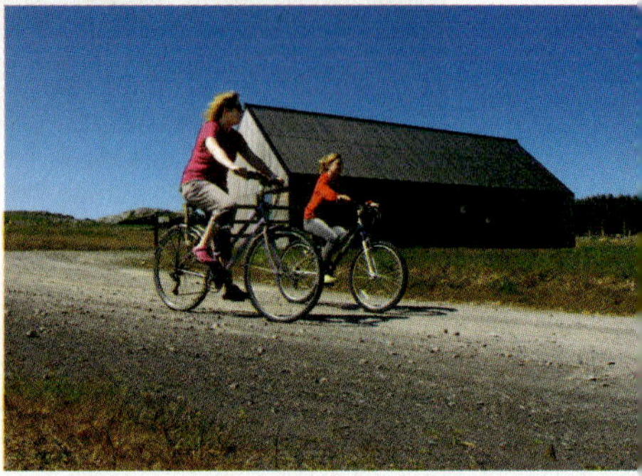
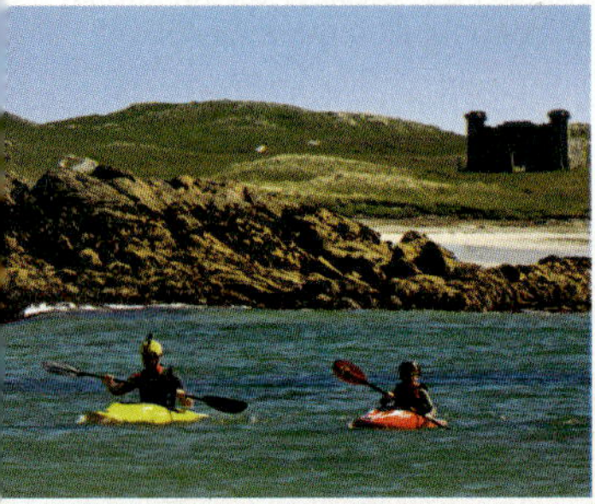
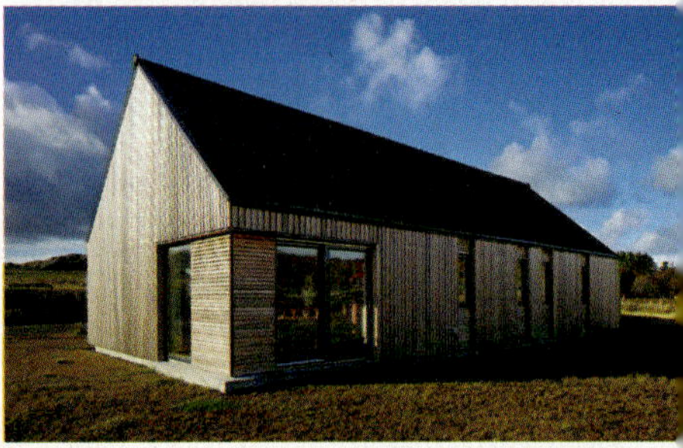
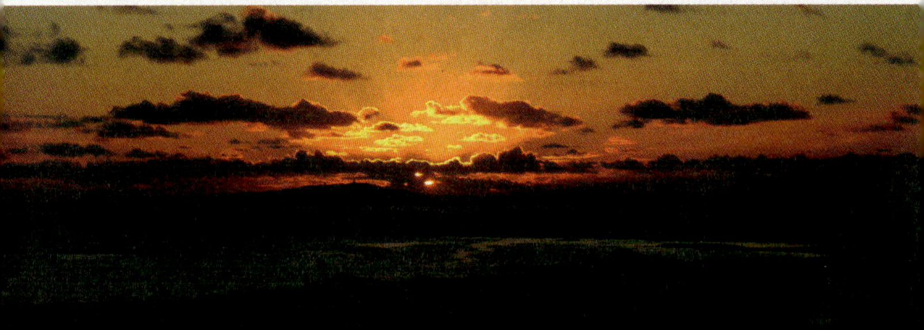

MILLHOUSE HOSTEL

SCOTLAND

Tiree is an idyllic Hebridean Island, perfect for outdoor pursuits, wildlife enthusiasts, and those yet to experience the total tranquility of stunning white beaches and crystal clear seas.

A warm welcome and excellent facilities await you at Millhouse. There are bikes for hire to explore the island, visit the lighthouse museum, 'ping' the ringing stone, find the standing stones, wonder at the Machair flowers or watch the seals. Watersports take place on adjacent Loch Bhasapol, and the secluded Cornaig beach is a ten minute walk away. There is a resident RSPB warden on the island and a bird hide near the hostel. For walkers, Millhouse is on the Tiree Pilgrimage route linking the ancient chapels and monuments around the island.

STB 4 star hostel with free Wifi.

DETAILS

- **Open** - Mar-Oct, open in winter by arrangement, open all day (quiet after 11.30pm, check out 9.30am).
- **Number of beds** - Hostel 16 : 2 x 2/3, 2 x 5. Farmhouse 10: 3 x 4 (limit 10)
- **Booking** - Advisable, please check vacancies before boarding the ferry
- **Price per night** - Twin £25pp single night, £22pppn 2 or more nights. Dorm £21pp single night, £19pppn 2 or more nights. Family £50 to £65 per room.
- **Public Transport** - Caledonian MacBrayne ferry from Oban to Tiree or Flybe flight from Glasgow. Local Ring and Ride bus 01879 220419.
- **Directions** - From ferry turn right at T junction, then left at next fork. Continue for 4 miles to Millhouse Hostel

CONTACT: Judith Boyd
Tel: 01879 220435
tireemillhouse@yahoo.co.uk   www.tireemillhouse.co.uk
Cornaigmore, Isle of Tiree, Argyll, PA77 6XA

IONA HOSTEL

SCOTTLAND

'BEST ECO-HOSTEL IN SCOTLAND' (GTBS). Tucked into the rocky outcrops at the north end of the island, Iona Hostel has spectacular views to Staffa and the Treshnish Isles, and beyond Rhum to the Black Cuillins of Skye. The hostel is situated on the working croft of Lagandorain (the hollow of the otter).

This land has been worked for countless generations, creating the familiar Hebridean patchwork of wildflower meadow, crops and grazing land, home to an amazing variety of plants and birds. It offers quiet sanctuary for those that seek it, within easy reach of island activities.

Whether travelling on your own, with friends, or as part of one of our many visiting groups, Iona Hostel offers you a warm welcome - with the best views this side of heaven. 4 star STB. Green Tourism Gold Award. We regret no dogs.

DETAILS

- **Open** - All year, closed 11am-1pm for cleaning - no curfew
- **Number of beds** - 21: 1 x 2, 2 x 4, 1 x 5, 1 x 6.
- **Booking** - Strongly advised
- **Price per night** - £21.00 adult / £17.50 under 10s (bedding included).
- **Public Transport** - Caledonian Macbrayne ferry service from Oban or Mull 08705 650000. For buses on Mull 01546 604695. Taxi service on Iona 0781 0325990.

- **Directions** - You cannot bring your car onto Iona, but there is free parking in Fionnphort on Mull at the Columba Centre. Iona Hostel is the last building at the north end of the island, 2 km from the pier and up beyond the abbey.

CONTACT: John MacLean
Tel: 01681 700781
info@ionahostel.co.uk   www.ionahostel.co.uk
Iona Hostel, Iona, Argyll, PA76 6SW

CRAIGNURE BUNKHOUSE

SCOTLAND

Craignure Bunkhouse is an eco-sensitive hostel in an atmospheric setting, close to Craignure Pier where the ferry arrives from Oban. Next to the bunkhouse is The Craignure Inn, a popular traditional inn offering food, drink and and a welcoming atmosphere. Craignure is the hub for the island bus services and tourist information. The bunkhouse has a biomass boiler and solar powered heating. There are two rooms of 6 beds and two rooms of 4 beds, each with an en suite shower. Each bunk has a locker, a reading light and USB port. The Convivial is a large communal room, with well equipped kitchen, ample dining space, plenty of books/games and a large Freesat television surrounded by comfortable couches and chairs. There is free WiFi throughout the building. Bedlinen is provided on arrival, and towels can be hired. Laundry, equipment/bike store and drying room are available. Mull has great beaches and a visit to Duart Castle, a sea trip to Staffa, ferry trip to Iona, or shopping trip Tobermory harbour town are all reccommended.

DETAILS

- **Open** - All year, closed 11am-4pm for cleaning.
- **Number of beds** - 20: 2x4, 2x6
- **Booking** - Booking through website or phone.
- **Price per night** - £19pp. 4 beds £70, 6 beds £100. Ask for whole hostel bookings.
- **Public Transport** - Ferries from Oban dock at Craignure Pier. Coaches and trains run frequently from Glasgow to Oban. Craignure is the hub for the island buses.
- **Directions** - From Craignure Peir, turn left and look out for the Craignure Inn 350 metres down the road. The bunkhouse is next door.

CONTACT: Sarah or Chris James
Tel: 01680 812043 Mob:07900 692973
info@craignure-bunkhouse.co.uk www.craignure-bunkhouse.co.uk/
Craignure Bunkhouse, Craignure, Isle Of Mull, Argyll And Bute, PA65 6AY

SHIELING HOLIDAYS

443

SCOTLAND

Right on the sea, with views to Ben Nevis. There are otters on site, and you may see porpoises, dolphins and eagles. Your accommodation is in shared Shielings, unique carpeted cottage tents, made on Mull, which are clean, bright and spacious, and have real beds for 2, 4, or 6 people. Or you can hire a Shieling to yourself or stay in a self catering cottage. There are super showers, and a communal Shieling with woodburning stove, TV, payphone and launderette. Free WiFi. Campfire. Bike hire.

Stroll to the ferry, pub, café, shops, and swimming pool. Walk to Duart Castle, home of the Clan Maclean. Catch the bus for Tobermory for Iona (where Columba brought Christianity to Scotland) and for Staffa (home of puffins, and inspiration for Mendelssohn's overture 'Fingal's Cave'). A perfect base for all Mull. You don't need a car.

DETAILS

- **Open** - April to October, 24 hours (reception 8am - 10pm)
- **Number of beds** - 18: 6 x 2, 1 x 6.
- **Booking** - Please email a booking enquiry from our website.
- **Price per night** - £14.00 pp. Under 15s £10. Bedding £3 pp.
- **Public Transport** - From Glasgow, rail or bus (0871 266 3333) at 12.00, ferry (01680 812343) at 16.00 from Oban, arrive Mull 16.46; back by 10.55 ferry, arrive Glasgow by 1600. Please check times before travel.
- **Directions** - Grid Ref 724 369. From ferry, left on the A849 to Iona. After 400 metres, left opposite church past old pier to reception by the sea - 800 metres in all.

CONTACT: David Gracie
Tel: 01680 812496
sales@shielingholidays.co.uk www.shielingholidays.co.uk
Craignure, Isle of Mull, Argyll, PA65 6AY

GLENCOE INDEPENDENT HOSTEL
SCOTLAND

Glencoe Independent Hostel, centred around an old highland croft in the heart of Glencoe, offers great value accommodation for groups, families and individuals. It is set in secluded and peaceful woodland midway between Glencoe village and the Clachaig Inn with immediate access to world class cycling, walking, climbing and kayaking. The hostel is 20 minutes from Glencoe Ski Centre and the West Highland Way and 40 minutes from Nevis Range. The hostel has 4 rooms, a lounge with open fire, cooking and dining facilities and offers private family and couples rooms when available. The Alpine bunkhouse sleeps 16 in 3 rooms, ideal for outdoor activity and school groups. Also available are luxury and economy caravans for 2 to 4 people and a log cabin for 2 to 3 people. The site has a top class drying room, bike storage, and mountains all around. Free WiFi in reception. Go Glencoe Guided walks now available too!

DETAILS

- **Open** - All year (phone in Nov and Dec), 9am - 9 pm
- **Number of beds** - Hostel: 26, bunkhouse: 16, 4 caravans of 2-4, log cabin: 2-3.
- **Booking** - Booking advised in summer. 30% non refundable deposit (min. £10).
- **Price per night** - From £12.50 to £22 per person.
- **Public Transport** - 1.5 miles from bus stop in Glencoe Village (crossroads). Citylink buses 914, 915 and 916 from Skye, Fort William, Glasgow. Bus 44 from Fort William and Kinlochleven. For West Highland Way take White Corries near Kingshouse Hotel to Glencoe Crossroads (20 mins) then 1.5 miles' walk.
- **Directions** - From A82 south, take right turn for Clachaig Inn, 1 mile after pub on left. From north, take left turn for Kinlochleven, then immediate right to Glencoe Village. 1 mile out of village on right.

CONTACT: Keith or Davina
Tel: 01855 811906
info@glencoehostel.co.uk www.glencoehostel.co.uk
Glencoe Independent Hostel, Glencoe, Argyll, PH49 4HX

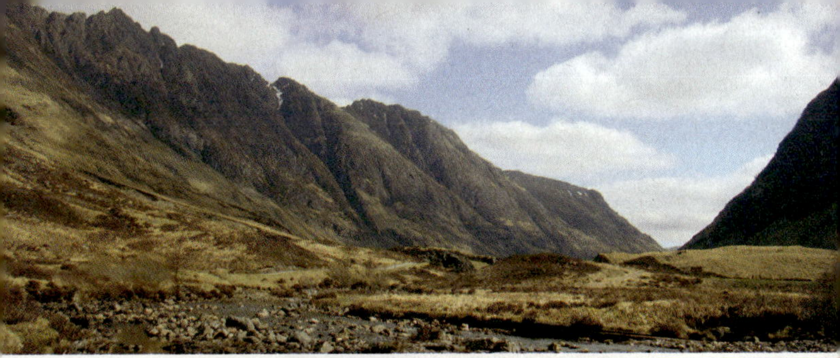

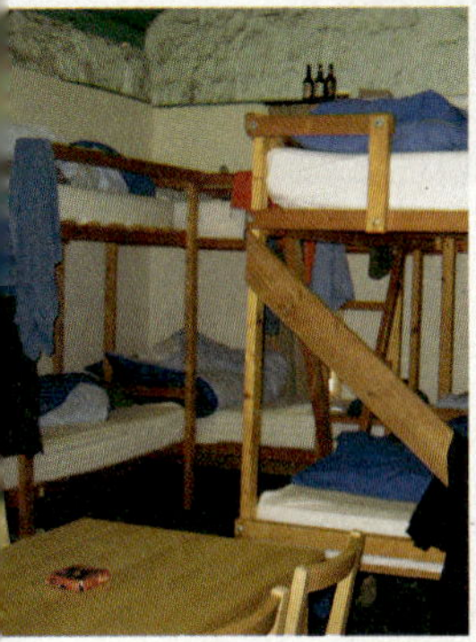

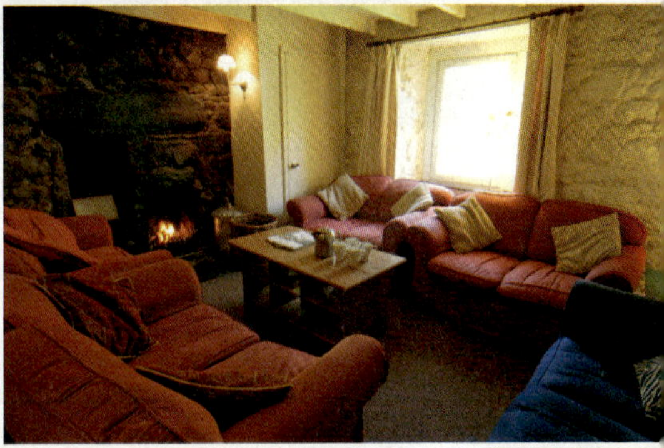

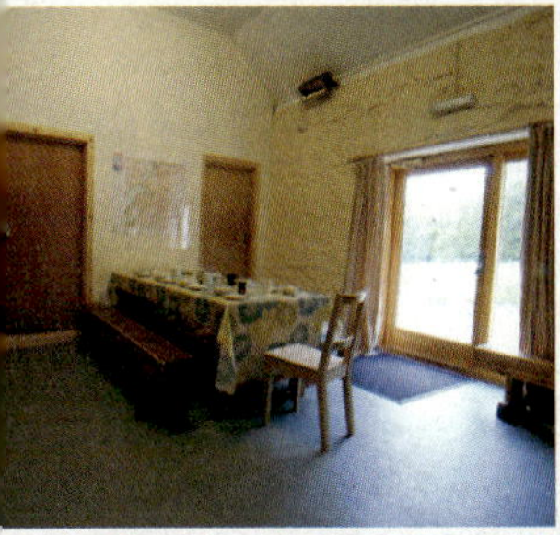

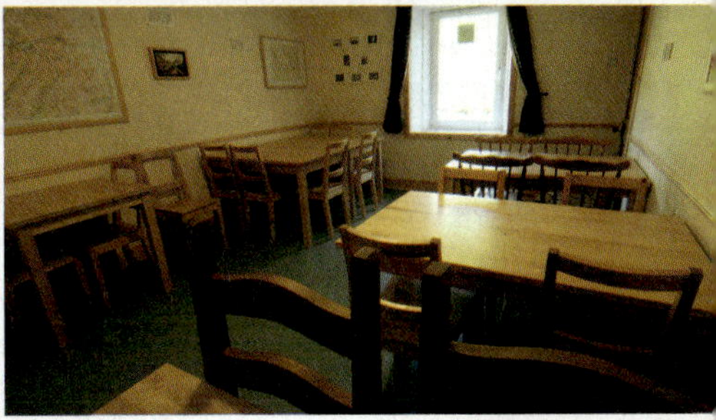

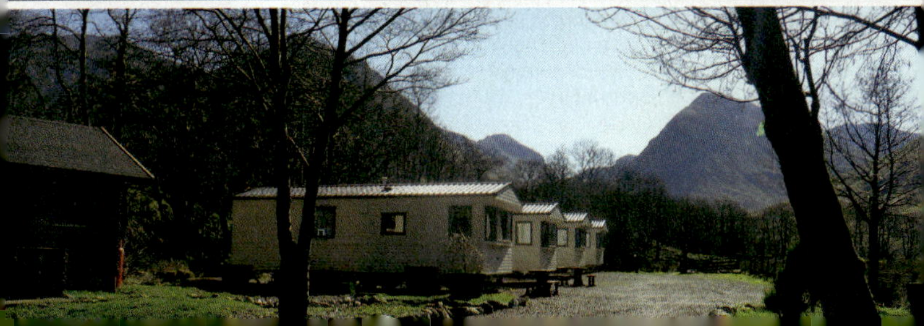

FORT WILLIAM BACKPACKERS

SCOTLAND

Deep in the Highlands, surrounded by spectacular mountain scenery lies Fort William, a mecca for those with a spirit of adventure. You can start (or end) the 'West Highland Way' in Fort William, hike or bike along mountain trails, go for a boat trip on the sea loch or just take it easy amidst the wonderful scenery. Even in winter Fort William stays busy with skiing, snow-boarding, mountaineering and ice-climbing. Nestling on a hillside above the town, with wonderful views, this characterful and comfy hostel provides everything you'll need after a day in the hills. In the evening put your feet up in the elegant lounge in front of a real fire or stroll down to the choice of local pubs. Ben Nevis, Britain's highest mountain, is just around the corner and below it is Glen Nevis, perhaps Scotland's prettiest glen, with wonderful waterfalls and ancient pine forest. Dramatic and eerie, Glencoe awaits a few miles away for an excellent day trip.

DETAILS

- **Open** - All year, all day. Reception 7am-noon and 5pm-10.30pm (times may vary)
- **Number of beds** - 38
- **Booking** - First night's payment required to confirm booking.
- **Price per night** - From £17 per person. ID required for check-in.
- **Public Transport** - Train and bus stations are only 5/10 minute walk from hostel.
- **Directions** - From north on the A82 go right at roundabout towards town centre. Turn left onto Victoria Road, then left at fork onto Alma Road. From south on the A82 go straight over first roundabout. At second roundabout go right onto Belford Road following Inverness signs, then turn right up Victoria Road then into Alma Road at left fork. From stations walk past supermarket, turn left before the underpass, heading onto the Belford Road. The hostel is just a bit further up, on Alma Road, on the right.

CONTACT: Receptionist
Tel: 01397 700 711
info@fortwilliambackpackers.com www.fortwilliambackpackers.com
Alma Road, Fort William, PH33 6HB

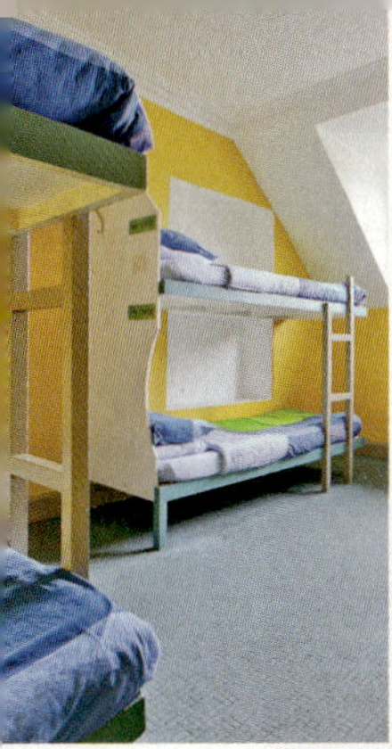
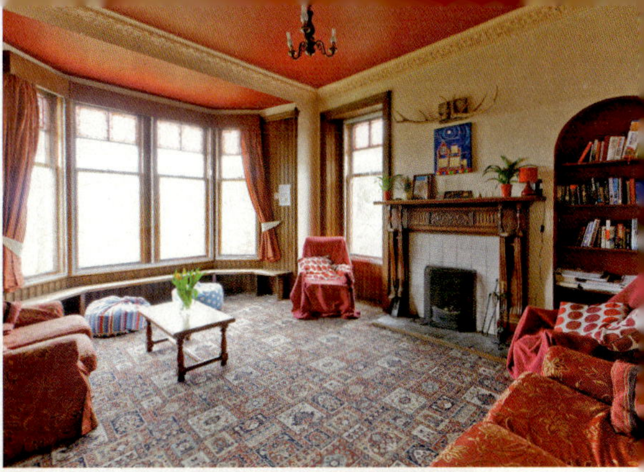
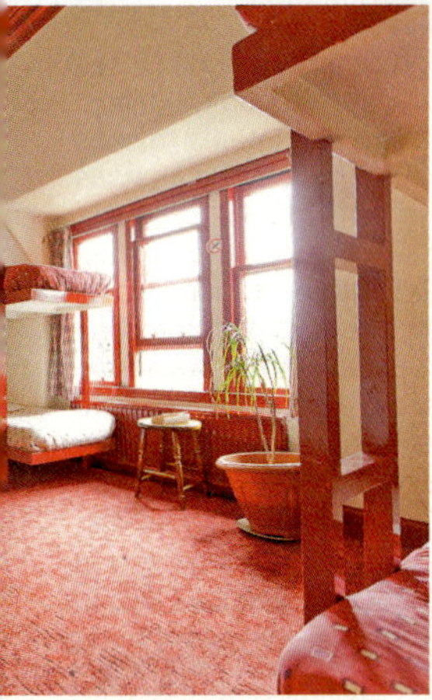
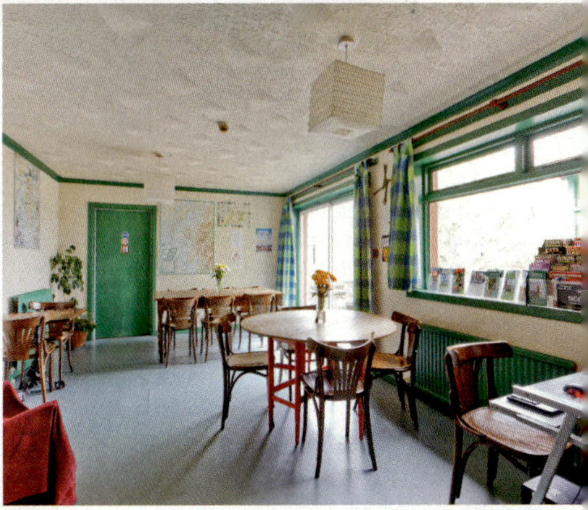
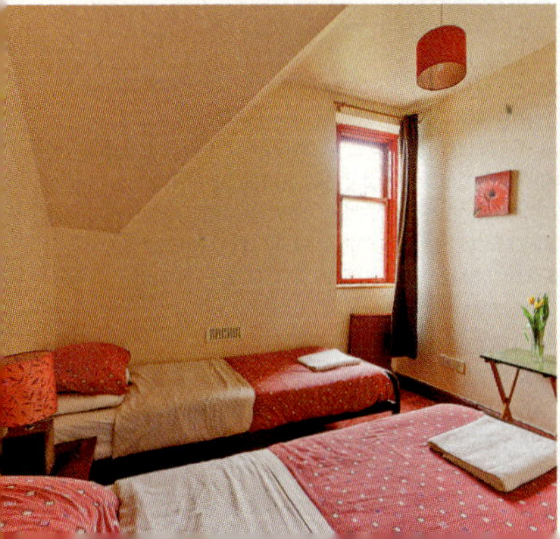
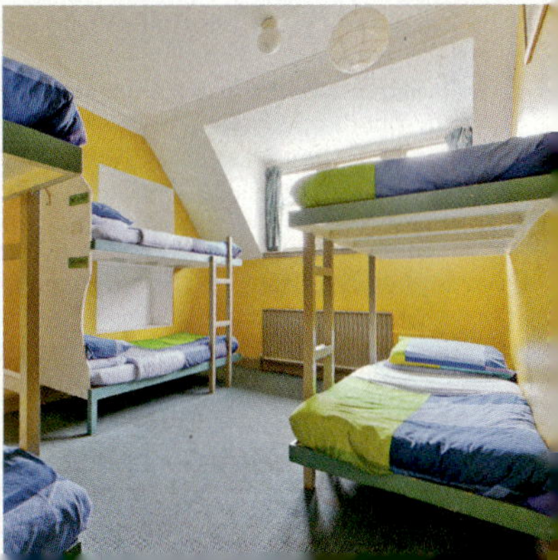

CALLUNA

SCOTLAND

Situated within fifteen minutes' walk of Fort William High Street, Calluna is ideal for short or long stays, for individuals or groups. The modern accommodation consists of one six-bed flat, an alpine loft (4 beds) and two apartments (8 beds each). Bedding is supplied, along with spacious kitchens, comfortable lounges and efficient drying rooms.

On the spot advice from Alan Kimber (mountain guide) and an on-site indoor bouldering wall, make this an ideal all weather climbing venue. Waterproofs, boots, axes, crampons for hire and mountaineering courses are also available (see website for details). Calluna is well known for peace, quiet and fine views over Loch Linnhe to the hills of Ardgour. A popular base for climbing and canoeing groups, families and individual globe trotters. Plenty of parking for mini-buses and trailers and secure lock up for bicycles. Lecture room available.

DETAILS

- **Open** - Christmas to October, , 24 hours (keys supplied)
- **Number of beds** - 18: Flat: 1x2, 1x4. Loft: 1x4. Apartments 1&2 2x4, 2x2, 2x2 (twin)
- **Booking** - Phone or email beforehand
- **Price per night** - Dorm beds £16 a night and twin beds £19pp a night.
- **Public Transport** - Fort William train and coach/bus stations are 20 mins' walk away. Alan & Sue offer a free lift from the stations when available - just phone.
- **Directions** - From A82 roundabout (by the Loch and West End Hotel), go uphill on Lundavra Rd, after 500 metres turn left uphill onto Connochie Rd (between four-storey flats). Follow for 200 metres uphill (do not take right turns). Look for our sign.

CONTACT: Alan or Sue
Tel: 01397 700451, Fax: 01397 700489
info@fortwilliamholiday.co.uk www.fortwilliamholiday.co.uk
Calluna, Connochie Road, Fort William, PH33 6JX

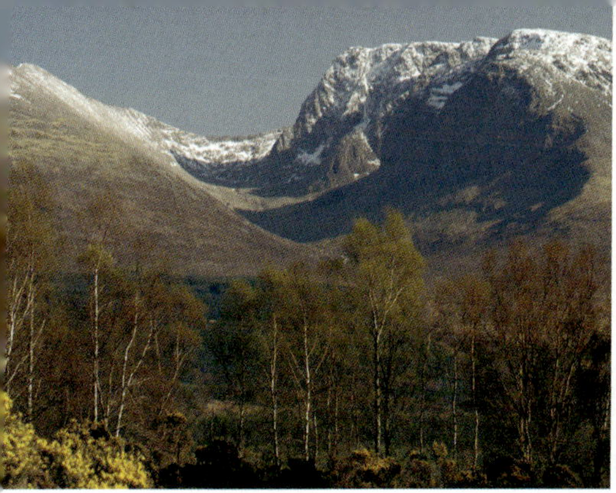
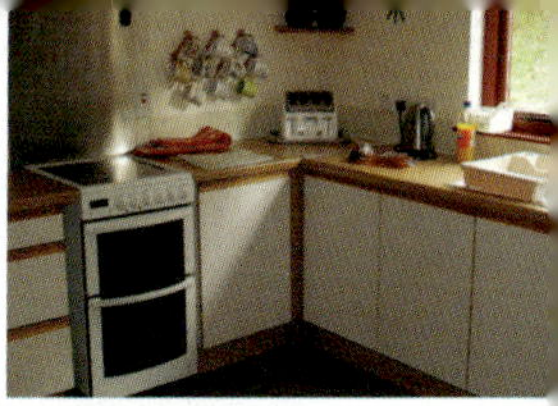
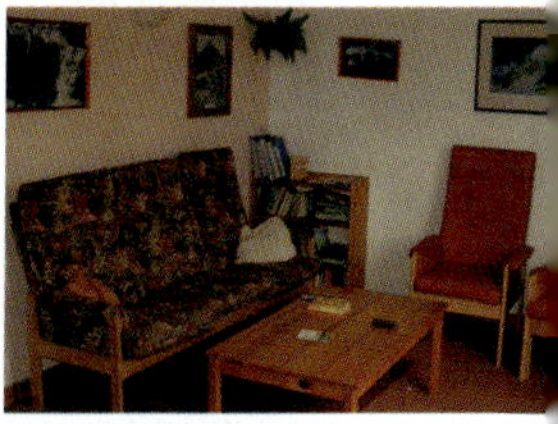
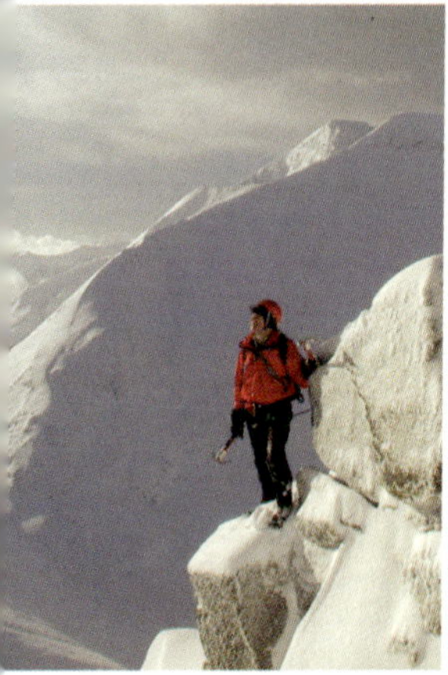
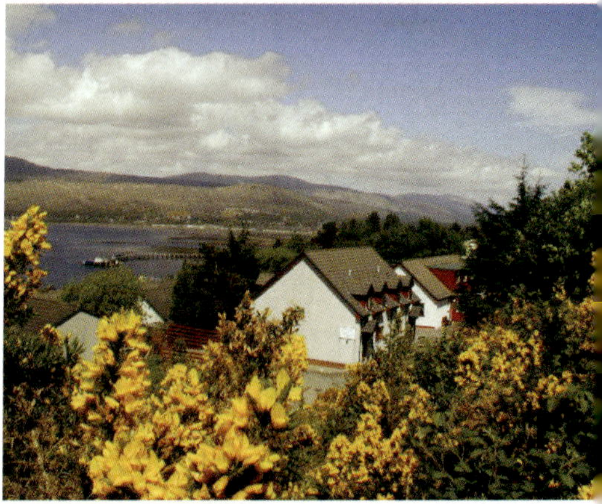
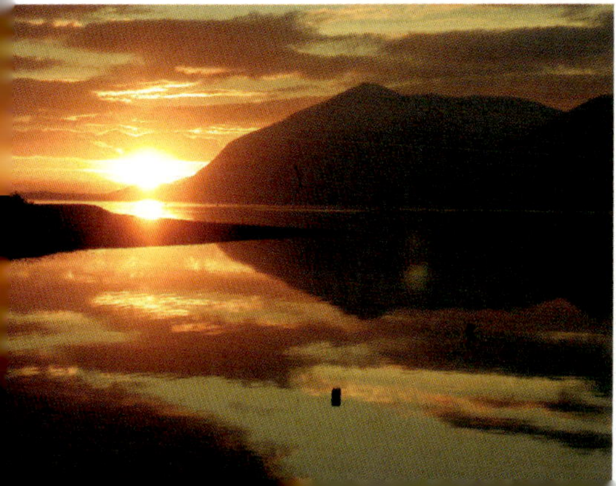
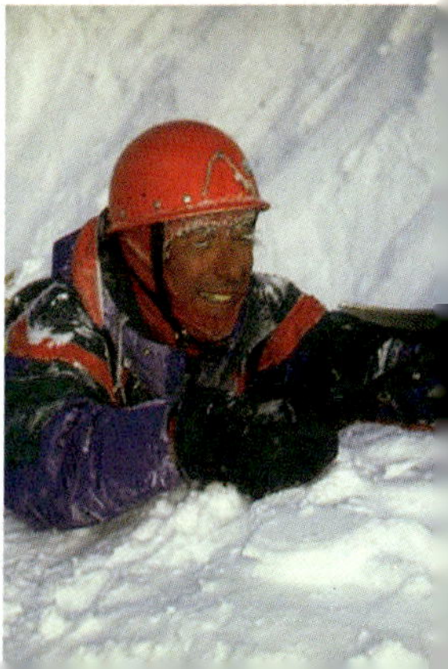

SMIDDY BUNKHOUSE

SCOTLAND

Find a friendly welcome at this comfortable, mountain hostel with a loch-side location overlooking the Caledonian Canal. The pine clad interior has a cosy, friendly atmosphere. Stunning mountains and water on the doorstep with the meeting of the West Highland Way and Great Glen Way only yards away. Hot showers. Fully equipped kitchens available at all times (local shop open until 11pm daily). Use of 2 efficient drying / laundry rooms. All bedding provided. Fully heated for all year round use. Lockable bike & canoe stores. Ample off road parking. Outdoor information, daily weather & snow reports. Advice/instruction/guiding available from resident mountain and water based instructors for: winter and summer walking/climbing; river, loch and sea kayaking; dinghy sailing. Hire of sea and river kayaks/open canoes, dinghy and other equipment. AALS licensed & DofE Approved Activity Provider (Assessor available). Group and family accommodation. Meeting / lecture room available by arrangement.

DETAILS

- **Open** - All year, all day (with key).
- **Number of beds** - 24: 3x4, 2x6.
- **Booking** - Book on-line or telephone / e-mail.
- **Price per night** - £15 - £20 (seasonal) pp (incl. bedding).
- **Public Transport** - Two minutes' walk from Corpach Railway Station-the Mallaig Line. Three miles - 2 stops out from Fort William (trains from Glasgow and London).
- **Directions** - Take A82 north out of Fort William towards Inverness. After one mile take A830 west towards Mallaig and follow for 2 miles to village of Corpach. Turn left before shops, signposted 'Snowgoose Mountain Centre'. The hostel is 30yds on left.

CONTACT: John or Tina
Tel: 01397 772467
enquiry@highland-mountain-guides.co.uk   www.highland-mountain-guides.co.uk
Snowgoose Mountain Centre, Station Road, Corpach, Fort William, PH33 7JH

DISCOVERY

Snowgoose
Mountain Centre
OUTDOOR
ACTION
ADVENTURE

BANK STREET LODGE

SCOTLAND

Bank Street Lodge is situated 100 metres from Fort William High Street which has numerous shops, pubs, restaurants and banks. There is a fully equipped kitchen with cooker, fridge, microwave, cutlery and crockery provided. The common room lounge has a TV, it also provides tables and chairs for eating self prepared meals, and a snack vending machine.

All bedding is provided. Some rooms are en suite (twins, doubles and family). WiFi is also now available in our lounge/TV room. The Stables Restaurant, at the front of the building, serves fine food for lunches and dinners (also breakfast from May to September) - treat yourself! Fort William is an ideal base from which to enjoy walking, climbing, cycling or mountain biking. The world-renowned Nevis Range Mountain Bike Trails and Ski Centre are only a short distance from the town centre. Three star STB rating.

DETAILS

- **Open** - All year, 24 hour reception
- **Number of beds** - 43: 6 x 4, 4 x 3, 1 x 7
- **Booking** - Booking advised. Deposit required for long stays or groups.
- **Price per night** - From £17 to £20.00 per person. Group rates available.
- **Public Transport** - Train and bus stations at Fort William, 500 metres from Lodge.
- **Directions** - Head for town centre via the underpass, turn left after Tesco supermarket on Bank Street, then head up the hill for 150 metres. Hostel is above the Stables Restaurant. Car parking is available.

CONTACT: Reception
Tel: 01397 700070, Fax: 01397 705569
bankstreetlodge@btconnect.com www.bankstreetlodge.co.uk
Bank Street, Fort William, PH33 6AY

FARR COTTAGE
LODGE

453

SCOTLAND

Farr Cottage is a 4 star hostel in Corpach just 4 miles from Fort William, the outdoor capital of the UK. It has a breath-taking view of Ben Nevis and views across Loch Linnhe. There is a full range of in-house facilities including freesat TV with DVD player in the lounge, free WiFi, licensed bar, self-catering facilities, drying room and a laundry service. The hostel has central heating and hot showers. Bike storage, bike hire and free onsite parking are available. Some pet friendly rooms are available please ring for details. Breakfast and picnic lunches can be provided when pre-ordered. The hostel organises many outdoor pursuits including white water rafting, canyoning, climbing, abseiling, skiing, snowboarding, fishing, and golf. Check website for special offers and details of music nights and events nights. Farr Cottage's professional team are geared to meet your needs and requirements.

DETAILS

- **Open** - Closed 14 Dec to 15 Jan unless 4 or more book. Reception 4:30pm - 10pm
- **Number of beds** - Cottage 30: 2 x double, 2 x 8,1 x 10. Fully self-contained.
- **Booking** - Advance booking advised.
- **Price per night** - £16.50pp in mixed dorms, From £17pp in double room. Group rates available. Contact Kirsty for Winter special - Nov till end of March.
- **Public Transport** - Corpach train station is 200m from the hostel. The nearest Citylink service is three miles away at Fort William. Taxi fare from Fort William £7.50.
- **Directions** - Follow the A82 north from Fort William centre towards Inverness for 1.5 miles. Turn left at the A830 to Mallaig. Follow this road for 1.5 miles into Corpach. We are on the right.

CONTACT: Cliff or Kirsty
Tel: 01397 772315 Mob: 07973828833, Fax: 07969960503
mail@farrcottage.com www.farrcottage.com
Corpach, Fort William, PH33 7LR

454 ÀITE CRUINNICHIDH
SCOTLAND

Àite Cruinnichidh, 15 miles northeast of Fort William, occupies a unique sheltered spot adjacent to the Monessie Gorge; explore remote glens, mountain passes and lochs. Numerous easy walks within minutes of the hostel and seven magnificent canoeing rivers within 20 miles. The location is also ideal for climbing (rock and ice), mountain biking, skiing or just relaxing. A warm, peaceful, friendly, country hostel in a converted barn, Àite Cruinnichidh has been renovated to high standards and sleeps 32 in five rooms of four, one of six, one twin and one double/family room en suite. All bedding supplied. A fully equipped kitchen/dining room, sitting room, excellent showers. Additional facilities: sauna suite, garden, seminar room, use of maps, advice on walking/cycling routes. Groups and individuals welcome. We do not have wheelchair access but we are glad to accommodate people with all forms of disability whenever we can.

DETAILS

- **Open** - All year, all day
- **Number of beds** - 32: 1x6, 5x4, 1x twin, 1x family/double en suite.
- **Booking** - Booking advised, 50% deposit.
- **Price per night** - From £16 per person
- **Public Transport** - Roy Bridge train station and bus stop (2 miles) has several trains and buses to and from Fort William daily. Pick up available from Roy Bridge with advanced notice.
- **Directions** - From Fort William follow A82 for 10 miles to Spean Bridge, turn right onto A86 for 3 miles to Roy Bridge. Pass though village and continue for 2 miles. The hostel is on right 100m after Glenspean Lodge Hotel on left.

CONTACT: Gavin or Nicola
Tel: 01397 712315
gavin@highland-hostel.co.uk www.highland-hostel.co.uk
1 Achluachrach, By Roy Bridge, Near Fort William, PH31 4AW

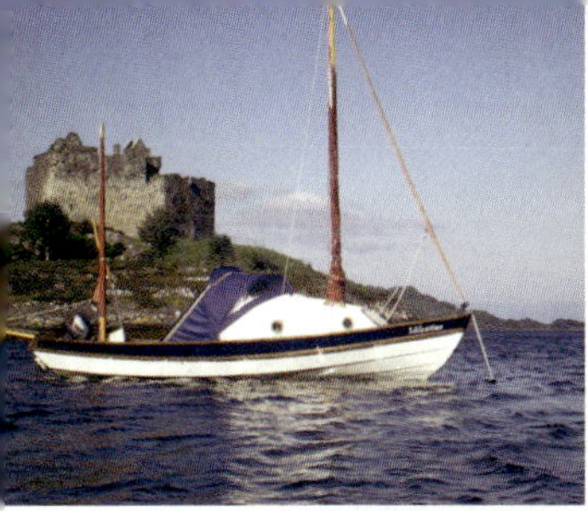

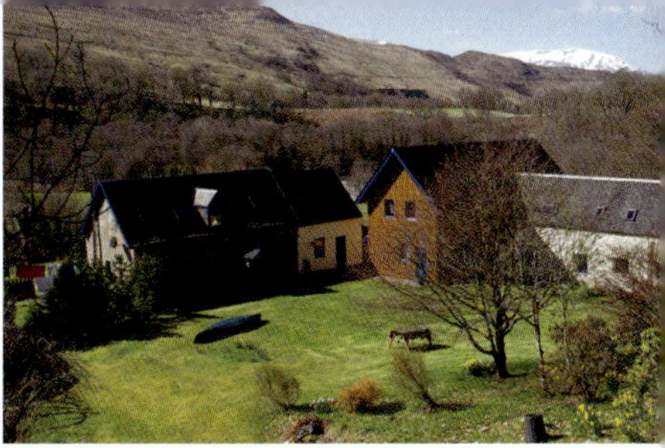

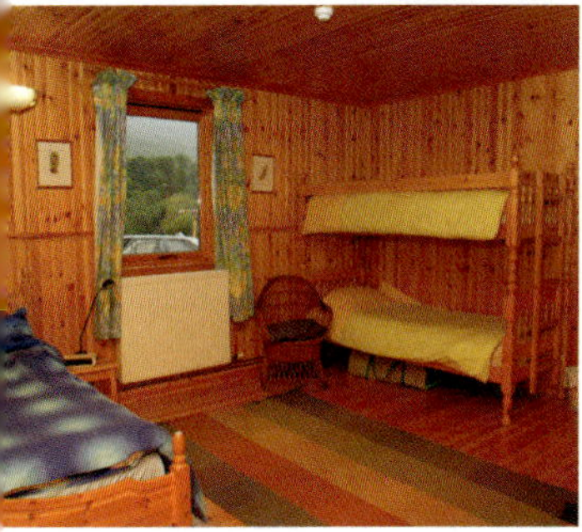

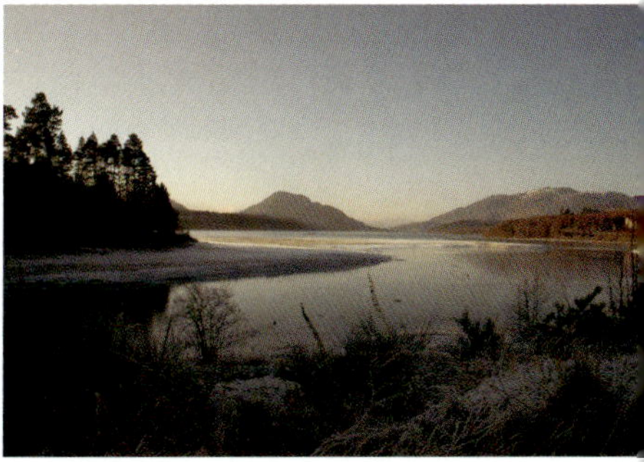

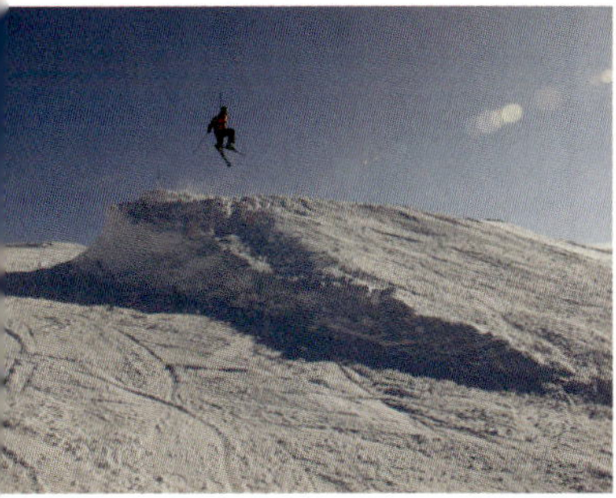

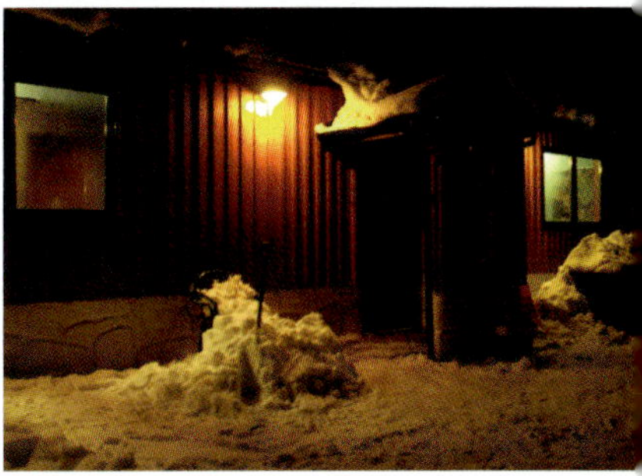

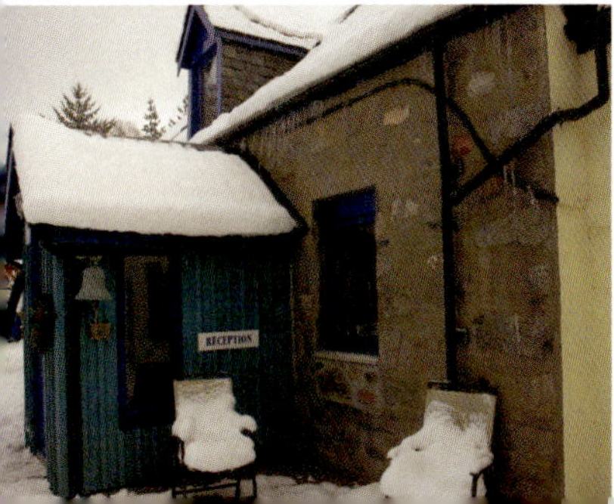
RECEPTION

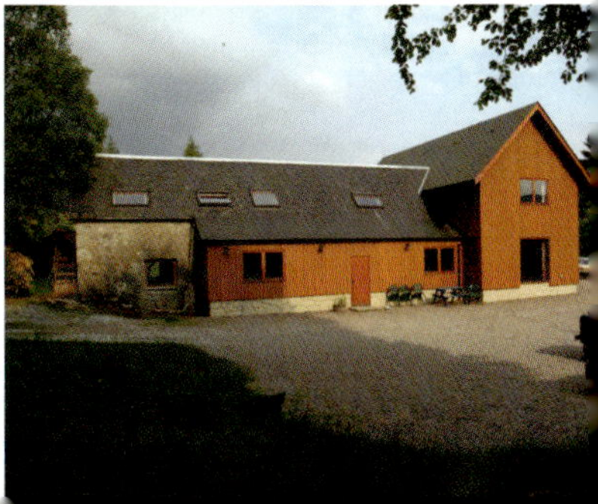

INSH HALL LODGE

SCOTLAND

Situated between Loch Insh and the foothills of Glenfeshie, Insh Hall Lodge provides comfortable double, twin and family rooms on a B&B basis. Rooms are equipped with bed linen and TVs. Facilities include large meeting room, laundry/drying room, sauna and mini gym, outdoor volleyball and basketball, as well as private car parking. Meals are available in the Boathouse Restaurant situated by the shore, 120 yds from the lodge.

Loch Insh Watersports provides a range of accessible watersports on-site. This is also the starting point for many local walks, lochside trails and cycle routes. Loch Insh is on Sustrans Route 7 Cycle Way. Anyone staying two nights or more between April and October has free use of the water sports equipment or between November and March has free use of dry ski slope - from 8.30 to 10.00 and from 4.00 to 5.30pm.

DETAILS

- **Open** - All year. All day
- **Number of beds** - 50+: Double, twin or family rooms en suite.
- **Booking** - Booking is recommended but not always required. Deposit taken.
- **Price per night** - From £34 per room.
- **Public Transport** - Trains at Aviemore and Kingussie (7 miles from Loch Insh). Nearest airport is Inverness, approximately one hour north of Loch Insh.
- **Directions** - Situated near Kincraig, 7 miles south of Aviemore, 7 miles north of Kingussie on the B9152, follow signs for Loch Insh Watersports. Local bus routes from Aviemore to Kincraig, approx. 1 mile from the Lodge.

CONTACT: Receptionist
Tel: 01540 651272, Fax: 01540 651208
office@lochinsh.com   www.lochinsh.com
Insh Hall, Kincraig, Inverness-shire, PH21 1NU

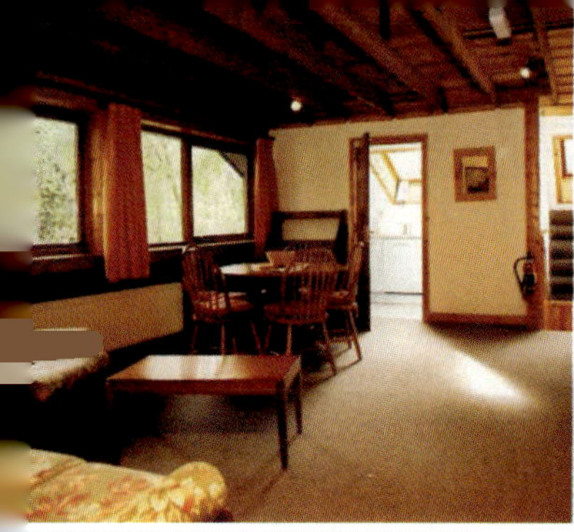
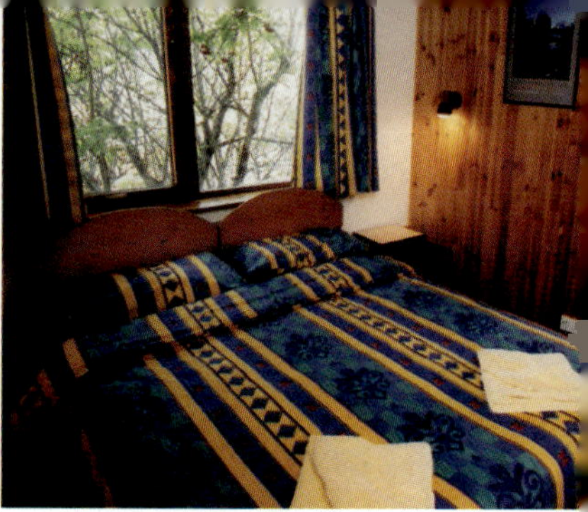
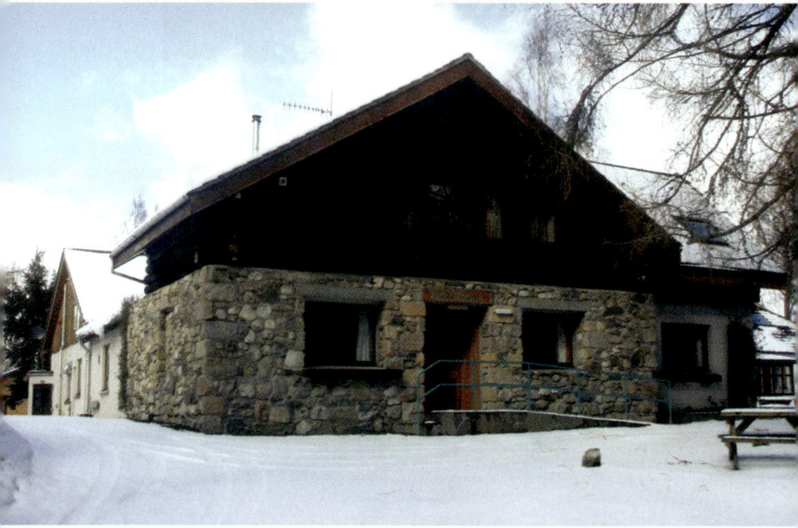
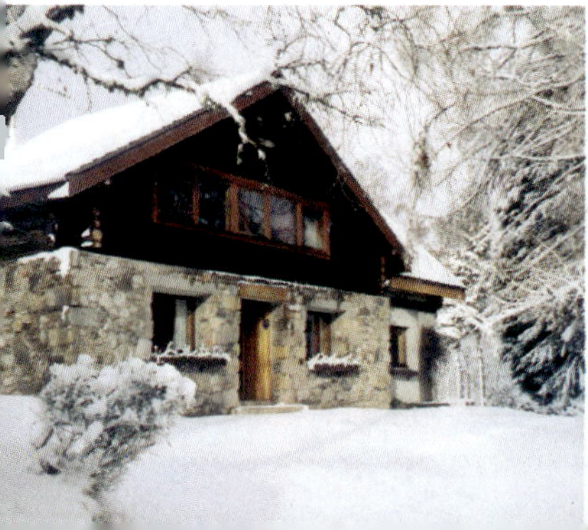
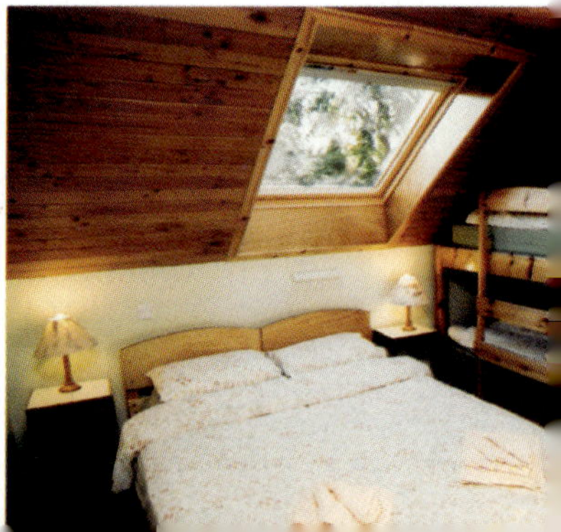

ABERNETHY BUNKHOUSE

SCOTLAND

Sharing a car park with the Speyside Way and just yards from the river, the converted Nethy Station offers all that a group of 10-20 could expect from a bunkhouse. It is well equipped, fully central heated and has two public areas. Most rooms have triple bunks and there is a 2 bunk room with unusual access: we call it Narnia, as you get there through a wardrobe! There is also 'The Shed'.

Whether you self-cater or we cook for you as a group, you will have access to the kitchen at all times. We never ask people to share the building so you may sleep, walk, ski, board, hike, ride, fish, etc. at your own convenience.

The bunkhouse is only 200 yards from the centre of Nethy Bridge with its shop, butcher, pub and interpretive centre and half way between two winter sports areas. Dogs are welcome but please do not let them sleep on the beds!

DETAILS

- **Open** - All year, anytime
- **Number of beds** - 24: 2x9: 3x2.
- **Booking** - Essential (with deposit)
- **Price per night** - £14.50pp May-Sep. £15.50pp Oct–Apr. Minimum of 10 people.
- **Public Transport** - Take train or Citylink coach to Aviemore. Local buses are available from Aviemore to Nethy Bridge Post Office, phone 01479 811566.
- **Directions** - GR 002 207. Hostel is adjacent to the Speyside Way. From the B970, with Post Office on your right, go over the bridge and turn left immediately. Go past the butcher turn second right.

CONTACT: Patricia or Richard
Tel: 01479 821370, Fax: 441479821370
info@nethy.org www.nethy.org
Station Road, Nethy Bridge, PH25 3DN

ARDENBEG BUNKHOUSE

SCOTLAND

459

Part of the award-winning Craggan Outdoors activity centre, Ardenbeg offers good value self-catering accommodation across rooms of four, five, six & eight bunks, along with two well appointed kitchen / dining / common room areas, four bathrooms and a large private garden with BBQ, picnic tables & a children's play area.

The property is situated on a quiet residential street in Grantown-on-Spey, the historic capital of Strathspey. As well as the wide range of outdoor activities on offer through Craggan Outdoors (see www.cragganoutdoors.co.uk), Ardenbeg is perfectly situated - 15 minutes from Aviemore, 45 minutes from Inverness, 2 hours from Aberdeen, 3 hours from the Central Belt - to enjoy all that the Cairngorms National Park & wider central Highlands has to offer.

DETAILS

- **Open** - Year round. Access 24 hours
- **Number of beds** - 23: 1x4, 1x5, 1x6, 1x8.
- **Booking** - In advance to avoid disappointment
- **Price per night** - From £15.50 to £24 per person per night, subject to number of people & duration of stay.
- **Public Transport** - Rail: Aviemore. Bus: stop on the High Street in Grantown. Air: Inverness
- **Directions** - Once in Grantown-on-Spey, find the Co-op on the High Street, & then take the road that runs beside the Co-op (keeping it on your right), & turn left after 100 yards into Grant Road. Ardenbeg is the fifth building on the right.

CONTACT: Keith & Jill Ballam
Tel: 01479 873283 / 01479 872824
info@cragganoutdoors.co.uk www.cragganoutdoors.co.uk
Grant Road, Grantown-on-Spey, Moray PH26 3LD

FINDHORN VILLAGE HOSTEL

460 — SCOTLAND

Located in the heart of the coastal village of Findhorn, in the Moray Coast Area of Outstanding Natural Beauty, Findhorn Village Hostel is just a stone's throw from the beautiful bay and a short walk to the dunes and the Findhorn Foundation Eco Village. Extensive sandy beaches, great wildlife sites and even the Cairngorm mountains and Speyside distilleries are within reach of the village. The hostel provides self catering accommodation in the former village school which can be booked exclusively by groups but is open to individuals in the summer months. The hostel has a well equipped kitchen and communal area, TV and DVD, modern showers and central heating. Visitors are accommodated in two 10 bed bunk rooms each with it's own two bed "leaders room" attached. The communal areas provide plenty of space for large groups but can be rearranged into a more intimate setting for individuals.

DETAILS

- **Open** - All year- groups, May-Sept individuals, ,
- **Number of beds** - 24: 2x10 2x2
- **Booking** - Essential via website. Group bookings £50 deposit. Bookings must be paid in full one month in advance. Individuals should pay in full on booking.
- **Price per night** - £16pp individuals. £13.50pp groups. Minimum group charge £135 (10 people). Groups are subject to a £24 charge for cleaning.
- **Public Transport** - Trains and intercity busses to Forres. Bus No 34 runs hourly (except Sundays) from Forres to Findhorn (until 18.15) and stops by the Church.
- **Directions** - B9011 into Findhorn. at the end of the one-way system through the village take a left turn. Findhorn Village Centre is directly ahead.

CONTACT: Karin
Tel: 01309 692339
findhornvillagecentre@gmail.com www.findhornvillagehostel.com
Church Place, Findhorn, Forres, Moray, IV36 3YR

CULLEN HARBOUR HOSTEL
461
SCOTLAND

Cullen Harbour Hostel's special location on the shores of the Moray Firth offers guests a relaxing break with the sound of the sea at night and lovely coastal walks by day. Accommodation at the hostel is spacious and uncluttered with the best solid single beds, power shower, and separate bathroom. It has been awarded 4 stars by VisitScotland. The kitchen has a solid fuel Rayburn cooker and comfortable sitting area. There is a large laundry area and drying room. Cullen is at one end of the Speyside Way and on the National Cycle Route 1.

Outdoor activity groups enjoy sea kayaking, surfing, rock climbing and wildlife watching. Dolphins are seen from the hostel. Children enjoy the sandy harbour and rock pools. Pubs and food are readily available.

DETAILS

- **Open** - All year, all day but please check in initially by 21.30
- **Number of beds** - 14: 2x6, 1x4 (family room)
- **Booking** - Not essential for individuals. For groups and advanced bookings a deposit is required.
- **Price per night** - £16 pp. Four-bed family room with en-suite shower, linen included: £80 for four, £65 for three and £50 for two.
- **Public Transport** - Cullen village is easily reached by buses from Inverness or Aberdeen, or trains to Elgin or Keith and then by bus to Cullen. Car journeys from Inverness or Aberdeen take 1.5 hours.
- **Directions** - The hostel is found immediately adjacent to the harbour, a 5 min walk downhill from Cullen village square.

CONTACT: Ruth or Howard
Tel: 01542 841997, Mob: 07432 591201(Ruth) 07912 079416(Howard)
ruth@cullenharbourholidays.com www.cullenharbourholidays.com
The Sailors Store, Portlong Rd, Cullen, AB56 4AG

RATTRAY HEAD ECO-HOSTEL

SCOTLAND — 462

Rattray Head Eco-Hostel is a former lighthouse shore station among huge dunes on an isolated 11 mile long sandy beach. Come and relax in this gorgeous most easterly part of mainland Scotland, and enjoy one of its driest, sunniest, midge-free areas.

The 1892 granite building has been renovated to form a modern, non-smoking, dog-friendly coastal retreat. The hostel has self-catering kitchens, bunkrooms, and double and family bedrooms. It is part of the SIH network and has a Visit Scotland 3 star grading.

The North Sea Cycle Route (Sustrans 1) is 17 miles inland and passes through historic Aberdeenshire with stone circles, castle ruins and golf courses.

DETAILS

- **Open** - All year, phone in winter, check-in 4–8pm, check-out 11am. No curfew.
- **Number of beds** - 22: 1x2, 5x4
- **Booking** - Booking is available with first night as deposit.
- **Price per night** - Bunk £16pp, Triple £19pp, Double/Twin £24pp. Includes bedding and drinks.
- **Public Transport** - Airport, coach and train stations at Aberdeen (43 miles). Buses 60, 63 run frequently between Aberdeen and Peterhead. Bus 69 runs hourly between Peterhead and Fraserburgh. Taxi from Peterhead about £23.
- **Directions** - NK103577 Rattray is signed from the A90 Peterhead to Fraserburgh road. The hostel is at the end of the lane near the lighthouse, about 3 miles from the A90.

CONTACT: Rob and Val
Tel: 01346 532236, Fax: 01346532236
hostel@rattrayhead.net www.rattrayhead.net/hostel
Lighthouse Cottages, Rattray Head, Peterhead, Aberdeenshire, AB42 3HA

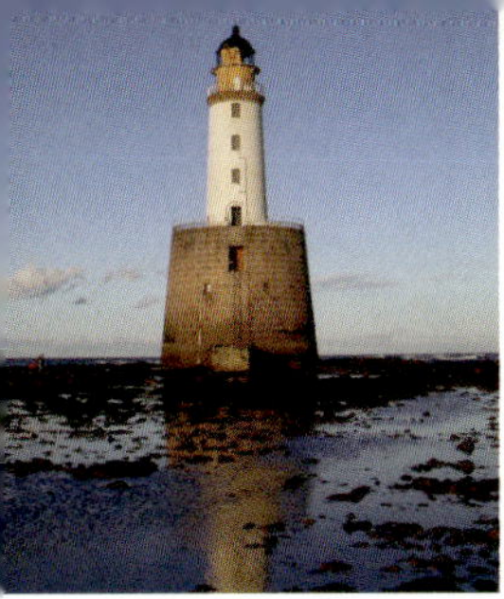
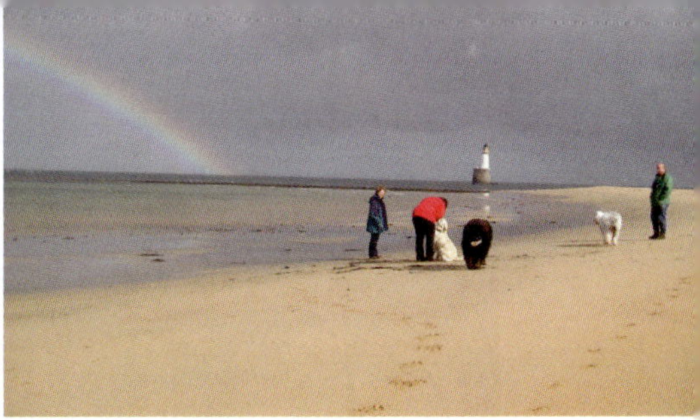
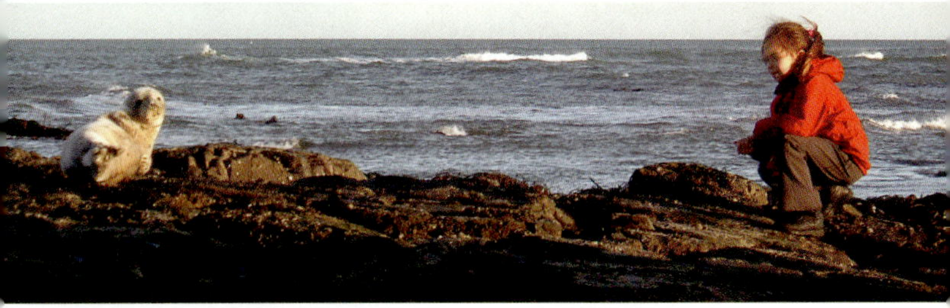
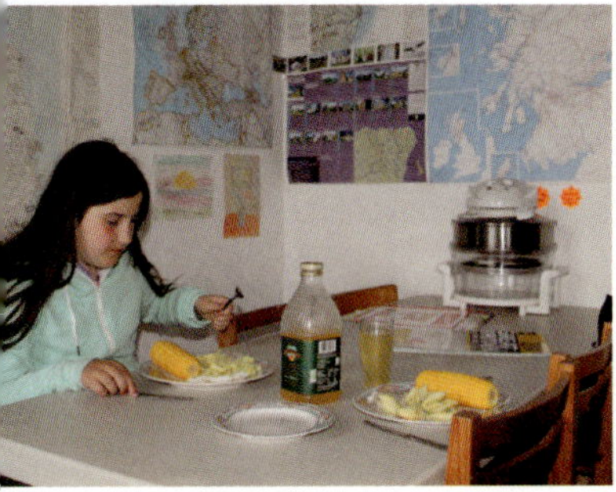
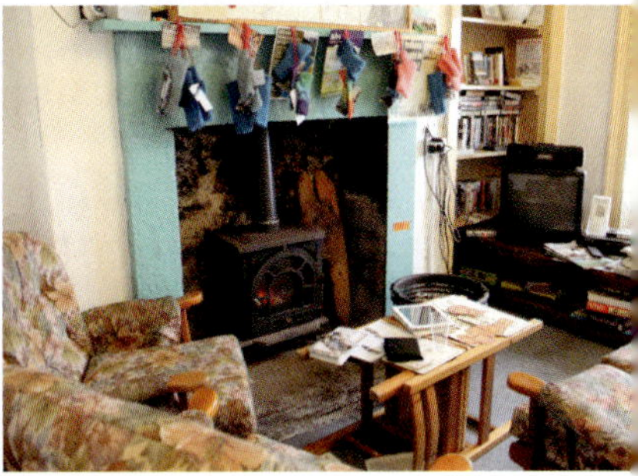
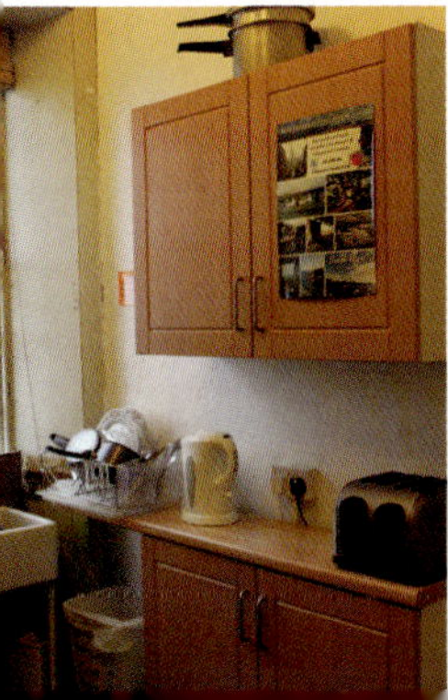
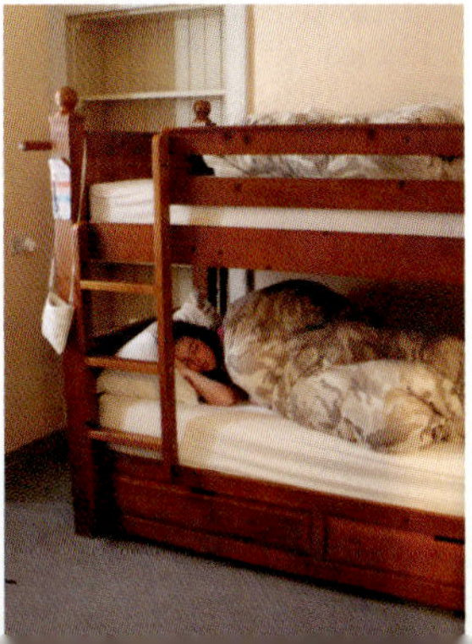
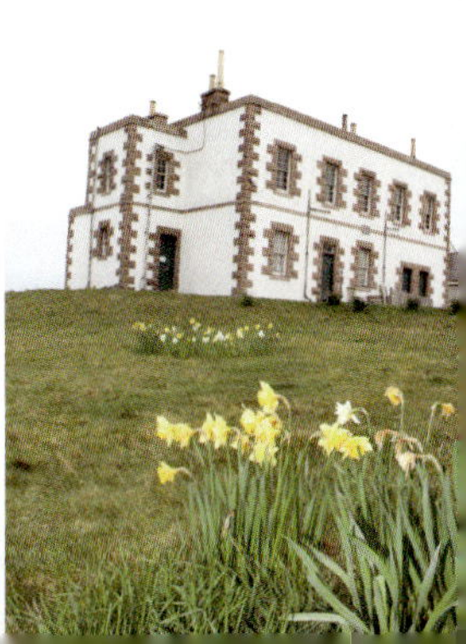

INVERNESS STUDENT HOTEL

SCOTLAND

Set amongst some of Scotland's most fascinating attractions, the bustling town centre of Inverness soon gives way to lochs, hills, forests and glens. Close to Inverness Castle, the cosy and friendly Student Hotel enjoys panoramic views of the town and the mountains beyond. After a hard day's Nessie hunting, the hostel provides the perfect place to unwind, just yards from the city's varied night-life and a few minutes' walk from bus and train stations. Relax in the fabulous lounge with real log fire and drink as much free tea, coffee & hot chocolate as you like. Knowledgeable staff can give you tips on what to see and do in the area and free WiFi is available. Visit the beautiful ancient pine forest of Glen Affric, tranquil but deeply historic Culloden Battlefield, the 4,000 year old standing stones at Clava Cairns or stroll down the riverbank to the waterfront to try to glimpse the wild dolphins in the nearby Moray Firth. Famous Loch Ness lies just a few miles upstream and of course has its own special wild animal.

DETAILS

- **Open** - All year, all day, reception 7am - 10.30pm.
- **Number of beds** - 57.
- **Booking** - First night's payment required to confirm booking.
- **Price per night** - From £15 per night. ID required for check-in.
- **Public Transport** - Inverness train station and bus station are a mere 10 minute walk from the hostel. Alternatively jump in a taxi for around £5.
- **Directions** - From train/bus station left onto Academy St, take right down Inglis St. then right onto High Street, turn left onto Castle St past the castle. Continue up Culduthel Road and hostel is on right. By road take B861 over the river then follow the road round into Castle Street/Cuthuthel Road the hostel is on the right

CONTACT: Receptionist
Tel: 01463 236 556
info@invernessstudenthotel.com www.invernessstudenthotel.com
8 Culduthel Road, Inverness, IV2 4AB

BIRD MAP OF SCOTLAND
Chalkboard Magic
unicorn
CHAMPION
SCOTLAND
GUINNESS
DRAUGHT

SLOCHD MHOR LODGE

SCOTLAND

Slochd Mhor Lodge is perfectly situated in spectacular Strathspey in the Cairngorms National Park, halfway between the villages of Carrbridge and Tomatin. The Lodge is on an 'off road' section of the No 7 Sustrans cycle route, surrounded by hills and forests. This is perfect walking country and in winter there are nordic ski trails from the doorstep. Slochd Mhor Lodge offers a genuine welcome in warm cosy surroundings with full central heating. Fully equipped kitchen and a spacious dining area together with large lounge/lecture room with woodburner, TV, WiFi, books and games. Other facilities include a drying room and laundry facilities, some en suite rooms, bedroom, shower and toilet suitable for wheel-chair users, on-site cycle shop/workshop, MT bike hire and nordic ski hire. Locked bike shed. Free range eggs when available. Coffee and tea. Outside seating and BBQ area. Ample parking. VisitScotland 4 star graded. Silver Green Business Award. Cyclists and Walkers Welcome.

DETAILS

- **Open** - All year, new arrivals 5-9pm. Checked in gets key.
- **Number of beds** - 22: 1x10, 1x6, 2x5, 1x2. Max 22 people.
- **Booking** - Booking recommended
- **Price per night** - £21, £20 for 2+ nights. Family rooms sleep 5 from £21 each. 2-12 yrs £15, under 2s free. Prices include bedding and linen. Towels extra. Sole use rates available for Christmas, New Year, clubs, meetings, courses etc
- **Public Transport** - Nearest bus and train station Carrbridge (4miles). City Link London/Edinburgh and Glasgow/Inverness stop at Aviemore (11 miles).
- **Directions** - Northbound on A9, after mileage board 'Inverness 23' travel 1.5 miles, take first left marked 'Slochd', then first right after ¼ mile into large car park.

CONTACT: Liz or Ian
Tel: +44 (0)1479 841666
Slochd666@aol.com www.slochd.co.uk
Slochd, Carrbridge, Inverness-shire, PH23 3AY

MORAG'S LODGE
LOCH NESS
SCOTLAND

467

Morag's Lodge is a multi-award winning hostel just a minute's walk from the bustling village of Fort Augustus on Loch Ness. The perfect base to explore the Loch Ness area and an ideal stop off on the Great Glen Way.

The Lodge offers great budget accommodation for backpackers, independent travellers and groups. It has a range of dorms, twins, doubles and private family rooms most of which are en suite. The fantastic facilities include a fully licensed bar, home-cooked meals, drying room, WiFi, self-catering kitchen and bike hire. There is ample car parking. FINALST "Best Holiday Accommodation" Highlands & Islands Tourism Awards 2014 WINNER 'Best Self Catering Accommodation' Highlands and Islands Tourism Awards 2012 WINNER 'Team of the Year' Hospitality Assured Business Excellence Awards 2012. Member of Europe's Famous Hostels, 4 Star VisitScotland, Green Tourism Silver Award.

DETAILS

- **Open** - All year. All day. Check-in from 4.30pm (earlier by arrangement)
- **Number of beds** - 75: 1x7, 6x6, 6x4, 4x2/3
- **Booking** - Booking recommended.
- **Price per night** - From £22pp in dorm beds. Doubles/twins from £25pp. Family rooms from £62.
- **Public Transport** - Bus stop for Fort William and Inverness only 200m away.
- **Directions** - From Inverness, arrive at Fort Augustus, turn first right up Bunoich Brae. From Fort William, go through village past petrol station and car park. Take next left up Bunoich Brae.

CONTACT: Claire
Tel: 01320 366289
info@moragslodge.com   www.moragslodge.com
Bunoich Brae, Fort Augustus, Inverness-shire, PH32 4DG

LOCH NESS BACKPACKERS LODGE
SCOTLAND

Loch Ness Backpackers is a warm and friendly little hostel with a relaxed atmosphere, good music and no curfew. It has grown from an 18th century farm cottage and barn and provides a warm open fire to greet you on cold nights. The house forms the main area of the hostel with reception, bar and restaurant, lounge, dining room, kitchen and toilets/showers on the ground floor, and two dormitories and one double room in the upstairs area. A converted barn (the bunkhouse) contains four more dormitories, toilets/showers. There are two comfortable family rooms. There is also a great BBQ area, garden and car park. Loch Ness Backpackers is within easy walking distance of Loch Ness, Urquhart Castle, three pubs, restaurants, a supermarket, a fish and chip shop, post office, bank, gift shops and bus stops. A perfect location for activity or relaxation amongst spectacular scenery. Horse riding, fishing on the loch and mountain biking can all be arranged locally (great bikes available for hire).

DETAILS

- **Open** - All year, all day
- **Number of beds** - House 16: Bunkhouse 24: (1x2, 2 x family room, 6 x dorms).
- **Booking** - Check availability on website or by phone.
- **Price per night** - From £17 per person. Discount applied to group bookings or long term stays.
- **Public Transport** - Nearest trains at Inverness. Rapsons and Citylink buses all pass close to the hostel.
- **Directions** - Near the A82 Inverness to Fort William road. Turn off is next to the stone bridge in Lewiston near the Poachers pub

CONTACT: Wendy and Neil MacIntosh
Tel: 07985 988015
neil@borlum.go-plus.net   www.lochness-backpackers.com
Borlum Bridge, East Lewiston, Drumnadrochit, Inverness, IV63 6UJ

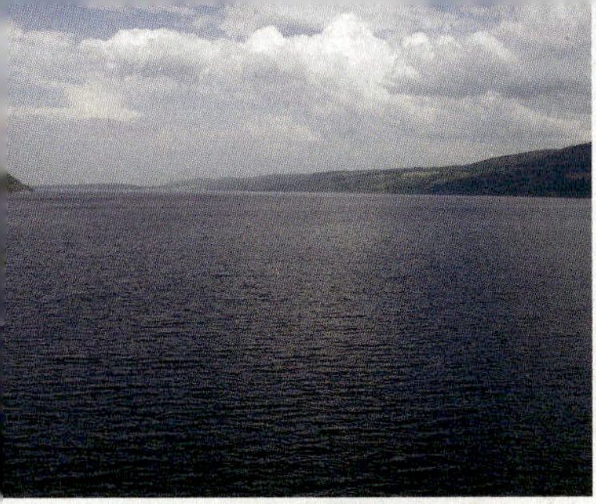
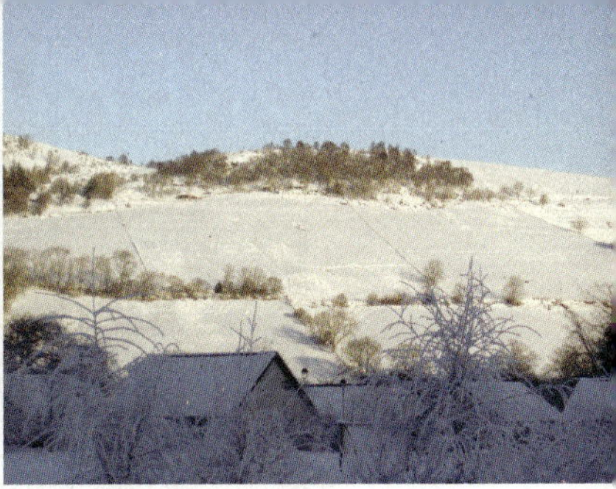
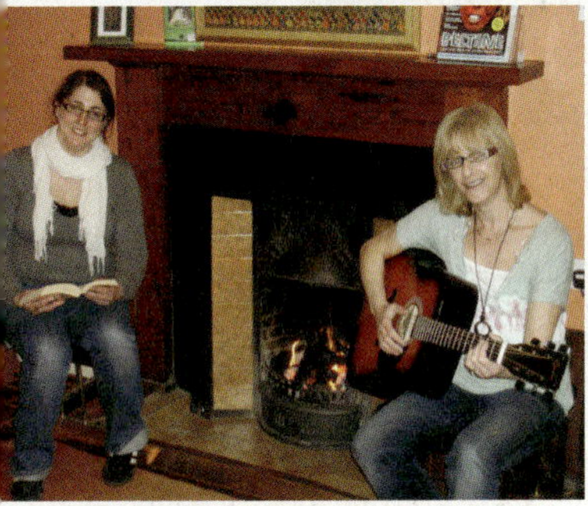
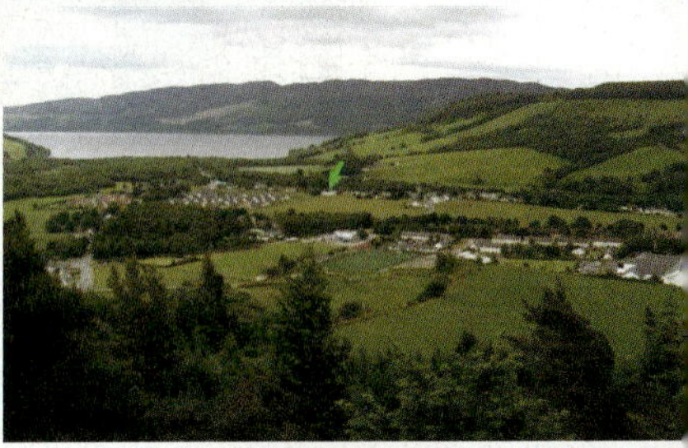
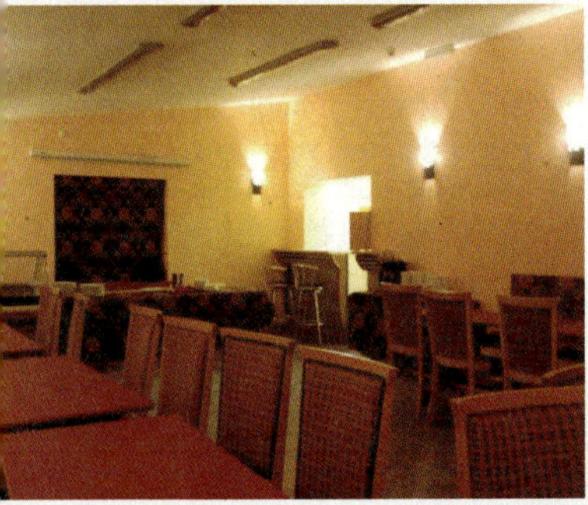
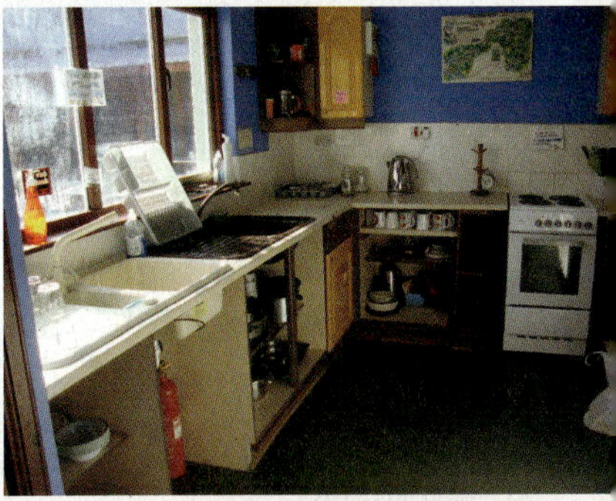
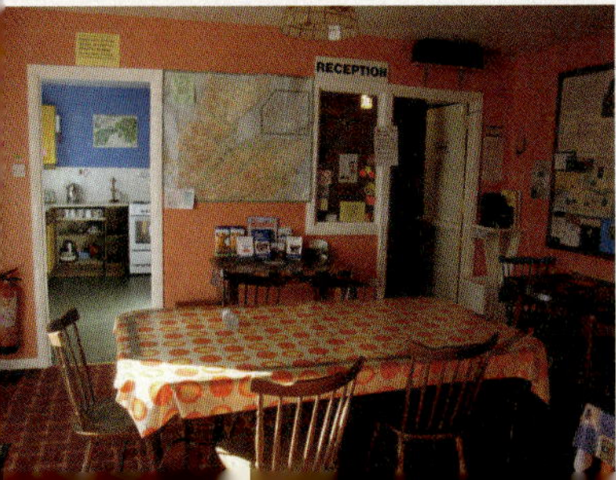
RECEPTION
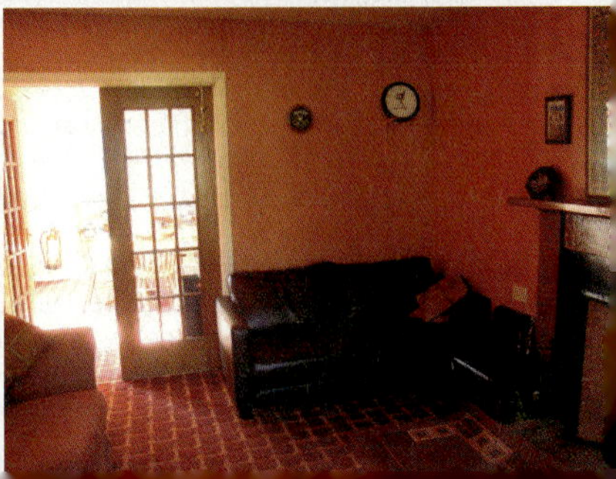

GREAT GLEN HOSTEL

SCOTLAND

Nestled between mountains and lochs in the heart of the "Outdoor Capital of the UK", 20 miles north of Fort William and 10 miles south of Loch Ness, the Great Glen Hostel is an ideal location whether you're touring the Highlands, bagging Munros or paddling rivers and lochs, and it is only a few minutes' walk from the Great Glen Way.

The hostel provides comfortable accommodation in twin, family and dormitory rooms. Hostel facilities include a self-catering kitchen, drying room, laundry, bike and canoe storage, free internet access, hot showers and a hostel store.

The whole hostel is available for exclusive rental for groups throughout the year.

DETAILS

- **Open** - Open all year, all day. Please call first Nov-March.
- **Number of beds** - 49: 3 x 2, 1 x 3, 4 x 5, 2 x 6, 1 x 8
- **Booking** - Booking recommended. Please telephone in advance or book online
- **Price per night** - Dorm beds from £17. Twin rooms from £20 per person. Whole hostel available for exclusive hire from £350 per night.
- **Public Transport** - Citylink bus services between Glasgow and the Isle of Skye, and between Fort William and Inverness will stop nearby. Nearest railway station: Spean Bridge. Nearest airport: Inverness.
- **Directions** - We are located 11 miles north of Spean Bridge and 3 miles south of Invergarry on the A82 in a small settlement called South Laggan. Citylink buses stop 100m north of the hostel on the A82. If you are walking the Great Glen Way, stay on the Way until you see signs directing you to the hostel.

CONTACT: Clem or Kirsty
Tel: 01809 501430
bookings@greatglenhostel.com   www.greatglenhostel.com
South Laggan, Spean Bridge, Invernesshire, PH34 4EA

ARIUNDLE BUNKHOUSE

SCOTLAND — 471

The Ariundle Centre is located at the beginning of the Ariundle Oakwoods, close to glorious walks, bird song, climbing, cycling, canoeing and fishing. It is a friendly family run business with a licensed restaurant, tea room, craft shop and bunkhouse. The 4 star bunkhouse sleeps 26 people, the rooms are large and airy and there is a drying area and self-catering facilities. Linen is supplied, towels can be hired for 50p. The bunkhouse is ideal for walkers and climbers. Groups, individuals and families are all welcome and family rooms are available. Cooked breakfasts, morning coffee, light lunches and scrumptious home baking are available in the restaurant. The sandwiches and baking make ideal packed lunches and home cooked ready meals are available to warm up in the bunkhouse. Candlelit suppers are served using local products, sometimes with a local musician to entertain. The Centre can cater for parties or weddings with guests sleeping in the bunkhouse. The village of Strontian has a petrol station and a well stocked shop.

DETAILS

- **Open** - All year.
- **Number of beds** - 26: 2x8, 2x4,1x2
- **Booking** - Advance bookings accepted all year
- **Price per night** - From £18 pp. Cont. b/fst £4. Bed & Breakfast £26. Grp. discount for advance payment.
- **Public Transport** - 1 mile from the nearest public transport.
- **Directions** - Travelling from north, east or south take the A82 to the Corran Ferry and then follow the road to Strontian. (Turn left when you come off the ferry).

CONTACT: Kate Campbell
Tel: 01967 402279
ariundle@aol.com www.ariundlecentre.co.uk
Ariundle Centre, Strontian, PH36 4JA

GLENFINNAN SLEEPING CAR

472 SCOTLAND

Glenfinnan sleeping car provides unique, comfortable accommodation in an historic railway carriage adjacent to Glenfinnan Station. An ideal location for the mountains of Lochaber, Rough Bounds, Moidart and Ardgour.

Glenfinnan makes a great starting point for bothy expeditions and is a useful stopping-off point on the route to Skye. Why not use it also for extended stays using road or rail for trips to fishing, golf, ferries, cruises, and beach locations?

The sleeping car has a fully equipped kitchen, showers, a drying room and total hydro-electric heating. The adjacent dining coach provides excellent meals to give you a break from self-catering.

Your overnight stay includes free admission to the railway museum housed in the station buildings.

DETAILS

- **Open** - All year, 24 hours
- **Number of beds** - 10
- **Booking** - Booking preferred and advisable to avoid disappointment.
- **Price per night** - £14 pppn, £120 for exclusive use of whole coach.
- **Public Transport** - Bunkhouse is adjacent to Glenfinnan Railway Station on the West Highland Line (Glasgow-Fort William-Mallaig) and is 100m from a bus stop.
- **Directions** - On the A830, 15 miles from Fort William and 30 miles from Mallaig with ferry connections to the Small Isles and Skye.

CONTACT: John or Hege
Tel: 01397 722295, Fax: 01397 722334
glenfinnan@btconnect.com   www.glenfinnanstationmuseum.co.uk
Glenfinnan Station, Glenfinnan, nr Fort William, PH37 4LT

SHEENA'S
BACKPACKERS LODGE SCOTLAND

473

The Backpackers Lodge, the oldest original croft house in Mallaig, offers a homely base from which you can explore the Inner Hebrides, the famous white sands of Morar and the remote peninsula of Knoydart.

Mallaig is a working fishing village with all the excitement of the boats landing. You can see the seals playing in the harbour waiting for the boats, whale and dolphin watching trips are available from the harbour. The hostel provides excellent budget accommodation with two rooms each with six beds, full central heating and fully equipped kitchen/common room with free WiFi. Scottish Tourist Board three star. All hot water and heating provided by renewable energy.

On site is the Tea Garden Café (open from 9am to 6pm March to November and 9am to 6.30pm June, July and August) serving quality meals, snacks, speciality coffee and home baking. See website for pictures of the restaurant and the beautiful countryside around.

DETAILS

- **Open** - All year, 24 hours.
- **Number of beds** - 12: 2 x 6
- **Booking** - Telephone ahead for availability and bookings.
- **Price per night** - £17.50 per person
- **Public Transport** - Mallaig has a train station and services by Citylink coaches. For information on local buses phone 01967 431272.
- **Directions** - From railway station turn right, hostel is two buildings along.

CONTACT: Norman Payne
Tel: 01687 462764, Fax: 01687462708
backpackers@btinternet.com www.mallaigbackpackers.co.uk
Harbour View, Mallaig, Inverness-shire, PH41 4PU

GLEBE BARN

SCOTLAND

Situated on the extraordinary Isle of Eigg in a charmingly converted 19th century building, the Glebe Barn offers 4 Star, homely hostel accommodation within 1 mile of the well stocked island shop and café/restaurant. The hostel boasts outstanding sea views, a well equipped kitchen, cozy log fire and wide range of books and games for all ages. Sleeping up to 22 in a combination of twin, triple, family and dormitory rooms, Glebe Barn is perfect for individuals, families or large groups. If you fancy more privacy an adjoining 2 person mezzanine apartment is also available. What better place than Eigg to relax or energise. A haven for nature and wildlife lovers, photographers or outdoor enthusiasts, with stunning beaches and coastal landscapes, regular traditional music sessions and exquisite local produce and cuisine, Eigg can make a magical Hebridean holiday.

DETAILS

- **Open** - Groups all year round; individuals from April to October. Open all day
- **Number of beds** - 22: 1 x 2, 2 x 3, 1 x 6, 1 x 8.
- **Booking** - Booking essential prior to boarding ferry. Deposit required.
- **Price per night** - Dorm bed £18 (1-2 nights), £16 (3+ nights). Twin room £40 (1-2 nights), £36 (3+ nights). Triple room £57 (1-2 nights), £51 (3+ nights). Exclusive use of the building (min 14 persons) £18pppn (1-2 nights), £16pppn (3+ nights).
- **Public Transport** - The early train from Fort William meets the ferry at Arisaig or Mallaig. Daily summer sailings. There is an Island mini-bus, or a taxi 01687 482404.
- **Directions** - 1 mile from ferry pier. Take the shore road that forks right from the ferry pier. Pass a white cottage close to the road & continue uphill away from the bay. Take the track, signed Glebe Barn, on the right before reaching the Church.

CONTACT: Tamsin or Stu
Tel: 01687 315099
admin@glebebarn.co.uk   www.glebebarn.co.uk
Isle of Eigg, PH42 4RL

KINTAIL LODGE BUNKHOUSES

475
SCOTLAND

Kintail Lodge stands at the foot of the Five Sisters of Kintail, right on the shores of Loch Duich. It is an ideal base for touring Skye and the Western Highlands or for bagging some of the 30 Munros in the area. In the grounds of the hotel there are two budget accommodation units which are especially popular with walkers, climbers and fishermen. The Wee Bunk House has a cosy room with bunks to sleep 6 people and a snack kitchen containing fridge, hot rings, kettle, microwave and basic cooking utensils. There is a shower room with a toilet and the building is wheelchair friendly. The Trekkers' Lodge sleeps 6 people in two twin rooms and two single rooms, each with their own washbasin. There are 2 shower rooms with toilets and a snack kitchen equipped as in the Wee Bunkhouse. After a long day in the hills you can unwind in the relaxed atmosphere of the traditional Kintail Bar, where good food is served and beer is plentiful, or enjoy the lochside garden and patio. Packed lunches available.

DETAILS

- **Open** - All year with winter restrictions. ,All day (restricted winter hours).
- **Number of beds** - Trekkers' Lodge 6: 2x2, 2x1, Wee Bunkhouse 6: 1x6.
- **Booking** - Book by phone or email with credit card details.
- **Price per night** - £16.50pp, 3+ nights £16.00pp. Sole use of Trekkers' Lodge £95. Sole use of Wee Bunkhouse £85. Duvet and towel £6.50. Full scottish breakfast in the hotel £14.50. Continental breakfast in the hotel £9.50.
- **Public Transport** - See Citylink website. Inverness to Skye or Glasgow to Skye.
- **Directions** - Kintail Lodge is situated on the A87 between Invergarry and the Isle of Skye Bridge.

CONTACT: Reception
Tel: 01599 511275
reception@kintaillodgehotel.co.uk www.kintaillodgehotel.co.uk
Kintail Lodge Hotel, Glenshiel, Kyle of Lochalsh, Ross-shire, IV40 8HL

STATIONMASTERS HOSTEL

SCOTLAND

Set in the peaceful village of Strome Ferry, The Stationmaster's Hostel offers a warm welcome to everyone. With only 20 beds, it is relaxed and friendly. There are woodland walks within walking distance and the hostel overlooks beautiful Loch Carron where otters and other wildlife are regularly sighted. An excellent base from which to explore the Isle of Skye, Glenelg, Torridon and the Applecross Peninsula. Eilean Donan Castle, wildlife boat trips and the picturesque village of Plockton are all within a 15 minute drive. Strome Ferry is a small village, so there are no shops or pubs within walking distance. However the nearest shops can be found in Balmacara, Kyle of Lochalsh and Lochcarron (10 miles away). The hostel has excellent kitchen facilities, a common room with pool table, family and twin/double rooms and a basic breakfast is included. Pubs and restaurants can be found in Plockton, 7 miles away by car or train.

DETAILS

- **Open** - March - October. Group Bookings all year, check in 3pm – 8pm
- **Number of beds** - 20: Private, family and dorm.
- **Booking** - Booking recommended. 10% deposit required for group bookings.
- **Price per night** - £18 dorm bed, £20pp quad, £22.50pp triple, £25pp double/twin, £35 single. Get in touch for exclusive use rates.
- **Public Transport** - Train: from Inverness take the Kyle of Lochalsh line to Strome Ferry. Turn left out of the station, hostel is on the right hand side 30 metres along the road. Bus: to Kyle of Lochalsh, change to the train and follow instructions as above.
- **Directions** - By Car: turn off the A890 at the sign for Strome Ferry. Hostel is located at the bottom of the hill on the left hand side just before the jetty.

CONTACT: Kath or Ewan (9am-8pm)
Tel: 01599 577212
beds@stationmastershostel.co.uk www.stationmastershostel.co.uk
Stationmaster's Hostel, Stromeferry, Ross-Shire, IV53 8UJ

FLORA MACDONALD [477]
HOSTEL
SCOTLAND

Flora Macdonald Hostel offers clean, comfortable accommodation in the magnificent surroundings of the Sleat Peninsular in the south of the isle. In this region, also known as the Garden of Skye, visitors may see golden eagles, sea eagles, red and roe deer, otters and lots of other wildlife. It is also of enormous interest to geology students. The owner Peter Macdonald, a direct descendent of the Lords of the Isles, the Macdonald Chiefs and Robert the Bruce, is a local historian happy to share his knowledge of the area, and breeds rare Eriskay ponies on the family croft. The hostel has solid pine bunks in rooms sleeping 2,3,4, 7 or 8 people. It is centrally heated and has a modern well equipped kitchen, free WiFi, a drying room with washer and tumble dryer and a conservatory with seating so you can enjoy the views. Three miles from the nearest shop, please bring all your supplies.

DETAILS

- **Open** - March-October, 9am to 9pm.
- **Number of beds** - 24: 1x8, 1x7, 1x4, 1x3, 1x2
- **Booking** - Booking is not essential but strongly advised. Deposits required with all bookings, at least 1 week in advance. Preference to group bookings.
- **Price per night** - £17 dorm beds, private rooms from £42. Cash only. 20% reduction for block bookings and individual stays in excess of 7 nights.
- **Public Transport** - Regular bus service between Broadford and Armadale (bus stop at end of hostel road by the church).
- **Directions** - 3 miles from Armadale opposite Kilmore church, 22 miles from Skye bridge on the A851.

CONTACT: Peter Macdonald
Tel: 01471 844272 or 01471 844440
thefloramacdonaldhostel@btconnect.com   www.skye-hostel.co.uk
Kilmore Sleat, By Armadale, Isle of Skye, IV44 8RG

SKYE BACKPACKERS

Skye Backpackers sits in the picturesque fishing village of Kyleakin, skirted by mountains and sea. It's a small, cosy hostel with an open fire in the lounge and a lovely backyard garden. Whether you are coming to Skye to tackle the mighty mountains, meet the legendary faeries or simply want somewhere relaxed and comfortable to chill out, Skye Backpackers has everything you will need to ensure that you make the most of your time on this magical island.

The hostel has dorm, double and twin rooms and all beds come complete with sheets, duvets and 2 comfy pillows. There is also a fully equipped self-catering kitchen, a sunny dining area, as much free tea, coffee & hot chocolate as you can drink and free WiFi. Friendly & knowledgeable staff know all of the best places to visit and are on hand for you to ask them to help you plan your Skye adventure.

DETAILS

- **Open** - All year, all day. Reception 7am-12noon and 5pm-10pm (times may vary)
- **Number of beds** - 39
- **Booking** - Booking in advance not always essential, first night's payment required.
- **Price per night** - From £12 per night. ID required for check-in.
- **Public Transport** - Trains at Kyle of Lochalsh, only a short bus ride (approx 10 mins) from the hostel. The bus drops opposite the hostel.
- **Directions** - From Kyle of Lochalsh go over the Skye Bridge then take first exit at roundabout, which takes you into Kyleakin. The hostel is on the right hand side after the Kings Arms Hotel. Park in the car park opposite hostel or in the grounds.

CONTACT: Receptionist
Tel: 01599 534510
info@skyebackpackers.com   www.skyebackpackers.com
Benmhor, Kyleakin, Isle of Skye, IV41 8PH

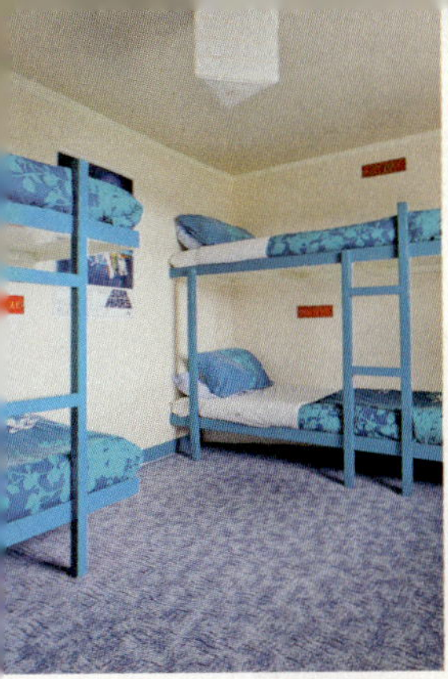

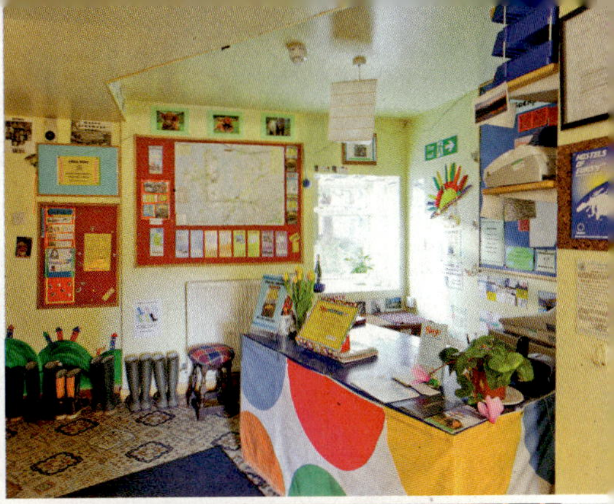

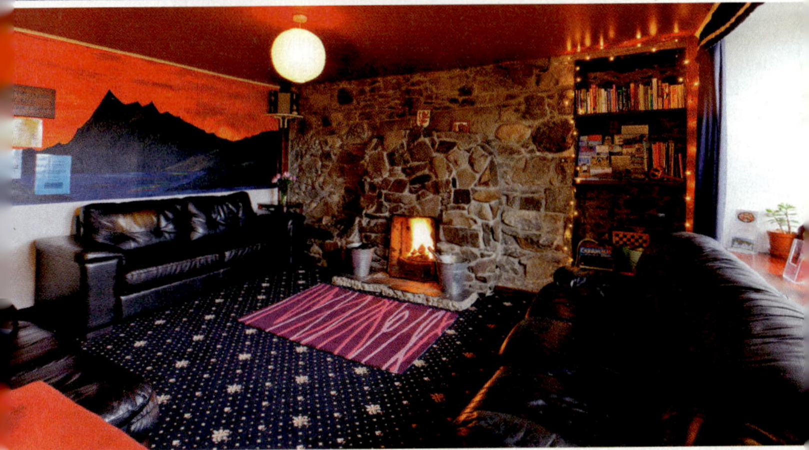

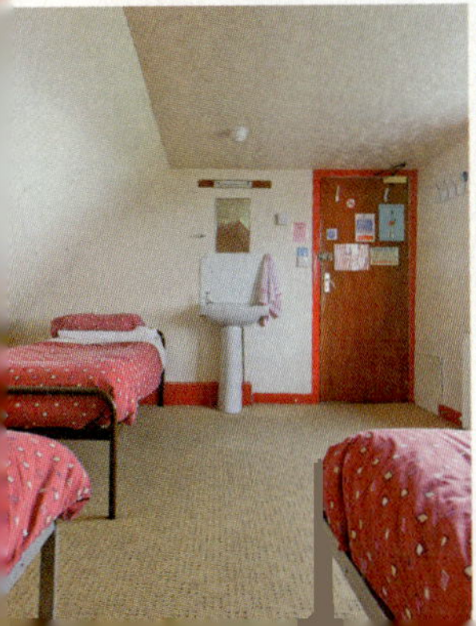

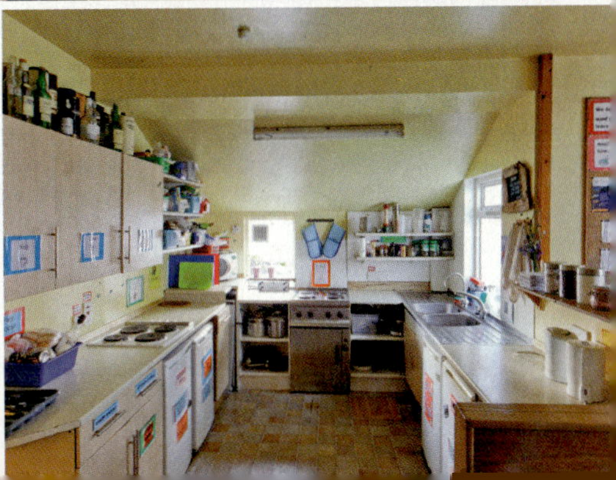

BROADFORD BACKPACKERS

SCOTLAND

Ideally located for enjoying the Isle of Skye, this child-friendly hostel is clean and cosy, with helpful staff for advice and information. There is a large kitchen for self-catering and a pleasant dining room overlooking the garden. The communal area has a TV and comfortable seating with plenty of board games and tea or coffee. Put in a lovely house cat and you've got yourself a home away from home. There are family rooms sleeping 4 (a double and two single beds), private double and twin rooms and small dorms sleeping 6 or 3. There is a bathroom with bath, a large garden and on-site parking. Cots and high chairs are available. Bedding and linen is provided and towels can be hired. From the hostel it is a short walk to the supermarket, shops, restaurants, beach and regular public transport, which connects Broadford with the rest of Skye and the mainland. Broadford Backpackers makes a perfect base for hiking, climbing, mountain biking and enjoying the spectacular scenery of Skye.

DETAILS

- **Open** - All year, From 9.00 am to 10.30 pm
- **Number of beds** - 38:1x7, 1x6, 1x4, 2x3, 2 x family, 2 x dbl, 1 x twin
- **Booking** - To book please telephone or email
- **Price per night** - Low Season: Dorm £15pp, Double /Twin £40. High Season: Dorm £18.80, Double /Twin £47
- **Public Transport** - Either: ferry from Mallaig to Armadale and a short bus ride; or any bus that is going to Skye will stop at Broadford (regular buses from Glasgow and Inverness); or train to Kyle of Lochalsh and then a short bus ride.
- **Directions** - From west on A87, in Broadford turn right onto High Road, then hostel is on right after 0.3 mile.

CONTACT:
Tel: 01471 820333
broadfordbackpackers@gmail.com broadfordbackpackers.blogspot.co.uk
High Road, Broadford, Isle of Skye, IV49 9AA

SKYEWALKER HOSTEL

481

SCOTLAND

Come and visit the award winning, family run Skyewalker Hostel, rated 4 star by VisitScotland. Experience a warm welcome and true Scottish hospitality. Ideally situated as a base for exploring the island and offering a very high standard of clean, cosy accommodation at a budget price. Rooms range from sociable, dormitory accommodation to twin en suite rooms and the amazing Jedi Huts! The comfortable lounge comes complete with guitars and games and there is a modern, fully equipped self-catering kitchen for guests to use. Outside, a large garden has a BBQ area, giant chess, fantastic glass chill-out dome and free car park. The local bar is a five minute walk from the hostel, taking in great views of the magnificent Cuillin Mountains. A short walk takes you to the sandy beach at Fiskavaig Bay and the world famous and very popular, Talisker Distillery is a five minute journey by car. See the website for more info on the hostel or Skye.

DETAILS

- **Open** - 1st April - 30th Sept (or all year for group bookings). Check in between 3pm and 9pm.
- **Number of beds** - 50
- **Booking** - Book early to save disappointment. Online booking available.
- **Price per night** - From £17.00 per person.
- **Public Transport** - Two local buses run each weekday from Portree via Sligachan to Portnalong and back. Citylink coaches from the mainland and north Skye drop off at Sligachan. Please note there is no bus to/from the hostel on Sundays.
- **Directions** - From Sligachan (in the centre of Skye), take A863 for 5 miles to the turn off for Carbost which takes you onto the B8009. Proceed through Carbost to Portnalong. Alternatively, follow the green signs from Sligachan! GR 348 348

CONTACT: Brian or Lisa
Tel: 01478 640250
enquiries@skyewalkerhostel.com   www.skyewalkerhostel.com
Old School, Portnalong, Isle of Skye, IV47 8SL

DUNARD HOSTEL

SCOTLAND

Dunard is a warm, friendly, family-run hostel on the beautiful island of Barra in Scotland's Outer Hebrides. The hostel has a cosy living room with a lovely fire, hot showers and spacious kitchen. There are bunk, twin and family bedrooms. Situated in Castlebay, the hostel has views over the castle to beaches and islands beyond. Close to the ferry terminal, a handful of shops, and bars which often fill with live music. During the summer the island is alive for 'Feis Bharraidh' a gaelic festival of music, song and dance. Take time and explore this truly beautiful island with stunning white beaches, quiet bays where otters hunt and seals bask on rocks, dunes and meadows carpeted in flowers, and wild windswept hills home to golden eagles. Join one of our friendly guided sea kayaking trips and paddle amongst sheltered islands for really close-up wildlife encounters, hire a sit-on-top kayak, or experience the ultimate adventure of coasteering, (no experience needed). www.clearwaterpaddling.com

DETAILS

- **Open** - All year, except Christmas and New Year, all day.
- **Number of beds** - 18: 3x4 3x2
- **Booking** - Booking advised particularly in summer. Booking essential for groups.
- **Price per night** - £17 per person bunk room and twin cabin. £19 pp twin room. £58 per family room (sleeps 4). £305 sole use.
- **Public Transport** - The hostel is a 3 minute walk from the ferry terminal in Castlebay. If using a local bus ask to be dropped at the hostel.
- **Directions** - From ferry terminal in Castlebay head up hill, turn left and we are the third house past the old school (200m from Terminal).

CONTACT: Katie or Chris
Tel: 01871 810443
info@dunardhostel.co.uk www.dunardhostel.co.uk
Dunard, Castlebay, Isle of Barra, Western Isles, HS9 5XD

Nº5 DRINISHADER

483

SCOTLAND

Nº5 Drinishader is located on the Isle of Harris, Outer Hebrides, 5 miles from Tarbert and 8 miles from the white sandy beaches. Situated above Drinishader Harbour, overlooking the beautiful East Loch Tarbert, the hostel and self-catering units provide a variety of accommodation for individuals, families and groups as well as activities. The hostel has a cosy lounge with open fire, a well-equipped kitchen, shower, wc and comfortable beds. Pick-up services from Tarbert can be arranged for a small cost if there are no bus services. There is a shop/post office nearby and you can pre-order fresh, delicious home-made bread and cakes to be delivered to your breakfast table. Among the activities guests enjoy are coastal/hill walking, cycling, kayaking, boat trips, sightseeing, bird/wild life watching or simply chilling out. Bed and breakfast and evening meals are available. Croft camping will be available from 2015. For full information on activities for 2015 please visit the website

DETAILS

- **Open** - All year, 0700-2300
- **Number of beds** - 20
- **Booking** - Advisable to confirm beds, may require deposit.
- **Price per night** - From £20 per person. Reductions for families, groups and longer stay.
- **Public Transport** - Caledonian MacBrayne ferries (01876 500337) from Ullapool to Stornoway or from Uig (Skye) to Tarbert. Drinishader is a 10 min bus journey from Tarbert (01851 705050). Bus stop at hostel. There are 5 buses each day.
- **Directions** - From Tarbert follow the A859 south. After 3.5km turn left along the Golden Road. The hostel is located just above the small harbour in Drinishader.

CONTACT: Alyson & Donald
Tel: 01859 511255, Fax: 0783323189
info@number5.biz www.number5.biz
Drinishader, Isle of Harris, HS3 3DX

HEB HOSTEL

SCOTLAND

The Heb Hostel is a family-run backpackers' hostel in the heart of Stornoway on the enchanting Isle of Lewis. It is an ideal stop/stay for travellers visiting the Hebrides. Surfers, cyclists, walkers, families and groups are all welcome.

Clean, comfortable, friendly and relaxed - Heb Hostel aims to provide you with a quality stay at budget prices.

There are many facilities, including a common room with TV, peat fire, local guides and information.

DETAILS

- **Open** - All year, all day. New arrivals phone for access code if warden not around.
- **Number of beds** - 26: 1x8, 2x7, 1x4 (family dorm).
- **Booking** - Booking is not essential but may be advisable at busier times. Deposits are only required for groups. Payment is due on arrival by cash or cheque.
- **Price per night** - £18 per person per night. Family dorm £72 for a family, £80 for adults only
- **Public Transport** - By plane: from Glasgow, Edinburgh or Inverness (Flybe), Aberdeen (Eastern Airways), Inverness & Benbecula (Highland Airways). By ferry (Caledonian McBrayne) Ullapool to Stornoway (Lewis), Uig (Skye) to Tarbert (Harris) or Berneray (Uists) to Leverburgh (Harris)
- **Directions** - From bus station: exit front door, cross South Beach St and walk up Kenneth St. Pass 1st intersection and we are 2nd on the right. From ferry terminal come out main exit, turn left, follow pedestrian walk-way to the bus station. From Airport take bus to Stornoway bus station.

CONTACT: Christine Macintosh
Tel: 01851 709889
christine@hebhostel.com www.hebhostel.com
25 Kenneth St, Stornoway, Isle of Lewis, HS1 2DR

LAXDALE BUNKHOUSE

SCOTLAND

Laxdale Bunkhouse is contained within Laxdale Holiday Park which is a small family-run park set in peaceful tree-lined surroundings. Located 1.5 miles away from the town of Stornoway this is an ideal centre from which to tour the islands of Lewis and Harris. Built in 1998, the bunkhouse has four bedrooms with four bunks in each room and caters for backpackers, families or groups looking for convenient, low cost accommodation. There is a drying room, a spacious fully equipped dining kitchen which provides two cookers, fridge and microwave and a comfortable TV lounge in which to relax. Toilets and showers are located within the building and are suitable for the disabled. Outside there is a covered veranda, picnic table and BBQ area. Sole use booking of the bunkhouse is available or you can book a room for your own use or book by the bed. Wigwams were new additions in 2014.

DETAILS

- **Open** - All year, 8am - 10pm
- **Number of beds** - 16: 4x4.
- **Booking** - July and August booking advisable one week in advance.
- **Price per night** - £17 adult, £15 child, £64 room (3 or less people) £240 sole use.
- **Public Transport** - Buses every 30 mins stop close to hostel. Taxi fare from town centre approximately £5.00.
- **Directions** - From Stornoway ferry terminal take the A857. Take the second turning on the left past the hospital. Follow camping signs for one mile out of town. The bunkhouse is located inside the holiday park. From Tarbert or Leverburgh take A859 for 40 miles to Stornoway. Turn left at the roundabout and 2nd left after hospital then as above.

CONTACT: Gordon Macleod
Tel: 01851 706966 / 01851 703234
info@laxdaleholidaypark.com www.laxdaleholidaypark.com
Laxdale Holiday Park, 6 Laxdale Lane, Stornoway, Isle of Lewis, HS2 0DR

GERRY'S HOSTEL

Gerry's Hostel is situated in an excellent mountaineering and wilderness area on the most scenic railway in Britain. It is on the Cape Wrath Trail, the T.G.O. Challenge Route, and is 0.5 miles from Coulin Pass at Craig.

The photo shows the hostel, looking North West. The hostel has a comfortable common room with log fire, library and self-catering kitchen. Meals are available 15 minutes' drive away.

Come and go as you please. No smoking inside or out.

Accommodation for non-smokers.

DETAILS

- **Open** - All year (check by phone), check in 5pm to 8.30pm (later by arrangement only.)
- **Number of beds** - 20: 1 x 10 : 2 x 5. Double and twin also.
- **Booking** - Prepay to secure bed, or phone.
- **Price per night** - From £16 pp, discount for long stay/large groups. Sheet hire £1 per stay.
- **Public Transport** - Achnashellach station is 4km west of the hostel. Nearest Citylink coaches drop off at Inverness. Local bus between Inverness and Lochcarron garage: Wednesday and Saterday 3pm.
- **Directions** - GR 037 493. 95 miles north of Fort William, 50 miles west of Inverness on A890.

CONTACT: Gerry Howkins
Tel: 01520 766232, Fax: 441520766232
gerryshostel@gmail.com www.gerryshostel-achnashellach.co.uk
Craig, Achnashellach, Strathcarron, Wester-Ross, Scotland, IV54 8YU

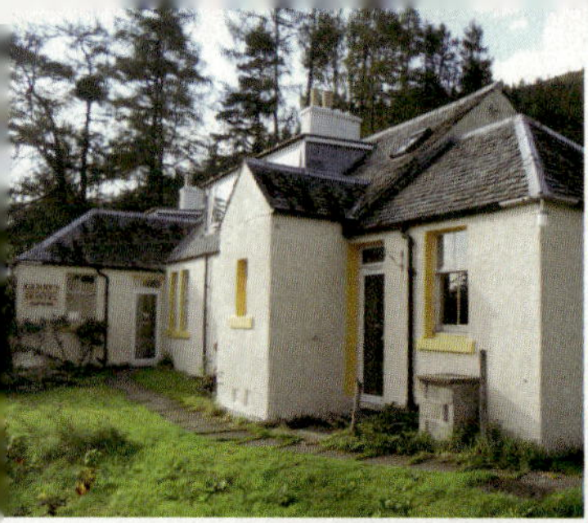

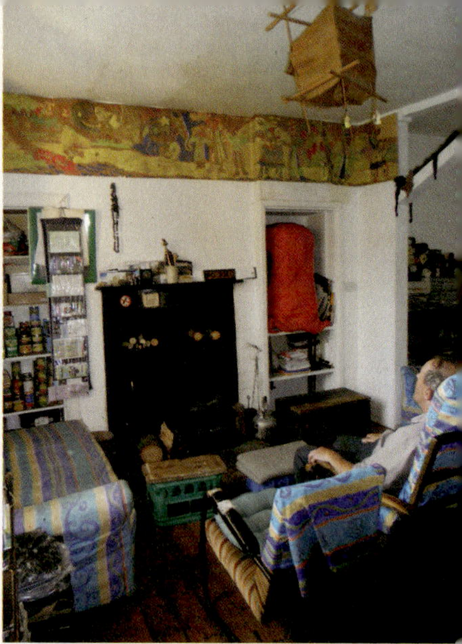

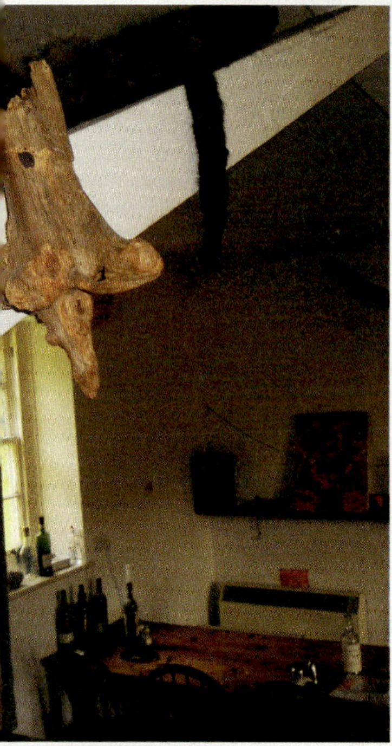

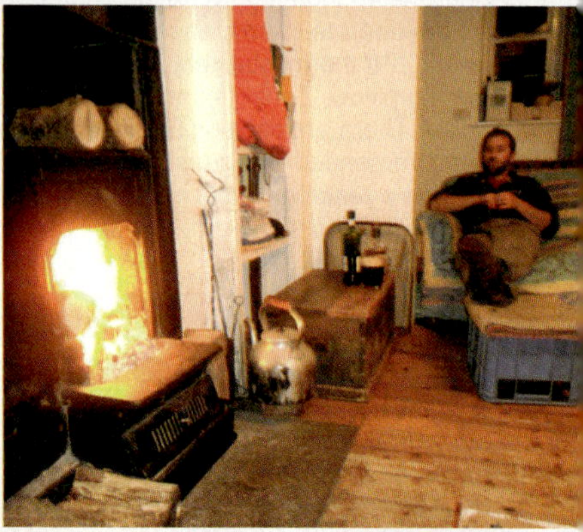

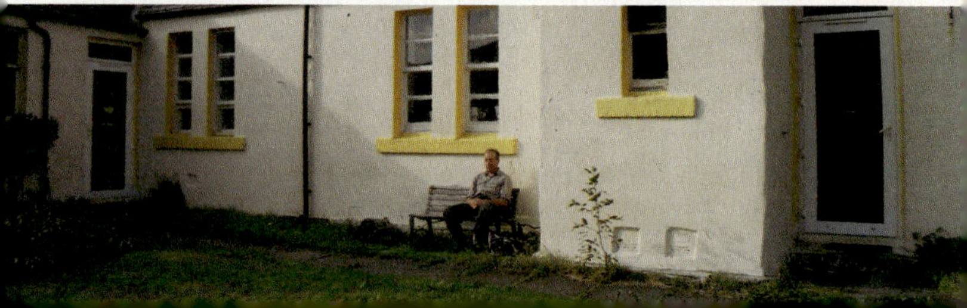

LEDGOWAN LODGE
SCOTLAND — HOTEL & BUNKHOUSE

Ledgowan Lodge is a traditional country house hotel with cosy log fires, original features and friendly bar open to residents and non-residents. The bunkhouse is adjacent to the hotel and bunkhouse guests have full use of the hotel's facilities. Ledgowan Lodge is perfectly situated for the hill walker, climber or anyone wanting low cost basic overnight accommodation. It is within easy driving distance of the Torridon and Fannich Mountain ranges and Fionn Bheinn Mountain is on the doorstep. The bunkhouse sleeps ten adults in five separate rooms, each with a set of bunk beds, hand basin, chest of drawers and thermostatically controlled heating. There is a one off charge for providing pillow, 2 sheets and blankets. There is a bathroom with shower and a toilet. There are cooking facilities and a refrigerator for self catering, but it is recommended that guests socialise within the hotel where the welcome provides a restaurant, bar meals, real fires and lively conversation. There is ample car parking in the grounds and an excellent drying room within the hotel. Camping available.

DETAILS

- **Open** - All year, all day
- **Number of beds** - 10: 5 x 2
- **Booking** - Book by phone or email.
- **Price per night** - £15.50pp. £31 for sole use of 2 bed bunkroom. Linen £7 (one off charge). Camper vans and tents £6pp.
- **Public Transport** - Achnasheen Station is one mile from the hotel/ bunkhouse.
- **Directions** - On the A890, 1 mile south of Achnasheen

CONTACT: Reception
Tel: 01445 720252
info@ledgowanlodge.co.uk www.ledgowanlodge.co.uk
Ledgowan Lodge Hotel, Achnasheen, Ross-shire, Scottish Highlands, IV22 2EJ

KINLOCHEWE BUNKHOUSE

489
SCOTLAND

Walkers, climbers and mountain bikers enjoying the Torridon Mountains and wilderness areas will be delighted to find the Kinlochewe Hotel with its warm, welcoming bar and bunkhouse accommodation. There are over 20 Munros within 20 miles of Kinlochewe and the hotel provides a great base from which to explore them. The hotel bar is open all the year round, and serves excellent home-made food at affordable prices, a selection of real ales and over 70 malt whiskies. The bunkhouse is ideal for outdoor enthusiasts with a well-equipped self-catering kitchen, an efficient drying room, toilets and hot showers. There is one dormitory with 12 bunks (this makes it unsuitable for children). Each bunk has an individual locker and a pillow with pillowcase is provided (please bring your own sleeping bags, towels and padlock for the locker).

DETAILS

- **Open** - All year, 8am - midnight
- **Number of beds** - 12.
- **Booking** - Essential for groups. Advisable for individuals.
- **Price per night** - £16.50 per person. Special offer: reduction for group bookings with sole occupancy for 2 nights or more
- **Public Transport** - Nearest train station is in Achnasheen (10 miles away). In summer trains run four times a day (twice a day on Sundays) from Inverness and the lunchtime train can be met by the local Dial-a-Bus which comes to Kinlochewe. Phone 01520 722205 for further details. On Tuesdays, Thursdays and Fridays the 5pm Westerbus from Inverness to Gairloch stops outside the bunkhouse at 6.45pm.
- **Directions** - Kinlochewe is situated at the junction of the A832 Garve to Gairloch road and the A896 north from Torridon.

CONTACT: Andrew and Gail Staddon
Tel: 01445 760253
bookings@kinlochewehotel.co.uk   www.kinlochewehotel.co.uk
Kinlochewe by Achnasheen, Wester Ross, IV22 2PA

SAIL MHOR CROFT

SCOTLAND

Sail Mhor Croft is a small rural hostel which is situated at Dundonnell on the shores of Little Loch Broom. The mountain range of An Teallach, which has the reputation of being one of the finest ridge walks in Great Britain, is right on the doorstep and the area is a haven for walkers of all experience as well as for photographers. Whether you wish to climb the summits, walk along the loch side, visit a beautiful sandy beach or just soak up the tranquillity of the area, you know the scenery cannot be beaten anywhere in the country.

The hostel offers accommodation for up to 16 persons in three dorms which are fitted with anti-midge screens. Guests have a choice of using our self-catering facilities or we can provide a full breakfast. It is advisable to ring in advance in order to book yourself a bed, the next self-catering hostel is many miles away.

DETAILS

- **Open** - All year except Xmas, New Year and January, flexible hours
- **Number of beds** - 16: 2 x 4: 1 x 8
- **Booking** - Always phone in advance. Groups should book as soon as possible.
- **Price per night** - £16.00 per person self-catering. £21 with cooked breakfast. £210.00 per night sole use.
- **Public Transport** - Nearest train station is Inverness (60 miles). Nearest City Link bus drop off is Braemore Junction (15 miles). Wester bus passes the hostel 3 times a week; Mon, Wed and Sat. It also provides a service between Gairloch and Ullapool on Thursday afternoon.
- **Directions** - GR 064 893 (sheet 19) 1.5 miles west of Dundonnell Hotel on A832.

CONTACT: Dave or Lynda
Tel: 01854 633224
dave.lynda@sailmhor.co.uk www.sailmhor.co.uk
Camusnagaul, Dundonnell, Ross-shire, IV23 2QT

BADRALLACH
BOTHY AND CAMPSITE SCOTLAND

On the tranquil shores of Little Loch Broom overlooking An Teallach, one of Scotland's finest mountain ranges, Badrallach Bothy and Camp Site, with its welcoming traditional buildings, offers a fine base for walking and climbing in the hills of Wester Ross, Caithness and Sutherland. You can fish in the rivers, hill lochs and sea, or simply watch the flora and fauna including many orchids, golden eagles, otters, porpoises, pine martens, deer and wild goats. Guests often sit around the peat stove in the gas light (there is now electric here too) and discuss life over a dram or two. Hot showers, spotless sanitary accommodation (STB graded 4 star excellent), an unbelievable price (thanks to S.N.H) and the total peace makes the bothy and camp site (12 tents only) one that visitors return to year after year. There is also a 4 star cottage and B&B, with breakfast/dinner served in our new eco-crofthouse. Hire canoes, kites, bikes, boats and blokarts.

DETAILS

- **Open** - 23 March-30 September 2015, access all day.
- **Number of beds** - 12 plus bedspaces (Alpine style platforms). We have had 20 at a squeeze, mats & sleeping bags required.
- **Booking** - Recommended.
- **Price per night** - £8pp, £2 per vehicle. £100 sole use (£150 Xmas & New Year).
- **Public Transport** - Westerbus (01445 712255) operate Mon/Wed/Sat between Inverness/Gairloch and drops at road end Dundonnell, 7 miles from hostel. Pick-up can be arranged.
- **Directions** - GR 065 915   Located on the shore of Little Loch Broom 7 miles along a single track road off the A832, one mile east of the Dundonnell Hotel.

CONTACT: Mr / Mrs Stott,
Tel: 01854 633281
mail@badrallach.com www.badrallach.com
Croft No 9, Badrallach, Dundonnell, Ross-shire, IV23 2QP

INCHNADAMPH LODGE

SCOTLAND

Situated at the heart of the dramatic Assynt mountains, Inchnadamph Lodge has been tastefully converted to provide luxury hostel accommodation at a budget price. Twin, family and dormitory (4-8 people) rooms are available and a continental-style breakfast is included. There is a large self-catering kitchen, a games room, a lounge and a dining room (both with real fires). Bar meals are usually available at the Inchnadamph Hotel just across the river.

Based at the foot of Ben More Assynt, and overlooking Loch Assynt, visitors are free to explore one of the wildest areas in the Highlands. Mountains can be climbed from the door, there are caves and other exciting geological features in the Traligill river valley, and a wide diversity of birds, plants, animals can be found. Nearby lochs are popular for trout fly fishing. Details and photos on the website.

DETAILS

- **Open** - Mid March to Mid November, 24 hours
- **Number of beds** - 38: 8x2: 7x2: 4x2 (dormitory) 12 (twin/double).
- **Booking** - Strongly advised. No vacancies June 2015. From Nov-March booking is required as the hostel may be closed.
- **Price per night** - £18-£20 (dormitory), £26-£30 (twin room) incl. continental breakfast and linen. Group discounts.
- **Public Transport** - Transport is available to the door from Inverness 6 days a week, by coach to Ullapool and minibus to Inchnadamph. Times vary - call for details.
- **Directions** - Inchnadamph is 25 miles north of Ullapool on the Lochinver/Durness road. The lodge is the big white building across the river from the hotel.

CONTACT: Chris
Tel: 01571 822218
info@inch-lodge.co.uk   www.inch-lodge.co.uk
Inchnadamph, Assynt, Nr Lochinver, Sutherland, IV27 4HL

BLACK ISLE BERRIES BUNKHOUSE

SCOTLAND

Situated on a working fruit farm, Black Isle Berries Bunkhouse was completed in December 2013 and provides good-quality, warm, friendly and comfortable accommodation for all outdoor enthusiasts at a reasonable price. Whether you are looking for a stopping off point or somewhere to use as a base the bunkhouse is ideally located for all the Highlands have to offer such as kayaking, cycling, mountaineering and more. The Black Isle is great for cycling, wildlife watching (including the Moray Firth Dolphins) or visiting the beach. The bunkhouse has a well equipped kitchen/dining/seating area. There are four bedrooms sleeping a maximum of 3 and 4 people. A family/disabled access room sleeps up to 5 and is en suite. There are plenty of showers for everyone else! A single room is available for group leaders only - please ask for details. Ample car parking and a large drying room and bike shed are opposite the bunkhouse. Well placed for those following the LEJOG route.

DETAILS

- **Open** - All year. Check in 4pm - 7pm (earlier or later by arrangement)
- **Number of beds** - 21:1x3, 2x4, 2x5
- **Booking** - Booking recommended Mar - Oct, Booking essential Nov - Feb
- **Price per night** - £19/bed; 3 bed room £51/night; 4 bed room £68/night; 5 bed room £85/night; family room £90
- **Public Transport** - Bus stops for Inverness, the west and the north 0.5km away
- **Directions** - From Inverness, the west or north follow the road to the Tore roundabout where you should take the A832 signposted to Fortrose. Go past the filling station on your left and we are approx. 500yds further along the road on the left.

CONTACT: Lynn Fraser
Tel: 07891 578998
ih@blackislebunkhouse.co.uk www.blackislebunkhouse.co.uk
Ryefield Farm, Tore, Ross-shire, IV6 7SB

BLACK ROCK BUNKHOUSE

SCOTLAND

Situated in beautiful Glenglass and sheltered by Ben Wyvis, this comfortable bunkhouse is named after the breathtaking Black Rock Gorge. It is an ideal base for touring the Highlands and seeing wildlife, including seals in the Cromarty Firth and dolphins at Cromarty. The bunkhouse is at the eastern end of a hikers' route across Scotland and on the Lands End to John O'Groats route for walkers and cyclists. The Highland Games are held throughout the area. The village has a general shop, Post Office, bus service and an inn (serving good bar meals and breakfasts) 250m away.

Available to groups or individuals, accommodation is in four rooms of four and one room for one. Sleeping bags and liners are provided free of charge. There is a self-catering kitchen and dining area with TV. Showers and launderette facilities are available on site. There is also a camping ground. All areas of the bunkhouse are easily accessible by wheelchair and suitable for the disabled.

DETAILS

- **Open** - April 1st to October 31st, 24hr access. New arrivals 12noon - 9pm
- **Number of beds** - 17 : 4 x 4, 1 x 1.
- **Booking** - Not always essential. Deposit of 1 night's fee to secure booking.
- **Price per night** - £13 - £15 per person. 10% off for groups of 8+.
- **Public Transport** - Nearest train station Dingwall (6 miles). Nearest Citylink drop off Inverness (15 miles). There are local buses hourly.
- **Directions** - Follow A9 north from Inverness, 2 miles north of Cromarty Firth bridge take left turn for Evanton. Follow camping signs.

CONTACT: Lillian
Tel: 01349 830917
enquires@blackrockscotland.co.uk www.blackrockscotland.co.uk
Evanton, Dingwall, Ross-shire, IV16 9UN

BUNKHOUSE
@ INVERSHIN HOTEL SCOTLAND

A small hotel in the north Highlands run by a young family. The bunkhouse is situated within the hotel and consists of 4 rooms which share a shower room and toilet. Guests can use the large, comfortable, reception area and the cosy wee bar where the fire is always lit, and enjoy an evening meal and a real cask ale. Situated on the main route north if wanting to avoid the A9, and ideally placed to reach the far north, as well as both east and west coasts. Cyclists, walkers, bikers, fishers, munro baggers, families, groups, and lone travellers are all welcome. Breakfast: tea/coffee, cereal, toast, homemade jam/marmalade,(£5) or fully cooked (£10), is served in the conservatory with views overlooking the Kyle of Sutherland. Bed linen is included but not towels. There are no self-catering facilities available, however breakfast and a small selection of home cooked meals in the evening are available. New for 2015 - Discount for parties of 6 or more, please enquire when booking. Some spots at the back of the hotel for campers. Free WiFi within the hotel public areas.

DETAILS
- **Open** - April - end October. Check in from 4pm
- **Number of beds** - 10 1x double, 1x twin, 2x triple (bunkbeds)
- **Booking** - Please call for any booking enquiries or questions.
- **Price per night** - £20pp. Breakfast: £5 or £10. Discount for groups 6 or more.
- **Public Transport** - Train daily to Inverness from Invershin station (30 secs' walk from hotel). The local bus to Tain stops outside the hotel. Connecting buses to Inverness from Tain. Approx 1 hour 20 minutes drive from Inverness Airport.
- **Directions** - On the A836 from Bonar Bridge to Lairg beside the railway bridge.

CONTACT: Angus or Cheryl
Tel: 01549 421 202
enquiries@invershin.com www.invershin.com
Invershin Hotel, Lairg, Sutherland, IV27 4ET

SLEEPERZZZ.COM
SCOTLAND

Stay on a first class train in Rogart in the heart of the Highlands halfway between Inverness and John O'Groats. The two railway carriages have been tastefully converted, with many original features. One sleeps 8 and one is subdivided to sleep 4 and 2. There are two beds per room, and a kitchen, dining room, sitting room, showers and toilets. They are heated and non-smoking. All bedding is included. There is also a cosy showman's wagon which sleeps up to 3 and a converted bus which also sleeps up to 3. Four trains per day in each direction serve this small crofting community which has a shop, post office and pub with restaurant. Glenmorangie and Clynelish distilleries, Dunrobin Castle and Helmsdale's Heritage Centre are easy to reach by train or car.

See the silver salmon leap at Lairg and the seabirds and seals in Loch Fleet. Or just enjoy the peace of Rogart. The climate is good and the midges are less prevalent than in the west! Families welcome. Free use of bikes for guests.

DETAILS
- **Open** - March to September inclusive, 24 hours
- **Number of beds** - 20: 1 x 8, 1 x 4, 2 x 3, 1 x 2.
- **Booking** - Booking is advisable
- **Price per night** - From £17 per person, 12yrs and under £12 per person. (10% discount if you arrive by cycle or train).
- **Public Transport** - Wick to Inverness trains stop at the door.
- **Directions** - We are at the railway station, 4 miles from the A9 trunk road, 54 miles north of Inverness.

CONTACT: Kate
Tel: 01408 641343   Mobile/Text: 07833 641226
kate@sleeperzzz.com   www.sleeperzzz.com
Rogart Station, Pittentrail, Sutherland, Highlands, IV28 3XA

HELMSDALE HOSTEL

497
SCOTLAND

Set in the scenic coastal village of Helmsdale (halfway between Inverness and John O'Groats), the hostel offers spacious en suite accommodation including fully equipped kitchen and comfortable lounge area with log burning stove plus a large garden area. On the main Land's End to John O'Groats route, the hostel is popular with 'end to enders' and walkers exploring the Far North Marilyn hills such as Morven and Scaraben. An ideal stop when travelling to and from Orkney and great location for beach walks, archaeology, geology, mountain biking, horse riding, fishing, bird and wildlife watching. Dogs welcome on request (private rooms only). Groups are welcome and there is a discount for sole use of the hostel

DETAILS

- **Open** - Open 1 May – 30 Sep 2015 (April-Oct for groups). Open during the day.
- **Number of beds** - 24: 2x8, 2x4
- **Booking** - Advance booking not essential - book on line, by email or phone.
- **Price per night** - Adults from £18.50. Children from £10. En suite rooms from £45. During April & October sole use of the hostel is available for groups for £300 per night with a minimum of 3 nights booking.
- **Public Transport** - Helmsdale is served by the City Link bus service and is on the railway line from Inverness to Thurso.
- **Directions** - The hostel is situated on the corner of the A9 and Old Caithness Road. From bus: walk up the slope for 100 metres. The Hostel is after the old church on your left. (200 metres). From train: Cross over the old bridge, turn right along Dunrobin Street, then left up Stafford Street. Hostel is 200m up the slope on the left.

CONTACT: Irene
Tel: 07971 516287 or 07778 377078
irene.drummond@btinternet.com www.helmsdalehostel.co.uk
Helmsdale Hostel, Stafford Street, Helmsdale, Sutherland, KW8 6JR

CORNMILL BUNKHOUSE

SCOTLAND

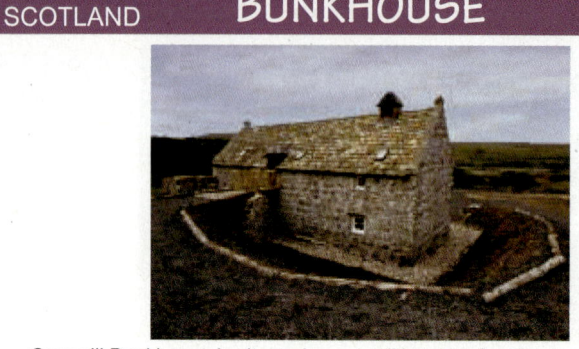

Cornmill Bunkhouse is situated on a traditional croft which has been in the family for many generations. The croft runs ewes, spring-calving cows, and grows winter feed and woodland. The mill was built in the early 1800s and was active until around 1926. It has been converted into 4 star affordable and comfortable accommodation for individuals or groups. The bunkhouse can sleep up to 14 people. It has a large self catering kitchen and open-plan sitting room on the first floor, in which the old grinding wheel now serves as a coffee table. There is level access to the first floor at the rear of the building, with an easy going stair down to the ground floor, which has two bunk rooms, a disabled access toilet/wetroom and a toilet with a shower. The first bunk room sleeps 8. The second sleeps 6 and has a patio door looking onto the workings of the old mill with its large wooden cog driving wheels. Activities can be organised for groups including Laser Tagging, Shooting and Clippage. Hen and Stag parties welcome. Come and enjoy this historic setting. 4 star tourist board graded.

DETAILS
- **Open** - All year, advanced notice required 1st Oct - 1st April, all day
- **Number of beds** - 14: 1x8,1x6
- **Booking** - Please enquire for availability by phone or email.
- **Price per night** - £15 per person. Discounts available for group bookings.
- **Public Transport** - Forsinard railway station is only 10 miles away. The line runs from Inverness to Wick, stopping at Forsinard three times a day.
- **Directions** - The Cornmill Bunkhouse is located on the A897, 6 miles from Melvich, 20 miles to Thurso, 42 miles to John O'Groats and 34 miles to Helmsdale.

CONTACT: Sandy Murray
Tel: 01641 571219   Mob: 07808 197350
sandy.murray2@btinternet.com   www.achumore.co.uk
Cornmill Bunkhouse, Achumore, Strathhalladale, Sutherland, KW13 6YT

KYLE OF TONGUE
HOSTEL & HOLIDAY PARK SCOTLAND

Kyle of Tongue Hostel is a stone lodge, magnificently situated on the romantic shores of the Kyle of Tongue on the north coast of Scotland. It has supreme panoramic views of Castle Varich, Ben Hope and the queen of Scottish mountains - Ben Loyal.

The hostel is relaxed and welcoming with irresistible home baking on offer. Beautifully furnished, like a boutique hotel, but with all the friendliness of a hostel. There are comfortable private bedrooms, roomy shared dormitories and relaxing communal areas. Relax in the lounge, well equipped dining area or the spacious self-catering kitchen. There is a drying room and bike shed for your outdoor gear and an onsite well stocked mini shop. Camping also available.

The atmosphere of this remote area is quite special. To truly leave the hustle and bustle of life behind, you must escape to the very edge of Scotland

DETAILS
- **Open** - Open all year, Check in from 4pm
- **Number of beds** - 36
- **Booking** - Book via e-mail or telephone
- **Price per night** - Dormitory beds from £16, Private rooms from £39
- **Public Transport** - Train station - 37 miles. Public bus routes through Tongue, Ferry terminal (Scrabster) - 45 miles
- **Directions** - Situated on the A838 road in the village of Tongue, in the north of Scotland within the Scottish Highlands

CONTACT: Richard Mackay
Tel: 01847611789, Fax: 01847611224
kothostelandhp@btinternet.com   www.tonguehostelandholidaypark.co.uk
Kyle of Tongue Hostel & Holiday Park, Tongue, By Lairg, Sutherland, IV27 4XH

HAMNAVOE HOSTEL

SCOTLAND

On the Stromness waterfront, a short distance from the ferry terminal, Hamnavoe Hostel makes an ideal base for your visit to Orkney. It has single, twin, twin en suite and family rooms. The rooms have easy access to the shower, bathroom and toilet on each floor. All bedrooms are fitted with hand basins, pine bunk beds and have stunning views out across Hamnavoe. The light and airy kitchen is well appointed with two cookers, microwave, double fridge, fridge freezer and a large dining table allowing you to enjoy your meals whilst taking in the fantastic views of the Stromness harbour and marina. The lounge has comfortable seating, freeview TV, DVD's and a stock of books. The laundry room has a coin operated washing machine and tumble drier. The hostel has WiFi internet connection throughout. Entry to the hostel is by a coded door lock and individual rooms have keys. Free long stay car park is available in front of the hostel. Come and visit the nearby islands of Graemsay and Hoy, check out the World Heritage Sites or just relax in the tranquillity of island life.

DETAILS

- **Open** - All year, all day, no curfew, check in from 2pm and check out by 10am. Reconfirm your booking by 7pm on the scheduled date of arrival.
- **Number of beds** - 13: 1x4, 1x1, 4x2.
- **Booking** - Book with deposit of first night, re-confirm by 7pm on the arrival day.
- **Price per night** - From £20pp. Private rooms £22.
- **Public Transport** - Orkney Ferries run to Stromness ferry terminal. There is a regular bus service to and from the town of Stronmness from the terminal.
- **Directions** - On the waterfront a short walk from Stromness ferry terminal.

CONTACT: Mr George Argo
Tel: 01856 851202
info@hamnavoehostel.co.uk www.hamnavoehostel.co.uk
10a North End Road, Stromness, Orkney, KW16 3AG

BROWN'S
HOSTEL AND HOUSES SCOTLAND

501

Brown's Hostel and Houses make ideal bases for your stay in Orkney, situated close to all amenities and just 3-5 minutes' walk from the bus and ferry terminal. Stromness is a small friendly town full of character, has a museum, art centre, scuba diving, free fishing, golf, festivals etc. The hostel is within walking/cycling distance of the historical sites at Maeshowe, Standing Stones, Ring of Brodgar, Skara Brae etc.

Self catering accommodation is offered nightly or weekly. Facilities include fully equipped kitchens and sitting rooms and accommodation is in single, double, twin, triple and family rooms from the smaller to the very comfortable en suite bedrooms, all with bed linen and towels provided. All properties have computer/internet access and WiFi. There is a shed for cycle storage and free car parking up the lane.

DETAILS

- **Open** - All year, all day. No curfew, keys provided.
- **Number of beds** - 28: 3x1; 4x2; 3x3; 2x4
- **Booking** - Booking advisable especially if wanting private rooms.
- **Price per night** - From £18.
- **Public Transport** - Train or bus to Thurso, bus 2 miles to Scrabster then boat to Stromness. Alternatively from Gills Bay to St Margarets Hope by boat or John O'Groats by boat to Burwick then bus to Stromness via Kirkwall.
- **Directions** - Brown's accommodation is just three minutes' walk along the street from the Stromness ferry terminal and bus stop.

CONTACT: Sylvia Brown
Tel: 01856 850661
info@brownsorkney.co.uk www.brownsorkney.co.uk
45/47 Victoria Street, Stromness, Orkney, KW16 3BS

HOY CENTRE

SCOTLAND

Surrounded by magnificent scenery, the Hoy Centre is ideally situated for a peaceful and relaxing holiday and is an ideal venue for outdoor education trips, weddings, workshops, clubs or family gatherings. It offers high quality, four star accommodation, all rooms are en suite with shower, twin beds and a bunk bed, chairs, lockers and bedding. One room is equipped for wheelchair access and the centre is all on one level. It has a well equipped kitchen, comfortable lounge area, a spacious dining hall and washing and drying facilities. Under floor heating ensures a comfortable temperature at all times.

Hoy is an RSPB reserve comprising 3,500ha of upland heath and cliffs with a large variety of wildlife including arctic hares. Off the west coast is The Old Man of Hoy - Orkney's most famous landmark and a great place to see puffins. The dramatic hills and cliffs offer excellent walking and climbing. Nearest shop is 20 miles so guests need to bring their own provisions. Catering is available for groups. The centre has VisitScotland, Walkers and Groups Welcome awards.

DETAILS

- **Open** - All year, from 10.00am to 8.00pm or by arrangement with the warden.
- **Number of beds** - 32: 8x4.
- **Booking** - Preferred. Groups send 25% deposit, balance 28 days prior to arrival
- **Price per night** - For prices contact 01856 3535
- **Public Transport** - Short walk from Moaness Pier (pedestrian ferry from Stromness) www.orkneyferries.co.uk (01856 872044). Taxis/minibuses are available.
- **Directions** - Car ferry arrives from Houton to Lyness, which is 16km from centre.

CONTACT: Leisure and Lifelong Learning
Tel: 01856 873535 ext 2430
leisure.culture@orkney.gov.uk   www.orkney.gov.uk/Service-Directory/S/hoy-centre.htm
Hoy Centre, Hoy, Orkney, KW16 3NJ

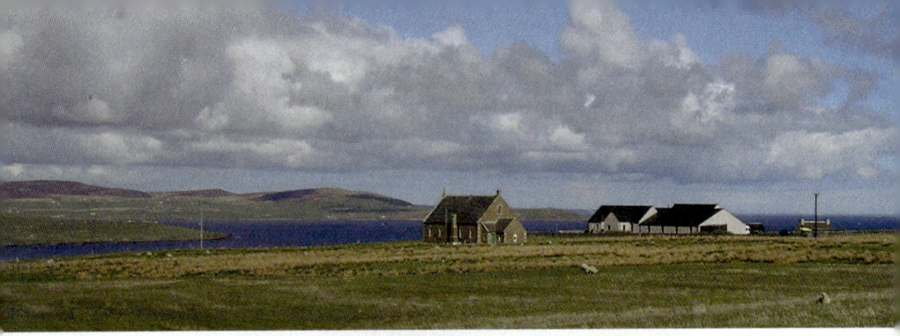

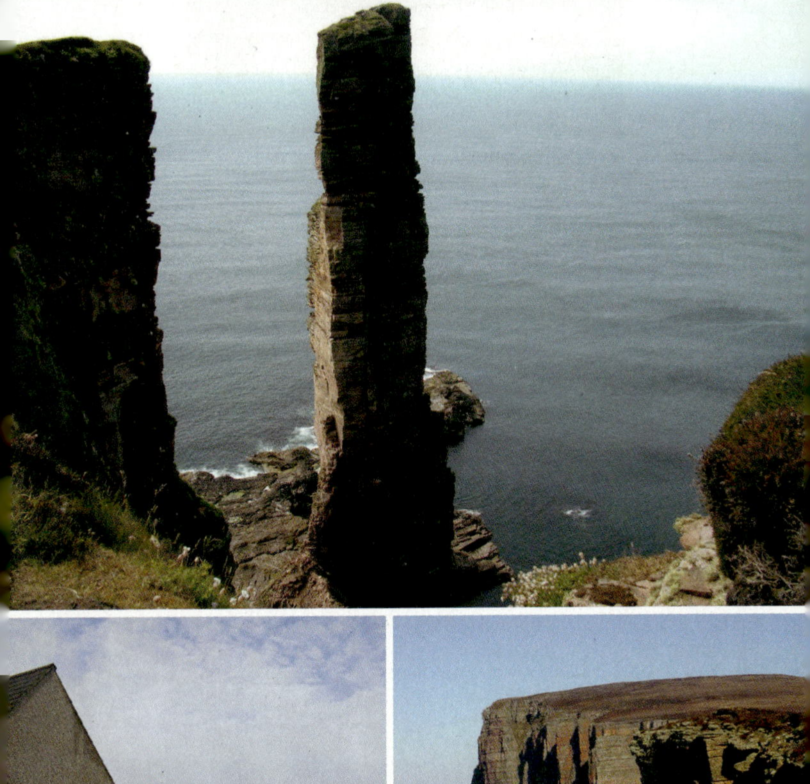

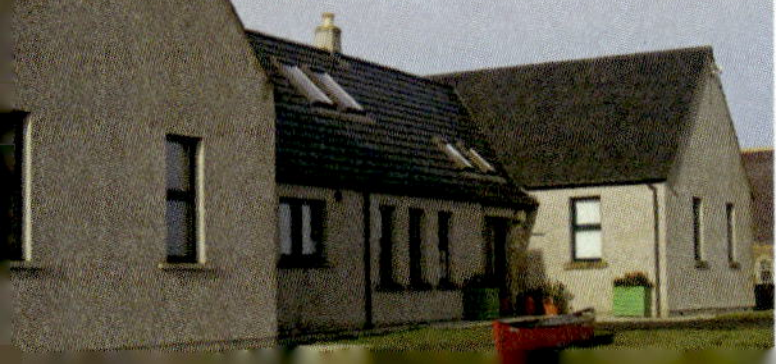

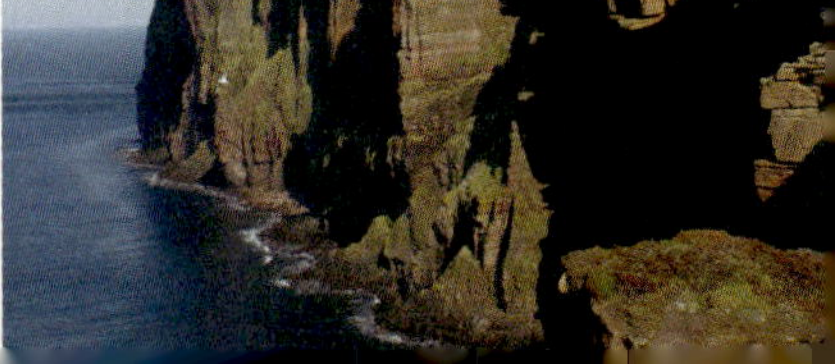

RACKWICK OUTDOOR CENTRE

SCOTLAND

Rackwick Outdoor Centre is in the scenic Rackwick Valley in the north of Hoy. Much of north Hoy is owned by the RSPB, where a large variety of birds live and breed. Off the west coast of the reserve towers The Old Man of Hoy, a 137m sea stack, Orkney's most famous landmark and a great place to see puffins. Local wild flowers and bird life make this a must for naturalists to visit.

The centre overlooks Rackwick Bay considered one of the most beautiful places in Orkney. The hostel sleeps 8 in two rooms, two pairs of bunks per room. All bedding is provided. There's a small kitchen with a good range of utensils, and a separate eating area. Free car parking and storage to the rear of the hostel for bikes. Walkers and Cyclist Welcome Scheme awarded.

DETAILS

- **Open** - April to September, Signing in by arrangement with warden.
- **Number of beds** - 8: 2x4
- **Booking** - Booking is preferred. 25% deposit required for groups with balance payable 28 days prior to arrival.
- **Price per night** - Prices on enquiry. You can book the whole hostel or a family room.
- **Public Transport** - Passenger ferry from Stromness to Moaness Pier (about 10 km away). Private hire and taxis are normally available at the pier, or alternatively the walk to the hostel is via the scenic Rackwick valley which takes approximately 2 hours. Car ferry from Kirkwall to Lyness, about 21 km away. (Orkney ferries 01856 872 044/www.orkneyferries.co.uk).
- **Directions** - In Rackwick village on the NW coast, OS sheet7 GR199998.

CONTACT: Leisure and Lifelong Learning
Tel: 01856 873535 ext. 2430
leisure.culture@orkney.gov.uk www.orkney.gov.uk/Service-Directory
Rackwick, Hoy, Orkney, KW16 3NJ

BIRSAY
OUTDOOR CENTRE
SCOTLAND

505

Birsay Hostel in the northwest corner of the Orkney mainland offers comfortable accommodation for up to 28 in 5 bedrooms. It is an ideal venue for outdoor education trips, weddings, workshops, clubs or family gatherings. It has a well equipped kitchen, dining area and small lounge, drying room, disabled access, and all bed linen is provided. There is a camp site in the extensive grounds with a level firm grassy site for touring caravans, motor homes and tents. Dogs allowed on the camp site but not the hostel. The centre is close to spectacular coastline including the RSPB reserve of Marwick Head. Nearby at the Brough of Birsay you can see the remains of early Christian and Norse settlements on a tidal island, The centre is convenient for visiting Orkney's 5,500 year old Neolithic Heartland (UNESCO World Heritage site), with the Ring of Brodgar, the Standing Stones of Stenness, the Tomb of Maeshowe and Skara Brae.

DETAILS

- **Open** - All year excl. Christmas and New Year, 10am to 8pm or by arrangement.
- **Number of beds** - 28: 2x4, 1x2, 1x6, 1x12 plus camping.
- **Booking** - Bookings preferred. For group bookings 25% deposit required with balance payable 28 days prior to arrival.
- **Price per night** - Prices available on enquiry. We also have private rooms and sole use of hostel available - contact for details.
- **Public Transport** - For buses from Kirkwall and Stromness contact Orkney Coaches (01856 870555). Ferries from Scrabster, (Northlink Ferries 01856 872044), to Gills Bay, (Pentland Ferries 01856 831226). Foot passenger ferries from John O'Groats, summer only (John O'Groats Ferry 01955 611353)
- **Directions** - OS sheet 7 GR 253267.

CONTACT: Leisure and Lifelong Learning
Tel: 01856 873535 ext. 2430
leisure.culture@orkney.gov.uk www.orkney.gov.uk
Birsay, Orkney, KW17 2LY

ORCADES HOSTEL

SCOTLAND

Welcome to Orcades Hostel in Kirkwall. A warm and friendly welcome awaits you at this modern, comfortable 4 star hostel which makes an excellent base for exploring the beautiful Orkney isles.

The family who run the hostel have carefully considered the guest's comfort to create a homely feel. Accommodation is in doubles, twins, 4, 5 and 6 bedded rooms (mixed or single sex). All of the bedrooms have en suite toilet/shower rooms, TVs and all bedding is provided. There is a stylish kitchen fully equipped, including oils and spices for cooking. The lounge has a DVD player, XBOX 360, lots of board games and books and free internet access. There is WiFi throughout the building. Drying facilities, bike storage and lockers are available. Stag and hen groups are not welcome.

DETAILS

- **Open** - All year. Check in after 2pm. Check out by 10.30am on day of departure.
- **Number of beds** - 36+: doubles, twin, 4, 5 and 6 bed rooms
- **Booking** - Book by email or phone. Credit or debit card details must be given to secure bookings.
- **Price per night** - £20 pppn in a shared room, £26 pp in a double or twin room (£52 for the room), £40 for single occupancy of a double/twin room. Winter rates available
- **Public Transport** - Kirkwall is the centre for buses on mainland Orkney and the harbour is the hub for ferries to the Northern Isles.
- **Directions** - Take Pickaquoy Rd from roundabout at the west side of the waterfront. Proceed for 300m, turn left onto Muddisdale Rd, and hostel is after 500m.

CONTACT: Erik or Sandra
Tel: 01856 873745
orcadeshostel@hotmail.co.uk www.orcadeshostel.com
Muddisdale Road, Kirkwall, KW15 1RS

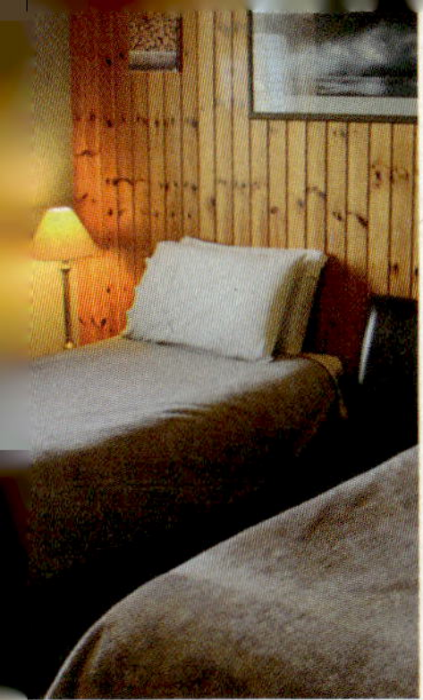
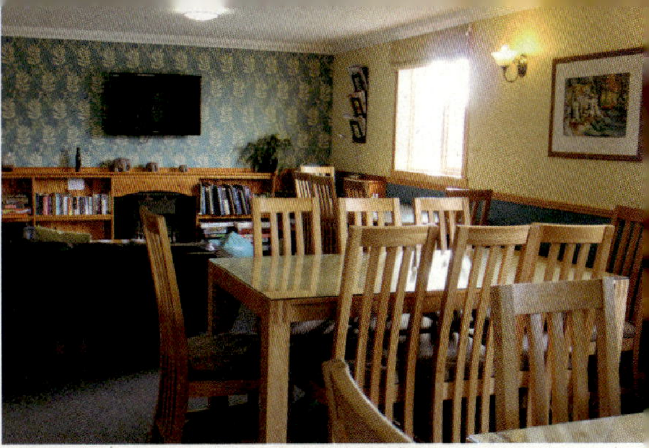
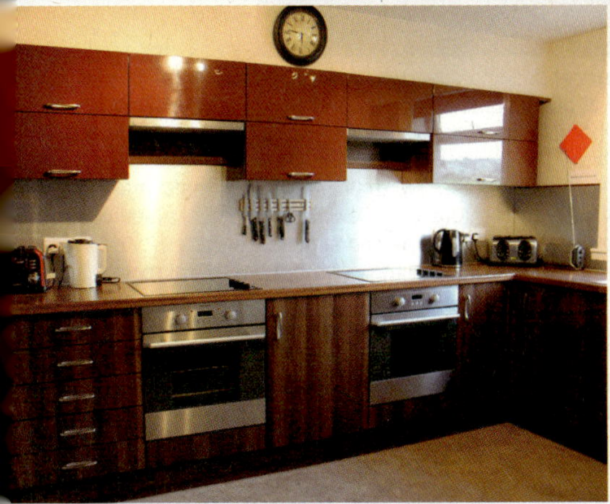
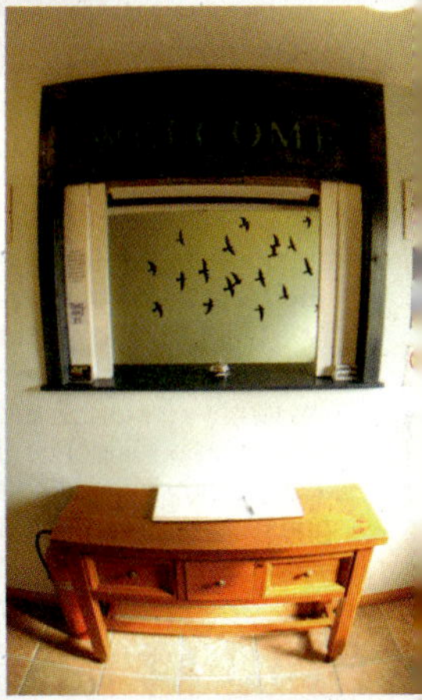
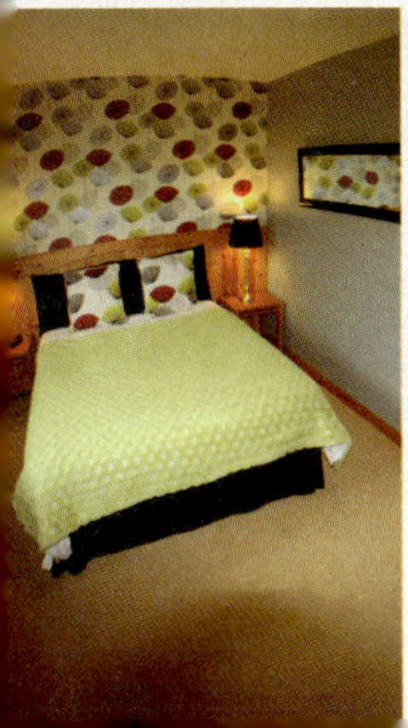
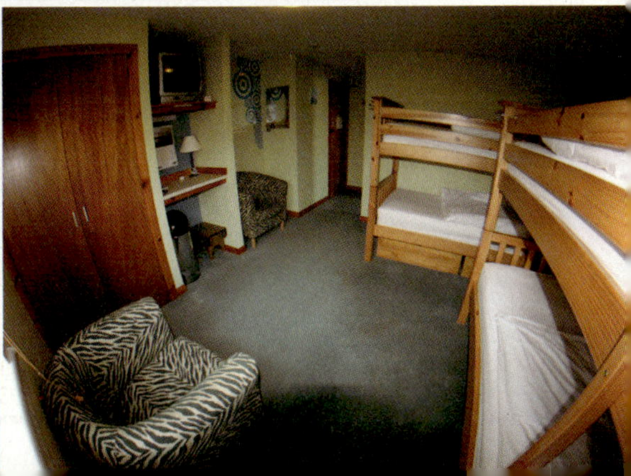

KIRKWALL PEEDIE HOSTEL

SCOTLAND

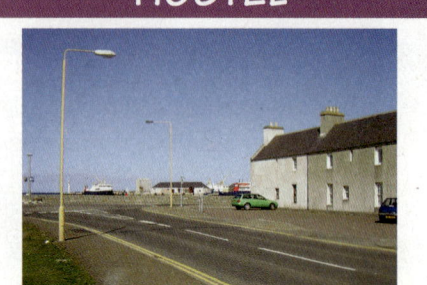

A 4 star hostel in a quaint old building overlooking the harbour in the town of Kirkwall and within easy strolling distance of the Main Street and many local attractions. Kirkwall is the heart of the Orkney Archipelago and the hub of nearly all transport within the isles. The hostel is 200m from the island's main bus station and 200m from the inner and outer North Isles ferry terminals, making it the ideal base for your Orkney adventure. It is close to many local amenities, including pubs, restaurants, shops and supermarkets.

The hostel has two single rooms, four twin rooms, two 4 bed dorm rooms (or family rooms). Shared facilities include three kitchens and three shower/bathrooms, a resident's lounge and free WiFi throughout. All rooms are heated. Each room has its own key and the hostel and its facilities are open 24/7 giving guests complete freedom during their stay. Also available are a 2 bed Bothy (small one bedroom bungalow) and a 4 bed holiday flat, " The Hoose", newly refurbished to a very high standard.

DETAILS

- **Open** - March to October, all day
- **Number of beds** - 24 2x1, 4x2, 2x4 plus Bothy (sleeps 2) plus Hoos (sleeps 4)
- **Booking** - Bookings can be made by phone, email or letter.
- **Price per night** - £15 pp. (supplement for single occupancy)
- **Public Transport** - 200m to North Isle & Shapinsay ferries. 200m to bus station. Bus from airport stops at the hostel by request. Courtesy bus from Northlink ferries stops at the hostel.
- **Directions** - Situated on the sea front on Ayre Road, overlooking Kirkwall harbour.

CONTACT: Chris Wild
Tel: 01856 875477
kirkwallhostel@btconnect.com www.kirkwallhostel.co.uk
1 Ayre Houses, Ayre Road, Kirkwall, Orkney, KW15 1QX

AYRES ROCK HOSTEL

509
SCOTLAND

Sanday is the perfect place to take time out, with long stretches of unspoilt sandy beaches, an abundance of birds, seals and other wildlife, glittering seas, clear air and spectacular skies. Those lucky enough to live here enjoy a rare quality of life in a small, friendly and safe community.

Ayre's Rock Hostel has accreditation by VisitScotland and is rated at 4 stars. There are two twin rooms and one family en suite room. A brand new conservatory and lounge area with expansive views over the Holms of Ire & Westray offers a comfortable place to relax after a day's exploration. A kitchen is available for self-catering, continental breakfast is included. One and two berth camping pods are available. Evening meals can be provided by arrangement. Takeaways are also available from the Ayre's Rock Chip Shop every Saturday.

DETAILS

- **Open** - All year, 8am to 10pm
- **Number of beds** - 8 : 2x2, 1x4.
- **Booking** - Book by phone or email.
- **Price per night** - From £17.50pp. Twin room single occupancy £20. Group bookings from £50. C'ping pods from £10pp. Cooked b'fast £5, evening meals from £10.
- **Public Transport** - Direct ferry from Kirkwall Pier to the Loth terminal in Sanday takes 1 hr 20 minutes. Passenger fares approx £14 rtn. Flying direct from Kirkwall airport to Sanday takes 11 minutes and a return flight approx £65. For local buses and taxi phone 01857 600410.
- **Directions** - 6 miles from Loth ferry terminal and 2 miles from Sanday air field.

CONTACT: Julie or Paul
Tel: 01857 600410, Fax: 01857 600410
allanpaul67@googlemail.com www.ayres-rock-hostel-orkney.com
Ayre, Coo Road, Sanday, Orkney KW17 2AY

OBSERVATORY HOSTEL

SCOTLAND

The North Ronaldsay Bird Observatory is situated at the south west corner of the island with outstanding views and an adjacent shell sand beach. Seals and the unique seaweed-eating sheep are abundant along the coast which skirts the 34 acres of croft managed by the observatory. The observatory sees spectacular bird migration through the island in spring and autumn. It offers a special attraction for those interested in wildlife, but welcomes all visitors. The Observatory Hostel consists of three dormitories and a self-catering kitchen in a converted barn and byre of the croft. The Byre sleeps four in two bunks and has en suite washing, shower and toilet facilities, great for family use. The Barn also sleeps four and shares facilities with the Bøl which has a single bunk sleeping two. Adjacent is the Observatory Guest House (3 star) which has a lounge bar and meals which are available to hostellers. Camping and shop on site.

DETAILS

- **Open** - All year, 24 hours, open all day, no curfews.
- **Number of beds** - 10: 2x4, 1x2; house: 8: 2x4 and private rooms.
- **Booking** - Advance booking essential.
- **Price per night** - Hostel £17.50-£18.50. Half board in hostel from £37. Guest house private rooms £55.50-£72.50 half board.
- **Public Transport** - Loganair flights from Kirkwall (Orkney) leave daily. Ferry from Kirkwall on Fridays and between May-Sept also on Tuesdays (subject to tides and weather). Small boats may be chartered. Orkney can be reached by vehicle ferries from Aberdeen, Thurso (Scrabster) and Gill's Bay, and a passenger summer service from John O'Groats.
- **Directions** - Situated at the south west corner of the island

CONTACT: Duty Warden
Tel: 01857 633200
bookings@nrbo.prestel.co.uk www.nrbo.co.uk
NRBO, North Ronaldsay, Orkney Islands, KW17 2BE

GARDIESFAULD HOSTEL

SCOTLAND

Gardiesfauld Hostel is on Unst, the most northerly of the Shetland Isles. The island has spectacular cliffs sculpted by the Atlantic Ocean on the west and secluded, sandy beaches on the east with rocky outcrops where seals and otters appear. The Gulf Stream provides a moderate climate and offers an invigorating chance to relax in a community where crime is unknown. During the summer enjoy long hours of daylight and the twilight of the "simmer dim" while in winter the long nights provide the backdrop for a vibrant cultural life. Situated on the picturesque shore at Uyeasound, this refurbished hostel combines superb facilities with a relaxed atmosphere. There is a kitchen, dining room, lounge, conservatory, coin operated laundry, showers (coin operated) and rooms with en suite facilities. A 5 berth caravan site has also been added.

DETAILS

- **Open** - April to October. Open in winter for pre-bookings, all day
- **Number of beds** - 35: 1 x 11, 2 x 6, 2 x 5, 1 x 2
- **Booking** - Book by phone or email
- **Price per night** - Adults £15pp, children (under 16) £8pp. Camping from £6 a tent, caravan hook ups £15
- **Public Transport** - Ferry from Aberdeen to Shetland (Northlink Ferries). The bus meets the ferry and continues to Unst. Ask for Uyeasound. Flights to Lerwick (BA). From Fetlar catch 7:55am ferry from Oddsta (Bus meets ferry)
- **Directions** - Take the A970 north from Lerwick to Voe then the A968 north to Toft. Take the ferry from Toft to Ulsta in Yell. Take the A968 north to Gutcher. Take the ferry from Gutcher to Belmont. Follow the A968 north and head into Uyeasound (B9084). Follow the road to the pier and look out for the hostel sign board.

CONTACT: Warden
Tel: 01957 755279
enquiries@gardiesfauld.shetland.co.uk www.gardiesfauld.shetland.co.uk
Uyeasound, Unst, Shetland, ZE2 9DW

SHETLAND
CAMPING BÖD NETWORK
SCOTLAND

The Shetland camping böd network offers low cost accommodation in nine historic buildings with fantastic scenery - giving the opportunity to tour these beautiful islands, staying in böds en route. Due to the böd's historic nature, no two buildings are the same and facilities vary. The smallest böd sleeps four and the largest sixteen. Electricity, hot water and showers are available in six of the nine buildings and solid fuel stoves and mains water in all. Each böd has a story to tell, for example Voe Sail Loft was once a knitwear workshop, where the jumpers for Sir Edmund Hillary's expedition to reach the peak of Mount Everest in 1953 were produced. Seven out of nine have local meals available within two miles and seven out of nine have (variable) facilities for less able people. Under 16s must be accompanied by an adult. No pets allowed. Explore Shetland, bed down in a böd. For further info log onto: www.camping-bods.co.uk

DETAILS

- **Open** - 1st March – 31st October. Böds are unmanned. Contact custodian up to 9pm on day of entry.
- **Number of beds** - 4 to 16 (depending on böd).
- **Booking** - Booking is not essential however, as böds are unmanned it is best to book in advance to ensure the custodian is available before arrival.
- **Price per night** - £8 to £10 pppn. Group discounts are also available.
- **Public Transport** - Information on public transport within Shetland: www.shetland.gov.uk/transport/ Information on cycle and car hire: http://visit.shetland.org/car-and-bike-hire
- **Directions** - Ferry from Aberdeen to Shetland (NorthLink). Flights to Shetland from Orkney, Inverness, Aberdeen, Edinburgh and Glasgow (Flybe).

CONTACT: Reception
Tel: 01595 694688
info@shetlandamenity.org www.camping-bods.co.uk
For info: Shetland Amenity Trust, Garthspool, Lerwick, Shetland, ZE1 0NY

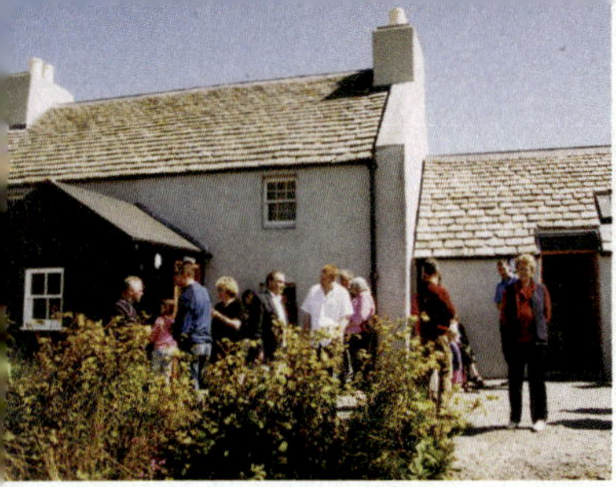
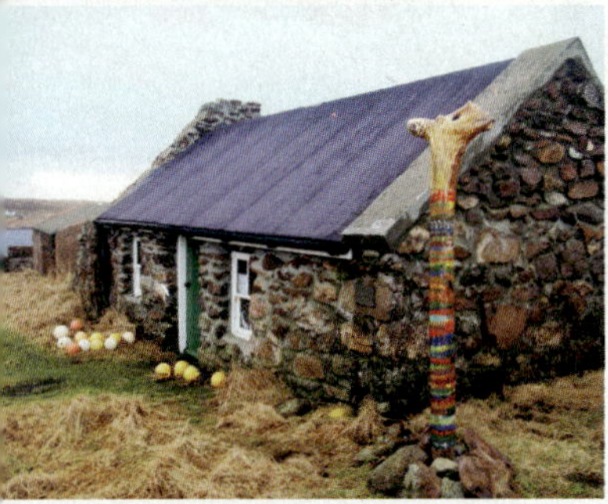
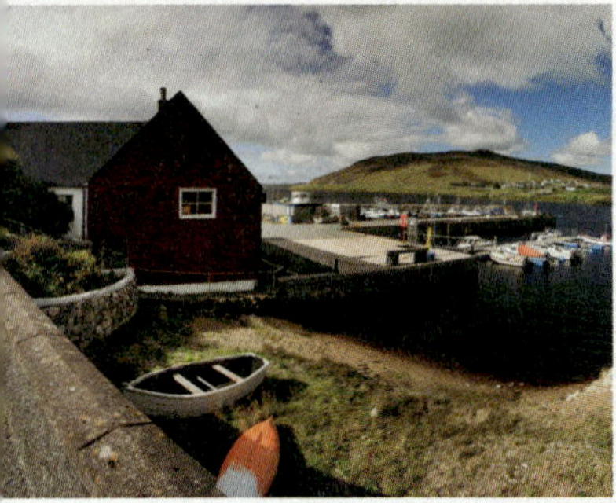
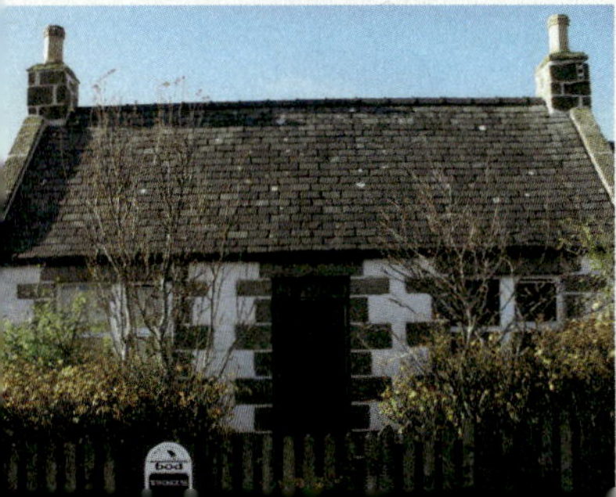
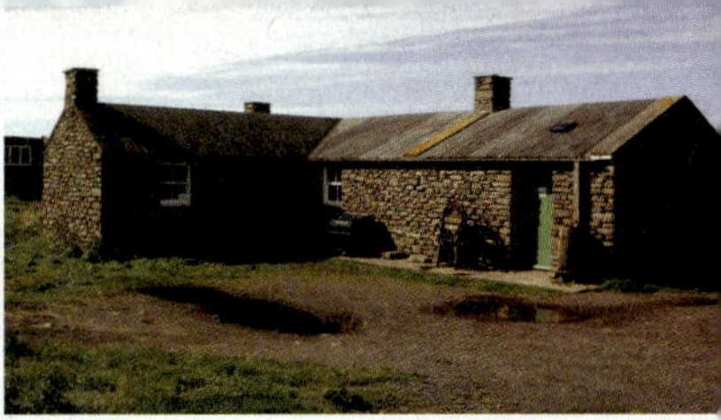
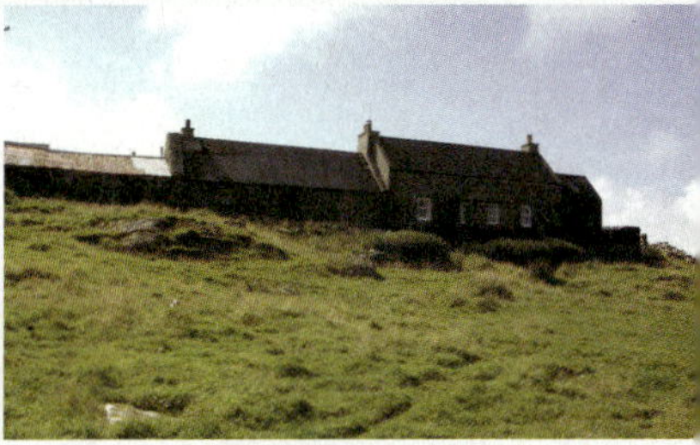
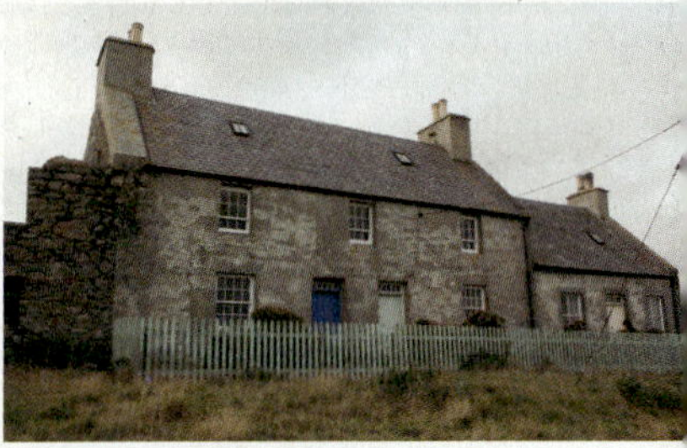
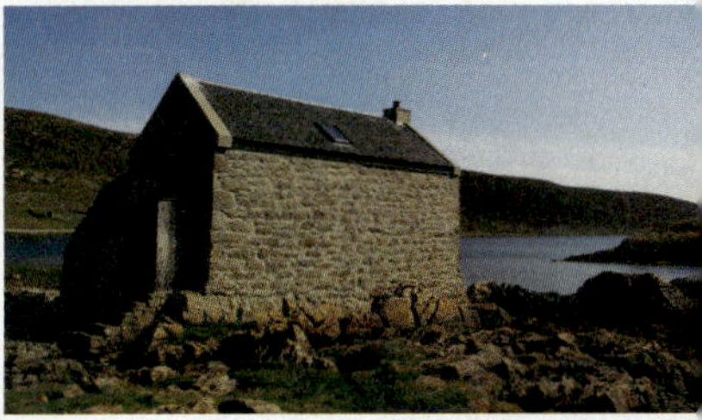
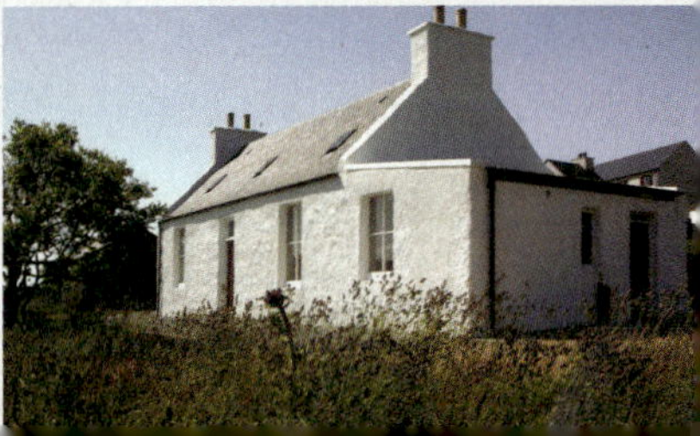

Lakeland Camping Barns

Find us on Facebook

www.lakelandcampingbarns.co.uk

Dry camping in prime locations around the English Lake District. Camping barns offer the opportunity to stay in restored farm buildings at affordable prices. Experience Cumbria's stunning lakes and lofty peaks literally from your doorstep. All the barns are unique and offer differing facilities. Visit our website to take our virtual tours.

We look forward to welcoming you and your families and friends in 2015.

Barn	Facilities	Page
St John's-in-the-Vale Camping Barn		240
Tarn Flatt Camping Barn		252
Bents Camping Barn		201
Catbells Camping Barn		245
Swallow Barn Camping Barn		250
Murt Barn Camping Barn		
Cragg Barn Camping Barn		249
Dinah Hoggus Camping Barn		
Fell End Camping Barn		212
Hudscales Camping Barn		253
Wythmoor Farm Camping Barn		227

SYMBOLS

- Breakfast bookable in advance
- Shop (miles)
- Pub (miles)
- Shower
- Pets by arrangement
- Electric lighting
- Toilets not in main building
- Hot water
- Campfire
- Powerpoints
- Disabled facilities
- Wood burning stove
- BBQ aea
- Cooking facilites
- Heating

COME AND STAY DIFFERENT IN SWISS HOSTELS!

BOOK NOW!

Quality independent Hostels and low budget hotels in Switzerland. We offer accommodation for individual travellers, families and groups. Checking-in at one of over 30 Swiss Hostels, we will make

OVER 30 HOSTELS IN SWITZERLAND

7050	Arosa, Mountain Lodge Arosa, info@arosamountainlodge.ch	0041 81 378 84 23
6677	Aurigeno, Baracca Backpacker, info@baracca-backpacker.ch	0041 79 207 15 54
3011	Bern, Backpackers Hotel Glocke, info@bernbackpackers.ch	0041 31 311 37 71
2560	Biel/Nidau, Lago Lodge, sleep@lagolodge.ch	0041 32 331 37 32
8784	Braunwald, Adrenalin Backpackers Hostel, info@adrenalin.gl	0041 79 347 29 05
3901	Brig/Rothwald, Berggasthaus Wasenalp, info@wasenalp.ch	0041 27 923 23 70
1874	Champéry, Le Petit Baroudeur Backpacker, info@lebaroudeur.ch	0041 24 479 14 07
7002	Chur, JBN Just be Nice Hostel, info@justbenice.ch	0041 81 284 10 10
7075	Churwalden, Basis Hostel, hostelbasis@krone-churwalden.ch	0041 81 356 22 31
7215	Fanas, Gästehaus Alpina Fanas, gasthausalpina@gmail.com	0041 81 325 12 75
1202	Geneva, City Hostel Geneva, info@cityhostel.ch	0041 22 901 15 00
1202	Geneva, Geneva Hostel, info@genevahostel.ch	0041 22 732 62 60
3826	Gimmelwald, Mountain Hostel, mountainhostel@tcnet.ch	0041 33 855 17 04
3818	Grindelwald, Mountain Hostel Grindelwald, info@mountainhostel.ch	0041 33 854 38 38
1882	Gryon, Chalet Martin, info@gryon.com	0041 79 724 63 74
6086	Hasliberg-Reuti, C'est la Vie Hostel, info@cestlavie.ch	0041 79 765 02 53
3800	Interlaken, Backpackers Villa Sonnenhof, mail@villa.ch	0041 33 826 71 71
3800	Interlaken, Happy Inn Lodge, info@happy-inn.com	0041 33 822 32 25
3800	Interlaken, River Lodge, welcome@riverlodge.ch	0041 33 822 44 24
3800	Interlaken/Matten, Balmer's Herberge, mail@balmers.com	0041 33 822 19 61

you feel home with our friendly and helpful staff.
People of all ages welcome. No membership required.

swiss hostels

BOOK ONLINE: WWW.SWISSHOSTELS.COM

3807 Iseltwald, Lake Lodge Iseltwald, lakelodge.iseltwald@gmail.com	0041 33 845 11 20
7250 Klosters, Adventure Hostel Klosters, info@ramadventure.ch	0041 81 422 12 29
7031 Laax-Cons, Backpacker Deluxe Hotel Capricorn, info@caprilounge.ch	0041 81 921 21 20
3550 Langnau i.E., Emme Lodge, info@emmelodge.ch	0041 34 402 45 26
1007 Lausanne, GuestHouse & Backpacker, info@lausanne-guesthouse.ch	0041 21 601 80 00
3822 Lauterbrunnen, Valley Hostel, info@valleyhostel.ch	0041 33 855 20 08
6005 Luzern, Backpacker's Lucerne, info@backpackerslucerne.ch	0041 41 360 04 20
6010 Luzern, Bellpark Hostel, info@bellparkhostel.ch	0041 41 360 25 15
4310 Rheinfelden, Hostel Tabakhüsli, welcome@hostel-tabakhuesli.ch	0041 61 813 32 16
9400 Rorschach, Herberge See Rorschach, info@herberge-rorschach.ch	0041 71 844 97 12
6430 Schwyz, hirschen backpackers.hotel.pub, info@hirschen-schwyz.ch	0041 41 811 12 76
7500 St.Moritz, Randolins Backpackers, welcome@randolins-backpackers.ch	0041 81 830 83 83
9657 Unterwasser/Toggenburg, Säntis Lodge, saentis@beutler-hotels.ch	0041 71 998 50 25
1800 Vevey, Vevey Hotel & Guesthouse, reservation@veveyhotel.com	0041 21 922 35 32
6484 Wassen, Gotthardbackpacker, mgentsch@bluemail.ch	0041 79 306 54 23
8400 Winterthur, Depot 195, info@depot195.ch	0041 52 203 13 63
8001 Zürich, City Backpacker - Hotel Biber, sleep@city-backpacker.ch	0041 44 251 90 15
8004 Zürich, Langstars, info@langstars.com	0041 43 317 96 55
3770 Zweisimmen, Vista Resort Hostel, info@hotelvista.ch	0041 33 729 80 80

Photos: Jungfrau Region & maennlichen.ch

GET YOUR FREE 10% HOSTEL DISCOUNT CARD

CASTLE NEUSCHWANSTEIN, FÜSSEN

BACKPACKER GERMANY NETWORK

60 TOP QUALITY
INDEPENDENT HOSTELS
THROUGHOUT GERMANY

WWW.GERMAN-HOSTELS.DE

TRAVEL ESSENTIALS FOR NEW ZEALAND

BBH Accommodation Guide

It's FREE and POST FREE to you!

Order Online

- 260+ places to stay
- Great value accommodation
- Available from **BBH** hostels and i-Sites (visitor centres) all over NZ.

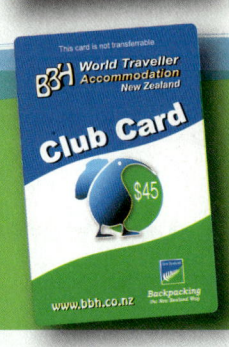

BBH Club Card

Frequent Sleepers Sleep Cheaper!

$45 Order online or from any BBH hostel.

- $3+ / night saving on accommodation
- Save on transport & activity
- Claim a $15 online booking rebate (see website for details)

Visitor Vehicle Insurance

3rd party insurance for touring around New Zealand. Designed with the traveller in mind.

BOOK ONLINE
www.bbh.co.nz

Hostel info • Job vacancies •
Online ratings • Vehicles buy/sell •
Vehicle / Travel insurance •
Noticeboard • Club Card discounts

Estab. 1987

Wake up Ready...
...to Explore

Great Hostels for an Irish adventure

Book online at
www.hostels-ireland.com

The network of Irish Tourist Board Approved Hostels all over Ireland

INDEPENDENT HOLIDAY HOSTELS OF IRELAND

WELCOME TO IHUK

"We continue to get lots of enquiries through IHUK, more importantly usually groups of nice peope"
Sue, Springhill Farm

"We like the constant interaction between the hostels and the IHUK network"
John Adams, Mid Wales Bunkhouse

The IHUK marketing package offers great value for money"
Andrew Donaldson, Comrie Croft

BENEFITS
FOR IHUK MEMBERS

Members are listed on our website, in this guide and on the Long Distance Walkers website.

Our group booking service promotes your accommodation to group leaders and enables them to easily get in touch with you.

We actively promote your accommodation on our Twitter, Facebook, YouTube and Pinterest pages.

Active message boards host conversations between members and our weekly emails keep you in touch with their views and other news.

IHUK signs let guests know your accommodation is in the IHUK network.

Official **IH** Member
Independent Hostels UK
The largest network of hostels, bunkhouses & group accommodation in England, Scotland and Wales

WHAT IS IHUK ?

523

Independent Hostels UK is the largest network of bunkhouses, hostels and group accommodation centres in the UK.

The network's website is viewed by 140,000 individuals each year and the guidebook, is distributed via bookshops, Tourist Information Centres, hostels and at shows and events.

For more details visit
www.independenthostels.co.uk/advertise-your-hostel
or phone 01629 580427

BECOME A TRAVEL WRITER

524

NEEDED:- Outdoor enthusiasts, bloggers, travel writers and photographers, to stay at Independent Hostels across the UK.

Write about the area and your adventures in exchange for a free night.

IndependentHostels.co.uk/travel-writer

INDEX

1912 CENTRE	106	BRIDGES YOUTH HOSTEL	118
ABERDARON FARM BKH	380	BRISTOL BACKPACKERS	74
ABERNETHY BUNKHOUSE	458	BROADFORD BACKPACKERS	480
ABERSOCH SGUBOR UNNOS	378	BROOK HOUSE BARN	128
AIRTON BARN	188	BROUGHTON BUNKHOUSE	117
ÀITE CRUINNICHIDH	454	BROWN'S HOSTEL	501
ALBATROSS BACKPACKERS	270	BRYNCARNEDD COTTAGES	339
ALL STRETTON BUNKHOUSE	120	BUNKHOUSE @ INVERSHIN	495
ALLENDALE BUNKHOUSE	259	BUNKHOUSE AT WARREN FM	318
ALNWICK YOUTH HOSTEL	274	BUNKHOUSE PLUS	76
ALPHA HOSTEL	94	BUSHEY HEATH FARM	166
AMBLESIDE BACKPACKERS	220	BUTE BACKPACKERS	407
ANGLESEY OUTDOOR CEN	384	BY THE WAY HOSTEL	416
ARDENBEG BUNKHOUSE	459	CABAN CYSGU BUNKHOUSE	366
ARETE OUTDOOR CENTRE	332	CAERHAFOD LODGE	320
ARIUNDLE BUNKHOUSE	471	CALLANDER HOSTEL	412
ARNSIDE INDEP. HOSTEL	211	CALLUNA	448
AYRES ROCK HOSTEL	509	CAMPBELL ROOM	68
BACKPACKERS PLUS OBAN	428	CAMPBELTOWN BPKS	404
BADRALLACH BOTHY	491	CARLISLE CITY HOSTEL	256
BALA BACKPACKERS	354	CASTLE CREAVIE HAY BARN	392
BALA BUNKHOUSE	353	CASTLE ROCK HOSTEL	401
BALMAHA BUNKHOUSE	410	CATBELLS CAMPING BARN	245
BANK HOUSE FARM HOSTEL	182	CHATTON PARK BUNKHOUSE	286
BANK STREET LODGE	452	CHITCOMBE FARM	69
BARN FARM BARNS	140	CLINK261	100
BARRINGTON BUNKHOUSE	260	CLINK78	98
BASE LODGE	67	CLYNGWYN BUNKHOUSE	304
BATH YMCA	72	COED OWEN BUNKHOUSE	295
BEILI NEUADD BUNKHOUSE	334	COLL BUNKHOUSE	438
BENTS CAMPING BARN	201	COLONSAY BACKPACKERS	436
BERROW HOUSE BUNKH	110	COMRIE CROFT	414
BIG MOSE BASECAMP	119	CONWY VALLEY BPKS BARN	368
BIRSAY OUTDOOR CENTRE	505	CORNMILL BUNKHOUSE	498
BLACK ISLE BERRIES	493	CORRAN HOUSE	434
BLACK ROCK BUNKHOUSE	494	CORRIS HOSTEL	350
BLINDWELL BUNKHOUSE	66	COTE GHYLL MILL	184
BLUEBELL FARM BUNKBARN	284	COURT HILL CENTRE	86
BLYTHESWOOD HOSTEL	55	CRAGG BARN CAMPING B.	249
BRAEMAR LODGE	425	CRAIG Y NOS CASTLE	306
BRAICH GOCH BUNKHOUSEN	348	CRAIGNURE BUNKHOUSE	442
BRANCASTER ACT CENTRE)	130	CROFT FARM WATERPARK	107
BRECON BUNKHOUSE	302	CULLEN HARBOUR HOSTEL	461

INDEX

CWM PENNANT HOSTEL	374
DALEHEAD BUNKHOUSE	158
DALES BIKE CENTRE	198
DALESBRIDGE	193
DARTMOOR EXPED. CENTRE	50
DAVID DONALD BASE	77
DEEPDALE BACKPACKERS	134
DEEPDALE GRANARY	133
DEMESNE FARM BUNKH.	267
DENTON HOUSE	242
DERWENTWATER HOSTEL	238
DOLGOCH HOSTEL	330
DOVER CASTLE HOSTEL	96
DRAGONS BACK	301
DUDDON SANDS HOSTEL	213
DUNARD HOSTEL	482
ECOCAMP GLENSHEE	424
EDMUNDBYERS Y. HOSTEL	83
ELMSCOTT HOSTEL	60
ELTERWATER HOSTEL	237
EMBASSIE BACKPACKERS	172
EURO HOSTEL GLASGOW	402
EXETER GLOBE	56
FALMOUTH BACKPACKERS	44
FARR COTTAGE LODGE	453
FELL END BUNKHOUSE	200
FELL END CAMPING BARN	212
FELL HOUSE COTTAGE	261
FELLDYKE BUNKHOUSE	251
FINDHORN VILLAGE HOSTEL	460
FISHER-GILL CAMPING BARN	236
FLAT HOLM FARMHOUSE	292
FLORA MACDONALD HOSTEL	477
FOREST VIEW HOSTEL	276
FORT WILLIAM BPKS	446
FOUNDRY ADVENT. CENTRE	162
FOX TOR BUNKHOUSE	52
FOXHOLES CASTLE BUNKH.	116
GALFORD SPRINGS	53
GALLOWAY YURTS	393
GARDIESFAULD HOSTEL	511
GERRY'S HOSTEL	486
GIBBS HILL FARM HOSTEL	266
GILFACH WEN BARN	314
GLEBE BARN	474
GLENCOE INDEP HOSTEL	444
GLENFINNAN SLEEPING CAR	472
GLENORCHY CENTRE	136
GOBLIN COMBE LODGE	71
GRASMERE INDEP. HOSTEL	232
GRASSINGTON BUNKBARN	189
GREAT GLEN HOSTEL	470
GREAT LANGDALE BUNKH.	229
GREENGILL BARN	208
GREENHEAD HOSTEL	262
GULABIN LODGE	420
GUMBER BOTHY	82
HABITAT @ BALLATER	426
HAGGIS HOSTELS	398
HAGGS BANK BUNKHOUSE	257
HAMILTON BACKPACKERS	323
HAMNAVOE HOSTEL	500
HARDINGSDOWN BUNKH.	312
HARDRAW OLD SCHOOL	196
HARFORD BUNKHOUSE	47
HARLOW INTER. HOSTEL	95
HATTERS BIRMINGHAM	126
HATTERS LIVERPOOL	174
HATTERS ON HILTON STREET	169
HATTERS ON NEWTON ST.	171
HAWSE END CENTRE	246
HAYE FARM SLEEPING BARN	109
HEB HOSTEL	484
HEBDEN BRIDGE HOSTEL	175
HELMSDALE HOSTEL	497
HENDRE ISAF BASECAMP	359
HERDING HILL FARM	263
HIGH HOUSE	248
HIGH STREET HOSTEL	397
HIGH WRAY BASECAMP	218
HILLSIDE FARM BUNKBARN	255
HOMESTEAD	156
HOUGHTON NORTH ACCOM.	272
HOY CENTRE	502
HUDSCALES CAMPING BARN	253
HUNSTANTON BPKS & YHA	132

INDEX

HYB BUNKHOUSE	352
IFFERDALE FARM BUNKH.	406
IGLOO BACKPACKERS	127
ILAM BUNKHOUSE	144
INCHNADAMPH LODGE	492
INGLETON YH GRETA TOWER	194
INSH HALL LODGE	456
INVERARAY HOSTEL	409
INVERNESS STUDENT HOTEL	464
IONA HOSTEL	441
JEREMY INGLIS HOSTEL	430
JERSEY ACCOMMODATION	38
JOHN HUNT BASE	160
KENDAL HOSTEL	226
KETTLEWELL HOSTEL	191
KILMORY LODGE BUNKH.	403
KINLOCHEWE BUNKHOUSE	489
KINTAIL LODGE BUNKH.	475
KIPPS BRIGHTON	88
KiPPS CANTERBURY	92
KIRK YETHOLM FOFN HOUSE	395
KIRKBY STEPHEN HOSTEL	204
KIRKWALL PEEDIE HOSTEL	508
KYLE OF TONGUE HOSTEL	499
L & A OUTDOOR CENTRE	309
LAKE DISTRICT BPKS	224
LAND'S END HOSTEL	39
LAWRENNY HOSTEL	315
LAXDALE BUNKHOUSE	485
LEDGOWAN LODGE	488
LLANDUDNO HOSTEL	370
LLANGOLLEN HOSTEL	356
LLEDR HOUSE	360
LOCH NESS BACKPACKERS	468
LONGRIGG RESI. CENTRE	202
LOW GILLERTHWAITE FC	247
LOWER PENDERLEATH	43
LOWICK SCHOOL BUNKH.	216
LUDLOW MASCALL CENTRE	114
MAENTWROG BUNKHOUSE	382
MAES-Y-MOR	342
MAGGS HOWE CAMPING B.	241
MARTHROWN OF MABIE	390
MAUGHOLD VENTURE	287
MENDIP BUNKHOUSE	70
MID WALES BUNKHOUSE	336
MILLHOUSE HOSTEL	440
MONKTON WYLD COURT	75
MOORSIDE FM. BUNKHOUSE	152
MORAG'S LODGE LOCH NESS	467
MULLACOTT FARM C. BARN	61
N°5 DRINISHADER	483
NANTYR OUTDOOR CENTRE	355
NEW ING LODGE	206
NEW INN BUNKHOUSE	338
NINEBANKS	258
NORTHSHOREBUDE	58
NOSDA STUDIO HOSTEL	293
OBAN BACKPACKERS	432
OBSERVATORY HOSTEL	510
OCEAN BACKPACKERS	62
OLD RED LION	135
OLD SCHOOL HOSTEL	322
OLD WEATHER STATION	344
ORCADES HOSTEL	506
OUTDOOR ALTERNATIVE	385
PALACE FARM HOSTEL	90
PANTYRATHRO INT. HOSTEL	313
PEMBROKESHIRE ADV. CEN.	316
PENTRE BACH BUNKHOUSE	373
PENZANCE BACKPACKERS	40
PIGGERY POKE HOSTEL	324
PINDALE FARM OUTDOOR C.	154
PITLOCHRY BPKS HOTEL	418
PLAS CURIG HOSTEL	362
PLAS DOLAU COUNTRY H.	340
PLASNEWYDD BUNKHOUSE	343
PLATT'S FARM BUNKHOUSE	372
PLYMOUTH GLOBE BPKS	48
PROSEN HOSTEL	422
PUTTENHAM ECO C. BARN	84
RACKWICK OUT. CENTRE	504
RATTRAY HEAD ECO-HOSTEL	462
RHOSSILI BUNKHOUSE	310
RICHMOND CAMPING BARN	199
RICKYARD BUNKHOUSE	298

INDEX

RIVER HOUSE HOSTEL	294	THE LONG BARN	326
ROCK AND RAPID BUNKH.	64	THE OLD SCHOOL BUNKH.	195
ROOKHOW CENTRE	214	THE OLD SMITHY C. BARN	170
ROYAL MILE BACKPACKERS	400	THE PRIVETT CENTRE	81
ROYAL OAK BUNKBARN	151	THE RECKONING HOUSE	138
RYDAL HALL YOUTH CENTRE	228	THE STABLES BUNKHOUSE	164
SAFESTAY YORK	177	THE WAIN HOUSE	300
SAIL MHOR CROFT	490	THE WHITE HORSE INN BUNH.	243
SCARBOROUGH Y. HOSTEL	176	THORNEY HOW IND. HOSTEL	230
SHACKLETON LODGE	222	THORPE FARM BUNKHOUSES	148
SHAGGY SHEEP	325	TOAD HALL	346
SHEEN BUNKHOUSE	142	TOMLINSON'S BUNKHOUSE	273
SHEENA'S BPKS LODGE	473	TORRAN BAY HOSTEL	408
SHEPHERD'S CROOK	234	TOTTERS	383
SHETLAND CAMPING BöDS	512	TRAVEL JOY HOSTEL	102
SHIELING HOLIDAYS	443	TREGEDNA LODGE	46
SHINING CLIFF HOSTEL	150	TRERICKET MILL BUNKROOM	303
SKIDDAW HOUSE	244	TROSSACHS TRYST	411
SKYE BACKPACKERS	478	TY'N CORNEL HOSTEL	328
SKYEWALKER HOSTEL	481	TYDDYN BYCHAN	358
SLACK HOUSE FARM	264	TYN Y BERTH MOU. CENTRE	347
SLEEPERZZZ.COM	496	UNDERBANK CAMPING BARN	167
SLOCHD MHOR LODGE	466	UPPER BOOTH C. BARN	153
SMARTCITYHOSTELS EDIN.	398	UPPER NEESTON LODGES	319
SMIDDY BUNKHOUSE	450	WANDERING DUCK	168
SNOWDON HOUSE BUNKH.	364	WAYFARERS INDEP. HOSTEL	254
SNOWDON LODGE HOSTEL	376	WELL ROAD CENTRE	394
SPARROWHAWK BPKS	54	WERN WATKIN BUNKHOUSE	296
SPRINGHILL BUNKHOUSE	280	WEST END OUT. CENTRE	186
SPRINGHILL FARM BUNKH.	125	WESTER CAPUTH STEADING	417
ST JOHN'S-IN-THE-VALE CB	240	WETHERDOWN LODGE	80
ST MICHAELS CENTRE	146	WHARFESIDE HOUSE	190
STACKPOLE OUT. CENTRE	317	WHITBY BACKPACKERS	180
STATIONMASTERS HOSTEL	476	WHITEFIELDS COTTAGE	192
STOKES BARN BUNKHOUSES	122	WOMERTON FARM BUNKH.	124
STONECROFT LODGE	333	WOODLANDS BUNKHOUSE	308
STOUR VALLEY BUNKHOUSE	104	WOODSIDE LODGES BUNKH.	112
SWALLOW BARN C. BARN.	250	WOOLER YOUTH HOSTEL	283
SWANAGE AUBERGE BUNKH	78	WYTHMOOR FARM C. BARN	227
TACKROOM BUNKHOUSE	282	YE OLD FERRIE INN	108
TARN FLATT CAMPING BARN	252	YEALAND OLD SCHOOL	210
TARSET TOR BUNKHOUSE	268	YMCA CORNWALL PENZANCE	42
THE HIDES	278	YORK RACECOURSE CENTRE	178
THE JONAS CENTRE	197		